Critical Essays in Music Education

Critical Essays in Music Education

Edited by

Marvelene C. Moore

University of Tennessee, Knoxville, USA

ASHGATE

Published by
Ashgate Publishing Limited
Wey Court East
Union Road
Farnham
Surrey GU9 7PT
England

Ashgate Publishing Company
Suite 420
101 Cherry Street
Burlington
VT 05401-4405
USA

www.ashgate.com

British Library Cataloguing in Publication Data
Critical essays in music education.
    1. Music–Instruction and study.
    I. Moore, Marvelene C.
    780.7'1-dc22

Library of Congress Control Number: 2011929909

ISBN 9780754629429

Printed and bound in Great Britain by
TJ International Ltd, Padstow, Cornwall.

Contents

PART V MULTICULTURAL AND WORLD MUSIC

Acknowledgements

The editor and publishers wish to thank the following for permission to use copyright material.

Association for Childhood Education International for the essay: Mary Palmer (2002), 'Musical Connections', in P.A. Crawford and K.G. Burriss (eds), *It's Elementary! Special Topics in Elementary Education*, Olney, MD: Association for Childhood Education International, pp. 127–30. Reprinted by permission of Mary Palmer and the Association for Childhood Education International, 17904 Georgia Avenue, Suite 215, Olney, MD. Copyright © 2002 by the Association.

Australian Scholarly Publishing for the essays: David Forrest (2009), 'Music for Children and Young People', in Martin Comte (ed.), *Musical Dimensions: A Festschrift for Doreen Bridges*, Melbourne, Australia: Australian Scholarly Publishing, pp. 178–91; Marvelene C. Moore (2009), 'A Case for Multiculturalism in the General Music Classroom', in Martin Comte (ed.), *Musical Dimensions: A Festschrift for Doreen Bridges*, Melbourne, Australia: Australian Scholarly Publishing, pp. 235–40.

Australian Society for Music Education for the essay: Martin Comte (2005), 'Music Education: Giving Children a Voice', *Australian Society for Music Education Monograph*, **7**, pp. 5–22. Copyright © 2005 Australian Society for Music Education Incorporated.

Center for Black Music Research for the essay: Rosita M. Sands (1996), 'What Prospective Music Teachers Need to Know about Black Music', *Black Music Research Journal*, **16**, pp. 225–38.

GIA Publications, Inc. for the essays: Edwin E. Gordon (2007), 'Measurement and Evaluation in Music', in *Learning Sequences in Music: A Contemporary Music Learning Theory*, Chicago: GIA Publications, pp. 303–44. Copyright © 1980, 1984, 1988, 1993, 1997, 2003, 2007 by GIA Publications, Inc.; Glenn E. Nierman (2007), 'The Development and Validation of a Measurement Tool for Assessing Students' Ability to Keep a Steady Beat', in Timothy S. Brophy *et al.* (eds), *Assessment in Music Education: Integrating Curriculum, Theory and Practice*, Chicago: GIA Publications, pp. 289–95. Copyright © 2008 by GIA Publications, Inc., www.giamusic.com. All rights reserved.

Greek Society for Music Education for the essay: Polyvios Androutsos (2007), 'Praxial Philosophy and Educational Praxis', *Musical Pedagogics*, **4**, pp. 20–34.

International Journal of Education and the Arts for the essay: Bo Wah Leung and Eddie C.K. Leung (2010), 'Teacher–Artist Partnership in Teaching Cantonese Opera in Hong Kong Schools: Student Transformation', *International Journal of Education and the Arts*, **11**, pp. 1–26.

J. David Boyle and Rudolf E. Radocy for their essay: J. David Boyle and Rudolf E. Radocy (1987), 'Measuring Musical Aptitude and Ability', in *Measurement and Evaluation of Musical Experiences*, New York: Schirmer Books, pp. 139–56.

MENC: The National Association for Music Education for the essay: Paul R. Lehman (2000), 'The Power of the National Standards for Music Education', in Bennett Reimer (ed.), *Performing with Understanding*, Reston, VA: MENC, pp. 3–9.

Music Educators National Conference for the essays: Liora Bresler and Robert E. Stake (1992), 'Qualitative Research Methodology in Music Education', in Richard Colwell (ed.), *Handbook of Research on Music Teaching and Learning*, New York: Schirmer Books, pp. 75–90; Edward P. Asmus and Rudolf E. Radocy (1992), 'Quantitative Analysis', in Richard Colwell (ed.), *Handbook of Research on Music Teaching and Learning*, New York: Schirmer Books, pp. 141–83; Peter Costanza and Timothy Russell (1992), 'Methodologies in Music Education', in Richard Colwell (ed.), *Handbook of Research on Music Teaching and Learning*, New York: Schirmer Books, pp. 498–508; Joyce Jordan (1992), 'Multicultural Music Education in a Pluralistic Society', in Richard Colwell (ed.), *Handbook of Research in Music Teaching and Learning*, New York: Schirmer Books, pp. 735–48.

Oxford University Press for the essays: David J. Elliott (1995), 'Musicing', in *Music Matters: A New Philosophy of Music Education*, New York: Oxford University Press, pp. 49–77; Peter R. Webster (2002), 'Computer-Based Technology and Music Teaching and Learning', in Richard Colwell and Carol P. Richardson (eds), *The New Handbook of Research of Music Teaching and Learning*, New York: Oxford University Press, pp. 416–39. Copyright © 2002 MENC; Richard Colwell (2002), 'Assessment's Potential in Music Education', in Richard Colwell and Carol P. Richardson (eds), *The New Handbook of Research on Music Teaching and Learning*, New York: Oxford Press, pp. 1128–58. Copyright © 2002 MENC; Robert A. Cutietta (2001), 'Measuring Musical Talent', in *Raising Musical Kids*, New York: Oxford Press, pp. 38–43.

Pearson Education, Inc. for the essay: Bennett Reimer (1970), 'Alternative Views about Art on Which a Philosophy Can Be Based', in *Philosophy of Music Education*, New York: Prentice Hall, pp. 12–27. Copyright © 1970 by Prentice-Hall, Inc., Eaglewood Cliffs, New Jersey.

Sage Publications for the essays: Colin Durrant (2009), 'Communicating and Accentuating the Aesthetic and Expressive Dimension in Choral Conducting', *International Journal of Music Education*, **27**, pp. 326–40. Copyright © 2009 International Society for Music Education; Charles Leonhard (1965), 'Philosophy of Music Education', *Music Educators Journal*, **52**, pp. 58–61, 177; Michael L. Mark (1982), 'The Evolution of Music Education Philosophy from Utilitarian to Aesthetic', *Journal of Research in Music Education*, **30**, pp. 15–21; Judith A. Jellison and Patricia J. Flowers (1991), 'Talking about Music: Interviews with Disabled and Nondisabled Children', *Journal of Research in Music Education*, **39**, pp. 322–33; Clifford K. Madsen, Jayne M. Standley and Jane W. Cassidy (1989), 'Demonstration and Recognition of High and Low Contrasts in Teacher Intensity', *Journal of Research in Music Education*, **37**, pp. 85–92; Marie McCarthy (1995), 'On "American Music for American Children": The Contribution of Charles L. Seeger', *Journal of Research in Music Education*, **43**, pp. 270–87;

James L. Byo (2004), 'Teaching Problem Solving in Practice', *Music Educators Journal*, **91**, pp. 35–39; Bryan Burton and Peter Dunbar-Hall (2002), 'Teaching about and through Native American Musics: An Excursion into the Cultural Politics of Music Education', *Research Studies in Music Education*, **19**, pp. 56–64. Copyright © 2002 Calloway International Resource Centre for Music Education; Terese M. Volk (1993), 'The History and Development of Multicultural Music Education as Evidenced in the *Music Educators Journal*, 1967–1992', *Journal of Research in Music Education*, **41**, pp. 137–55.

Taylor & Francis for the essay: Patricia Shehan Campbell (2001), 'Unsafe Suppositions? Cutting across Cultures on Questions of Music's Transmission', *Music Education Research*, **3**, pp. 215–26. Copyright © 2001 Taylor & Francis; Scott C. Shuler (1988), 'Arts Education and the Curriculum: Joining the Mainstream', *Design for Arts in Education*, **90**, pp. 17–24.

Every effort has been made to trace all the copyright holders, but if any have been inadvertently overlooked the publishers will be pleased to make the necessary arrangement at the first opportunity.

Introduction

The field of music education is very broad and varied and as complex as any academic discipline. Its scope extends from research to pedagogy to performance and success in the field requires competence in knowledge of philosophy, curriculum, assessment, evaluation and music diversity. It encompasses many challenging components and rewarding practices which include transmission of knowledge and aesthetics of music, competence in performance, grasp of appropriate music literature (based on age, ability, interest) and expertise in establishing an atmosphere where creativity and composing can thrive. Further, the field of music education is concerned with the teaching and learning of music from pre-primary through secondary levels, university undergraduate and graduate levels and throughout adulthood. Every domain that comprises the 'whole' person can be affected and developed through engagement in music including the cognitive (the intellectual), the affective (the emotional) and the psycho motor (the physical) domains. Consequently, opportunities for participation in music should be made available to all whether in the school, community or the home and should be taught, or at the least, instruction should be supervised by qualified, certified music educators. A brief look back at the beginnings of music education will provide greater insight on its importance and evolution.

Historical Overview

Evidence of instruction in music and its importance to the development of the individual can be verified around 400 BC in the writings of the Greek philosopher Plato in 'Republic and Laws' where he describes the ideal educational system consisting of music and gymnastics (Mark and Gary, 2007, p. 12). Further in his doctrine of the Ethos, he placed emphasis on music as an agent for developing moral character. In progressing towards the Middle Ages, we find that music occupies an important place in education as one of the seven liberal arts, including arithmetic, astronomy, geometry, grammar, logic and rhetoric, which were offered in institutions of higher learning in England, France and Italy. However, music was not regarded for its aesthetic properties or sonority. Rather, it was valued for its mathematic qualities (Mark and Gary, 2007, p. 20). In the 1500s and into the seventeenth century, music education was reserved as study for the cultured and educated and as such was taught in the conservatories, to young women of the upper class and boys who were interested in pursuing music as a profession (Hoffer, 1993, pp. 78–9).

In the eighteenth century in Europe, a new philosophy in general education surfaced that focused on educating the masses which impacted the development of music education for years to come. In fact, specific patterns of mass education emerged during this time in France, England, Prussia, Japan and America (Cox and Stevens, 2010). Williams (1997, p. 120) in his publication on the development of modern education notes that:

By the mid-1800s, states outside Europe began to institute compulsory schooling – Haiti, Argentina, Massachusetts in the United States, then Japan. European nations continued to enact compulsory schooling statutes – Norway and Sweden, then finally in the late 1800s, the industrial leaders, France, the Netherlands, and Britain [required the same].

These movements are significant in the history of music education because they ultimately led to a debate on course subjects that should comprise a curriculum in the education of the masses which later included music.

As in most countries, throughout the eighteenth and nineteenth centuries, music education evolved from issues and concerns related to religion, politics and humanism. For instance, in the United States around the eighteenth century, music education began in an effort to improve singing in the church among the colonists. This interest contributed to the development of the singing schools, a two-day to two-week course in vocal instruction and music reading. In England, it was the National Song Book that was used in music instruction throughout the country to promote patriotism in its disputes with other countries. Likewise, in Australia, soldiers were well versed on patriotic and nationalistic songs when sent to the Sudan and South Africa. In Canada, immigrants were required to learn English through singing; in China the influence of John Curwen was seen through the use of the tonic sol-fa system in the congregational singing; in Spain, music was a dominant force in its expansion in Latin America, it was Jesuit missionaries who taught the Argentineans to read music and in Cuba a school of Cuban composers of Western art music was established (Cox and Stevens, 2010, p. 5). In reference to the connection of humanism to the historical development of music education the following can be cited. In the nineteenth century, it was the British who promoted the idea of music education as an agent in developing ideal citizens through the work of Arthur Somervell, a British school inspector. Further, the Chinese, Australians, Canadians and Japanese were advocates of music in education for the sake of building social harmony and moral character. At the same time the Canadians and Japanese advanced this theory of music education (Cox and Stevens, 2010).

Concurrent to the development of music education in the nineteenth century was the expansion of appropriate pedagogy for teaching music to large groups of students, basically singing and sight reading. The source of sight singing of course, goes back to the teachings of Guido d'Arezzo on which G.L. Bocquillon Wilheim of France based his 'fixed do' system of music instruction. His technique spread to Argentina and in England, John Hullah was so inspired by him that he adopted the 'fixed do' technique of teaching sight reading which later reached Australia, Canada and Ireland. However, it was Sarah Glover who was responsible for the change to 'moveable do' in England along with John Curwen, which was carried by missionaries to many parts of the world (Cox and Stevens, 2010). Further signs of an emphasis on pedagogy emerged in the work of Johann Heinrich Pestalozzi, a Swiss educator whose process for instruction emphasized direct sense experience. He promoted the philosophy of practice before theory and made a clear distinction between 'real and book' knowledge (Leonhard and House, 1972, p. 58). Notable European music educators like George Nageli and Joseph H. Naef, became advocates of Pestalozzi's approach to instruction, which was adopted in other European countries (Hoffer, 1993, p. 80). At the same time in the United States, Lowell Mason, through his efforts and pedgogical techniques based on those of Pestalozzi in instructing primary age children in music, was able to secure a place for music education at the primary level in the Boston public schools (Hoffer, 1993, p. 80).

In the twentieth century, music education acquired a more prominent place in the school curriculum and was regarded as a core curriculum discipline in many countries of the world. Further, the emphasis shifted from teaching the masses through 'a' type of methodology, to meeting individual needs of students by applying eclectic methods, strategies and techniques to music instruction. During this period the need for maximum development of the 'whole' child, the cognitive, affective, psycho motor domains was advanced through the efforts of John Dewey and other notable educators, psychologists and music educators. Although instruction in music was designed to bring about greater understanding of the medium and proficiency in performance, there were those who also supported the inclusion of music as part of an 'interdisciplinary' design. In a framework of this type, music was and is often today relegated to enhancing learning of academic subjects. Other aspects of music learning and curriculum that came to the forefront at this time were performance standards, assessment and evaluation and the beginnings of interest in music for lifelong learning. In the United States other events occurred that contributed to the growth and development of music education in the country. They were: (1) the Child's Bill of Rights (1950) – a philosophy centred around the student (http://www.MENC.org/resources/view/child-s-bill-of-rights); (2) the Tanglewood Symposium (1967) – emphasis on an eclectic curriculum that promoted urban and multicultural music and emphasis on music instruction for special needs children (Mark in Madsen, 2000, pp. 8–9); (3) National Standards for Arts Education (1994) – created by MENC: The National Association for Music Education to establish standards for music teaching and learning which could be assessed and evaluated (Consortium of National Arts Education Association, 1994, pp. 11–18); and (4) the Housewright Symposium (1999) – an extension of the Tanglewood Symposium that addressed the philosophies and practices of music education that would provide direction for the profession by the year 2020 (Hinckley, 2000 in Madsen, 2000, p. 1). Further, in this century there was a movement towards inclusion of folk music from world cultures in the curriculum and in instruction. As a result students in the Western and European countries for example, gained greater exposure to music of the East and those in the East became acquainted with Western and European folk and ethnic music. This movement coupled with the advancements in technology led to unlimited accessibility to music of the world.

In the twenty-first century, music education was concerned with issues similar to those of previous centuries coupled with a heightened interest in the challenges of providing equal access in music for all ages, abilities and ethnicities and meeting the demands for the inclusion of technology. The focus of the century also reflects an interest in ensuring a place for music in the lives of all people as a lifelong learning pursuit. In addition, a substantial number of music educators exhibit an interest in research and conducting inquiry in diverse areas of the profession which include philosophical conceptualization, student responses to music (how they learn), performance behaviour, evaluation, music teacher education and world music to name a few. The music education profession calls for:

- establishing a sound belief system on which music can be justified and taught, philosophy;
- well-constructed plans for instruction, curriculum;
- solid and innovative teaching methods and procedures, pedagogy;
- valid measurements of student performance, assessment and effective pedagogy, evaluation;

- inclusion of non-traditional, multicultural and world music in all segments of the profession.

Importance of This Publication

This volume of critical essays in music education is vital for the preservation, safeguard and continuation of the profession. It serves as a chronicle of writings by scholars throughout the world who are experts in specific areas of the profession. The volume represents a comprehensive collection of their works in areas that are of interest and importance to music educators, applied music teachers, professors and students at all levels. It reflects a oneness of purpose in providing an overview of the profession with its varied divisions while focusing on specific topics within the field. The publication is an essential reference that: (1) documents the uniqueness of the discipline, yet displays its collaborative properties; (2) assists in imparting knowledge of and instruction in music; and (3) supports research and advocacy in its justification of music for all. The result is a valuable and comprehensive source.

Selection of Essays

The essays in this volume were selected from refereed research journals and reputable monographs. They were chosen for inclusion in the publication because they are representative of the categories commonly linked with music education. They exemplify distinguished writings in philosophy, research, curriculum and pedagogy, assessment and evaluation and multicultural and world music.

Philosophy

The section on philosophy is the 'heart beat' of music education because it is the foundation on which the profession evolves. It gives purpose to actions, and aids in determining goals, establishing objectives, formulating procedure and designing assessment and performance standards. To augment these tenets, four major topics are presented: (1) articulating beliefs about music in 'Praxial Philosophy and Educational Praxis' by Polyvios Androutsos and 'Philosophy of Music Education' by Charles Leonhard; (2) new ways of describing philosophical thought, represented by 'Musicing' by David Elliott and 'Music Education: Giving Children a Voice' by Martin Comte; (3) viewing philosophy in relation to societal needs, addressed in 'The Evolution of Music Education Philosophy from Utilitarian to Aesthetic' by Michael Mark, and (4) music as aesthetic education, represented by 'Alternative Views about Art on Which a Philosophy Can Be Based' by Bennett Reimer and 'Communicating and Accentuating the Aesthetic and Expressive Dimension in Choral Conducting' by Colin Durrant.

Research

One of the most effective ways to keep abreast of the latest findings in teaching and learning in music education is to examine research in an area of interest and importance to the individual that has been thoroughly investigated by scholars. Bennett Reimer concurs that information on appropriate methodology, proper music literature, relevant music experiences and well-designed curricula could be enhanced significantly if information in the areas were based on clear cut knowledge acquired from examination of research (Reimer, quoted in Madison, 1966, p. 461). In the research category, attention is given to documentation of knowledge applicable to instructional settings in music. The essays focus on describing the research design of qualitative inquiry and delineating characteristics of this approach to research, particularly 'Qualitative Research Methodology in Music Education' by Liora Bresler and Robert Stake, as compared to quantitative research with its emphasis on numbers, statistics and analysis of raw data as in 'Quantitative Analysis' by Edward Asmus and Rudolf Radocy. Further valuable information is provided on evaluation in music in 'Measurement and Evaluation in Music' by Edwin Gordon; student responses to music and learning by special needs and non-special needs students in 'Talking about Music: Interviews with Disabled and Nondisabled Children' by Judith Jellison and Patricia Flowers; factors that influence teacher effectiveness in 'Demonstration and Recognition of High and Low Contrasts in Teacher Intensity' by Clifford Madsen *et al.*; and a historical account of contributions made to the field of children's music in 'On "American Music for American Children": The Contribution of Charles L. Seeger' by Marie McCarthy.

Pedagogy/Curriculum

Curriculum and pedagogy are grouped conjointly since collectively they form the core of music education. Together they create a road map for selecting desired learning experiences and end results. Planning a comprehensive music programme and devising instructional strategies and techniques are the lifeline of successful teaching. According to Harry E. Price (1998, p. xv), music educators 'need to identify good teaching practices, carefully define them, utilize them, and attempt to teach people to use them'. The essays in this part centre around curriculum design: 'Arts Education and the Curriculum: Joining the Mainstream' by Scott Shuler, and various methodologies for successful teaching: 'Methodologies in Music Education' by Peter Costanza and Timothy Russell; 'Music for Children and Young People' by David Forrest; 'Teacher–Artist Partnership in Teaching Cantonese Opera in Hong Kong Schools: Student Transformation' by Bo Wah Leung and Eddie Leung; 'Musical Connections' by Mary Palmer; and 'Computer-Based Technology and Music Teaching and Learning' by Peter Webster.

Assessment and Evaluation

Assessment and evaluation are important components of music education. They are essential for determining the progress of students (assessment) and the effectiveness and value of a music programme (evaluation). These measurement devices play a key role in determining aptitude, measuring music talent and achievement and the extent of progression towards meeting objectives and desired outcomes. Tools for measuring the success of a music programme and student aptitude and achievement may include establishing standards by which a programme can be reviewed, utilizing standardized tests and teacher made tests and identifying measurements designed for self-assessment. In this collection of essays, the authors focus on the study and measurement of music aptitude: 'Measuring Musical Aptitude and Ability' by J. David Boyle and Rudolph Radocy; 'Assessment's Potential in Music Education' by Richard Colwell; 'Measuring Musical Talent' by Robert Cutietta; 'The Power of National Standards' by Paul Lehman; 'The Development and Validation of a Measurement Tool for Assessing Students' Ability to Keep a Steady Beat' by Glenn Nierman; and on individual solutions to problems encountered in music in 'Teaching Problem Solving in Practice' by James Byo.

Multicultural and World Music

Everywhere people reside whether in schools, communities, homes, churches, in groups or alone, there surfaces a need to make music. As it relates to the cultural context, participation in some form of music activity becomes a part of the human experience and often functions for social, religious and political purposes. Further, music in many cultures serves to link generations to the past. It is a reflection of their life and often provides a historical perspective on current behaviour within ethnic groups. In its broadest sense, multicultural music education is an approach to teaching and learning that incorporates the music of many ethnic groups along with the study of history, customs and social issues. Regardless of how it is defined, music that promotes understanding among people and joy within the participant is a 'must' for inclusion in the music programme. The authors of the essays in this category approach multicultural music in diverse ways: (1) by defining the what, why and how of multicultural music in 'Multicultural Music Education in a Pluralistic Society' by Joyce Jordan and 'A Case for Multiculturalism in the General Music Classroom' by Marvelene Moore; (2) approaching it from a historical standpoint, in 'The History and Development of Multicultural Music Education as Evidenced in the *Music Educators Journal*, 1967–1992' by Terese Volk; (3) as a means of oral transmission in 'Unsafe Suppositions? Crossing Cultures on Issues of Music's Transmission' by Patricia Shehan Campbell; and (4) by providing details on teaching specific music cultures, in 'Teaching about and through Native American Musics: An Excursion into the Cultural Politics of Music Education' by Bryan Burton and Peter Dunbar-Hall, and 'What Prospective Music Teachers Need to Know about Black Music' by Rosita Sands.

Philosophy of Music Education

'Praxial Philosophy and Educational Praxis' by Polyvios Androutsos

In this essay (Chapter 1) Polyvios Androutsos investigates the relationship between praxial philosophy and curriculum and pedagogy in music education. He defines praxial as a Greek derivative which denotes action and he ponders whether philosophy can result in action in an educational setting. In response to this query, he points to the work of David Elliott in *Music Matters* where Elliott emphasizes the importance of making music, which is referred to as 'musicing'. Both Androutsos and Elliott concur that a purely listening-based music programme consisting of surface listening does not reflect music in action nor the praxial philosophy. On the other hand, Androutsos points out the limitations that affect application of a praxial philosophy including time constraints for instruction; lack of basic equipment; evaluation and assessment issues; and improper music teacher education preparation. Androutsos (Chapter 1) leaves this inquiry with additional questions that revolve around theory (philosophy) and practice. They include: 'Are theory and practice unrelated? Does theory influence practice or does practice generate theory? ... Should philosophy guide practice, not the other way around?' (p. 8).

The essay by Androutsos is important to the field of music education because it reaches to the core of important issues in music; building philosophy and transferring it to the stage of active engagement in music performance in diverse ways. It represents in-depth thought on music making grounded on a philosophical base.

'Music Education: Giving Children a Voice' by Martin Comte

'Music Education: Giving Children a Voice,' by Martin Comte (Chapter 2) focuses on a number of facets of music education in relation to perceived needs and to the future of the field. Its implications for music education are worldwide, readily apparent and will strike a chord with music educators in many countries. Comte (Chapter 2) states that the essay addresses three major imperatives facing music education in the twenty-first century:

- The imperative of developing an Australian theory of music education.
- The imperative of engaging in advocacy more strategically.
- The imperative of confronting the insidious aspects of technology whilst at the same time acknowledging that we are living in an increasingly technological age. (p. 13)

Comte (Chapter 2) argues that each of these imperatives requires a paradigm shift on the part of music educators if children are not to lose their voice – 'their voice for music' (p. 14). It is argued that to a significant degree the media have already displaced the role of music educators by playing a *de facto* role in the musical upbringing of the majority of children. The writer also opens up the debate on the future of schooling and implications of an increased emphasis on e-learning with its social implications for music making (or a lack thereof) by children. Children are singing less and less and more broadly, this is symptomatic of a kind of social de-voicing in which our voices are being de-humanized and replaced by 'synthetic' voices. The writer argues that music educators must exert due influence on the developers and marketers of the new technologies that are robbing children of their voice. For if they do not children and music in schools will be swamped with more and more new programmes of dubious value. The author forces the reader to take a long, hard look at the influences of technology on the future of music education. He describes engagement in music in the future as a sedentary exercise void of the 'sense of experience' and dominated by manipulation of tools on an electronic device, absent of human contact. Further he voices concern for the absence of children's voices in singing which has been a natural expression of music in times past as heard in the handclapping games, jump rope games, ring games and ethereal sounds of children's voices in choirs directed by music specialists. The writings serve as a wake-up call for music educators to create a balanced programme in music that includes singing to experience the unique aesthetic nature of music that only it can bring about while researching ways of adapting and incorporating technology more effectively in instruction and performance. He concludes his debate by declaring that music educators must not allow the children's voices to be silenced.

'Communicating and Accentuating the Aesthetic and Expressive Dimension in Choral Conducting' by Colin Durrant

This essay (Chapter 3) provides a very interesting way of viewing choral conducting with an emphasis on communicating aesthetics through gesture. In the first part of the essay, the author begins with a discussion on the role of the conductor; from dictator to facilitator. He continues with a description of what is implied in (1) communicating, (2) communication and musical meaning, (3) gesture, (4) gesture and dance and (5) gesture and meaning. His purpose is to enlighten conductors of all ages, but especially young conductors, to the role of becoming a leader and a communicator in rehearsals through gestures rather than an absolute ruler. He concludes that meaningful, expressive gestures profoundly affect communication and vocal outcomes in a positive way and diminish the use of verbal instruction. In the second part of the essay, the author conveys the results of a research study which documents that simply consideration of gesture in communicating meaning helps to bring about this event. The study was conducted by Durrant and Varvarigou with school teachers and music student teachers who did not consider themselves competent as conductors. All participated in professional development courses that focused on communication and gesture, implemented and extended over a five-month period of time. Data from the research were collected through observation of the participants' perceptions and reflections on their progress and responses on questionnaires. The research study further confirmed that the greater the musical knowledge, the greater the ability to communicate effectively, referring to technical knowing, aural skills and knowing how the music should progress. Musical knowledge specifically refers to: (1) knowledge of literature appropriate for the various choral ensembles; (2) understanding of the voice and how to maintain its health; (3) understanding of the inner workings of the music that characterizes it expressive qualities; and (4) the ability to hear and communicate to the singers what has been heard in order to produce the desired sound (Apfelstadt, 1997; Decker and Kirk, 1988; Durrant 2003; Fuelberth, 2003). The essay can be very helpful to young conductors who are often preoccupied with their conducting pattern and neglect the very thing they are trying to portray, the beauty and expressive nature of music; the aesthetic.

'Musicing' by David J. Elliott

The essay on 'Musicing' by David Elliott (Chapter 4) is a unique, yet reasonable way of thinking about what constitutes making music. Elliott refers to it as *musicing*, used as a verb instead of an object. He describes musicing as the act of deliberate doing, performing, and proceeds to ask the question then, what is music and what is musicianship? Elliott (Chapter 4) explores these questions by identifying four categories of musicianship and describes them in detail in the essay. They are 'formal musical knowledge, informal musical knowledge, impressionistic musical knowledge, and supervisory musical knowledge' (p. 51). He sees his theory on musicing as having direct implications to the why of music, what of music and how of music. He believes firmly that making music is knowledge in-action; the art of playing instruments and singing. Elliott (Chapter 4) further believes that it is necessary to frame music teaching and learning in a way that is 'true to the nature and value of MUSIC and musicianship' (p. 70).

This interesting view on music teaching, learning and performing requires that the music teacher takes a look at the teaching environment, the manner in which practice is approached, how students discover their problems in music and resolve them and how evaluation can be attained without sacrificing the true essence of music. This type of scrutiny on viewing and expressing music would be beneficial for all music educators, regardless of their particular area of expertise.

'Philosophy of Music Education' by Charles Leonhard

This essay (Chapter 5) provides a comprehensive look at the importance of philosophy to the field of music education. Leonhard believes that a sound philosophy gives a view into the music programme and provides the teachers with a basis on which to establish instruction. In this essay, he offers a definition of music education: efforts to teach music to individuals at all levels, and descriptions of a music educator: teacher, professor and administrator. He recounts that historically music educators have been distrustful of philosophy and have focused their energies on the practical aspect of music teaching. However, in recent years, they have come to recognize the value of having a sound philosophy because of its capacity to give direction for instruction. Leonhard focuses his attention in this essay on opposing philosophical systems: realism, a traditional position in philosophy and pragmaticism, a more contemporary belief system. He references Broudy as a realist and McMurray as a pragmatist and discusses their positions on philosophy in detail. After a thorough discourse on the opposing philosophies, Leonhard suggest that because of the complexities involved in creating a philosophy, professionals at all levels should be involved in the process of constructing a set of sound beliefs about music in education.

The essay contributes significantly to music education in that it accommodates diverse ways of thinking about music and teaching. Regardless of the theory adopted, the core issue of philosophy centres around the value of music and the role music plays in the lives of humans.

'The Evolution of Music Education Philosophy from Utilitarian to Aesthetic' by Michael L. Mark

This essay (Chapter 6) is an interesting account of the unfolding of philosophical thought on aesthetics as justification for music in education. Mark takes the reader back to the Greek period where he points out the beginnings of viewing music for its value to human beings rather than its utilitarian uses as evidenced in the Middle Ages, in Europe among prominent educators of the nineteenth century and in early America with its uses in religion and the church. He notes the departure from this way of thinking with John Dewey and Progressive Education. However, when progressivism waned an urgent need emerged for educators to re-define the role of music and examine it on the basis of its aesthetic qualities. This gave rise to reputable thinkers like Allen Britton, Bennett Reimer, Charles Leonhard and many others. Later, however worldly events of the mid-twentieth century gave rise to the need to relate music to culture and society resulting primarily from the Tanglewood Symposium. Mark adds that soon after this time, Reimer's book on *A Philosophy of Music Education*, published in 1970 challenged educators to construct a philosophy based on reasons for music education to be regarded as aesthetic in its nature and value (Reimer from Mark, p. 91), an established way of viewing music education to this day.

Mark's contributions to the field of music education through his historical investigations have been highly regarded and well documented in many publications. He is esteemed as one of the foremost experts on historical events in music education and this essay is no exception. In a very succinct way he described the events surrounding the movement from thinking about music education as aesthetic, to music for utilitarian purposes to re-emphasizing music for its aesthetic properties.

'Alternative Views about Art on Which Philosophy Can Be Based' by Bennett Reimer

In Chapter 7 Reimer presents five points in discussing ways in which music educators may view art on which to formulate a philosophy. The first is to be selective when considering views on aesthetics; not all can or should be investigated. Second, the selection should be broad enough to include all aspects of music and music education but specific enough to focus on tangible guidelines. Third, the view must focus on the art of music. Fourth, one must be able to derive implications for education. Fifth, the view must reflect some connection to the society. Of the many aesthetic viewpoints that exist today, Reimer believes that one of the three aesthetics theories as categorised by Leonard B. Meyer (Referentialism, Absolute Formalism and Absolute Expressionism) communicates most effectively the value and nature of music, Absolute Expressionism. Reimer implies that absolute expressionism reflects the position that the 'message is in the medium'. In other words, the intrinsic value of music is what defines it. In describing each aesthetic theory, Reimer also discusses the implication of the theory to music teaching and supplements his discussions with figures that further illustrate his points. Through his discourse, Reimer makes his position clear on the importance of music in education, its place in the lives of human beings and defends his position with passion.

The essay has profound significance to music education because of its position on the need to formulate philosophy in music education based on the essence of music and its aesthetic qualities. It assists the teacher in establishing a sound foundation for curriculum planning and pedagogy and for articulating the need for students to engage in music making.

Review of Essays, Chapters in Books, Research Studies

Research in Music Education

'Qualitative Research Methodology in Music Education' by Liora Bresler and Robert E. Stake
Bresler and Stake (Chapter 8) do an outstanding job of defining, describing and reviewing components of qualitative research and conduct a comparative analysis of qualitative research with quantitative inquiry. They identify the types of investigations that characterize qualitative research as case study, field study, ethnographic research, naturalistic, phenomenological, interpretive, symbolic, interactionist and descriptive. They further point out four research strategies that relate to qualitative investigation: '1) noninterventionist observation in natural settings; 2) emphasis on interpretation of both emic issues (those of the participants) and etic issues (those of the writer); 3) highly contextual description of people and events; and 4) validation of information through triangulation.'(p. 114). Bresler and Stake go on to give a

perspective on the roots of qualitative research, ethnography and biography of the individuals who are perceived as originators of the movement. In the comparison of qualitative and quantitative research, the authors distinguish the two by depicting quantitative research as making generalizations about diverse conditions and attempts to fit situations into a statistical model. Conversely, they view qualitative research as multidimensional: holistic, empirical, descriptive, interpretive, emphatic with collection of data emerging from immediate validation of observations and interpretations.

Of particular importance in the study is the section on qualitative research in music education. Here the authors give examples of studies that have been conducted in the United Kingdom and the United States and the efforts of the investigators to examine musical activities of children. Both Bresler and Stake acknowledge the impact of technology on music instruction and education and suggest that one of the most effective ways of examining the impact is through case studies. The study concludes with a discussion on methods and criteria for managing qualitative research that include helpful suggestions on data collection, data analysis and criteria for quality research. At the very end of the study, the authors summarize qualitative research with a discussion of its strengths and weaknesses.

This is a very useful study in the field of music education, especially for the novice researcher, because it provides basic information on what constitutes qualitative research, how to conduct research of this type, methods and criteria basic to the inquiry and reasons for and against engaging in this form of investigation.

'Quantitative Analysis' by Edward P. Asmus and Rudolf E. Radocy

Edward Asmus and Rudolf Radocy (Chapter 9) give an excellent detailed analysis of quantitative research as it relates to music. The authors begin the essay with an introduction comprised of the definition of research, an explanation of quantitative methods and the meaning of quantification. Of particular interest is the manner in which the authors relate the resistance of some music educators to engage in quantification with music because of the aesthetic, intangible nature of the medium. However, they argue that music research through quantification is of greater significance in documentation through the use of numbers. Asmus and Radocy continue their discussion by identifying significant components of quantitative research such as measurement, statistical principles, variables, univariate tests – one dependent variable, univariate tests – two or more independent variables, multivariate factorial designs correlation, extensions of correlation, statistical based modelling, multidimensional scaling, non-parametric statistics, graphic data analysis methods and the appropriate time to use specific statistics; a very exhaustive list of components useful for conducting inquiry through the quantitative method. The reader should pay close attention to their discussion on measurement; the source of quantities needed for an accurate explanation on the differences between reliability and validity. Further, it would be an advantage to the reader to acquire an understanding of the diverse methods of analysis consisting of ANOVA (Analysis of Variance), MANOVA (Mulitvariate Analysis of Variance), and MANCOVA (Multivariate Analysis of Variance & Covariance) which are helpful designs for collecting data.

The essay is well written and explains each component on quantitative research in detail. It is extremely valuable in assisting the young professional music educator in understanding and applying basic principles of this method and assisting professionals at the university level in supervising graduate students in qualitative inquiry. Further, it serves as a useful tool in assessing students' musical behaviour in the classroom and evaluation of teacher instruction.

'Measurement and Evaluation in Music' by Edwin E. Gordon

Edwin Gordon (Chapter 10) provides an interesting and thorough discourse on the meaning and difference of measurement and evaluation in music. In this essay from his book, *Learning Sequences in Music*, he focuses on ways of determining the music achievement of students. He firmly believes that measurement and evaluation must be used in combination in order to analyzes objectively students' progression in music from one level to another and improve teacher instruction. Gordon defines measurement as an objective standard and evaluation as a subjective enterprise and he gives several examples of both. Gordon positions himself as an advocate for creating sequential objectives for which tests can be created, either teacher-made or published to measure and evaluate students' music performance. He goes into great detail in discussing teacher-made tests. He believes that the most popular form of these tests is the rating scale because it can be more easily constructed by the teacher in establishing levels of difficulty. Other teacher-made tests discussed in the essay are multiple choice and essay. In his views on published tests, Gordon is actually referring to standardized tests, which infers that the test has an established way to be administered and a standardized means of interpreting the scores accompanied by a percentile ranking. Measurements of standard deviation are also explained with a sample formula given to determine the degree of deviation.

This essay is extremely useful for music teachers at all levels. Over the years, teachers have struggled with devising appropriate measurement and evaluation tools for determining students' growth and development, level of understanding and performance of music. Gordon has provided valuable information on how testing and examination of students' musical behaviour can be accomplished successfully and serve as documentation of their performance when relating such information to parents, administrators and politicians.

'Talking about Music: Interviews with Disabled and Nondisabled Children' by Judith A. Jellison and Patricia J. Flowers

Throughout the twentieth century, but particularly in the 1970s–1980s in the United States, music educators have grappled with the issue of the most effective way of providing quality music and art experiences for the disabled. The issues range from addressing the music needs of the disabled in separate instructional settings to devising a programme of 'mainstreaming' where the disabled and non-disabled students are integrated into regular music classes. This issue was legally addressed in the United States with the passage of the Education for All Handicapped Children Act of 1975 (Public Law 94–142). This act legalized a process called 'normalization', that of making experiences accessible to the disabled that are available to non-disabled students.

In this research study, Jellison and Flowers (Chapter 11) compare the behavioural responses of the disabled and non-disabled students in the areas of preferences, experiences and performance of skills when engaging in music activities in the classroom. It was conducted in 1991 when the concept of integrating disabled students with non-disabled ones was relatively new. The procedure described by Jellison and Flowers involved interviewing 228 students in specific age categories, 3–5 years, 6–8, 9–11 and 12–14. Of the 228 students, seventy-three were identified as disabled and the remainder as non-disabled. Specific questions were formulated that all interviewers asked the students. There were eleven questions. The interviewers were undergraduate students from three major universities in the United States who asked each student a specific number of questions. A few are as follows: What is your favourite song? Can you clap a steady beat? Have you ever played an instrument? The results of the study were very striking in documenting few differences in responses between the disabled and non-disabled students except in the category of verbal responses in which the non-disabled were more vocal. Of particular interest was the issue of socialization. It is common knowledge that most students tend to form groups and cliques comprised of others of their kind. However, the study points out that these barriers can be reduced when the teacher structures groupings that include students from both classifications.

The study is very helpful to music educators who struggle with strategies for teaching music in integrated situations of the disabled and non-disabled. Further, it serves as support for educators who are advocates of music for disabled students as well as others who are considered disenfranchised and different from the so-called 'norm'.

'Demonstration and Recognition of High and Low Contrasts in Teacher Intensity' by Clifford K. Madsen, Jayne M. Standley and Jane W. Cassidy
Music educators who are engaged in teacher preparation of pre-service teachers consistently field questions from student teachers on techniques for acquiring and maintaining the attention of students. Even the most experienced music teachers may encounter this challenge especially in the twenty-first-century classroom where computers and other electronic devices may be common distractions among students. Therefore, the study conducted by Madsen, Standley and Cassidy (Chapter 12) is timely in providing suggestions for keeping the classroom alive with participation of students who pay attention and exhibit interest in making and studying music. The authors believe that in order to prepare teachers for maintaining a high level of attentiveness, it is imperative to identify observable, quantifiable traits that characterize expert teachers in this area with enthusiasm being the main trait. The study identifies eight teacher behaviours of enthusiasm based on the measurement of tools of Mary Lynn Collins, (a reputable researcher in teacher behaviour), that engaged subjects in rating levels of teacher enthusiasm: low; medium; and high. The study sought to document whether high and low contrasts in teacher intensity could be quickly taught and then demonstrated by prospective music education student teachers and whether subjects untrained in the concept of intensity could recognize these contrasts in others. The authors concluded that it was indeed possible to teach intensity to prospective student teachers and documented their findings in the study with evidence provided by high levels of reliability and validity and supplemented with formulas and tables.

The authors believe that since their study supported the connection of high intensity to teacher effectiveness, further study should be conducted in all areas related to the topic including: (1) student attentiveness; (2) subject matter acquisition; (3) the degree of intensity associated with subject matter; (4) various levels of social and peer interaction that contribute to intensity; and (5) the general level of teacher 'on task'. The significance of this research lies in the contribution it makes in developing effective music teachers who are knowledgeable in subject matter and exhibit exceptional qualities of intensity, and enthusiasm. The authors demonstrate that enthusiasm can be taught and show how easily a lack of it can be perceived by students whether consciously or unconsciously. Further, the authors have provided a paradigm for university professors engaged in teacher education to assist in training and producing effective pre-service music teachers. In addition to giving information on what characterises a successful teacher, they document their claims.

'On "American Music for American Children": The Contribution of Charles L. Seeger' by Marie McCarthy
Charles L. Seeger is regarded by some as one of the world's leading musicologists and music educators. He contributed significantly to advancing cultural music and music diversity in the school curricula in the United States and broadening the concept and meaning of American music. One of his most memorable contributions to music education is the essay he presented at an MENC conference in 1942 where he defended the importance of American songs for American Children in the curriculum. In her essay, Marie McCarthy (Chapter 13) gives a historical account of Seeger's contributions to the profession and his legacy to the field of music education. She studies Seeger's essays in depth and determines that they can be viewed on five levels: (1) as a redefinition of school music; (2) as a revelation of the depth and length of Seeger's thoughts and work on the place of music in culture, society and education; (3) as a historical perspective on Seeger's voyage from the classical realm of music of the nineteenth century to a new perspective on music rooted in the culture and society; (4) to separate American music from the European music concept; and (5) as debates that ensued as a result of his pursuit of American music for American children. The author chronicles the life of Charles Seeger by describing his work as a music educator, discussing his investigation of the relationship of music to culture and his efforts in making connections with music, culture and education. Not only did he communicate his views on the place of American music in schools but how it should be taught. He was an advocate for oral transmission which reflected the way music was most often learned and performed in the culture. This essay is important to the field of music education, especially in the United States, because it serves as documentation for the place of culture and music in the curriculum and in the classroom. Further, it corroborates the need to transmit (teach) music from a culture in the manner in which it is experienced, learned, performed and enjoyed among the people. It further documents the 'making America movement' which sought to purge folk music from the schools in favour of Western classical music, a position that Seeger abhorred. The essay portrays him as a revolutionary figure in music education, playing an important role in introducing American music in the schools during the middle of the twentieth century. The essay is also a model of the principal issues to address when conducting historical research on an individual. It is an excellent example of scholarly inquiry into the life of a prominent scholar and lesser known music educator.

Pedagogy and Curriculum in Music Education

'Methodologies in Music Education' by Peter Costanza and Timothy Russell
Of the five areas of music education discussed in this publication, it is pedagogy that forms the core of the profession. An individual may possess the most capable skills in research, exhibit great mental agility as a thinker, devise convincing measurement tools and promote the ideals of inclusion of world and popular music in curricula, but without skill in the application of these domains the work lies dormant. Therefore, pedagogy is vital to the life of the profession. It requires effective application of the aforementioned areas, knowledge and

skill in incorporating appropriate strategies and development of a style of instruction. The authors of the study, Peter Costanza and Timothy Russell (Chapter 14) feel it is necessary to define clearly the processes that constitute pedagogy which will hopefully increase teacher effectiveness. They make a distinction between techniques, methods, curricula and methodologies. Further, they believe it is necessary to do so in order to dispel the notion that they are all the same.

Peter Costanza and Timothy Russell (Chapter 14) define the terms in the following way:

> Technique: a teaching activity or strategy use to achieve an objective
> Method: 'a procedure or process for obtaining an objective ...
> Curriculum: a plan or course of study that describes what is to be taught ...
> Methodology: a body of techniques, methods, and curricula that is based on a philosophical system ... (p. 256)

In the essay, the authors focus on examining selected research on techniques, methods, curriculum and methodologies in: (1) general music education including Dalcroze, Orff, Kodály, Gordon and general music textbook series; (2) choral music; (3) instrumental music, band and strings; and (4) trends in music education methodologies, modelling and initiation, individualized instruction, discovery method and comprehensive musicianship. Their investigation led them to conclude that after reviewing the research of Gordon (1989a); Landis and Carder (1972); Olson (1964); Palmer (1974); Reimer (1989); Siemens (1969); the Dalcroze, Kodály and Orff methods, they all have a significant effect on music learning, but no one method was more effective than the other. In choral music, the authors reviewed the works of Gonzo (1973), Hylton (1983) and Stockton (1983), and reached the conclusion that research in methods and technique were fractional and limited in scope. As it pertains to instrumental music, the authors were neither very complimentary of the results of their findings in this area. While the work of Costanza and Russell is very helpful in presenting a picture of the state of methodologies in music education in the early 1990s, improvements have been made in the research conducted by professionals current in the field for example, Kerschner, Abril, Campbell, Sands, Legette and many others. Further, research investigated by the authors was conducted in the 1980s. Currently, with the emphasis on meeting the needs of individual students, competency based education, establishing measurable standards and inclusion, to name a few, improvements have been made in techniques, methods, curricula design and implementation and methodologies in providing quality music instruction for students. The essay is helpful in giving music educators a historical view on the development of pedagogy in providing ways of improving music offerings in the schools.

'Music for Children and Young People' by David Forrest

The essay by Forrest (Chapter 15) reflects his work in researching the contributions of the Russian composer Dmitri Kabalevsky and reviewing his collection of music entitled *Piano Music for Children*. During his lifetime, Kabalevsky composed over 250 compositions with approximately half of them written for children or including children's material. His compositions were either song collections or solo piano compositions. The essay (Chapter 15) also provides information on the collection of music based on the definition of children's music as described by I.B. Aliev, a Russian writer and supporter of music and the arts for young people. Further, it provides support for the work of Doreen Bridges, a music educator who advocated for the place of the piano in the musical experience of children (p. 267). Children's music in this essay (Chapter 15), as described by Aliev, is regarded as:

> works written to be performed by children; songs and instrumental works written for children's broadcasts, for plays performed in children's theatres, and for children's films; works based on subjects drawn from the life of children but performed by professional musicians, and not specifically designed for an audience of children; and music for educational purposes. (pp. 267–68)

Each category of children's music is well defined and discussed by Forrest with a repertory list of Kabalevsky's works for each.

The essay is important to music education in that it provides a framework for the discussion and determines what constitutes children's music, particularly those characteristics that typify compositions for children. The essay references Kabalevsky's (1972) seminal education text for children: *About the Three Whales and Many Other Things: A Book about Music* in which he articulates his philosophical stand on the place of music in the educational and social development of children.

'Teacher–Artist Partnership in Teaching Cantonese Opera in Hong Kong Schools: Student Transformation' by Bo Wah Leung and Eddie C.K. Leung

The study by Leung and Leung (Chapter 16) examines an approach to teaching that combines instruction by music educators with the assistance of the teaching-artist. For some years the debate has ensued throughout the world, on the value and place of the teaching-artist in a school setting. The debate in teacher education has centred around whether the teaching-artist possesses the necessary pedagogical skills to instruct students in a group setting. This study documents the effectiveness of the teaching-artists, who are experts in Cantonese opera, in motivating Chinese students to learn about a valued historical Chinese form of music and culture. The study examines whether students will become more highly provoked and inspired to learn Cantonese opera through a teacher–artist partnership approach with students in the primary and secondary schools in Hong Kong. The partnership arrangement was created because of the ability of the teaching-artist to provide authentic indigenous music experiences for the students in the hope that they would be motivated to learn about an ancient genre.

Results of the study documented the necessity to begin exposure and instruction at a very early age (as one would for study in any area to build awareness, appreciation and possibly preference) in the opera before self-consciousness about learning an ancient art sets in as it would potentially among older students. The findings displayed a definite difference between the motivation level of the primary and secondary students. The primary students were more receptive of Cantonese opera as part of their music instruction because they were younger and self-consciousness was not an influencing issue. In addition, their interest in learning about Cantonese opera was heightened and they appeared to acquire a value of it. While on the other hand, students at the secondary level exhibited negative behaviour towards learning about and performing the art form.

The study provides sound support for the theory of beginning exposure and instruction in a concept or idea at a very early age, while students find it easier to learn new things, before negative opinions have been formed and prior to students questioning unnecessarily the relevance of a concept to their lives. It further documents the advantage of adopting a pedagogical approach where the educator and teaching-artist can collaborate and form a partnership to provide authentic, quality music instruction for students.

'Musical Connections' by Mary Palmer

This excellent essay builds a case for music in the curriculum and the importance of inclusion of music when teaching other disciplines. Palmer (Chapter 17) views involvement in music as an effective and motivational alternative to students spending an inordinate amount of time at the computer. She contends that music has certain properties that can strengthen students' academic achievement and cites several sources in support of her position including Howard Gardner (1983) who has identified music as the eight intelligences and Hackett and Lindeman (2001) who maintain that music stimulates learning in all subjects and that students who receive arts instruction excel in all subjects. She states that in the elementary school, in particular, music can be approached in a variety of ways, which she refers to as Brain Breaks, Esprit de Corps and Curriculum Enhancement, addressed in detail in the essay. She believes that music is a powerful medium for making life-long connections that should not be left to the music teacher alone in the elementary school. Rather, through the integration of music and dance with other academic subjects, students will excel in the academics and the arts.

This essay is important to the field of Music Education because it documents the need for music in the lives of young children. Music and dance for them are synonymous to life, which are formed early, thus making these critical years for engagement with music and other arts a must. Further, the content of this essay is based on 'real life' experiences that link theory and practice witnessed and researched by the author.

'Arts Education and the Curriculum: Joining the Mainstream' by Scott C. Shuler

'The key to becoming a partner in the new order lies in achieving a curricular status equivalent to that of subjects held sacred by the American public' (Chapter 18, p. 313) is the essence of this essay. The author advances the notion that if art is to advance in importance and respect; it is up to the arts educator to bring this to fruition by promoting and advocating that the arts are as necessary as other subjects. Scott C. Shuler believes that in order to become a partner in 'the new order' (created by the current economic crisis in the world, especially in the United States), arts educators should strive to achieve a curricula status equal to that held dear by the public; in other words, arts educators must change the public perception of music as extra curricula to curricula. Shuler makes a strong case for the arts educator being accountable for the state of the arts in their communities and schools. He suggests that preparation for being advocates begins in teacher education programmes where courses should include skill development in advocacy. He makes an interesting observation on the necessity of arts educators to promote a balance of teaching theory and performance in the curriculum and in their classes. Shuler (Chapter 18) states that,

> Arts educators, however, seem to have developed just such a limited public image. Large ensemble performances, school musicals, and art exhibits are often the only results of arts programs that the public ever sees, thus, many citizens have concluded that the sole purpose of public school arts programs is to train performers. That image must be changed. (pp. 316–17)

This is a thought-provoking essay that should be read by all arts educators. Though published in 1988, it has relevance for today. Shuler is currently president of MENC (The National Association of Music Education).

'Computer-Based Technology and Music Teaching and Learning' by Peter R. Webster
The essay on technology by Webster (Chapter 19) is a very comprehensive look at the future of technology in music education in the twenty-first century. Webster recounts the warnings of educators in previous years about 'jumping on the bandwagon' of computer use and not being so eager to embrace it. However, one of the most respected and insightful music educators of the twentieth century, Paul Lehman, took a different position in his message to music educators as quoted by Webster (Chapter 19),

> The computer revolution in music education won't begin until we rethink what we want education to be. Only then can we clarify our goals and bring them into focus. Only then can we know how to use the computer. Only then can we know what we want in educational software. At the very least we must have software that is genuinely interactive and genuinely individualized. There are hundreds of ways to misuse computers in education and only a few ways to use them properly. (Lehman, 1985, quoted on p. 321)

Webster agrees with Lehman and warns that in order for music educators to take advantage of funds allocated for computer hardware and software, the best information should be acquired on making maximum and effective use of the resources. In taking this position, Webster is in agreement with Shuler about the necessity for music educators to be proactive and responsible for bringing about change in perception and realistic needs of the profession; in essence, we need to know what we are about and how to best achieve it. In the concluding part of the essay, Webster voices his excitement about the growth of resources available on technology and music but warns about the necessity to assist in-service teachers in acquiring this knowledge and applying it to the classroom. He expresses concern for the inability of music teachers to evaluate the uses of technology and reiterates that additional research is needed.

Webster was exactly correct about the implications for use of technology in the music classroom. Today we find Promethean ActivBoard, iPod, Bose Sound dock, iMac, MacBook, iTunes, Finale, Music Maestro, ActivInsprie Electric, programmable piano – Yamaha, Cable in the Classroom (School TV station), Digital camera, Digital camcorder, ActivExpressions, ActivSlate, ActivWand, to name a few. In addition to the valuable content contained in the essay, it is a fine example of how an essay should be written; well organized with clearly defined categories and examples, a comprehensive introduction and summary; and an extensive list of sources. This essay is a useful resource for arts educators.

Assessment and Evaluation in Music Education

'Measuring Musical Aptitude and Ability' by J. David Boyle and Rudolf E. Radocy
In this essay, J. David Boyle and Rudolf E. Radocy (Chapter 20) begin with a definition of aptitude that can be described as capacity or anything that can measure future success in music. He goes further to discuss what may be measured in a musical aptitude test that basically centres on discrimination, primarily aural discrimination. Although interest in creating aptitude tests waned between World War I and II and the late 1960s, Boyle and

Radocy have examined those that exist today and made some recommendations for their use. They are the Seashore Measures of Musical Talent; the Wing Standardized Test of Musical Intelligence; the Bentley Measures of Musical Abilities; Gordon's Music Aptitude Profile; and Primary Measures of Music Audition and Intermediate Measures of Music Audiation. Boyle and Radocy believe that Gordon's Music Aptitude Profile is one of the most comprehensive tests that assist in determining music abilities of students in grades 4 through 12. Boyle and Radocy close their discussion with a reminder to the reader that there is not just one criterion for choosing an aptitude test. The choice is based on what the test giver wants to measure. In addition, aptitude is not based on musical ability alone, but may include other variables, such as intelligence. Boyle and Radocy's essay is particularly profitable to music educators who are expected to document the music ability of their students for parents and administrators. In an age where competition for funding is at its height, record of students' music ability and achievement may provide the music educator with an advantage.

'Teaching Problem Solving in Practice' by James L. Byo

James L. Byo (Chapter 21) addresses the issues of problem-solving by recounting that too many young musicians have not developed the independence to solve problems in their practice when faced with difficulty. He acknowledges that in their practice, musicians may concentrate on building flexibility and endurance, improve and maintain their ability to sight read but do not feel competent when they try to solve problems. Byo (Chapter 21) gives several scenarios where young musicians when faced with a problem while practising on their instrument, either slowed down, stopped, hesitated or played through the piece saying and recounting to themselves that it just does not sound good (p. 365). He suggests that first the teacher should ask, 'What do I want my students to look like as accomplished learners?' (p. 366) and begin developing strategies to assist students in this area. In the narrative, he offers suggestions for achieving this goal through his Work Place Practice Protocol outline, Practices Protocol: Lesson Task and Practice Protocol: Ensemble or Lesson Assignment. These protocols provide a starting and ending point, and sequential steps in between that will address a student's problem. They include, sufficient time devoted by the teacher, to instruct students in problem-solving and a plan for assessing their progress.

Anyone who teaches music whether in a group or privately, can benefit from Byo's approach to assisting students in problem-solving. As music teachers we perpetuate the notion that we want our students to become independent learners and that music is an ideal medium for acquiring this skill. Byo presents the music teacher with the opportunity to do so.

'Assessment's Potential in Music Education' by Richard Colwell

In his essay on assessment (Chapter 22), Richard Colwell reminds us that education and evaluation are two of the most important issues we face He even goes so far as to say that concerns for education are more important than many matters in society including, national defence, foreign policy and immigration to name a few. However, some would argue that in the twenty-first century, the economy appears to be the most important issue worldwide. In the field of education, he identifies standards and accountability as being of paramount importance, resulting from the focus on increased funding for education and the interest of society in providing a quality education for its youth. This essay (Chapter 22) focuses on standards and accountability by documenting research developments 'in assessment in education and in music teaching and learning' (p. 371). It is an extensive account of these subjects and addresses numerous issues pertaining to them. It begins with an overview of issues that may blur discussion on assessment and continues with information on presently published tests, unpublished tests, assessment tools, evaluation, taxonomy of objectives and new devices in assessment that attempt to provide clarity on the issues. Colwell (Chapter 22) continues with a discussion on eight topics of importance to his views on assessment: (1) recently published tests; (2) unpublished measurements; (3) criteria for use of rubrics as an assessment device; (4) programme evaluation; (5) types of validity; (6) educational taxonomies; (7) technology in assessment; and (8) future of assessment (p. 372).

Colwell's essay is of utmost importance to music education because of its thorough examination of the many facets of assessment in music. Further, it provides direction and information necessary for constructing a viable assessment plan. In today's societies, arts educators are being required to document the performance and achievement of their students like never before. Further, in some countries, the success of student learning and performance, as documented on standardized tests, is the determining factor in the future employment of arts (music) educators. Although the essay contains information helpful to teachers, it requires an elevated degree of knowledge on assessment in order to interpret the content and attain maximum benefit from Colwell's writings.

'Measuring Musical Talent' by Robert A. Cutietta

Robert A. Cutietta (Chapter 23) makes a case for the use of aptitude tests in determining a student's promise for becoming musical. However, like Boyle, he advised against using aptitude tests as the only measure of musical ability. He further reminds the reader of the difference between aptitude and talent and cautions against viewing the two as the same. He organizes his discussion around four issues: why test, uses for tests, norms in tests and availability of tests. Cutietta believes that the primary reason for administering aptitude tests is to identify students who possess outstanding musical promise and second to identify those who do not. He supports the use of standardized tests and provides a step by step model for applying the results. In reference to teacher made tests, he considers them time consuming and often difficult to construct. Cutietta (Chapter 23) concludes this essay by providing further advice to the reader about the use and interpretation of tests: 'Take all the information available to you, add some common sense regarding your child, and trust your gut reaction. This combination will produce the best possible results' (p. 408).

This essay can be useful to both the music educator and the parent. It will assist the music educator in immediately identifying students who have exceptional ability in music and planning for instruction and exposure that will assist them in working towards their maximum potential. The essay provides information needed for parents to help them in determining the extent of investment they wish to make in nurturing their child's musical development, or not depending on the collection of information they have at their disposal.

'The Power of the National Standards for Music Education' by Paul R. Lehman

According to Paul R. Lehman (Chapter 24), formulating the National Standards for Arts Education (The Standards) was a somewhat challenging task because of the need to consider the variety of teaching strategies implemented by the large population of music teachers in the United States. Because of this necessity, Lehman makes it clear that the standards are in line with what teachers already do and that there is little need to restructure a curriculum in order to implement them. The Standards are simply a framework for all music teaching. Teachers' responses to the Standards however, have been varied. They have responded either favourably or been unwilling to broaden their perspective on their inclusion. On the other hand music teacher organizations were very positive and proactive on the application of the Standards to curriculum and teaching and offered their assistance in implementation. Lehman believes that solutions to better understanding of the Standards and their application to teaching lie in creating workshops and professional development meetings where information on the Standards could be acquired and teachers could pose questions. In the essay, Lehman (Chapter 24) cites ten benefits for having the standards: (1) benefit students; (2) focus efforts; (3) clarify expectations; (4) bring equity; (5) move music beyond entertainment; (6) give a basis for claiming resources; (7) give a basis for insisting on qualified teachers; (8) give a basis for assessment; (9) give music a place at the curricula table; and (10) provide vision (pp. 412–14).

The Standards are important to the field of music education because they provide direction for organising, sequencing and teaching goals to be accomplished by students and give the profession ammunition for building a case on the importance of music in education.

'The Development and Validation of a Measurement Tool for Assessing Students' Ability to Keep a Steady Beat' by Glenn E. Nierman
In this essay Glenn E. Nierman (Chapter 25) discusses the importance of being able to diagnose a learner's potential ability to master successfully a music skill or concept. He believes that in order for this to occur, attitudes about music aptitude must change as well as beliefs about its construct. He further de-bunks the notion that assessment and evaluation be regarded as tools for punitive purposes nor viewed as the sole bases for deciding who may or may not participate in a music programme. Rather, he supports the notion that aptitude tests should be used as a measurement tool that provides music educators with objective information that can be used to predict and to diagnose better ways of meeting individual learners' needs. Further, he refers to them as important, necessary and a normal part of the learning process, a part of helping teachers and learners solve problems surrounding a particular learning episode and achieve success in music. Nierman equates failure to diagnose a student's capabilities before initiating instruction as analogous to a medical doctor prescribing a remedy for an illness before proper examination of the patient. He targets the ability to keep a steady beat as a basic skill, underlying understanding, performance and successful engagement in music. His interest in the importance of this skill led him to devise a tool for assessing the ability of 167 fifth and sixth graders to keep a steady beat. He constructed an assessment tool that measured the students' success in internalizing the steady pulse for a period of time after it was heard at various tempi. In the final analysis, the test yielded an acceptable reliability coefficient (0.7532) and a suitable construct validity in measuring the students' 'performance'. This suggests that the test would be a useful tool for music educators to determine student aptitude in performing, identifying and articulating a steady beat.

Multicultural and World Music

'Teaching about and through Native American Musics: An Excursion into the Cultural Politics of Music Education' by Bryan Burton and Peter Dunbar-Hall

Bryan Burton and Peter Dunbar-Hall begin the essay (Chapter 26) with a statement by Tsianina Lomawaima, a Muskogee-Creek, Native American of the United States to set forth the cultural political issues in his discussion:

> Educating Native Americans. Those three words encapsulate a 500 year-old battle for power to define what education is – the power to set its goals, define its policies, and enforce its practices – and second, the power to define who native people are and who they are not. European and American colonial governments, operating through denominations of the Christian Church, first defined 'education' for Native Americans as the cleansing, uplifting and thoroughly aggressive and penetrating force that would Christianise, civilise and individualise a heathen, barbaric and tribal world. (Tsianina Lomawaima, 1995, quoted on p. 425)

The issues surround the definition and control of pedagogy, implication of the value of indigenous ways of knowing and post-colonial critique of education as it pertains to teaching multicultural music in the classroom and Native American music in particular. When making reference to post-colonialism, the authors are referring to the omission of ways of thinking that are contrary to the accepted established ones in teaching music which are based on Eurocentric pedagogy with the absence of ways of learning of indigenous peoples. They agree with Mitchell (2002) that education and society are in a cultural war with deep roots in religion, ideology, class differences, ethnicities and gender differences to name a few, which has an effect on music teaching and learning that we classify as multicultural music. In their discussions they denote three practices of music educators who are truly interested in Native American music: (1) greater interest in the inclusion of Native American music in the curriculum on the part of researchers with disregard to strategies for its instruction; (2) discourse on contemporary practices of Native American music with reference to post-colonial thinking; and (3) comments on how investigating Native American music can create a dialogue about post-colonialism in the classroom. Burton and Dunbar-Hall discuss these practices under the headings, Native American Musics in Music Education; Native American Musics: Some Explanatory Notes; and Post-Colonial Applications of Native American Musics in Music Education. They conclude the essay by declaring that there exists a mixture of traditional and contemporary sounds in colonized people that reflects the tension between continuation of the traditional and assimilation of the present. This essay represents issues pertaining to most attempts in teaching multicultural and world music, in particular music of a culture not based in Western traditions. It implies that when teaching multicultural music, music educators should make every effort to acquire knowledge about the culture, teach music from the cultural perspectives; when teaching songs, sing in the vernacular of the culture with appropriate vocalization; teach the meaning of the music; and present the culture in a positive non-stereotypical way. The essay provides 'food for thought' when embarking on the study of multicultural music and preparing for instruction.

'Unsafe Suppositions? Cutting across Cultures on Questions of Music's Transmission' by
Patricia Shehan Campbell
Patricia Shehan Campbell (Chapter 27) provides a well-defined essay on the need to acquire
a pedagogical template by which the transmission, delivery and acquisition (teaching and
learning) of ethnic music transcends cultural boundaries. In the essay, the author presents
formal and informal steps for learning about culture and performing music from diverse
cultures. The issue of cross-cultural music learning is investigated through children's songs:
Balinese gamelan; Bulgarian traditional music; and Filipino Kulinlang. Campbell (Chapter
27) approaches the examination of the music through what she describes as principles of
comparison for transmission. They include:

> the aural-oral techniques of demonstration and imitation; the visual-kinaesthetic network; the
> spectrum of holistic to analytical reception of skills and knowledge; the necessity of eye–hand
> coordination and the perception of gestural patterns for instrumentalists; and the role of the expert or
> more experienced musician. (p. 435)

Campbell (Chapter 27) believes that prior to this discussion however, framing issues should
be considered. She describes them as: '(i) the idiographic [individual, unique] study of
transmission versus an approach that envelops cross cultural comparison and their ... fear
of universal principles, and (ii) the spectrum of formal and informal processes by which
culture is acquired and learned' (p. 436). The framing issues are important because they aid
in the understanding of the transmission of music discussed throughout the essay. The essay
concludes with the suggestion that indeed the comparisons of transmission could well serve as
a template for the transmission of music and guide for acceptable pedagogy. She suggests that
as a result of ethnographic and observational studies music educators may move beyond their
limited view of how cultures make sense of their music, how they transfer it to their young,
how their young safeguard it and how a culture's way of life can be viewed by the way they
transmit their music. She advises the reader to investigate different teaching practices from
those of their teachers and consider the application of a broader template for instruction.
    Campbell advocates an overarching, broad pattern for teaching music cultures that embraces
individual, unique modes of learning and performing.

'Multicultural Music Education in a Pluralistic Society' by Joyce Jordan
In this essay (Chapter 28), Joyce Jordan seems to attribute the rise of multicultural music
education in the United States to the need for addressing the challenges of bilingual/bicultural
education and social awareness in the schools and the communities. She provides an
interesting account on the historical background, dating from 1916 with the creation of music
classes by Satis Coleman at Columbia University who provided opportunities for her students
to construct instruments performed in selected world cultures. However, Jordan believes that
the momentum for the multicultural movement in the United States occurred around 1929
at an international conference in Switzerland, sponsored by the Music Supervisors National
Conference. She continues on her historical journey with a discussion on the passage of
legislation in the 1970s that impacted multicultural education at the elementary and secondary
levels but did little to advance the course in higher education. Jordan moves from the historical
perspective to a search for a philosophical base that includes a discussion on misconceptions
about diversity to establishing a suitable framework on which pedagogical principles can

be established. The essay contains an extensive section on curriculum development in multicultural music education at the elementary and secondary level and in higher education. In this section, she describes studies conducted by music educators throughout the world where student negative responses to learning about indigenous music (including their own) were similar, indicating a need to instruct students about the music of their culture. In the concluding part of the essay, Jordan (Chapter 28) identifies major issues in multicultural music to investigate in future studies. They pertain to improved instruction in multicultural music for pre-service and in-service teachers, efforts of cross-cultural exposure on music perceptions, determining the age of readiness for study of world music, a review of the effectiveness of different approaches to experiencing multicultural music and 'the question of bimusical and multimusical capacity' (p. 456).

   Jordan does an excellent job of presenting an overview of the state of multicultural music education as it existed in the early part of the twentieth century and making implications for further research inquiry for the twenty-first century. This essay is an insightful overview on multicultural music education.

'A Case for Multiculturalism in the General Music Classroom' by Marvelene C. Moore

The essay by Marvelene C. Moore (Chapter 29) addresses practical issues on the inclusion of multicultural music in education, specifically in general music. She believes that all too often, students in the general music classroom are presented with music that purports to be representative of specific cultures when in fact it is often based in Western classical music. Frequently, the music is a version composed in the style of the music culture, but presented as being authentic. In reference to the curriculum, she believes that informed parents should play a major role in determining the degree to which Western music is included in a school's curriculum balanced with music common to that of the community in which the school resides. In Moore's opinion (Chapter 29), when given the opportunity to develop a curriculum, designers must ask and answer the following questions: (1) What is multicultural music education? (2) Why multicultural music education? (3) How can multicultural music be taught? (p. 461). In response to these questions, she gives a broad definition of multicultural music that is international in scope and emphasizes the need to consider ethnic origin, class, religion, age and gender in construction of philosophy and practice. She goes on to relate important music benefits that can be derived from an immersion in music cultures from broadening students' exposure to learning and performing music as it is taught in a culture. Moore (Chapter 29) also cites social and personal gains for example, acquiring a greater understanding of self through study of one's music culture and that of other ethnic groups (p. 462). In response to the question of teaching multicultural music, Moore recommends delivering instruction and providing music experiences that are accompanied by attention to accuracy, integrity, authenticity and other issues pertaining to the ethnic group. She concludes the essay by encouraging music educators, to rid themselves of the melting pot theory and approach the study of each culture as though it was a necessary part of a mosaic.

   Moore's practical approach to the place of multicultural music in the school's general music curriculum is valuable reading for professors engaged in teacher education programmes and for students in methods courses and pre-service training. Her ideas are basic to success in teaching about music cultures and developing curriculum.

'What Prospective Music Teachers Need to Know about Black Music' by Rosita M. Sands
Rosita M. Sands begins the essay (Chapter 30) by providing valuable information on the changing make-up of the population of American schools characterized by diverse cultures and ethnic groups. She comments further on the current composition of students in American schools of the twentieth and twenty-first centuries, due in part to the influx of immigrants to the United States from non-Western countries. Sands (Chapter 30) supports her characterization with a similar observation made by Gollnick and Chinn in the publication, *Multicultural Education in a Pluralistic Society*:

> Students who will make up our future schools will represent much greater diversity than is currently seen ... Children will be inexorably more Asian-American, more Hispanic (but not more Cuban-American), more African-American, and less white. By the end of this century, over 30 percent of the school population will be composed of students of color. (Gollnick and Chinn, 1990, quoted on p. 467)

Sands continues that these changes present implications for curriculum content and pedagogical practices. Her primary interest however, is to provide pertinent information on the place of Black music in the multicultural arena. She approaches the discussion in two extensive parts in the essay labelled, What Teachers Need to Know about Black Music and Sources of Information [on Black music]. The essay concludes with a final pronouncement to music educators that if Black music (or music of any ethnic culture) is included in a school's curriculum or music programme, it must be valued. She proclaims that without this element, Black music will remain in the realm of the underrepresented.

This essay is important because it presents the subject of 'Black music' as an inherently multicultural, yet unified body of music – a perspective that may not be widely acknowledged across the profession of music educators. It expands the subject matter by contending that this body of music represents an international body of music that exists across geographic regions of the world, across multiple cultures, across multiple national and ethnic groups and across musical styles and genres – all of which are connected because they are part of the African Diaspora.

Further, the essay introduces readers to conceptual understandings that are fundamental across this repertoire of music, such as an understanding of Black music genres as representing both a product of distinctive characteristics as well as a process of making music, and the importance of understanding the symbiotic relationship that exists between functions served by the music and characteristics of the music.

Finally, the essay provides some practical information about the pedagogy of this body of music, including general guidelines for teaching and performing the music and recommendations of resources and study opportunities for increasing teachers' and students' knowledge of the music. While the essay's focus is on the education of prospective teachers, the information contained in the essay could certainly be of value to in-service teachers as well.

The History and Development of Multicultural Music Education as Evidenced in the Music Educators Journal, 1967–1992' by Terese M. Volk
Terese M. Volk opens her essay (Chapter 31) with an account of a speech given by Egon Kraus at the 1966 International Society for Music Education (ISME) conference, published in the January 1967 issue of the *Music Educators Journal*. She regards this speech as paramount

to the multicultural movement in its challenge to music educators to embrace and incorporate the music cultures in all areas of the profession in future endeavours. To meet the challenge, Kraus (cited in Chapter 31) outlined eight problems that music educators must solve and asked for: (1) proper regard for foreign musical cultures in music teaching at all educational levels; (2) methodological realization of the music of foreign cultures, past and present; (3) renewal of ear training, rhythmic training, and music theory with a view to inclusion of the music of foreign cultures; (4) reviewing of school music textbooks and study materials (also with regard to prejudice and national and racial resentments; and (5) preparation of pedagogically suitable works on the music of foreign cultures with special attention to authentic sound recordings (p. 482). The purpose of this essay is to chronicle the Music Educators National Conference's (MENC) commitment to meeting Kraus' challenge through its publication, primarily, the *Music Educators Journal* (MEJ). Volk chose the MEJ for two reasons: one, it is the leading journal of the largest music teacher education organization in the United States. Two, the journal is the most popular means of communication between (a) public school teachers and university professors and (b) teachers and administrators and other music education professionals. In addition to essays in the MEJ, the author acquired information from conference programmes, music reports, announcements of MENC advertisements and activities and MENC book reviews. She concludes by highlighting the efforts MENC has made to meet the challenge set forth by Kraus and be at the forefront of promoting and supporting multicultural music in the major publication, conference, pre-conference symposia and supplemental materials.

The essay will benefit music educators in many ways. First, it gives them a perspective on the beginnings of multiculturalism in music education, charts the progress thus far and provides implications for future action. Further, it directs the teacher to resources containing materials that are currently useful for classroom instruction. It also provides direction for researchers who are interested in 'shedding additional light' on the subject of multicultural music education. Lastly, it contains over 100 bibliographic references.

Acknowledgements

The author is grateful for the contributions of colleagues and former students in the collection of materials for the publication. Special thanks are extended to Dr Glenn Nierman, University of Nebraska and former University of Tennessee graduate assistants: Kevin Crowe, Allison Hill, Laura Taliaferro and Ally Tarwarter for assistance in acquisition of hard copies of essays and research studies.

Appreciation is expressed to the Ashgate Publishing Company staff for their guidance and direction in producing the manuscript.

Bibliography

Apfelstadt, H. (1997), 'Applying Leadership Models in Teaching Choral Conductors', *Choral Journal of the American Choral Directors' Association*, **37**, pp. 23–30.

Consortium of National Arts Education Associations (1994), *National Standards for Arts Education: Dance, Music, Theatre, Visual Arts*, Reston, VA: MENC.

Cox, G. and Stevens, R. (eds) (2010), *The Origins and Foundations of Music Education: CrossCultural Historical Studies of Music in Compulsory Schooling*, New York: Continuum International.

Decker, H. and Kirk, C. (1988), *Choral Conducting: Focus on Communication*, Englewood Cliffs, NJ: Prentice Hall.

Durrant, C. (2003), *Choral Conducting: Philosophy and Practice*, New York: Routledge.

Fuelberth, R.J. (2003), 'The Effect of Conducting Gesture on Singers' Perceptions of Inappropriate Vocal Tension: A Pilot Study', *International Journal of Research in Choral Singing*, **1**, pp. 3–12.

Gardner, H. (1983), *Frames of Mind: The Theory of Multiple Intelligences*, New York: Basic Books.

Gollnick, D.M. and Chinn, P.C. (1990), *Multicultural Education in a Pluralistic Society* (3rd edn), Columbus, OH: Merrill.

Gonzo, C. (1973), Research in choral music education, *Bulletin of the Council for Research in Music Education*, 35(2), pp. 1–9.

Gordon, E. (1989a), *Learning sequences in music: Skills, content and patterns. A music learning theory*, Chicago: GIA Publications.

Hackett, P. and Lindeman, C.A. (2001), *The Musical Classroom: Backgrounds, Models, and Skills for Elementary Teaching*, Upper Saddle River, NJ: Prentice Hall.

Hinckley, J. (2000), 'Introduction', in C.K. Madsen (ed.), *Vision 2020: The Housewright Symposium on the Future of Music Education*, Reston, VA: MENC, pp. 1–3.

Hoffer, C.R. (1993), *Introduction to Music Education* (2nd edn), Belmont, CA: Wadsworth Publishing.

Hylton, J. (1983), 'A Survey of Choral Music Education Research: 1972–1981', *Bulletin of the Council for Research in Music Education*, **76**, pp. 1–29.

Kabalevsky, D.B. (1972), *Pro treh kitov i pro mnogoe [About the Three Whales and Many Other Things: A Book about Music]* (2nd edn), Moscow: Detskayar Literatura.

Kraus, E. (1967), 'The Contribution of Music Education to the Understanding of Foreign Cultures, Past and Present', *Music Educators Journal*, **53,** pp. 30–32, 91.

Landis, B. and Carder, P. (1972), *The Eclectic Curriculum in American Music Education: Contributions of Dalcroze, Kodály and Orff*, Reston, VA: Music Educators National Conference.

Lehman, P.R. (1985), *The Class of 2001: Coping with the Computer Bandwagon*, Reston, VA: Music Educators National Conference.

Leonhard, C. and House, R.W. (1972), *Foundations and Principles of Music Education* (2nd edn), New York: McGraw-Hill.

Madison, T. H. (ed.) (1966), *Perspectives in Music Education*, Washington, D.C.: MENC.

Mark, M. (2000), 'MENC: From Tanglewood to the Present', in C.K. Madsen (ed.), *Vision 2020: The Housewright Symposium on the Future of Music Education*, Reston, VA: MENC, pp. 5–22.

Mark, M. and Gary, C.L. (2007), *A History of American Music Education* (3rd edn), Landham, MD: R and L Education.

Mitchell, D. (2000), *Cultural geography: A critical introduction*, Oxford: Blackwell.

Olson, R.G. (1964), 'A Comparison of Two Pedagogical Approaches Adapted to the Acquisition of Melodic Sensitivity in Sixth Grade Children: The Orff Method and the Traditional Approach', unpublished doctoral dissertation, Indiana University, Bloomington.

Palmer, M.H. (1974), 'The Relative Effectiveness of the Richards and Gordon Approaches to Rhythm Reading for Fourth Grade Children', unpublished doctoral dissertation, University of Illinois, Urbana.

Price, H. (1998), *Music Education Research*, Reston, VA: MENC.

Reimer, B. (1970), *A Philosophy of Music Education*, Englewood Cliffs, NJ: Prentice-Hall.

Reimer, B. (1989), *A Philosophy of Music Education* (2nd edn), Englewood Cliffs: Prentice Hall.

Siemens, M.T. (1969), 'A Comparison of Orff and Traditional Instructional Methods in Music', *Journal of Research in Music Education*, **17**, pp. 272–85.

Stockton, J. (1983), 'An Experimental Study of Two Approaches to the Development of Aural Meter Discrimination among Students in a College Introductory Class', unpublished doctoral dissertation, Temple University, Philadelphia.

Tsianina Lomawaima, K. (1995), 'Educating Native Americans', in J. Banks and C. Banks (eds), *Handbook of Research on Multicultural Education*, New York: Macmillan, pp. 331–47

Williams, J. H. (1997), 'The Diffusion of the Modern School', in W.K. Cummings and N. F. McGinn (eds.), *International Handbook of Education and Development: Preparing Schools, Students and the Nations for the Twenty-First Century*, Oxford: Pergamon, pp. 119–36.

Part I
Philosophy

[1]

PRAXIAL PHILOSOPHY AND EDUCATIONAL PRAXIS

Polyvios Androutsos (Ph.D.)
Department of Music Science and Art
Macedonia University
Thessaloniki, Greece

In this article I will discuss some aspects and highlight some strengths and weaknesses of the application of praxial philosophy to the practice of music teaching. Of course one has to remember that philosophy is about values, and it isn't necessarily practical, but in the end one thing that is very essential is how and to what extent any philosophy works or could work in educational praxis.

Although I believe that a universal or even a unique philosophy for a field as complex as music education is probably not realistic, or maybe even not legitimate, or necessary, David Elliott's praxial philosophy represents a significant step forward. The word "praxial" comes from Greek, by which Aristotle meant "critically reflective action in a context". Based upon the praxial views of Aristotle and others who followed him, Elliott's praxial philosophy has brought in focus on the importance of "music making in general and musical performing in particular." Since praxis is truly the essence of "musicing," both in sonic qualities and social aspects, when Elliott's philosophy came out a decade ago it vigorously shook the ground and reminded music educators in a comprehensive and detailed way that teaching music is not the same as teaching about music.

With the term Music the Ancient Greeks for a long time meant the entirety of spiritual and intellectual achievement in every art that was under the protection of the Muses. The term Music as we use it today as an independent art was generalized in the 4th century B.C. (Michaelides, 1982: 217).

In Plato's thinking, music is not simply the organized motion of sounds by humans, but something deeper and versatile. It is the harmonious relationship between three forms of expression of the human existence: *Movement* (expression of the body), *Speech* (expression of thinking) and *Sounds* (expression of emotions). The Ancient Greek Drama was an unbreakable unity of *Speech, Movement* and *Music.* Music education in Ancient Greece included learning an instrument (mostly the lyre, which is like a small harp) in an empirical way close to a teacher (apprenticeship), singing (mostly along with the lyre) and dancing, expressing an education that had as a goal to harmonically mould the soul. The ancient Greek society made sure that music teaching was among the most basic subjects in the education of the youth.

Aristotle in his Politics (1340b20-33 and 1340a13-18) emphasized *active engagement in productive music making.* Productive music making brings students close to achieve progressive development of musicianship and that leads them to enjoyment, self-growth and self-esteem. And this is the most important point I believe in Elliott's philosophy. I think that this praxial philosophy highlights again some very important and well-established questions that our profession still needs to face today.

Because neither music education nor philosophies about it occur in a vacuum, the application of the praxial philosophy (or any other philosophy) to teaching practice faces a variety of obstacles, restraints, and challenges. Some of these challenges, lie in the realms of the ideological, cultural, political, and social, and will be discussed in this article. At a first glance, one might very well argue, for example, that the praxial philosophy probably will not work in most teaching situations given time and other types of constraints. Some of those will be examined and discussed below.

It was so convenient the way it used to be…

The way music was taught and is still taught in many places in the world encourages a practical split between listening-based –in many cases appreciation- general music programs and performance programs. The listening-based general music programs have been very convenient for many people in the school system. People like administrators, principals, policy makers and in many cases even music teachers find satisfaction with the status quo. Teacher-proof and student-proof curricula like the above mentioned, in many ways do not demand a lot in praxis. You can teach music in this way even if you do not have a music room. You do not really need instruments. You basically need only a CD-player and maybe a textbook or your own written material. You can safely evaluate student's achievement in linguistic ways, not having to think about the difficult task of evaluating musicianship. Your subject, "music" is evaluated and is part of the school system without any special demands, and it is similarly taught and evaluated as the other subjects. In this way almost the whole chain of the schooling system is satisfied. Nobody asks for more funds, or bothers for special equipment and the students are under "control" in a safe, conventional way. Principals are especially happy about this harmony and the only time that demand really something special from the music educator is when they ask him to prepare a program for a school celebration. This is when of course things are getting a little bit difficult, because this is a situation when a music educator could demand that the school should buy instruments, or provide a special room for rehearsals, arrange the schedule differently, so students can rehearse and so on. Many times nothing of all this happens, but the music educator finds ways to take students out of their classes to rehearse (making special agreements with the colleagues), gives up the idea of the instruments and orchestra and just puts together a choir to meet the needs of the school's celebration. But how close is the above example to what music teaching should really be? Only in the last case of the choir there is some action based music teaching and learning taking place and again the goal is not what it should be, it is just to meet the needs of the school's celebration. Bringing to light a philosophy, like Elliott's, that shakes the ground and proposes something completely different which is not very convenient for some or many of the links in the schooling chain, it is for sure that would bring many and different kinds of oppositions to it, not to mention the philosophical debates it aroused. And of course this philosophy has to face a lot of challenges.

Time and teacher working conditions constraints

To start with, in quite many countries, in general public schools, music is taught only once or at the most twice per week, which means that the music teacher has only 45 or 90 minutes to meet each class of students. For example in Greek Public Schools where music is an obligatory course, at the primary level in grades 3 and 4 music is taught for two 45 minute periods per week, while in grades 5 and 6 is taught for one 45 minute period per week. Only in some schools that are part of special programmes, grades 1 and 2 have music lessons by a music teacher. Otherwise music is supposed to be taught by the classroom teacher. In the secondary schools (grades 7 – 9), music is taught one 45 minute period per week, by a music teacher.

The first question that comes up is: how can it be possible for a music educator to implement successfully a praxial philosophy or I would even argue whatever philosophy in his/her teaching when time is so limited?

2

Another problem is of course the amount of students that attend the class. In classes with more than 30 students things are getting really difficult. This could partly be solved by dividing each class in smaller groups with the help of the person that is responsible for the schedule in the school.

Also many times music teachers have to work in 2 or 3 different schools to fill in hours in order for their schedule to be considered fulltime, and they have to face 20-25 teaching hours per week. At the secondary level this means at least 20 different classes that the teacher meets only once per week. This situation eventually could lead to burn out. How can this change? These two above examples do not have really anything to do with philosophy, but with the constraints of the schools scheduling and administration. These constraints though, have an impact on the implementation of a philosophy of music education.

Equipment constraints

In most public schools in Greece and maybe elsewhere, there are no special music classrooms. This means that the music teacher has to move from classroom to classroom and carry with him/her the needed equipment (instruments, CD-player, etc.). Many times there are no instruments available. Even though Praxialism does not mean teaching children to perform expertly or in other words to be professional performers, but is about teaching children to experience the profound values of deep musical joy and self-esteem that arises in gradually learning to make music, musical instruments are a prerequisite for this praxial philosophy to function properly.

In this case what can the music teacher do? Of course one "easy" solution is to focus on forming choirs, or even to make instruments out of garbage material. At the same time the music teacher has to fight for the necessary funds to purchase instruments. Many times even if the school directors are not keen on the idea of trying to find funds for that reason, parents associations can be very helpful in this direction.

Curriculum and teaching material constraints

As Runfola and Rutkowski, (1992, 704) successfully put forth the important question back in 1992: *"...a great deal of sophistication is needed in order to design, implement and evaluate effective curricula. This fact poses a dilemma to the profession: Should there be a national curriculum guide for general music developed by curriculum specialists and music education scholars that teachers could adapt to local needs, or should the general music curriculum be developed independently at the local level by teachers? In either case, are teachers being prepared to cope with and select from the diversity of information that is available to them? Is the inability to cope with information overload the reason why so many teachers latch onto an activities and/or techniques driven program?"*

And I would go further, how deep in educational praxis can really philosophers, curriculum specialists and music education scholars go in order to provide some realistic philosophies and programs that work in every day school reality? I believe such questions are still timely today and ask for answers.

By reading Elliott's excellent Chapter 10 in *Music Matters* regarding curriculum, one feels so liberated. On the one hand it is refreshing through the "curriculum as practicum" to be able to break free from the linear and hierarchical Tylerian Rationale that imposes the curriculum on teachers and students (Hanley, B., Montgomery, J., 2002: 116), as well as the structure-of-disciplines approach, but on the other hand can music teachers actually do –without help- what is so well illustrated in this chapter? Maybe some kind of mediators is needed to "filter" the philosophy and make it applicable to the music classroom? Should the curriculum designers undertake that task? Can music teachers do it on their own? (Here we have to bear in mind their working conditions mentioned above). Very important matters that have to do with teacher education play a significant role here.

It has to be noted here that Elliott offers many strategies for teaching throughout the chapters of *Music Matters*. But I think this is not enough for a teacher to be able to implement a praxial view. In practical terms should there not be books published aimed at all music specialists to help them deliver a very practical music curriculum with an increased understanding of children's learning? Some more than "what to do books" that are thoughtful, stimulating and direct in addressing the real questions of how to teach music meaningfully and effectively under the praxial prism?

In Greece we have had an integrated National Curriculum, "fixed" by the Pedagogical Institute of the Ministry of Education since the mid 70s.

Until recently in primary schools, music teaching included exercises in getting to know the elements of music, Orff instrumentation (where instruments are available), singing, basic music theory and listening and in secondary schools, music appreciation, history of music (with listening examples), and some singing. Also there are choral groups and sometimes orchestras in the schools that perform in different occasions and celebrations of the school life.

Of course teachers many times are doing something else than what the curriculum suggests. And that is because until recently there was no real help from the ministry on the curriculum application, in the form of providing proper teaching materials or lifelong teacher education courses, etc. The situation reminds of Regelski's (1999) characteristic reference to this distinction as the all too common gap between the intended and implemented curricula.

Even though the current situation in Greek public schools may seem dissuasive for future implementation of a praxial philosophy, there is a very positive recent change that could lead to it. Since the last months of 2001, there is a new National Music Curriculum in effect that is influenced largely from the British National Curriculum and things have really started changing. With its three basic axes being performing, creating (composing) and appraising, it comes quite close to the praxial philosophy, although it supports greatly a cross-thematic integration. Of course there is a long way to go. The pre-service teachers need to be educated and the in-service teachers need to be re-educated, so that they will be able to successfully implement the new curriculum. For the latter, the Ministry has a plan to re-educate a number of teachers that in their turn will function as multipliers that will undertake the responsibility to re-educate their colleagues. But for the pre-service teacher education the Ministry and the Pedagogical Institute will need to collaborate with the University Music Departments in order to accordingly shape the music teacher education programs. Also the presupposition that was put forth from the designers of the curriculum was that schools will have to acquire music rooms and instruments and also that new textbooks and supplementary material will be created.

I believe directing efforts in a similar plan could work also for implementing the praxial philosophy itself. Could this be manageable? Yes, but the changes should not refer to new cognitive approaches and syllabuses but to an overall different way of thinking and approaching music teaching and learning as for example is proposed in Elliott's philosophy.

After discussing the situation at the general public schools, now it is time to turn to an example of a kind of school that functions with a praxial attitude.

4

In the Greek public special music school programs, performance predominates, in western as well as in Greek traditional instruments. Throughout Greece there are more than 35 public special music schools for grades 7 to 12. The curriculum for these includes performance (with an emphasis on Greek traditional instruments: tampouras, kanonaki, santouri, oud, lute, percussion instruments, and the like), theory, harmony, analysis, form, music history, solfége, counterpoint, Byzantine music, etc. Whatever instrument the student will choose to study, he/she has also to study one of the traditional instruments (most of the time tampouras is the obligatory traditional instrument to study). Although there do exist the known problems when traditional music teaching and learning gets institutionalized, still, the study of the traditional instruments follows the apprenticeship way. Except from the above there is a constant participation of the students in different ensembles, like choirs, orchestras and traditional ensembles that rehearse regularly and hold performances in different occasions. The public special music school programs described above is offered as an example for an implementation of the praxial philosophy, since there are many tenets of this philosophy inbuilt in them.

Evaluation-Assessment constraints

The musical process folio assessment concept that is explained thoroughly in Elliott's *Music Matters* (1995: 282-285) could work, but this is not always the case. For example, a music teacher working in a private school, constructed a performance oriented curriculum, but the administration required that there should be written tests through the year and written exams in the end of the year, in order to give grades. And that is of course a characteristic paradigm of the traditional procedures that require teachers to freeze the teaching learning process to examine student achievement in "stop time" and out of context (Elliott, 1995: 265). How can a music teacher change this situation? How much can he/she intervene and try to change some of the strongest bureaucratic means that are corollaries of schooling? We know very well that conventional ways of evaluation are inappropriate in music education. How can this change?

In certain private schools it might be possible, easier than in the public sector to take away let's say the grades in music, but then, as it has happened in such circumstances, music loses its power as an "academic" subject and students –some times also the colleagues, teachers of the other subjects- do not respect it as a subject that is at least of equal value as the other subjects.

If somehow by a *miracle* music teachers could get away with the above, again there is one more step for success: They should be educated in order to be able to use the musical process folio assessment concept.

Music Teacher Education constraints

Praxial music education is not the current paradigm in many countries but there are many school and community-based music programs in the United States, Canada, the United Kingdom, Scandinavia and elsewhere that exemplify many of the conceptual and curricular tenets of the praxial philosophy (Elliott, 1995:286-287). Even more, many times essential characteristics of this philosophy and its proposed concept of curriculum can be found in the professional practices of many music educators (even though some times these educators are not aware of it, or they cannot explain their ways of teaching in philosophical or psychological terminology). For example, many music educators that use the Dalcroze, Orff, Kodály and Suzuki ap-

5

proaches in their teaching, create a learning environment where reflective music making (as Elliott conceives it) is emphasized.

It's quite easy to apply this philosophy in praxis in countries where a performance-oriented paradigm is already in function. In non-performance-oriented countries, the re-designing of curricula, teaching materials, and music teacher education would be required to implement praxial music education programs.

According to Elliott's line of thinking, teaching kids to gradually learn to sing, play, compose, improvise, listen (and so forth), brings joy, at every step, if teachers know how to teach musically. But this last part of the sentence has a heavy weight. *If teachers know how to teach musically.* It shows one of the directions that the music teacher education programs should put emphasis on.

Teachers most of the time tend to teach as they were taught (Gumm, 2003: 131-132). So in order for teachers to be able to implement something new, say the praxial philosophy in their teaching, they need to become familiar with it and to study it. So, there are two basic prerequisites in order for them to succeed in implementing the praxial philosophy: First, the music teacher education programs need to be re-designed and accommodate the praxial philosophy in their core and second these programs should also aim to improve the musicianship and educatorship of the pre-service teachers. For the in-service teachers one way for them might be to attend lifelong teacher education courses conducted by the University Music Departments or the Ministry of Education mechanisms, and/or to be re-educated by other teachers (multipliers) that have already undergone such an education.

I will definitely agree with Elliott (1992: 12) when he said that *"what is needed are reflective practitioners: teachers with the musicianship and educatorship to think-in-action, know-in-action, and reflect-in-action in relation to the fluid situations of music teaching and learning"*. But we need to educate such teachers!

Towards the future

All this discussion I believe highlights again some very vital, well-established questions that our profession still needs to face today as it used to do in the past.

To start with: Are theory and practice unrelated? Does theory influence practice or does practice generate theory? What about philosophy? Should philosophy guide practice, not the other way around? Is this how it should be? Maybe the teachers' needs and concerns should be heard and give constructive feedback to the proposed philosophies? In one way Elliott himself referred to this matter back in 1997: *"The praxial philosophy will also benefit from the theory-practice transactions that music educators are reflecting on more and more deeply in our professional forums"* (Elliott, 1997:33).

And to continue towards another direction, I will remind us what Jere Humphreys very well pointed out back in 1996 *"Yet, the overriding question remains: Should not the practice of philosophy be an evolutionary process by which people seek insights through systematic philosophical thinking, with no real hope of developing a definitive paradigm?"* and later on *"Neither a single philosophy nor a single work of history, no matter how distinguished, can treat its subject adequately in all respects. Cannot the new, written from a different perspective and viewing the subject through different lenses, stand beside the old, with each contributing in its own unique ways to an understanding of the events and issues under study? Put more simply, must one philosophy or one history replace another?"* (Humphreys, 1996:153). Also there are *"several music educators that have written that a multifaceted music education philosophy might better serve the profession"* (Humphreys, 1996).

Koopman (1998:15-16) shows very well in the end of his article, that music education can benefit largely by taking under consideration and be inspired by the best ideas that originate from both the praxial and the aesthetic views. The above claims are very much true I believe, but in any case the praxial philosophy is step forward, and it is closer to the essence of music and music praxis, than any other philosophy so far. It might not provide all the answers to all the questions, and it might be that it can't either. But even more important than that is the effort to go a step forward, towards a philosophy that better serves the profession.

In that sense Elliott's philosophy is dynamic not static. It is a valuable contribution to the ongoing process of philosophy building in music education. As Stubley (1996: 66) very well put it: *"Music Matters, in this sense, is a beginning, not an end"*.

This is very much true also because Elliott himself supports this process. I value the effort in this direction first of all by publishing in 2005 of the collection of essays titled *Praxial Music Education: Reflections and Dialogues*. Also the establishment of a relevant website is an important step. In his words *"The main reason is that all fields of study must continuously study and critically appraise their foundational beliefs if they are to avoid stagnation or death. Taken together, the combination of PME and this web site is an effort to contribute to critical thinking about the foundations of music education. Also, by opening MM to critical commentaries, my colleagues and I have an important opportunity to clarify our views with and for each other, and for music educators-at-large, and for students of music education who are developing their professional foundations."* (http://www.davidelliottmusic.com/ Intro,p.1).

Music Matters I believe was a landmark. Maybe Elliott's praxial philosophy will become music education's new philosophical paradigm. Everybody knows that there is no such a thing like *the best philosophy,* but I guess this is not the interesting point here. It has already and will affect probably even more music education practice to some extent, as well as it will influence -even more than it has already- future philosophical thinking and writing. But at all events history will show.

In this article I have tried to discuss and point out some difficulties that might entail with the application of praxial philosophy to the educational praxis. As Elliott early pointed out in *Music Matters* (1995: 10) *"[N]o philosophy can be perfectly applicable to all practical situations"*. This is definitely true, but of course it does not mean that one should give up and not try.

Talking from the perspective of the music teacher (I have taught music in primary, secondary schools and also in special schools-for special students) as well as from the perspective of the music teachers educator (which I am doing for several years at the university level), I am mostly concerned on how the implementation of such a philosophy in educational praxis could be successful.

I believe that the praxial philosophy will move forward our profession and in order to see its results in educational praxis we really have to work hard in this direction. As it was illustrated throughout this article, there are many restraints and challenges in this path, but as it was also shown in certain examples mentioned, there are ideas that sometimes offer easy solutions. Other times bigger changes need to take place, like say trying to change some of the negative corollaries of schooling. In any case I believe it's worth the effort, and as Regelski very well put it *"...the praxial tradition has considerable promise for serving as the theoretical or philosophical foundation of a music education that is, in every sense of the word "basic" to general education."* (Regelski, 1998:48).

7

Bibliography

Aristotle, *Politics* (1340b20-33, 1340a13-18), trans. Jonathan Barnes, ed. Stephen Everson (Cambridge: Cambridge University Press, 1988), pp. 192-193.

Aspin, D. N. (1996). Book review: 'Music Matters'. International Journal of Music Education, 27: 51-56.

Elliott, D. J. (2006) Home page http://www.davidelliottmusic.com/ .

Elliott, D. J. (Ed.). (2005). *Praxial Music Education: Reflections and Dialogues.* New York: Oxford University Press.

Elliott, D. J. (1997). "Continuing Matters: Myths, Realities, Rejoinders." Bulletin of the Council for Research in Music Education.

Elliott, D. J. (1997). "Consciousness, Culture and Curriculum." International Journal of Music Education 28 (Spring): 1-15.

Elliott, D. J. (1997). "Putting Matters in Perspective: Reflections on a New Philosophy." Quarterly Journal of Music Teaching and Learning 7 (Spring): 20-35.

Elliott, D. J. (1995). *Music Matters: A New Philosophy of Music Education.* New York: Oxford University Press.

Elliott, D. J. (1995). "Improvisation and Jazz: Implications for Music Teaching and Learning." International Journal of Music Education 26: 3-13.

Elliott, D. J. (1993). "On the Values of Music and Music Education." Philosophy of Music Education Review 1, no. 2 (Fall): 81-93.

Elliott, D. J. (1992). "Rethinking Music Teacher Education." Journal of Music Teacher Education 2, no. 1 (Fall): 6-15.

Gumm, A. (2003). *Music Teaching Style: Moving beyond tradition.* Galesville, MD: Meredith Music Publications.

Hanley, B., Montgomery, J. (2002). Contemporary Curriculum Practices and Their Theoretical Bases. In R. Colwell, C. Richardson, (Eds.), *The New Handbook of Research on Music Teaching and Learning* (pp. 113-143).

Humphreys, J. T. (1996). "Book Review of Music Matters: A New Philosophy of Music Education." Bulletin of Historical Research in Music Education 17 (January): 153-159.

Koopman, C. (1998). "Music Education: Aesthetic or Praxial?" Journal of Aesthetic Education 32, no. 3 (Fall):1-17.

LeBlanc, A. (1996). "Book review of Music Matters: A New Philosophy of Music Education." *Music Educators Journal,* 82, 4: 61-62.

Michaelides, S. (1982). *Encyclopaedia of Ancient Greek Music.* Instructional Institution of the National Bank of Greece. Athens, pp. 216-218.

Regelski, T. A. (1999). Action learning: Curriculum and instruction as and for praxis. In M. McCarthy (Ed.), *Music Education as praxis: Reflecting on music-making as human action.* The 1997 Charles Fowler Colloquium on Innovation in Arts Education, April 18-19, 1997 (pp. 99-120), College Park: University of Maryland.

8

Regelski, T. A. (1998). The Aristotelian Bases of Praxis for Music and Music Education as Praxis. *Philosophy of Music Education Review,* 6, 1: *22-59.*

Reimer, B. (1998). Aims, Concepts, and the Philosopher's Quest: Reflections on Koopman's "Conceptual Study". *Philosophy of Music Education Review,* 6, 1: 60-70.

Reimer, B. (1997). Should there be a universal philosophy of music education? *International Journal of Music Education,* 29: 4-21.

Reimer, B. (1996). David Elliott's 'New' Philosophy of Music Education: Music for Performers Only. *Bulletin of the Council for Research in Music Education* No. 128 (Spring): 59-89.

Runfola, M., Rutkowski, J. (1992). General Music Curriculum. In R. Colwell (Ed.), *Handbook of Research on Music Teaching and Learning* (pp. 697-705). New York: Schirmer Books.

Stubley, E. V. (1996). "Book Review of Music Matters: A New Philosophy of Music Education." *Philosophy of Music Education Review* 4, 1 (Spring): 63-67.

Swanwick, K. (1995). "Book Review of Music Matters: A New Philosophy of Music Education." *British Journal of Music Education,* 12, 3: 287-303.

Westbury, I. (2002). Theory, Research, and the Improvement of Music Education. In R. Colwell, C. Richardson, (Eds.), *The New Handbook of Research on Music Teaching and Learning* (pp. 144-161).

[2]

MUSIC EDUCATION: GIVING CHILDREN A VOICE

Martin Comte

I was extremely touched when asked to give the Jacinth Oliver Address at this conference. I was touched for many reasons, not least because the last time ASME held its national conference in Adelaide, way back in 1986, I was the Society's president, and there is something nice about being back in Adelaide again and once more having a small role to play in another successful conference.

But most of all I was touched because Jacinth Oliver was special to me. It was 14 years ago this month that, as a member of the ASME Executive, she came down from Canberra for a weekend meeting in Melbourne. We all had dinner at my home on the Friday night. The next morning, the person with whom Jacinth was staying telephoned to say that she was ill. My first thought was that this was the result of my cooking the night before! Jacinth did make it to the meeting later that day and mentioned that only that week she had undergone some medical tests, the results of which she would get on the following Monday. Two days later she was given the sad news that she had cancer of the liver. She lived for another 18 months and continued to give life her all.

It was Jacinth who argued so strongly for the need for Advocacy with a capital "A". It was to be the subject of her Ph.D. thesis. Not for her any playing around the edges. We needed to engage in advocacy much more systematically, she argued. We needed to see how others in non-related fields were doing it—not only in music, or in education, but in disparate fields.

It was Jacinth's vision that music educators around the country would become a real force for music, for education, and for children. Sadly, she did not live to test her dream. And sadly, no-one to date has put it in place for her.

It was because of my strong belief in what Jacinth was trying to teach us as a society that I subsequently proposed to our National Council that there should be a Jacinth Oliver Address at every national conference (a) in memory of Jacinth, and (b) in an attempt to further her cause of Advocacy. I don't profess to understand the realm of Advocacy as Jacinth did. But part of her passion for Advocacy and what we might achieve if we engaged in it much more effectively influenced me greatly.

In entitling this address *Giving Children a Voice* I do not intend to limit myself to an argument that *merely* stresses the importance of children singing. The concept of giving children a voice is much broader than this.

Essentially I would like to address what I see as three of many imperatives facing music education in the 21st century:

- The imperative of developing an Australian theory of music education.
- The imperative of engaging in advocacy more strategically.
- The imperative of confronting the insidious aspects of technology whilst at the same time acknowledging that we are living in an increasingly technological age.

Each of these imperatives requires, I believe, a *paradigm shift* on the part of Australian music educators. I shall argue that unless we make this shift and satisfactorily deal with these imperatives, children will lose their voice their voice for music.

I believe today that if we as music educators don't begin advocating to an extent that has not been done in the past, then those who would come after us will not be talking about music education later this century. We are at a crisis point. And I say this notwithstanding the excellent work that is being done in pockets of schools and by particular individuals around our country.

I read recently that by the middle of this century we will have to negotiate with our computers! Can you believe it! For me this is in the realm of fantasy–but so much of what we are now experiencing in the electronic age, the "e" age, was also once fantasy for me. I thought I had it made when my college provided me with an IBM golf ball typewriter in 1975. I couldn't imagine anything surpassing this in technology and innovation! These typewriters were even available in designer colours!

I often ponder who the real music educators are of today's children. I especially ponder it when I am reminded of the paucity of provision for music education in primary and secondary schools around the country. Certainly, it cannot be said that our schools *exclusively* provide children of today with their music education. Nor can it even be said that schools are the *chief* providers. I acknowledge that schools are generally regarded as having the chief *responsibility* for music education throughout a child's schooling. But *responsibility* is one thing, and *provision*–even *basic provision*–is quite another.

Alas, it is the Media that provide the majority of Australian children with their music education. At best, schools assist in the process. So poor is our track record in providing a sequential music program for children from Prep to 10, that if music education were to be abolished in the schools in which it is currently offered, the percentage of our nation's children who would grow up any the *less* musically educated would be insignificant!

I have no doubt that some of you would challenge this statement. But the truth is that the overwhelming majority of our children do not even receive a sequential music program throughout all of their *primary* school years, let alone the *secondary* years. By way of compensation, many schools enable children to experience a one-off performance each year. But this, even in the wildest flight of fantasy, cannot in any way be accepted as a *substitute* for a sustained, sequential, and ongoing music program. To point out the ridiculous, no school would regard a one-hour science demonstration or the viewing of a televised science documentary as a substitute for a school science program. But where music education is concerned, it is not uncommon for a one-off performance to be the main musical experience that children have in a year. I've met administrators and teachers whose attitude has been, "They've seen the performance. That's it for music education this year." In saying this let me stress that I am not decrying the importance of children experiencing such performances or, for that matter, the musical standard of such performances. In themselves they are excellent. But no one-off performance–not even a two-off performance–can be a satisfactory substitute for an ongoing education in music over 40 weeks.

But to return to the Media: in suggesting that the Media are the chief providers of music education, I am aware that many of you would question whether one could call this *music education*. Well, it seems to me that despite our protestations it is through the media that children are educated musically, regardless of whether we would want to question the quality of the music presented and listened to. The truth is, from birth children are responding to music that is principally provided by the media. The question is what should we as music educators be doing about it.

In a sense, what we do in schools is peripheral to the music education of the masses. It could be argued Kylie or Eminem, have more influence on young people than music educators and school music programs.

If we are to believe the report, *Australians and the Arts,* the so-called Saatchi & Saatchi Report, published in 2000 by the Australia Council, "There is a strong relationship", it says, "between the level of involvement people have in the arts when they are growing up and the value they place on the arts later in life" (p. 90). Consider this with another of the report's findings, namely: "The two types of involvement that appear to be most strongly linked to valuing the arts are encouragement from parents . . . and being involved in things outside of school" (p. 90). Surely this must make us question the value, or at least the efficacy, of school programs in the arts. To be fair, the report does add that "there appears to be a weaker [but note: weaker] relationship between whether a child enjoys the way the arts are taught at school and their eventual attitudes towards the arts" (p. 90). In other words, the importance of schools in relation to children valuing the arts is a weak third, *after* parental encouragement and outside influences.

I do not intend here to provide an argument for school music education. Let me say, simply, that it is certain that we do need an articulated theory of music education for Australian students; a theory that can stand up to robust interrogation. This is my first imperative. At this stage we do not have such a robust theory. What we have are many theories, some half-baked, and many philosophies, some of which contradict others: but we don't have a rigorous theory of music education that is applicable to Australian children today–children who will be alive well into this century.

In saying this I'm conscious that there is a sense in which, when we speak of our global civilization, one must ask whether we shouldn't be thinking of a global theory of music education as distinct from a nationalistic, Australian one, but one which, at the same time acknowledges our indigenous musical culture. I firmly believe that if we go global in such an endeavour we will only be contributing to the ever-increasing dehumanization of society. But of course this is not to say that an Australian theory of music education must not be developed within the context of our global and multicultural existence. There is, I find, a delightful irony in the tendency for cultures and societies that are forced to live closer and closer together to become more and more conscious of their mutual differences. It is important that *we* acknowledge and celebrate what is unique to *us* and what makes *us*, as Australians, *different*. This in turn must be reflected in our theory of music education. I was interested to read in the Saatchi & Saatchi Report that 68% of respondents agreed that 'It is important that the arts reflect who we are as Australians' (p. 88).

What, then, might an Australian theory of music education look like?

Firstly it must contain our belief statements about the nature of children. Then it must concern itself with the nature of learning and teaching, and notions of schooling and society. It must address issues concerning assessment and evaluation. Of course it must acknowledge the place of technology and the "e" society. It must consider what it means to be Australian. And, within the confines of being an Australian theory, it must be multinational and multicultural, radiating the best qualities of the collective heritage of two or three thousand years from East and West, as well as our own indigenous heritage And it must, to some extent, crystal-ball gaze as to where we might be heading in the future. Of course, there will be many more considerations, and in the process it will be essential for us as music educators to explore new ways of examining our beliefs that will allow us to move forward in order to engage children at a deeper level, to engage their whole being, and perhaps save civilization from what some see as its own destructive nemesis.

In developing an Australian theory of music education, one set in a global context, we should not restrict ourselves to the realm of the probable: it is the realm of the *improbable* that must exercise our minds–something which scholars in diverse fields now recognise. The impossible has already become possible in all realms of thought and action!

I thus look forward to us examining, as music educators, the discrepancy between the possibilities (the dreams) and the reality of our experience. But why, in the past, have we always experienced problems in this endeavour? There are many reasons, but they all have one thing in common: the belief that the task is purely administrative, or purely systemic, and that all we need to do is come up with ingenious structures or new institutions. We behave as though we need do no more that *discuss* exhaustively or more precisely–*argue* exhaustively or more precisely–key issues, without ever attempting to question our *motives* as music educators. As a consequence the values that we might have wanted to be secured by systemic changes get *lost* in the tangle of debates over those changes. In other words, what was to have been no more than a means to an end becomes the central topic of discussion. And this weakens our very capacity to agree and the means becomes the end, however inconclusive and temporary.

What our theory of music education should avoid doing is what so many schools and systems persist in doing. And that is base their programs on the theories or practices of Orff or Kodály. Isn't it ludicrous: this is the equivalent of teaching science as if Galileo and Copernicus were still the most important figures!

It saddens me that some people with the best of intentions have never got past the "happy clappy" syndrome. A bit like a Southern Evangelical Revival meeting. Many years ago when I was living in North America I remember listening on the radio to a religious program late one night and hearing a young person say "I'm so happy I've found Jesus that I could beat Christ out of this drum." I've seen a lot of music practitioners who have the same evangelical zeal. But after they've beaten the drum not much else happens. Except that they beat it again the next day, and even harder. At the same time, parenthetically, I must confess to finding something enticing in the notion of imbuing children with a feeling of 'happiness' such that they would want to beat their individual drums with such fervour. But music education is more than just beating drums, be they literal or metaphoric drums.

Of course, music education has gone through many stages in the last 50, even 100 years. Creativity has been big for a long time now. "Get children to compose" has been the catch-phrase. "Even get them to improvise." In itself this is a praiseworthy endeavour. But sadly, in the process, many music teachers have failed to make the distinction between "anything goes" or "anything is good enough" and the need for musical and aesthetic discrimination. And so often I have been disappointed to see teachers with such honourable intentions not knowing where to go after the initial experience. Sadly, it has become an issue of "more of the same", and not a case of sequential development leading children to a higher stage of understanding, valuing and skill acquisition.

One could write an interesting exposé of music educators. In addition to the happy clappies, there are those who emphasise the *passion* of music. There are those who emphasise the facts. There are those who believe that a study of theory is the best path to musical understanding. There are the smorgasbord music educators who believe in a bit of this and a bit of that and hope that it will add up to a balanced musical meal–and heck, even if it doesn't, at least we've had a fun time! And, of course, there are others.

Sometimes, to the outsider at least, prevailing methodologies and allegiances must seem little more than a cauldron of seething rivalries. Some might say a battlefield of ideologies! And so often, I find, these rivalries are held in check only by fragile alliances.

Having said that we need a robust theory of music education, the next challenge is what do we do with it?

But before I discuss this it seems to me that in addition to a Theory of Music education we might do well to have a Creed also. A sort of Ten Commandments of Music Education. I'm not going to seriously suggest any here. But knowing that I was coming to the City of Churches, I did, in an idle moment, play around with the Ten Commandments, the Biblical ones. Let me indulge myself in a bit of whimsy:

1. "You shall not have strange gods before me."
   Translation: Let's stop thinking that the answers to the problems besetting music education today will be found in outdated and outmoded methodologies. Fix your sights on the music.

2. "You shall not take the name of the Lord God in vain."
   Translation: Music educators must stop arguing as if a child's success in life depends principally on Music. It doesn't! But it would be a less fulfilling life if music were not there.

3. "Remember to keep holy the Lord's Day."
   Translation: Let's not forget that we also need to recharge our own batteries! We owe it to ourselves and our students to indulge ourselves in music. We should go to concerts more frequently! And we should practise our art more.

4. "Honour your mother and father."

Translation: Don't forget where our discipline comes from and how it fits into the bigger picture.

5. "You shall not kill."
   Translation: Don't kill kids learning and enjoyment of music just so that we can push our own obsessional wheelbarrow regardless of the result.

6. "You shall not commit Adultery."
   Translation: Music educators must stop getting into bed with every fad that comes along.

7. "You shall not steal."
   Translation: Music educators must stop pinching ideas relevant to other disciplines just so that they can be seen to compete with the other buggers by using their language. We too have our own language. And it's unique.

8. "You shall not bear false witness against a neighbour."
   Translation: We don't have to shoot our colleagues in the other arts in order to push our own barrow. Let's make them real allies.

9. "You shall not covet your neighbour's wife [or husband]."
   Translation: Let's stop thinking that all of the other learning areas have it better than us. Let's start looking into ourselves and seek consensus on what we have to offer.

10. "You shall not covet your neighbour's goods."
    Translation: Don't covert the dance educators or their success. Learn from them such that you have equal success. Support them. Advocate with them. And the same goes for drama and visual arts educators.

Now let's move on to what we must do once we have a robust theory of music education.

We must, as Jacinth Oliver was stressing 15 years ago, engage in advocacy of a new kind. And this is my second imperative. Jacinth wasn't referring to a "hit and miss" approach. There are many organisations outside the educational arena that could teach us about advocacy. We are, sadly, babes in the woods, even compared to some of the other disciplines or key learning areas, when it comes to advocacy.

We have tried just about everything in our attempts at advocacy. To be sure, we have enlisted the 'support' of every arts theorist who has come along. And we've also quoted a great deal of research (some of it of dubious value).

My belief is that unless we can show that music is part of our psyche as human beings, we won't get anywhere in the long term. Unless we can show that music is integral to our nature, is essential in defining what we are as human beings, then our quest is doomed. We might as well give up now.

But in addition, in advocating for music education, we also need to take a societal stance and argue the integral importance of music not only to our proper functioning as human beings in a society that is increasingly experiencing dehumanizing forces, but we must also argue the *vital* role of music in enabling society itself to function effectively, not only now, but into the future. It's a mammoth task. But it's a task worth undertaking if, like me, you are committed to the essential role of music for us as individuals and for our society.

But so far I've only referred to the 'content' aspect of advocacy: what it is that we need to argue. There are also other important issues: who do we say it to? And how? And in advocating our cause we need to identify allies who might assist us. And in doing this we must be united in the values that we want to hold on to–values that transcend the immediate and pragmatic needs of politicians and bureaucrats and even, dare I say it, the pragmatic needs of some music educators themselves.

When it comes to advocacy, even today music educators tend to look for *incremental* success in an age when incremental success is not valued, it has little currency and, some would argue, it has no future! As long as we only look for incremental success we will get nowhere. For there are those out there who do not even recognise incremental success. Maybe we have waited too patiently for something to happen. And maybe, when we have witnessed small advances (like, perhaps, Australia's National *Statements* and *Profiles* of the early 1990s) this has reinforced our patience. But I contend that the rate of change overall in our society is way ahead of the rate of change in music education, in arts education; the rate of societal change is way ahead of the rate of *provision* of music education nationally. And what is more, the gap is widening. Let us not fool ourselves that this is not so, despite the fact that we have the Australian *Statements* and *Profiles* and the curricula that have emerged from them, and despite the small pockets of success that we can all quote.

Some of you may want to jump in and argue that having music included in the so called 'national curriculum' was a *major* step forward. But has this really resulted in a change in the scope, nature, quality and provision of music programs in Australian schools? I doubt it. And certainly I have seen no research to convince me otherwise. The truth is, music education in the schools of our nation is not in a healthy state. The Saatchi & Saatchi Report indicates that 86% of those surveyed would feel more positive about the arts if there were 'better education and opportunities for kids in the arts' (p. 86). But, the report adds, "many Australians do not see or feel how the arts can be relevant in their lives and they feel that the arts are somehow removed from their live experience" (p. 20). And even more telling, as I have already noted, the report states: "There is also a strong relationship between a person receiving parental encouragement when they were young and eventually placing a high value on the arts. **This appears to exceed the influence of formal school education alone**" (my bold) (p. 21). If this is so, then how important it is that we educate in our schools *future* parents who will pass on a love of the arts to their children. Even at the beginning of the 21st century the report found that "Many children feel that peer pressures at school tend to cast artistic and creative achievements as 'uncool' or 'daggy' compared with sporting achievement (which can turn students into instant heroes)" (p. 23). Wouldn't it be wonderful if Ian Thorpe would go on television and say that the most valuable part of his schooling was music education!

Is there any persuasive evidence to suggest that, in relation to the size of the population, music programs–or a lack of them–in the 1920s, '30s and '40s–produced people who valued music less than young people of today? I doubt it! Is the concert/opera audience today any greater per head of population than it was 50, 60 or 70 years ago? I doubt it! The concert-going audience might have increased, but not at the exponential rate of population growth. The Saatchi & Saatchi Report notes that "many Australians do not feel welcome to enjoy the arts" and, further, "There is a perceived lack of relevant information and education about the arts" (p. 18). Almost three-quarters, 74%, of respondents indicated that they "would feel more positive about the arts by 'being able to understand the arts better'" (p. 86). This indicates, suggests the report, that "there is significant interest in learning about the arts outside of school" (p. 86). Only half of the respondents, 51%, agree that "the arts are an important part of my lifestyle" (p. 87). Only half! If we are to address these issues we need to advocate for music education like we have never advocated before.

The truth is, music education in schools is often a "hit and miss affair"–and has been so for a long time. Some, indeed, would say that it has *always* been thus. Ask a 20 year-old what they think of the music education they received in school. Ask the same of a 30 year-old. And a 40 year-old. A 50 year-old . . .

In practice, music education has been one of the most piecemeal aspects of the curriculum for a very long time. The truth is, we have grounds for questioning whether we've come very far in music education in over a century of State education. Strong words, I know.

Go around the country. Observe the band rotundas–in your town, in your suburb. What do they signify? Community involvement in music–both as performers and audience! Has this been replaced by school music? No! A resounding 'No'! But, sadly, these edifices to music-making in the community can no longer be equated with active music-making. These days they're generally used for anything but music making. This should be seen in the context of the findings of the so-called Nugent Report, *Securing Our Future* (1999), which stressed that "Encouraging a broad cross-section of attendees at major performing arts events is *critical* to the future success of the major performing arts" (p. 6). The report adds:

> More specifically, attendance should be encouraged from individuals:
> - **with diverse income backgrounds.** The major performing arts sector needs to shed its 'silver-tail' image and ensure attendance by the less affluent.
> - **with diverse education backgrounds.** The profile of attendees needs to be broadened to include more individuals who do not have a tertiary education.
> - **with diverse ethnic backgrounds.** Ways of engaging with, and encouraging the participation of individuals, regardless of their ethnic origins, need to be explored.
> - **from diverse age groups.** Young people, parents with children, as well as older people who are already strong supporters should be encouraged to participate; and
> - **of both genders.** Greater participation from men should be encouraged, while maintaining the support of women. (p. 6)

I ask again: are we doing anything better today than we were 100 years ago? I'm not sure. Convince me! More importantly, convince the decision-makers of the benefits of an education in music for children and for our society. We must convince those whose support we need. And in this regard, if we are to believe the Saatchi & Saatchi Report, we have the so-called silent majority, the general public, on our side, for it was reported that "The vast majority also agreed that 'the arts should be an important part of the education of every Australian kid" (p. 23).

In criticising the *status quo,* I'm very conscious that *we* are attending this conference because *we* are committed to music education. But sadly, overall, we represent an extremely small percentage of those entrusted to provide music education to Australian children. It is a pity, I believe, that ASME itself represents a similarly small percentage of those entrusted to provide music education to Australian children.

I often hear claims from different States or Territories that they are doing it better than the rest of Australia. Yet I've seen nothing that convinces me. Sometimes what is being said is little more than that the structures are there. And even where programs are being implemented, I sometimes question the relevance of them for today.

Even legislating for music education won't guarantee that we'll have any more success. There is already a sense in which it is legislated that children will receive a sequential education in music–or at least in the arts. But in practice it doesn't seem to have changed things. And, further, just as we can't legislate for happiness, we cannot legislate to ensure that children will be turned on to music–at least not the music that we traditionally have offered. In saying this I acknowledge all of the wonderful exceptions, including the excellent youth choirs and orchestras. But the number of children involved in them represents an extremely small percentage of Australian children.

Let us not forget that in advocating music education our most important allies are children themselves. We all have treasured statements from children regarding the joy they have experienced in music. Equally do we have treasured memories of particular situations in which children, to use one of *my* favourite statements from a child, "got inside the music."

For this reason I love the 1996 publication by the Music Educators National Conference in the USA, entitled *Kid's Voices.* It's a wonderful assemblage of *positive* comments by children. Here are just some of them, the voices of children from kindergarten to secondary school (and excuse me for indulging myself):

> When I sing, my heart goes wild. (p. 1)

> Sometimes music just picks you up off your feet and makes you dance. (p. 1)

> Some music can make a person want to jump out of their skin, while some music can make you want to rock yourself to sleep. (p. 1)

> Music has a power that can make you go places you never heard of. (p. 1)

> With music, you can make someone go from happy to sad in a split second. (p. 1)

> When I play my instrument, happiness goes through me. (p. 2)

I love to sing and make up songs everywhere I go. It makes my heart tingle. (p. 4)

Music makes me feel good inside. It makes me change from the inside out. (p. 4)

I like music because it makes me and my dog feel good about ourselves. My dog and I like to dance with the beat of the music. (p. 9)

Some things you can't have for a lifetime, but music you can have in your heart everywhere you go and forever. (p. 11)

I like music because it is something positive. There are not many positive things in the world, but I'm good at one of them. (p. 22)

If there wasn't any music on earth, do you know what I would do? I would get our 400 tractor, turn it on, and grab the gas level, and push it up and down and that is how I would make music if there wasn't any on the earth. (p. 29)

If music were taken away from me, it would be like someone taking away my colour, my feelings, my light. (p. 29)

Without music, people wouldn't dance. . . . Everybody would be in a bad mood. (p. 31)

What I like best about music is that you can make music just by using your mouth in a special way. (p. 32)

Music makes me feel like I can touch myself inside. I sing while I skateboard. (p. 38)

Music makes me want to walk on my hands. (p. 38)

I like having music in school, but I think you have to have the right music teacher to like it. (p. 42)

I like music because you can tell people what you think without talking. (p. 58)

Well, there are many more. But what a powerful tool for advocacy. Let the decision-makers argue against these statements—the very powerful voices of children.

The problem, as I've already suggested, is that we do not provide music education to the masses. Far from it. But this *must* be a major goal when we advocate music education.

I realise at the same time that there will always be some children who will choose music of their own volition. But they will forever be on the fringe. We as music educators must ensure that we advocate for inclusive, and not exclusive music education—music education that will be of universal benefit for all Australian children. I'm concerned not only with the students who haven't succeeded in our terms, but, even more so, with the large majority who have not even been given the opportunity to have failed. There are countless children who have not had the opportunity to reject school music because it has not been offered to them on an ongoing sequential basis. I am not interested, ultimately, in the education of the few if this must entail the exclusion of the many. But this is not to deny our obligation to the musically gifted and talented.

This brings me back again to the title of my talk: *Giving Children a Voice*. At best, we're only giving some children–relatively few children–a voice. Part of the reason is that we've put most of the effort into the wrong end of schooling. Twenty-five years ago I wrote a chapter for a book in which I argued that the way we approach music education in this country is 'arsyversy'. The word 'arsyversy' dates back to 1539 and means "back to front" or "upside down". Most of the specialists are in the secondary schools. I contend that they should be in the primary schools and kindergartens. This would be a much better way to go if we only have limited resources. Indeed, the report, *An Agenda for the Knowledge Nation* (2001), by the Australian Labor Party under the chairmanship of The Honourable Barry Jones, acknowledges that "A growing body of literature on early childhood development indicates that what happens in the first years of a child's life can strongly influence that child's performance at school . . . Investing in early learning . . . can therefore be one of the best investments we can make in improving social equity and raising our nation's future knowledge capacity" (p. 12).

If we are to give children a voice, we must accept that any theory or philosophy of music education that was developed in the 1960s, '70s, '80s and, dare I say it, even the '90s, will no longer be completely relevant for children today. Who, back in the '60s, '70s and '80s could have envisaged the impact that computer technology would have on our lives? Increasingly will we be living in the "e" age.

Schooling is going to change radically in the next 20 years. More and more children will be living in a telecommuting society: there will not be the need to leave home to go to an institutional building in order to be educated. We're already seeing it at the university level where courses are delivered on-line. Enroll in Australia but stay in Asia! Even some schools are experimenting with it. Indeed in *An Agenda for the Knowledge Nation* (2001), it is recommended that "Australia must aim to become a world leader in online education at all levels within the next few years" (p. 10). The ultimate implications of this for children getting together to make music are horrifying. I am delighted by the way that music gets a guernsey in the same report when it is recommended that the Commonwealth and the States should overhaul and modernize Australia's schools by among other things, "providing children, from Kindergarten through to Year 12 with a variety of experiences, encouraging a spirit of curiosity, excitement and their capacity for conceptual thinking to make linkages, form judgments, and to feel a sense of empowerment in a variety of disciplines, including language, music, art, sport, mathematics and communications" (p. 11). It is interesting that no mention is made of dance or drama.

Computers, and before them television, have affected our children's voices. The anthropologist Helena Norberg-Hodge undertook a study of people in Ladakh, a trans-Himalayan region of Kashmir. She was studying these people when radio and television came to their villages. Before radio, she said, "there was lots of dancing, singing, and theatre. People of all ages joined in. . . . Everyone knew how to sing, to act, to play music" (quoted in Locke, 1998, p. 147). Norberg-Hodge observed that when the media arrived, people became less inclined to sing their own songs and tell their own stories.

Instead, they sat and listened to what they saw as the far *better* singers and storytellers in the little box. She concluded that the idealised stars that we now see on TV "make people feel inferior and passive, and the here and now pales in comparison with the colourful excitement of faraway places" (quoted in Locke, 1998, p. 148). Does it sound familiar?

There is a sense, it seems to me, in which radio, television, and computers, have made talking a spectator sport. And similarly, singing and the making of music have become spectator sports. It's possible that we music educators are just too late in even *contemplating* addressing the situation. Passivity on the part of children is on the increase. Less and less are children interacting with others. And less and less, I suggest, are children singing.

Of course, by modern technostandards, we must admit that talking is inefficient compared to the use of e-mail and even text messaging on mobile phones. But so is maintaining a state symphony orchestra or a national opera company inefficient. How much longer will it be before the technocrats so influence our society that governments will find it political suicide to maintain such cultural organisations? And in saying this I am not suggesting that we abandon e-mail. It is now an intimate part of our technoculture and will become increasingly so. But I nonetheless reserve the right to decry the fact that it is interfering with oral discourse; it is interfering with face-to-face interaction. And the less children engage in oral discourse, the less they will want to sing. In fact, the less they will see a *use* for singing.

Nobody on the Internet knows your voice! And conceivably, increasingly we will not even care about someone's voice. Another horrifying thought! The digital voice is already commonplace.

Already children today represent a phenomenon that none of *us* experienced in our childhood. Increasingly young people are communicating through chat rooms–another "e" issue! No longer can they see and hear their communicants. Writing recently, John Locke, the linguist (not the philosopher), says:

> We . . . trade thoughts on a daily basis with people we do not know and will never meet. The social feedback mechanisms that were handed down by our evolutionary ancestors–systems that were designed and carefully tuned by hundreds of millennia of face-to-face interaction–are rarely used nowadays, and there is a potential for miscommunication and mistrust as never before in human history. (Locke, 1998, p.18)

Read any daily newspaper and you will even see advertisements for sex on-line. The mind boggles. I haven't worked out yet what the body does!

Locke (1998) adds: "Intimate talking, the social call of humans, is on the endangered behaviors list" (p. 19). Of course we music educators here today in Elder Hall know that, there are, thankfully, still lots of people "who long not for a 'conversation' over e-mail, but a vocal chat, complete with eye movements and gestures and the possibility that either party could touch or embrace . . . the other" (p. 19).

And so we have yet another challenge: how to harness new technologies for our own ends. And this is my third imperative.

Children today–but not just children–are increasingly suffering the symptoms of what Locke (1998) calls "a kind of functional 'de-voicing,' brought on by an insufficient diet of intimate talking" (p. 19). It's with us everywhere. As you know, it now costs us more to deal with a human being in the bank than it does to deal with a machine. We experience it also when we try to pay an account over the telephone and have to deal with a digital voice. Try speaking to a real live person and you will be lucky–and you will pay the price by having to wait for an inordinate amount of time. Because of the "e" age we are witnessing a pernicious kind of *social* de-voicing that has terrifying implications for music education.

Children today are losing their personal voices. Even some adults are losing their personal voices. Our voice is becoming a rare thing! We were even discouraged from using it at the conference dinner on Sunday night when the music was so loud that conversation was impeded. Because of new technologies, our children are becoming socially and vocally mute. As a society we can't afford for them to become musically mute.

I was recently travelling on a Melbourne tram–a 10 minute ride from the city to my home and I took down the following conversation by two very charming teenagers: "How was your day?" "Cool" "Right, right, right" "Yeah, right." "Yeah, Cool." "Got your wheels yet?" "Yeah, yeah, yeah." "Cool." "Yeah." "Yeah, yeah, yeah." "Geez." "Yeah." I may be wrong, but it seems to me that even the most banal of music is richer than this!

It goes without saying that the de-voicing of society has implications for us as music educators. If children are increasingly the products of this social condition, how much more difficult is it for us who want to enable children to use their voices to sing. Sadly, I think it is inevitable that increasingly we will have to *re-voice* children if we still want them to experience the joy of singing.

For let us not forget that there is a sense in which our voice is our personality! It can say a lot about us. We as music educators must not allow a situation to develop where children are increasingly *de-voiced* and as a consequence unable to use their voice to express nuances of emotion.

The more that children are *de-voiced,* the more music educators will have an up-hill battle in *re-voicing them:* opening-up for them the joy of singing and expression–the joy of communicating musically.

As all teachers know, and preschool and primary teachers especially, if we are to express ourselves personally, talking is the *least* we must do. And singing–not to mention other aspects of musical involvement–adds another dimension. The role of the music educator is of paramount importance in a society where, more and more, children are being *de-voiced.*

As a consequence of increasingly experiencing the world through their computer screen, children are experiencing the arts face-to-face less and less. More and more are they becoming passive consumers of music. And increasingly real live music ceases to be part of their lives. At least the one-off performance does offer children an opportunity to experience live music.

It is no coincidence that *Big Brother* is one of the most highly rated TV shows. I've watched it twice now. Why twice you might ask? Well I just wanted to convince myself that the first time was not an aberration! If *Big Brother* doesn't encourage voyeurism, I don't know what does. No wonder children are becoming voyeurs of life. The implications for the experience of music are just too dismal.

Ah, you might say, at least children have their pop idols. But there's a sense in which even they are a shadow, an anonymous mass. The real thing is disappearing. Many children are already living part of their lives in the virtual world. The challenge this presents for music educators is overwhelming.

But there is yet another reason why children must be given a voice: it is a political reason. For let us not forget that the arts have had a political role throughout history. Vaclav Havel, one of the 20th century's greatest thinkers, who was President of Czechoslovakia and then the Czech Republic, as well as a dissident and prominent playwright, has said that "A writer with an aversion to politics is like a scientist studying the holes in the ozone, while ignoring the fact that his boss is inventing chlorofluorocarbons" (Havel, 1997, p. 186). Children, I believe, need to understand the political power–and the political voice–of the arts regardless of whether they, or us, approve of the arts being used politically. Every art form is created and practiced within a particular political milieu and this in itself has ramifications for the experience of the art form, and for its creation and presentation. By ignoring this we accept, suggests Havel, "the perverted principle of specialization, according to which some . . . are here to understand the world and morality, without having to intervene in that world and turn morality into action; others are here to intervene in the world and behave morally, without being bound in any way to understand any of it" (pp. 186-187). Artists, musicians, have, I believe, a political responsibility. History in the 20th century has given us glaring examples of how the arts have been used politically and negatively and what the consequences are if artists don't exert their political and moral voice. We as music educators have a responsibility to develop children's political awareness–maybe, even, their political voice. But let me stress that I'm not suggesting that we provide music education *in order* to produce political activists. But equally, I *am* suggesting that children need to understand the political power of the arts–be it for good or for evil. For all educators, regardless of their specialization, are entrusted, I believe, with the education of the *whole* child.

Can you believe that in some quarters the fact that we are increasingly living in a world that is depersonalized and dehumanized is equated with the progress of civilization! It saddens me to think that children who have rarely experienced live music do not miss it. Now if that is not a challenge to us as music educators, I don't know what is.

We must be out there influencing the developers of the new technologies. And this is yet another challenge. For if we don't influence the developers of the new technologies and those who market them, we will be swamped with more and more new programs of dubious value. And to teachers in schools, who are under increasing pressures from diverse sources, it is sometimes very tempting to seize upon a quick fix.

A few days ago, indeed, on the very day that this conference opened, the *Australian Financial Review* reported that "the U.S. schools system was becoming a franchise for Coke and Pepsi." A school principal was reported as saying, "We have Coca-Cola machines in our hallways because they gave us $US10,000 to do it." And only last year, when President Bush was Governor of Texas, his then Education Secretary, "as Superintendent of Schools in Houston, Texas, signed a $US5 million deal to give Coke exclusive access to the city's school children" (p. 27). There was fortunately such a protest across the United States against this kind of intrusion, that in March this year Coca-Cola announced that it would "discourage its affiliated bottling companies from doing the high-pressure exclusive distribution deals with schools" (p. 27). And Coca-Cola isn't the only company on to this bandwagon. But what struck me as just as bad was mentioned in the same article, namely, that the makers of Prozac send speakers to talk to kids about how to deal with depression! As one U.S. Senator said, "The three Rs should not stand for retail, resale and rebate" (p. 27). But this is what can happen if education is taken out of the hands of the educators. And similarly, this is what can happen if music educators don't work alongside those who develop the new technologies, the new computer programs.

Maybe this entails that we, the music educators, must use our *intellectual voice* on behalf of children. What do I mean by our 'intellectual voice'? Let me quote Robin Prior and Joseph O'Connor (2000) who state:

> The intellectual voice is our capacity to evaluate, to take a step outside the feelings of the present, to compare and decide. It is not swayed either by instinct or blind conditioning. It is not about academic knowledge . . . or philosophy. It is reasonable, although not necessarily logical. It does not stand in contrast to emotions, but works with them. . . . You need a balance between emotion and reason . . . A strong intellectual voice is an essential part of that balance.

> The intellectual voice needs something to work on–like fire, it can't burn without fuel and it burns poorly on low-grade fuel. Serve it up conflicting and limiting beliefs, confused values and mistaken facts and it will do its best, but its conclusion will be as good as the fuel. The intellectual voice needs accurate information to work from. (p. 76)

Here, then, is another challenge for us. If children are to have a voice, I contend that we must use our intellectual voice on their behalf!

But we cannot do this effectively until we become united. There are too many voices and not a united, dominant one. Decision-makers have a smorgasbord of voices to choose from–and they will choose whichever one suits their political agenda.

As music educators we must grasp our responsibility in a new way. As Jacinth Oliver said so many years ago, we need to advocate–advocate on a united front. We need to embrace more fervently the fact that we are responsible for the destiny of music education; it is up to us whether children will have a voice in the future. It is up to us whether children will sing together in the future. If we don't accept the challenge bureaucrats will do it for us. And the "e" decision-makers will do it for us. And *they* don't make decisions based on the importance of music education: they have political or pecuniary interests–not artistic interests–at heart. Make no mistake: I am suggesting a definitive departure from our almost benign acceptance of the current situation in which music education is at best the poor country cousin; in which the status of music education is seen simply as an inconvenience that some need to work around. I know that Jacinth Oliver wanted us to take much more responsibility for our future.

I look forward to the day when our intellectuals and our politicians–when our decision-makers–tell us that our civilization is in danger not *simply* because of the greenhouse effect, or the depletion of this or that planet: no–I look forward to the day when we are told that our civilization is in danger because we have neglected the arts, we have neglected music, we have not provided a sustained and sequential education in music based on an articulated theory. I look forward to the day when our decision-makers tell us that we must give children a voice and enable them to use it.

We must acknowledge the problems besetting music education. But in doing so we should recognise them as opportunities for change. At the same time we must think laterally and recognise that the real obstacles to overcome are not the problems themselves, but rather the approaches to their solution.

It is a truism that in life change is the only constant. Music educators have been slow to acknowledge this. Let there be no doubt: I am arguing for a dramatic shift in our paradigms of music education. This will entail us questioning and changing our long-standing basic assumptions about music education. We need to be prepared to discard our long-held belief systems. We can no longer afford to support belief systems that are acted upon as if they are immutable or are unquestioningly accepted as "the way we do things." *An Agenda for the Knowledge Nation* stresses that overcoming obstacles to become an effective Knowledge Nation "will require changing the culture", adding that "we have no option. Time is running out" (p. 21).

In addition to a new theory of music education, we will, of course, need new methodologies–but not antiquated methodologies. And I speak of methodologies in the plural. I was fascinated a few weeks ago to hear the visiting American Episcopalian cleric, Bishop Spong, suggest that, in explaining the different religions, from Christianity, to Buddhism, to Hinduism, to Islam, that each of them might be seen as different doorways in a large house that lead along separate passage ways to the same central room in which is found God. Maybe, methodologies are a bit like this. Any one of a number might lead us to the same goal.

We must not let future generations of children adrift in a voiceless society. That is our challenge.

It is essential that music educators are in positions where they have the power to change the current trend whereby children are becoming de-voiced. We must influence and alter priorities if children are to get their voices back. There is a sense in which we all participated in the process that led to our de-voicing. Now we must re-voice ourselves through action.

Music educators, educators in general, must recognise the inevitability of change and conflict. It seems to me that to date music educators have not engaged in much debate regarding new ideological boundaries that influence public policy. But we must if we wish to be part of the debate. And if we don't, then we forfeit our cause.

On the ASME calendar that has just seen its last month (after 18 wonderful months), Elena Kats-Chernin, a friend of our society, is quoted as saying, "As a composer, I must have the ability to be flexible in response to changing environments around me." We music educators need to be just as flexible. And as Matthew Hindson says in the same calendar, "As Australians living at the turn of the 21st century, we can all create and shape the culture and society in which we live. Whether as composers, performers or just music lovers, let's embrace this unique opportunity." He neglected to mention music educators, so let me do it for him. For our role is at least equally as important as that of the others.

To finish, even if I'm misguided in what I've tried to say, I believe, from many discussions I had with her prior to her untimely death, that Jacinth Oliver would be pleased that at least I was fuelling the debate and offering an argument that could be publicly discussed and even torn apart. As music educators, let us challenge each other more in order that children may have a better voice. And, somewhat ironically, if children are to win back their voices, we as music educators will need to use certain technologies judiciously.

Let us give children a voice not for the sake of music education *per se:* let us give children a voice for the sake of the children themselves and the guarantee that the "e" generations will still *want* to sing. Let us do everything we can to ensure that children will always have a voice: a voice for themselves, a voice for their future, and a voice for making music.

Finally, let me leave you with this thought. Doesn't it strike you as odd that in the past few years the Government has spent infinitely more money on subsidising the wonder drug, Viagra, than it has on music education?

References

Australian Labor Party. (2001). *An Agenda for a Knowledge Nation.* Sydney: Chifley Research Centre.

Australia Council. (2000). *Australians and the Arts: What do the arts mean to Australians?* Surry Hills, NSW: Australia Council for the Arts.

Commonwealth of Australia. (1999). *Securing the Future: Major Performing Arts Inquiry Final Report.* (DOCITA 44/99). Canberra, ACT: Department of Communications, Information Technology and the Arts.

Hartcher, P. (2001, 6 July). US schools reject Coke's plan to 'teach the world'. *Australian Financial Review.*

Havel, V. (1997). *The Art of the Impossible: Politics as Morality in Practice,* (Translated from the Czech by Paul Wilson et al.). New York: Alfred A. Knopf.

Locke, J.L. (1998). *The De-Voicing of Society: Why We Don't Talk to Each Other Anymore.* New York: Simon and Schuster.

Music Educators National Conference. (1996). *Kids' Voices.* Reston, VA: MENC.

Prior, R. & O'Connor, J. (2000). *NLP & Relationships.* London: Thorsons.

[3]

Communicating and accentuating the aesthetic and expressive dimension in choral conducting

COLIN DURRANT
Institute of Education, University of London, UK

Abstract

This article considers the issues that are involved in effective choral conducting from an aesthetic dimension. Drawing upon research, theories and practice, it provides some insight into the nature of communication and the significance of gesture on vocal outcome as well as qualities of leadership concomitant with such musical activity. The article also reports on a research study that investigated the professional development of students and teachers in the area of choral conducting, focusing on their attitudes, skill acquisition and the importance attached to reflection on practice. The findings reveal that consideration of what counts as effective conducting gesture and communication skill can promote better conducting and, consequently, better, more expressive singing. In addition, the positive impact of self- and peer reflection on progress (both face-to-face and within a virtual learning environment) was also acknowledged. Certain suggestions for promoting effective musical leadership in the area of choral conducting are provided, in order to ground theoretical perspectives in practice.

Key words
aesthetic, choral conducting, expressive singing, leadership and communication

Introduction

The cognitive scientist Steven Pinker in his book *How the Mind Works* refers to music as an 'enigma' (1997, p. 528). In trying to investigate the meaning of life, he acknowledges that the arts are not biologically necessary and suggests that the more we try to explain the functions of music, the more we 'pass the enigma along'. As musicologists, we can examine the tensions and resolutions in melodies and harmonies, and the vivid concoction of auditory stimulation; as sociologists we can seek to explain the role of music in societies and cultures and, as psychologists, try to explain the effect it has on us. Those who are leaders of musical activity are given the responsibility of making music meaningful in some way or other – technically, emotionally and socially. However, it might also be salutary for us to be reminded of music's enigmatic nature – and it may be that we do not always need to explain meanings verbally or instructively. This article addresses some of the issues surrounding conductors' communication of that enigma, with particular reference to the aesthetic and expressive dimension of choral music.

Three critical ingredients of effective, communicative musical leadership, particularly in relation to choral conducting, established by Durrant (2003) are: (1) a philosophical under-pinning of the role; (2) musical and technical skills; and (3) inter-personal skills. Inter-personal skills will be explored in more detail here, but in relation to the musical outcomes, learning styles and behaviours, as well as an over-arching awareness of the role of the conductor as leader of musical events. Through analysis and discussion of the implications of some research studies together with reference to experience in the field, aspects of communication and leadership in conducting will be guided by: (1) gesture; (2) verbal and non-verbal inter-actions; (3) the music.

One of the more elusive phenomena in creating an effective and successful musical event concerns communication. Not the relaying of information, but, rather, imparting the subtle nuances of the character of a piece is integral to the communication system of those leading, directing and conducting music. Those who call themselves conductors (which should be all who lead music-making from the front in whatever context) have consciously taken on board a role that has connotations of musical leadership. This leadership is traditionally concerned with creating a performance according to the vision and musical insight of the one person who has taken on the mantle of leading, shaping and directing that event. Let us not forget that the word 'conductor' has a Latin derivation *conducare* – to lead (*ducare*) together (*con*). That person, then, will have particular and identifiable leadership characteristics.

Perceptions of the conductor's role

A traditional notion of the conductor is of a dictator, benevolent or otherwise, usually male, leading the musical activity with assured leadership. He (and it often is) has all the vision, knowledge of the score and the wherewithal to coerce the players, singers or those in his charge to follow his interpretation and demands on the re-creative endeavour (Durrant, 2003). This traditional model of operation is accompanied usually by verbal instruction, sometimes admonition, perhaps praise, propelled by the physical gesture associated with the acknowledged frame of conducting patterns. Often this is carried out with facial and other forms of expressive gesture to enlighten the performers in the expressive and aesthetic requirements of the composer and conductor. Potentially, the conductor holds the key to music's enigma.

These traditional notions of leading musical activity are often adopted in school, church and community contexts. The expectations of the role, from conductors themselves as well as from those they conduct, often mirror the traditional model. There is a perpetuating myth, as exposed by Lebrecht (1991), that the conductor has the appropriate knowledge, skill and character to command respect. The singers and players blindly follow, obeying each instruction without question – there being an expectation of that particular pattern of inter-actions. In an ensemble context it is clearly necessary for there to be a vision of the musical product; the process along the way involves a series of goals and sub-goals moving towards achieving that vision – towards the 'bull's-eye' (Thurman & Welch, 2000). Culturally and philosophically, we have to have leadership in an ensemble music-making context. In the same way in any organization, political, commercial or educational, we choose people with key attributes to lead us, inspire and motivate us, who command our loyalty and respect and admiration. Sometimes it works and sometimes not.

Conductors are able to command attention through a combination of musical skills, self-belief and personality. Matheopoulos (1982) and Lebrecht (1991), in order to demystify the conductor, explored the characteristics of well-known conductors, particularly their musician-ship and leadership skills. This was carried out largely through interviews with conductors themselves and also singers and players who had been conducted by them. In each case, there was a self-belief in the ability to execute the role. Leonard Bernstein was once asked by an aspiring young conductor if he thought he was good enough to become a professional conductor. Bernstein's reply was that if he didn't know that himself, he was not. This in itself confirms one of the attributes in the model of the effective choral conductor (Durrant, 2003), namely that a conductor will have 'an understanding of the conductor's role' – an inner knowing, if you like, of the self-possession of a leadership aptitude and responsibility that goes with the job. Yet, Simon Rattle, the current conductor of the Berlin Philharmonic Orchestra, in a film about their tour of Asia, mentioned his regular feelings of doubt about his own musical leadership – fearing that he might be 'found out'.

This section has recognized issues of self-efficacy and the conductor, while the next focuses on the behaviours that are appropriate in effectively communicating musical ideas in educational contexts.

Communication

While we can accept that communication must be integral to the conducting process and leadership role, exploration of the key issues concerning the nature of conductor behaviour might well provide insight into effective communication in a musical and educational context. In other words, how can those leading musical activity in schools and similar educational contexts become more efficient and effective? Does the teacher leading singing with young children need to act as a dictator? Does the conductor of a youth band need to rule with a rod of iron in order to achieve accurate playing? Does the conductor of an adult community chorus need to shout at them? While these may appear to represent extreme conditions and behaviours, in one respect these scenarios might be recognized as 'accepted' behaviours of conductors in particular contexts. Singers and players tacitly accept that this is the way con-ductors may or even ought to behave. However, in other educational contexts, we expect our teachers to behave in a less dictatorial manner and know that, in order to promote effective learning, we need to understand the ways in which learning occurs.

Communication is about interaction, exchange of ideas and consultation between people. Effective communication is key to leadership in all sorts of situations. Apfelstadt (1997) suggests that leadership is integral to the creation of an environment where quality singing can take place and makes a connection with communication. She proposes three categories of leadership characteristics: (1) 'musical'; (2) 'extra-musical'; (3) 'gestalt'. Here, leadership skills are not only concerned with musical outcomes, but also with combining the development of those with such attributes as confidence, initiative and enthusiasm for the task. Those conducting and leading our musical activities need, therefore, to be effective communicators. Musical outcomes, individual and collective development, together with building confidence and ultimately gaining mastery and self-esteem, are inextricably linked to conductors' behaviours (Donovan, 1994; Durrant, 2000, 2005; Watkins, 1986).

Communication and musical meaning

It seems odd to be writing about communication, particularly musical communication that relies on all sorts of non-verbal means, from the conducting gesture to facial expressions. Something inevitably will be missing – that other real-time dimension of experiencing some of the impact of effective and ineffective ways of communicating in the flesh – which can enhance understanding and impact on learning. In the same way that writing about the meaning of music itself cannot actually portray its meaning – otherwise we would not need the music – so writing about physical gesture and the elements of communicating musical ideas and expressions cannot give a full portrayal of musical communication. It seems a pity that we have to rely on the written word so much to give credence to our research in academia. Talking on music in the 2006 BBC Reith lecture, Daniel Barenboim said:

> I firmly believe that it is really impossible to speak really deeply about music. All we can do then is speak about our own reaction to the music … I will therefore attempt the impossible and maybe try and draw some connection between the inexpressible content of music and, maybe, the inexpressible content of life. (Barenboim, 2006)

If music is to represent the inexpressible, then our non-verbal messages as a conductor have the potential to communicate more than verbal instruction can in terms of emotional import and expressive interpretations. Even with linguistic text, music is the most absolute symbolic art form, according to Langer (1957), whose expressivity goes beyond the expressive potential of words. Poetry and drama rely on words to express their meanings; dance has gesture as its prime means of expression and is probably the nearest symbolic art form to music. Music has no literal meaning that can be explained sufficiently by verbal communication or instruction, but it does have meaning (Meyer, 1956), 'meaningfulness' and 'feelingfulness' (Swanwick, 1979). It is therefore deeply symbolic. Musical gesture symbolically suggested and notated in the score (by the composer) therefore calls for an aesthetic gestural living form to bring it to its aural manifestation (by the conductor and performers). This is generated by gestures, expressions and forms of communication from the conductor that lead the performers to an understanding of the musical import through reflection, musical and vocal skill, aural awareness, technical accuracy and aesthetic realization. The whole person is involved in the aesthetic communication. However, music and physical gestures are two very different symbolic modes, each used for artistic expression. How one is translated into the other is a complex action, processed cognitively and emotionally.

In terms of non-verbal communication, Mehrabian (1972) suggested that 55 percent of communication is transmitted by facial expression, arm–hand gestures and postural arrangements of the body, while 45 percent is transmitted vocally. Of that 45 percent, Mehrabian maintains that only 7 percent is perceived and produced 'in conscious awareness', 38 percent being perceived and produced 'outside conscious awareness' as part of the non-verbal context of spoken communication. The substance of communication, even verbally, is associated with variations in vocal pitch, volume, timbre and timing and pacing of speech rather than just the literal meaning of words. In turn, the vast array of communications drives and shapes our feelings and interpretations of feelings into meanings (Durrant, 2003). The implication for verbal instruction, therefore, as a prime means of communicating musical meaning, is significant. The conductor and teacher would do well to consider the appropriateness of other means of communicating – through conducting gesture, facial expression, vocal timbre and the like, many of which are processed and received outside conscious awareness. According to Thurman, 'the parts of human beings that process outside conscious awareness have enormous processing capacity and those parts are significantly developed by birth' (Thurman & Welch, 2000, p. 162). And these non-verbal communications between humans are interpreted for 'emotional significance' and 'interrelational significance' (Thurman & Welch, 2000, p. 162) outside conscious awareness.

It is therefore incumbent on the conductor to adopt a 'human-compatible', as opposed to 'human-antagonistic' style of behaviour in music-making processes in order to get the best out of the participants. This includes providing safe, free-from-threat learning and singing

330 INTERNATIONAL JOURNAL OF MUSIC EDUCATION 27(4)

environments as well as encouraging cooperative rather than competitive actions from participants. Hart (1983) has developed a theory of learning that is brain-centred and states – 'creating a brain-compatible ambiance calls for deliberately identifying and stripping away sources of threat' (p. 133). Many traditional modes of conducting behaviour are associated with 'telling off', belittling people and thus creating a threatening situation where effective learning is unlikely to take place (Durrant, 2003; Hart, 1983).

Gesture

While threatening situations are often verbal, there are also non-verbal means – inappropriate gestures and facial expressions – that can prevent learning and a growth of confidence and, ultimately, promote low self-esteem. The quality and nature of communication through gesture is fundamental in the choral conducting and musical learning context and contributes to the development of effective musical leadership. Given a normally equipped human being, gesture is used extensively to communicate. There are recognizable gestural signs that have specified meaning in particular cultures or countries (Morris, Collett, Marsh, & O'Shaughnessy, 1979). Generally, in our everyday lives we point to give direction, or for emphasis or in anger, we wave to greet or exit, we shape in order to enhance our description of something. We can open and extend our arms as a sign of welcome, or we can cross or fold them as a sign of non-committal or 'fed-up-ness'. There are distinct, specific and also covert meanings in gestures. The teacher standing in the front of a class with folded arms, together with a particular expression is giving a subliminal message to the students. A conductor beginning a choir rehearsal with arms extended, coupled with a warm smile, gives a message of welcome to the singers, as if to embrace them and invite them to sing.

Ford (2001) illustrates and reviews how gesture has been codified for rhetorical delivery, how certain gestures were associated with corresponding emotions or points in argument, establishing almost a biological basis for a universal gestural language. We use gesture outside conscious awareness as part of the human condition of communicating our thoughts, ideas and behaviours. He further categorizes types of gestures according to McNeill (1992), who suggests that gestures are closely linked to speech, but yet fundamentally different in their form of presentation of meaning. This concept relates to the Vygotskyian model of interlocking linguistic and non-verbal thought – 'the synthesis of image and word'. Gesture, then, is close to thought. One significant consideration for the conductor is the cooperative meanings of the image – the gesture – and the verbal instruction. The craft of conducting is to ensure the interpreted meanings of both coincide, otherwise the conducted will receive confusing subliminal messages.

Gesture and dance

Gesture is integral to dance and, in many cultures, movement and gesture have specified meaning. In the Pacific islands of Kiribati,[1] for example, traditional dance is a significant part of the preservation of the historical and cultural life of its people, whose very existence is threatened by rising sea levels. Even the Catholic mass is 'translated' into dances, in order to encourage better understanding of it (Whincup & Whincup, 2001). Not only do there appear to be representative gestures and movements in the dances of Kiribati, but the dances are controlled and precise with deeper spiritual, historical and cultural meaning. The dances are conducted, although the conductor does not himself dance, but as one conductor reflected:

> A well trained conductor … should have possessed that kind of spiritual/emotional inspiration to influence members of his group … I notice that the dancers always respond to me and automatically understand my signals even when I shout as a result of that emotional excitement. (Whincup & Whincup, 2001, p. 109)

The minutiae of each gesture and movement are significant, as reported by a participant:

> the arm, head and eye movements should always follow the rhythm of the song and illustrate the meaning of the word. For example, the arm stretched sideways with the forearm moving up and down, it illustrates the bird that flies up in the air. The arm horizontal, move forward or inward in a fast up or down movement illustrates the movement of the fish. (Whincup & Whincup, 2001, p. 114)

Gesture and meaning

Within the conducting framework, there are gestures that have indicative meaning – those that more obviously are signals. A cut-off or stop is usually unambiguous in normal conducting situations. Even signals to perform a phrase quietly are rarely misunderstood. These signals, or indicative gestures, are recognizable in that they correspond to similar signals in other non-musical contexts. A sign to halt from a policeman on traffic duty might be similar to the conductor's cut-off and is recognized easily, given due attention by those using the road or those performing. A sign to request quiet is often indicated as the first finger against the lips, or in conducting, a similar kind of retracting movement with the hand towards the mouth. Beating time and giving entries are, to some extent, literal or indicative gestures (Durrant, 2003). We recognize the movement of the beat and instinctively operate within that given pulse. This type of gesture is appropriate in certain pieces of music that need, for example, 'controlling' in terms of tempo security within a complex range of metres. (There are internationally accepted conducting patterns to indicate the musical metre, which can be found in any textbook on conducting methods.)

Visual association of the conducting pattern with the inner pulse and musical outcomes of the performer is a connection that is processed neurally and kinaesthetically. Other gestures are of the more connotative kind – those that may not be indicative of tempo or entry, but rather of the expressive character of the music. These gestures connect with the quality of sound, the expressive musical line and the elusive and non-discursive element of musical interpretation. This is concerned with imaginative and creative interplay between the symbolic modes of gesture and music (Hatten, 2004).

Various research studies in the area of conducting gesture have been carried out. Gumm (1993) outlined the purpose of gesture in communication: some gestures are for specific musical tasks, while others may communicate other unintended non-verbal messages. He points out the importance of conducting gesture in creating an appropriate learning environment. Fuelberth (2003) explored the effect of conducting gesture on singers' perceptions of inappropriate vocal tension. This highlights the impact, overt and covert, that conducting gesture can have, not only on vocal and musical outcome, but also on the vocal mechanism itself in terms of healthy voice use and vocal tension. Benge (1996) reported that the conducting skills of expressive conductors can communicate a vast array of information, thus recognizing the power and potential of the conducting gesture together with other forms of non-verbal communication. More recently, Mathers (2008) examined how various theories of expressive movement and non-verbal communication can impact upon conducting behaviour at all levels of experience to produce more expressive conducting gestures. Again, this confirms the potential impact of gesture on vocal outcome, attitude and environment.

332 INTERNATIONAL JOURNAL OF MUSIC EDUCATION 27(4)

Research study

In order to investigate further the relationship between communication and conducting gesture, a research study with school and student music teachers was carried out during continuing professional development courses in choral conducting[2] over three years (2006–08). These teachers self-perceived themselves as less-than-confident in their conducting skills (Durrant, 2006; Durrant & Varvarigou, 2008). Each course took place over four separate days over a period of five months with intervening time for practice and reflection. The study was essentially concerned with perceptions and reflections of their progress in relation to putting the strategies addressed into practice in their professional situations.

Using both observation (participant and non-participant) and questionnaires as the main methods of collecting data, it became noticeable that in the early stages of training in workshop situations, the conductors (school and student music teachers) assumed that conducting is essentially about beating time and much less about managing the aesthetic and expressive character of the music. In the first course of the study (during the spring and summer 2006), questionnaires ($N = 21$) were given at four points during the course (six hours × four separate days over a period of three months) in order to track participants' progress and attitudes towards choral conducting.

A qualitative design was considered the most appropriate for this evaluative, ongoing research, as the intention was for the course participants to reflect on their practice and for the tutors to monitor the development of each participant over time. The methods used were extensive observations through video snapshots of the workshop seminars, distribution of questionnaires and semi-structured interviews with some randomly selected participants. Questionnaires were issued and completed at the beginning of each workshop session in order to allow participants to reflect on their own progress, as well as make reference to comments that may have been received from the singers they conducted in their own situations in between sessions.

Further data was collected in the two subsequent courses with different students in 2007 and 2008, using essentially the same method with small modifications to the questionnaires and more sophisticated and developed technology. The outcomes of these investigations are more fully reported in Durrant & Varvarigou (2008). Questionnaires have their limitation in artistic contexts as the method necessitates that 'inner subjective realities are submitted to an external objective form' (Aldridge, 1990, p. 178). Observations can therefore elicit more insight into people's aesthetic responses and emotions to particular musical or other events and provide a triangulation of evidence. In these subsequent years, participants were encouraged to reflect on their own progress through video-recordings taken of their conducting sessions that were uploaded onto the Blackboard Virtual Learning Environment (Bb). Through Bb, they were also able to reflect on their own conducting as well as chat about their progress and development through the course: they were encouraged to develop their own narratives. The production of audio-visual material was considered an unobtrusive method of collecting data (Denscombe, 2003; Durrant & Varvarigou, 2008).

At the beginning of the courses, it was evident that the majority of participants thought that developing conducting skills meant knowing how to beat time – that this was the essential technique required. Fewer participants at this stage realized the significance of communication and leadership skills (Durrant & Varvarigou, 2008, p. 76). Concentrating on developing expressive and more efficient and effective gestures, in preference to an over-reliance on verbal instruction during the practical sessions of the course, participants were asked in subsequent sessions to reflect upon their conducting and the responses from the singers they conducted in the periods between the teaching sessions. These written comments included:

> '[singers were] more focused on my conducting gestures.'

> '[my] choir are much more attentive to gestures.'

> 'they are much more responsive to me – maybe because I am more aware of the conductor–choir relationship.'

> 'they are watching my gestures more carefully. Seem to be more responsive.'

Not only the conductors themselves, but singers and onlookers noticed differences – with reported comments in the questionnaires including:

> 'the singers have noticed. They are more attentive and responsive to my gestures.'

> 'they are happier to sing paying better attention.'

> 'two people came to me and said they found my conducting more expressive and they thought the choir responsive.'

The move away from their concern over the 'technical' towards the 'musical' and 'aesthetic' became apparent during the course, with a growing general recognition that leading through the finer points of gesture, as well as the nature and style of verbal and non-verbal communication, could make a difference to the vocal outcome and attitude of the singers (Benge, 1996). As two student conductors commented:

> 'Small changes in conductors' gestures can evoke large difference in singing by groups, but why does this happen? How?'

> 'After viewing the video of me conducting, I have come to realize how the slightest movements made by a conductor can have a major effect on the outcome of the vocal quality from the choir.'

The members of the class were encouraged to comment and feedback to the conductors (both face-to-face and online) on how their conducting style and gesture impacted on their engagement with the music both vocally and aesthetically. Such feedback validated the development of 'kinaesthetic' awareness of conducting. In essence, some of the comments outlined a growing awareness of the need to provide strategies for effective and expressive conducting, rather than being overly concerned with the technical aspects of beating time. Some more detailed reflections and comments from conducting students writing online included:

> 'The holistic view of the voice, emotion and communication has had an impact on my teaching beyond choral work …'

> 'My eye contact with the choir and facial expressions were positive and helped to establish a rapport with the singers as well as convey emotions in the music. Nevertheless, there were several flaws with my gestures. Initially, I was beating time with not only my arms, but my entire body and head, resulting in ambiguous beating overall. Due to unnecessary

334 INTERNATIONAL JOURNAL OF MUSIC EDUCATION 27(4)

movement of my arms and fingers, singers were not looking to my fingertips as the focal point for the beat.'

'Over the years I have got into some really bad conducting habits which I thought were good practice. Now I realize that I can probably improve the children's singing just by improving my conducting gestures.'

'Having watched the video I feel like I move way too much and so in the next session I will focus on doing less. By making my gestures more specific I hope to be able to indicate phrasing and dynamics to the singers.'

'... I can see immediately from the beginning of my video that I need to improve my eye contact with the singers. During the introduction to the piece my eyes are firmly fixed on the music which hinders the connection between us as musicians and will render my "understanding of and insight into the expressive content and dimensions" useless as the singers will be unable to benefit from a person with whom they remain unconnected. Through the piece my eyes lift more frequently and my gaze becomes more focused and enthusiastic, but I am aware that I need to develop the confidence to begin with an authoritative, directed and inclusive level of eye contact with the choir in order to improve as a conductor.'

The responses of the majority of participants highlighted the need to develop further their communication through expressive gesture and conducting technique together with efficient use of time in rehearsals. The positive impact of self- and peer reflection on progress was also acknowledged.

Conducting: the technical and expressive

While maintaining ensemble is clearly dependent on singing and playing together in time, there are other equally important roles that the conductor needs to take on board. Conducting gesture is not just beating time; there are, nevertheless, pieces of music where this will be paramount, particularly when the rhythmic momentum is integral to the musical meaning. It is essential that the conductor drives the music of, for example, the first movement of Bernstein's *Chichester Psalms* or the section in Britten's *Rejoice in the Lamb* – 'Let Nimrod the mighty hunter', where the metre irregularly moves through 7/8–6/8–9/8–5/8–11/8, as well as numerous other examples of music with a particular dynamic rhythmic character. However, a gentle folk song, such as 'Shenendoah' or 'Down by the Sally Gardens', requires expressive gestures that reflect the musical phrases rather than a pulsating beat. These songs express longing rather than excitement and so the aesthetic gesture of longing needs to be part of the kinaesthetic interpretation – the movement of the conducting gesture (McCoy, 1994). Feeling with movement is the essence, naturally, of 'kinaesthesia'. How we translate 'longing' (a human emotional state) into a gesture (a symbolic mode) is problematic. How singers then interpret gesture (one symbolic mode) into music (another symbolic mode) through vocal expression is indicative of the complex 'designed and crafted patterns of the visual, auditory, somatosensory-kinesthetic'[3] (Thurman & Welch, 2000, p. 167). The combination of these artistic symbolic modes generates aesthetic and emotional responses in humans (Thurman & Welch, 2000, p. 167).

As exemplified in the research study discussed previously, there is a tendency for conductors, particularly those of amateur and children's choral groups, to think that they have to do everything for their singers in terms of conducting cues, mouthing words, exaggerating beat patterns and often exaggerating facial expressions (Decker & Kirk, 1988; Durrant, 2003; Terry, 1991). This is often counter-productive and makes the singers over-reliant on the conductor; excessive mouthing of the words focuses singers' attention on the conductor's mouth rather than on the conductor's gesture. Perhaps such exaggerations are subliminal ways of keeping control, of not trusting singers (Durrant, 2003). This is a style of leadership revealed in gesture that suggests 'I am in charge' as opposed to 'I am facilitating'. Notwithstanding the need for conductors to take responsibility for rehearsing and performing, there are moments when conducting gestures get in the way of the aesthetic of the music. Again, this was validated by the research study. These over-exaggerated, controlling gestures and patterns, including exaggerated mouthing of words, are often 'un-aesthetic', as evidenced by general feedback the conductors gave to each other in the research study. For, if the conducting gesture is not gesturally aesthetic and in keeping with the expressive and aesthetic content of the music, then part of the aesthetic gestalt is destroyed for those being conducted and, ultimately, for those listening as well. The choral experience is aural certainly, but it is also visual. Beautiful sounds are promoted by beautiful gestures. Thurman and Welch (2000) refer to this as a 'bodymind'[4] connection, part of the theory on human compatible learning.

The impact of effective conducting gesture and communication on providing for aesthetic moments in music is revealed in the following account. A BBC Radio 3 series of programmes was devoted to the performances of the retired British mezzo-soprano Dame Janet Baker (BBC Radio 3, 2006). At one point in conversation, she recalled her experience of singing the role of Charlotte in Massenet's *Werther* in 1977. The opera was being performed with the English National Opera at the London Coliseum with Sir Charles Mackerras conducting. She talked of a moment of real 'connection' with the conductor and orchestra in one particular performance of the letter scene in Act 3. Unable to account for why on this particular occasion there was this particular 'connection', she simply referred to it as a moment of 'extraordinary life quality'. This is but one moment that music can generate, symbolizing all that is inexplicable in the human emotional world (Kivy, 1989; Langer, 1957). The emotional context of the opera's drama, the composed music symbolizing that emotion, the conductor's interpretation of the music, and the gestural and facial communication with the singers and orchestra all combined to create that aesthetic, special, poignant and memorable moment. Making special, lifting us out of the ordinary, the poignant moment, are all characteristics of musical encounter (Custodero, 2005) – in this case, a combination of musical interpretation and its communication through 'beautiful' gesture to enable 'beautiful' sounds to emerge.

Meaningful conducting: symbolic transformation

Attention to the musical score, be it a simple folk song or a more complex larger scale choral work, covers several types of knowing. There is a 'knowing that' – a cognitive awareness of the musical and technical aspects – a 'knowing how' – a kind of craft knowledge (Brown & McIntyre, 1993; Collingwood, 1938; Elbaz, 1983) that concerns the processes and contexts of the learners or singers in the encounter and how to deal with them. In addition, a 'knowing-in-action' (Schön, 1987) and 'tacit knowing' (Polanyi, 1983) suggest that we may know more than we can tell. Our understanding of musical concepts, as Barenboim suggested in his Reith lecture (2006), is a tacit knowing, uncovering a series of meanings through 'dwelling in' the musical experience. There is nothing like the experience to uncover meanings and make sense of ourselves within the musical world (Dewey, 1934; Durrant, 2003). Scruton (1983) determines that musical understanding is gained through experience of music in all its sensations and evocations of feelings, not just through appreciation of its structures. He applies this even to music that is considered 'absolute' – that has no intended extra-musical meanings outside its own rhetoric (Pinker's [1997] 'enigma'). Langer (1957) puts forward the notion that performers and listeners do not actually experience feelings and emotions portrayed in a piece of music, but, rather, understand those feelings and emotions through previous encounters with similar emotions. The act of performance is a symbolic transformation, a gestured expression of hearing and final imagination of tone – a collaborative venture, in the case of choral performance, between the composer, conductor and singers. The conductor is symbolically engaged in this transformation of the composer's imagination, ideas, rhythms and sonorities, which find embodiment in the performed music (Grey, 2006).

To illustrate this symbolic transformation within the collaborative venture: the requiem is a liturgical setting of a mass for the dead that has been set to music by many composers in the Western musical canon. Engaged in a performance of, say, the dynamic setting by Verdi, it is easy for conductors and singers to understand something of the emotions and feelings of those grieving for the loss of loved ones. Verdi wrote his *Requiem* in response to the death of his friend, the writer Manzoni, in order to represent vivid emotions – 'feeling into form' (Grey, 2006; Langer, 1957). However, conductors and singers do not have to share those emotions directly in order to perform the music effectively and expressively; rather, the conductor's role is to shape the music through gesture – symbolically transform – so that particular expressive character is understood by all those engaged in the experience. Many people engaged in a performance of Verdi's masterpiece will have some experience perhaps of grief, tragedy and hurt, and can connect with the expressive character presented through the lyrical melodies, chromatic harmonies, musical structures and indulgent orchestration. The conductor has the potential to make the event meaningful.

Conclusion

Evidence from the reported research study with school and student teachers confirms that communication and leadership skills are stronger when knowledge is secure. Musical knowledge in the context of choral conducting incorporates: (1) a knowledge of choral repertoire appropriate for the singers; (2) a knowledge of the voice, including some physiology in order to be able to promote healthy singing; (3) a knowledge of the expressive intentions of the music through its text and musical structures; (4) a technical knowledge that enables the conductor to hear and therefore to feed back to the singers, as appropriate, to enhance the musical and singing experience (Apfelstadt, 1997; Decker & Kirk, 1988; Durrant, 2003; Fuelberth, 2003). The craft skill or knowledge is the practical application of the technical knowledge, the aural skills, the detection of errors and the general shaping – knowing when and how to deal and progress with the music. According to Collingwood (1938), skilled craftsmen use knowledge as the means necessary to realize a given end, it being the mastery of these means that is the craftsmen's skill. Teachers and choral conductors have a range of appropriate knowledge to be able to realize their specific goals. In the rehearsal context, the mastery of the means is fundamental to competent and effective musical progression. However, while effective teachers and conductors will have the craft knowledge and will know how to proceed in order to attain technical goals, they will also have the vision to guide the rehearsal towards aesthetic goals (Durrant, 2003; Durrant & Varvarigou, 2008). The inextricable relationship between knowledge and vision with communication and leadership abilities ensures the efficacy of this process.

This discourse on the aesthetic dimension of choral conducting arises from my experience of being engaged in music education through: (1) conducting for most of my life; (2) the initial training and professional development of music teachers and choral conductors; (3) research; (4) the concern to improve the singing experiences of those who commit themselves to the activity; and (5) the desire to motivate and inspire those who are reluctant and less confident singers. It is my belief that the leader of these activities must have the communication, leadership and musical skills to make singing experience positive and effective vocally and aesthetically. Greater understanding of the conductor's role in this respect will enable greater understanding of the lives and loves of those who sing and those who listen.

Notes

1. These are a group of low-lying atolls on the equator and international dateline, sadly being threatened by rising sea levels.
2. This is ongoing, both as part of the postgraduate music education programme and professional development courses at the Institute of Education, University of London.
3. The visual arts – painting, sculpture, architecture; the auditory – music, poetry, spoken written and story arts; the somatosensory-kineasthetic – mime and dance.
4. A term used to denote the interdependency of all processing parts of the human body, which has its basis in the neuro-psycho-biological sciences (Durrant, 2003; Thurman & Welch, 2000).

References

Aldridge, D. (1990). Meaning and expression: The pursuit of aesthetics in research. *Holistic Medicine*, 5, 177–186.

Apfelstadt, H. (1997). Applying leadership models in teaching choral conductors. *Choral Journal of the American Choral Directors' Association*, *37*(8), 23–30.

Barenboim, D. (2006). In the beginning was sound [BBC Radio Reith lecture]. Retrieved 28 April 2006, from http://www.bbc.co.uk/radio4/reith2006/lecture1.shtml

BBC Radio 3 (2006) Celebrating Dame Janet Baker: German lieder plus. Performance on 3. Retrieved 26 April 2006, from http://www.bbc.co.uk/radio3/performanceon3/pip/u2pkz/

Benge, T. J. (1996). Movements utilized by conductors in the stimulation of expression and musicianship [doctorial dissertation, University of Southern California, 1995]. *Dissertation Abstracts International*, A, *58*(1), 0018.

Brown, S., & McIntyre, D. (1993). *Making sense of teaching.* Buckingham: Open University Press.

Collingwood, R. (1938). *The principles of art.* Oxford: Oxford University Press.

Custodero, L. (2005). Making sense of 'making special': Art and intimacy in musical lives and educational practice. *International Journal of Education & the Arts*, *6*(15). Retreived 2 September 2008, from http://ijea.asu.edu

Decker, H., & Kirk, C. (1988). *Choral conducting: Focus on communication.* Englewood Cliffs, NJ: Prentice Hall.

Denscombe, M. (2003). *The good research guide for small-scale social research projects* (2nd ed). Philadelphia, PA: Open University Press.

Dewey, J. (1934). *Art as experience.* New York: Capricorn Books.

Donovan, A. (1994). *The interaction of personality traits in applied music teaching.* Unpublished doctoral dissertation, University of Southern Mississippi.

Durrant, C. (2000). Making choral rehearsing seductive: Implications for practice and choral education. *Research Studies in Music Education*, *15*, 40–49.

Durrant, C. (2003). *Choral conducting: Philosophy and practice.* New York: Routledge.

Durrant, C. (2005). 'Stand still when you sing': Human compatible conducting and its impact on singing development. In D. Forrest (Ed.), *A celebration of voices: Conference proceedings of the Australian Society for Music Education ASME* (pp. 84–89). Mawson: Australian Society for Music Education.

Durrant, C. (2006). Completing the triangle: Professional development for the choral conductor. In M. Moore & B. W. Leung (Eds.), *Proceedings for the 15th International Seminar of Music in Schools and Teacher Education Commission of the International Society of Music Education* (pp. 175–183). Hong Kong: Hong Kong Institute of Education and ISME.

Durrant, C., & Varvarigou, M. (2008). Real time and virtual: Tracking the professional development and reflections of choral conductors. *Reflecting Education*, 4(1), 72–80.

Elbaz, F. (1983). *Teacher thinking: A study of practical knowledge*. London: Croom Helm.

Ford, J. (2001). Implications for non-verbal communication and conducting gesture. *Choral Journal of the American Choral Directors' Association*, 42(1), 17–23.

Fuelberth, R. J. (2003). The effect of conducting gesture on singers' perceptions of inappropriate vocal tension: A pilot study. *International Journal of Research in Choral Singing*, 1(1), 3–12.

Grey, C. (2006). *Feeling into form: Musical composition as embodiment in the philosophy of Susanne Langer*. Unpublished MA dissertation, Institute of Education, University of London.

Gumm, A. J. (1993). The development of a model and assessment instrument of choral music teaching styles. *Journal of Research in Music Education*, 41(3), 181–199.

Hart, L. (1983). *Human brain and human learning*. Arizona: Books for Educators.

Hatten, R. S. (2004). *Interpreting musical gestures, topics, and tropes*. Bloomington, IN: Indiana University Press.

Kivy, P. (1989). *Sound sentiment: An essay on the musical emotions*. Philadelphia, PA: Temple University Press.

Langer, S. (1957). *Philosophy in a new key* (3rd ed). Cambridge, MA: Harvard University Press.

Lebrecht, N. (1991). *The maestro myth*. London: Simon & Schuster.

Matheopoulos, H. (1982). *Maestro: Encounters with conductors of today*. London: Hutchinson.

Mathers, A. (2008). *How theories of expressive movement and non-verbal communication can enhance expressive conducting at all levels of entering behaviour*. Unpublished doctoral thesis, Monash University, Australia.

McCoy, C. (1994). Eurhythmics: Enhancing the music-body-mind connection in conductor training. *Choral Journal of the American Choral Directors' Association*, 35(5), 21–28.

McNeill, D. (1992). *Hand and mind: What gestures reveal about thought*. Chicago, IL: The University of Chicago Press.

Mehrabian, A. (1972). *Nonverbal communication*. Englewood Cliffs, NJ: Prentice Hall.

Meyer, L. (1956). *Emotion and meaning in music*. Chicago, IL: The University of Chicago Press.

Morris, D., Collett, P., Marsh, P., & O'Shaughnessy, M. (1979). *Gestures: Their origins and distribution*. London: Jonathan Cape.

Pinker, S. (1997). *How the mind works*. New York: W.W. Norton.

Polanyi, M. (1983). *The tacit dimension*. Gloucester, MA: Peter Smith.

Schön, D. (1987). *Educating the reflective practitioner*. San Fransisco, CA: Jossey-Bass.

Scruton, R. (1983). *The aesthetic understanding*. London: Methuen.

Swanwick, K. (1979). *A basis for music education*. Windsor: NFER/Nelson.

Terry, E. (1991). *The choral conductor's art*. London, ON: The Althouse Press.

Thurman, L., & Welch, G. (Eds.). (2000). *Bodymind and voice: Foundations of voice education*. Minneapolis, MN: The VoiceCare Network.

Watkins, R. (1986). *A descriptive study of high school choral directors' use of modeling, metaphorical language and musical/technical language related to student attentiveness*. Doctoral dissertation, University of Texas at Austin.

Whincup, T., & Whincup, J. (2001). *Akekeia! Traditional dance in Kiribati*. Wellington: Format.

Colin Durrant leads the postgraduate programme in Music Education at the Institute of Education, University of London. He currently conducts the University of London Chamber Choir and Imperial College Choir. He has published many articles on choral conducting and music education; his book *Choral Conducting: Philosophy and Practice* appeared in 2003 (published by Routledge). He has led teacher training and conducting workshops in the USA, Australia, China, Hong Kong, Taiwan and Malaysia as well as in Europe and the UK and was in 2009 one of the international adjudicators at the Singapore Youth

Music Festival. He is also a principal conducting tutor for the Association of British Choral Directors.
Address: Department of Arts and Humanities, Institute of Education, University of London, 20 Bedford Way, London WC1H 0AL, UK. [email: c.durrant@ioe.ac.uk]

Abstracts

Communiquer et accentuer la dimension esthétique et expressive dans la direction de chœur

Cet article étudie les questions impliquées dans la direction de choeur efficace dans une dimension esthétique. Utilisant la recherche, les théories et la pratique, il fournit un regard dans la nature de communication et la signification du geste sur les résultats vocaux aussi bien que des qualités de la direction cette activité musicale. L'article rend compte également d'une recherche qui a étudié le développement professionnel des étudiants et des professeurs dans le secteur de la direction chorale, se concentrant sur leurs attitudes, l'acquisition de compétence et l'importance adjoints à la réflexion sur la pratique. Les résultats indiquent que des considérations sur ce qui compte en tant que geste de conduite efficace et la compétence de communication peut favoriser conduire mieux et, par conséquent, mieux, un chant plus expressif. En outre, l'impact positif de l'individu et de la réflexion va de pair sur la progression (tête à tête et dans un environnement d'étude virtuel) a été également reconnu. Certaines suggestions pour favoriser la conduite musicale efficace dans le secteur de la direction de choeur sont fournies, afin de rectifier des perspectives théoriques dans la pratique.

Vermitteln und Hervorheben der Ästhetik und der ausdrucksvollen Dimensionen im Chordirigieren

Der Artikel beschäftigt sich mit dem komplexen Sachverhalt für ein erfolgreiches Chordirigieren, ausgehend von der ästhetischen Dimension. Aufbauend auf der Forschung, Theorie und Praxis, werden einige Einsichten in die Natur der Kommunikation und der Bedeutung der Gestik und der stimmlichen Ergebnisse vermittelt, aber ebenso über Führungsqualitäten die mit einer solchen musikalischen Aktivität verbunden sind. Der Artikel berichtet von einer Forschungsstudie, worin die professionelle Entwicklung von Studenten und Lehrern im Bereich des Chordirigierens, basierend auf deren Verhalten und Entwickeln von Fertigkeiten untersucht wurde, wie auch aufzuzeigen, wie wichtig Überlegungen über die Praxis sind. Der Befund deckt auf, dass das in Betracht ziehen was wirklich zählt, eine erfolgreiche Gestik beim Dirigieren und vermittelnde Fähigkeiten zu verbessertem Dirigieren, und als Konsequenz dazu, zu besserem und ausdrucksvollerem Singen führen. Ergänzend dazu wurde auch erkannt, dass Selbst- und Gruppenreflektion (beide, von Angesicht zu Angesicht und in einem sogenannten lernenden Umfeld) einen positiven Einfluss haben. Einige Vorschläge zur Förderung von effizienter, musikalischer Führung im Bereich des Chordirigierens werden angeboten, in dem Sinne, den Boden für theoretische Perspektiven in der Praxis zu bereiten.

Comunicar y acentuar las dimensiones estéticas y expresivas de la dirección coral

Este artículo considera desde una dimensión estética temas relacionados con la efectividad de la dirección coral. Basándose en la investigación, en teorías y en la práctica, aporta un punto de vista sobre la naturaleza de la comunicación y la importancia del gesto en el resultado

340 INTERNATIONAL JOURNAL OF MUSIC EDUCATION 27(4)

vocal, así como sobre las cualidades de liderazgo concomitantes con dicha actividad musical. Este artículo también informa sobre una investigación que estudió el desarrollo profesional de estudiantes y profesores en el área de la dirección coral, centrándose en sus actitudes, en la adquisición de destrezas y en la importancia asignada la reflexión sobre la práctica. Los resultados revelan que la consideración de qué cuenta como gesto de dirección efectivo y como destrezas comunicativas puede promover una mejor dirección y, consecuentemente, un canto mejor y más expresivo. Además, se reconoció el impacto positivo de la reflexión individual y entre pares sobre el progreso, tanto cara a cara como en un entorno de aprendizaje virtual. Se proporcionan sugerencias para promover un liderazgo musical efectivo en el área de la dirección coral, a fin de fundamentar las perspectivas teóricas en la práctica.

[4]

Musicing

David J. Elliott

To have "music" in the familiar sense of audible performances, someone must first take action to make music or "music!" Musical works are not only a matter of sounds, they are also a matter of *actions*. Put another way, musicing is an inceptional property of music as an auditory presence.[1]

The word *musicing* may sound odd at first. This is understandable. The aesthetic concept of music-as-object obscures the more fundamental reality of "music!" as a form of deliberate doing and making. But consider how easily people speak of dancing, drawing, or painting, or how we use the word *dance* in multiple ways to mean the dancing a dancer does, a gathering of dancers, or the outcome of a dancer's dancing.

Musicing is an important term. It serves to remind (and re-mind) us that long before there were musical compositions there was music making in the sense of singing and playing remembered renditions and improvisations; that many cultures still view music as something people do; and that even in the West where composers and composing are essential aspects of the musical tradition, compositions remain silent until interpreted and performed by music makers. Most of all, musicing reminds us that performing and improvising through singing and playing instruments lies at the heart of MUSIC as a diverse human practice. As the philosopher Nicholas Wolterstorff insists, "the basic reality of music is not works nor the composition of works but music making."[2]

From this viewpoint, the question "What is music?" subdivides first into two closely related questions: (1) What is the nature of musicing? and (2) What does it mean to be a music maker? This chapter begins to answer both questions. But since we cannot say everything at once, and since improvising is a kind of performing, and since composing, arranging, and conducting usually imply the presence of musical performers, it seems reasonable to start with an emphasis on performing. (Thus, I shall often use *musicing* interchangeably with *performing* in this chapter.) Note, however, that most themes in my discussion apply to all forms of music making. Later chapters will develop these themes in relation to improvising, composing, arranging, and conducting.

1. Orientation

When people such as Jessye Norman or our imaginary students Clara, Sara, and Tim perform a composition by singing or playing an instrument, what is occurring? To say they are engaged in an activity is not precise enough. A person can be active and still get nothing done. Doing implies intention; the word *activity* alone does not. When Clara, Sara, Tim, and Jessye Norman perform a composition, they are not acting aimlessly or accidentally, nor are they acting musically in the sense that someone might be acting impatiently. They are doing something intentionally, and they are getting something done. Performing involves doing and making. For to make something is always to do something, and doing something always involves making a difference of some kind in a situation or condition.[3]

The key word above is *intention*. In thinking about the nature of performing we must differentiate immediately between (1) involuntary physical movements, reflexes, and manifestations of character (e.g., "acting impatiently") and (2) intentional actions. To act is not merely to move or exhibit behavior. To act is to move deliberately, with control, to achieve intended ends. Actions are purpose-*full*. Actions include movements, but actions cannot be reduced to movements because movements can occur without intent (such as involuntary twitches, tics, and shudders[4]). As the philosopher Saul Ross puts it, "the characteristic of personal action is that it is the realization of intentions. Action is informed and determined by a conscious purpose."[5]

Musicing in the sense of musical performing is a particular form of intentional human action. Performing depends on the deliberate formulation of purposes in a definite context. A musicer acts by selecting a particular situation or condition with an intention in mind; by deploying, directing, and adjusting certain actions to make changes of certain kinds in sounds of a certain kind; and by judging when the intended changes have been achieved in relation to standards and traditions of musical practice. To perform music is to achieve intended changes of a musical kind through actions that are taken up deliberately, or at will.[6] What this means, in turn, is that *to perform music is to act thoughtfully and knowingly*. For selecting, deploying, directing, adjusting, and judging are definite forms of thinking and knowing.

In review, musical performing involves the following essential ingredients in combination:

1. a music maker, or music makers
2. some kind of knowledge that determines and informs the intentions of music makers, including knowledge of relevant standards and traditions of musical practice
3. the sounds that music makers make and act upon in relation to their musical knowledge
4. the instruments (including voices) of their work
5. the actions of performing (and/or improvising)
6. the musical product-in-view (i.e., a performance of a composition, or an improvisation)

7. the context (physical, cultural, and social) in which music makers interpret, perform, or improvise musical works

These reflections bring us to the central question of this chapter: Exactly what does it mean to act thoughtfully and knowingly as a music maker? To answer, we must address several fundamental matters of human *being,* including the concepts of consciousness, knowledge, and thought. In other words, we must begin with what it means to be a music maker in the most fundamental sense of an individual, conscious *self.*

2. Consciousness, Knowledge, and Thought

What is consciousness? Philosophers and cognitive scientists are not entirely sure. What is certain, however, is that while the traditional theory of consciousness called *dualism* is in wide disrepute, *materialism* is a theory of consciousness approaching consensus.[7] Among the assumptions of the old dualistic notion of consciousness are the following:[8]

1. Mind (or human consciousness) is mental and the body is physical. (Mind is composed of special "mental stuff" that is distinct from the "physical matter" of the brain.) Hence, mind and body are separate and distinct.
2. There is a central place in the mind where a Central Controller (or Mental Boss) sifts and sorts all information and directs all thinking.
3. Thinking and knowing are matters of speaking silently to oneself, or out loud, or in written symbols. Action is physical and therefore dumb.

In opposition to dualism, materialism holds that there is no special "mental stuff" distinct from the physical brain. The philosopher and cognitive scientist Daniel Dennett summarizes the basic tenet of materialism this way: "[T]he mind *is* the brain."[9] That is, the physical processes of the brain are responsible for all the characteristics of human consciousness, including thinking, knowing, feeling, imagining, attending, remembering, and intending. (Some readers may prefer the term *naturalism* to *materialism* because it captures the same idea more clearly: "that the mind-brain relationship is a natural one. Mental processes just are brain processes."[10]) Furthermore, there is likely no central place in the brain where all incoming and outgoing information is sifted, sorted, and interpreted by some kind of Central Controller. Instead, human consciousness is parallel and distributed; consciousness consists in many simultaneous streams of processing that operate throughout the brain.

Consciousness, then, is not an inscrutable process. It is neither a mystical power nor a secret compartment in the head. Consciousness is part of the human nervous system that, in turn, is the outcome of biological processes. As Mark Johnson suggests, it's not that the mind is in the body, it's that *the body is in the mind.*[11] Furthermore, as I detail later, each individual human consciousness (or self) is a product of both natural selection and cultural evolution.

The psychologist Mihalyi Csikszentmihalyi (pronounced Me-hi Chick-sent-me-

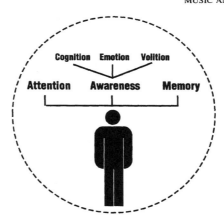

FIGURE 3.1. Consciousness, or Self

hi) maps consciousness in terms of three integrated subsystems: attention, awareness, and memory.[12] Awareness, in turn, consists in three capacities: cognition,
emotion, and volition (or intention). Cognition (from the Latin *cognoscere*, "to
know") means knowing in the widest sense of the term and includes all processes
involved in the verbal and nonverbal organization, retrieval, use, and application
of our apprehensions. Cognition refers to the various processes by which we recognize, relate, and deploy information from inside and outside ourselves. *Information* includes all the differentiated sights and sounds, all the recognized thoughts
and emotions, all the situations and events, that we encounter.[13] In sum, attention,
awareness, and memory constitute the human meaning-making system we call consciousness, and another word for human consciousness is *self*.

The "portrait" of the self in Figure 3.1 brings these thoughts together.

I wish to highlight three important themes. First, attention, awareness, and
memory interact. Our everyday phenomenological experience results from the integration of our powers of consciousness. There is likely no such thing as cognition
without emotion, emotion without cognition, or awareness without memory.

Second, every aspect of consciousness depends on attention. Attention is the
gateway to consciousness and is required to select, sort, retrieve, and evaluate all
overt and covert actions.[14] Csikszentmihalyi conceives attention as an energy supply that fuels thinking and knowing in all their various forms.[15] But there are
limitations on this energy supply.[16] We cannot pay attention to everything there is
to see, hear, or do.

Third, there is a consensus among scholars that thinking and knowing are not
one-dimensional phenomena: verbal expression is not the only form that thinking
and knowing can take. Instead, there are varieties of thinking and knowing. Aristotle made the same point long ago when he distinguished between theoretical
knowledge (*epistémé*), practical knowledge (*politiké*), and productive knowledge
(*techné*).[17] Aristotle believed that each form of knowledge depends on its own
dominant form of thinking and its own definite standards. In line with this tradition,

the philosopher Vernon Howard suggests that thinking exhibits itself in at least the following ways:[18] (1) in what people believe and assert; (2) in how people deliberate and decide; (3) in how people perform in various kinds of action; and (4) in how people generate and use images to guide and shape action. Moreover, says Howard, "whatever the dominant mode of thought, others inevitably get involved in surrounding and supporting ways."[19]

Contemporary theories of intelligence reflect this multidimensional view of thinking and knowing. For it stands to reason that if thinking and knowing come in a variety of forms, then human intelligence is not one-dimensional, but multidimensional. Howard Gardner's theory of multiple intelligences[20] (which posits musical intelligence as one of seven) and Robert Sternberg's triarchic theory of mind[21] are extensions of this multifarious way of thinking about thinking. "An intelligence," says Gardner, "is an ability to fashion products, or to solve problems, that are of significance within one or more cultural settings."[22] Part of Gardner's mission is to emphasize that abilities not typically considered intelligences in Western culture (e.g., musical and bodily-kinesthetic ones) should be counted on an equal footing with linguistic and mathematical abilities.[23] Gardner suggests that one helpful way to grasp his proposal "is to think of the various intelligences as *sets of know-how*—procedures for doing things."[24]

Gardner's reference to "know-how" echoes the writings of Jean Piaget and Gilbert Ryle, among others. In his influential book *The Concept of Mind*,[25] Ryle debunks dualism and its corollary that thinking and knowing are always and only verbal. In the process, Ryle makes important distinctions between nonverbal knowing-*how* (or procedural knowledge) and verbal knowing-*that* (or formal knowledge). These two basic classifications of knowledge are widely accepted by philosophers and cognitive scientists. Moreover, many scholars posit several additional categories of knowing.

In summary, the way has been opened for a more complete epistemology, one in which thinking and knowing (and intelligence) are not restricted to words and other symbols but are also manifested in *action*. With these ideas in mind, let us return to the nature of music making in general and performing in particular.

3. Musicianship

Music making is essentially a matter of *procedural* knowledge. I say "essentially" because it is reasonable to argue that at least four other kinds of musical knowledge contribute to the procedural essence of music making in a variety of ways. Following the cognitive psychologists Carl Bereiter and Marlene Scardamalia,[26] the names I shall give to these four kinds of knowing are: formal musical knowledge, informal musical knowledge, impressionistic musical knowledge, and supervisory musical knowledge. Taken together, these five forms of musical knowing constitute *musicianship*.

Let me rephrase what I have just written. Whenever a person (child through adult) is making music well, he or she is exhibiting a multidimensional form of knowledge called musicianship. Musicianship is demonstrated in actions, not

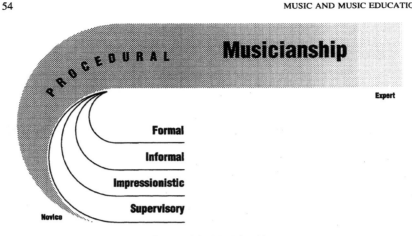

FIGURE 3.2. Musicianship

words. It is a form of practical knowledge, or reflective practice,[27] a matter of what Donald Schön calls "thinking-in-action" and "knowing-in-action."[28] But while musicianship is procedural in essence, four other kinds of musical knowledge contribute to this essence in surrounding and supporting ways.

A preliminary map of musicianship appears in Figure 3.2. More will be added in later chapters, including an explanation of the relationships between music making and music-listening know-how (or *listenership*).

The next several sections of this chapter explain the procedural essence of musicianship and the four other kinds of musical knowing that contribute to this essence. Before I proceed, however, there are a few overarching points that need highlighting.

In Chapter 2 I stated that MUSIC consists in many musical practices worldwide and that each musical practice pivots on the shared understandings of the musicers who are the practitioners of that practice. Thus, musicianship is not synonymous with what it takes to make and listen for the music of any one musical practice. *Musicianship is practice-specific.* That is to say, while the five kinds of knowledge that make up musicianship likely hold across most (if not all) musical practices, the precise contents of these knowledge categories are context-dependent. For example, the musicianship of a Dagomba master drummer differs in content (but not in its five-dimensional structure) from the musicianship of (say) a North Indian drummer, a jazz drummer, an opera singer, or a Bulgarian bagpiper. It is because the five component knowings of musicianship are practice-specific (or "situated") that musicianship differs from musical practice to practice.

What I am proposing, then, is that while musicianship is essentially local (or context-dependent), it is global to the extent that most (if not all) forms of musicianship involve the same five *kinds* of musical knowing. Of course, musicianship is also global in the most basic sense that all forms of music making are mainly directed toward the construction of successive and simultaneous musical sound patterns.[29] Music makers everywhere construct and chain musical patterns together,

make same-different comparisons among musical sound patterns, and vary, transform, and abstract musical patterns.[30] (This is not to say that musical works are
merely sound patterns. On the contrary, as I explain in later chapters, musical works
are always multilayered, or multidimensional. But all musical works obviously
depend on auditory patterns of some kind.) In sum, musicianship is what music
makers know how to do with practice-specific musical sound patterns in relation
to practice-specific musical knowings.

Let us now examine each knowledge component of musicianship in turn.

4. The Procedural Essence of Musicianship

An understanding of musicianship begins with an understanding of its procedural
nature. What does it mean to act thoughtfully and knowingly as a musical performer?

In the old dualistic view, actions follow from verbal thoughts in a two-step
sequence of think-act, think-act, ad infinitum. The first event is mental (speaking
silently to oneself), and the second event is physical (bodily movement). The dualistic assumption is that thinking and knowing are always verbal and that bodily
actions are nonverbal, or dumb.

Most philosophers and cognitive scientists today deny the dualistic view. Actions do not proceed by (1) verbally theorizing to oneself and then (2) physically
doing. If they did, says Ryle, then the first event (verbal thinking) would become
an action that would itself require a preceding act of theorizing, thereby leading
us to the absurdity (or infinite regress) that no one can act until he or she completes
an infinite number of verbal thoughts.[31] In the contemporary view, *actions are
nonverbal forms of thinking and knowing in and of themselves.* Ryle puts it this
way: "Overt intelligent performances are not clues to the workings of minds; they
are those workings."[32]

Consider the example of a surgeon operating on a patient. As Saul Ross explains, the surgeon's actions are theoretical and practical at the very same time:

> Each thrust of the scalpel, a movement which is done intentionally, is one wherein
> thought and action work together, not as two separate additive components nor as
> two consecutive events, one mental and the other material, but as one where the
> mental and the material components are interwoven. An action is a piece of overt
> behavior that cannot be detached or separated from the thought which motivates and
> directs it.[33]

John Macmurray agrees:

> The Self that reflects and the Self that acts is the same Self. . . . Action is not blind.
> When we turn reflection to action, we do not turn from consciousness to uncon-
> sciousness. When we act, sense, perception, and judgment are continuous activity,
> along with physical movement. . . . Action, then, is full concrete activity of the self
> in which all our capacities [all powers of consciousness] are employed.[34]

When we know how to do something competently, proficiently, or expertly, our knowledge is not manifested verbally but practically. During the continuous actions of singing or playing instruments *our musical knowledge is in our actions; our musical thinking and knowing are in our musical doing and making.* Thus, it is entirely appropriate to describe competent musical performers as thinking very hard and very deeply (but tacitly) as they perform (or improvise)—as they construct and chain musical patterns together; as they vary, transform, and abstract musical patterns; as they judge the quality of their musical constructions in relation to specific criteria and traditions of musical practice; and as they interpret the emotional expressiveness of musical patterns. In other words, a performer's musical understanding is exhibited not in what a performer says about what he or she does; a performer's musical understanding is exhibited in the quality of what she gets done in and through her actions of performing. Of course, it is entirely possible to reflect *on,* or speak to oneself about, one's actions as they proceed. Such "reflecting-on-action"[35] can and does occur. For the most part, however, performers think nonverbally *in* action, reflect-in-action, and know-in-action.

Let me develop these points through another example. If I tell you that I know how to ski, and if I explain the why-what-and-how of downhill skiing, will this convince you that I really know how to ski? I think not. You will want tangible proof of my skiing know-how. You will want to see me ski successfully on several occasions before you grant that, "Yes, David, you really do know how to ski." My words about skiing are not enough. The proof of my "skiership" lies in the effectiveness of my skiing actions.

The same holds for you as my evaluator. To understand and assess my performance as a downhill skier, you must also possess some degree of competency or proficiency in downhill skiing. As Gilbert Ryle insists: "[T]he knowledge that is required for understanding intelligent performances of a specific kind is some degree of competence in performances of that kind."[36] Knowing how to do something intelligently and knowing how to watch or listen to someone do something well are two sides of the same conscious coin: "The intelligent performer operates critically, the intelligent spectator follows critically. Roughly, execution and understanding are merely different exercises of knowledge of the tricks of the same trade. . . . [T]he capacity to appreciate a performance is one in type with the capacity to execute it."[37]

Note that the ability to follow an expert performance does not require the same *levels* of knowing involved in accomplishing that performance. (One need not be an Olympic-level skier to understand Olympic skiing.) What I am suggesting instead is that to understand and appreciate (or value knowledgeably) an intelligent performance, a spectator (or audience member) requires the same *kinds* of knowing as the performer(s), including a reasonable level of procedural knowledge in performances of that nature.[38]

Of course, nonparticipants may gain some knowledge and pleasure by reading about skiing, basketball, or cricket, or by watching these sports on television. But because sports are essentially concerned with athletic performances (or thinking-in-action), a discerning level of understanding and appreciation demands knowledge in kind. Without developing some competency in the procedural knowings that lie at the core of these pursuits, and a first hand knowledge of the circumstances in which these knowings apply, a spectator's perspectives on and relationships with these sports will remain moot in the most essential regard.

These ideas apply equally to musicianship. The proof of my musicianship lies in the quality of my music making, in what I get done as a performer (improviser, composer, arranger, or conductor). To understand and assess the quality of my musicianship as exhibited in my music making, my evaluators (and other listeners) must possess some degree of competency in musicing themselves. Rephrasing Ryle: Your capacity to understand (and therefore estimate properly the value of) my musical thinking-in-action is one in type with knowing how to think musically in action yourself.

Non–music makers may gain some knowledge and pleasure by reading about music or by listening to recordings. But as I shall continue to explain in this book, because the sounds of music are essentially a matter of artistic-cultural actions and performances, a discerning level of understanding and appreciation demands knowledge in kind. Without developing some competency in the procedural know-ings that lie at the core of musical practices and musical works, and a first hand knowledge of the circumstances in which these knowings apply, a listener's per-spectives on and relationships with music will remain moot in the most essential regard.

On the basis of the discussion so far, it seems fair to suggest that a person who knows how to do something competently possesses knowledge in the robust sense of a working understanding of a domain. Clearly, a working understanding includes known principles and the ability to make effective judgments about one's actions in relation to the applicable standards, traditions, obligations, and ethics of a given domain. But what shall we say about the role of verbal knowledge? Indeed, mention of "principles" and "judgments" implies the presence of verbal concepts.

This is partly correct—but only partly. For concepts need not be verbal. A concept (from *concipere,* "to conceive") is a thought or an idea of any degree of concreteness or abstraction. A concept is anything that enables consciousness to distinguish between and among phenomena, a cognitive unit that can manifest itself in words, in images of various kinds, or in practical actions. In short, our contem-porary understanding of the term *concept* goes well beyond the old classical notion of early psychology that restricts concepts to verbal abstractions alone.[39] Cogni-tive scientists now recognize various kinds of concepts, including verbal concepts, nonverbal practical concepts, fuzzy concepts, situational concepts, and social concepts.[40]

Jean Piaget foreshadowed these ideas in *The Origins of Intelligence in Children.* Piaget recognized that children make practical adaptations and judgments and solve problems in relation to their environments before they can speak or conceptualize in words.[41] In doing so, children develop and employ *practical* concepts, principles, and judgments. In Piaget's view, actions speak for themselves. Piaget elaborates: "There is no basic difference between verbal logic and the logic inherent in the coordination of actions, but the logic of actions is more profound and more prim-itive. It develops more rapidly and surmounts the difficulties it encounters more quickly, but they are the same difficulties of decentration as those which will appear later in the field of language."[42]

Practical concepts are far richer than words can capture. Compare bicycle riding to a written description of the physics involved in balancing a bike. The action of riding speaks more effectively than words about riding. More to the point, there is no reason to believe that riding a bicycle involves anything like speaking the laws of physics to ourselves while we ride along.

In musical terms, there is no reason to accept the dualistic supposition that musical performing involves anything like reading a set of rules in the mind before or during the actions of performing. As Hubert Dreyfus emphasizes, although a verbal explanation may enable the audience to conceive certain aspects of a performance for itself, a verbal formalization is "in no way an explanation of [a] performance."[43] At best, words can only describe what may be going on; they cannot explain what is actually going on in performers while they perform or improvise.

While it is true, then, that verbal concepts and principles play an important role in learning to make music (as I explain in the next section of this chapter), the actions of music making can be seen, fundamentally, as the "em-body-ment" of musical thinking, knowing, and understanding.

There is an important parallel here. Whereas the development of verbal thinking depends heavily on verbal concepts, practical thinking-in-action depends heavily on nonverbal, practical concepts. Just as verbal concepts emerge, develop, and are utilized in the realm of language, practical concepts emerge, develop, and are utilized in action.[44] This helps explain why models of action are so effective in learning how to do something. Models and demonstrations are practical concepts. Practical concepts inform the actions of students in much the same way that verbal concepts inform verbal thinking. Again, practical concepts can never be fully translated into verbal statements. They are too complex. This is why Sparshott emphasizes that the artist's procedural knowledge "is neither verbalizable nor mechanical, and hence neither reducible nor subordinated to propositional knowledge."[45] Sparshott continues: "It is the novice, and not the skilled practitioner, whose knowledge is contained in precepts he can recite, and many of his failures come about because his skill does not run beyond his grasp of general truths."[46]

In broader perspective, materialism holds that there is likely no hierarchy of commands at work in consciousness when we engage in ongoing actions.[47] Actions are not controlled with verbal messages sent by a Central Controller from a Central Command Center in the brain as dualistic theories maintain.[48] There are no grounds for believing in such things. Our conscious processes do not operate in linear, stepwise fashion. Again, consciousness is a matter of many parallel streams of processing in which multiple goals are simultaneously on the alert for means of expression.

"Means of expression" include actions as well as words. And means of expression are, themselves, on the alert for employment opportunities. Our conscious processes are a matter of back-and-forth interactions among the intentions we want to express, our individual ways of expressing these intentions, and the contexts in which we act. During the overall action of musical performing, consciousness makes a continuous series of parallel adjustments in relation to our musical knowledge (tacit and verbal) and the context in which we express our musical thinking-in-action.

I conclude this section with four supplementary reflections on the procedural dimension of musicianship and the kind of thinking-knowing it involves.

Consider that the actions of musical performers and improvisers (like the actions of surgeons and dancers) are not natural (or innate). They are cultural actions.[49] Cultural actions require the elaboration, extension, and very often the reconstruction of everyday movement patterns. For example, there is nothing routine about the way a musician holds a violin in Western classical practices, or the way an African master drummer uses his drumming hands, or the way a singer achieves bel canto. Ordinary efforts and movements become part of artistic musical actions by virtue of the thinking a performer does in and about his attempts to perform the musical works of a particular musical practice.

Second, the actions of musical performing involve different costs and benefits and different levels of risk for success. Performing therefore requires us to make personal judgments in action. Contrast this with a task that follows a predetermined set of steps. For example, preparing an aircraft for takeoff requires step-by-step algorithmic thinking in checklist fashion. (Similarly, some rudimentary aspects of musical performing require the integration of movement sequences through step-by-step reflecting-on-action, especially during the early stages of learning.) But a competent, proficient, or expert performer must continuously reflect upon, judge, and adjust his or her thinking-in-action on the basis of internalized sets of practical or heuristic understandings.

Third, the actions of performing are most often prepared, informed, or practiced before final public performances. (This also holds, to a large extent, for improvising.) Practice sessions and rehearsals may therefore be thought of in terms of bringing about and editing numerous "drafts" of a "final-draft" performance. As I explain in Chapters 7 and 9, each draft rehearsal of a composition involves generating, selecting, and refining one's concept or *interpretation* of a given musical composition as a whole. In other words, there is a substantial and critical difference between merely being able to produce tones and rhythms and knowing how to *perform* musical works. The difference, of course, is *musicianship*.

Fourth, while preparing a composition for performance, performers inevitably think deductively and inductively. For example, to decide the most effective bowings and articulations for an orchestral composition, a violinist employs deductive strategies. In addition, inferences must be drawn from particular details to similar instances. The same holds for a singer's analysis and interpretation of the relationships between a choral composition and its text. A performer accomplishes such thinking in relation to verbal and practical knowledge of the musical context concerned, including his or her previous experience in that practice. What this means, in turn, is that a *person's performance of a given composition is a robust representation of his or her level of musical understanding of that work and the musical practice of which it is a piece.*

In this view, differences in accuracy and interpretation across performances of a given composition reflect differences in individual musical thinking and knowing. In singing or playing a composition, performers think partly in relation to sound patterns and action patterns defined by a score (or a remembered performance). But they also think in relation to less clearly stipulated guidelines, including histories and standards of musical practice, possibilities of interpretation, the feed-back that arises in a specific context, and their own musical judgments and intuitions. Such judgments are more individualized than evaluations of, for example, mathematical correctness, because part of the artistry (or deep musical understanding) we often expect from musical performers includes their ability to personalize their performances by creating original and significant interpretations of given compositions.

We can draw several conclusions at this point. First, an artistic performance of a composition requires many forms of thinking and knowing, ranging on a wide continuum from the most convergent to the most divergent, from the most tacit to the most verbally explicit, from the most practical to the most abstract. Second, performing musically in relation to the standards and traditions of a musical domain engages a person's entire system of conscious powers: attention, awareness, cognition, emotion, intention, and memory. Third, although competent music making demands many types of thinking and knowing, it is nonverbal and procedural in essence. Knowing *how* to make music musically and knowing *that* performing involves this-and-that are two different modes of knowing. Procedural knowledge and formal knowledge are logically separable.[50] Artistic musical success validates musicianship; logical evidence validates formal knowledge about music. Donald Schön summarizes the differences between procedural knowledge and formal knowledge:

> Whatever language we may employ . . . our descriptions of knowing-in-action are always *constructions*. They are always attempts to put into explicit, symbolic form a kind of intelligence that begins by being tacit and spontaneous. Our descriptions are conjectures that need to be tested against observation of their originals—which, in at least one respect, they are bound to distort. For knowing-in-action is dynamic, and "facts," "procedures," "rules," and "theories" are static.[51]

I have separated procedural musical knowledge from other forms of musical knowing (including verbal knowledge) for the sake of clarity. I reconnect them now.

5. Formal Musical Knowledge

Formal knowledge includes verbal facts, concepts, descriptions, theories—in short, all textbook-type information about music. (Equivalent terms are propositional knowledge, declarative knowledge, or knowing-*that*.)

In domains such as the performing arts and athletics, where thinking effectively in action is what counts, the relationship between procedural knowledge and formal knowledge can be highly variable. Many students grasp principles nonverbally in the process of music making and in the course of seeing and hearing models (practical concepts) of how to perform artistically. Other students require "talk" before they can think-in-action. Most students grasp principles both nonverbally and verbally. Some students will be full of verbal information about what they do; others will advance their musicianship to a significant level without it.

Most musical practices are sufficiently complex that music makers (including teachers and students) must consult sources of formal musical knowledge at various times. Verbal concepts about music history, music theory, and vocal and instrumental performance practices can influence, guide, shape, and refine a learner's musical thinking-in-action. By itself, however, formal musical knowledge is inert and unmusical. It must be converted into procedural knowing-in-action to achieve its potential. Accordingly, verbal concepts about musical pieces and procedures ought to be viewed as nothing more or less than resource materials for improving the reliability, portability, accuracy, authenticity, sensitivity, and expressiveness of musical thinking-in-action. In this view, the issue of prime importance to music educators is not whether to make use of formal musical knowledge but when and how.

This praxial philosophy of music education holds that formal knowledge ought to be filtered into the teaching-learning situation parenthetically and contextually. Verbal concepts about musical works and music making ought to emerge from and be discussed in relation to ongoing efforts to solve authentic musical problems through active music making. This contextualization of formal knowledge enables students to understand its value immediately and artistically. This, in turn, enables students to convert formal musical knowledge into musical knowing-in-action. As procedural knowledge develops in educational settings that approximate genuine musical practices, actions come to embody formal knowledge, including knowledge of musical notation.

The issue of notation deserves separate comment. Part of the musicianship of many (but not all) musical practices worldwide is knowledge about notation and knowledge of how to decode and encode musical sound patterns in staff notation, graphic notation, hand signs, or rhythmic syllables. But "music literacy,"[52] or the ability to decode and encode a system of musical notation, is not equivalent to musicianship. It is only one part of the formal and procedural dimensions of musicianship. Moreover, literacy should also be taught and learned parenthetically and contextually—as a coding problem to be gradually reduced within the larger process of *musical* problem solving through active music making.

Speaking more broadly, imparting formal musical knowledge in the process of active musical problem solving requires the use of various "languages." As Vernon Howard suggests, the term "languages" includes everything from the theoretical and technical terminology of a musical practice to practice-specific jargon to similes and metaphors to diagrammatic conceptions.[53]

For example, at one point in my development as a young trombonist I recall my teacher setting me the musical problem (or challenge) of performing a slow jazz ballad. This ballad required a very smooth, legato style. With a few carefully chosen words about breath support and articulation (formal knowledge), and a brief model of legato playing (practical concept), my teacher coached me toward performing the ballad musically—that is, in relation to the criteria and traditions of the jazz practice (the musical whole) of which the selected ballad was a part. In the course of trying to solve this musical problem, I grasped the principles I needed to think-in-action by converting formal knowledge into procedural knowledge. This legato aspect of my musicianship developed as an aside (in parenthetical relation) to the central thrust of my effort: learning to make music artistically in relation to the norms and ideals of a specific musical practice. In other words, the larger wheel of thinking-in-action meshed with the smaller ''legato wheel'' to propel me forward in my musical efforts. Subsequent reflecting in and on my musical performing made this small but important part of my procedural knowledge effective, reliable, and tacit.

Clearly, the procedural essence of musicianship is not acquired by slavishly repeating movements or memorizing verbal concepts about musical works. Instead, and with the guidance of educated teachers, students learn to *reflect on* the causes of their musical successes and failures in the course of their focused actions. Students learn how to *target their attention* to different aspects of their musical thinking-in-action in relation to practical and formal concepts. As Donald Schön explains, such reflecting-on-action usually occurs in the medium of words spoken silently to oneself (or aloud to others).[54] In contrast, reflecting-in-action—monitoring the effectiveness of our musical thinking-in-action in the present moment—is a nonverbal form of critical thinking. It enables us to adjust our thinking-in-action in relation to our grasp of musical goals, standards, traditions, and working principles. Schön adds the following:

> Like knowing-in-action, reflection-in-action is a process we can deliver without being able to say what we are doing. . . . Clearly, it is one thing to be able to reflect-in-action and quite another to be able to reflect *on* our reflection-in-action so as to produce a good verbal description of it; and it is still another thing to be able to reflect on the resulting description.[55]

While reflecting on their musical actions, students compare their music making to that of other musicers (peers, teachers, and musical heroes past and present). Students notice (or should be encouraged to discern) why, when, and how music making proceeds well or poorly. Such discernments lead to further understandings (tacit and verbal) of principles, standards, and histories of music making.

It follows that while formal knowledge about music and music making is necessary to become a music teacher, critic, or musicologist, it is neither a necessary prerequisite nor a sufficient corequisite for achieving competent, proficient, or expert levels of musicianship. True, many brilliant performers (improvisers, composers) talk and write eloquently about music and musical artistry. But many others do not. In sum, the acquisition of formal musical knowledge is a proper but secondary goal of music education.

6. Informal Musical Knowledge

Although widely recognized by cognitive scientists, informal knowledge is just beginning to receive rigorous study. As Bereiter and Scardamalia explain it, informal knowledge is the savvy or practical common sense developed by people who know how to do things well in specific domains of practice.[56]

Many popular films rest on oversimplified contrasts between formal and informal knowledge. Typically, the informal knowledge of the old country doctor wins out over the bookish stupidity of the young hotshot fresh out of medical school. But formal knowledge is not at odds with informal knowledge; it is simply different. Bereiter and Scardamalia suggest that formal knowledge is to informal knowledge as the tip of an iceberg is to its foundation.[57] Indeed, informal knowledge is hard to get at. It is not available in textbooks. Even experts have difficulty saying how they know what they know in the informal sense. When questioned, experts often refer to this kind of knowledge loosely as "experience." But a closer look reveals that informal knowledge involves at least three related ingredients. In musical terms, these ingredients can be explained this way: Informal musical knowledge involves the ability to reflect *critically* in action. Reflecting critically depends, in turn, on knowing when and how to make musical *judgments*. And knowing how to make musical judgments depends on an understanding of the musical situation or *context:* the standards and traditions of practice that ground and surround a particular kind of music making and music listening.

Critical reflecting-in-action is fundamental to musicianship because music making is not a simple matter of habits, behaviors, routines, or physical skills. (These common ways of talking about musical performance are as inaccurate as they are widespread. They rest on a dualistic misunderstanding of the cognitive nature of music making.) Indeed, it is not the case that for every action of music making there is a verifiable principle that always works and that can always be reduced to words. Principles of music making, like chess strategies, do not guarantee success. They are always provisional. The effectiveness, flexibility, and portability of musicianship hinges on the critical selection and deployment of all forms of musical knowing.[58]

Underlying the critical selection and deployment of musical knowings is "strategic musical judgment" (Howard's term[59]): the disposition and the ability to make musical judgments in action. This ingredient of informal musical knowledge develops through active musical problem solving. It grows by listening intently for the musical sounds one is performing and interpreting; weighing musical choices in action; adjusting one's musical thinking-in-action according to one's choices; assessing the artistic results of one's choices; and considering alternative strategies during continuing efforts to make music well.[60]

To give these ideas a human face, consider the informal musical knowledge of an African master drummer. In his *African Rhythm and African Sensibility* (1979), John Miller Chernoff explains how the Dagomba drumming practiced in Ghana interweaves diverse rhythmic patterns in a complex polymetric structure. The way the drummers in a Dagomba drum ensemble repeat, accentuate, and improvise contrasting patterns exerts a kind of pressure on the many rhythmic parts that make up the musical whole. This pressure creates rhythmic tension and drive. At its best, African musicians call the music "sweet."[61]

Making the music "sweet," says Chernoff, is a matter of knowing how and learning how to be "cool."[62] Less successful drummers tend to be "hot." They play impulsively. In the terms I am using, they have yet to develop the informal knowledge component of Dagomba musicianship.

The master drummer knows how to be patient. He knows the importance of waiting for the right moment in the ongoing texture of rhythms to make his contribution.[63] He improvises with respect for what the other drummers are doing.[64] (The master drummer is the one who has "cooled his heart."[65]) He pays attention to what the dancers are dancing. In the terms of this book, the master drummer knows how to reflect critically in action. He makes strategic judgments on the basis of his "situated knowledge" of the standards and traditions of Dagomba drumming. He is in tune with both the musical and social occasion that he is influencing and motivating. He has achieved this situational savvy from making music (and from observing others make music) in the authentic contexts of his Dagomba practice. In addition, his music making reflects and informs the social practices of his community. For, as Chernoff says, "we should be conscious of the fact that music making in Africa is above all an occasion for the demonstration of character."[66]

(At this point, the reader may wish to stop and reflect on the ways that informal musical knowledge manifests itself differently in different musical practices.)

Informal musical knowledge derives from two sources. One source is a person's individual (and usually partial) interpretations of the formal knowledge of a musical practice (if such is available). But the most important source is one's own musical reflecting-in-action. The informal knowledge component of musicianship crystallizes in a student's efforts to develop practical solutions to realistic musical problems in relation to the standards, traditions, history, and lore of a musical context. The process resembles the way a chess player learns: not by repeating moves over and over in isolation but by solving real chess problems in the context of playing real chess games (or practice games).

In sum, informal musical knowledge (like procedural musical knowledge) is distinctive in being closely tied to learning and working in the local conditions of a practice. Informal musical knowledge is *situated* knowledge: it is knowledge that arises and develops chiefly from musical problem finding and musical problem solving in a genuine musical context, or a close approximation of a real musical practice.

7. Impressionistic Musical Knowledge

"Intuition" comes closest to what we mean by "impressionistic knowledge."[67] It is what experts know as a strongly felt sense that one line of action is better than another, or not quite right.

At root, impressionistic knowledge is a matter of cognitive emotions or knowledgeable feelings for a particular kind of doing and making. Israel Scheffler and Paul Wagner use the terms "cognitive emotion"[68] and "mindful feeling"[69] to break down the walls people tend to build between thinking and feeling. As I have emphasized, consciousness is integrated. There is likely no such thing as thinking without feeling or feeling without thinking. Thinking and feeling are hybrids, neither completely emotive nor completely cognitive in content. Accordingly, says Wagner, the words *emotion* and *feeling* are vague and clumsy ways of referring to a wide assortment of experiences and events.[70] (Psychologists prefer the term *affect*.)

For example, while fear can be induced through direct chemical intervention (fear as bodily sensation), fear is most often a cognitive emotion resulting from a cognitive evaluation (tacit or verbal) of a particular situation. Indeed, people often have good reasons for being afraid of someone or something.[71] (Recall that cognition does not always require or imply the presence of verbal thinking. Our integrated powers of consciousness can appraise our circumstances tacitly in action and in-the-moment.)

Generally speaking, emotions tend to be cognitive. Emotions such as surprise, sadness, anger, jealousy, pride, sorrow, certainty, and doubt are always *about* something. Emotions arise from our personal knowledge and beliefs (tacit and verbal) about people, objects, situations, events, and ideas. Thinking and feeling (cognition and affect) are interdependent.

Music makers acquire nonverbal impressions, or an affective sense of things, while doing, making, and reflecting in specific musical contexts. These impressions influence a student's subsequent efforts and decisions. To develop musicianship is, in part, to advance a student's feel for or affective awareness of what "counts" in musical situations. Musicianship includes educated or knowledgeable feelings for the nature of music making and the nature of musical works in the contexts of definite music cultures. This is what I mean by impressionistic musical knowledge.

Consider the example of a young singer like our student Sara Band who is learning how to perform Kabalevsky's song *Good Night*.[72] As an advanced beginner, Sara is starting to reflect in and on her musical actions. Implicit in Sara's musical thinking-in-action is an emerging sensibility about how her singing ought to be carried out. Her affective sense of what ought to be done musically (which is informed by her procedural, formal, and informal musical knowings) works for her as she sings. In other words (and following the previous work of Nelson Goodman, Israel Scheffler, and Paul Wagner), I suggest that cognitive musical emotions fulfill a selective function by facilitating choices among patterns and by "defining their salient features, focusing attention accordingly."[73] Cognitive emotions play an essential role in helping music makers evaluate, decide, judge, generate, and select musical options in the actions of music making.

Notice, again, that impressionistic musical knowledge (like procedural and informal knowledge) is situated knowledge. It cannot be taught or learned in abstraction from the actions and contexts of actual music making. Impressionistic musical knowledge develops through critical musical problem solving in relation to natural music making challenges (for example, compositions to interpret and perform, improvisations to make).

The concept of impressionistic musical knowledge helps explain why a proficient performer might well say that he or she "feels" how to sing a certain phrase in a certain way or "senses" what to do without being able to say exactly why. Impressionistic musical knowledge is no less rational or intelligent for being affective. It is about specific musical matters. In short, cognitive musical emotions are artistically thought-*full*.

Impressionistic musical knowledge makes an essential contribution to musicianship. It helps us assess, categorize, and "place" our musical actions. It contributes to the ability to reflect in and on our actions. And it is especially important in grounding our ability to make critical musical judgments in action.

8. Supervisory Musical Knowledge

Supervisory knowledge is sometimes called metaknowledge or metacognition. This form of musical knowing includes the disposition and ability to monitor, adjust, balance, manage, oversee, and otherwise regulate one's musical thinking both in action ("in-the-moment") and over the long-term development of one's musicianship.

The immediate importance of supervisory musical knowledge becomes clear when we compare musical performing and improvising to reading a book or adding a sum. In reading and arithmetic, thinking and knowing usually operate in predictable (or closed) contexts. In performing and improvising, thinking- and knowing-in-action usually occur in less certain (or open) circumstances. The same holds for other reflective practices (such as teaching and athletics) in which the ability to act appropriately and optimally under pressure (in balanced relation to guidance from one's overall assessment of a given situation) is essential to succeeding.

In broad terms, I suggest that supervisory musical knowledge (knowing how to manage, guide, and advance one's musicianship in and over time) combines the following: (1) an overarching sense of musical-personal judgment; (2) an understanding of (if not a devotion to) the musical obligations and ethics of a given practice (see Chapter 7); and (3) a particular kind of imagination that Vernon Howard calls "heuristic imagination":[74] the ability to project and hold pertinent images in one's mind before, during, and after one's musical efforts. Indeed, while "imagination" has several aspects (as I detail in Chapter 9), the practical process of musical image making (or "imagination in action"[75]) is a key component of supervisory musical knowledge. Howard offers several examples of this point:

> "mental rehearsal": going over things "in the mind's eye" before or after doing them; forming or holding particular ends-in-view such as . . . the aural image of a desired sound, a game plan, or correction to be made in practice; metaphoric imagery—"Imagine the throat as a tall dome across which the voice travels," . . . ; and aspect perception— . . . the hidden fifth in a musical progression. In these and many other ways, mental imagery constitutes a "mind set" or selective predilection to specific patterns of thought, action, and perception.[76]

Howard observes that imagination-in-action goes hand-in-glove with the ability and disposition to continuously retarget one's attention forward to new musical challenges (or ends) as one develops the ability (or means) to meet current challenges: "Improved facility at the keyboard, for example, enables one not only to perform a musical passage up to some preconceived [or imagined] standard of phraseology, but to reconceive the phraseology itself—to project [or imagine] a new standard."[77]

Finally, a student who uses heuristic imagination as part of his musical self-management procedures may be more likely to identify with, care for, and enjoy what and how he is musicing. This is so because holding appropriate musical images, goals, and standards in mind as references for the quality of one's moment-to-moment efforts prevents rehearsals and practice sessions from degenerating into mindless drill and drudgery. As Howard says:

> The implicit distinction here is between critical foresight and mere preconception or slavish adherence to habit or routine. Only in imagination can we confront past experience with present challenge by holding ends *in* view as well as the past in *re-*view. In so doing, imagination focuses the whence and the whither of our efforts in critical overview, supporting the will by showing the way. . . .
>
> [T]he imagination sustains critical hindsight and foresight, not so much as a matter of "inspiration," but rather as of *control* within a means-ends continuum linking the necessary skills to the propelling disposition to do well.[78]

Supervisory musical knowledge is yet another kind of situated knowledge. It develops primarily in educational contexts centered on musical actions, interactions, and transactions with life-like musical challenges. To some extent, supervisory knowledge also results from talking to one's teachers, peers, and oneself about the strengths and weaknesses of one's musicianship. But its ultimate application (and test) occurs during efforts to monitor and coordinate all other forms of musical knowing in the pursuit of artistic musical outcomes.

Notice, in review, that four of the five kinds of knowledge that constitute musicianship—procedural, informal, impressionistic, and supervisory musical knowledge—are essentially nonverbal and situated. These commonalities hold several important implications for music teaching and learning that I expand upon later. At this point I wish only to link and underline the following points.

To make and listen for music intelligently requires musicianship. Developing musicianship is essentially a matter of induction; students must enter and become part of the musical practices (or music cultures) they intend to learn. This is so because musicianship is context-dependent. The musicianship underlying any practice of music making and listening has its roots in specific communities of practitioners who share and advance a specific tradition of musical thinking. Musical practices swirl around the efforts of practitioners who originate, maintain, and refine established ways and means of musicing, as well as cherished musical histories, legends, and lore.

Of course, the extent to which practitioners formalize and regulate the criteria and traditions of their musical practices varies greatly around the world. Many musical practices survive orally and aurally. Many other practices depend on complex formal institutions (such as university music schools) to protect, maintain, research, teach, and certify practitioners in their traditions and standards of musicianship. Either way, effective music teaching and learning requires a definite type of teaching-learning situation that inducts learners into musical practices as authentically as possible (see Chapters 10 and 11). John Dewey placed a high value on teaching and learning conceived as "induction" in this sense: "The customs, methods, and working standards . . . of the calling constitute a 'tradition,' and . . . initiation into the tradition is the means by which the powers of learners are released and directed."[79]

Note Dewey's words: "released and directed." Standards and traditions of musical practice nurture musicianship, musical achievement, and musical enjoyment by releasing or pushing musical thinking forward as much as they define what communities of music makers and listeners currently understand and value. They mark the existing boundaries of musical practices. Even new musical practices depend on shared ways of making and listening for musical works, on shared norms and ideals, and on the tradition that begins to form around the initial musical works of innovative practitioners.

Standards and traditions define (formally and informally) what counts as musical in a specific context of musicing and listening. Thus, musical standards and traditions function in two ways. They ask musicers and listeners to respect and work within current boundaries. At the same time, they invite musicers and listeners to go beyond current understandings and values to create highly original musical works and, perhaps, whole new musical practices. Indeed, just as the real products of apple trees are not apples but new apple trees, the eventual outcomes of musical practices are not only new musical works but new musical practices.

9. Musicianship as Musical Understanding

Some people want to claim that musical understanding is distinct from knowing how to make music well. The claim is false. It rests on the dualistic assumption that verbal knowledge about music represents true understanding, while the ability to make music well is a mechanical skill or behavior. Such notions fail to appreciate the rich and complex nature of music making as knowledge-in-action. Howard Gardner agrees:

> A word about understanding in the arts is in order. If the notion of understanding is introduced in too literal a fashion in the arts, it may be taken as cognate to the mastery of certain concepts like "style" or "rhythm" or "the Renaissance." As I have noted throughout this book, however, any notion of understanding ought to center on the capacities exhibited and the operations carried out by masters of a domain, and each domain features its own characteristic constraints and opportunities.
>
> Such a perspective reveals that, in the arts, production ought to lie at the center of any artistic experience.[80]

This book's praxial philosophy of music education holds that musicianship equals musical understanding. Musicianship (which always includes listenership) is a form of working understanding. The word *understanding* points to something deeper than formal knowledge about musical works. It implies a related network of knowings, not always linear or verbal, but weblike and procedural in essence. The word *working* suggests a practical, situated form of knowing—knowing anchored in the contexts and purposes of specific musical practices.

David Perkins suggests that all forms of understanding share at least five characteristics.[81] Musicianship exhibits all five characteristics. First, musicianship is a *relational* form of knowing. It is gridlike. Competent, proficient, and artistic music makers know how different aspects of musicing relate to one another in terms of cause-effect, whole-part, form-function, comparison-contrast, and production-interpretation.[82] More broadly, to possess musicianship is to comprehend how the components of one's thinking and knowing relate to the goals, ideals, standards, and histories that define particular musical communities and thereby give one's musical efforts meaning.[83]

Second, musicianship is *coherent*. At an expert level, the various strands of tacit and verbal knowings that make up this multidimensional form of understanding weave together in a seamless fabric of fluid thinking-in-action. Musicianship is not only unified in itself, it is effective in achieving the practical ends of musical excellence and creativity as artistic music makers actually know them.[84]

Third, musicianship includes what Perkins calls "standards of coherence,"[85] or what this chapter calls *standards of practice*. Standards of musical excellence, originality, and significance anchor and define the contents of musicianship. In doing so, standards also serve to guide the development of musicianship. For as the various components of musicianship grow and weave together, knowledge of musical criteria directs music makers toward new goals and new possibilities of music making within a given genre.

Fourth, musicianship is a *productive* form of knowledge. As in all forms of working understanding, the relevant test of musicianship is the way it "plays out in action in response to the demands and opportunities of the moment."[86] What this chapter calls the *procedural* essence of musicianship David Perkins terms "generative use":[87] the demonstration of understanding in practical achievement.

Fifth, musicianship is *open*. Like all forms of genuine understanding, musicianship is not an end but a continuous process. It grows in the ways that a complex web weaves inward and outward. It develops as each of its five knowledge components mature and interweave with each other.

For all these reasons, I recommend *praxis* to summarize the essential nature of music making and musicianship. As I noted in Chapter 1, Aristotle used *praxis* to mean informed and deliberative "doing-action" in which doers (as ethical practitioners) are not merely concerned with completing tasks correctly (*techné*), but with "right action": enlightened, critical, and "situated" action. *Praxis* means action committed to achieving goals (*telos*) in relation to standards, traditions, images, and purposes (*eidos*) viewed as Ideals that are themselves open to renewal, reformulation, and improvement. In *praxis* (and in knowledgeable music making as I have attempted to describe it), the feedback that arises from one's reflections is used to improve one's expertise and to refine (or redefine) the goals that guide one's making and doing.[88] Put another way, to act artistically as a music maker is to engage in music making and music listening (and MUSIC) as *praxis*.

Contrast this praxial view with more common descriptions of music making as a skill, craft, technique, or psychomotor behavior. If laypeople understood the original meaning of "skill" (from the Old Norse *skil* for understanding, or competence), then we might make a case for retaining its usage. But the original sense of the word has been almost completely lost. Nowadays *skill* means many things, including manual dexterity, a trade, a general ability, a habit, a routine, or the ability to follow rules in algorithmic fashion. In short, *skill* fails to communicate the fact that competent music making depends on a legitimate and complex form of *knowledge* that partakes of consciousness as a whole (attention, cognition, emotion, intention, and memory).

More broadly, the tendency to describe music making in terms of knowledge *and* skill assumes a dualistic sense of mind. It implies, wrongly, that verbal knowledge is primary in music making, that musical actions always follow from verbal thoughts, and, therefore, that the actions of musicing are essentially mind-less.

Craft (from the German word *Kraft*) is ambiguous, suggesting strength, manual dexterity, and informed ability.[89] While it is true that *craft* is sometimes used in the larger sense of practical knowledge,[90] its old-fashioned association with manual dexterity persists. Accordingly, musical craftsmanship is inadequate to communicate the fact that music making depends on a wide range of tacit and verbal knowings, especially knowings of an informal, impressionistic, and supervisory kind.

The suggestion that music making pivots on techniques will not do either. Technique (from *techné*) is narrowly concerned with the technology of making. True, the procedural dimension of musicianship includes techniques, as well as routines, procedures, facilities, and abilities. But in music making done well, the procedural essence of musicianship always involves several other forms of thinking and knowing linked to specific goals, ideas, and values of musical doing and making (as *praxis* implies).

In summary, many common ways of conceiving music making and musicianship tend to misrepresent and diminish their true natures. This book's philosophy urges the view that musicianship equals musical understanding and that musicianship (which always includes listenership) is a multipartite form of working understanding (or *praxis*) that is procedural and situated in essence. Stated another way, artistic music making and intelligent music listening involve a multidimensional, relational, coherent, generative, open, and educable form of knowing called musicianship.

10. Levels of Musicianship

Because musicianship is open—because it is not an all-or-nothing matter—there must be various levels or stages of musicianship to achieve. Since the possibilities are numerous, and since *Music Matters* is a philosophy of music education (not a psychology of musical development), my only intent in the following is to supplement this discussion with a general outline of how musicianship may progress. In doing so, I combine the themes of this chapter with a five-level scheme of expertise suggested elsewhere by Dreyfus and Dreyfus.[91] Later chapters will reference this scheme as the concept of musicianship continues to unfold.

Before continuing, please note that the five-level progression I present is not tied to "age-level characteristics" as traditionally defined by mathematical, linguistic, or other kinds of nonmusical measures. Accordingly, a musical artist can be a child or adult, depending on what that person knows how to do musically. Note, also, that a person can evidence his or her level of musicianship in several ways: by performing, improvising, composing, arranging, and/or conducting (all of which involve listening). For ease of discussion, however, I describe the five levels—novice, advanced beginner, competency, proficiency, and expert— in terms of musical performing.

1. *Novices* may have some formal knowledge about musical works. They may

even possess a few tacit and verbal principles of action that they can follow in step-by-step fashion. But their musical thinking is essentially trial-and-error; it is not yet thinking-in-action. Novices have little (if any) informal, impressionistic, or supervisory musical knowledge because they have not yet had time to "situate" themselves in the context of the musical practice(s) they are striving to learn. As a result, novices are typically unable to see the musical forest for the trees. Their focus is local, not global. Novices tend to be so absorbed in *reducing* immediate problems that they have no attention left for musical problem *solving*. This local focus and lack of surplus attention prevents novices from making music in a reliable and reflective way.

2. Unlike the novice, an *advanced beginner* like Sara Band (see Chapter 1) has small degrees of musical knowledge in each of the five categories that make up musicianship. Sara has begun to weave these knowings together in action. (She has begun to *proceduralize* her musical knowings.) For these reasons, Sara has small amounts of surplus attention that she can deploy to move back and forth between local and global levels of musical thinking-in-action. But the advanced beginner cannot yet think reliably or fluently. Her reflecting-on-action still absorbs too much of her attention and awareness at the local level of detail.

3. The *competent* music student is one who has succeeded in proceduralizing a variety of tacit and verbal knowings from each of the five knowledge categories. He is able to reflect-in-action by monitoring the features and outcomes of what he is doing in relation to standards of musical practice. He understands these demands formally and informally. He can solve many musical problems if they are pointed out to him by his teacher.

The more global intents of students at the competent level of musicianship act like a magnet to draw their actions forward from in-front. (The local concerns of novices push them along from behind.) Still, a major part of what competent students lack is the ability to *find* musical problems on their own. Competent students have yet to develop the musical problem-finding ability they require to integrate and enhance their musicianship.

4. Someone like Clara Nette is said to possess a *proficient* level of musicianship. Her attention is almost completely free of reflections on her actions. Her musicing is characterized by fluent thinking-in-action and reflecting-in-action. Clara's informal, impressionistic, and supervisory musical knowings inform her thinking-in-action as she attends to the significant features of the compositions she is interpreting and performing.

5. The *musical expert or artist* possesses what Dreyfus and Dreyfus call "deep situational understanding."[92] An expert level of musicianship is distinguished by the full development and integration of procedural, formal, informal, impressionistic, and supervisory musical knowledge. The artist's level of thinking-in-action is so rich that he or she not only solves all problems of musical execution in a composition, she deliberately searches for and finds increasingly subtle opportunities for (or problems of) artistic expression. As I explain in Chapter 9, creative music makers develop what Bereiter and Scardamallia call knowledge of creative "promisingness"[93] and the disposition to use this aspect of their informal musical knowledge to achieve creative musical results.

11. Implications for Music Education

This chapter holds several implications for the why-what-and-how of music teaching and learning.

On the most fundamental level, it is clear that music making in the sense of singing and playing instruments lies at the heart of what MUSIC is and that music making is a matter of musical knowledge-in-action, or musicianship. Music education ought to be centrally concerned with teaching and learning musicianship, which, as I have explained, involves several related forms of thinking and knowing. In this sense, what music educators do is the same as what all teachers do. For thinking and knowing lie at the heart of all educational efforts. Teachers in every subject area focus on the outcomes of student thinking in relation to domain-specific standards of accuracy, appropriateness, and originality. At the same time, what music educators do is unique. For developing musicianship is a matter of teaching a multidimensional form of "sound-artistic" thinking that is procedural and context-dependent.

The next question, of course, is how we organize and carry out music teaching and learning in ways that are true to the nature and value of MUSIC and musicianship. It will take the whole of this book to answer. Let me begin by proposing several first principles of music teaching and learning that are implicit in the themes of this chapter. In doing so, I continue to focus on performing for ease of explanation, but the principles outlined apply to the development of musicianship as manifested in all forms of musicing.

• *The teaching-learning context.* The prime principle that follows from the philosophical themes of this chapter concerns the nature of the teaching-learning environment. Recall that musicianship is practice-specific and that four of its five knowledge components are essentially nonverbal and situational. What this means is that musicianship develops only through active music making in curricular situations that teachers deliberately design to approximate the salient conditions of genuine musical practices. The name I give to this kind of teaching-learning environment is *curriculum-as-practicum.* In Chapters 10 and 11 I detail the practicum concept of curriculum that follows from this praxial philosophy of music education. At this point it is enough to emphasize that the musical authenticity of the teaching-learning situation is a crucial determinate of what music students learn and how deeply they learn. In other words, knowledge cannot be separated from the context in which it is learned and used.[94] In essence, then, developing musicianship is a matter of inducting students into particular music cultures.

• *Progressive musical problem solving.* Inducting students into musical practices depends on selecting significant musical challenges that confront students with genuine musical problems to solve in context: in relation to the demands and traditions of carefully selected musical practices. By a musical challenge I mean an authentic and engaging musical work (or project) to be performed (improvised, composed, arranged, or conducted).

Musicianship advances and integrates to the degree that teachers require their students to meet increasingly significant musical challenges on a continuous basis. By increasingly significant musical challenges I mean either completely new compositions to perform (improvise, compose, arrange, or conduct) or aspects of musical works that are already familiar to learners in some respects but not yet in others. Progressive problem solving[95] requires students to take more and more musical details into account during successive encounters with familiar and unfamiliar challenges. To engage in progressive musical problem solving is to work at the edge of one's musicianship.

• *Targeting surplus attention.* Ericsson and Smith observe that "research on expertise may be one of the most rapidly expanding areas within cognitive psychology and cognitive science."[96] Recent contributions to this research suggest that most students can achieve the rudiments of most forms of know-how through repeated attempts and moderate effort.[97] But since competency, proficiency, and expertise occur less frequently, there is clearly something more involved in advancing beyond a novice level. What is this something more?

As the rudimentary knowings of musicianship begin to develop through active music making, more of the energy resource called attention is released for further investment. Bereiter and Scardamallia suggest that advancing beyond a novice level to competency, proficiency, and artistry depends on what students learn to do with the surplus attention that becomes available as their thinking-in-action improves.[98] Students have three choices. They can spend their surplus attention on: (1) issues unrelated to musicianship; (2) musical problem reduction; or (3) musical problem solving and problem finding.

Students who advance their musical thinking beyond a novice level are those who learn how to reinvest their surplus attention (and, therefore, their powers of cognition, emotion, intention, and memory) in progressive musical problem solving. Improving musicianship does not depend on the slavish repetition of isolated movements or the memorization of verbal concepts. Moving from beginning to advanced levels of musicianship depends on learning to target and solve significant problems in the music one is making and the ways one is making music through performing, improvising, composing, arranging, or conducting.

• *Problem finding.* Donald Schön points out that problem solving in ordinary talk assumes that there is already a well-defined problem that learners can identify and go about solving.[99] But this is not always the case in music making and music listening. An important part of what music students need to learn is how to locate what counts and what needs to be done musically in relation to a given musical challenge. Finding what counts depends, in turn, on learning the expectations and ideals of the musical practice that apply to one's musicing and listening.

• *Problem reduction.* There is an important distinction between problem reduction and problem solving. Suppose, for example, that Sara is having difficulty singing a particular composition because of the demands it makes on her breath control. To advance, Sara must reduce (or eliminate) her breath management problem in terms of the amount of attention it takes up in her conscious awareness. Suppose Sara starts to reduce her breath control problem with the help of practical and verbal concepts provided by her teacher. At this juncture, Sara has a choice to make. The wrong choice is to invest her surplus attention in further breath control management (problem reduction) instead of musical problem solving (e.g., learning to phrase a melodic line expressively).

Musical problem reduction is necessary and intelligent. But in order for musicianship to develop, problem reduction cannot be confused with musical problem solving.[100] Part of what music students need to learn is how to decide when to pursue problem reduction and when to pursue musical problem solving. In general, problem reduction can and should proceed parenthetically—as an aside to the ongoing process of learning to make music well.

It follows from this discussion (and from the research of Bereiter and Scardamallia in particular[101]) that the development of musicianship involves a specific kind of learning process that learners can both engage in and learn how to carry out themselves. This learning process depends on the pursuit of increasingly challenging musical projects using musicianship that is never quite sufficient to meet all the requirements of a given musical challenge. Within this process, students must learn when and how to invest their surplus attention in musical problem finding and problem solving.

Carefully chosen musical challenges expose what students do not yet know how to achieve. With the guidance of music teachers who have achieved competent, proficient, or expert levels of musicianship themselves, music students learn how to meet successive musical challenges by drawing upon and developing various dimensions of their own musicianship. This learning process is promoted by a learning context in which individual advances are observed and shared by students who are taught as (and who therefore learn to see themselves as) authentic music makers. In this context, students learn to expect members of their class and school music community to succeed not merely in problem reduction but in meaningful and significant music making.

Music educators who conceive the development of musicianship as a progressive process in which students and teachers engage in finding, solving, and meeting genuine musical challenges together will not find musical performing elitist. (The same holds for all forms of music making.) Teachers and students will find the achievement of competent, proficient, and expert levels of performing (improvising, composing, arranging, and conducting) central to the development of individual musicianship and, therefore, central to the individual self. A musically excellent teaching-learning community is one in which to pursue and comply with standards and traditions of musical artistry is to grow. What this means, in turn, is that the boundaries of musicianship are not limited to individuals. They also apply to musical organizations (e.g., class and school choirs, class and school wind ensembles, string orchestras, jazz ensembles, composition workshops, guitar ensembles, woodwind ensembles) and to school music education programs as a whole.

• *Music teachers and music students.* The philosophical themes of this chapter suggest that the music educator's role is principally one of mentoring, coaching, and modeling for music students conceived as apprentice musical practitioners. That is to say, all music students (including all general music students) ought to be viewed and taught in the same basic way: as reflective musical practitioners engaged in the kind of cognitive apprenticeship we call music education.[102] Indeed, the fundamental natures of MUSIC and MUSICIANSHIP point to the conclusion that authentic music making (which always involves listening intelligently for the music one is making) ought to be the focus of all music education curricula.

During the interactions of music teaching and learning, music teachers shift back and forth between the products and the processes of students' musical thinking. We analyze what and how our apprentice practitioners are thinking-in-action. Music educators are diagnosticians of musical thinking. We consider what our students are giving attention to, what they fail to notice and understand, what they find difficult to solve, what they feel right or wrong about musically, and so on. On the basis of these analyses, we target students' attention and guide their thinking-in-action by using different languages of instruction including modeling, demonstrating, explaining in words, gestures, diagrams, and metaphors.[103]

Implicit in this view of the music teacher and the music student is the conviction that musicianship is educable. Unless there are serious congenital deficiencies, it seems reasonable to posit that the innate powers of consciousness that contribute to musical intelligence make it possible for most students to learn how to make music to a competent (if not a proficient) degree. True, some children have extraordinary levels of musical intelligence that enable them to develop the musicianship of their music cultures more quickly, deeply, and broadly than others. But even a high level of innate musical intelligence does not promote musicianship. That is, a child with a high degree of musical intelligence can be, but still may not learn to be, musically competent.[104] To achieve a competent, proficient, or artistic level of musical thinking requires the development of a practice-specific form of understanding called musicianship.

• *Evaluation.* Like all forms of thinking and knowing, musicing can be done well or poorly, brilliantly or ineptly. In terms of evaluation, the primary point to make now is that a student's level of musical understanding demonstrates itself primarily in the quality of his or her music making, not in what a student can tell us about musical works. For example, if Clara knows how to perform a variety of compositions proficiently and reliably (according to relevant standards of musical practice), then Clara can be said to possess a proficient level of musicianship. The quality of Clara's music making evidences her musical understanding of the musical works she is interpreting and performing and her understanding of the musical practices of which these works are individual pieces.

The ability to generalize about a musical composition using verbal concepts often helps a student perform musically. But verbal information (or formal knowledge) about music is no substitute for the ultra-specific nonverbal conception of musical works that a student exhibits when he or she performs (improvises, composes, arranges, or conducts) intelligently. Having a concept of something is not limited to the ability to match a word with a phenomenon. Knowing musical concepts is something a student evidences practically in the consistency and quality of her musical thinking-in-action. (Just because musicing is nonverbal in essence does not mean it is nonconceptual.)

An unfortunate legacy of dualistic thinking is the false belief that to really possess musical understanding one must possess a storehouse of verbal information about musical works. The corollary of this belief is that pencil-and-paper tests of verbal concepts are measures of musicianship. This is also false. Tests of formal musical knowledge are just that: decontextualized gauges of one aspect of musicianship. And by itself, formal musical knowledge will not get any music making done.

I am not at all suggesting that verbal knowledge about music is unimportant in music education. Verbal explanations may alleviate or reveal students' misunderstandings and lead to improvements in their musical thinking-in-action. In addition, verbal explanations can help to contextualize the teaching and learning of musicianship. What I am urging, however, is that a musical performance ought to be valued for what it is: an embodiment of a student's musical understanding of a given work and its related practice. The same holds for all other kinds of musical outcomes (improvisations, compositions, and musical arrangements). As I detail in later chapters, a performance of a work is especially valuable in assessing musical achievement. This is so, I suggest, because a performance provides authentic and tangible evidence of a person's moment-to-moment musical understanding (including his or her music-listening ability) with regard to all relevant dimensions of a musical work and the musical practice in which it is embedded.

A full explanation of the values of music making in music education must wait for Chapter 5. But even at this point, one thing seems clear: The values of musicing in music education cannot be tied to its use as an educational means. Authentic music making is a valid and valuable educational end for all students. For in real life, people do not learn how to make music just to improve their ability to listen to music. Instead, music making is something people find worth doing for the sake of musicing itself.

Questions for Discussion and Review

1. What does *musicing* refer to in this chapter? Explain why music teachers may find *musicing* a helpful term and/or a problematic term.

2. Explain the basic distinctions between activity and action. What qualifies music performing as a specific form of action? Summarize the essential ingredients involved in any act of music performing.

3. What is consciousness? (Include a brief comparison between dualism and materialism). What other terms do scholars use for consciousness? What does this book mean by *information*? Explain the functions of attention and cognition.

4. This chapter proposes that musicianship involves at least five forms of musical thinking and knowing. Summarize the main characteristics of each. Explain why musicianship is procedural in essence. Explain why musicianship is "context-specific."

5. Explain the reasons behind this chapter's contention that musicianship equals musical understanding.

6. Analyze the words and concepts people use (in interviews, conversations, and commentaries) to explain how musicians, athletes, and other kinds of "reflective practitioners" do what they do. In what ways do these popular discussions match, conflict with, or extend the several kinds of knowing explained in this chapter?

7. Distinguish between (1) producing sounds and (2) performing music. Some people believe that musical performing is a skill, a technique, or a craft. Explain why you agree or disagree.

8. This chapter proposes several practical principles for the development of musicianship. Summarize five (or more) of these principles. On the basis of (1) your own music teaching experiences and/or (2) your observations of other music teachers in action and/or (3) your study of the videotape listed in the supplementary sources, give an example of each of these principles in action.

Supplementary Sources

V. A. Howard. "Introduction." In *Varieties of Thinking*, ed. V. A. Howard. New York: Routledge, 1990. A succinct overview of "thinking."

Gilbert Ryle. *The Concept of Mind*. New York: Penguin Books, 1949. Chapter 2 explains Ryle's classic distinction between knowing-how and knowing-that.

Mihalyi Csikszentmihalyi. *Flow: The Psychology of Optimal Experience*. New York: Harper and Row, 1990. Chapter 2 explains the "anatomy of consciousness."

V. A. Howard. *Learning By All Means: Lessons From the Arts*. New York: Peter Lang, 1992. Chapter 2, "Music as Educating Imagination," examines the role of imagination in music performance.

Doreen Rao. *ACDA on Location, Vol. 1: The Children's Choir*. Lawton, Okla.: American Choral Directors' Association, Educational Videotape Series, 1988. This video provides several examples of the "first principles" explained at the end of this chapter. Please keep in mind, however, that the philosophical themes and practical proposals explained thus far apply to all forms of music performing and, indeed, to the teaching and learning of most (if not all) forms of musicing. This video exemplifies just one of many (many!) possible ways of implementing just some of the themes in this chapter.

Eleanor V. Stubley. "Philosophical Foundations." In *Handbook of Research on Music Teaching and Learning*, ed. Richard Colwell, pp. 3–20. New York: Schirmer Books, 1992. A broad examination of knowledge in relation to music and music education.

John Seely Brown, Allan Collins, and Paul Duguid. "Situated Cognition and the Culture of Learning." *Educational Researcher* 18, no. 1 (January–February 1989): 32–42. An explanation of "situated cognition."

Daniel C. Dennett. *Consciousness Explained*. Boston: Little, Brown, 1991. Chapter 2, "Explaining Consciousness," offers a concise introduction to the case against dualism and the argument for materialism.

Notes

1. The original source of this idea is Walhout, "The Nature and Function of Art," pp. 18–20. Note also that Christopher Small uses the term *musicking* in his *Music of the Common Tongue: Survival and Celebration in Afro-American Music* (New York: Riverrun Press, 1987), p. 50.

2. Wolterstorff, "The Work," p. 121.

3. For a development of this point, see Sparshott, *Theory*, pp. 34–35.

4. Saul Ross, "Epistemology, Intentional Action and Physical Education," in *Philosophy of Sport and Physical Activity*, ed. P. J. Galasso (Toronto: Canadian Scholars' Press, 1988), p. 124.

5. Ibid.

6. S. Hampshire, *Thought and Action* (London: Chatto and Windus, 1965), p. 154.

7. Daniel C. Dennett, *Consciousness Explained* (Boston: Little, Brown, 1991), pp. 33, 106.

8. For the full case against dualism, see Dennett, *Consciousness*, p. 33ff.

9. Ibid., p. 33.

10. Owen Flanagan, *Consciousness Reconsidered* (Cambridge, Mass.: MIT Press, 1992), p. xi.

11. Mark Johnson develops this theme in *The Body in the Mind: The Bodily Basis of Meaning, Imagination, and Reason* (Chicago: University of Chicago Press, 1987). See also Dennett, *Consciousness*, pp. 25–39.

12. Mihalyi Csikszentmihalyi and Isabella Csikszentmihalyi, eds., *Optimal Experience: Psychological Studies of Flow in Consciousness* (Cambridge: Cambridge University Press, 1988), p. 17.

13. Mihalyi Csikszentmihalyi, *Flow: The Psychology of Optimal Experience* (New York: Harper and Row, 1990), p. 29.

14. Csikszentmihalyi, *Flow*, p. 31.

15. Csikszentmihalyi and Csikszentmihalyi, *Optimal*, pp. 17–19.

16. Ibid., p. 19.

17. Vernon Howard provides a synthesis of Aristotle's perspective and an overview of his thinking in the "Introduction" to *Varieties of Thinking*, ed. V. A. Howard (New York: Routledge, 1990), pp. 1–14.

18. Ibid. p. 6.

19. Ibid., p. 11.

20. Howard Gardner, *Frames of Mind: The Theory of Multiple Intelligences* (New York: Basic Books, 1983).

21. R. J. Sternberg, *The Triarchic Mind: A New Theory of Human Intelligence* (New York: Viking, 1988).

22. Howard Gardner, "Symposium on the Theory of Multiple Intelligences," in *Thinking: The Second International Conference,* ed. D. N. Perkins, Jack Lockhead, and John Bishop (Hillsdale, N.J.: Erlbaum, 1987), p. 80.

23. Robert J. Sternberg, *Metaphors of Mind* (New York: Cambridge University Press, 1990), p. 266.

24. Gardner, *Frames of Mind,* p. 69.

25. Gilbert Ryle, *The Concept of Mind* (New York: Penguin Books, 1949).

26. Carl Bereiter and Marlene Scardamalia, *Surpassing Ourselves: An Inquiry Into the Nature and Implications of Expertise* (La Salle, Ill.: Open Court Publishing, 1993), pp. 43–75.

27. The concepts of reflective practice, reflective practitioner, and reflective practicum are originally presented in Donald A. Schön, *The Reflective Practitioner: How Professionals Think in Action* (New York: Basic Books, 1983), and in his *Educating the Reflective Practitioner: Toward a New Design for Teaching and Learning in the Professions* (San Francisco: Jossey-Bass, 1987).

28. Schön, *Educating,* p. 22ff.

29. Here I follow Serafine's use of the terms *simultaneous* and *successive* as explained in her *Music as Cognition,* p. 74.

30. The terms *chain, transform,* and *abstract* are original to Serafine, *Music as Cognition,* pp. 74–88.

31. Ryle, *Concept of Mind,* pp. 30–32.

32. Ibid., p. 57.

33. Ross, "Epistemology," pp. 134–35.

34. John Macmurray, *The Self as Agent* (Atlantic Heights, N.J.: Humanities Press, 1957), p. 86.

35. Schön, *Educating,* p. 31.

36. Ryle, *Concept of Mind,* p. 53.

37. Ibid., pp. 54–55.

38. Ibid., p. 55. This is a rewording of Ryle, who says: "the ability to appreciate a performance does not involve the same degree of competence as the ability to execute it."

39. Reimer's philosophy defines "a concept" in the early "classical" way. See Reimer, *A Philosophy* (1989), pp. 80–84. I argue against Reimer's outdated notion of a concept in my "Music Education as Aesthetic Education," p. 57.

40. See, for example, Edward E. Smith, "Concepts and Thought," in *The Psychology of Human Thought,* ed. Robert J. Sternberg and Edward E. Smith (Cambridge: Cambridge University Press, 1988), pp. 19–49; and, K. Nelson, *Making Sense: The Acquisition of Shared Meaning* (Orlando, Fla.: Academic Press, 1985).

41. Jean Piaget, *The Origins of Intelligence in Children* (New York: International Universities Press, 1952), p. 359.

42. Jean Piaget, *Six Psychological Studies* (New York: Random House, 1967), p. 79.

43. Hubert L. Dreyfus, *What Computers Can't Do: The Limits of Artificial Intelligence* (New York: Harper and Row, 1979), p. 190.

44. Ross, "Epistemology," p. 93.

45. Sparshott, *Theory*, p. 32.

46. Ibid.

47. Dennett, *Consciousness*, p. 243.

48. Ibid., p. 252.

49. The concept of cultural actions is explained in two sources. See P. C. W. Van Wieringen, "Discussion: Self-Organization or Representation? Let's Have Both," in *Cognition and Action in Skilled Behavior*, ed. A. M. Colley and J. R. Beech (Amsterdam: North Holland, 1988); and A. M. Colley and J. R. Beech, *Acquisition and Performance of Cognitive Skills* (Chichester, Eng.: John Wiley, 1989), p. 174.

50. Vernon Howard explains this distinction in his *Artistry: The Work of Artists* (Indianapolis: Hackett Publishing, 1982), p. 49.

51. Schön, *Educating*, p. 25.

52. Some writers use *music literacy* as a synonym for *musical understanding* and *musicianship*. This usage is misleading on two counts. First, *literacy* gives the false impression that knowing how to read music notation is the core of what it takes to be a competent or proficient music maker. More broadly, *music literacy* gives the false impression that musical understanding is essentially a matter of formal musical knowledge. I therefore eschew the use of *musical literacy* for anything more than references to coding and decoding music notation.

53. For a detailed discussion of the "languages of craft," see Howard, *Artistry*, pp. 59–109.

54. Schön, *Educating*, pp. 25–31.

55. Ibid., p. 31.

56. Bereiter and Scardamalia, *Surpassing Ourselves*, pp. 51–54.

57. Ibid.

58. Howard, *Artistry*, p. 182.

59. Ibid.

60. Ibid., pp. 182–85.

61. John Miller Chernoff, *African Rhythm and African Sensibility* (Chicago: University of Chicago Press, 1979), pp. 102, 106.

62. Ibid., pp. 106–07. '

63. Ibid., p. 114.

64. Ibid., p. 108.

65. Ibid., p. 107.

66. Ibid., p. 151.

67. See Bereiter and Scardamalia, *Surpassing Ourselves*, pp. 54–58, and Harry S. Broudy, "Types of Knowledge and Purposes of Education," in *Schooling and the Acquisition of Knowledge*, ed. Richard C. Anderson, R. J. Spiro, and W. E. Montague (Hillsdale, N.J.: Erlbaum, 1977), pp. 1–18.

68. Israel Scheffler, "In Praise of Cognitive Emotions," *Teachers College Record* 79, no. 2 (1977), pp. 171–86.

69. Paul A. Wagner, "Will Education Contain Fewer Surprises for Students in the Future?," in *Varieties of Thinking*, ed. V. A. Howard (New York: Routledge, 1990), p. 161.

70. Ibid., p. 162.

71. Ibid., p. 161.

72. *Good Night*. A Russian folk song arranged by Doreen Rao for unison treble voices and piano (New York: Boosey and Hawkes, 1990), OCTB-6631.

73. Scheffler, "In Praise of Cognitive Emotions," p. 178. Also see Wagner, "Will Education Contain Fewer Surprises," p. 164. Wagner references related writings by Nelson

Notes   323

Goodman and Israel Scheffler to establish the point that cognition and emotion are inter-dependent.

74. V. A. Howard, *Learning by All Means: Lessons From the Arts* (New York: Peter Lang, 1992), p. 14.

75. Ibid., p. 13.

76. Ibid., p. 14.

77. Ibid., p. 15.

78. Ibid., pp. 16–19.

79. R. D. Archambault, ed., *John Dewey on Education: Selected Writings* (Chicago: University of Chicago Press, 1974), p. 151.

80. Howard Gardner, *The Unschooled Mind* (New York: Basic Books, 1991), pp. 238–39.

81. D. N. Perkins, "Art as Understanding," *Journal of Aesthetic Education* 22, no. 1 (Spring 1988): 114 ff.

82. Ibid.

83. Ibid.

84. Ibid., p. 115.

85. Ibid.

86. Ibid., p. 116.

87. Ibid.

88. I am grateful to Thomas Regelski for alerting me to the following sources on these points: Andrew Harrison, *Making and Thinking: A Study of Intelligent Activities* (Indianapolis: Hackett, 1978), and Randall R. Dipert, *Artifacts, Art Works, and Agency* (Philadelphia: Temple University Press, 1993).

89. See C. B. Fethe, "Hand and Eye: The Role of Craft in R. G. Collingwood's Aesthetic Theory," *British Journal of Aesthetics* 22, no. 1 (Winter 1982): 37–51; and Arnold Whittick, "Towards Precise Distinctions of Art and Craft," *British Journal of Aesthetics* 24, no. 1 (Winter 1984): 47–52.

90. Howard, *Artistry*, p. 26.

91. Hubert Dreyfus and Stuart E. Dreyfus, *Mind Over Machine: The Power of Human Intuition and Expertise in the Era of the Computer* (New York: Free Press, 1986), p. 21ff.

92. Ibid., p. 32.

93. Bereiter and Scardamalia, *Surpassing Ourselves*, p. 125ff.

94. Here I follow a basic principle of situated cognition as explained by John Seely Brown, Allan Collins, and Paul Duguid, "Situated Cognition and the Culture of Learning," *Educational Researcher* 18, no. 1 (January–February 1989): 32–42.

95. The term *progressive problem solving* is original to Bereiter and Scardamalia, *Surpassing Ourselves*, p. 96.

96. K. Anders Ericsson and Jacqui Smith, "Prospects and Limits of the Empirical Study of Expertise: An Introduction," in *Toward a General Theory of Expertise*, ed. K. Anders Ericsson and Jacqui Smith (Cambridge: Cambridge University Press, 1991), p. 1.

97. Bereiter and Scardamalia, *Surpassing Ourselves*, pp. 77–82.

98. Ibid.

99. The ideas underlying problem finding and problem setting are discussed in Schön, *Educating*, pp. 4, 42–43.

100. Bereiter and Scardamalia, *Surpassing Ourselves*, pp. 99–101.

101. Ibid., pp. 91–98.

102. The term *reflective practitioner* is original to Schön, *The Reflective Practitioner*. The term *cognitive apprenticeship* is found in Brown, Collins, and Duguid, "Situated Cognition and the Culture of Learning."

324

103. Howard, *Artistry*, pp. 59–109.

104. D. N. Perkins, ''Creativity and the Quest for Mechanism,'' in *The Psychology of Human Thought,* ed. Robert J. Sternberg and Edward E. Smith (New York: Cambridge University Press, 1988), p. 319.

References

Reimer, Bennett. *A Philosophy of Music Education.* Englewood Cliffs, N.J.: Prentice Hall, 1970, 1989.

Serafine, Mary Louise. *Music as Cognition: The Development of Thought in Sound.* New York: Columbia University Press, 1988.

Sparshott, Francis E. *The Theory of the Arts* Princeton, N.J.: Princeton University Press, 1982.

Walhout, David. "The Nature and Function of Art." *Journal of Aesthetics and Art Criticism* 26, no. 1 (Winter 1986): 16–25.

Wolterstorff, Nicholas. "The Work of Making a Work of Music." In *What Is Music? An Introduction to the Philosophy of Music.* Edited by Philip A. Alperson. New York: Haven Publications, 1987.

[5]

PHILOSOPHY OF MUSIC EDUCATION

by Charles Leonhard

■ When we speak of a philosophy of music education, we refer to a system of basic beliefs which underlies and provides a basis for the operation of the musical enterprise in an educational setting. A philosophy should serve as a source of insight into the total music program and should assist music teachers in determining what the musical enterprise is all about, what it is trying to accomplish and how it should operate. A definitive philosophy is useful, even essential, for an operation as important and complex as music education because concepts, theory and practice rely on one another.

The phrase "music education" is conceived as including all deliberate efforts to educate people in music regardless of the level or area of specialization. Thus, the term "music educator," as used in this paper, does not refer solely to persons associated with the music program in the public schools; it encompasses all college music teachers and administrators and private teachers.

Traditionally Americans have been suspicious of philosophy and have prided themselves on being practical people. Likewise, music teachers often grow impatient with theoretical considerations and commonly accept practice more readily than theory. The growing complexity of the technology of our society and the increasing reliance of the society on theory and basic principles is, however, causing a dramatic change in attitudes toward philosophy. Everyone realizes, for example, that a precise theory preceded the splitting of the atom and the development of atomic energy. The achievement would have been inconceivable without an underlying basis in theory.

Music educators have lately begun to realize that systematic philosophy is one of the most practical things a teacher can have. When problems arise for which he has no ready answers, he can turn to his philosophical foundation for clues to appropriate solutions. Having a reasoned philosophy enables a teacher to behave rationally rather than on naive impulse or ingrained habit. Theory and practice have a relationship of mutual dependence: practice checks the soundness of theory by putting it to work and testing it out; theory checks the soundness of practice.

Even though music educators have in recent years grown more receptive to philosophy, there exists no comprehensive philosophy of music education. Furthermore, practice in music education is only slightly affected by such philosophy as does exist.

The situation is further complicated due to the fact that by the very nature of its practitioners and their preparation music education tends to operate on the periphery of the educational enterprise. Even if music education operated in the mainstream of education, there is no assurance that any sounder theoretical position would ensue because the theoretical position of American education is unstable and inconsistent. No one philosophic system is dominant in education today. Our educational system has traces of a number of philosophic systems including Idealism, Realism, Experimentalism, Pragmatism and Instrumentalism. Existentialism and Linguistic Analysis represent philosophic approaches which may in the future influence education.

While each of these philosophic systems has implications for education and for music education, no one has constructed a comprehensive philosophy of music education based on any one of them. Furthermore, it is difficult, if not impossible, to construct an eclectic philosophy of either education or music education which can reconcile the conflicting points of view embodied in these systems.

The conflict among these philosophic systems can be illustrated by consideration of the question of the nature of ultimate reality. Idealism and Realism hold in common the belief that there is a dimension to the cosmos which holds ultimate sanction over us, that an ultimate reality exists and prescribes certain values for men to hold and cherish for all time and in all places. An Idealistic or Realistic philosopher seeks to determine what this *Good* consists in. The school operating on an Idealistic or Realistic theory has the mission of helping young people learn and conform to those prescriptions.

Experimentalism, Pragmatism, Instrumentalism and Existentialism take a different view of the question of reality. They hold that values are not imposed on men from without. Values are what men decide they are. The Experimentalist, for example, makes the decision on the basis of consequences, the Existentialist on the basis of individual choice. The business of the school is to help young people undergo meaningful experience and arrive at a system of values that will be beneficial to society, in the case of Experimentalism, or satisfying to the individual, in the case of Existentialism.

The difficulty of reconciliation among philosophic systems should be apparent. Even if we should accept a position from philosophy on the question of reality and value, we have only begun. The problem of developing a philosophy of music education necessarily involves structuring a theory on the meaning of music, the valuation of music and the role of music in human living.

A background paper submitted to the Seminar on Comprehensive Musicianship,
Northwestern University, April 1965, sponsored by the Contemporary Music Project.

If one follows a philosophic system, the system itself may provide more or less direct implications for a theory of musical meaning and value but no major exponent of a philosophic system with the exception of John Dewey has dealt systematically with both areas. As a result, one who would develop a philosophy for music education must develop systematic reconcilable positions not only in educational philosophy, but also in aesthetics.

While some systematic positions in aesthetics are related more or less directly to general systems of philosophy, there are frequent inconsistencies which make it difficult to subsume a philosophic position and an aesthetic position under the same tent.

Having defined the meaning of the phrase philosophy of music education and having delineated some of the complex problems involved in developing a philosophy, we turn to a consideration of the present philosophical status of the music education enterprise.

Until recently and, perhaps even today, the dominant orientation toward the music program, at least as reflected in the professional literature, has been based on a system of instrumental values. This concept of instrumental values was derived from an inaccurate interpretation of a doctrine advocated by John Dewey, called Instrumentalism.

Instrumentalism as advocated by Dewey holds that knowledge is an instrument for accomplishing a purpose and that the truth and value of knowledge is demonstrated only when that knowledge proves to be useful in accomplishing that purpose. Instrumentalism has important implications for sequence in learning: information should be made available to the student when it is relevant to his purpose and not before.

A derivation of this doctrine has been used for many years in an attempt to justify the music program in the public schools on the grounds that music makes a contribution to ends that are essentially unrelated to music.

While musicians and music teachers usually have firm convictions about the value of music in the schools, they are faced with the problem of justifying to administrators, boards of education and parents the inclusion of music in the curriculum. They have found that many people are skeptical about the worth of musical instruction, and as a result have felt constrained to develop arguments that would be convincing to those people.

These efforts usually begin with the aims of general education as developed by some authoritative body and move on to the claim that music can contribute to the achievement of those aims. Without doubt the aims most frequently used in this way have been those commonly referred to as the Seven Cardinal Principles.

It may well have been a historical accident that the publication of this statement in 1918 coincided with the beginning of the great expansion of the music program in the public schools. When the need for an argument to bolster the claim of music was great, the seven cardinal principles were available. In any event, these principles were for years the foundation stone for justifying the music program.

Professional books on music education, courses of study for school systems and publications of professional organizations contain statements such as these: Music education contributes to the health of the student. Music education aims to develop wholesome ideals of conduct. Music education contributes to the development of citizenship.

Music education aims to develop good work habits.[1]

While reliance on statements of the instrumental values of music may well have convinced some reluctant administrator more fully to support the music program, those values cannot stand close scrutiny because they are not directly related to music and are not unique to music. In fact, many other areas of the curriculum are in a position to make a more powerful contribution to these values than is music.

Furthermore, reliance on instrumental values has often taken the focus of music teachers' efforts away from musical achievement, and provided cover for minimal musical learning and low musical standards. If one is teaching music for citizenship, health or recreation, it matters little what kind of music one teaches or how well he teaches it.

In recent years the intellectual leadership of music education has become increasingly skeptical of the worth of a philosophy for music education based on instrumental values such as these. Evidence of discontent has appeared in articles in professional journals and in statements of speakers at professional meetings. Furthermore, many people have become aware of an increasing alienation between music education in the public schools and music programs at the college level which has resulted in a growing dichotomy in the music education enterprise based on educational level. This condition is due at least partially to the fact that public school programs were emphasizing instrumental values of musical experience while college programs were promoting music for its own sake.

Other factors have been influen-

[1]See, for example, *The Function of Music in the Secondary School Curriculum* (Washington: Music Educators National Conference, 1952).

tial in this rising discontent with a philosophy of music education based on instrumental values. First, there has been a tremendous increase in the number of students entering graduate programs in music education and a significant improvement in the quality of those programs. Music educators are becoming increasingly sophisticated and learned not only in music but in philosophy and psychology. They understand the need for a comprehensive philosophy of music education and are no longer satisfied with having no basic beliefs or a naive theoretical framework.

A second factor has been the upheaval that struck the entire educational enterprise as a result of the successful launching of Sputnik which dramatized the educational advances of the Soviet Union. The resulting unprecedented emphasis on science and its related academic subjects, often to the detriment of education in the humanities and the arts, has brought forcefully to attention the necessity for musicians and music teachers at both public school and college levels to close ranks and join forces in preserving and extending the music program at all levels.

The ferment into which music education has been catapulted has resulted in encouraging advances. Music educators at all levels are examining their programs and procedures with unprecedented care. The need for emphasis on objectives directly related to music, the need for structure and sequence in the music program, the need for systematic evaluation of the results of the music program are all receiving increased recognition. Efforts, long overdue, are being made to begin the development of a philosophy of music education that will be relevant, comprehensive and applicable to all levels of music education.

A highly significant development occurred in 1954 with the organization of the Commission on Basic Concepts by the Music Educators National Conference. This Commission resulted from a growing recognition that music education needed a soundly based theoretical foundation and that specialists from without the ranks of music educators were essential to the development of such a foundation.

The work of the Commission resulted in a decision by the National Society for the Study of Education to devote its 1958 yearbook to music education. A distinguished group of authors from disciplines related to music education contributed papers which were published in 1958 under the title *Basic Concepts in Music Education,* The Fifty-Seventh Yearbook of the National Society for the Study of Education, Part I.[2]

While the entire book has real significance for the development of a philosophy of music education, the contributions of McMurray and Broudy have been selected for summary treatment here. They provide excellent examples of the possibilities and limitations of drawing implications for music education from an established philosophic system. Broudy represents a traditional philosophic position, Realism; McMurray represents a contemporary position, Pragmatism.

Broudy—Realism

The concept of connoisseurship is central to Broudy's views on music education. He treats from a Realistic rationale these questions:

▶ What are the components of the musical experience?

▶ How is musical experience related to other types of experience?

▶ Which phases of musical experience can be improved by instruction?

▶ How can we set up standards for musical judgment?

▶ What kind of outcomes can we expect from music education?

▶ What kind of a program of general music education does Realism imply?

These questions are all basic to a philosophy of music education and, although all his answers do not seem to be directly grounded in the Realistic orientation, his views are provocative and meaningful in the formulation of a philosophy of music education.

His statement on the program of music education for general education contains the essence of Realistic views on music education, and is, therefore, quoted.

"As regards the program, the key concept we have employed is that of connoisseurship. Growth in taste and appreciation has been held to be correlative with growth in musical skill, knowledge and the ability to comprehend and discriminate the musical qualities. If this is so, then the program can be formal, systematic and deliberately instituted and conducted, for both knowledge and skill can be taught systematically. It also makes sense to speak of a method of teaching music if there are skill and knowledge to be taught, and if there are gradations of this knowledge and skill in the learner.

"The concept of connoisseurship encourages the use of materials that the experts of successive ages have regarded as good and important. It does not exclude the contemporary and experimental, but it does evaluate them in terms of musical *knowledge* and *cultivated* taste.

"Further, this view sees value in having the learner aware of the continuity of the musical tradition. Thus the study of the twelfth century chant aids the listener when he hears it used or simulated in a contemporary work; and its presence in the contemporary work expands the understanding of it in its original form."[3]

McMurray—Pragmatism

At the outset McMurray raises the question as to the appropriateness of educators turning to philosophy as a source of basic concepts. He points out the lack of consensus among philosophers about the rightness of such a procedure but indicates that, in his opinion, the philosophic method can assist in the critical refinement of conclusions resulting from experience.

He defines pragmatism as a "theory about human action as guided by cognition of consequences, a theory of deliberate or rational self control, of intellectually achieved continuity in behavior."[4]

Rejecting the instrumental approach to determining the objectives of music education, he recom-

---

[2]*Basic Concepts in Music Education,* The Fifty-seventh Yearbook of the National Society for the Study of Education, Part I (Chicago: The University of Chicago Press, 1958).

[3]Harry S. Broudy, "A Realistic Philosophy of Music Education," *Basic Concepts in Music Education, Ibid.,* p. 86.
[4]Foster McMurray, "Pragmatism in Music Education," *Basic Concepts in Music Education,* p. 33.

mends that music educators find a generalized statement of the purposes of general education and then show how music education fits into the over-all scheme.

He suggests as a pragmatist that "the aim of general education is to use our accumulated knowledge, values and skills to acquaint everyone with those more subtle forces in his world which influence his life, with the hope that, if he learns of their existence and their force, he can control his relations with the environment to gain more of the good and less of the preventable bad outcomes."[5]

Moving from this statement of the aim of general education, he suggests that the aim of music education might be "to help everyone to further awareness of patterns of sound as an aesthetic component in the world of experience; to increase each person's capacity to control the availability of aesthetic richness through music; and to transform the public musical culture into a recognized part of each person's environment."[6]

McMurray raises some provocative questions concerning music programs and provides answers based in pragmatism. In answer to a question as to whether a music teacher should judge his success on the basis of his pupils gaining a new and increased liking for music he says:

"A music teacher should neither attempt nor expect to teach his pupils a new and stronger liking for music. In his contribution to a pupil's general education, at least, this strengthening of positive appreciation is no part of his job. A teacher's job is only to show his pupils what is to be found in music when obstacles to perception are removed and when the learned capacity to attend and to hear has been developed. If, when a pupil has truly learned to hear more of what is potentially there, he does not value highly the new content, then that evaluation is his own rightful concern and no one else's."[7]

With regard to musical performance he questions performance being a primary means to aesthetic sensitivity, and emphasizes the need for experience other than per-

formance if the student is to develop his full sensitivity to the aesthetic content of music. He does, however, cite two reasons for including musical performance in general education: 1) training in performance helps the student see what is involved in music making; and 2) it helps him hear music in its full reality.

Contributions such as those of McMurray and Broudy have unquestioned value for music educators in developing a philosophy of music education, but there are difficulties involved in asking educational philosophers to furnish music educators with beliefs about music and its place in the educational system. In the first place, one cannot depend upon educational philosophers having sufficient understanding of music and music education to perceive accurately the problems of music educators. Furthermore, there is the very real question of what music educators should do with statements of this kind. Are music educators qualified to evaluate such statements critically? Should they accept all the ideas and opinions expressed by McMurray and Broudy, for example, or should they accept only those with which they agree?

I suggest that our efforts to develop a philosophy of music education have proceeded in the wrong direction on at least two counts. In the first place, we have appealed principally to educational philosophy to give us our direction when the questions that arise in our at-

tempts to validate our beliefs about music are more nearly answered in systematic aesthetic theory. Secondly, whatever discipline we have appealed to—philosophy, psychology or aesthetics—we have started with the general theory and tried to draw inferences, often naively, for music education rather than starting, as I believe we should, with our own theoretical and practical problems, proceeding to systematize and evaluate our beliefs and then seeking to verify our beliefs through an appeal to aesthetic theory.

Music teachers would seem to be in a unique position to gain insights into music, into varying responses to music and into the development of responsiveness to music. No one else is as close to the problems of musical perception and musical learning as the music teacher. Should we not then set about developing a theoretical orientation for music education ourselves? Are we not in a position to make a potentially significant and unique contribution to both educational and esthetic theory?

I submit that it is the responsibility of music educators themselves to systematize and verify their principles and to develop a theoretical rationale for music education.

The first step may well be the recognition that we do not have a comprehensive philosophy of music education, that our efforts to borrow a theoretical foundation for music education from traditional or

[5]*Ibid.*, p. 41.
[6]*Ibid.*
[7]*Ibid.*, p. 43.

educational philosophy have not paid off. The next step would logically be the identification and definition of the theoretical problems of music education. This would lead to discussion of beliefs and principles which music educators use in attacking those problems.

The kind of thinking and discussion involved would lead us to a determination of areas of agreement and disagreement on principles and beliefs in a language that would be intelligible and meaningful to music educators and in a context that would be relevant to a consideration of their problems.

Once the theoretical problems of music education have been defined, it would seem reasonable for music educators to turn to a serious study of aesthetics. With their theoretical problems defined and sufficient background in aesthetics, music educators could then enter into a true and productive partnership with aestheticians and educational philosophers. The philosophers could assist music educators in a critical examination of their beliefs and principles; music educators could furnish unique data and concepts to the philosophers.[8]

Developing a philosophy of music education is a complex proposition. It requires deliberate cooperation among music educators at all levels, musicologists, theorists, composers, performers, critics, aestheticians and philosophers. I suggest the following program to initiate the development of such a theory:

▸ Requirement of courses in aesthetics for all undergraduate and graduate degrees in music and music education.

▸ The establishment of a specialization in the aesthetics of music in graduate degree programs.

▸ The creation in major institutions of professorships in the philosophy of music education.

▸ The organization of a series of seminars and conferences by educational institutions and professional organizations involving music educators, composers, musicologists, critics, aestheticians and philosophers in discussion of the theoretical problems of music education.

The author is Professor of Music, University of Illinois, Urbana.

[8]For a detailed discussion of the relationship of esthetic theory to music education, see Robert C. Smith, *Esthetic Theory and the Appraisal of Practices in Music Education*, Unpublished doctoral dissertation (Urbana: University of Illinois, 1964).

[6]

The Evolution of Music Education Philosophy from Utilitarian to Aesthetic

Michael L. Mark *Towson State University, Towson, Maryland*

Throughout Western history, various philosophies of music education have been articulated by intellectual, political, and religious leaders. A common factor in the various philosophies is the relationship between music education and society. Since the middle of the 20th century, writers on music education philosophy have been mostly music educators, rather than societal leaders. They have, for the most part, abandoned the many historical justifications of the profession in favor of aesthetic philosophy. The utilitarian values of music education that have formed its historical philosophical basis have been rejected during the last 30 years because they have little to do with music. Music is now taught for the sake of music, and the link that has historically connected aesthetics with societal needs has been broken.

Philosophies of music education have been articulated by many societal leaders throughout history. A review of those with whom music educators are generally familiar reveals that the writers understood the aesthetic value of music, but did not think of it, in itself, as justification for music education. Justification was based on the fact that the aesthetic development of the individual influenced behavior in such a way that a better citizen (in terms of cultural, civic, religious, or other values) was expected to be developed.

The literature of ancient Greece contains many statements describing the role of music education in the development of the individual. Plato strongly emphasized the necessity for music (meaning all of the arts) in education to maintain traditional cultural values and to develop the ideal citizen. Discussion of the topic is found in his *Protagoras*(Hamilton & Cairns, Eds., 1961, p. 322), *Laws* (1961, pp. 1,251–1,257, 1,264–1,267, 1,294, 1,343, 1,370–1,374, 1,300–1,303, 1,386–1,387, 1,394–1,396, 1,400), and *Republic*(1961, pp. 623, 643–647, 654–656, 753–754). Aristotle cited historical precedents for music education, saying that music is

16 MARK

valued for "intellectual enjoyment in leisure" and that it "...is a sort of education in which parents should train their sons, not as being useful or necessary, but because it is liberal or noble." (Ross, Ed., 1921, 1,383:30). The Greek scholar Athenaeus, discussing Damon, said, "...Damon of Athens and his school say that songs and dances are the result of the soul's being in a kind of motion; those songs which are noble and beautiful produce noble and beautiful souls, whereas the contrary kind produce the contrary" (Gulick, trans., 1937, p. 389). Roman authors also discussed music education in reference to the development of the citizen. The orator Quintilian stated that music was a necessasy part of the ideal training program for orators, who were among the most respected members of the Roman intelligentsia (Smail, 1936, pp. 47–55). The Roman statesman and scholar Boethius, in summarizing the musical practices of the ancient world, reviewed many of the viewpoints held by Greek and Roman schools of thought about the influence of music on the development of the individual and the relationship of the influence to society (Bower, 1967, pp. 31–44).

The Middle Ages also produced many leaders concerned about music education. During a period of retreat from the greater world by the Holy Roman Empire and of church dominance over civic and governmental affairs, the basis of music education was the need for individuals to be religiously influenced by music. Again, music education was seen as a tool for the formation of the adult who would best fulfill those functions expected of him or her by the society of which he was a part. Charlemagne established a basic curriculum that included music throughout the Carolingian Empire in his decree "that there should be schools for boys who can read. The Psalms, the notation, the chant, and arithmetic and grammar [ought to be taught] in all monasteries and episcopacies..." In the same decree, he specified that all clerics were to learn the Roman chant thoroughly (Ellard, 1956, pp. 54–55). Seven centuries later the Protestant Reformation continued to confirm the value of music in the development of the citizen, beginning with the writings of Martin Luther.

Many well known European educators who influenced American education advocated music education. Comenius (who was also a minister) was specific about how and why music and art were to be taught. (Monroe, 1908, pp. 48–49; Comenius, 1923, pp. 194–202, 259, 261, 268, 274). Pestalozzi recognized the need for music education for the development of, among other things, a peaceful and serene family life, and of nationalistic feelings in children (Green, 1916, pp. 228–229). Froebel advocated music education (and other arts) as a means of developing an understanding of the universe and man's place in it (1908, pp. 225–229). This goal was not unlike that of the classical quadrivium, in which music, as a mathematical subject, was expected to reveal the nature of the universe and the relationship of man to it. Spencer presented an argument for the power of music to further emotional development. He stated, "...music must take rank as the highest of the fine arts—as the one which, more than any other, ministers to human welfare." (1951, p. 76; 1980, pp. 28–33, 70–81).

JRME 17

MUSIC EDUCATION IN AMERICA

Music was not a part of the normal educational program in colonial America, but was considered an important aspect of life in the theocratic New England colonies. The New England ministers spoke and wrote of it frequently, often in impassioned tones. One of the most influential ministers, Cotton Mather, wrote that music was a natural part of worship and religion (Swan, Ed., 1977, pp. 10–11). Over a century later, Lowell Mason justified music education on the same basis and wrote about the benefits of music instruction for moral character development. He added other justifications—improved health and development of intellectual discipline (1834). It was on the basis of those same factors that the special committee of the Boston School Committee considered music as a school subject. The committee's report stated:

> Judged then by this triple standard, intellectually, morally, and physically, vocal music seems to have a natural place in every system of instruction which aspires, as should every system, to develop man's whole nature.... Now the defect of our present system, admirable as that system is, is this, that it aims to develop the intellectual part of man's nature solely, when for all the true purposes of life, it is of more importance, a hundred fold, to feel rightly, than to think profoundly (*Boston Music Gazette*, 1838).

The Boston School Committee adopted music as a curricular subject on the basis of the recommendations contained in the report. This was a turning point in music education history because the way was now prepared for music to become a regular component of the public school curriculum, which it did in most American school systems during the course of the next century. Music was usually adopted by local boards of education on essentially the same justifications as those accepted in Boston in 1838. Horace Mann, the first secretary of the Massachusetts Board of Education, reported in 1844 that music instruction was successful in Massachusetts; his judgment was based on the threefold standard of morality, intellect, and health (1891, pp. 445–463). Although his judgment may have been subjective, he spoke for the state's board of education and the citizens of Massachusetts, and he influenced educational policy-making bodies in many other states.

Early in his career, John Dewey wrote about aesthetic feeling, saying that "the end of art is to produce a perfect harmonized self" (1887, p. 274), thus restating Plato's justification for education in the arts. Dewey said in 1897, "We need to return more to the Greek conception, which defined education as the attaching of pleasure and pain to the right objects and ideals in the right way" (pp. 329–330). Dewey was concerned about the development of the individual as a social being. The introduction of the *Progressive Music Series*, derived from Dewey's philosophy, stated:

> The general aim of education is to train the child to become a capable, useful, and contented member of society. The development of a fine character and of the desire to be of service to humanity are results that lie

uppermost in the minds of the leaders of educational thought. Every school subject is valued in proportion to its contribution to these desirable ends. Music, because of its powerful influence upon the very innermost recesses of our subjective life, because of its wonderfully stimulating effect upon our physical, mental, and spiritual nature, and because of its well-nigh universality of appeal, contributes directly to both of the fundamental purposes of education. By many of the advanced educators of the present day, therefore, music, next to the "three R's," is considered the most important subject in the public school curriculum (1916, p. 9).

In 1954, Benjamin Willis, superintendent of schools in Chicago, stated:

At the risk of underemphasizing many of the other important functions of music in the curriculum at all levels of education today, I believe I would put *education for citizenship* as its most important function. This concept is a very logical and necessary base from which many of the other values to be derived from music as a part of education, can follow. This is music's most important stake in education" (Morgan, 1955, p. 3).

The societal and educational changes brought about by the decline of progressive education, World War II, the Cold War, the repercussions of Sputnik, the dawn of the age of technology, and other events resulted in the need for music educators to redefine their profession in order to identify their place in the emerging technological society. Music Educators National Conference addressed itself to the need by appointing the Commission on Basic Concepts in 1954. The purpose of the commission was to articulate the philosophical and theoretical foundations of music education. The commission's work was published in *Basic Concepts in Music Education* (Henry, Ed., 1958). Although meant to serve as a basis for future development, it is ironic that, with the exception of one author, *Basic Concepts* was the philosophical culmination, in the United States at least, of thousands of years of utilitarian philosophy. Several authors discussed music education philosophy in utilitarian terms. They include Madison (p. 21), Mueller (pp. 120–122), McKay (pp. 138–139), Burmeister (pp. 218–219, 234), House (p. 238), and Gaston (pp. 272–274). *Basic Concepts* also contained an article by Allen Britton, who articulated a different philosophy, which later came to be called "aesthetic education." It was characterized by total emphasis on the aesthetic development of the child and rejection of extramusical values as part of the philosophical justification of music education. Few authors have addressed themselves to music education philosophy since the publication of *Basic Concepts*. The very small body of literature suggests that educational philosophy, the historical basis of music education philosophy, was replaced by aesthetic philosophy. Aesthetics had been, until that time, the philosophical basis of the art of music, rather than of music education. Where earlier writers had sought to link the two philosophies in order to indicate how aesthetic development led to societal fulfillment, the philosophy of aesthetic education concentrated only on aesthetics, breaking the link with societal needs. Bennett Reimer stated in *A Philosophy of Music Education*:

> If music education in the present era could be characterized by a single, overriding purpose, one would have to say this field is trying to become "aesthetic education." What is needed in order to fulfill this purpose is a philosophy which shows how and why music education is aesthetic in its nature and value (1970, p. 2).

Britton wrote in *Basic Concepts in Music Education*:

> Music, as one of the seven liberal arts, has formed an integral part of the educational system of western civilization from Hellenic times to the present. Thus, the position of music in education historically speaking, is one of great strength. Unfortunately, this fact seems to be one of which most educators, including music educators, remain unaware. As a result, the defense of music in the curriculum is often approached as if something new were being dealt with. Lacking the assurance which a knowledge of history could provide, many who seek to justify the present place of music in American schools tend to place too heavy a reliance upon ancillary values which music may certainly serve but which cannot, in the end, constitute its justification. Plato, of course, is the original offender in this regard, and his general view that the essential value of music lies in its social usefulness seems to be as alive today as ever (1958, p. 195).

Charles Leonhard agreed with Britton. He wrote:

> While reliance on statements of the instrumental value of music may well have convinced some reluctant adminstrator more fully to support the music program, those values cannot stand close scrutiny, because they are not directly related to music and are not unique to music. In fact, many other areas of the curriculum are in a position to make a more powerful contribution to these values than is music (1965, p. 43).

The Tanglewood Symposium in 1967 appeared to be an attempt to counter the new philosophy. Its purpose was to explore the present and future relationship between music education and society. The resulting document, the *Documentary Report of the Tanglewood Symposium,* presented many viewpoints of the relationship. However, the summarizing statement, "The Tanglewood Declaration," dealt for the most part with the place of music in the curriculum, rather than with societal needs that can be met by music education. Only one of the eight articles of the declaration referred to individual student needs. The inference might be drawn that the concern for the development of a citizen who is in some way different because of music education was not of the highest priority to the symposium participants.

Little has been written on music education philosophy since the publication of Reimer's work in 1970. One concludes from the lack of current literature, from the impact of Reimer's work, and from the emphasis on the subject at local, state, and national conferences, that aesthetic education is recognized to be the prevailing philosophy.

20 MARK

SUMMARY

Music education philosophy developed over 2,000 years. The developmental process was not evolutionary because the philosophy remained essentially the same from Plato's time to mid 20th century. Developmental factors, indicated in the large body of literature of music education philosophy, resulted from differences between societies in various cultures over an extended period of time. In every case, the philosophical justification for music education was its effect on the development of the citizen and its ability to influence people to be more effective citizens. Around the middle of the 20th century, music education philosophers no longer expressed the need to relate aesthetic development to societal needs and goals. From that time on, the prevailing philosophy of aesthetic education has supported the teaching of music for aesthetic development without expressing the value to society of the aesthetically developed individual.

REFERENCES

Aristotle. *Politica, Book 7.* In W. D. Ross (Ed.), *The Works of Aristotle,* vol. 10. London: Oxford University Press, 1921.

Athenaeus. *The Deipnosophists.* (C. B. Gulick, trans.). Cambridge, Massachusetts: Harvard University Press, 1937.

Boston Musical Gazette, 18, Nov. 28, Dec. 12, 26, 1938.

Bower, C. M. Boethius' "The principles of music," an introduction, translation and commentary. (Doctoral dissertation, George Peabody College for Teachers, 1967). *Dissertation Abstracts International,* 1967, *28,* 2279A. (University Microfilms, no. 67–15,005).

Charlemagne. *Monumenta Germania historica,* Leges II, Capitulari regum Francorum I. In G. Ellard. Master Alcuin, liturgist. Chicago: Loyola University Press, 1956.

Comenius, J. A. *The great didactic.* (M. W. Keatinge, trans. and Ed.). London: A. & G. Black, Ltd., 1923).

Dewey, J. The aesthetic element in education. In *Addresses and proceedings of the National Education Association.* Washington, D. C.: National Education Association, 1897.

Dewey, J. *Psychology,* 1887. In *The early works of John Dewey: Psychology.* Carbondale: Southern Illinois University Press, 1967.

Froebel, F. *The education of man.* New York: D. Appleton and Company, 1908.

Green, J. A., Ed. *Pestalozzi's educational writings.* New York: Longmans, Green & Co., 1916.

Henry, N. B., Ed. *Basic concepts in music education.* Chicago: National Society for the Study of Education, 1958.

Leonhard, C. The philosophy of music education—present and future. In *Comprehensive musicianship: The foundation for college education in music.* Washington, D. C.: Music Educators National Conference, 1965.

Mann, H. *Life and works of Horace Mann: Annual reports of the secretary of the board of education of Massachusetts for the years 1839–1844.* Boston: Lee and Shepherd Publishers, 1891.

Mason, L. *Manual of the Boston Academy of Music for instruction in the elements of vocal music on the system of Pestalozzi.* Boston: Boston Academy of Music, 1834.

Mather, C. *The accomplished singer.* Boston, 1721. In Swan, J. C. (Ed.), *Music in*

Boston. Boston: Trustees of the Public Library of the City of Boston, 1977.

Monroe, W. S. *Comenius' school of infancy.* Boston: D. C. Heath & Co., Publishers, 1908.

Parker, H.; McConathy, O.; Birge, E. B.; and Miessner, O. *The progressive music series,* teacher's manual, vol. 2. Boston: Silver, Burdett and Company, 1916.

Plato. *Protagoras, Laws, Republic.* (E. Hamilton and H. Cairns, Eds.). Princeton, New Jersey: Princeton University Press, 1961.

Reimer, B. *A philosophy of music education.* Englewood Cliffs, New Jersey: Prentice-Hall, 1970.

Smail, W. M., trans. *Quintilian on education,* book 1. Oxford, England: Clarendon Press, 1938.

Spencer, H. *Education: Intellectual, moral, and physical.* New York: D. Appelton and Company, 1890.

Spencer, H. *Literary style and music.* New York: Philosophical Library, 1951.

June 1, 1981

[7]

alternative views about art on which a philosophy can be based

Bennett Reimer

In the long, tortuous history of aesthetics thousands of views have been expressed about art. To one who examines these views with any degree of objectivity it becomes evident that here, if no place else, is a perfect example of truth being relative. So strong is this impression, so overwhelming its effect, that one is tempted to throw up his hands in despair, turn his back on the entire field of aesthetics, and proclaim that in aesthetic education one might as well do whatever strikes his fancy, since there probably exists plenty of justification for whatever this happens to be.

To yield to this temptation, however, is to give oneself up to ineffectuality. Of course there is no immutable truth in aesthetics. Of course there is no single or simple answer to every question. Of course there is no one guideline which will insure satisfactory results of action. The question is, can one accept this condition and at the same time develop a point of view which helps one's efforts to be as consistent, as effective, as useful for one's purposes as intelligence and modesty allow?

There is really no alternative but to answer "yes." Everything we do in this world is done in the face of imperfect and partial knowledge.

But it is possible—in fact, it is necessary—to adopt some working premises and to use them (not be used *by* them) as guidelines to action, knowing full well that they may be altered or even dropped as conditions change. To refuse to work from a critically accepted position about the nature of one's subject is to avoid one of the central imperatives of human life, which is to carve out, from all existing possibilities, the most reasonable possibilities for one's purposes. Not to do so dooms one to intellectual and operational paralysis. To do so blindly and irrevocably insures the same fate. Searching out a convincing, useful, coherent point of view, adopting it as a base of operations, examining it and sharpening it and tightening it while using it, opening it to new ideas and altering it as seems necessary, can help one to act with purpose, with impact, with some measure of meaningfulness.

The problem, of course, is to determine the best possible point of view. Several principles can help us do so. First, the field of aesthetics must be approached in a highly selective way. It would be beside the point (and quite impossible) to investigate indiscriminately the writings of every aesthetician in history, or every aesthetician of this century, or every aesthetician alive today, looking for leads to a philosophy of music education. Instead, the search must start with an acquaintance with the field of music education; its problems, its needs, its history, its present status. Aesthetics must be used by the music educator to serve his purposes. Otherwise he is likely to lose himself in the history and problems of aesthetics, never to emerge with a workable philosophy. A philosophy should articulate a consistent and helpful statement about the nature and value of music and music education. Only those portions of aesthetics useful for this purpose need be used.

Second, the point of view adopted should be sufficiently broad to take into account all major aspects of music and music education, but sufficiently focused to provide tangible guidelines for thought and action. No single aesthetician has supplied the breadth of conception needed for our purpose, although, as will be seen, some have been of unusual help. It will be necessary to identify an aesthetic position which includes major thinkers and which at the same time has an identifiable structure of ideas which can be handled without being overwhelming in complexity.

Third, the point of view should be particularly pertinent to the art of music, but at the same time capable of yielding insights into the nature of all the arts. Some aesthetic theories are heavily slanted toward the non-musical arts, and while they offer insights into music they do so only secondarily. An example would be the psychoanalytic theory of Carl G. Jung, which is immensely fruitful of ideas about literature, poetry and the visual arts, but which has little to say about music. (2, pp. 140–54; 1, pp. 347–48).*[1] Obviously this situation should be reversed for our purposes, although a view confined to a single art, even music, would be unacceptable also.

Fourth, the view being sought must contain rich implications for education. It would be of little use to adopt a theory which offered few leads to teaching and learning music and the other arts, no matter how strong the theory might be in other matters. Existentialist aesthetics, for example, has provided powerful insights into the nature of art and its role in human life. (1, pp. 363–76).[2] But helpful as these insights are, they do not seem to lend themselves directly or abundantly to problems of mass education. It would be difficult, therefore, to depend on this particular view for a philosophy of music education.

Finally, any aesthetic position to be used as a basis for a philosophy must be relevant to the society in which we live and to the general conditions under which American education operates. Important as Marxism-Leninism has been in history, for example (1, pp. 355–63) it is quite peripheral to our concerns. The same can be said about Freudian aesthetics and Oriental aesthetics and Medieval aesthetics. All of these, and others, can be of use for particular purposes, but they can not be the foundation on which our philosophy is to be built.

Of all existing aesthetic viewpoints,[3] one in particular fulfills the principles outlined above and does so with unusual power. This view is presented by Leonard B. Meyer (7) as one of three related aesthetic theories; Absolute Formalism, Absolute Expressionism and Referentialism. An explanation of each of these theories will set the stage for the choice to be made as to which will best serve as the basis for a philosophy, and for our systematic examination of the implications of using this theory as a base of operations.

The words "Absolutism" and "Referentialism" tell one where to go to find the meaning and value of a work of art. The Absolutist says that in order to find an art work's meaning, you must go to the work itself and attend to the qualities which make the work a created thing. In

---

* References in parentheses refer to the Supplementary Readings at the ends of the chapters in this book.

1 An excellent introduction to the monumental work of Jung is Carl G. Jung, ed., *Man and his Symbols* (Garden City, New York: Doubleday & Company, Inc., 1964).

2 Also see Arturo B. Fallico, *Art and Existentialism* (Englewood Cliffs, N.J.: Prentice-Hall, Inc., 1962).

3 All the major "isms" in aesthetics are reviewed in Monroe C. Beardsley, *Aesthetics* (New York: The Macmillan Company, 1966).

music, you would go to the sounds themselves, and attend to what those sounds do.

The Referentialist disagrees. According to his view, the meaning and value of a work of art exist outside of the work itself. In order to find the art work's meaning you must go to the ideas, emotions, attitudes, events, which the work *refers* you to in the world outside the art work. The function of the art work is to remind you of, or tell you about, or help you understand, or make you experience, something which is extra-artistic; that is, something which is outside the created thing and the artistic qualities which make it a created thing. In music, the sounds should serve as a reminder of, or a clue to, or a sign of something extra-musical; something separate from the sounds and what the sounds are doing. To the degree that the music is successful in referring you to a non-musical experience it is a successful piece of music. To the degree that the experience is an important or valuable one the music is itself important or valuable.

The most clear-cut example of Referentialism is the Communist theory of art, called "Socialist Realism." This view, which is the official aesthetic doctrine of Marxism-Leninism, regards art as a servant of social and political needs. The function of art is to further the cause of the state by influencing attitudes toward social problems and by illuminating the needs of the state and the proper actions to be taken to fulfill those needs. As stated in the Statute of the Union of Soviet Writers:

> Socialist Realism is the fundamental method of Soviet Litera-
> ture and criticism [and of all art]: it demands of the artist a
> true, historically concrete representation of reality in its revo-
> lutionary development. Further, it ought to contribute to the
> ideological transformation and education of the workers in the
> spirit of socialism.[4]

According to Socialist Realism, and for any referential theory of art, the key factor of value is the non-aesthetic goodness of the art work's "message." If a particular art work has no identifiable, non-artistic message (a piece of "pure" instrumental music, for example), it must be regarded as merely a titillation of the senses with no value beyond that of sheer decoration. Of course any message in the art work must be presented attractively, but the artistic attractiveness only serves to make the message more vivid, more powerfully felt. To the extent that artistic interest becomes the central value of the work and non-artistic aspects are diminished in importance, the work is decadent and useless.

---

4 Beardsley, *Aesthetics*, p. 360.

The message in an art work, according to Referentialism, need not be an intellectual or practical one: it can also be an "emotional" one. If a work makes people feel a particular, desirable, useful emotion, it would fulfill the conditions for "good" art. The emotion must be identifiable; it must be unambiguous and concrete, and it must be the kind which serves some non-artistic end, such as closer identification with fellow workers, or higher regard for the community, or deeper sympathy for those less fortunate, etc. If the emotion in a work is not of this specific, non-artistically directed kind; if it is, instead, an integral and inseparable part of the artistic qualities in the work and is therefore experienced as an ineffable sense of feeling, the work is to that extent, again, decadent and useless.

The notion that art works arouse non-artistic emotions and that one must carefully choose which of these emotions *should* be aroused is as old as Plato, who felt that the kinds of music used by the general public should be severely limited so that their moral fiber would not be weakened through the effects of hearing voluptuous tunes. The strongest statement of this position in modern times is that of Leo Tolstoy. It will repay us to take a brief look at Tolstoy's views, in making very explicit the consequences of taking a thoroughgoing referentialist viewpoint.

For Tolstoy, the function of art is to transmit specific emotions from the artist to the recipient in the most direct and most powerful way the artist can devise. If the artist can transmit an emotion which is individual; that is, which is a particular, precise, concrete emotion: if the emotion is transmitted clearly and unambiguously, so there is no question about what the recipient should feel: and if the artist sincerely feels the emotion himself and has the need to express it, the work of art is likely to be a good one. (4, pp. 140–41). All these principles illustrate the emotional dimension of Referentialism.

But in addition to transmitting a specific emotion and doing it well, the quality of the art work also depends on the desirability of the particular emotion transmitted. If it is a "bad" emotion the art work will be pernicious in its effects. If it is a "good" emotion the art work will be beneficent in its effects. So, inevitably, for Tolstoy and for any referentialist, one must judge a work of art on the basis of its non-artistic subject matter—its content of reference to the world which is outside the work and which is separate from the work's artistic qualities. One can specify good and bad emotions according to one's view of what is good and what is bad in life. According to Tolstoy, good emotions are those which lead toward Christian brotherhood. Unfortunately, very few art works fulfill his criteria of goodness. "In modern painting, strange to say, works of this kind, directly transmitting the Christian feeling of love of God and of one's neighbor are hardly to be found, especially among the works of the celebrated painters."[5]

Tolstoy finds very few art works in any medium that satisfy his demands for good art, although occasionally a few crop up—*Uncle Tom's Cabin,* Millet's "The Man with the Hoe," china dolls and other ornaments which are easily comprehensible to everyone, etc. In music his position is illustrated most strikingly. The best examples of music are marches and dances, which approach the condition of having a distinct, easily understood message. The popular songs of the various nations are also great art, but in "learned" music there are precious few examples from which to choose—the Violin Aria by Bach, the E-flat Major Nocturne of Chopin, some scattered selections from Haydn, Mozart, Schubert. Beethoven is perhaps the poorest of composers and the weakest of his compositions is the Ninth Symphony. This is so because

> not only do I not see how the feelings transmitted by this work could unite people not specially trained to submit themselves to its complex hypnotism, but I am unable to imagine to myself a crowd of normal people who could understand anything of this long, confused, and artificial production, except short snatches which are lost in a sea of what is incomprehensible. And therefore, whether I like it or not, I am compelled to conclude that this work belongs to the rank of bad art.[6]

But Beethoven is in good company, for in the same classification (along with paintings which display "all that odious female nudity")[7]

> belongs almost all the chamber and opera music of our times, beginning especially from Beethoven (Schumann, Berlioz, Liszt, Wagner), by its subject matter devoted to the expression of feelings accessible only to people who have developed in themselves an unhealthy, nervous irritation evoked by this exclusive, artificial, and complex music.[8]

The reason for dwelling a bit on Tolstoy's aesthetic views is that they present the most thorough statement of Referentialism available, and can serve as a foil against which the other views to be presented can

---

5 Leo N. Tolstoy, *What Is Art?,* trans. Aylmer Maude (Indianapolis: The Liberal Arts Press, Inc., 1960), p. 152. Reprinted by permission of The Liberal Arts Press Division of The Bobbs-Merrill Company, Inc.

6 Tolstoy, *What Is Art?,* p. 158.

7 Tolstoy, *What Is Art?,* p. 153.

8 Tolstoy, *What Is Art?,* p. 157.

be compared. Another very obvious example of Referentialism should be noted, this one in musical aesthetics, because it also will help keep straight the three viewpoints to be explained here. This is the view of the English aesthetician Deryck Cooke. (3).

Mr. Cooke is in agreement with Tolstoy that music is by nature a language and that, as with any good language, the meaning of the terms used in the language can be specified. This notion will be explored in several places throughout this book, so no explanation will be made at this point. It need only be noted that the conception of art as "language" (by which is meant a system of symbols having conventional referents) is a purely referential one and leads inevitably to a search for the proper "meanings" of the language's terms. While Cooke recognizes the difficulty of stipulating precise referents for musical "language terms," the difficulty, according to him, can be overcome by intellectual effort. As a step in this direction he analyzes the notes of the major, minor and chromatic scales, and several basic melodic patterns, to find the emotional referent of each. To the extent that he succeeds in doing so, according to his theory, he succeeds in revealing the meanings hidden in the musical sounds. The task, obviously, is one of translation; of "breaking the code" so to speak. (3, p. 34).

After long analyses of the use of various intervals and note patterns, Mr. Cooke offers his conclusions as to their referents. A selection of these follows:

> Minor Second: . . . spiritless anguish, context of finality.
> Minor Third: . . . stoic acceptance, tragedy.
> Major Third: . . . joy.
> Sharp Fourth: . . . devilish and inimical forces.
> Major Seventh: . . . violent longing, aspiration in a context of finality.
> Ascending 1-(2)-3-(4)-5 (major): . . . an outgoing, active, assertive emotion of joy.
> Ascending 1-(2)-3-(4)-5 (minor): . . . an outgoing feeling of pain—an assertion of sorrow, a complaint, a protest against misfortune.
> Descending 5-(4)-3-(2)-1 (minor): . . . an "incoming" painful emotion, in a context of finality: acceptance of, or yielding to grief: discouragement and depression; passive suffering; and the despair connected with death.[9]

---

[9] Deryck Cooke, *The Language of Music* (London, Oxford University Press, 1959), pp. 90, 115, 122, 133. Quotations reprinted by permission of Oxford University Press.

The use of these translations by the knowledgable listener should allow, according to Cooke, for full participation in music's meaning. Is this oversimplifying the case? Not according to Cooke, for

> Actually, the process of musical communication is funda-mentally a very simple one, which only appears complicated because of its complicated apparatus. There is nothing more involved about it than there is in any form of emotional ex-pression—say, a physical movement or a vocal utterance.[10]

Beethoven's music, for example, would not be needed if Beethoven could personally communicate his inner joy by jumping or shouting in the presence of an audience. To convert his emotion into permanent form he used sounds, so that many people, even after his death, could ex-perience with him the joy that he felt. (3, p. 209). Music, then, is essentially a giving vent to emotions through sounds.

While the examples of Referentialism given here are obviously extreme ones, many opinions about and practices in aesthetic education share some of the same assumptions, even if not as consistently or strongly. For example, the idea that when non-aesthetic subject matter exists in a work of art (fruit in a painting, political theories in a novel, a story or "program" in music) the art work is "about" that subject matter, is a referentialist assumption. If one isolates the subject matter; say, the story of *Til Eulenspiegel,* and teaches about it as if the story was what the music is about, one is acting as a Referentialist. If one adds a story or message to an art work which contains none; say, Mozart's *Eine kleine Nachtmusik,* one is, again, acting as a Referentialist. The same applies to "emotional" content. Teaching about love and its mean-ing as the content of the *Liebestod,* or identifying the content of Beetho-ven's Funeral March as "sadness," and teaching about sadness and its roots, its implications, etc., are practices compatible with Referentialism.

Music educators and others concerned with the arts in the schools will recognize that referentialist assumptions are in operation in much that is done in the teaching of art. The isolating of and teaching about the meaning of the words in vocal music; the same process in program music; the searching out of a "message" in absolute music; the attempt to add a story or picture to music, either verbally or visually; the search for the right emotion-words with which to characterize music; the com-paring of musical works with works in other art forms according to similarities in subject matter; these and many other practices attest to the presence of Referentialism in music education.

---

10 Cooke, *The Language of Music,* p. 209.

What is the value of art, according to the referentialist point of view? Obviously, the values of art and of being involved with art are non-artistic values. Art works serve many purposes, all of them extra-aesthetic. If one can share these values one becomes a better citizen, a better worker, a better human being, to the extent that art influences one in non-artistic ways and these influences are assumed to be beneficial. Of course, there is the danger that harmful works of art will have harmful effects, so care must be taken in the choice of art works. This is why societies which operate under a referentialist aesthetic must exercise a high degree of control over the artistic diet of their citizens. Teachers, if they are Referentialists, are in the position of having to make decisions as to which art works are proper for their students and which improper, these judgments being based on the non-artistic effects of the art works' subject matter.

As with teaching practices based on Referentialism, music educators will have no difficulty recognizing the referentialist basis for many of the value claims made for music education. Studying music makes one a better person in many ways: it improves learning skills; it imparts moral uplift; it fulfills a wide variety of social needs; it provides a healthy outlet for repressed emotions; it encourages self-discipline; it provides a challenge to focus efforts upon; it gives a basis for worthy use of leisure time; it improves health in countless ways; it is assumed to be, in short, a most effective way to make people better people—non-aesthetically.

Let us return now to the aesthetic point of view called Absolutism. It will be recalled that this view asserts that the meaning and value of a work of art are to be found in the qualities which make the work a created thing—the very qualities which the Referentialist insists are only the bearers of meanings *outside* themselves. In music, according to Absolutism, the sounds and what they do are inherently meaningful, and if one is to share their "meaning" one must attend to the sounds and not to anything the sounds might remind one of in the extra-aesthetic realm outside the music.

At the opposite end of the aesthetic spectrum from the Referentialist is the Absolutist who is also a Formalist. The Absolute Formalist asserts that the "meaning" of an art work is like no other meaning in all the experience of man. Aesthetic events, such as sounds in music, mean *only themselves:* the meaning is *sui generis,* completely and essentially different from anything in the world which is non-musical:

> . . . to appreciate a work of art we need bring with us nothing
> from life, no knowledge of its ideas and affairs, no familiarity
> with its emotions. Art transports us from the world of man's
> activity to a world of aesthetic exaltation. For a moment we

are shut off from human interests; our anticipations and memories are arrested; we are lifted above the stream of life.[11]

The experience of art, for the Formalist, is primarily an intellectual one; it is the recognition and appreciation of form for its own sake.
This recognition and appreciation, while intellectual in character, is
called by Formalists an "emotion"—usually, the "aesthetic emotion." But
this so-called "emotion" is a unique one—it has no counterpart in other
emotional experiences:

> . . . he who contemplates a work of art, inhabit(s) a world
> with an intense and peculiar significance of its own; that sig-
> nificance is unrelated to the significance of life. In this world
> the emotions of life find no place. It is a world with emotions
> of its own.[12]

The Formalist does not deny that many art works contain references to the world outside the work. But he insists that all such
references are *totally irrelevant* to the art work's meaning:

> . . . no one who has a real understanding of the art of paint-
> ing attaches any importance to what we call the subject of a
> picture—what is represented . . . all depends on *how* it is
> presented, *nothing* on what. Rembrandt expressed his pro-
> foundest feelings just as well when he painted a carcass hang-
> ing up in a butcher's shop as when he painted the Crucifixion
> or his mistress.[13]

In music, since it is capable of being entirely untainted with non-
aesthetic subject matter, the Formalist finds the clearest example of
artistic meaning. In a complete reversal of Referentialism, the Formalist
claims that "Definite feelings and emotions are unsusceptible of being
embodied in music."[14] Instead, "The ideas which a composer expresses
are mainly and primarily of a purely musical nature."[15] There is no
correspondence whatsoever between the beauty we find in the non-artistic

---

[11] Clive Bell, *Art* (New York: G. P. Putnam's Sons, 1914), p. 25. Quotations reprinted by permission of Putnam's, Professor Quentin Bell and Chatto & Windus
Ltd., London.

[12] Bell, *Art*, pp. 26, 27.

[13] Roger Fry, *The Artist and Psycho-Analysis*, Hogarth Essays (London: Hogarth
Press, 1924), p. 308. Reprinted by permission of Mrs. Pamela Diamand and the
Hogarth Press.

[14] Eduard Hanslick, *The Beautiful in Music*, trans. Gustav Cohen (Indianapolis:
The Liberal Arts Press, Inc., 1957), p. 21. Reprinted by permission of The
Liberal Arts Press Division of The Bobbs-Merrill Company, Inc.

[15] Hanslick, *The Beautiful in Music*, p. 23.

world and the beauty we find in art, for art's beauty is a separate kind. This is especially the case in music, in which the nature of the beautiful ". . . is specifically musical. By this we mean that the beautiful is not contingent upon nor in need of any subject introduced from without, but that it consists wholly of sounds artistically combined."[16]

Unfortunately, it is given to few people to be able to enjoy the peculiar, special, esoteric kind of experience which the contemplation of formal relationships offers. According to the Formalist, most people, being inherently incapable of pure aesthetic enjoyment, satisfy themselves with non-aesthetic reactions to art works; that is, with reactions to the referents of the works. This completely misses the point of art, of course, but the Formalist assumes that this is to be expected. Given the special nature of the aesthetic and the general insensitivity of most people, we should not be too concerned if art's value is available on only a limited basis, and we should not have any illusions that most people will ever understand that the real value of art is quite different from what they think it is.

The further removed from the events and objects of life, the purer the appeal to the intellect which can apprehend fine distinctions in formal relations, the more exquisite the arrangement of aesthetic properties, the freer from ordinary emotions not directly dependent on form, the better the art work and the more aesthetic the experience of it. In the rarified realm of pure form, untouched by the homeliness of ordinary life, the Formalist finds his satisfaction and his delight. He does not expect to find much company there.

Pure Formalism, as pure Referentialism, represents an extreme view of the nature and value of art. However, as some beliefs and practices in aesthetic education are based on assumptions of Referentialism, many are based on Formalist suppositions. The practice of isolating the formal elements of art works and studying them for their own sake is the counterpart of separating out the referential elements. The study of art as a "discipline," with primary attention given to the accumulation of information or the development of skills, is formalistic in flavor. That the major value of music education is intellectual; that the study of "the fundamentals" is, in and of itself, a beneficial thing; that musical experience consists primarily of using the mind to ferret out all possible tonal relationships; that music, or art in general, transports one from the real world into the ethereal world of the aesthetic; all these are assumptions compatible with Formalism.

Perhaps the most widespread application of Formalism to music

---

16 Hanslick, *The Beautiful in Music*, p. 47.

education is the policy of teaching the talented and entertaining the remaining masses. Music education in recent history has focused major effort on developing the musical skills of children with talent, and in this it has achieved a high level of success. And why, after all, should one worry about the general population, which is never going to be aesthetically educated anyhow? As with all special abilities, artistic enjoyment is possible for a few, and these are the ones who can benefit from serious music education. As for music in general education, let it be pleasant, let it be attractive, let it be amusing, but don't expect authentic musical learning to take place. Teachers who care to devote themselves to music education for the masses, whether through missionary zeal or lack of musical ability, are certainly welcome to do so, but they should not expect to be regarded with the same respect as those who are engaged in serious music teaching. It is not surprising, given the pervasiveness of this formalistic view, however subliminal it might be, that music education has achieved so much in the performance program and so little in the general music program. It is also not surprising, in view of the educational reform movement in our times, that the entire profession has become alarmed over this situation and determined to improve upon it.

While Referentialism and Formalism are contradictory in the major aspects of their theories, both contain a measure of truth. One can agree with the Referentialist that art works are affected by their subject matter. One can also agree that art and feelings are intimately connected. Perhaps it is so that art can serve non-artistic ends. But how are these ideas reconciled with the equally convincing ideas that art works can be entirely devoid of subject matter and in any case always transcend subject matter; that aesthetic reactions are not identical to ordinary emotions; that art's value is inherently aesthetic rather than non-aesthetic?

When considering each of these two viewpoints separately it is difficult (perhaps impossible) to give full assent to either. There is no evidence to support the Referentialist's claim that artists or art lovers are better citizens, behave more morally, are more socially adjusted, are healthier, etc. The use of art as propaganda—no matter whether for good or bad causes—perverts the nature of the artistic impulse. To translate the "meaning" of art into non-artistic terms, whether cognitive or emotional, is to violate the meaningfulness of aesthetic experience. And to justify the arts in education on the basis of values least characteristic of art is to miss the point of what art really does have to offer.

At the same time it is not possible to regard art, with the Formalist, as an intellectual exercise. Surely art is intimately connected to life rather than totally distinct from it. The sense of significance we get from art is a sense applicable to the significance of human life, and the beauty or truth we find in art has some relation to the beauty or truth of life as lived and known. To assume that art is a fragile thing, suitable for some people but irrelevant for most, and that education should reflect this exclusiveness, disregards the power and pervasiveness of art in human life and the obligation of education to share life's goods fully.

So while each view contains some truth, each also contains major falsehoods which prevent their use as a basis for a philosophy. Somehow their contributions to understanding must be preserved while their limitations are overcome.

This brings us to a third aesthetic theory, Absolute Expressionism, which, it will be argued in this book, does in fact include the elements of truth found in both Referentialism and Formalism. But Expressionism is not in any sense a combination of the other two. It is a distinctive, coherent viewpoint, requiring systematic explanation if its major tenets are to be understood. These tenets, it is believed, will be found to be as widely acceptable by aestheticians, artists and educators as any available in aesthetic theory. Further, the views of Absolute Expressionism seem to be most suitable to mass education in a democratic society; most true to the nature of art, as art is conceived in our times; and most germinal of guidelines for teaching and learning music and the other arts in all aspects of educational programs.

The remainder of this book will be devoted to an explanation of Expressionism and its application to music education. A brief overview at this point will introduce the major issues which need to be explored.

First, and most basic, is the clear distinction between Absolutism and Referentialism. The Absolute Expressionist agrees with the Absolute Formalist that the meaning and value of art are to be found in the aesthetic qualities of art works. In this there is an irreconcilable conflict with the referentialist view of art's meaning as a function of subject matter. But while Expressionism cannot accept non-artistic meaning as central to art, it also cannot accept the formalist notion of the intellectual, removed-from-life nature of aesthetic experience. How can it be maintained that the experience of art is *aesthetic* experience, that art's meaning is *aesthetic* meaning, that art's value is *aesthetic* value, and at the same time claim that art can exert a strong effect on the quality of human life? This is the key question, for it states the two conditions which must be met if an aesthetic theory is to be both convincing and useful. First, the nature of art as art must be affirmed. Second, the relation of art to life must be recognized.

The answer to this question has been given in many different ways by many different writers on art. A summary of their views might be stated as follows: the aesthetic components in a work of art are similar in quality to the quality inherent in all human experience. When one shares the qualities contained in an art work's aesthetic content, one is also sharing in the qualities of which all human experience is made. The relation between the qualities of the art work and the qualities of human experience is felt by the perceiver of the work as "significance." To the degree that an art work contains aesthetic qualities which are convincing, vital, keen, and to the degree that these qualities can be experienced by the perceiver. the significance of the experience—the relation of the aesthetic qualities to the qualities of life—will be convincing, vital, keen. The residue of sharing the significant aesthetic qualities of the art work is a deeper sense of the nature of human life.

Many words have been used in aesthetics to explain this notion. The following is a summary of the more common ones:

Art:
is expressive of	
is analogous to	subjective reality
is isomorphic with	the quality of experience
corresponds to	the emotive life
is a counterpart of	the patterns of feeling
has the same patterns as	the life of feeling
is a semblance of	sentience
gives images of	the depth of existence
gives insights into	the human personality
gives experience of	the realm of affect
gives understanding of	the patterns of consciousness
gives revelations of	the significance of experience
brings to consciousness	
makes conceivable	

All these terms convey the same sense; that the experience of art is related to the experience of life at the deepest levels of life's significance. One can share the insights of art not by going outside of art to non-artistic references, *but by going deeper into the aesthetic qualities the art work contains.* It is in the aesthetic content of the art work that insights can be found, and the deeper the experience of the aesthetic qualities the deeper can be the sense of significance gained. If the experience of art is to be significant for life, the experience of art must be aesthetic experience.

What is the value of such experience? If it is true that experiences of art yield insights into human subjective reality, the arts may be conceived as a means to self-understanding, a way by which a human's sense of his nature can be explored, clarified, grasped. Many words have

been used to describe the value of insight into one's nature as a responsive organism: "self-unification" (John Dewey); "personal identity"
(Susanne K. Langer); "individualization" (Leonard B. Meyer); "indi-
viduation" (Carl G. Jung); "self-actualization" (Abraham H. Maslow);
"integration of the personality" (Paul Tillich). All these terms signify
the humanising value of self-knowledge. There are few deeper values
than this. And the arts are one of the most effective means known to man
to realize this value.

All these statements must be explained and their relevance to music
education shown. In what follows, the meaning of Expressionism will be
explored as it is manifested in the most important areas of aesthetics:
the relation of art and feeling; the process of aesthetic creation; the complex but central problem of aesthetic meaning; and the content of
aesthetic experience. This will be followed by a discussion of the particular nature of the art of music. At that point, the implicit and explicit
references made throughout the book to education will be applied to
the three major aspects of the music education program; general music,
performance, and music among the other arts.

QUESTIONS FOR DISCUSSION

1. Why would it be dangerous to start with the field of aesthetics
   and try to work out a philosophy of music education on the
   basis of what aesthetics suggests? What role can aesthetics play
   in the formation of a philosophy?
2. According to Referentialism, where does one find the value of
   art? Give examples. How would one teach art in order to help
   people find its referential value? Give examples.
3. According to Formalism, where does one find the value of art?
   Give examples. How would one teach art for its formal values?
   Give examples.
4. What seems true and what seems false about Referentialism and
   about Formalism? Can one be both a Referentialist and a Formalist at the same time?
5. What are some practices in music education other than those
   mentioned in this chapter which seem to be based on 1) Referentialist assumptions, 2) Formalist assumptions?
6. Can you think of terms other than the ones suggested in this
   chapter which state the same idea that art (is expressive of)
   (the realm of human feeling)?

SUPPLEMENTARY READINGS

A. General writings on aesthetics

    1. Beardsley, Monroe C., *Aesthetics*. New York: The Macmillan Company, 1966. This is a most useful history of aesthetics, comprehensive but succinct.

    2. Rader, Melvin, ed., *A Modern Book of Esthetics*. New York: Holt, Rinehart & Winston, Inc., 1962. Perhaps the most widely used collection of essays on the main topics in aesthetics.

B. Referentialism

    3. Cooke, Deryck, *The Language of Music*. London: Oxford University Press, 1959.

    4. Tolstoy, Leo N., *What Is Art?*, trans. Aylmer Maude. Indianapolis: The Liberal Arts Press, Inc., 1960.

C. Formalism

    5. Bell, Clive, *Art*. New York: G. P. Putnam's Sons, 1914.

    6. Hanslick, Eduard, *The Beautiful in Music*, trans. Gustav Cohen. Indianapolis: The Liberal Arts Press, Inc., 1957.

D. Expressionism

    7. Meyer, Leonard B., *Emotion and Meaning in Music*. Chicago: The University of Chicago Press, 1956, pp. 1–6. The first section of Meyer's book presents the three views and his intentions in exploring them.

    Supplementary readings on Expressionism will be given for the next 5 chapters. For an introduction, see Beardsley (1, pp. 342–55) on "Semiotic Approaches."

Part II
Research

[8]

QUALITATIVE RESEARCH METHODOLOGY
IN MUSIC EDUCATION

Liora Bresler and Robert E. Stake

UNIVERSITY OF ILLINOIS AT URBANA-CHAMPAIGN

A freckled third grader approaches the music teacher in the corridor and hands her a stack of 3 x 5 cards. "Thirty-six," he announces proudly. Back in her office Rebecca Grant puts the cards in an envelope on which she neatly writes, "Daniel Wang, 36," and posts it on the wall near three other envelopes. This latest is Daniel's entry in the Composer's Facts competition, this week featuring Aaron Copland. Were curious eyes to pry, they would find information about Copland's birthdate, milestones, compositions, and books. Winners will get musical handbags, musical rulers, musical paraphernalia which Rebecca orders (and pays for with her own money) from a mail-order firm specializing in music items.[1]

• • •

Public Act 84-126, effective August 1, 1985, amended The School Code of Illinois to include, for the first time in state history, a requirement that the goals for learning be identified and assessed. The fine arts were one of the six primary areas designated. Broad goals for Illinois school children include understanding the sensory, formal, technical, and expressive qualities for each of the arts; demonstrating the basic skills necessary to participate in the creation and performance of the arts; and identifying significant works in the arts from major historical periods and how they reflect societies, cultures, and civilizations, past and present.

Achievement of the goals would be assessed by paper and pencil tests. Music specialists, classroom teachers, and principals expressed anger and frustration about these new mandated tests. Among the main complaints were the loss and redirection of instructional time, the lack of empathy about teaching within existing constraints, the lack of responsiveness to teacher concerns, and the lack of financial support to help the teachers learn new skills. Mark Denman, principal in East Park, reacted as follows:

"It is not fair for the state to dictate this. Unless they teach us how to teach these areas it's not realistic. You can't just legislate improvement. You can't just say we are going to raise test scores. You've got to build the groundwork. You can't impose change from the top. You've got to ignite the interest of the staff. Oftentimes people in the

State Department of Education will say: 'Do this, this, and this.' But we have no money to do it. We were not asked if we wanted to do it. We were not asked how we could do it. We work for years to improve something, then funding runs out and nothing further happens. So people are discouraged [shaking his head]. I know the intents of legislators are very good, but . . . "

• • •

It is a chilly Tuesday morning when Ms. Casieri and myself (in the role of observer, and not a very experienced one) are sitting in a half-full bus, with a group of third and fourth graders, on the way to the Civic Center to hear Humperdinck's *Hansel und Gretel*. When we are seated, a blue light is turned on, a series of Shhh's spreads in waves. The chaos subsides, an intense diminuendo, with some uncontrollable giggles as leftovers. The striking silence makes me uneasy, seems to invite a reaction. But no. The lights go down. The piano sounds.

Today's performance is a shortened version of the opera, 60 minutes rather than the 2 original hours. It is performed by a junior group of opera members, the orchestra parts transcribed to piano. An accomplished young woman plays flawlessly the difficult virtuoso part—rhythm and notes, articulations and phrasing, matching dynamics. There is much humor and jest as Hansel and Gretel tease and chase each other. Children laugh *with* the singers, an honest laugh. A good channel to release the tension of the unfamiliar—singing culture, the new form.

• • •

In this chapter we review the basic theory and method of qualitative research in music education. Qualitative approaches come with various names and descriptions: case study, field study, ethnographic research, naturalistic, phenomenological, interpretive, symbolic interactionist, or just plain descriptive. We use "qualitative research" as a general term to refer to several research strategies that share certain characteristics: (1) *noninterventionist* observation in natural settings; (2) emphasis on *interpretation* of both emic issues (those of the participants) and etic issues (those of the writer); (3) highly *contextual description* of people and events; and (4) validation of information through triangulation. These constructs will be developed later in this chapter.

Educational researchers in America have increasingly come to value what researchers elsewhere have long emphasized: the personal and political nature of education. Part of the awareness is reflected in an increased interest in the unique circumstances of school programs and performances. The study of uniqueness can be handled in a disciplined and scholarly way with qualitative inquiry. The classroom community and societal contexts become more than abstract variables.

Our chapter begins with an overview of the intellectual and methodological roots of qualitative research, its basic assumptions and goals, plus identification of kinds of research questions of central interest. In the next section, we examine qualitative research in music. First, we examine models in pedagogy, ethnomusicology, and musical biography. Then we review key studies, focusing on their unique contributions to the field, their aims and objectives, and their primary issues and findings. Of special interest is the compatibility of research methods to the training of musicians regarding teaching as art form and classroom interaction as kinetic performance. We then focus on methods and criteria of qualitative studies. We conclude by pointing to some future directions and possibilities offered by qualitative research to the field of music education.

ROOTS OF QUALITATIVE METHODOLOGY

Just as music and education can be traced back across the centuries ultimately to the crude and custom-driven habits of primitive societies, qualitative inquiry has its roots in the intuitive and survivalist behavior of early peoples. For ages we have operated on hunches and emotions, increasingly using those that brought us safety and satisfaction. Gradually we saw the wisdom of what we already were doing by observing, questioning, keeping records and interpreting, respecting the experience and rumination of elders. Gradually we formed rules for study and names for our sciences. Music educators, too, increasingly drew from philosophers and social scientists to codify research procedures.

Intellectual Roots

The intellectual roots of qualitative methodology lie in the idealist movement—in particular, William Dilthey (1900) and Max Weber (1949), who found their philosophical origins in Kantian thinking. Immanuel Kant (1969) distinguished objects and events as they appear in experience from objects and events as they are in themselves, independent of the forms imposed on them by our cognitive faculties. The for-

mer he called "phenomena"; the latter, "noumena." All we can ever know, Kant argued, are phenomena. Rather than knowing the world directly, we sense, interpret, and explain it to ourselves. All experience is mediated by mind, and all human intellect is imbued with and limited to human interpretation and representation.

Phenomenologists follow Kant in the claim that immediate experiences and sensory observations are always interpreted or classified under general concepts. Their appeal to phenomena is therefore not an appeal to simple, uninterpreted data of sensory experience. Meaning is the target of phenomenology. Phenomenologists do not assume they know what things mean to others. Emphasizing the subjective aspects, they attempt to gain entry into the conceptual world of themselves and others. Giving accounts of their reality construction, phenomenologists believe that these inward construals derive from a developing understanding of self, others, and things. The relationships between these are not "givens" but dialectical, context bound, and processual.

Qualitative researchers tend to be phenomenological in their orientation. Most maintain that knowledge is a human construction. They reason as follows: Although knowledge starts with sensory experience of external stimuli, these sensations are immediately given meaning by the recipient. Though meaning originates in outside action, only the inside interpretation is known. As far as we can tell, nothing about the stimuli is registered in awareness and memory other than our interpretations of it. This registration is not necessarily conscious or rational.

In our minds, new perceptions of stimulation mix with old, and with complexes of perception, some of which we call generalizations. Some aspects of knowledge seem generated entirely from internal deliberation, without immediate external stimulation—but no aspects are purely of the external world, devoid of human construction.

Concepts of Reality The aim of qualitative research is not to discover reality, for by phenomenological reasoning this is impossible. The aim is to construct a clearer experiential memory and to help people obtain a more sophisticated account of things. Sophistication is partly a matter of withstanding disciplined skepticism. Science strives to build universal understanding. The understanding reached by each individual will of course be to some degree unique to the beholder, but much will be held in common. Though the comprehension we seek is of our own making, it is a collective making. Each of us seeks a well-tuned comprehension, one bearing up under further human constructions: scrutiny and challenge.

The qualitative researcher chooses which realities to investigate. For researcher data or interpretation of findings, not every person's personal reality is of equal use. Society deems some interpretations better than others. People have ways of agreeing on which are the best explanations. Of course they are not always right. There is no reason to think that among people fully committed to a constructed reality all constructions are of equal value. One can believe in relativity, contextuality, and constructivism, without believing all views are of equal merit. Personal civility or political ideology may call for respecting every view, but scientific study does not.[2]

Researchers interested in the uniqueness of particular teaching or learning find value in qualitative studies because the design allows or demands extra attention to physical, temporal, historical, social, political, economic, and aesthetic contexts. Contextual epistemology requires in-depth studies, leaving less time for the refinement of theme and construct. It is true that naturalistic and phenomenological case studies are likely to be undertaken by researchers with constructivist persuasions. Why this is is not clear, but it probably would be a mistake to conclude that more than a realist logic, a constructivist logic promotes contextualist epistemology or case-specific study. It is not uncommon to find case study researchers espousing a constructivist view of reality, but the two persuasions are not one and the same.

Cultural sciences need *descriptive* as well as explanatory and predictive powers. At the beginning, middle, and end of a program of research, the researcher at times needs to concentrate on interpretive understanding (*verstehen*). The process of *verstehen* involves the ability to empathize, to recreate the experience of others within oneself.

Dilthey and Weber perceived understanding as hermeneutic, resulting from a process of interpretation. The hermeneutic experience (encounter with a work of art) is historical, linguistic, dialectical. Understanding the meaning of any particular part of a text (a word or a sentence) requires an understanding of the meaning of the whole and vice versa. Thus, achieving a meaningful interpretation requires back and forth movement between parts and whole. Understanding cannot be pursued in the absence of context and interpretive framework. The hermeneutic perspective means that human experience is context bound and that there can be no context-free or neutral scientific language with which to express what happens in the social world. At best we could have laws applying to only a limited context for a limited time.

Ethnography and Biography

The roots of qualitative research methods can be traced to ethnography and sociological fieldwork as well as literary criticism, biography, and journalism. From the end of the nineteenth century, anthropologists advocated and practiced spending extensive periods of time in the natural setting, studying cultures with the intent of learning how the culture was perceived and understood by its members (cf. Boas and Malinowski). Bronislaw Malinowski, who found himself in New Guinea and unable to return to Poland because of the outbreak of World War I, was the first social anthropologist to spend long periods in a native village to observe what was going on. He was also the first professional anthropologist to dwell on how he obtained his data and what the fieldwork experience was like. Malinowski maintained that a theory of culture had to be grounded in particular human experiences, based on observation, and inductively sought.

Case study and ethnographic methods have been part of sociology's history since the 1920s and 1930s when University of Chicago sociologists, under the influence of Robert Park, W. I. Thomas, and Herbert Blumer, were trained in the interpretive approach to human group life (Bogdan and Biklin, 1982; Denzin, 1989). Sociologists in succeeding generations turned away from the method, giving their attention to problems of measurement, validity, and reliability; survey methodologies; and laboratory experiments. Educational researchers recently have witnessed a surge of interest in interpretive approaches to the study of culture, biography, and human life. Central to this view has been the argument that societies, cultures, and the expressions of human experience can be read as social text, that is, the structures of representation that require symbolic statement (Denzin, 1989).

Literary models provide another important model for qualitative methodology. Eisner (1979, 1991) advocates the paradigmatic use of qualitative inquiry found in the arts and the world of art critics. Artists inquire in a qualitative mode both in the formulation of ends and in the use of means to achieve such ends. The art critic's task is to render the essentially ineffable qualities constituting works of art into a language that will help others perceive the world more deeply.

Thomas Barone (1987, 1990) follows Eisner in referring to works of art as relying on a continuum of scientific texts. All texts, claims Barone, are modes of fiction (borrowing the Geertz meaning of fiction—something fashioned). Each brings with it researcher/author subjectivity and personal bias, ideology, and visions, but with fictional works these are more visible, explicit. Barone reminds us that novelists do not spin their imaginary webs from within a world of pure illusion and fantasy, but that "since Henry Fielding, they also have relied upon observation of the minutae of human activity, observing social phenomena" (1987, p. 455). Often a novelist will construct a story out of the qualitative phenomena confronted in everyday experience: Sometimes they will intentionally transport themselves into the field to investigate facets of their emerging story's milieu, as did Dickens who, in preparation for *The Life Adventures of Nicholas Nickelby*, gained admittance to a notorious Yorkshire boarding school by assuming the false identity of someone seeking a school for the son of a widowed friend. The fictionalization process of the novelist, says Barone, is a rigorous and disciplined undertaking, a qualitative problem-solving process that even proceeds through several identifiable stages. A thesis, or central insight, is gradually constructed from patterned relationships between qualitative phenomena. A similar relationship between thesis and particulars exists in accomplished worlds of literary-style fiction such as autobiography, new journalism, and educational criticism. The crafting of an educational criticism closely resembles the dialectical problem-solving process of the novelist.

Rorty (1982) believes that all qualitative inquiry is continuous with literature. For Rorty, books serve the important role of advancing social and political goals of liberalism by promoting a genuine sense of human solidarity (Rorty, 1989).

Literature has been a methodological force. Biography

and autobiography have become a topic of renewed interest in literary criticism (cf. Elbaz, 1987; Cockshut, 1984), as well as in sociology (cf. Denzin, 1989) and anthropology (cf. Geertz, 1988). Feminist views have had an important influence in this discussion (cf. Jelinek, 1980; Spacks, 1976; Grumet, 1988). Jean-Paul Sartre recognized the force of literature in the preface to *The Family Idiot, Gustave Flaubert,* Vol. 1, 1821–1857 (1981):

What, at this point in time, can we know about man? It seemed to me that this question could only be answered by studying a specific case. . . . For a man is never an individual; it would be more fitting to call him a *universal singular*. Summed up and for this reason universalized by his epoch, he in turn resumes it by reproducing himself in it as singularity. Universal by the singular universality of human history, singular by the universalizing singularity of his projects, he requires simultaneous examination from both ends. (pp. ix—x)

Biography has always been an important part of musicology and music history, with oral history gaining interest. While sociology focuses on *interpretive biography*—the creation of literary, narrative accounts and representations of lived experience (Denzin, 1989)—the traditional use of biographies in music centers around life-events, especially family, patrons, and mentoring, a written account or history of an individual.

A second kind of biography (e.g., Von Gunden, 1983) is essentially a musical analysis, where biographical information of the composer and philosophy are brought in to interpret the music. Here, listening to musical works itself provides data, extending the examination of archives (e.g., documents, letters) and in-depth interviews of author and composer. Immersed in the music, the interviews, or observation data, the music education researcher attempts to find new patterns and meanings.

Qualitative vs. Quantitative Research

The quantitative research tradition, grounded in the positivist urge for a science of society, fostered adaptation of the methodology of the physical sciences to investigate social and human worlds. From the theological to the metaphysical, twentieth-century positivism saw culmination of progress and human knowledge through scientific methods. Objects of study in the social sciences are to be treated in the same way that physical scientists treat physical things. The role of the social scientist is that of recorder and theory builder for a reality existing outside human experience.

Another assumption in positivist thinking was that in regard to values, social investigation can and should be a *neutral* activity. Hence, social scientists should eliminate all bias and value-laden preconception and not be emotionally involved with their subject matter. Knowledge derived from social investigation would eventually result in the same sort of technological mastery over the social world as physical science had for the physical world. The aims of practical application would be achieved by the discovery of social laws that point at relationships among social objects, aiming, like

physical laws, at context-free social laws (Hempel, 1966; Popper, 1969).

Dilthey and Weber challenged the positivist point of view, arguing that social studies has a different ontological and epistemological status. They claimed that there we are both the subject and the object of inquiry: The subject matter concerns the product of human minds and as such is inseparably connected to our minds, bringing along all our subjectivities, cognitions, emotions, and values. Furthermore, the complexity of the social world and cultures makes it impossible to discover laws as in the physical sciences. Rather than a series of overarching causal laws, they said, emphasis must be on understanding the individual case or type.[3]

Philosophically, we are dealing here with two paradigms. The *quantitative paradigm* supports investigation of how reality exists independently of us. Ontological questions concerning what is can be kept separate from the epistemological questions about how we come to know "what is." According to that paradigm, knowledge and truth are questions of correspondence—what is true is what corresponds to reality. Done well, the activity of investigation does not affect what is being investigated.

In the *qualitative paradigm* there is a range of positions, from the idealist belief that social and human reality are created, to the milder conviction that this reality is shaped by our minds. But all the positions posit a degree of mind involvement with subject matter not acceptable to the quantitative, positivist, realist tradition. The idea that the process of investigation can be separated from what is being investigated is possible only within that realist perspective. In the realist view, an investigation is directed toward an external referent. In the idealist view, the process is external as well as internal, a part of the investigator's active participation in shaping the world (cf. Peshkin, 1988).

In actual life, no research study is purely qualitative or quantitative. In each qualitative study, enumeration and recognition of differences in amount have a place. And in each quantitative study, natural language description and interpretation are expected. The distinction as we see it is an epistemological distinction that can be identified as the distinction between inquiry for making explanations versus inquiry for promoting understanding. This distinction has best been developed by the Finnish philosopher of science Georg Hendrik von Wright (1971), who emphasized the epistemological distinction between formal explanations and experiential understanding.

Quantitative study was nourished by the scientific search for grand theory seeking generalizations that hold over diverse situations, trying to eliminate the merely situational, letting contextual effects "balance each other out." Quantitative researchers try to nullify context in order to find the most general and pervasive explanatory relationships. Research in education, including music education, has been dominated by this universalist approach, this grand search for explanation. Quantification occurs in order to permit simultaneous study of a large number of dissimilar cases, in order to put the researcher in a position to make formal generalizations about teaching and learning. Proposition-shaped knowledge obviously can be important.

It is apparent that much important knowledge about education (e.g., the calendar, the practice facilities) is situational. Qualitative researchers have a great interest in the uniqueness of the individual case, the variety of perceptions of that case, and the different intentionalities of the actors who populate that case. These interests force the researcher to find easy-access situations for repeated observations, to limit attention to small numbers of teachers and students, to rely little on objective measurement, and to probe in unexpected directions. Fixed designs are less necessary and can be less productive for providing understanding of particular cases. Still, in a discipline governed strongly by an existing composition or score, the musician may find the structures of quantitativism attractive and the open-field behavior of the qualitative researcher too improvisational.

Qualitative researchers are not devoid of interest in generalization but it does not dominate their thinking. Often the qualitative researchers' commitments to multiple interpretations become manifest in a desire to assist practitioners to interpret the situations for themselves. The intent of research then may become the provision of vicarious experience for report readers who will draw their own generalizations, combining previous experience with new. It often is research specially designed to assist practice. The choice of epistemological role for research and the immediacy of its assistance to practice should be part of our distinction between quantitative and qualitative inquiries.

Qualitative researchers too have interest in frequency, typicality, and generalizability (cf. Stake, Bresler, and Mabry, in press). Still, their craft is distinguished by a too-holistic viewing of phenomena. They examine multiple situations but each at close quarters, not forcing them into comparisons, not fixated on common variables. It is not uncommon for a qualitative researcher to ask in midstudy: "Of all things, what is it that is most important to be learned from this case?" In music education, we have need for formal generalizations and need for experiential understandings of particular situations. We need high-quality research, both quantitative and qualitative.

CHARACTERISTICS OF QUALITATIVE RESEARCH

1. It is holistic. Its contexts are well studied. It is case oriented (a case may be a student, a teacher, a classroom, a curriculum, any "bounded system"). It is relatively noncomparative, seeking more to understand its case than to understand how it differs from others.
2. It is empirical. It is field oriented, the field being the natural settings of the case. Its emphasis is on observables, including observations by informants. It strives to be naturalistic, noninterventionistic. There is a preference for natural language description. The researcher is the key instrument. For qualitative research, researchers

typically spend considerable time in schools, homes, neighborhoods, and other locales learning about educational concerns. Data are collected on the premises. Qualitative researchers go to the particular settings because they are concerned with context. Action can be better understood when it is observed in the natural setting.

3. It is descriptive. Data take the form of words and graphics more than numbers. The written results of the research contain quotations to illustrate and substantiate the presentation.
4. It is interpretive. Its researchers rely on intuition with many important criteria not specified. Its on-site observers strive to keep attention free to recognize problem-relevant events. It is attuned to the fact that research is a researcher-subject interaction. Qualitative research is concerned with the different meanings that actions and events carry for different members.
5. It is empathic. It attends to the presumed intentions of those being observed. It seeks actor frames of reference, value commitments. Though planned, its design is emergent, responsive. Its issues are emic issues, progressively focused. Its reporting provides vicarious experience.
6. Some researchers emphasize working from bottom up (e.g., Glaser and Strauss's term "grounded theory," 1967). Indeed, the direction of the issues and foci often emerge during data collection. The picture takes shape as the parts are examined.
7. When done well, its observations and immediate interpretations are validated. Triangulation, the checking of data against multiple sources and methods, is routine. There is a deliberate effort to disconfirm one's own interpretations. The reports assist readers to make their own interpretations, as well as to recognize subjectivity.[4]

QUALITATIVE RESEARCH IN MUSIC EDUCATION

The first decades of research in music education, much as in general education, were characterized by adherence to quantitative models. Little research employed qualitative strategies to illuminate education problems. The late 1960s affected research mores too. National foci on educational equity and back-to-basics curricula swung concern to values, feelings, and minority perspectives. Many recognized that we did not know enough about the educational experience of children "not making it." In general education, qualitative emphasis on understanding the perspective of all participants challenged the idea that the views of those in power are worth more than others. Student perspectives (Jackson, 1968) and the viewing of school as a system of discipline (Dreeben, 1968; Foucault, 1977; Henry, 1966) were widely considered. Concern about student achievement yielded some to concern for what students were actually doing in school. All this stimulated the need for different content, goals, and methods. It opened up educational researchers to qualitative approaches.

Music education, too, followed that route, perhaps delayed by a decade or so. The emphasis in formal music education research on quantitative methodology is reflected in books, reports, journal papers, and dissertations. But researchers and practitioners, teachers and conductors, have always used qualitative observations. To establish pedagogy requires illusive observation of students in order to pinpoint problems and suggest remedies. In an ancient example considered to be the first music pedagogy book, *L'Art de Toucher le Clavicin,* Francois Couperin expressed pedagogical assertions based on observations of student behavior: "It will be necessary to place some additional support under the feet of young people, varying in height as they grow, so that their feet not dangling in the air, may keep the body properly balanced." "With regard to making grimaces, it is possible to break oneself of this habit by placing a mirror on the reading-desk of the Spinet or harpsichord" (p. xx). "It is better and more seemly not to beat time with the head, the body, nor with the feet" (p. xx). The discipline of Couperin's observations and analysis is not known. Should we consider his writings research based?

As Couperin's book illustrates, pedagogical books on performance and conducting are designed to foster learning and remedy problems more than to arrive at causal explanations or understandings of the situation. Use of pictures to express good and bad technique is quite common (Kohut and Grant, 1990). Performance, like some aspects of pedagogy, involves a self-synchronous process of constant listening (either in one's own playing or in ensemble) and comparing it to the score. Through score preparation, the performer not only knows individual details—parts and sections of the score—but also develops a conception of the complete work. The style of performance best suited to any given work; a sound knowledge of music theory, harmonic analysis, and musical form; musicological knowledge to relate the piece to the composer's other works, as well as to other works of the period; all of these shape a performance.

Ethnomusicology is a field in music that draws its intellectual roots and methods from anthropology as well as from musicology. Merriam (1964) and Nettl (1983, 1987) discuss two major approaches in ethnomusicology. The first, a comparative study of musical systems and cultures, is standardized musicology, aiming to record and analyze music in order to produce an accurate structural analysis of the music investigated. Here, the study is primarily based upon a fact-gathering descriptive approach, dealing with such questions as the modes of Persian or Indian music, names of instruments, how they are made, and who owns them.

The second approach, aiming to understand music in the context of human behavior, is an anthropological speciality. Here, the field-worker tries to approximate the anthropologist, for the concern is with much broader questions of the use and function of music, the role and status of musicians, the concepts that lie behind music behavior, and other similar questions (Merriam, 1967; Nettl, 1987). The emphasis is

on music but not on music divorced from its total context: The investigator attempts to emerge from the study with a broad and generally complete knowledge of both the culture and the music, as well as the way music fits into and is used within the wider context (Merriam, 1964, p. 42). This second approach is typically a field-oriented naturalistic study. The researcher stays at the site for a considerable amount of time, getting immersed in the culture. The issues, a combination of emic and etic, are progressively focused. The direction of the issues and foci often emerge during and after data collection.[5] With few exceptions (Keil, 1966; Oliver, 1960), ethnomusicological studies typically examine other cultures. Few ethnomusicological studies examine familiar music in familiar settings.

Even though these kinds of knowledge have not, until recently, entered the established domains of music education research, the methods of observation, the interview, the use of archival material, and immersion in the case have long been important tools in music education, and in performance and musicology as well. A pioneering work that drew upon these methods, done within the formal boundaries of music education research, was the Pillsbury Foundation Study (Moorhead and Pond, 1941, 1942, 1944, 1951). Initiated by people outside the field of music education (conductor Leopold Stokowski and composer Donald Pond), the Pillsbury Study was dedicated to the discovery of children's musical development through analysis of free, unhampered musical play. Amazed at the spontaneous outpouring of music in young children, Pond wanted to understand how and why children become musically expressive. Thinking along Deweian lines, he wanted to provide them with opportunities and materials so that they might function in their own ways as musicians. In the study, Pond made a conscious attempt to set aside adult notions about elements of music, processes of learning music, and ways of assessing musical development.

The Pillsbury Study was conducted with 3- to 6-year-old children attending a kindergarten designed specifically for research into musical creativity: an environment full of enticing instruments (e.g., sarong, Chinese and Burmese gongs, Indian drums, and tom-toms) and supportive, musically knowledgeable (but not intrusive) adults. The methods of study involved in-depth observation and analysis. Since the context of sound was of major importance, the observations included such activities as speech and physical movement. All sounds produced were considered musical or "embryonically of musical value." In his reports, Pond provided such examples as when a child calls from the sandbox, "I want a red spoon," in a rhythmic and tonal pattern or a child riding on a tricycle sings over and over to himself in unvarying rhythm, "I ran over a whole basket of cherries." The final report (Moorhead and Pond, 1951), was a set of three short case studies of individual children selected for individual differences and approaches. Data included biographical information such as age, personal, family, and school history.

Some naturalistic studies are taxonomic; others are not. Moorhead and Pond worked toward classification of the musical products. A classification of instrumental music, for example, included flexible and asymmetrical measures, exploring wide intervals, tone colors, and pitch contrast. Another category of sonic physical activity, "insistent and savage," was based on rigid and symmetrical rhythms, indifferent to melody and color variety. Pond distinguished between two types of spontaneous vocal utterances: "song," private rhythmically and melodically complex entities, and "chant," a more public utterance, often spontaneously improvised by groups of children. Social-personal context was seen to be highly relevant; most chants were developed first by one child, continued by that child or undertaken by others to form repartee series. Pond raised issues such as: Are these rhythmic patterns fundamental to the child's musical consciousness? What are the relationships between rhythmic patterns and physical rhythms?

The Moorhead and Pond study was holistic, case oriented, noncomparative. The authors sought more to understand each child than to understand how children differ from each other. The natural setting was stressed, with an emphasis on observables. Moorhead and Pond did not try to intervene but rather to observe, describe, and understand.

The Pillsbury Study set a new direction for investigation of free musical activities and improvisation. For music education research, it provided methodological direction and legitimation of the use of naturalistic methods. In the late 1970s and 1980s, music education saw a spurt of qualitative works, independently done in different locations and universities across the country. Jean Bamberger of Massachusetts Institute of Technology (1977) examined two subjects' perceptions of a melody, noting the strategies used by each to compose a melody and the relationship between perceptions, models, strategies, and the completed melody. A protocol analysis employing an innovative computer-based recording system to study compositional process was included.

Most reported qualitative studies have been dissertations, works of solitary, inexperienced researchers, backed by little financial resource (cf. Gerber, 1975; Freundlich, 1978; Cohen, 1980; Lewers, 1980; L'Roy, 1983; Thiel, 1984; Garrison, 1985; Krueger, 1985; Upitis, 1985; Bresler, 1987; DeLorenzo, 1987; Harwood, 1987). Observing spontaneous musical behavior of children, Douglas Freundlich (1978) of Harvard explored two fifth-grade children's musical thinking, especially focusing on spontaneous solutions to musical problems. Students were to improvise on a simple diatonic xylophone within a traditional musical frame of standard 12-bar blues. The data were collected in the context of a structured "jam session." The research was qualitative not because the situation was loosely structured but because the researcher was refining his interpretation with every observation. Freundlich found that development proceeded down from the chorus-as-a-whole and up from a self-generated two-bar motif. Addressing improvisation's pedagogical value, Freundlich pointed out that the child can generate authentic musical ideas without reference to notation, and that musical concepts furnished by the improvisation procedure are logically organized.

Veronica Cohen (1980) of the University of Illinois also examined the generation of musical ideas in a loosely structured situation. Discussing her methods, Cohen noted the following:

This is not a conventional study in which the researcher set up a plan and then followed it, reporting in what ways it was successful or not. Instead, borrowing on the naturalistic, exploratory and yet scientific tradition exemplified in some of the most important of Piaget's studies, it searched through observations over many years . . . focusing finally on a few of two children's musical productions that held the most promise for revealing the underlying structure and dynamics of children's spontaneous music. (p. 1)

Data collection included a 3-year period of general background observation and immersion in children's free musical play in the kindergarten, followed by a rigorous and detailed study of videotaped data involving two kindergarten children. Cohen discussed the role of intuition and accumulated knowledge of the whole field of music in making the thousands of decisions in data collection in the field. "The researcher becomes the chief instrument who selects, interprets and synthesizes evidence in order to break through to the mind of the child" (p. 2). Engagement in musical dialogues with children was a focus. Descriptors included the role of kindergarten music, teacher special interest, and the *participant-observer* role of the researcher. Cohen reported that she was constantly involved in planning the music curriculum, taught demonstration classes for university students, demonstrated ways of interacting with children at the music center, and discussed and analyzed children's work for classroom teachers, parents, and university students.

Cohen investigated musical gestures, noting how the children organize sounds into "musical ideas." Using videotapes for data collection, Cohen found that such behavior could be nicely placed into three broad categories: exploration, mastery, and generation of musical gestures. She speculated that even at this early age children tended to specialize: some almost always engaged in "mastery" activities (reproduction of known melodies) whereas others "improvised" their own gestures.

Influences of culture and society on the musical behavior of children is a relatively sociology-based area studied by qualitative researchers. In Israel, Devorah Kalekin-Fishman (1981, 1986) investigated the nature of music in kindergartens, examining it from teacher as well as from child perspectives. A kindergarten was chosen as the case because it is here the child encounters society as officially organized by educators and is exposed to conceptual frameworks deliberately arranged to fit at least a dozen years of life in educational organizations. Kalekin-Fishman made intensive observations and conducted semistructured interviews. An analysis of sonal patterns in kindergartens in Germany and Israel showed that with minimal framing (intended pitch and intended rhythm), children produced varieties of typified music making. The framing, however, was not that most commonly employed by kindergarten teachers, who usually have a relatively narrow field of musical knowledge.

Ethnomusicology provides an important model for music education research. At the University of Wisconsin, Madison, Virginia Garrison (1985) examined the transmission process of folk music, a process that is as vital to that tradition as is its product, the music. If folk music is to be included in formal music educational settings, then it is important that those social and musical aspects of the folk music tradition that are essential to that tradition are identified. In order to investigate the transmission process and the effect of changed instructional context on that process, Garrison used ethnomusicological methods of extensive and intensive naturalistic observations of 72 practicing fiddlers and 49 beginning fiddling students in a variety of contexts for a period of 6 years, as well as open-ended interviews and photography.

In a similar vein, Eve Harwood (1987) of the University of Illinois opened her dissertation discussing the difficulty researchers have studying music of a culture different from their own. Whereas at one time it was considered sufficient to analyze musical artifacts in the form of tape recordings and transcriptions, using terms appropriate to traditional western musicology, modern ethnomusicology holds that understanding and describing the cultural context in which music making occurs is a necessary part of understanding the music of a given group. An outsider's analytical tools and observations are not necessarily invalid, but an insider's view of what is significant about the music are thought to illuminate our understanding in a unique way.

In the case of North American children, folklorists and musicians were collecting children's repertoires before 1900, but little scholarship had been directed toward the singers themselves. Harwood's study was based on the assumption that children's music and musical world are distinct from adult counterparts, that what is considered beautiful, attractive, or good to sing and is cherished by children may be different. Not a naturalistic study, Harwood's procedures included semistructured interviews in which the 15 children sang all the songs they could remember, discussed how they had learned each song, and described their singing habits and preferences. A parent of each child answered questions regarding the child's singing habits and preferences and the musical life of the family. Interviews and singing were taped and transcribed, and a fieldwork journal of impressions and visual observations was kept. In conclusion, Harwood once again asserted the need to study children's music as one would that of any outside culture, attempting to appreciate both the insider's and the outsider's view of the material.

In the studies just reviewed, researchers examined relatively uncharted territories in order to understand musical activities in context. The study of innovation is another such uncharted territory. Qualitative methodology not only allows but features the study of contexts. One innovation has been the introduction of instructional computer programming that many music educators claim dramatically affects the music education scene. Case studies are one of many ways to examine accommodation of computers into music classes.

At Stanford, Liora Bresler (1987) studied the integration of computers into a college-level introductory music theory class. The learning environment into which the computer is integrated is far too complex to be condensed to one or even several variables. Complications ranged from implicit and explicit curricula of the music theory class to multiple goals and values of instructors, program designers, and students, all interacting with beliefs, musical aspirations, and perceptions of the innovation. Intensive observations of student work at the computer and unstructured and semistructured interviews with the participants provided the main data, supplemented with questionnaires, computer logs, and collection of materials (e.g., syllabi, tests, and students' composition answer sheets).

Even though initially the class seemed an ideal setting for the use of computers for education (e.g., perfect match between contents of software and curriculum-individualized instruction for a musically heterogeneous population; stable teaching over a number of years), the results fell well short of expectations. Many important issues such as the relevance of music practice to the computer program and the aesthetics of music in the computer program emerged at the site.

Focusing on social and cultural contexts, Saville Kushner (1985) of the University of East Anglia studied an innovative, 3-year course for third- and fourth-year students at the Guildhall School of Music and Drama in London. The course, a response to fundamental misgivings about the education of musicians in conservatoires, arranged student performances and workshops in a range of unconventional community sites. Rather than judging the merits of the training, Kushner was commissioned to collect information that participants would find useful in making such judgments. His report was rich in description of program development over time, noting student and teacher perception and audience response. Through vignettes and vivid pictures, it conveyed conservatory life, its inside rivalries, competitions, participant experiences, implicit and explicit goals, and values. The personal debates about destination, the dreams, the dilemmas—so personal, yet so common to performance-oriented people—captured a reality pertinent to musical lives, innovations, and experiences. The portrayal of student perspectives, including those at the lower social strata, captured personal and cultural meanings of music, confusion over what the role of the professional musician should be, as well as the social context of repertoire.

Case studies are typically confined to one setting. A series of eight case studies portraying ordinary arts instruction in the United States was conducted by the Center for Instructional Research and Curriculum Evaluation (CIRCE) at the University of Illinois under the auspices of the National Arts Education Research Center, funded by the National Endowment for the Arts (see Stake, Bresler, and Mabry, in press). Described in detail were the fundamental differences in program offering for music education specialists and general classroom teachers, not only in curricula and pedagogy, but in impact on scheduling, resources, and use of curricular organizers as well. One etic (original design) issue was the role of community resources and performances. Classroom observations brought out the "hidden curriculum"—art as relief from schoolwork and the regularity with which music was presented without background or interpretation, whether for class participation or as background activity to eating, doing worksheets, or reading. As usual, the emphasis was not on what ought to be, but the study did provide researcher interpretation as to what is needed.

In another federally funded project, the Elementary Subjects Study (funded by the U.S. Department of Education) at Michigan State University, music and the visual arts were studied along with mathematics, science, social studies, and literature. The program focused on conceptual understanding, higher order thinking and problem solving in elementary school teaching through a series of case studies of music and visual arts instruction (May, 1990). Research questions included the following: What content is taught when teaching for conceptual understanding and higher level learning? How do teachers negotiate curricular decisions? How do teachers concentrate their teaching to use their limited resources best? In what ways is good teaching subject matter specific?

Some research in music is done by nonmusicians, where music is but one subject among several others, chosen to highlight larger patterns. Such was a study by Benjamin Bloom (1985), who was interested in the development of talent in a variety of domains—music, math, sculpture, athletics—and the roles of families, teachers, and schools in discovering, developing, and encouraging unusually high levels of competence. The commonalities of music with other domains, as well as its unique properties, were presented by Sosniak (1985).

Music Concepts to Aid Qualitative Study

Extensive use of observation in natural settings with little intervention encourages us to discern the complexity of music education. Taped interviews can capture participant voices, views, and struggles. Qualitative methodology promotes the pursuit of questions like, What music do teachers cherish and participate in outside of school? How are school reform and the accountability movement affecting how teachers perceive the teaching of music? What are children's assumptions about music, about what is beautiful, attractive, or well formed? What musical events are to be found in prekindergarten settings? In school settings? In jam sessions? Are there ways that teachers are using MTV for legitimate music instruction? Qualitative researchers can examine events that reflect latent as well as manifest learnings. They can study interrelationships of school, home, media, and culture as they shape musical skills and attitudes. They do this by studying individual cases, problems, settings.

Capturing reality in its complexity opens up research studies to additional modes of representation: vignettes, photographs, audio-and videotapes, films, and various artifacts of performing and teaching music.

Using tapes to capture musical nuances and qualities in performances as well as intonations of "everyday speech" is useful for musicians, for whom intonation, rhythm, and pitch are specially meaningful.

Having discussed the content and representations that qualitative methodology offers music education research, we now want to draw attention to the symbiotic relation between musicianship and intellectual inquiry—noting that much can be developed along qualitative lines. Musical approach can be an asset in qualitative research in general education. Music educators who turn to research in education can use their musical background to contribute to structural conceptualizations and analysis of school life and teaching.

Teaching and classroom life should sometimes be regarded through aesthetic lenses (cf. Eisner, 1979; Goodman, 1968; Brophy and Good, 1986; Kagan, 1989). Here, it is important to make the distinction between an artwork and a phenomenon analyzed through aesthetic parameters (Dewey, 1958). As Eisner has stated, we can pay attention to the aesthetic qualities of a teaching performance in order to perceive what is later described as its qualitative aspects or its feelingful character. The performance itself may not be artistic; that is, it may not have coherence and unity and might not be particularly inventive. Nevertheless, it still can have aesthetic properties. The opposite of aesthetic is anaesthetic, the thwarting of feeling. Objects, situations, or events that are aesthetic evoke or elicit feeling. Whether the situation of performance is artistic, it can be argued, is another matter (Eisner, private communication, 1990).

Art affords us the unique experience of apprehending the result of one individual's (the artist's) inquiry into the structure of reality and the structure of a medium (Olson, 1978; Arnheim, 1986; Eisner, 1988). Teachers, like artists, create articulated, planned experiences[6] and the portrayal of experience can be disciplined by qualitative methods. Analysis of a lesson, like a work of art in general and a musical work in particular, can benefit by allusion to arts' structural properties: rhythm, line, orchestration, texture, form. Lessons can create drama—introduction, building of tension, and resolution. Formal qualities play a major role in the educational communication, interacting with specific messages and contents to create the impact. These properties help provide standards for teaching, drawing attention to coherence, sequentiality, and comprehension.

Let us examine some musical parameters that we have found helpful for conceptualizing qualitative research, particularly in examining curricula and pedagogies. (1) *Form* relates to the organization of parts and whole, arrangement of repetition and variation, unity and variety. Teaching uses and builds on these. A number of educational models point to the importance of form in teaching: setting up introductory anticipation, development and closure, or the creation of suspense, a dramatic climax and resolution as the summing up of the lesson, or a topic. Every lesson has a form, created by the interplay of new and old material, repetition and variation. A lesson may be conceptualized as a Baroque suite—a series of little, related movements (except for parameters like tonality and orchestration)—or as a classical sonata form, tightly organized, fully developed, and well balanced. (2) *Style.* Just as categorization of musical style[7] is useful for perception and analysis, so is the categorization of teaching style. Parameters of style are qualitative lenses for classroom life, pedagogies, and curricular materials.

Form and style are broad categories, referring to complexes or syndromes. The qualities of melody (or line), tempo and rhythm, orchestration and texture, are more specific. (3) *Tempo* is the pace, quick and slow and all the gradations in between. *Rhythm* refers to relationships of tempi over time as well as to temporal patterns. What are the paces of the lesson? How fast do the ideas flow? How rapidly does the teacher change topic, focus, and assignment? How does this pace raise anticipation, or a sense of development and evaluation? (4) *Orchestration* refers to the character of the interplay among players or participants. What is the character of interplay between teacher and students? How does the teacher get the students to take more initiative? Presentations can be didactic, the teacher assuming the soloist's role, dominating the presentation. Alternatively, the teacher assumes the conductor's role, facilitating student dialogue, yet maintaining control over content and form. Classroom life can take the form of chamber ensembles, a measure of student leadership and autonomy. Orchestration reveals the "colors" of voices in the classroom, for example some extroverted (brass v. string instruments) in higher registers, intense, and interacting. (5) *Melody* refers to the "plot line," its direction ascending, descending, or flat. Is the unit of thought a long one or are there many shorter units? What are the interrelations of the shorter idea units to the whole lesson? Are they complementary, autonomous, or unified? What is the inner form (in terms of anticipation and drama) within each of these plot lines? (6) *Texture* refers to the interrelations of simultaneous lines and their development over time during the lesson. Under the category of texture, the presentation of topics, such as at a board meeting, can be homophonic or contrapuntal, several voices echoing, confronting, ignoring each other.

These music concepts, as well as special concepts of education, are expected content and representation in qualitative music education research. Most important are their contributions to expressivity. Though unobtrusive, the researcher interacts with teaching and learning phenomena, bringing unique experience and scholarship into interpretation. Along with relatively uncontestable descriptions, traces of the researcher's deepest personal understandings are presented. The character and the art form of the researcher are not hidden.

METHODS AND CRITERIA

The primary task of the researcher is interpretation (with interpretations presented eventually not just as findings but as assertions; (Erickson, 1986). The most obvious work of the qualitative researcher is data gathering in the field. The

ethic of qualitative research calls for abundant description, sufficient for readers to participate in verification of the researcher's interpretations and to make some of their own (Stake, 1978). Thus, most of the methodological advice in the literature has to do with data gathering. If we were limited to a single recommendation we would name Schatzman and Strauss (1973), *Field Research: Strategies for a Natural Sociology.*

Data Collection

The examples of music education research described earlier identify the main methods for qualitative research: intensive observation in natural settings, examination of documents and other artifacts, and interview. Even when audio- or videotaped, the principal "instrument" is the researcher, a constant arbiter of what is important, of the need for further data, for probing, and for small or large redesign of the study. The design of the study is said to be emergent or progressively focused (Strauss, 1987). The design is based not only on a strong sense of the research questions or issues at hand (Smith, 1978) but on the growing body of interpreted observations in the classroom or wherever.

When assuming the more common nonparticipant role, the researcher observes ordinary activities and habitat, the people, the exercise of authority and responsibility, the expression of intent, the productivity, and especially the milieu. Believing that important understandings are situationally rooted, the researcher carefully describes the contacts, noting not just space and time characteristics, but social, economic, political, historical, and aesthetic contexts. The nonparticipating observer is as invisible and nonintrusive as possible, often even refraining from appearing to record what is going on.

In a participant-observer role the researcher engages in the ordinary activities of the group or program being studied but tries not to redirect those activities. Participation may be marginal, perhaps the role of helpmate with some sharing of interests and problems (Spindler, 1982), or more extensive, such as the teacher as researcher in her own classroom or the researcher as consultant providing inservice training to teachers (Cohen, 1980; Stake and Easley, 1978; Stanley, 1990; Wagner, 1990). The growing interest in action research (teacher as researcher; Carr and Kemmis, 1986) is apparent in recent meetings of the American Education Research Association. Here especially, but even in the more passive roles, as interpreter, the researcher is seen as an interactive force in events.

Document review is an essential component of data collection (Andre, 1983). Needed data on inspiration, obligation, and constraint on personal or group action are often disclosed in formal and informal documents. Many useful documents are fugitive records, stored in places no one can remember, making it necessary for the researcher to look through countless papers to find a useful one. Often the information needed is a marginal notation or not even a document at all, such as an inscription on a trophy or notes on a calendar. Browsing is a common activity for the researcher, with half a mind for the research question but another half just trying to comprehend what sort of place it is.

Interviews are conducted not as surveys of how people feel but primarily to obtain observations that the researcher is unable to make directly, secondly to capture multiple realities or perceptions of any given situation, and, finally, to assist in interpreting what is happening. When standardized information is needed from large numbers of people, the written survey is more efficient, but most qualitative researchers want to probe more deeply than is possible with questionnaires. With a structured interview the researcher assumes questions are comprehensible and consistent in meaning across respondents. Semistructured interviews, with topics or questions predetermined, allow latitude for probing and following the interviewee's sense of what is important. Unfortunately, they are costly to administer and time-consuming in analysis. The degree of structure for individual questions, for the interview as a whole, or for the project as a whole are key decisions to be made and remade (Mishler, 1986).

The qualitative researcher seeks to be unobtrusive, knowing that the more attention is drawn to the study, the more posturing there will be and less ordinary activity available for observation. Even interviewing and testing are interventions, drawing attention to the presence and purpose of the research. The researcher takes advantage of indications of accretion and use, such as graffiti on walls or repair records for tape recorders. Gene Webb and his Northwestern colleagues provided many examples of unobtrusive measures (Webb, Campbell, Schwartz, and Sechrest, 1966), but one of the authors, Don Campbell, later expressed the concern that heavy use of such methods persuade readers that social scientists are covert and deceptive, undermining the credibility of all research. Researchers, often in effect guests at the work space and in the private spaces of others, should be considerate. With its probing orientation, qualitative research easily intrudes into the personal affairs of others. Making the report anonymous is often insufficient to avoid the risk of harming people. Handling data is an ethical as much as a technical matter (Rainwater and Pittman, 1969).

Data Analysis

Techniques vary widely. Both qualitative and quantitative analyses of data are used by the qualitative researcher. Quantitative analysis is used more to work toward generalization across specifics observed in the field. It proceeds largely by coding, classifying, and aggregating observations (Miles and Huberman, 1984). Thus, for example, teaching episodes are increasingly seen to be of perhaps three kinds, and the length of student deliberation in choosing a musical instrument is treated statistically. Uniqueness of each particular situation is given little attention: the typical, aggregate, and generalizable are given more attention. Such an approach is often followed in policy analysis (Yin, 1984).

Qualitative analysis is organized more around the notes and stories the researcher keeps, increasingly focused on a small number of issues or themes. The researcher selects the most revealing instances, identifies vignettes, and composes narratives from day to day, then uses an even smaller selection of them in the final presentation (Goetz and LeCompte, 1984). The choice of what to report is subjective, evolving, emphasizing more what contributes to the understanding of the particulars observed than relating to cases and situations elsewhere, usually giving no more than minor attention to comparisons, not worrying much about typicality or representativeness. Thus, the integrity, complexity, and contextuality of individual cases are probed. Readers fit them in among cases they have known. If theory building is the ultimate intent of the researcher here, qualitative analysis paces it not by years but by decades.

Multiple case studies require a kind of analysis that remains largely unformalized. One tries to preserve the uniqueness of the individual case, yet produce cross-site conclusions. The usual reporting procedure is to present a long or short summary of each case, then chapters on understanding the aggregate (Huberman and Miles, 1984). Panels of interpreters, some of whom may not have observed at any sites, are often useful for enriching and challenging the interpretations—but require more comprehensive site summaries than site-visiting researchers usually provide for themselves. For self-use, panel, or instructional purposes, such summaries provide a synthesis of what the researcher knows about the site, tentative findings, and quality of data supporting them, even indicating what is still left to find out, and perhaps indicating an agenda for the next wave of data collection (Bogdan and Taylor, 1984).

For most qualitative projects, data analysis is an informal and often overwhelming task. There are too many data to keep records of and too few that support prevailing impressions. The researcher works with those seeming most likely to advance understanding, describing them in detail, and frequently restating the issue being pursued. Data analysis is an art form.

Criteria of Quality

The characteristics of quality in quantitative studies are widely agreed upon: representativeness of the sample, reliability and validity of measurement, objectivity in interpretation, and the probabilities of Type I and Type II errors, to name several (Campbell and Stanley, 1966). No such summary of characteristics of quality has been developed for qualitative research. Many of the same concepts are worthy of consideration, but when purposes are different (e.g., a low interest in broad generalization), then the criteria will be different. Whether the alternative purposes are legitimate is a question that researchers continue to debate (Smith and Heshusius, 1986).

The most important criterion for any research is that it is about something important, important to readers as well as to researchers. Researchers are given great respect for recognizing what needs to be studied, and they should not abuse that privilege. Perhaps an overly large share of music education research is the psychological study of musical skills and knowledge; perhaps too little is the study of curriculum change and that of music teaching. Still, the health of any research enterprise depends more on intellectual curiosity, studying what needs to be better understood, rather than on what can be funded or will be pleasing to patrons and readers.

In a response to critics of naturalistic inquiry, Lincoln and Guba (1985, 1988) asked methodologists and philosophers of science for evidence that well-crafted research grounded in qualitative and phenomenological traditions *could* be judged and found (1) systematically congruent with the context, that is, valid; (2) not subject to aberrations in research process or instrumentation, that is, reliable; and (3) not open to charges of bias, prejudice, or political advocacy of the investigators. Lincoln and Guba rejected these more quantitative or positivist criteria on grounds that they were incompatible with the axioms of naturalistic research. They saw the naturalist's criteria to be (1) credibility (rather than internal validity), (2) transferability (rather than external validity or generalizability), (3) dependability (rather than reliability), and (4) confirmability (rather than objectivity). These alternative terms were advocated primarily to make clear the inappropriateness of conventional criteria for qualitative research (House, 1980).

To illustrate these criteria, consider a naturalistic case study of a program for training teachers of introductory band. As does a quantitative researcher, the qualitative researcher unconsciously or deliberately takes into account the experience, sophistication, curiosity, and concerns of the eventual audience and seeks to say mostly what will be credible to them. But unlike the quantitative researcher, the qualitative researcher intends to build upon the uniqueness of personal understanding, offering for each reader a credible account and a vicarious experience for substantiation or modification of existing generalizations.

Transferability refers to the extent to which the research facilitates inferences by readers regarding their own situations and responsibilities. Such are petite generalizations rather than the grand generalizations of the theory builder, relatively context free, and a basis for general policy. Good transfer is based on similarity of situations, intuitively weighted as to what is important and unimportant in the match.

Our campus researcher seeks to describe band director trainees meaningfully to readers, with observations transferable to their situations. Rather than measuring with instrument or frequency count, he observes and portrays the band teacher training experience, clearly describing people, dialogue, settings, expressions of intent and frustration, and so on so as to enable the reader to associate this new vicarious experience with previous experience, recognizing ordinary use of both reasoning and intuition in clarifying views and improving understanding.

Confirmability is a sophisticated way of suggesting accuracy. With qualitative data we seldom have an accurate impression the first time we look; we have to confirm or triangulate[8] (Denzin, 1970), and when we can we have others,

including our readers, confirm the finding. The researcher is not content to note available confirmatory evidence but deliberately seeks new facts that might refute the present facts (Popper, 1969). What are facts? It always happens that several important facts are in some degree interpretations (e.g., a professor's apparent lack of interest in band appearance, particularly synchronous movement—whether or not she confirms it), the meanings differing from observer to observer. The researcher triangulates the observations, working toward some common perception, but expects and reports on certain differences in perception (for example, between male and female faculty members) and goes out of his way to relate certain ways he, with background and value commitment showing, interacted with the scene and arrived at assertions. With different backgrounds, the readers too interpret the account differently. Confirmability is an aim, not an ideal, to be tempered by the indefiniteness of reality and by sticking with questions that matter.

Drawn by his persuasion toward constructed reality, our quantitative researcher finds it of little use to hypothesize some "true account" of the band director training program, an account independent of human observers, an ideal to which actual accounts might be compared. Even those parts of the account most agreed upon are not good grounds for considering "validity"—for many of those easily confirmed facts are of little interest and one way to get confirmation is to omit things, even important things, that people see differently. The account should be dependable among relatively neutral readers, portraying much of what they would have seen, had they been there, and omitting most of what they would have found irrelevant and distracting. The researcher is greatly privileged in what to attend to, but the audience can invalidate, at least for their purposes, the account as off-the-mark and incomplete.

Complete objectivity is unattainable and unsought in this research paradigm (Dilthey, 1900; Barone, 1990). The researcher seeks to diminish subjectivity that interferes with comprehension and to exploit subjectivity for deeper interpretation (Peshkin, 1988). He exposes himself, preferably with grace. Although most readers have little interest in reading the researcher's track record, autobiographical and opinion statements are useful footnotes for deliberately revealing lack of experience, alliances, and value positions. And to carry the handling of subjectivity further, the competent qualitative researcher finds ways of including contrary views and alternative explanations.

The criteria for high-quality inquiry and for high-quality reports are not one and the same. The inquiry process belongs largely to the researcher. Each of the data gathering and analysis methods has its own criteria, sources for which we have footnoted. The criteria for reports (reports being communications requiring both a sender and a receiver) lie in the hands of both the researcher and the user of the research. With quantitative measurement, it is not the test or instrument that has validity, it is each use of the measurements that is valid or invalid (Cronbach, 1971). Similarly with qualitative research, the meanings arrived at by individual readers and the applications to new practice are the ultimate indexes of validity of the reports (Howe and Eisenhart, 1990). A final assertion might be that in the program studied here, band directors are reconsidering their roles in protection and perpetuation of local culture. If readers misinterpret this as indicating the graduates thus are hostile to change, the finding should be considered invalid. The researcher can do much to increase the quality of his work, but it serves no more than to facilitate cautious and insightful use of his accounts.

Strengths and Weaknesses

As summarized by Miles and Huberman (1984), the weakest aspect of qualitative research is its contribution to basic research generalizations and policy study—but such is not its intent. Its purpose is to facilitate understanding of the particular. Still, by charging the researcher with spontaneous responsibility in the field, it lacks good protection against

1. excessive subjectivity in observations,
2. imprecise language in descriptions,
3. vague descriptions of the research design,
4. unwieldy and voluminous reports,
5. implication of generalizability when little is warranted,
6. cost and time overrun, and
7. unethical intrusion into personal lives.

But the strengths of qualitative study are impressive as well. We would summarize those strengths as

1. a holistic, systemic purview, emphasizing inner workings and contexts;
2. a strong, empirical commitment to triangulated description of teaching;
3. an obligation and opportunity to get the most from fieldwork interpretations; and

4. a sense of empathy enhancing the utility of use for applied practice in education.

These features have not characterized the majority of the music education research in our journals. Certainly it would be a mistake were all the issues and developments of music education to be studied naturalistically—but that imbalance is far away.

To close this chapter we would like to quote from Kushner's (1985) case study, his final words:

As can be read throughout this report, the participating students are formidable critics and evaluators—and no one has been spared their scrutiny. MPCS offers a rare occasion in music training for trainees to support each other in a discussion forum and they use it with effect. Guildhall tutors, guest speakers, professional collaborators, prospective employers, those who seek to advise and the principal himself, have all found themselves having to defend statements they have made to MPCS groups in the face of often considerable pressure. There is no evidence on this course, at least, for the often-heard assertion that music students are inarticulate or reticent. This may be both heartening and worrying for the conservatoire facing the prospect of trying to integrate an educational curriculum with a training curriculum. The implications of curriculum integration go beyond finding appropriate slots on a timetable for optional sessions. If there is a vision of new practice enshrined in the Project then it might prove increasingly hard to protect other teaching areas in the School from the consequences of that vision. . . . To date the Project has undoubtedly enjoyed many successes—but it is still a curriculum 'fledgling' enjoying the attention and tolerance needed to nurture it. Its musical products are of a quality which still worry Peter, in educational terms its aims and outcome are still hit-and-miss. There is no certainty that the course will interest conservatoire students other than those (still small) numbers who opt to join and remain on the course. And, of course, MPCS has not had to withstand confrontation with critics one of the few experiences so far denied it.

Notes

1. Vignettes quoted herein are from Stake, Bresler, and Mabry, *Custom and Cherishing*, to be published by the Music Educators National Conference.
2. Guba and Lincoln (1981) have identified gradations of belief in an independent versus a constructed reality. One's belief is linked to belief in how we come to know what we know—but ontology and epistemology are not interdeterminate. Belief in independent reality does not fix one's belief in a simple world, the worlds of Stravinsky's Firebird or seasonal fund drives. Nor does belief in constructionism fix belief in a heterogenous, particularist world. Realists too believe that generalizations are regularly limited by local condition. "Do teachers always prefer authoritarian milieus or only under certain conditions?" Though idealists, relativists, situationalists, contextualists, and other champions of local knowledge often resist broad generalizations and are found to support constructivist ontology, their support for a contextualist epistemology is a correlate, not a derivative, of that ontology.
3. Rorty's perspective on both idealism and positivism moves us toward the role of literature in qualitative methodology. Kant and Hegel, claims Rorty (1989), went only halfway in their repu-

diation of the idea that truth is "out there." They were willing to view the world of empirical science as a made world, to see matter as constructed by mind. But they persisted in seeing mind, spirit, the depths of the human self, as having an intrinsic nature, one that could be known by a kind of nonempirical superscience called philosophy. Thus, only half of truth, the bottom, scientific half, was made. The truth about mind, the providence of philosophy, was still a matter of discovery rather than creation. The idealists confused the idea that nothing has intrinsic nature with the idea that space and time are unreal, that human beings cause the spatiotemporal world to exist. Claiming that truth is not out there, Rorty says that where there are no sentences, there is no truth, that sentences are elements of human languages, and that human languages, as whole vocabularies, are human creations.

4. See naturalistic generalizations, Stake and Trumbull (1982).
5. According to the emic approach, the issues, concepts, and meanings are of the people under study. In the etic approach, researchers apply their own concepts to understand the social behavior of the people being studied (Taylor and Bogdan, 1984). The emic categories of meaning are called first-order

concepts. The etic categories are called second-order concepts, since they are "constructs of the constructs made by actors on the social scene" (Schultz, 1962).

6. The fact that some teachers teach artistically does not necessitate that they articulate it. We find teachers who provide meaningful aesthetic experience in their lessons, yet seem unable to articulate it, just as some musicians create excellent music but find it difficult (and unnecessary) to talk about it. Time and again we are confronted with the difference between "know how" and "know about."

7. Pathos/Dyonsian/Romantic versus Ethos/Apolonian/Classic is a distinction of musical idiom prominent since Plato. Ethos, associated with restraint and serenity, canon and norm, implies belief in absolute, unalterable values. Pathos, associated with strong feeling, motion, and action implies the personal quest (cf. Sachs, 1946).

8. The term "triangulation" was coined by Webb et al. (1965), an internal index to provide convergent evidence, "the onslaught of a series of imperfect measures." Triangulation is supposed to support a finding by showing that independent measures (checking with different sources, applying different methods, corroborated by different researchers, and examined through different theories) of it agree with it, or at least, don't contradict it.

References

Andre, M. (1983). Use of content analysis in educational evaluation. *Discourse, 4*(1).

Arnheim, R. (1986). *New essays on the psychology of art.* Los Angeles: University of California Press.

Bamberger, J. (1977). Intuitive and formal musical knowing. In Stanley S. Madeja (Ed.), *The arts, cognition, and basic skills.* St. Louis: CEMREL.

Bamberger, J. (1978). In search of a tune. In D. Perkins and B. Leondar (Eds.), *The arts and cognition.* Baltimore: Johns Hopkins.

Barone, T. (1987). Research out of the shadows: A reply to Rist. *Curriculum Inquiry, 17*(4), 453–463.

Barone, T. (1990). *Rethinking the meaning of vigor: Toward a literary tradition of educational inquiry.* Paper presented at the annual meeting of the American Education Research Association, Boston.

Berg, B. L. (1989). *Qualitative research methods for the social sciences.* Boston: Allyn & Bacon.

Bloom, B. (Ed.). (1985). *Developing talent in young people.* New York: Balantine.

Bogdan, R., and Biklen, S. K. (1982). *Qualitative research for education: An introduction to theory and methods.* Boston: Allyn & Bacon.

Bogdan, R., and Taylor, S. (1984). *Introduction to qualitative research methodology.* New York: John Wiley.

Brand, M. (1987). A review of participant observation: Study of a fourth grade music classroom—Cynthia Rhodes Thiel. *Bulletin of the Council for Research in Music Education, 92.*

Bresler, L. (1987). The role of the computer in a music theory class: Integration, barriers and learning. Unpublished doctoral dissertation, Stanford University, Stanford.

Brophy, J., and Good, T. L. (1986). Teacher behavior and student achievement. In M. C. Wittrock (Ed.), *Handbook of research on teaching* (3rd ed.). New York: Macmillan.

Campbell, D. T., and Stanley, J. C. (1966). Closing down the conversation: The end of the quantitative/qualitative debate among educational inquirers. *Educational Researcher, 1*(4), 20–24.

Carr, W., and Kemmis, S. (1986). *Becoming critical: Education, knowledge and action research.* London: Falmer.

Cockshut, A. O. J. (1984). *The art of autobiography.* New Haven: Yale University Press.

Cohen, V. (1980). The emergence of musical gestures in kindergarten children. Unpublished doctoral dissertation, University of Illinois at Urbana-Champaign.

Couperin, F. (1933). *L'Art de toucher le clavecin.* Wiesbaden, Germany: Breitkopf & Hartel. (Originally published in 1717).

Cronbach, L. J. (1971). Test validation. In R. L. Thorndike (Ed.). *Educational measurement,* 2nd ed. (pp. 443–507). Washington: American Council on Education.

DeLorenzo, L. (1987). An exploratory field of sixth grade students' creative music problem solving processes in the general music class. Unpublished doctoral dissertation, Teachers College, Columbia University, New York.

Denzin, N. K. (1970). *The research act.* New York: Aldine.

Denzin, N. K. (1989). *Interpretative biography.* Beverly Hills: Sage.

Dewey, J. (1958). *Art as experience.* New York: Putnam's.

Dilthey, W. (1900/1976). *Selected writings.* (H. P. Rickman, Ed. and Trans.). Cambridge: Cambridge University Press.

Dilthey, W. (1910). *The construction of the historical world of the human studies. (Der Aufbauder Welt in den Geisteswissenschaften).* Gesammelte Schriften I-VII. Leipzig: B. G. Teubner, 1914–1927.

Dreeben, R. (1968). *On what is learned in school.* Reading: Addison-Wesley.

Eisner, E. (1979). *The educational imagination: On the design and evaluation of school programs.* New York: Macmillan.

Eisner, E. (1988). The primacy of experience and the politics of method. *Educational Researcher, 17*(5), 15–20.

Eisner, E. (1991). *The enlightened eye: Qualitative inquiry and the enactment of educational practice.* New York: Macmillan.

Elbaz, R. (1987). *The changing nature of the self: A critical study of the autobiographical discourse.* Iowa City: University of Iowa Press.

Erickson, F. (1986). Qualitative methods in research on teaching. In Merlin C. Wittrock (Ed.), *Handbook on teaching* (3rd ed.). New York: Macmillan.

Foucault, M. (1977) *Discipline and punish: The birth of the prison.* (Trans. A. Sheridan). New York: Pantheon Books.

Freundlich, D. (1978). The development of musical thinking case-studies in improvisation. Unpublished doctoral dissertation, Harvard University, Cambridge.

Garrison, V. (1985). *Traditional and non-traditional teaching and learning practices in folk music.* Unpublished doctoral dissertation, University of Wisconsin, Madison.

Gerber, L. (1975). An examination of three early childhood programs in relation to early childhood music education. Unpublished doctoral dissertation, University of Illinois at Urbana-Champaign.

Geertz, C. (1973). *The interpretation of cultures.* New York: Basic Books.

Geertz, C. (1988). *Works and lives: The anthropologist as author.* Stanford: Stanford University Press.

Glaser, G. A., and Strauss, A. L. (1967). *The discovery of grounded theory: Strategies for qualitative research.* Chicago: Aldine.

Goetz, J. P., and LeCompte, M. D. (1984). *Ethnography and qualitative design in educational research*. San Francisco: Academic Press.

Goodman, N. (1968). *The languages of art*. Indianapolis: Hackett.

Grumet, M. (1988). *Bitter milk: Women and teaching*. Amherst: University of Massachusetts Press.

Guba, E., and Lincoln, Y. (1981). *Effective evaluation*. San Francisco: Jossey-Bass.

Habermas, J. (1971). *Knowledge and human interests*. (J. J. Shapiro, Trans.). Boston: Beacon Press.

Hamilton, D. (1977). Making sense of curriculum evaluation: Continuities and discontinuities in an educational idea. *Review of Research in Education, 5,* 318–347.

Harwood, E. (1987). The memorized song repertoire of children in grades four and five. Unpublished doctoral dissertation, University of Illinois at Urbana-Champaign.

Hempel, C. (1966). *Philosophy of natural sciences*. London: Prentice Hall.

Henry, J. (1966). *On education*. New York: Random House.

House, E. (1980). *Evaluating with validity*. Beverly Hills: Sage.

Howe, K., and Eisenhart, M. (1990). Standards for qualitative (and quantitative) research: A prolegomenon. *Educational Researcher, 19*(4), pp. 2–9.

Huberman, A. M., and Miles, M. B. (1984). *Innovation up close: How school improvement works*. New York: Plenum.

Jackson, P. (1968). *Life in classrooms*. New York: Holt, Reinhart & Winston.

Jelinek, E. C. (Ed.). (1980). *Women's autobiography: Essays in criticism*. Bloomington: Indiana University Press.

Kagan, D. M. (1989). The heuristic value of regarding classroom instruction as an aesthetic medium. *Educational Researcher, 18*(6), 11–18.

Kalekin-Fishman, D. (1981). Ts'lilim ufikuach: R'chisshath mussag hamusika b'ganei Y'lakim [Sounds and control: The acquisition of the concept of music in the kindergarten.] *Mah'beroth L'mehkar ul'vikoreth [Notebooks of Research and Criticism], 6* 5–16.

Kalekin-Fishman, D. (1986). Music and not-music in kindergartens. *Journal of Research in Music Education, 34*(1), 54–68.

Kant, I. (1969). *Kritik der Urteilskraft* (S. H. Bergman, Trans.). Copyright by The Bialik Institute, Jerusalem.

Keil, C. (1966). *Urban blues*. Chicago: University of Chicago.

Klofas, J. J., and Cutshall, C. R. (1985). The social archeology of a juvenile facility: Unobtrusive methods in the study of institutional culture. *Qualitative Sociology, 8*(4), pp. 368–387.

Kohut, D., and Grant, J. (1990). *Learning to conduct and rehearse*. Englewood Cliffs: Prentice Hall.

Krueger, P. J. (1985). Influences of the hidden curriculum upon the perspectives of music student teachers. Unpublished doctoral dissertation, University of Wisconsin, Madison.

Krueger, P. J. (1987). Ethnographic research methodology in music education. *Journal of Research in Music Education, 35*(2), pp. 69–77.

Kushner, S. (1985). Working dreams: Innovation in a conservatoire. University of East Anglia, United Kingdom.

Kushner, S. (1989). St. Joseph's Hospice: A music performance and communication skills evaluation case study. Unpublished report, University of East Anglia, United Kingdom.

L'Roy, D. (1983). The development of occupational identity in undergraduate music education majors. Unpublished doctoral dissertation, North Texas State University, Denton.

Lewers, J. M. (1980). Rehearsal as the search for expressiveness: Implications for music reading in the high school mixed chorus. Unpublished doctoral dissertation, Teachers College, Columbia University, New York.

Lincoln, Y. S., and Guba, E. G. (1985). *Naturalistic inquiry*. New York: Sage.

Lincoln, Y. S., and Guba, E. G. (1986). But is it rigorous? Trustworthiness and authenticity in naturalistic evaluation. In D. D. William (Ed.), *Naturalistic evaluation: New directions for program evaluation*, No. 30. San Francisco: Jossey-Bass.

Lincoln, Y. S., and Guba, E. G. (1988). *Criteria for assessing naturalistic inquiries as reports*. Paper presented at the annual meeting of the American Education Research Association, New Orleans.

May, W. (1990). Teaching for understanding in the arts. *Quarterly, 1*(1 & 2), 5–16.

Merriam, A. (1964). *The anthropology of music*. Chicago: Northwestern University Press.

Merriam, A. (1967). *Ethnomusicology of the Flathead Indians*. Chicago: Aldine.

Miles, M. B., and Huberman, A. M. (1984). *Qualitative data analysis: A sourcebook of new methods*. Beverly Hills: Sage.

Mishler, E. G. (1986). *Research interviewing*. Cambridge: Harvard University Press.

Moorhead, G., and Pond D. (1941, 1942, 1944, 1951). *Music of young children* (Vols. 1–4). Vancouver: Pillsbury Foundation.

Nash, R. J. (1987). The convergence of anthropology and education. In G. Spindler (Ed.), *Education and cultural process*. Prospect: Waveland.

Nettl, B. (1983). *Twenty-nine issues and concepts*. Urbana: University of Illinois Press.

Nettl, B. (1987). *The radif of Persian music: Studies of structure and cultural context*. Champaign: Elephant & Cat.

Olson, D. (1978). The arts as basic skills: Three cognitive functions of symbols. In S. S. Madeja (Ed.), *The arts, cognition, and basic skills* (pp. 59–81). St. Louis: CEMREL.

Peshkin, A. (1988). In search of subjectivity—One's own. *Educational Researcher, 17*(7), 17–21.

Popper, K. (1959). *The logic of scientific discovery*. New York: Basic Books.

Popper, K. (1969). *Conjectures and refutations*. London: Routledge & Kegan Paul.

Rainwater, L., and Pittman, D. (1969). Ethical problems in studying a politically sensitive and deviant community. In G. J. McCall and J. L. Simmons (Eds.), *Issues in participant observation*. Reading: Addison-Wesley.

Rorty, R. (1982). *Consequences of pragmatism*. Minneapolis: University of Minnesota Press.

Rorty, R. (1989). *Contingency, irony and solidarity*. Cambridge: Cambridge University Press.

Sartre, J.-P. (1981). *The family idiot: Gustave Flaubert* (Vol. 1 1821–1857). Chicago: University of Chicago Press. (Originally published 1971).

Schatzman, L., and Strauss, A. (1973). *Field research: Strategies for a natural sociology*. Englewood Cliffs: Prentice Hall.

Schutz, A. (1962). *Collected Papers, Vol. I: The problem of social reality* (M. Natanson, Ed.). The Hague: Martinus Nijhoff.

Smith, J. K., and Heshusius, L. (1986). Closing down the conversation: The end of the quantitative—qualitative debate among educational inquirers. *Educational Researcher,* 4–12.

Smith, L. M. (1978). An evolving logic of participant observation, educational ethnography and other case studies. In L. Shulman (Ed.), *Review of research in education* (Vol. 6). Chicago: Peacock.

Sosniak, L. A. (1985). Learning to be a concert pianist. In B. Bloom (Ed.), *Developing talent in young people* (pp. 19–67). New York: Ballantine.

Spacks, P. (1976). *Imagining a self: Autobiography and novel in eighteenth-century England.* Cambridge: Harvard University Press.

Spindler, G. (Ed.). (1963). *Education and culture.* New York: Holt, Reinhart, & Winston.

Spindler, G. (1982). *Doing the ethnography of schooling.* New York: Holt, Rinehart & Winston.

Stake, R. E. (1978). The case study method in social inquiry. *Educational Researcher, 7*(2), 5–8.

Stake, R. E., Bresler, L., and Mabry, L. (in press). *Custom and cherishing.* Reston: Music Educators National Conference.

Stake, R. E., Easley, J., Denny, T., Smith, M. L., Peskin, A., Welch, W. W., Walker, R., Serano, R. G., Sanders, J. R., Stufflebeam, D. L., Hill-Burnett, J., Hoke, G., Dawson, B., and Day, J. A. (1978). *Case studies in science education.* Washington: U.S. Government Printing Office.

Stake, R. E., and Trumbull, D. (1982). Naturalistic generalizations. *Review Journal of Philosophy & Social Science, VII*(1, 2).

Stanley, J. (1990). Doing democracy: Cato Park School and the study of education in school settings. Paper presented at the annual meeting of the American Education Research Association, Boston.

Strauss, A. (1987). *Qualitative analysis for social scientists.* Cambridge: Cambridge University Press; Parlett & Hamilton.

Thiel, C. R. (1984). Participant observation: Study of a fourth grade music classroom. Unpublished doctoral dissertation, University of Illinois at Urbana-Champaign.

Upitis, R. (1985). Children's understanding of rhythm: The relationship between development and musical training. Unpublished doctoral dissertation, Harvard University, Cambridge.

Von Gunden, H. (1983). *The music of Pauline Oliveros.* London: Scarecrow.

Von Wright, G. (1971). *Explanation and understanding.* London: Routledge & Kegan Paul.

Wagner, J. (1990). Field research as a full participant in schools and other settings. Paper presented at the annual meeting of the American Education Research Association, Boston.

Webb, E., Campbell, D. T., Schwartz, R. D., and Sechrest, L. (1966). *Unobtrusive measures: Nonreactive research in the social sciences.* Chicago: Rand McNally.

Webb, E., Campbell, D. T., Schwartz, R. D., and Sechrest, L. (1981). *Nonreactive measures in the social sciences.* Boston: Houghton Mifflin.

Weber, M. (1949). *Methodology of the social sciences.* (E. Shils and H. Finch, Trans.). Glencoe: Free Press.

Yin, R. K. (1984). *Case studies in research design: Design and methods.* Beverly Hills: Sage.

Zeller, N. (1987). A rhetoric for naturalistic inquiry. Unpublished doctoral dissertation, Indiana University, Bloomington.

[9]

QUANTITATIVE ANALYSIS

Edward P. Asmus
UNIVERSITY OF UTAH

Rudolf E. Radocy
UNIVERSITY OF KANSAS

Research is a systematic process by which investigators gather information, organize it in a meaningful way, and analyze and interpret it. Much information is expressible as quantities or numeric judgments. Researchers may combine and manipulate numbers in a myriad of ways to gain insights and reach conclusions regarding their problems, questions, and hypotheses. After briefly overviewing quantification and measurement, this chapter presents univariate and multivariate statistical techniques for the analysis of research data. The chapter is not a statistical treatise or a critique of the state of the quantitative art in music education research. It is intended to guide the reader in understanding, questioning, and applying basic aspects of quantitative techniques.

Quantification

Quantitative methods greatly enhance the study of musical processes by providing the accuracy and rigor required to produce conclusions upon which the researcher and others can rely (Lehman, 1968). Phelps (1986) points out that researchers who develop their research in a manner that produces quantitative data are in a better initial position to produce research that is significant to the field of music education.

Quantification is the assignment of a number to represent an amount or a perceived degree of something. That is, the association of numbers with behaviors, objects, or events. The units of weight necessary to balance a scale quantify a person's body weight. The height of an enclosed column of mercury quantifies the thermal activity in air. An adjudicator's rating quantifies the apparent quality of a musical performance. Virtually anything is quantifiable, whether in terms of some logical counting unit or some sensory impression. The degree of objectivity varies with the method of quantification. Such variance is a matter of measurement theory in general, and validity in particular.

Quantification has met considerable resistance in music education. The general outlook is that music is so complex and deals with aesthetic elements that are so far beyond tangible matters that it is impossible to quantify musical behaviors, objects, or events. Whybrew (1971, p. 3) has claimed that the precision and objectivity of quantification appear to some as "antithetical" to the aesthetic nature of music. Nevertheless, a significant body of knowledge abut musical phenomena has arisen through the use of quantitative methods. The application of quantitative methods to music has been strongly supported at least since the 1930s. In 1936 Carl Seashore wrote the following:

Musical performance as a form of behavior lends itself surprisingly well to objective study and measurement. However, it requires a rather cataclysmic readjustment in attitude to pass from the traditional introspectional and emotional attitude of the musician to the laboratory attitude of exact measurement and painstaking analysis. (p. 7)

Today, music educators commonly use quantitative methods for such tasks as grading, student evaluation, contest and festival ratings, auditioning students for ensembles, and assigning chairs in an ensemble.

Why Quantitative Research Techniques?

Research is a multifaceted enterprise, and there are many ways to investigate. Numerical expression enhances the precision and specificity of phenomena under investigation. Numbers enable a researcher to describe in specific terms the subject matter under investigation and the results of the investigation. Furthermore, with the aid of statistical techniques, numbers and the resulting quantifications are important tools for framing and answering precise questions.

Quantitative methods have evolved for assigning numeric values to virtually all aspects of music and for the thorough, robust analysis of these values. As Madsen and Madsen (1978, p. 50) have pointed out, "It is the quantification of specific responses and subsequent logical methods of analysis that provide the background for experimental research."

MEASUREMENT: THE SOURCE OF QUANTITIES

The foundation of quantitative methods in research is measurement (Wilks, 1961). Measurement increases the precision and objectivity of observations whose results may be analyzed through statistical methods (Leonhard, 1958). It is the basic means humankind has used for understanding the universe (Finkelstein, 1982). This section discusses measurement because it is the source of quantities, and it imposes certain constraints on the manipulation of the quantities produced.

Definition

S. S. Stevens (1975, pp. 46–47), defined "measurement" as "the assignment of numbers to objects or events according to rule." Payne (1982, p. 1182) stresses that measurement must be more than counting; it must allow "the comparison of something with a unit or standard or quantity of that same thing, in order to represent the magnitude of the variable being measured." Boyle and Radocy (1987, p. 6) simply refer to measurement as quantifying data. Obviously, some observed object or event is expressed numerically. Fortunately for music education research, measurement does not always require using standard counting units, for example, centimeters, hertz, points, lengths of the king's foot. Impressions, judgments, and sensations may be quantified (Radocy, 1986; Stevens, 1975).

Stevens (1959, p.18) described measurement as "the business of pinning numbers on things." Initially, only physical measurements were made by science, which resulted in classical measurement theory being based on additive quantities. Modern measurement theory is predicated on the "correspondence between a set of manifestations of a property and the relations between them and a set of numbers and the relations between them" (Finkelstein, 1982, p. 5).

Good measurement must (1) be operationally defined, (2) be reproducible, and (3) produce valid results. The goal of measurement is to assign numbers in an objective, empirical manner to objects, behaviors, or events for the purpose of their accurate description (Finkelstein, 1982). Care during

the measurement process is essential to research, as it forms the foundation for all quantitative methods.

Levels of Measurement

The rules that are applied in the measurement of an object, behavior, or event yield numeric values with specific characteristics. On the basis of these characteristics, a set of numeric values can be placed into different levels of measurement. The levels of measurement, ordered from lowest to highest, are nominal, ordinal, interval, and ratio levels.

At the *nominal level* of measurement the numbers are labels for identifying some classification, as in coding all male subjects as "1" and all female subjects as "2." These numbers provide a means for placing objects or events into particular categories (Moore, 1988). Examples of nominal variables are gender, social security numbers, the numbers on players' football jerseys, and the numbering of individual musicians in a marching band.

The *ordinal level* indicates the position of an item in a set of items ordered from smallest to largest. Ordinal measurement provides no indication of how much more or less one object or event has than another object or event. A common illustration in music is the seating in a band or orchestra, where the principal in a given section presumably plays better than the other section members, but there is no specification of how much better.

The *interval level* of measurement describes the degree to which one unit may differ from another unit on a particular property. Examples of interval variables are scores on music aptitude tests, the number of members in various bands, and scores on music achievement tests.

An interval measure has some arbitrary zero point and a unit interval of constant size. A score of zero on an achievement test and zero degrees on a Fahrenheit or Celsius thermometer exemplify arbitrary zero points: A student who could answer no questions correctly might know something about the subject matter, and the temperature can fall "below zero." Test points and degrees of temperature exemplify measurement units that are presumed to be psychologically or physically equal: It is just as far from a score of 10 to 12 as it is from 55 to 57, and the number of degrees separating Fahrenheit temperatures of 21° and 27° is equal to the number of degrees separating 73° and 79°. It is not legitimate to say that a test score of 50 represents a performance that is "twice as good" as a test score of 25, or that a temperature of 80° is "twice as hot" as a temperature of 40°. Ratio comparisons such as these require a zero point that is a genuine absence of the property in question.

The *ratio level* of measurement describes a unit on the basis of the ratio of the unit's possession of a property in relation to another unit. That is, it describes a unit in terms of its having so many times as much of the property as another unit. Examples of ratio variables are loudness, the proportion of students in a class who passed an examination, and pupil-teacher ratio.

An "absolute" zero is found in ratio measurement. A temperature of 200° on the Kelvin scale is "twice as hot" physically as a temperature of 100°; 0° here is the theoretical absence of heat, a point at which molecular motion ceases. A measure of sound power where no sound results in a power measurement of zero is an example of a ratio scale.

Each succeeding level in the ordered levels of measurement must contain the basic empirical operations of all previous levels (Table 11-1) (Stevens, 1959). Knowing the numbered seat assignment of a member of a hundred-voice choir does not allow the determination of the individual's score on a music achievement test. However, knowing that student's music achievement score will allow the assignment of the student's rank in the class, which may then result in the student's placement into a particular numbered seat. From this, it can be noticed that some data can be expressed at different levels of measurement (Stevens, 1959). For example, the members of a choir may be numbered for identity and ease in keeping records of robe assignments—a nominal level of measurement. This choir may be the first-place choir at a contest where the choirs were ranked—an ordinal level of measurement. The choir may also have received a 99 out of a possible 100 score at the contest—an interval level of measurement. Finally, the choir may also be said to have received a score twice as good as that for their previous performance—a ratio measurement.

There is a relationship between the level of measurement and applicable statistics. In general, the lower the level of measurement, the more limited is the number of available statistical procedures. Asher (1976) has argued that educational researchers should strive for the interval level of measurement because of the variety of analyses available and the ability to test higher-order relationships between variables. However, advances in nonparametric statistics and multivariate analysis have allowed a much greater breadth of analysis than available one decade ago. Indeed, a significant body of relationship in music education has resulted from research that has utilized only nominal and ordinal scales. The complexity inherent in music learning suggests that the researcher should strive for interval measurement because, in

comparison with nominal and ordinal data, interval data are more precise and allow use of a wider variety of statistical techniques.

Precision in an Imprecise Enterprise

Music has been said to be a very subjective enterprise. *Subjectivity* implies that there are personal biases and prejudices in operation that may have significant influence on the obtained data. The music researcher should strive for as much objectivity as possible because this will yield data that are the most consistent and sound. The researcher selecting the most appropriate measurement method is involved in evaluating the issues related to reliability and validity.

Reliability In simple terms, reliability is the consistency with which a measuring technique measures. More specifically, as Stanley's (1971) authoritative treatise makes clear, reliability is the portion of variance in the measured property that is attributable to differences in the property itself, rather than to differences in the application of the technique on different occasions, or to other diverse sources of variance due to "error." Reliability affects the precision of measurement as well as the credence that a researcher may give results, so reporting reliability estimates is an important part of presenting the results of quantitative research.

There are several ways to estimate reliability, based on observed consistency across time or within a set of items or observers. Stanley (1971) reviews the "classic" techniques, and Boyle and Radocy (1987) refer to ways appropriate for performance measures. Music education researchers need to be cognizant that reliability is not limited to paper and pencil tests.

Reliability is usually estimated by determining the level of agreement between tests or among observers (Asher, 1976, pp. 93–94). The level of agreement can be determined statistically by the *correlation ratio*. The correlation ratio is a value ranging from -1 to $+1$ where 0 indicates no relationship, -1 indicates a perfect negative relationship, and $+1$

TABLE 11-1. Characteristics of Various Levels of Measurement

Scale	Basic Empirical Operations	Example	Measures of Location	Measures of Dispersion	Correlation	Significance Test
Nominal	Determination of equality	Numbering of players—1, 2, 3, . . .	Mode	—	Contingency correlation	Chi-square
Ordinal	Determination of greater or less	Ranking in music competitions	Median	Percentiles	Rank-order correlation	Sign test Run test
Interval	Determination of the equality of intervals of differences	Score on musical aptitude test	Arithmetic mean	Standard deviation	Correlation ratio	t test F test
Ratio	Determination of the equality of ratios	Loudness in sones	Geometric or harmonic mean	Percent	variation	

Note: Patterned after S. S. Stevens (1959).

indicates a perfect positive relationship. To calculate a correlation ratio, two matched sets of values are necessary. It is through the type of values the two sets contain that different methods for estimating reliability are derived. *Equivalence* is the agreement between two tests that measure the same attribute. *Internal consistency* is obtained from different subsets of items contained within a measure. Reliability, in its pure sense, is the stability of the measure across time, which may be ascertained by determining the agreement between two different administrations of the same test at some time interval.

Validity Validity refers to the extent to which a measurement technique measures what it is supposed to measure. According to Asher (1976, p. 97), validity is an indication of how effective, truthful, and genuine a measurement is. The validity of a measure may be determined from three primary perspectives: content validity, criterion-related validity, and construct validity.

Content validity is the test's effectiveness in providing a substantive measure of what the test is supposed to measure. *Criterion-related validity* is the level of agreement between a particular test and another indicator known to measure the particular trait of interest. Criterion-related validity may be considered further as *concurrent validity,* when the criterion measure is administered at nearly the same time as the test in question, or *predictive validity,* when the criterion is some future performance, such as eventual classroom or musical achievement. *Construct validity* is the effectiveness of a test to measure specific traits underlying the test (Ebel and Frisbie, 1986). Cronbach (1971, p. 462) indicates that the word "concepts" could be substituted for "constructs," but constructs is more indicative "that the categories are deliberate creations chosen to organize experience into general law-like statements." This has led some to suggest that construct validity is essentially concerned with the scientific variables measured by a test (Asher, 1976).

Music teachers concerned with whether a standardized test truly measures the objectives of their teaching are involved in establishing content validity. A researcher who wishes to determine if a test of auditory acuity is as effective at measuring pitch discrimination as the *Seashore Measures of Musical Talents* (Seashore, Lewis, and Saetveit, 1939/1960) pitch subtest is concerned with criterion-related validity. A researcher who wishes to determine whether a melodic perception test is also measuring rhythm and tonal memory is concerned with construct validity.

Subjectivity Subjectivity is inevitable in measurement and research because people are making judgments regarding what to measure, how to measure, and what the measures mean. Although a multiple-choice achievement test that has high reliability and empirical evidence of validity is more "objective" than a judge assigning ratings at a music festival, there is also subjectivity in writing the test items and in interpreting what the scores mean. The objective-subjective aspect of measurement is a continuum of various degrees: It is not a dichotomy.

Indirect Measurement A measure is conceptually direct when a property is measured in terms of itself. Measuring length in terms of length, as in measuring the length of one side of a room with a carpenter's rule, is an example. In contrast, measuring rhythm perception by judging the precision with which a student claps a pattern after hearing it exemplifies *indirect measurement*. Indirect measures are inevitable in quantifying musical behavior because much behavior is covert and overt behavior often is interpreted as evidence of some knowledge or attitude. Indirect measures abound and include written tests, judgment procedures, and electrical and mechanical measures.

Measurement Types in Music

There are many ways to classify types of measurement applicable to quantitative research in music education. Boyle's (1974) classification of musical test behaviors into performance, reading/writing, listening, and "other cognitive" is useful, as is the Johnson and Hess (1970) grouping of subjects' response behaviors and ways to elicit their responses. Another particularly useful classification scheme for conceptualizing music education research possibilities is the division of measurements into psychomusic tests and mechanized measures.

Psychomusic tests examine some psychomusical construct or psychoacoustical property as it is observed through some indicator created by a subject's conscious efforts, such as a test score or a performance. Psychomusic tests include measures of achievement in general music, musical performance skill, pitch discrimination, musical aptitude, attitude toward music, and sight singing.

Mechanized measurement, which includes electronic measures, employs one or more devices to obtain data from a subject; it does not require that a subject actively complete a form or report, or perform. Examples include monitoring physiological aspects, such as heartbeat and blood pressure, employing stroboscopic devices to monitor a subject's intonation during performance, analyzing a complex tone's frequency components and relative intensities and phases, and studying a room's reverberant properties.

Presumably, mechanized measurement is more reliable and "objective" than most psychomusical measures. A series of stroboscopic readings may be more consistent and easier to "read" than a series of subjective human judgments regarding a performer's intonation. Mechanized measurement avoids inherent problems of error that may be induced in the recording of a subject's response. For instance, a subject may mismark an answer sheet by simply responding to item 5 in the location of item 6. This is avoided by mechanical systems. The greater the error in a measurement, the lower the reliability (Lord and Novick, 1968).

STATISTICAL PRINCIPLES

Strictly speaking, one may quantify without employing statistics, but most quantitative research needs to describe characteristics and draw inferences. Statistical treatments must be appropriate for the research questions and the data. This section reviews basic principles regarding descriptive and inferential statistics, hypothesis testing, and specific properties of statistics.

Descriptive vs. Inferential Statistics

The primary difference between descriptive and inferential statistics is the use to which the statistics will be put. If the purpose is to describe the data, then *descriptive statistics* are used (Borg and Gall, 1979, p. 406). If the purpose is to make inferences about a population of individuals from data gathered from a sample of this population, then *inferential statistics* are used (Best and Kahn, 1989, p. 222). Practically, most research studies begin with descriptive statistics and then, once overall characteristics of the data are known, inferential statistics are applied to determine the characteristics of the population. In some cases, after inferential statistics have been applied, interesting phenomena are noted for particular samples whose data are then treated with descriptive statistics to determine the characteristics of these samples.

The purpose of descriptive statistics is to describe and summarize relatively large amounts of data (Sax, 1979, p. 370), thus reducing the data to a few statistics that simplify interpretation (Borg and Gall, 1979, p. 406). They often describe central tendencies and variability in the data, as well as simply relate how much of what exists. Analysis of the results of a classroom achievement test, a listing of the numbers of students enrolled in particular music classes, grade point averages for all members of a student body, and demographic data exemplify some uses of descriptive statistics.

Inferential statistics are employed to make judgments about some group beyond those subjects who contribute data. A general music class may be considered representative of other general music classes; a set of trumpet mouthpieces may be considered representative of available mouthpieces. On the basis of probabilities and known or surmised properties of the particular sample, a researcher infers characteristics of the larger group. In short, one "draws an inference."

A *statistic* is a numerical characteristic obtained from a sample. A *parameter* is a numerical characteristic obtained from a population. It is the role of inferential statistics to estimate the parameters of a population on the basis of observations derived from a sample (Best and Kahn, 1989, pp. 222–223).

Usually samples are drawn from a population utilizing random sampling techniques. The purpose of random sampling is to produce values for which margins of error can be determined statistically when the sampled values are generalized to a larger population (Borg and Gall, 1979, p. 182). Random sampling provides the most efficient means of providing data that can be generalized to the larger population from which the sample was drawn.

The Elements of Statistics

Populations All members of a particular group of interest comprise the population. Fifth-grade instrumental music stu-

dents in a city's schools, clarinet reeds available in a music store, learning-disabled students in music classes, string students taught by a Suzuki-based method, or virtually any logical group are populations. Populations may be huge, as in the population of all 6-year-olds, or tiny, as in the population of all students in one school who have absolute pitch. Generalization to a population is implicit in much music education research. In order for researchers to generalize to a specific population, all members of the population need a relatively equal chance to contribute to the data from which the inferences are drawn.

Samples A sample is a subset of a population. A group of voters carefully chosen from "representative" precincts by a polling organization is a sample of a population of voters. The subjects of research in which inferences are to be made are a sample of the population of interest.

Ideally, a sample is obtained in a way that gives each and every member of the population an equal chance of being selected. This is a *random sample*. Selecting subjects on the basis of random number tables, computerized random number generators, tossing fair dice, or drawing numbered slips of paper from a thoroughly mixed set are legitimate applications of randomization. Merely scanning a list of names or looking over a set of objects and in effect saying, "Let's take this one, and that one; we'll eliminate that one . . ." is not a random process. A random sample of sufficient number allows a researcher to generalize results to the population with confidence.

Truly random samples are almost always impossible to obtain. Some reasons include the necessity to work with volunteer subjects, a need to use intact classrooms or ensembles rather than mix subjects across groups, proscriptions caused by informed-consent aspects of using human subjects, and selective loss of subjects. Many samples employed in quantitative research thus are ersatz random samples: samples chosen on the basis of who is available, but deemed to be representative or like the members of some larger population. Researchers must use their training and experience to make an informed decision as to the representativeness of the sample. Many applications of inferential statistics proceed as if the sample were random.

Samples could be obviously nonrandom to a degree where there is no point in claiming that they are representative of a population in any way. Using the first 15 students one meets on campus as somehow representative of the student body clearly is using a nonrandom sample. So is a researcher's employing a group of the general population to answer questions about specific musical phenomena because they are available, without the researcher's having any knowledge of their musical backgrounds.

Sample Size One somewhat controversial issue is sample size. In general, the larger the size of a representative sample, the more stable and representative are the results of the inference. Classical statistical texts (e.g., Li, 1964) clearly show that larger sample sizes enhance the probability of finding a difference between experimental treatments when one "truly" exists in the population. They restrict the range within which some "true" value is likely to fall. Of course, with sufficiently large samples, even population differences that lack any "practical" significance will be statistically significant (Heller and Radocy, 1983).

How large is large enough? Kirk (1982, p. 8) indicates that adequate sample size is a function of experimental effects and the number of treatments, error variance in the population from which the sample comes, and the probability of making a false judgment about the outcome of a statistical test. Since some of these properties are not always known in advance, Kirk also presents procedures for estimating certain sample sizes. Consistent rules of thumb are hard to find. The Bruning and Kintz (1977) statistical "cookbook" recommends 10 to 15 subjects per experimental group. Cohen's (1988) treatise provides various means for estimating minimal sample sizes.

Drawing Inferences

Das and Giri (1986) identify three main characteristics of the inferential process: (1) the inferences are made with observations that are not exact but that are subject to variation making them probabilistic in nature, (2) methods are specified for the appropriate collection of data so that the assumptions for particular statistical methods are satisfied, and (3) techniques for the proper interpretation of the statistical results are devised.

Null Hypotheses Inferences are drawn on the basis of the outcomes of statistical tests. What is tested is a statement of no cause and effect, or no relationship, a *null hypothesis*. The null hypothesis results from a *hypothesis*, a tentative statement of cause and effect or relationship. In turn, the hypothesis is implied by questions that the researcher is trying to answer. Research questions, hypotheses, and null hypotheses are not always stated explicitly in a research report, but are implied by what the researcher investigates and how. Questions are implied in the form of, "What is the effect of _____ on _____?"

Hypotheses lead to deliberate statements of no cause and effect, or no relationship. These null hypotheses are directly testable through techniques of inferential statistics. An example of a null hypothesis statement is, "There is no difference in students' knowledge of excerpts between the beginning of the music appreciation course and the end."

Conceptually, a researcher tests a null hypothesis by judging whether an observed outcome of a statistical test is sufficiently likely to belong to a distribution of events—a distribution that will occur if the null hypothesis is true; that is, there "really" is no difference or relationship in the population. If the observed outcome is not too extreme, in accordance with statistical probabilities, it is deemed to belong to the distribution that exists if the null hypothesis is true. If the observed outcome is too extreme, it is considered to be too unlikely to belong to that distribution—it probably belongs to another and the null hypothesis probably is false. Just

what is "too extreme" is a matter of judgment of just how far from the center of a hypothesized distribution the outcome is.

Statistical Significance The necessary degree of extremity is a matter of statistical significance. Essentially, *statistical significance* is the likelihood that the observed result occurred by chance alone. To say that an outcome is significant at or beyond a certain level is to specify the odds. A researcher claiming statistical significance at the .05 level ($p \leq$ .05) is saying that the null hypothesis will be rejected 95 times out of 100. Although some researchers have claimed that results are significant at the .10 level ($p \leq$ .10) or even at the .20 level ($p \leq$ .20), it is rare that a researcher claims statistical significance unless the .05 level ($p \leq$ .05) is attained. If the outcome of an experiment may cause a major revision to existing instructional procedures or lead to considerable reallocation of resources, the researcher may require a greater significance level, such as the .01 level or the .001 level.

Statistically significant occurrences are deemed unlikely to have occurred by chance alone, in accordance with a set of statistical probabilities and a researcher's interpretative judgment. Practical significance does not necessarily follow. Large samples, for instance, are prone to produce small but statistically significant differences that have no practical importance. Basically, practical significance comes down to "So what?" (Heller and Radocy, 1983).

Correct Decision vs. Error Although statistical techniques are powerful tools for assessing population characteristics in accordance with sample characteristics, they are not infallible. The correct decision versus error issue may be conceptualized as an interaction of two dimensions. One dimension is reality; that is, whether the null hypothesis is in fact true or false. The other dimension is the researcher's decision to retain or reject the null hypothesis. If the researcher retains a null hypothesis that is in fact true *or* rejects a null hypothesis that is in fact false, that researcher makes a correct decision. If the researcher rejects a null hypothesis that is in fact true, that researcher commits a Type I or alpha error. The researcher who fails to reject a null hypothesis that is in fact false commits a Type II or beta error. Establishing a more stringent criterion for statistical significance, which essentially reduces the number of outcomes that will be deemed too extreme to occur by chance alone, reduces the likelihood of Type I error. Increasing the sample size reduces the likelihood of Type II error.

Parametric vs. Nonparametric Statistics

Parameters are values such as means and variances of some population. *Parametric statistics* are based on distributions of possible outcomes with known parameters. *Nonparametric statistics,* also called "distribution-free" statistics, are based on distributions with unknown parameters. Parametric statistics are applicable to data with at least interval level of measurement while nonparametric statistics are applicable to data with nominal and ordinal levels of measurement (Best, 1981, p. 221). Parametric statistics are more numerous and tend to be more powerful and more frequently used. Nonparametric statistics do not require the same number of assumptions about the underlying population as are required by parametric statistics.

Parametric statistics make a greater number of assumptions about the population parameters. First, the data are at least at the interval level of measurement. Second, the data of the population are normally distributed. Third, the distribution of the data for the various samples is generally the same. To be normally distributed means that the data when graphed create the well-known bell-shaped curve of the normal distribution (Figure 11–1). When the distributions of the various samples are approximately equal, the samples are said to have the characteristic of homogeneity of variance.

Nonparametric statistics require that observations are independent and that measurement is at the nominal or ordinal levels (Madsen and Madsen, 1978, p. 78). Nonparametric tests do not assume that the population is normally distributed, and they do not assume homogeneity of variance in the samples (Rainbow and Froehlich, 1987, p. 230). Siegel and Castellan (1988, p. xv) cite four advantages of using nonparametric statistics: (1) the tests are distribution free in that they do not assume that the data are normally distributed, (2) they can employ ordinal data that are simply ranks, (3) these statistics are simple to calculate, and (4) they are appropriate in the study of small samples.

Puri and Sen (1971, p. 1) point out that researchers seldom know the underlying distribution of a population, and that the use of parametric statistics in situations where the underlying distribution is not normal is highly suspect. However, Borg and Gall (1979, p. 464) recommend the use of parametric statistics when the researcher has interval scores but has neither normally distributed scores nor homogeneity of variance among the samples because (1) the outcome of a parametric technique is affected very little by moderate departure from the technique's theoretical assumptions; (2) nonparametric statistics are generally less powerful; and (3) for many educational research problems, suitable nonparametric tests are not available.

The decision to employ parametric or nonparametric methods depends on the data as well as a researcher's beliefs. Nominal or ordinal data of small sample sizes may be handled more appropriately with nonparametric methods. A researcher who is satisfied that there is no reason to question the propriety of parametric statistics in a particular situation should employ parametric statistics. Assuredly, the researcher should not do both: The researcher either believes that the conditions for parametric statistics are satisfied or does not believe it.

VARIABLES

A *variable,* in the broad sense, is something that does not remain the same under all conditions; that is, it varies. Variables are characterized according to the functions they serve in the research design and in the applicable statistical tests.

Independent Variables

In quantitative research, researchers often compare two or more levels of an *independent variable* on a dependent variable. For example, the effects of two or more instructional approaches could be compared. When investigators are free to decide what will be done and when, they are able to "manipulate" an independent variable. In cases where they must accept previously existing conditions, such as subjects' gender or ethnicity, the independent variable is labeled as an "assigned" variable. The reader should be aware that other labels do exist.

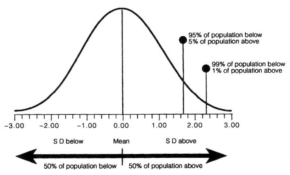

FIGURE 11–1. The Normal Curve with Reference of Population Percentages.

148 • RESEARCH MODES AND TECHNIQUES

Dependent Variables

Dependent variables presumably "depend" on the effect of independent variables. Changes between pretest and posttest scores exemplify dependent variables. If a researcher is studying the effects of instruction, different forms of instruction constitute an independent variable, and some measure of the result of instruction constitutes a dependent variable. Many quantitative studies contain just one dependent variable, in which case the use of univariate statistics is appropriate. Other studies, especially many contemporary ones, feature simultaneous investigation of the effects of independent variables on more than one dependent variable. In those studies, multivariate statistical techniques are mandatory.

Statistical Conceptualization

In cases where changes in the dependent variable are conceived as resulting from the manipulation of an independent variable, as when attitudes might change as a result of exposure to music across time, or where they are conceived as resulting from a "natural" or assigned independent variable, as when differences in musical taste might be due to gender, there is an underlying *factorial model:* An independent variable clearly is a causal agent or factor that determines what happens to a dependent variable.

In cases where the variables are conceived as a set of relationships—as, for example, where one might relate scores on a measure of musical ability with scores on a test of academic achievement—there is an underlying *regression model.* Here, depending on the research question, either variable could be "independent" or "dependent." The conception is of related variables, or predictor and criterion variables. For example, Hedden (1982) related a set of predictor variables— attitude toward music, self-concept in music, musical background, academic achievement, and gender—to a criterion variable of musical achievement.

"Other" Variables

Many variables exist that are neither independent nor dependent; most of them are irrelevant. Most research in music education need not be concerned with changing conditions of cosmic ray penetration, eye color, shoe size, hair length, position or rate of the Humboldt current, or subjects' prior exposure to Boolean algebra, for example. However, nuisance or confounding variables could influence a dependent variable. An example would be home musical background in a study of contrasting approaches to teaching instrumental music. Nuisance variables can be controlled by statistical techniques, random selection of subjects, or changing an experimental design and its associated statistical treatment to incorporate a nuisance variable as another independent variable.

Univariate vs. Multivariate Statistics

The distinction between univariate and multivariate statistics varies somewhat from author to author, but the generally distinguishing feature is that *univariate statistics* are used in analyzing the characteristics of one dependent variable (Hair, Anderson, Tatham, and Grablowsky, 1984, p. 5; Harris, 1985, p. 5; Kachigan, 1986, pp. 4–5). *Multivariate statistics,* on the other hand, are used in simultaneously analyzing a number of dependent variables. Multivariate statistics frequently provide a simplification of the data by summarizing the data with relatively few parameters (Chatfield and Collins, 1980, pp. 6–7). Not only do these procedures allow for the testing of hypotheses, but a number are exploratory in nature and can generate hypotheses as well as test hypotheses.

The study of musical processes usually involves multiple variables that could be expected to be affected by some factor. For instance, a 10-week experimental treatment in which fourth-grade students received a particular music-teaching method for 30 minutes each day might be expected to affect both rhythm and pitch skills. With traditional statistical procedures used in music research separate analyses would be performed on each of these skills to determine if the skills had been positively influenced by the treatment. Analyzing each skill separately involves the application of univariate statistics. Unfortunately, the use of separate univariate statistics in such cases increases the possibility of producing a significant result that is actually due to chance (Harris, 1985, pp. 6–7). Thus the research is subject to Type I error. Multivariate statistics provides a means around such problems by providing an overall test to determine first whether the experimental treatment actually produced a significant effect on both skills, and, if so, subanalyses can be performed to determine if the significant effect occurred for each of the skills separately.

Multivariate statistics are an assortment of descriptive and inferential procedures for analyzing the simultaneous effects of phenomena on a number of variables. There exists a multivariate analogue of virtually every univariate procedure. Most research in music will become increasingly involved in the application of multivariate procedures because of the complex nature of music processes. This is most appropriate because multivariate statistics have been claimed to produce more interesting results and to be more scientifically productive (Kachigan, 1986, p. 5). To avoid the use of multivariate statistics will result in research with a greater probability of error and research that does not provide the full range of insights that multivariate statistics provide. Harris (1985, p. 5) has stated that "if researchers were sufficiently narrowminded or theories and research techniques so well developed or nature so simple as to dictate a single independent variable and a single outcome measure as appropriate in each study, there would be no need for multivariate techniques."

As with univariate statistics, there are both parametric and nonparametric multivariate statistical procedures. For the parametric case, the distribution that forms the foundation for multivariate statistics is the multivariate normal distribution (Muirhead, 1982, p. 1). This distribution is an extension of the normal distribution to more than one variable. As in the univariate case, most sampled measurements tend to be normally distributed.

UNIVARIATE TESTS: ONE INDEPENDENT VARIABLE

Chi-Square Tests

The family of chi-square tests essentially compares an observed classification of frequencies with an expected classification. For example, in a study of elementary students' tempo perceptions, Kuhn and Booth (1988) used chi-square to determine whether the numbers of subjects who classified musical examples as going slower, staying the same, or going faster were significantly different from a chance distribution of the three tempo change classifications.

The assumptions of chi-square include independence of each observation from each other observation, placement of any observation in one and only one cell in the table formed by the classifications of observed and expected, and a sufficiently large sample size (Hays, 1988, p. 772). According to Wike (1971), if the total number of observations exceeds the total number of subjects, some subjects are contributing to more than one observation, and the independence criterion is violated. Sufficient sample size is controversial, but Wike suggests that the total sample size should exceed 20 and the expected frequency in any classification should be at least five. There are various adaptations for smaller numbers and for situations where subjects contribute more than one observation; the Siegel (1956) treatise and Wike's book are good sources of additional information.

t Tests

A widely applicable set of parametric statistical tests is based on a family of statistical distributions called the *t* distributions. Essentially, the researcher compares an observed *t* value with a hypothesized *t* value of zero; if the observed outcome is too far away from zero in accordance with the probabilities of the hypothesized *t* distribution, the null hypothesis is rejected. In using a *t* test, one assumes that all samples are drawn randomly from normally distributed populations with equivalent variances. In practice, these assumptions often are violated.

An *"independent"* t test compares two samples that are not matched in any way. The two groups represent two levels of an independent variable, and the *t* value is computed from the measures of the dependent variable. For example, Darrow, Haack, and Kuribayashi (1987) used independent *t* tests in comparing preferences for particular musical examples of two groups of subjects who differed in musical experience.

A *"related measures"* t test compares two matched groups. Often, the groups are "matched" because they are two sets of scores from the same group of people, as in a comparison of pretest and posttest scores. Price and Swanson (1990) used this type of related measures (matched, dependent, paired) *t* test in comparing their subjects' pretest and posttest scores on cognitive knowledge, attitudes, and preferences.

A less commonly applied *t* test is a test to compare an observed sample mean with a hypothesized population mean. An investigator might compare a mean score on a standardized musical achievement test administered in his or her school with a hypothesized mean equivalent to a published norm to see if the school's mean was "better" or "worse" than a hypothesized national mean.

A multiplicity of *t* tests that are testing a series of null hypotheses with data obtained in the same study may be unwise, not only from the standpoint of efficiency but because of increasing the probability of Type I or alpha error. Fortunately, the *t* test is a special case of a large family of more efficient statistical techniques known as analysis of variance.

Analysis of Variance

The family of *t* distributions is mathematically related to another family of statistical distributions, the *F* distributions. Mathematicians can show that $t^2 = F$. Therefore, a *t* test may be conceived as a special case of analysis of variance, which relies on the *F* distribution, where there are only two sets of measures to compare. The *analysis of variance* (ANOVA) is much more flexible because it can account for more than two levels of an independent variable and be extended to account for more than one independent variable simultaneously, and, through multivariate techniques, even more than one dependent variable simultaneously.

The assumptions of the analysis of variance are that the samples are obtained randomly from normally distributed populations, with equivalent variances. In practice, the randomization is critical; the other criteria may be "bent" a little (Li, 1964).

Types of ANOVA An ANOVA may be employed to analyze the difference between separate groups and repeated measures of the same group. If a subject can be in one and only one group, the comparison is between separate groups, each of which represents a level of an independent variable. If the same subjects experience different levels of an independent variable, there are *repeated measures* involved. A *mixed design* is one in which any particular subject experiences just one level of one (or more) independent variable(s) while simultaneously experiencing all levels of one (or more) other independent variable(s). For example, in a music preference study, all students in a junior high school can listen to each of five musical styles; the style variable is a repeated measure. If the investigator is interested in differential effects of gender, the gender variable is an independent variable where each subject can be at just one level.

The analysis of variance indicates via one or more *F* tests whether there is a significant difference between or among the levels of the independent variable. When two or more independent variables are studied simultaneously, F tests also are applied to any possible interaction(s); these are discussed below in the context of factorial designs. The original F tests do not indicate where the significance lies. If there are only two levels, the location of any significant difference is obvious. Otherwise, further testing is necessary.

Post-ANOVA Comparisons Opinions differ regarding multiple comparison tests to follow a significant F value. Kirk (1982) distinguishes between orthogonal and nonorthogonal comparisons and between a priori (planned) comparisons and a posteriori (data snooping) comparisons. Orthogonal comparisons use nonoverlapping information. In general, if there are k levels of the independent variable, there are $k - 1$ orthogonal comparisons. With four groups, for example, the possible comparisons for significant differences between two levels involve the differences between groups 1 and 2, 1 and 3, 1 and 4, 2 and 3, 2 and 4, and 3 and 4. Three pairwise comparisons—the difference between 1 and 2 as compared with the difference between 3 and 4, the difference between 1 and 3 as compared with the difference between 2 and 4, and the difference between 1 and 4 as compared with the difference between 2 and 3—are orthogonal. The other possible comparisons are nonorthogonal; for example, comparing the difference between group 1 and group 2 as compared with the difference between group 1 and group 3 involves group 1 in each difference, so it is nonorthogonal. *Planned comparisons* are hypothesized before the experiment. *A posteriori comparisons* emerge from the data.

In order to reduce the likelihood that some comparisons will be significant by chance alone, various adjustments to the significance level may be necessary, so statisticians have created a family of multiple comparison measures. Kirk describes four situations. When comparisons are limited to planned orthogonal comparisons, a modified form of the t test that incorporates part of the analysis of variance summary (the mean square for error variance) is appropriate. Dunn's test is appropriate for all planned comparisons, whether or not they are orthogonal. For a posteriori comparisons and mixtures of planned and unplanned comparisons, possibilities include Fisher's LSD (least significant difference) test, Tukey's HSD (honestly significant difference) test, Scheffé's test, the Newman-Keuls test, Duncan's new multiple range test, and Dunnett's test. In general, planned orthogonal comparisons are more powerful than the others. Computational procedures differ, and some tests are more versatile regarding the possibility of comparing combinations of levels within an independent variable.

An ANOVA Example The results of an ANOVA are presented in a *source table.* Gfeller, Darrow, and Hedden (1990), in a study of mainstreaming status among music educators, presented a fully documented source table, which appears here as Table 11–2. The grouping variable, or factor, of music education type contained three levels: instrumental, vocal, and general music educator. The dependent variable was the teachers' perception of the instructional support

TABLE 11–2. ANOVA Source Table of Gfeller, Darrow, and Hedden (1990)

Source of Variance	Sum of Squares	df	Mean Squares	F	p
Between groups	186.43	2	93.21	4.84	.010
Within groups	1,327.57	69	19.24		
Total	1,514.00	71			

they were receiving. In the source table, the mean squares are obtained by dividing the sum of squares by the corresponding degrees of freedom. The F value is obtained by dividing the between-groups mean squares with the within-groups mean squares. Note that there was a significant difference at the .01 level between the types of teachers as indicated by p in the table. The post hoc analysis was performed using the Newman Keuls Multiple Range Test (Table 11–3). This analysis indicates that the instrumental music educators have a higher opinion of the instructional support they receive for mainstreaming than do the other music educators.

Analysis of Covariance

A research design may not always control for effects of extraneous or "nuisance" variables. For example, in a study comparing the relative efficacies of two methods of teaching beginning instrumentalists, the two groups might differ significantly in their initial music aptitude, despite randomization. In a study where the researcher must necessarily work with intact groups, the students in one classroom may have some inherent advantage, such as parents who encourage and support private music lessons. Aptitude and parental support variables occasionally may be built into the experimental design as additional independent variables, but when that is not feasible, statistical control may be attained via *analysis of covariance,* where the additional variable functions as a *covariate.* The covariate varies along with the other variables, and its effects are parceled out mathematically; in effect, the researcher is able to indicate the effects of the independent variable with any effects of the covariate under statistical control. Analysis of covariance may be extended to factorial designs, with more than one independent variable and/or covariate, and to multivariate designs, with more than one independent variable, dependent variable, and/or covariate.

TABLE 11–3. Newman Keuls Multiple Range Test of Gfeller, Darrow, and Hedden (1990)

Elementary Music Educators	Vocal Music Educators	Instrumental Music Educators
20.60	22.26	24.81

Note: Rule under values indicates nonsignificance. All other comparisons significant ($p < .01$).

UNIVARIATE TESTS—TWO OR MORE INDEPENDENT VARIABLES

Factorial Design Concepts

The number of independent variables or factors and their associated levels determine which ANOVA model is appropriate. The model extends the partitioning of the total sums of squares beyond the within-treatments and between-treatments sums of squares done by the one-way ANOVA. The *F* value is still the ratio of the sums of squares of interest divided by the sums of squares within treatments now designated as *error* (Edwards, 1968, p. 120).

Figure 11–2 presents three different experiments that all use musical achievement as the dependent variable. In the first experiment, it is desired to determine the effect of three levels of musical aptitude, the single independent variable or factor, on musical achievement. This experimental design would require a *one-way ANOVA*. The second experiment is designed with a two-level factor of gender and a three-level factor of musical aptitude level. This experimental design, because it involves two factors, requires a *two-way ANOVA*. The third experiment extends the second by including a third factor of grade level, which requires a *three-way ANOVA*. ANOVAs with more than one factor may also be referred to by the number of levels of each factor. The second experiment would be referred to as a 2 × 3 ANOVA while the third experiment would be referred to as a 2 × 3 × 3 ANOVA.

The two-way ANOVA required by the second experiment in Figure 11–2 can further partition the between-treatment sums of squares into the *main effects* for each of the factors of gender and musical aptitude as well as for the interaction of these two factors. In this case, the partitioning of the treatment sums of squares yields sums of squares for the gender main effect, the musical aptitude main effect, and the gender × musical aptitude (gender by musical aptitude) *interaction*. An *F* ratio can be produced for each partition by dividing with the appropriate error team. The error term in this case is the within-treatment sums of squares. Thus, tests can be applied to determine if a significant difference exists in musical achievement attributable to gender, musical aptitude, or the interaction between gender and musical aptitude.

A significant interaction in a multiway ANOVA indicates that the effect of the various levels of the factors involved is not uniform. In the case of the second experiment in Figure 11–2, a significant gender × musical aptitude interaction might indicate that girls of high aptitude achieve more than boys of high aptitude while girls of low aptitude achieve less than boys of low aptitude. The opposite also could be true. It would be necessary to plot the means for the cells of the interaction, as in Figure 11–3 (p. 152), to determine the nature of the significant interaction. In this case, our initial supposition is indicated by the graph of the interaction. In general, a plot of significant interaction will reveal prominent nonparallel lines, although the lines may not always intersect.

The concepts presented for the second example can be extended for other multiway ANOVAs. Consider the characteristics of the three-way ANOVA of the third experiment in Figure 11–2. The between-treatments sums of squares can be partitioned into three main effects: gender, musical aptitude, and grade level. In addition, the following combinations of factors produce interactions that can be tested: gender × musical aptitude, gender × grade level, musical aptitude × grade level (two-way interactions), and gender × musical aptitude × grade level (three-way interaction).

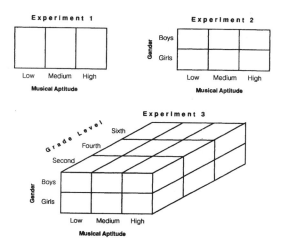

FIGURE 11–2. Three Experimental Designs in Music.

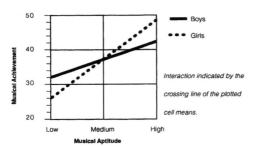

FIGURE 11–3. Hypothetical Interaction Effects for Experiment 2.

Simple Effects

In the example provided by Experiment 2, we may find that there are significant differences due to the main effects of both gender and musical aptitude. For the main effect of gender, there are only two means: one for the boys and one for the girls. Thus, the gender main effect states that the girls and boys performed significantly differently from each other on musical achievement, the dependent variable. For the main effect of musical aptitude, there are three means, one for each of the three musical aptitude levels. A number of methods are available to determine how these means differ through both post hoc and a priori methods. The multiple comparisons that are required to account for the differences among all the means have come to be called *simple effects*.

Simple effects are of two types: planned and unplanned (Kachigan, 1986, p. 306). Comparisons planned prior to data analysis are also known as *a priori comparisons*. Comparisons determined after the completion of an ANOVA where significant differences for the main and interaction effects have been noted are unplanned comparisons also known as *post hoc comparisons*.

A Priori Comparisons   The most accepted method for analyzing simple effects that are preplanned is through the testing of *orthogonal comparisons* (Kachigan, 1986, p. 306). Orthogonal comparisons are established by the assignment of weights to the means so that the sum of all the weights is equal to zero. For instance, in Experiment 2 of Figure 11–2 we might have obtained a significant musical aptitude main effect. This effect has three means. To compare the low aptitude mean ($\bar{x}_l$) with the medium aptitude mean ($\bar{x}_m$), we would subtract the second mean from the first mean. This in mathematical formulation would be:

$$\bar{x}_l - \bar{x}_m$$

which is equivalent to

$$(+1)\,\bar{x}_l + (-1)\,\bar{x}_m .$$

Removing the mean symbols leaves the two weights

$$+1 \text{ and } -1,$$

which also sum to zero. Orthogonal contrasts are created in just this manner. They also provide the ability to compare, say, the high musical aptitude mean ($\bar{x}_h$) against the average of the low and medium level musical aptitude means. This comparison would be mathematically displayed as

$$\bar{x}_h - \frac{\bar{x}_l + \bar{x}_m}{2} = \bar{x}_h - \frac{\bar{x}_l}{2} - \frac{\bar{x}_m}{2},$$

which would have the weights of

$$+1 \quad -\frac{1}{2} \quad -\frac{1}{2},$$

which also sum to zero.

Two contrasts, to be orthogonal to each other, must have the products of their respective coefficient weights sum to zero. The number of possible orthogonal contrasts is one less than the number of levels in the ANOVA effect of interest. For our musical aptitude effect of Experiment 2, there are three levels, which means that two orthogonal comparisons are possible. It is possible, however, to create a number of different sets of orthogonal comparisons. Table 11–4 presents a number of possibilities for the musical aptitude effect. Note that constants have been used in some of the contrasts to avoid fractions.

The test of the significance of an orthogonal contrast is done by testing whether the sum of the products of each weight times its respective mean is equal to zero. The test requires that the sum (W) of all the Weight (w) × Mean ($\bar{x}$) products is calculated as

$$W = w_1\,\bar{x}_1 + w_2\,\bar{x}_2 + \cdots + w_k\,\bar{x}_k .$$

The standard error (s_w) for the sum of all the Weight × Mean products is then calculated as

$$s_w = s\,\sqrt{\sum \frac{w_i^2}{n_i}},$$

where

s = square root of the within-treatment or error mean square,
w_i^2 = squared weight in a contrast, and
n_i = the sample size for a mean in the contrast.

TABLE 11–4. Possible Orthogonal Contrasts for Musical Aptitude

Contrast	Low Mean	Medium Mean	High Mean
1	2	−1	−1
2	0	1	−1
1	−1	−1	2
2	1	−1	0

The test is distributed as *t* with the same degrees of freedom as for the within-treatment sums of squares and an alpha twice that selected for the original ANOVA

$$t = \frac{W}{s_w}.$$

An equivalent interval to test this value is

$$W \pm (\alpha/2^t \, df) (s_w)$$

where

$1 - \alpha/2^t$ df = critical value of *t* for a particular confidence level with the same degrees of freedom as for the within-treatment sum of squares.

The value of using orthogonal contrasts is that both the significance levels of each comparison and the entire set of comparisons are known (Kachigan, 1986, p. 310). If for each of our musical aptitude comparisons we use a significance level of .05, the probability for the entire set is .95 × .95 = .85 that the set is without a Type I error or the probability of one Type I error in the set is .15 (1 − .85). For post hoc, that is unplanned comparisons, the probability in the set of comparisons is not known.

Post Hoc Comparisons Duncan's (1955) multiple range test provides one method for the post hoc determination of which of the differences of the means are significant. Use of post hoc methods assumes that there were no hypothesized differences prior to the implementation of the experiment. The method involves ordering all the means from lowest to highest in a table and calculating the standard error of the mean. A statistical table is then employed to find a multiplier value based on the degrees of freedom for the within-treatment partitioning of the sums of squares. Multipliers are found for two through to the total number of levels. The standard error of the mean and the multipliers are then multiplied. This forms the *shortest significant ranges*. The lowest mean is then subtracted from the highest mean. If this value is larger than the shortest significant range for the spread of levels covered by the lowest to the highest mean, then a significant difference between means has been identified. This process continues comparing the next smallest mean to the highest mean until no difference is noted. A line is drawn under the means from the highest mean to the point where no difference occurs. This entire procedure is then repeated comparing the next highest mean to the smallest values and so on until all significant mean differences have been identified.

Scheffé (1953) proposed another post hoc method for testing any and all comparisons of a set of means. In this procedure a table of all comparisons of interest is created. For the musical aptitude levels of Experiment 2 in Figure 11–2, a table similar to Table 11–5 might result. In the first row of

TABLE 11–5. Scheffé Contrast Vectors for Comparing Means in Experiment 2

Comparison	Means			Sum of Squared Weights
	Low	Medium	High	
Low vs. medium	1	−1	0	2
Low vs. high	1	0	−1	2
Medium vs. high	0	1	−1	2
Low vs. medium + high	2	−1	−1	6
High vs. low + medium	−1	−1	2	6

Table 11–5, the low mean is compared to the medium mean by using the weights 1 and −1 respectively while 0 is assigned to the high-aptitude level as it is not being considered in this contrast. The sum of the squared weights is obtained by squaring each of the weights in the row and adding them together. To test a particular contrast, the difference between the sum of the scores for one compared treatment group is subtracted from the sum of the other and this result is squared. The squared difference between the group sums is then divided by the sum of the squared weights from the table. The resulting value is divided by the error mean square from the analysis of variance producing *F*. To determine the significance of this *F*, the number of means minus one is used as the degrees of freedom for the numerator and the within-treatment degrees of freedom is used for the denominator degrees of freedom. With these values, the tabled value for a desired significance level is identified. This value is then multiplied by the number of means minus one to produce *F′*. To be significant, *F* must be greater than or equal to *F′*.

Symbolically, the Scheffé test amounts to:

$$MS_{D_i} = \frac{D_i^{\,2}}{n\Sigma \, w_{.i}^{\,2}}$$

$$F = \frac{MS_{D_i}}{s^2}$$

$$F' = (k - 1)F_{(k - 1),dfw},$$

where

$D_i^{\,2}$ = squared difference of the sum of scores for the contrasted means,
$\Sigma w_{.i}^{\,2}$ = sum of the squared weights for the contrast,
n = number of subjects in a treatment level,
k = total number of treatment levels, and
dfw = within-treatment or error mean square degrees of freedom.

Cell Size

The power of an analysis of variance is predicated on the number of subjects that are contained within each of the cells of the experimental design. All things being equal, the greater the number of individuals within a cell, the greater the power. This is related to the assumptions of homogeneity of variance and the measured values being normally distributed. The larger the sample for each cell, the greater the probability that the sampled values for the cell will have these characteristics. The researcher must be cautioned about including too many independent variables within an analysis as the sample size within the cells may become very small. This usually occurs when a researcher decides on a particular analysis of variance after the data are collected rather than before. To avoid such problems, the experiment should be planned carefully in advance to ensure that the number of subjects in each cell will be as equal as possible and as large as feasible. Practically, factorial experiments with fewer than 10 subjects in each cell should be avoided.

Randomized Block Designs

The full factorial designs considered above take the total sample of subjects and randomly assign each subject to one of the treatment level combinations. If one of the treatment, or condition, levels is related to the dependent variable, then a *randomized block design* could be formed. The benefit of the randomized block design is that the error variance—that is, the denominator in the ratio—is reduced, which makes it more likely that a significant ratio will be obtained (Kachigan, 1986, p. 299).

In the randomized block design, blocks are formed of subjects with similar characteristics on a trait. The number of subjects in the block must be equal to the number of treatments, and all subjects in a block must have homogeneous characteristics on the trait related to the dependent variable. Consider an experiment where the dependent variable was

rhythm learning after a 10-week instructional period. Five different treatments were used: (1) Orff method, (2) Kodály method, (3) Education Through Music method, (4) Gordon method, and (5) no-contact control group. The experimenters were interested in the relative effectiveness of these methods in teaching rhythm and, in addition, were interested in determining if a differential effect occurred for various musical aptitude levels. Musical aptitude should be related to rhythm achievement. Therefore, blocks could be formed of high, medium, and low musical aptitude. Because the number of subjects in a block is equal to the number of treatments, there would be five students in each of the three blocks, requiring a total of 15 students. The blocks would be formed by ranking the students according to musical aptitude and placing the first five in the high block, the second five in the medium block, and the last five in the low block. The subjects within each block would be randomly assigned to one of the five treatment conditions.

The statistical treatment of such data is summarized in Table 11–6. The variance in the data is partitioned into total, treatment, blocks, and block × treatment. The block × treatment is used as the error term in the ratios for treatment and block main effects. The fictitious results of this experiment indicate a significant effect for treatment and a significant effect for aptitude. Further analysis for simple effects would be necessary to identify exactly where the differences between means lie.

Repeated Measures Designs

It often occurs that an experiment is designed in which the subjects are measured more than once during the course

TABLE 11–6. A Fictitious Example of a Randomized Block Design

Block	Treatment					Block
Musical Aptitude	Orff	Kodály	ETM	Gordon	Control	Means
Low	22.00	19.00	14.00	26.00	14.00	19.00
Medium	34.00	24.00	19.00	37.00	11.00	25.00
High	39.00	33.00	28.00	42.00	23.00	33.00
Treatment means	31.67	25.33	20.33	35.00	16.00	25.67

Source	SS	df	MS	F	*p* <
Treatment	735.33	4	183.83	6.66	0.012
Block (musical aptitude)	493.33	2	246.67	8.94	0.002
Treatment × Block	220.67	8	27.58		
Total	1449.33	14			

General Form

Source	SS	df	MS	F
t Treatments	$\Sigma n_j (\bar{x}_{.j} - \bar{x}_{..})^2$	$t - 1$	SS_t / df_t	MS_t / MS_e
b Blocks	$\Sigma n_i (\bar{x}_{i.} - \bar{x}_{..})^2$	$b - 1$	SS_b / df_b	MS_b / MS_e
$t \times b$ Error	$SS_{total} - SS_t - SS_b$	$(t-1)(b-1)$	$SS_{t \times b} / df_{t \times b}$	
Total	$\Sigma\Sigma(x_{ij} - \bar{x}_{..})$	$tb - 1$		

$\bar{x}_{..}$ = grand mean	x_{ij} = a cell value
$\bar{x}_{.j}$ = a treatment mean	n_j = number of cells for a treatment
$\bar{x}_{i.}$ = a block mean	n_i = number of cells for a block

of an experiment. This may occur if all the sampled subjects are provided each of the various treatments or when the researcher desires to determine the effects of a treatment a number of times during the experiment. The appropriate analysis of this form of experiment is called repeated measures ANOVA.

Repeated measures ANOVA is a special case of the randomized block design in which each block is a subject. In repeated measures situations, the subject is not randomly assigned to a treatment, but rather is subjected to all treatments. Consider an experiment in which it is desired to know the effects of extraneous sound on an individual's ability to do simple math problems. Four sound conditions exist: (1) silence, (2) sedative music, (3) stimulative music, (4) random pitch durations. In this experiment 10 subjects are tested doing simple math problems during each of the sound conditions.

Data for such an experiment are presented in Table 11–7. Note that the only ratio of interest is the main effect for sound condition. A between-subjects main effect also can be tested using the within-subjects mean square as the denominator in the ratio. Note that the formulas used in deriving the conditions main effect are the same as that used in determining the treatment main effects in the fictitious randomized block design example. To identify exactly where the means differed between the conditions, simple effects would have to be tested.

Other Designs

Analysis of variance provides a very flexible means for analyzing data from virtually all types of experiments and is treated much more extensively in texts by Glass and Hopkins (1984), Hays (1988), Winer (1971), and Winkler and Hays (1975). Full factorial models, randomized blocks, and repeated-measures designs have common applications in music research. Other designs, such as the *nested designs*, where a grouping variable such as type of ensemble, band or chorus, may be nested under school, require different variance partitioning than previously described designs. It is also possible to have various combinations of the types of models presented here, which are known as mixed models. The researcher should consult one of the texts cited for detailed descriptions of how to analyze data from such models.

MULTIVARIATE FACTORIAL DESIGNS

Fundamental Concepts

Frequently a researcher is interested in more than one dependent variable within an experimental design. Referring back to the experiments in Figure 11–2, you may recall these designs all have musical achievement as the one dependent

TABLE 11–7. A Fictitious Example of a Repeated Measures Design

Subject	Silence	Sedative	Stimulative	Random	Subject Means
			Sound Condition		
1	15.00	14.00	8.00	17.00	13.50
2	7.00	9.00	5.00	11.00	8.00
3	12.00	10.00	9.00	15.00	11.50
4	19.00	17.00	10.00	22.00	17.00
5	13.00	14.00	7.00	15.00	12.25
Condition means	13.20	12.80	7.80	16.00	12.45

Source	SS	df	MS	F	p <
Between subjects	170.20	4	42.55	18.11	0.001
Within subjects	202.75	15	13.52		
Sound conditions	174.55	3	58.18	24.76	0.001
Error	28.20	12	2.35		
Total	372.95	19			

General Form

Source	SS	df	MS	F
Between n subjects	$\Sigma n_i\,(\bar{x}_{i.} - \bar{x}_{..})^2$	$n - 1$	SS_b / df_b	MS_b / MS_e
Within subjects	$\Sigma\Sigma_{(x_{ij} - \bar{x}_{i.})}$	$n(t - 1)$	SS_w / df_w	
t Treatments	$\Sigma n_j (\bar{x}_{.j} - \bar{x}_{..})^2$	$t - 1$	SS_t / df_t	MS_t / MS_e
Error	$SS_{total} - SS_t - SS_b$	$(t - 1)(n - 1)$	$SS_{t \times b} / df_{t \times b}$	
Total	$\Sigma\Sigma_{(x_{ij} - \bar{x}_{..})}$	$tn - 1$		

$\bar{x}_{..}$ = grand mean		x_{ij} = a cell value	
$\bar{x}_{.j}$ = a treatment mean		$n_{.j}$ = number of cells for a treatment	
$\bar{x}_{i.}$ = a subject's mean		n_i = number of cells for a subject	

variable. This made univariate ANOVA models the most appropriate for these designs. If the researcher now desired to include two different measures of musical achievement, one being knowledge of musical concepts and the other musical performance skill, the univariate ANOVA would no longer be appropriate. The family of statistical models most appropriate for this new situation would be *multivariate analysis of variance* (MANOVA).

It has been common practice to analyze data from situations such as those just described with two separate univariate ANOVAs. This, however, leads to the great probability of obtaining a significant difference due simply to chance. MANOVA protects from this possibility by first simultaneously testing to determine whether there are any differences across the various dependent variables. MANOVA has the additional benefit of not only providing tests of significance about the dependent variables of interest, but also being able to provide an indication of the pattern of relationships between the dependent variables (Sheth, 1984).

MANOVA

One-way and multiway experimental designs with more than one dependent variable can be analyzed with MANOVA. The overall null hypothesis is tested by reducing the number of measures to a single value by applying a linear combining rule (Harris, 1985, p. 19). The weights of the combining rule are applied in such a way as to produce the largest possible value. It is this value that tests the overall null hypothesis. This set of weights is the discriminant function, which will be discussed in the "Discriminant Analysis" section below.

Overall Test A number of overall tests of MANOVA results exist. Wilks's lambda is the most commonly employed. Harris (1985, p. 169) identifies four reasons for this: (1) historical precedence, (2) it provides a fairly good approximation to the distribution of *F*, (3) it is a more powerful test under certain circumstances, and (4) the discriminant functions on which Wilks's lambda is based are easier to compute than are characteristic roots. In addition, Harris notes that Wilks's lambda has been shown to be more robust against violations of the multivariate normal and homogeneity of variance assumptions of MANOVA than is the greatest characteristic root criterion (p. 170). Many computer programs, such as SPSS^x MANOVA (SPSS, 1988), provide these statistics along with their approximations in the output.

Subanalyses Once a significant overall test has been identified, it is common to then look at the univariate subanalyses of variance in which each dependent variable is analyzed separately. This allows the researcher to identify which of the dependent variables is producing significant differences for the particular effect. Computer programs that compute MANOVA generally provide this output whether the overall test is significant or not. In addition to separate, independent univariate subanalyses, some programs provide step-down

subanalyses in which the variance of preceding variables to have been analyzed with ANOVA is removed from the following variables yet to be analyzed. In this manner, the effect of a theoretical ordering of variables on following variables can be determined. For instance, in our Experiment 2 example with the two dependent variables of music knowledge and music skill, it might be desirable to determine if overall differences of the musical aptitude main effect are independent between knowledge and performance. The analysis could be arranged so that the performance subanalysis ANOVA occurred first, with the knowledge subanalysis last. The step-down process would first test the separate, independent ANOVA for performance and remove the performance-related variance from the data prior to testing the final knowledge ANOVA. If the knowledge step-down ANOVA was not significant but the separate performance ANOVA was, it could be concluded that musical aptitude has a profound effect on musical performance achievement. In addition, musical performance achievement is shown to be strongly related to the acquisition of musical knowledge. This is because when the variance of musical aptitude and performance is removed prior to testing musical knowledge, musical knowledge is no longer significant. Of course, this is a hypothetical example, but it does show MANOVA's capacity to provide the researcher with a wealth of information about not only the effects of interest, but the relationships between the dependent variables as well.

MANOVA Example As part of a study on the effectiveness of two forms of instruction on aural and instrumental performance skills, Kendall (1988) reported a MANOVA. The 3 × 2 factorial design included three levels of musical aptitude (above average, average, and below average) and two types of treatment (comprehensive and modeling). The analysis included four dependent variables: Instrumental Eye-to-Hand Coordination Test (IETHCT), Verbal Association Test (VAT), Instrumental Performance Test (IPT), and the Melodic/Rhythmic Sight-Reading Test (MRSRT). An extended source table that includes the multivariate and the univariate ANOVAs for the significant multivariate effect is presented in Table 11–8. As can be seen, there was one significant multivariate main effect for treatment—the type of instruction received. The subanalyses indicate that the effects were attributable to the Verbal Association Test and the Melodic/Rhythmic Sight-Reading Test. Kendall found through inspection of the means that the comprehensive treatment was more effective on these two dependent variables than the modeling treatment.

MANCOVA

As in the univariate case, there is a multivariate analog to the analysis of covariance, the *multivariate analysis of covariance* or MANCOVA. The need for MANCOVA is to provide statistical control for factors that might influence the set of dependent variables of interest. For instance, achievement

TABLE 11–8. MANOVA and Subanalyses from Kendal (1988)

Source	Wilks's Lambda	Hypothesis Mean Square	Error Mean Square	F	p <
Treatment	.425			22.65	.001
IETHCT		314.07	864.74	0.36	NS
VAT		1,433.93	320.32	4.48	.030
IPT		220.11	718.61	0.31	NS
MRSRT		16,869.63	219.40	76.89	1.001
Music aptitude level	.825			1.69	NS
Treatment × Music Aptitude Level	.934			0.58	NS

Note: The degrees of freedom were not completely reported so are not included here.
Abbreviations: IETHCT = Instrumental Eye-to-Hand Coordination Test; VAT = Verbal Association Test; IPT = Instrumental Performance Test; MRSRT = Melodic/Rhythmic Sight-Reading Test.

has been found to be influenced by socioeconomic status. This relationship could be applied to the Experiment 2 of Figure 11–2 where there were two forms of musical achievement measured: knowledge and performance. The influence of socioeconomic status can be removed from the dependent variables prior to testing for main and interaction effects of gender and musical aptitude. This is done by removing the variance that overlaps between the two achievement dependent variables and socioeconomic status, the *covariate.* The result is a clearer picture of the true effects of gender and musical aptitude on the two dependent variables.

MANCOVA can be extended further to include more than one covariate. For instance, a researcher may desire to remove the effect not only of socioeconomic status, but also of home music environment prior to testing the gender and musical aptitude effects. Such procedures allow a great deal of statistical control over the data analysis. However, it is the researcher's responsibility to assure that the initial design is not flawed in some manner that would introduce systematic bias. When the research situation does not allow for early design control of experimental bias, then MANCOVA provides a means for reducing this bias in the data analysis.

Computing Resources

Most major statistical computer packages now provide programs or subroutines for performing complex MANOVA and MANCOVA analyses. Such programs may come under the title of *general linear model.* The choice of computer programs is dependent on the availability of programs to the researcher, the researcher's knowledge of the particular statistical package, the particular procedures that the researcher desires to apply, and the output the program produces. Today's powerful computing environments make the extreme calculating complexity of multivariate statistics no more difficult or time-consuming than simple univariate statistics. The researcher, however, should not choose to use a particular statistical procedure and then design a research study. Rather, the research study should be designed and

then the appropriate statistical procedures should be selected.

CORRELATION

In addition to studying the effects of independent variables on dependent variables and describing populations in various ways, researchers may wish to show relationships among variables or sets of variables. Correlation techniques facilitate quantification of relationships.

In simple terms, a *correlation coefficient,* which may range from -1.00 to $+1.00$, shows the size and direction of a relationship between two sets of scores. The larger the absolute value of the number, the stronger the relationship, whether it be positive or negative. The most common type of correlation, the one most researchers would assume another researcher is talking about without any further qualification, is the Pearson product-moment correlation. The two variables must be measured at at least the interval level, and homoscedasticity is assumed. *Homoscedasticity* essentially means that if all of the scores on one variable are categorized into classes in terms of the other variable, the scores within the classes are normally distributed and the variances of the scores within the various categories are equal. Furthermore, the observations are assumed to be independent, and the underlying relationship is assumed to be linear. In a linear relationship, as one variable changes, the other changes in such a way that a straight line describes the relationship. In a curvilinear relationship, the changes must be described by a curved line or series of line segments that alternate in direction. For a visual depiction of both linear and curvilinear relationships, see the graphing section below.

Two sets of ranks (ordinal measures) may be described by *rank-order correlation,* also known as Spearman's rho. Two sets of dichotomies may be related through *tetrachoric correlation;* one dichotomy and a continuous variable featuring interval measurement may be related through *point-biserial correlation.* Point-biserial correlation is commonly used in psychometrics to express the relationship between answering a particular single item correctly, a dichotomy, and overall test score, the continuous variable.

The relationships between a number of variables can be depicted in a correlation matrix. The correlation matrix is a diagonal matrix in that the values of the lower left portion of the matrix are replicated in the upper right. Hedden (1982), in a study of the predictors of musical achievement for general music students, reported a correlation matrix for one of the participating schools composed of the major variables of the study: Attitude Toward Music Scale (ATMS), Self-Concept in Music Scale (SCIM), Music Background Scale (MB), Iowa Test of Basic Skills (ITBS), students' gender, and Music Achievement Test (MAT). This correlation matrix is reproduced as a complete diagonal matrix in Table 11–9. The lower-left portion of the matrix is not filled in because the correlation for any one variable, say, gender, with another variable, say, MAT, is the same as the correlation for MAT with gender.

EXTENSIONS OF CORRELATION

The concept of the interrelationship among a set of variables has produced a great number of valuable statistical tools. These tools all utilize the variance shared between variables and the variance unique to particular variables to further the understanding of the relationships between the variables and to provide tests of hypotheses about these relationships.

Partial Correlation

It can happen that a researcher wants to know the degree of relationship between variables when the effect of a third variable is removed. In such situations, the researcher is interested in the *partial correlation*. The partial correlation is the correlation between two variables when the common variance of one or more variables is removed. This provides another form of statistical control by removing unwanted variance to provide a clearer view of the relationship between two variables.

The *partial correlation coefficient* can be mathematically defined as

$$r_{12\,3} = \frac{r_{12} - r_{13}\,r_{23}}{\sqrt{(1 - r^2_{13})(1 - r^2_{23})}},$$

where

r_{12} = correlation between variables 1 and 2,
r_{13} = correlation between variables 1 and 3, and
r_{23} = correlation between variables 2 and 3.

This partial correlation indicates the relationship between the variables 1 and 2 with the effect of variable 3 removed. Figure 11–4 presents a graphic means of showing this relationship using a Venn diagram. It should be noted that the complete pattern of relationships within the Venn diagram can be determined from such procedures and that these procedures can be extended to indicate the relationship between two variables with the effect of any number of variables removed.

Kendall (1988) provides correlations for three variables related to aural perception and instrumental performance: a measure of student ability to perform on an instrument heard melodic patterns, a measure of student ability to respond in solfege to heard melodic patterns, and a measure of instrumental performance (Table 11–10). A research question could be, "What is the relationship between ability to perform heard melodic patterns and solfege response ability when the variance associated with instrumental performance ability is removed from the relationship?" To answer this question, a partial correlation coefficient would be appropriate. The results of this analysis in Table 11–10 indicate that the partial correlation drops to .59 from the original bivariate correlation of .63 when the variance associated with instrumental performance ability is removed. The difference between the variances (r^2) of the bivariate correlation and the partial correlation indicates that the variance associated with instrumental performance ability in the relationship between the ability to perform heard melodic patterns and the ability to solfege heard melodic patterns is approximately 5 percent.

TABLE 11–9. Full Diagonal Correlation
Matrix from Hedden (1982)

Variable	ATMS	SCIM	MB	ITBS	Gender	MAT
ATMS	1.000	.642	.461	.226	.373	.352
SCIM		1.000	.603	.400	.085	.472
MB			1.000	.535	.159	.450
ITBS				1.000	−.040	.505
Gender					1.000	.034
MAT						1.000

Abbreviations: ATMS = Attitude Toward Music Scale; SCIM = Self-Concept in Music Scale; MB = Music Background Scale; ITBS = Iowa Test of Basic Skills; MAT = Music Achievement Test.

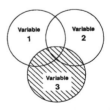

FIGURE 11–4. Partial Correlation between Variables 1 and 2 Controlling for 3.

TABLE 11–10. Example of Partial Correlation Using the Data of Kendal (1988)

	Correlation Matrix					r	r^2
	Heard/Played	Heard/Solfege	Instrumental Performance				
Heard/Played (P)	1.00			Bivariate (r_{PS})		0.63	0.40
Heard/Solfege (S)	0.63	1.00		Partial $(r_{IP\ S})$		0.59	0.35
Instrumental Performance (I)	0.40	0.28	1.00	Difference			0.05

Multiple Regression

Multiple regression is the extension of the case of a correlation between two variables to the case where there are a number of variables being related to a single variable. In multiple regression, the set of variables being related to a single variable are known as the *predictor variables*. The single variable to which the independent variables are being related is the *criterion variable*.

Multiple regression extends the bivariate regression

$$y = a + bx,$$

where the value y is predicted by a value of the predictor variable x multiplied by a weight and added to a constant, the *y intercept* in which only one variable x is involved, to

$$y = a + b_1x_1 + b_2x_2 + ... + b_kx_k,$$

where for a number of k variables there are corresponding weights. Thus, a single variable is predicted by a number of other variables.

The results of multiple regression produce a statistic of the degree of relationship between the predictor variables and the criterion variable, the multiple correlation coefficient (R). This statistic ranges from -1 to $+1$ and is interpreted in a manner similar to that used to interpret the simple bivariate correlation. As with the bivariate correlation, when R is squared (R^2), the proportion of variance in the criterion variable accounted for by the predictor variables is revealed. This variance can be tested with an F test. In addition, *beta weights,* the coefficients of the standardized predictor variables, are provided that indicate the relative importance of the predictor variables in predicting the dependent variable. The absolute values of the betas indicate the order of importance of the predictor variables for predicting the criterion. However, these values indicate only the relative importance of the predictor variables and not their absolute contributions to the prediction because their importance depends on other variables included in the analysis. This is because beta weights are related to partial correlation coefficients in that their value is a function not only of the correlation between the criterion variable and the particular predictor variable, but also of the correlations between all of the predictor variables.

The set of independent, or predictor, variables for a particular criterion variable can be analyzed in a number of different ways. The most obvious is to have all predictor variables simultaneously regressed on the criterion variable. Another method is to start with just one predictor variable and the criterion variable, after which another predictor variable is added, and another, until all predictor variables are included. The order of predictor variable entry can be determined on theoretical grounds, or it can be determined statistically. In either case, the amount of variance by which the prediction of the criterion variable is increased (or decreased) with the addition of a predictor variable can be tested. The testing of variance can be used as one basis for selecting which predictor variable should next enter the prediction equation. The variable that is the next largest contributor to the explained variance in the relationship of the predictor variables to the criterion could be selected.

The addition of predictor variables to the regression equation is called *forward stepping. Backward stepping* is also possible where the analysis begins with all predictor variables included in the regression equation and succeeding variables are removed from the equation on the basis of the smallest contribution to the prediction of the criterion variable or on some theoretical basis. A variety of other methods are available, and combinations of these methods are possible. The researcher must select the method that provides the analysis appropriate to the particular research study.

In a study of the factors that contribute to various aspects of work performed in first-year college theory courses, Harrison (1990a) reported a series of multiple regressions using the various aspects of the theory work as the dependent variables. Harrison used a forward-stepping procedure that determined "the best linear combination of statistically significant predictor variables ($p < .05$)" (p. 180). Table 11–11 (p. 160) contains the multiple regression analysis for the written work criterion variable for first-semester college students. In the table, Harrison provides a thorough compilation of the important statistics available for multiple regression. For this variable, the math score on the *Scholastic Aptitude Test* (SAT) is the most important predictor variable, which accounts for 19 percent of the variance (R^2 change), followed in order by high school grade-point average, accounting for an additional 6 percent of the variance, and whether the student was an instrumentalist, accounting for an additional 2 percent of the variance. The total amount of variance in theory written work grade accounted for by these three variables is 27 percent (R^2).

TABLE 11–11. Multiple Regression Predicting First-Semester Written Theory Work Grade from Harrison (1990a)

Variables	r	R	R^2	R^2 Change	F Change	$p <$	B	Beta Weights
SAT math	.43	.43	.19	.19	36.37	.001	.01	.32
HS GPA	.41	.50	.25	.06	12.41	.001	1.92	.26
Instrument	−.15	.52*	.27	.02	5.43	.022	−1.05	−.16

* = .0001 level.

Multiple regression is a very flexible analytical procedure. It can be used not only to identify the degree of relationship between a set of predictor variables and a criterion variable, but also to produce analyses of variance. Researchers who are interested in such uses and a more detailed discussion should consult the text by Kerlinger and Pedhazur (1982) as well as Chapter 15 of this handbook.

Discriminant Analysis

Discriminant analysis is used to study the case where there is a set of continuous independent variables predicting a single discrete grouping variable (Goodstein, 1987). For instance, a researcher may be interested in predicting the beginning band instrument on which students would be the most successful from a set of independent variables such as motivation, preferred sound quality, pitch acuity, parental desire, musical aptitude, physical capabilities, and parental support. This situation would require the use of discriminant analysis.

The particular variables used as independent variables are selected because they are believed to have some relationship with the single categorical dependent variable (Kachigan, 1986, p. 360). This parallels the process that would be used for the selection of the predictor variables for multiple regression. Whereas the calculation of the multiple-regression model centered on the determination of the set of weights for the predictor variables, discriminant analysis involves the determination of the discriminant function. The *discriminant function* is a set of weighted predictor variables for classifying a person or object into one of the groups of the dependent variable. The discriminant function is calculated in such a way as to minimize the classification error. It would hold that the larger the difference between the groups of the dependent variable on the measured independent variables, the fewer classification errors will be made.

The number of discriminant functions necessary to fully characterize the model will be equal to the number of groups in the dependent variable minus one. The process of calculating each of the discriminant functions is based first on determining the discriminant function that will have the greatest success in classifying the persons or objects into one of the dependent groups. Then, the next most successful function is calculated, and so on until all discriminant functions have been calculated. Each discriminant function, then, contains the set of weights that maximally separates persons or objects into one of the dependent variable's groups. Note that the reason for needing only one discriminant function less than the number of groups is that in the two-group case, if we know the person or persons classified into one group, all people left are classified into the other group—the fundamental principle of *degrees of freedom*.

Discriminant functions can be tested for their significance in differentiating the dependent variable groups beyond that expected by chance. The multivariate indicators of this significance are the same as frequently produced by the output of MANOVA: Mahalanobis D^2, Wilks Lambda, and Rao V. This is not surprising since a MANOVA determines the significant differences between groups on continuous variables. Indeed, Tatsuoka and Lohnes (1988, p. 210) have indicated that discriminant analysis is now used more in determining differences between groups than in its original use of classifying persons or objects into groups. This important relationship allows the researcher to gain additional insight into the group relationships of a MANOVA.

An additional method of evaluating the quality of the discriminant functions is to determine their accuracy of classification. The predicted and actual group memberships of a dependent variable can be compared. This process yields the proportion of people or objects correctly classified and the proportion misclassified.

As with multiple regression, the squared standardized discriminant function coefficients or beta weights can be analyzed to determine the relative importance of each independent variable in the classification of the persons or objects into a particular dependent group. The analysis of these weights provides significant insights about the independent variables and the groups of the dependent variable.

May (1985) studied the effects of grade level, gender, and race on first-, second-, and third-graders' musical preferences. As a follow-up to a MANOVA, May presented a table of discriminant analyses for each of these grouping variables. Table 11–12 presents the primary discriminant information for the grade-level effect. As can be seen, only function 1 was significant at $p < .05$ and accounted for 63 percent of the variance in the analysis.

Canonical Correlation

Canonical correlation provides a means of analyzing the relationship between two sets of continuous variables. Usually, one set of variables is considered to be the independent

TABLE 11–12. Discriminant Function Subanalysis for Grade Level from May (1985)

	Function 1	Function 2
Eigenvalue	.101	.060
Percent of variance	62.91	37.09
Canonical correlation	.303	.267
Wilks lambda	.857	.944
Chi-square	86.651	32.397
df	48	23
p	< .0005	< .0902

or predictor variables of the other set of dependent or criterion variables. The process can be conceived as an extension of multiple regression where there are two sets of weighted combinations of variables, one for the predictor variables and one for the criterion variables. The canonical correlation is the correlation between the derived predictor variables and the derived criterion variables. The derived variables are called *canonical variates*. In a manner similar to the calculation of the beta weights of multiple regression, *canonical weights* are derived that maximize the canonical correlation. The number of sets of possible canonical variates is equal to the number of variables in the smaller set of variables minus one.

The squared canonical correlation is the amount of variance shared by the derived canonical variates. The canonical correlation coefficients can be tested for significance. The squared canonical weights show the relative contribution of the individual variables to a derived variable in a manner parallel to the squared standardized regression weights of multiple regression. The amount of variance accounted for by a weighted combination of the original predictor variables in the opposite weighted combination of original criterion variables is not symmetrical. That is, the proportion of variance accounted for in the criterion variables by the predictor variables does not have to be equal. The predictor variables may account for more or less of the variance in the criterion variables than the criterion variables may account for in the predictor variables. This is because we are dealing with the original variables and not the derived canonical variates. The canonical correlation is based on the derived canonical variates, so its square indicates the proportion of variance accounted for by the canonical variates symmetrically. For a detailed example of canonical correlation, see May (1985).

Factor Analysis

Factor analysis is a family of techniques that can be used to study the underlying relationships between a large number of variables. The raw material for factor analysis is the correlation matrix or covariance matrix, which indicates the bivariate interrelationships of a variable set. Three primary techniques are under the factor analysis umbrella: principle components analysis, common factor analysis, and maximum likelihood factor analysis. Principle components analy-

sis creates underlying components that accommodate all the variance within a correlation matrix. Common factor analysis produces underlying factors that are based on the common or shared variance of the variables. Maximum likelihood factor analysis estimates the population parameters from sample statistics and can provide statistical tests of factor models.

Factor analysis can be utilized for a wide variety of research activities, including identifying underlying traits within a data set, developing theory, testing hypotheses, and data set reduction, among others. Having such wide applicability in the research process makes it a very powerful tool.

The various methods for performing factor analysis all attempt to define a smaller set of derived variables extracted from the data submitted for analysis. These derived variables are called factors or components depending on the type of factoring method used. The factors then can be interpreted on the basis of the weights each of the measured variables is assigned on each of the factors. Scores for each subject can be calculated for each factor based on the obtained weights. *Factor scores* then may be used for further statistical analysis.

The steps involved in performing a factor analysis are as follows: (1) determine the substantive reasons for performing a factor analysis, (2) obtain data with sufficient sample size to assure stability of the intercorrelation matrix between all the variables to be factored, (3) select the appropriate factoring method, (4) determine the appropriate number of factors to represent the data, (5) select the appropriate method of factor rotation to derive the weights upon which the interpretations will be based, (6) interpret the derived factors, and (7) compute the factor scores, if desired.

Principal Components Principal components analysis utilizes all the variance associated with the variables without partitioning the variance into constituent parts. The resulting components contain the variance unique to each variable, the variance each variable has in common with the other variables, and variance attributable to error (Asmus, 1989a). The principal components model is most appropriate when the variables being analyzed are believed to be quite different from each other and are considered to have large amounts of unique variance. The principal components model is useful for data reduction purposes in which it is desired to have the reduced set of derived variables account for the greatest amount of variance in the calculated factor scores.

Common Factor Analysis Common factor analysis explains the interrelationships between a set of variables by using only the variance that the variables have in common. Unlike the principal components model, this requires considerably fewer factors than the number of variables (Cureton and D'Agostino, 1983, p. 2). The common factor model partitions the variance associated with a variable into that which is common among the variables, that which is unique to the particular variable, and that which is associated with error. The common factor model is most appropriate when the variables being analyzed are similar to each other, as in a set of items to evaluate musical performance.

Maximum Likelihood Factor Analysis Maximum likelihood factor analysis uses sample statistics to estimate the population parameters of the factoring results. The procedure involves finding the population parameter values that are most likely to have produced the data (Harnett, 1982, p. 333; Lunneborg and Abbot, 1983, p. 222). Gorsuch (1983, p. 127) indicates that as the sample size increases toward that of the population the maximum likelihood estimate will converge to the population parameter, and that across samples the parameter estimates will be the most consistent possible. The maximum likelihood method allows testing hypotheses about the factors extracted through the use of chi-square tests. When the number of factors are tested for, a significant chi-square indicates that there is still significant covariance in the residual matrix (Gorsuch, 1983, p. 129). That is, too few factors have been extracted to this point. Maximum likelihood factor analysis has been developed for use only with large samples. The maximum likelihood model is most appropriate where it is desired to draw conclusions about a population from a large representative sampling of members of that population.

Confirmatory factor analysis extends the maximum likelihood model to allow the testing of a number of hypotheses beyond the number of factors. The most prominent applications have been in testing hypothesized factor structure, in testing the validity of a test or battery of tests, and in causal path analysis (Gorsuch, 1983, pp. 133–140).

Computing a Factor Analysis A factor analysis is based on a correlation matrix. It is imperative that the correlation matrix be as stable as possible, which is to say that the sample size on which the correlation matrix is based should be as large as possible. The subject to variable ratio should never be less than 3:1 and should exceed 5:1 (Asmus, 1989a, p. 4). Sample

sizes in excess of 250 tend to produce stable correlation matrices because of the relatively small error term for correlations with samples larger than this value. The measure of sampling adequacy, an indicator available in some computer packages, should never be lower than .5 (Kaiser and Rice, 1974).

Duke and Prickett (1987), as part of a study of applied music instruction, presented a correlation matrix that included the 10 items of a music teaching evaluation form used by 143 observers. This correlation matrix will be factor analyzed to show the steps involved in the factor analytic process. Duke and Prickett's correlation matrix has a subject to variable ratio of 14.3:1 and yields a measure of sampling adequacy of .847. These figures indicate that the correlation matrix had sufficient sample size to warrant factor analysis.

The items of the Duke and Prickett measure were adapted from Moore's (1976) evaluative instrument. All the items were selected to assess important aspects of the domain of music teaching in a private applied music setting. Because of this, it could be expected that there would be considerable variance shared between the items. This suggests that common factor analysis would be the most appropriate factor model for these data. The reason for factoring these data is not only to provide and exemplify the factor analysis process, but to provide some indication of the underlying constructs that are evaluated by the measure. Thus, because of the large common variance expected and because of the exploratory nature of the analysis, common factor analysis will be applied.

One of the most difficult decisions in performing a factor analysis is to determine how many factors best represent the data. Such decisions are usually based on previous research or theory, the eigenvalue-of-one criterion, a scree test in common factor analysis, and interpretation of the resulting factors (Asmus, 1989a, pp. 13–14). In Moore's (1976) original evaluation instrument, the items were divided into three categories: teacher interaction, musicianship, and creativity. In the table overlaying the scree test in Figure 11–5, it can be

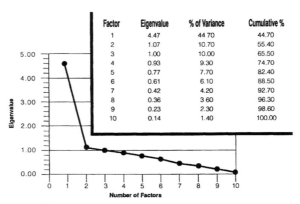

FIGURE 11–5. Scree Test of Duke and Prickett (1987) Data.

seen that three factors are indicated by eigenvalues of one or greater. The scree test of Figure 11–5 does not indicate any significant drop in the plotted line between the eigenvalues after the second eigenvalue so it yields little assistance in determining the number of factors. However, because of Moore's division of items into three categories and the eigenvalue-of-one criterion's indicating three potential factors, the number of factors in the analysis was constrained to three, which accounted for 65.5 percent of the variance in the correlation matrix.

The next decision in the factoring process is to determine the appropriate form of rotation to obtain simple structure. Simple structure maximizes the loading of a variable on one factor while minimizing the variable's loadings on the other factors (Asmus, 1989a, p. 19). Two major forms of rotation are available: orthogonal and oblique. Orthogonal rotation keeps the factors independent of each other and is most appropriate when it is believed that the resulting factors will indeed be independent or when it is desired to have the final factors maximally separated. Oblique rotation allows the factors to be related to each other. In the case of the Duke and Prickett data, the resulting factors logically should be related to each other because the items were selected to evaluate the

single concept of music teaching. Many types of orthogonal and oblique rotations are available. In a practical sense, the researcher is usually limited to those available in the computer statistical package being used. In the present case, SPSS[x] (SPSS, 1988) was the statistical package that provided oblimin oblique rotation for the analysis (Table 11–13). For a capsulated description of the major rotations, see Asmus (1989a).

The *factor pattern matrix* provides the relative weights for the variables on each of the derived factors. Interpretation of the factors is made in light of these weights along with the correlations of the variables with the factor that are presented in the *factor structure matrix*. The absolute values of the pattern weights are usually used to develop the initial conceptualization of a factor. Note that student participation and student attitude have relatively strong weights on the first factor and low weights on the other factors. This factor was labeled "Student Involvement." The second factor had strong weights on items that were interpreted to represent "Teacher Approach With Students." The final factor was interpreted as "Technical Aspects of Instruction."

A few items have relatively strong loadings on more than one factor; that is, the items *cross load*. Overall lesson effec-

TABLE 11–13. Factor Results of Duke and Prickett Data

Variables	Student Involvement	Teacher Approach With Students	Technical Aspects of Instruction
Pattern matrix			
Student participation (StPar)	0.747	−0.169	0.076
Student's attitude (StAtt)	0.588	−0.204	0.042
Quality of instruction (Instr)	0.044	−0.293	−0.001
Overall lesson effectiveness (OvEff)	0.280	−0.469	0.308
Attitude toward students (T-Att)	0.031	−0.849	0.041
Reinforcement effectiveness (Reinf)	−0.041	−1.004	−0.055
Lesson organization (Org)	0.141	0.045	0.931
Teacher's musicianship (Qual)	0.321	−0.087	0.432
Clarity of presentation (Clar)	−0.134	−0.082	0.281
Teacher's creativity (Creat)	0.113	0.008	0.199
Structure matrix			
Student participation (StPar)	0.843	−0.522	0.430
Student's attitude (StAtt)	0.687	−0.472	0.362
Quality of instruction (Instr)	0.165	−0.310	0.184
Overall lesson effectiveness (OvEff)	0.580	−0.764	0.677
Attitude toward students (T-Att)	0.397	−0.886	0.545
Reinforcement effectiveness (Reinf)	0.356	−0.956	0.515
Lesson organization (Org)	0.441	−0.554	0.953
Teacher's musicianship (Qual)	0.505	−0.471	0.592
Clarity of presentation (Clar)	−0.004	−0.189	0.283
Teacher's creativity (Creat)	0.178	−0.154	0.233
Factor Correlation Matrix			
Student involvement	1.000		
Teacher approach with students	−0.414	1.000	
Technical aspects of instruction	0.342	−0.581	1.000

tiveness, for instance, has fairly strong loadings on all factors. Logically a good lesson not only would involve the teacher's approach with students, the factor upon which this item loads most heavily, but also would incorporate significant student involvement and good technical aspects of instruction. Similarly, it is logical that the teacher's musicianship not only would load on the technical aspects of instruction, but also would influence student involvement—a fact long claimed by music teachers.

The factor structure matrix reveals many strong correlations of the items across the factors. This indicates that the derived factors are strongly related. As can be seen in the factor correlation matrix, the factors are indeed related to a considerable degree. Teacher approach, because of its negative weights, is inversely related to student involvement and the technical aspects of instruction. Student involvement, on the other hand, has a fairly substantial relationship with the technical aspects of teaching.

STATISTICAL BASED MODELING

Modeling

The conceptualization of theory generally produces a mental model of the interrelationships between the variables accommodated by the theory (Hanneman, 1988). Visual representations of the model help clarify the theory further. Such models can be evaluated statistically and, through modern computer systems, can be represented and manipulated in graphic form (Asmus, 1989b). The development of theory in music education has been a concern of many in the profession. The statistical methods available for evaluating theoretical models provide powerful tools for the testing and refinement of such theory.

The foundation of statistical based modeling is causation implied in the interrelationships between variables described by a theoretical model. The statistical correlation of variables provides the basis for explaining this causation. Although scientists and philosophers have debated the efficacy of such a position, several authors have clearly articulated the ratio-

nale for using intercorrelations to establish causation (Simon, 1985; Wright, 1921).

Statistical based modeling can be used to both test and develop theory. When theory is being tested, a formal model is established and then the causal links within the model are statistically tested. When theory is being developed, a formal model is evaluated statistically. Then, causal links are added or deleted until a model evolves that has satisfactory statistical and conceptual prowess. Two major types of statistical based modeling are available to researchers: *measured variable modeling* and *latent trait modeling*. In the former, variables that have been measured from a sample are used to form a model. In the latter, the underlying constructs of variables are used as the basis for the model.

Measured Variable Modeling

There are two forms of measured variable modeling: *causal analysis* and *path analysis*. Both are based on multiple regression of real-world data. That is, a variable identified as being caused by other variables in a theoretical model becomes the criterion variable in a multiple regression. The variables that cause the criterion variable are the predictor variables in this regression. The difference between causal and path analyses is that causal analysis uses the unstandardized regression coefficients or beta (*b*) weights to indicate the contribution of a causal variable to a dependent variable while path analysis uses the standardized regression coefficients or Beta (β) weights to indicate this contribution (Blalock, 1985).

Figure 11–6 presents a path model developed from a correlation matrix of variables extracted from a larger matrix presented by Harrison (1990b) in a study of music theory grade prediction. Harrison calculated the matrix from 121 first-year college music majors. Two types of variables exist within the system. *Exogenous variables*, caused by variables outside the system and linked with the curved line, are represented by total years of experience on musical instruments and whether or not the student had piano experience. *Endogenous variables* are caused by variables inside the system and are linked by the straight lines. The values in the figure

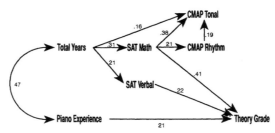

FIGURE 11–6. Path Analysis of Selected Variables from Harrison (1990b). (CMAP = College Musical Aptitude Profile; SAT = Scholastic Aptitude Test.)

are the path coefficients or β weights from the multiple regressions of a variable and its linked causal variables (Table 11–14).

The model was developed by placing the variables in their time ordering. Total years and piano experience would have been primarily determined prior to a student's having taken the SAT in late high school; the SAT would have been taken before the College Musical Aptitude Profile (CMAP; Schleuter, 1978), and the theory grade was assigned after the students had taken the CMAP. As Harrison found, music theory grade has no linkages from the two CMAP variables. Music theory grade is significantly predicted by the two SAT scores and whether or not the student had piano experience. These variables account for 38 percent of the theory grade. The strongest of the linkages is that between SAT math and the theory grade, as indicated by the path coefficient of .41. In the model, two variables play a pivotal role: SAT math and total years of experience. SAT math has substantial linkages with the CMAP variables and the theory grade while total years of experience has strong linkages with the SAT variables and the CMAP tonal variable. Does participation in music influence overall academic achievement? This model may suggest that this is so.

Latent Trait Modeling

Measuring the Unmeasurable Many in the field of music have claimed that a variety of important musical concepts are simply unmeasurable. *Latent trait modeling* provides a means of accounting for these "unmeasurable" concepts in complex systems. As with the measured variable modeling described earlier, latent trait modeling begins with a conceptual model that is depicted graphically. Then, through appropriate specification, the model can be tested using maximum likelihood principles.

A *latent trait* or *latent variable* is estimated from one or

more indicators of the hypothetical factor (Cooley, 1978; Jöreskog, 1979). Latent traits are underlying variables that can be conceived as the factors produced by factor analysis. Indeed, latent trait modeling can be considered a blend of multiple regression and factor analysis (Ecob and Cuttance, 1987). The procedure involves the development of structural equations that incorporate latent variables. A general computer program named LISREL (Jöreskog and Sörbom, 1989; SPSS, 1988) provides estimates of the coefficients in these structural equations (Jöreskog, 1982).

There are considerable benefits for the use of latent traits in music education research. Latent traits provide a means for accommodating concepts that are difficult to measure. Many variables in music education research contain considerable measurement error. Latent traits provide a means for compensating for this error (Jöreskog, 1979). Latent trait modeling also provides much greater information about the variables that have been measured, their interrelationships, error, and the theoretical model being investigated.

A Latent Trait Model of Theoretical Understanding The selected subset of Harrison's (1990b) correlation matrix used in demonstrating the concepts of measured variable modeling can be applied in demonstrating latent trait modeling. The model tested is presented in Figure 11–7 (p. 166). The figure follows the conventions that latent traits are indicated by ovals and measured variables are indicated by rectangles. In the model, three latent variables predict the dependent latent variable of theoretical understanding. The three independent latent variables are musical background, scholastic achievement, and musical aptitude. Note that the measured variables' paths do not point toward their associated latent variable. Rather, the opposite is true. This indicates that the latent variables are underlying causes of the observed variables or are intervening variables in a causal chain (Jöreskog, 1982, pp. 83–84). In the present model, the arrows from outside the model pointing toward variables or traits in the

TABLE 11–14. Path Analysis Multiple Regressions of Harrison's (1990b) Data.

Paths									
to	from	Beta	t	$p <$	R	R^2	df	F	$p <$
Theory Grade									
SAT	Math	0.41	4.80	0.00	0.62	0.38	3,117	23.75	0.01
SAT	Vrbl	0.22	2.68	0.01					
Piano	Exp	0.21	2.82	0.01					
CMAPT	Tonal								
SAT	Math	0.38	4.55	0.00	0.53	0.28	3,117	15.42	0.01
	Rhy	0.19	2.31	0.02					
CMAP									
Totl	Yr	0.16	1.99	0.05					
CMAP	Rhy								
SAT	Math	0.21	2.34	0.02	0.21	0.04	1,119	5.49	0.02
SAT	Math								
Totl	Yr	0.31	3.56	0.00	0.31	0.10	1,119	12.65	0.01
SAT	Vrbl								
Tot	Yr	0.21	2.34	0.02	0.21	0.04	1,119	5.49	0.02

Abbreviations: SAT = Scholastic Aptitude Test; CMAP = College Musical Aptitude Profile.

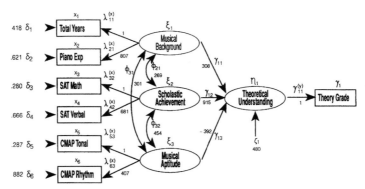

FIGURE 11–7. Latent Trait Model of Theoretical Understanding from Harrison's (1990b) Data.

model indicate measurement error. The various symbology used in latent trait modeling as it is implemented in LISREL is defined in Table 11–15.

The relationship between latent trait modeling and factor analysis is evident in the results of a maximum likelihood factor analysis with oblimin rotation of Harrison's data (Table 11–16). Note that the three factors, which account for 69.9

TABLE 11–15. LISREL Symbol Glossary

Symbol	Character	Description
η	eta	Vector of latent dependent variables
ξ	xi	Vector of latent independent variables
ζ	zetz	Vector of residuals (errors—random disturbances)
β	Beta	Matrix of the direct effects of latent dependent variables on other latent dependent variables
γ	Gamma	Direct effects of latent independent variables on the latent dependent variables
ε	epsilon	Vector of error terms
δ	delta	Vector of error terms
y		Observed dependent variable
x		Observed independent variable
Φ	Phi	Covariance matrix of the latent independent variables
Ψ	Psi	Covariance matrix of the residuals
Θ_ε	Theta$_\varepsilon$	Covariance matrix of the ε error terms
Θ_δ	Theta$_\delta$	Covariance matrix of the δ error terms
$\lambda^{(x)}_{bi}$	lambda$_{bi}$	Path arrow from ξ_i to x_b
$\lambda^{(y)}_{ag}$	lambda$_{ag}$	Path arrow from η_g to y_a
β_{gh}	beta$_{gh}$	Path arrow from η_h to η_g
γ_{gi}	gamma$_{gi}$	Path arrow from ξ_i to η_g
ϕ_{ij}	phi$_{ij}$	Path arrow from ξ_j to ξ_i
Ψ_{gh}	psi$_{gh}$	Path arrow from ζ_h to ζ_g
$\theta^{(\delta)}_{ab}$	theta$^{(\delta)}_{ab}$	Path arrow from δ_b to δ_a
$\theta^{(\varepsilon)}_{cd}$	theta$^{(\varepsilon)}_{cd}$	Path arrow from ε_d to ε_c

percent of the variance, are musical background, musical aptitude, and scholastic achievement. These are the same independent latent traits used in the latent trait model. Theory grade loads with the scholastic achievement variables as would be expected from the previous path analysis of these variables.

The overall goodness of fit for the latent trait model is tested with chi-square. In this case, the fit is quite good ($\chi^2 = 8.91$, $df = 9$, $p < .445$). The model accounts for 52 percent of the variance in the latent trait of theoretical understanding. The model indicates that scholastic achievement has significant impact upon theoretical understanding, musical background has considerably less influence, and musical aptitude is inversely related to theoretical understanding of first-year college music majors. Note that a number of the measured independent variables have error terms that are quite large. The ability of latent trait modeling to compensate for this error is demonstrated as the model does statistically fit the data and accounts for a significant proportion of the variance in theoretical understanding.

MULTIDIMENSIONAL SCALING

Scaling Concepts

Multidimensional scaling refers to a number of methods that provide spatial representations of the relationships between variables on a map (Green, Carmone, and Smith, 1989; Kruskal and Wish, 1978). The map's geometric representation of the data, usually in a Euclidean space of few dimensions, provides a visual means of interpreting the interrelationships of the variables and the variables' dimensionality (Young, 1987). The same mathematical models as employed by factor and discriminant analysis form the basis of multidimensional scaling (Nunnally, 1978). However, multidimen-

TABLE 11–16. Maximum Likelihood Factor Analysis of Harrison's (1990b) Data

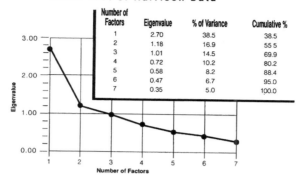

Scree Test of Harrison Data

Number of Factors	Eigenvalue	% of Variance	Cumulative %
1	2.70	38.5	38.5
2	1.18	16.9	55.5
3	1.01	14.5	69.9
4	0.72	10.2	80.2
5	0.58	8.2	88.4
6	0.47	6.7	95.0
7	0.35	5.0	100.0

	Pattern Matrix			Structure Matrix		
	Musical Background	Musical Aptitude	Scholastic Achievement	Musical Background	Musical Aptitude	Scholastic Achievement
Piano Experience	1.03	−0.22	−0.09	0.99	0.22	0.19
Total Years	0.41	0.14	0.17	0.50	0.34	0.36
SAT Verbal	−0.10	0.03	0.63	0.24	0.55	0.79
SAT Math	−0.02	0.22	0.69	0.09	0.31	0.62
Theory Grade	0.16	−0.11	0.73	0.34	0.29	0.72
CMAP Tonal	0.02	0.98	−0.09	0.27	0.94	0.39
CMAP Rhythm	0.02	0.28	0.07	0.11	0.31	0.20
Factor Correlation Matrix						
Musical Background	1.00					
Scholastic Achievement	0.28	1.00				
Musical Aptitude	0.29	0.49	1.00			

Abbreviations: CMAP = College Musical Aptitude Profile; SAT = Scholasti c Achievement Test.

sional scaling emphasizes the visual analysis of the variables in a space that reflects the variables' perceived similarities (Miller, 1989, p. 62).

Multidimensional scaling methods employ proximities of variables as input (Kruskal and Wish, 1978). The *proximities* are numbers that represent perceived similarities or differences among the variables. Typically, data are obtained by asking subjects to judge the similarity between two psychological objects. Computational methods are available that allow the use of data reflecting most levels of measurement. However, ordinal data tend to be most commonly employed. Correlations can be considered proximities as they may be conceived as indices of similarity or differences and are appropriate for analysis with multidimensional scaling (Kruskal and Wish, 1978, pp. 10–11).

Miller (1989) cites a number of advantages for multidimensional scaling: It has enormous data reduction power, subjects can easily make the similarity judgments often used for multidimensional scaling, it is easier to visualize and inter-

pret than factor analysis, the dimensions do not require specification prior to the analysis, in more complex stimulus domains it may sort out those attributes that are not important in making the required judgments, data of ordinal and nominal levels can be analyzed, and the data need not be related linearly.

An Application of Multidimensional Scaling

Larson (1977) presented the results of an investigation into undergraduate music majors' aural skills of melodic error detection; melodic dictation; and melodic sight singing in diatonic, chromatic, and atonal pitch categories. As part of his results, Larson presented a matrix of intercorrelations among the various aural tasks. An application of multidimensional scaling can be demonstrated by using Larson's correlations as proximity indices because they do indicate the similarity of the various aural tasks. The purpose

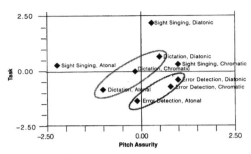

FIGURE 11–8. Multidimensional Scaling Solution of Larson's (1977) Data.

of scaling these data will be (1) to determine the similarities of the nine aural task combinations and (2) to identify the major dimensions characterized by the scaling procedures.

Figure 11–8 presents the variables as points in the two-dimensional Euclidean space of a solution that accounts for 99.1 percent of the variance in the scaled data. The center vertical and horizontal axes represent the two dimensions of the solution. The vertical dimension was interpreted as "task" while the horizontal dimension was interpreted as "pitch assurity." These interpretations were based on the variables' location along the two center axes. The error detection variables cluster along a diagonal plane, as do the dictation variables, and, with the exception of chromatic sight-singing, the sight-singing variables do as well. The tasks appear to be ordered from easy to difficult, with sight singing being the easiest and error detection being the most difficult. Another grouping of the variables can also be made. The atonal variables form a grouping in a diagonal plane opposite to those marked in the figure. The diatonic variables also group well in a similar diagonal plane. With the exception of chromatic sight singing, the chromatic variables form along this diagonal plane. As in the diagonal task planes, the pitch variables appear to be ordered from easy to difficult, with diatonic pitch tasks being the easiest and atonal pitch tasks being the most difficult. The chromatic sight-singing variable defies the overall logic of the map presented here. It could be that sight singing, a production task, interacts differently with pitch structure than the listening tasks of dictation and error detection.

NONPARAMETRIC STATISTICS

Fundamental Concepts

Nonparametric statistical tests have great value in music education as they are based on much less stringent assumptions than parametric statistics described to this point. The primary assumptions of nonparametric statistics are that the observations are independent and that there is underlying continuity to the variable in some cases (Conover, 1980; Gibbons, 1985; Siegel and Castellan, 1988). No assumption is made about the underlying distribution of the population from which the sample was drawn. Nonparametric statistics require only nominal or ordinal data. Parametric statistics, by contrast, require interval or ratio level data, make assumptions about the specific population distribution, and make inferences about population parameters.

Gibbons (1985, p. 29) suggests that nonparametric statistics should be chosen over parametric statistics when the assumptions required by parametric statistics are not satisfied by the data, when the fewest number of assumptions are met by the data, when sample size is small, and when a particular nonparametric test will provide a more adequate test of the null hypothesis. The mathematical simplicity of nonparametric tests adds to their attractiveness in that not only is their calculation simpler, but it is more likely that the user will understand and apply the tests appropriately (Conover, 1980).

Nonparametric Statistical Tests

Selection of the appropriate nonparametric statistical test depends on the particular null hypothesis being tested and the data's level of measurement. There are fewer nonparametric statistical tests than parametric tests. However, statistics are available for most situations involving traditional experimental designs. The nonparametric tests described here focus on tests relating to a single sample, related samples, independent samples, and measures of association. Single-sample tests are for those situations where only one group of subjects has been measured. Related samples are for when two samples have been measured but the samples are related in some way such as the same group being measured twice. Independent samples are two or more measured samples that are not related in any systematic way. Measures of association provide a means for determining the similarity or difference between two measures. For an easy-to-follow description of how to calculate the majority of statistics described here, the reader is directed to the work of Moore in the text by Madsen and Moore (1978) *Experimental Research in Music: Workbook in Design and Statistical Tests.*

One-Sample Tests In the case of research in which the entire set of observations on a variable are to be analyzed, the family of nonparametric one-sample tests may be appropriate.

CHI-SQUARE GOODNESS-OF-FIT TEST. The chi-square goodness-of-fit test determines whether an observed number of cases in each of a number of categories is the same as that expected by some theory. The procedure requires independent observations of a variable with the observations grouped into categories. The statistic assumes that the sample is random and that the variable has at least nominal level of measurement.

Suppose an elementary music teacher had taught a unit on tempo. The instructional goal was to have at least 70 percent

TABLE 11–17. Chi-Square Goodness-of-Fit Test
on Fictitious Data

Category	Observed	Expected	Residual
Faster	78	70.00	8.00
No Change	15	15.00	.00
Slower	7	15.00	−8.00
Total	100		

	Chi-Square	D.F.	Significance
	5.181	2	.075

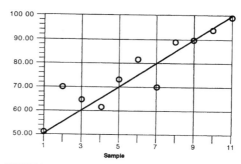

FIGURE 11–9. Fictitious Random Sampling of 11 Scores for a
Band History Test.

of the 100 students able to identify a change to faster when it occurred in music. The teacher assumed that 15 percent of the remaining group would not be able to detect any change and that the other 15 percent would indicate that the piece went slower when it indeed went faster. The teacher gave a single-item exam to determine the student's attainment. The data of this fictitious situation are presented in Table 11–17.

Note that in Table 11–17 the chi-square value has degrees of freedom equal to the number of categories minus one. The significance level in our fictitious sample is .075; this is larger than the .05 value of significance traditionally used as the lower bound of significance. Therefore, the statistic indicates no significant difference between the data's observed distribution and the expected distribution. The teacher's assumption that 70 percent of the students would be able to correctly identify an increase of tempo, with 15 percent not being able to detect a tempo change and 15 percent wrongly identifying a decrease in tempo, is supported by the chi-square goodness-of-fit test.

KOLMOGOROV GOODNESS-OF-FIT TEST. Goodness-of-fit tests determine if a random sample of some population matches an expected distribution. That is, goodness-of-fit tests test the null hypothesis that the unknown distribution of the sample is indeed known (Conover, 1980, p. 344). The example cited for the chi-square goodness-of-fit test actually tested the teacher's belief (hypothesis) that 70 percent of the class would be able to correctly identify increases in tempo, 15 percent would be unable to detect any change, and 15 percent would detect a decrease in tempo (a known distribution).

The Kolmogorov goodness-of-fit test provides a means for determining goodness of fit with ordinal data and provides a means for establishing a confidence region for the unknown distribution function. This test has benefits over the chi-square test when sample size is small and appears to be a more powerful test in general. The Kolmogorov test assumes that the data were drawn from a random sample and have some unknown distribution.

Suppose, for example, that a band director gave the 72 band students in the band a test to measure their knowledge of the historical aspects of the music that was being studied. A random sampling of 11 students' scores was taken to determine if the scores were distributed evenly between the minimum score of the class (50) and the maximum score of the

class (100). Figure 11–9 presents the data for the 11 randomly selected students with the hypothesized distribution of the scores plotted as a solid line. Note that distributions that are spread in such a manner are known as uniform distributions. The Kolmogorov goodness-of-fit test for this sample was .494 with an alpha level of .967. Thus, the band director can be statistically certain that the distribution of scores is uniform between the minimum and maximum of this test as based on this sample.

BINOMIAL TEST. The binomial test is used with dichotomous data, that is, data having each individual data point in one of only two categories. For instance, a question is answered either right or wrong, a student listens to the music or does not, or a trumpet student knows the fingerings or does not. Such data are tested with the binomial distribution, which indicates the probability p that the first of two possible events will occur and that the opposite event will occur with probability $q = 1 - p$. The binomial test has great versatility and can be applied in a considerable number of situations (Conover, 1980, p. 96).

The data for the binomial test are the outcomes of a number of trials where the result can be only one thing or another such as right or wrong, good or bad. Each of the trials is assumed to be independent of the others. The outcome of a trial is assumed to have the same probability for each and every trial.

Kuhn and Booth (1988) presented the results of a study on the influence of ornamented or plain melodic activity on tempo perception. In a series of tables they presented binomial comparisons of 95 elementary students' responses to various test items. The items required the students to listen to two musical examples and respond by indicating whether the second example was faster or slower than the first example or whether the tempos were the same (pp. 143–144). To demonstrate the use of binomial comparisons, the data of test item 2 will be used. Students responses for this item, in which there was no change in the second example, were 18 indicating slower, 53 indicating no change, and 24 indicating faster.

Figure 11–10 presents the various possible binomial comparisons for these data where the comparisons were tested for an even distribution of students in each of the two possible categories. That is, the test proportion was .50 or 50:50. Note that both the comparisons made with the correct no-change category are significantly different ($p < .05$) from being the expected proportion of .50. The comparison between the incorrect categories of faster and slower are not significantly different from the expected 50:50 proportion. The fourth pie chart was not contained in the Kuhn and Booth tables, but demonstrates a practical application of this test for music classroom situations. Consider a situation where it was desired that 70 percent of all the elementary students taking a tempo perception test would correctly identify that no change had occurred to the Kuhn and Booth item. After the number of students answering incorrectly either faster or slower were added together, the resulting value could be tested with the number of students answering the item correctly to determine whether the students had attained the 70 percent criterion. As can be seen, the number of correct responses does not achieve the 70 percent criterion level as indicated by the probability value p being less than .05.

Contingency Tables   A contingency table is a matrix of frequency data representing two or more categorical variables. Consider the situation where a high school music program wishes to know the makeup of their students by sex (male or female) and primary ensemble participation (band, chorus,

orchestra). The data could be displayed in a matrix such as the following, with sex across the rows of the matrix and ensemble type down the columns of the matrix:

	Band	Chorus	Orchestra
Male	34	30	12
Female	42	67	29

Contingency tables are usually described by their number of rows and number of columns; this is a 2 × 3 contingency table. As can easily be noted, contingency tables display a large amount of information based on nominal data. Additional information could be displayed in such a table, including various percentages based on the number in the rows, the number in the columns, or the total number contained in the table.

CHI-SQUARE TEST FOR INDEPENDENCE. Statistics are also available to determine various characteristics of a contingency table. Chief among these is the chi-square test for independence. The statistic assumes that the sample has been drawn at random and that each observation can be categorized into only one of the cells in the matrix. The hypothesis tested by this statistic is that the two categorical variables that make up the table are independent of each other.

Flowers and Dunne-Sousa (1990) reported a study of 93 preschool "children's abilities to echo short pitch patterns in relation to maintenance of a tonal center in self-chosen and taught songs" (p. 102). Within the report, a 3 × 3 contingency table is presented of students' age by self-chosen song category: modulating, somewhat modulating, and not modulating from the tonal center. Data presented in this table are used to provide an example of the results from a common computer program (CROSSTABS from SPSS[X], 1988) that demonstrates the amount of information that can be obtained from such frequency counts (Table 11–18). The table is an exact copy of the output from the SPSS[X] computer program. Note that the area at the top left of the display describes the content of each of the cells. The top-most value in each cell is the frequency for that particular combination of age and self-chosen song. The reader is encouraged to compare the table presented in the excellent article by Flowers and Dunne-Sousa with the computer output presented here. The authors reported the chi-square test for independence for this contingency table, which is contained at the bottom of Table 11–18. Note the significant chi-square value indicating that the two categorical variables are not independent. Rather, age is related to the ability to sing a self-chosen song on the tonal center. This led Flowers and Dunne-Sousa to conclude that "as would be expected, 3-year-olds comprised the largest proportion of modulating singers" (p. 107).

MEASURES OF ASSOCIATION FOR CONTINGENCY TABLES. The smallest form of contingency tables to which the chi-square test of independence can be applied is the 2 × 2 table. When a researcher wishes to establish the degree of association or relationship between the two categorical variables that define the contingency table, the *phi coefficient* is the most ap-

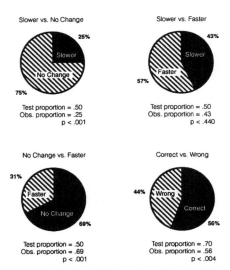

Slower vs. No Change

25%

Slower

No Change

75%

Test proportion = .50
Obs. proportion = .25
p < .001

Slower vs. Faster

43%

Slower

Faster

57%

Test proportion = .50
Obs. proportion = .43
p < .440

No Change vs. Faster

31%

Faster

No Change

69%

Test proportion = .50
Obs. proportion = .69
p < .001

Correct vs. Wrong

44%

Wrong

Correct

56%

Test proportion = .70
Obs. proportion = .56
p < .004

FIGURE 11–10. Binomial Comparisons Using the Data of Kuhn and Booth (1988).

TABLE 11–18. 3 × 3 Contingency Table Using the Data of Flowers and Dunne-Sousa (1990): Age (Preschool Students Age) by SONG (Type of Song Selected)

AGE	Count Row Pct Col Pct Tot Pct	Modulating 1	Somewhat Modulating 2	Not Modulating 3	Row Total
3 years old	3	13 68.4 31.0 14.4	5 26.3 14.7 5.6	1 5.3 7.1 1.1	19 21.1
4 years old	4	10 33.3 23.8 11.1	11 36.7 32.4 12.2	9 30.0 64.3 10.0	30 33.3
5 years old	5	19 46.3 45.2 21.1	18 43.9 52.9 20.0	4 9.8 28.6 4.4	41 45.6
Column Total		42 46.7	34 37.8	14 15.6	90 100.0

Chi-Square	Value	DF	Significance
Pearson	10.35247	4	.03489

propriate. This coefficient is a special case of the Pearson product-moment correlation (Conover, 1980). It is normally calculated from the chi-square value, which will always be positive. Therefore, the phi coefficient is a value that ranges from 0, independence or no association, to +1, dependence or perfect association.

For tables larger than 2 × 2, *Cramer's V* provides an appropriate statistic. It is a slightly modified form of the phi coefficient that accounts for a greater number of rows or columns. Cramer's V, because it is usually calculated from the phi coefficient, will also have a value that ranges from 0, independence, to +1, dependence. Cramer's V obtained from Flowers and Dunne-Sousa's (1990) data is .24.

The contingency coefficient provides another index of association. Its lowest value is 0, but its maximum value varies with the size of the table. The larger the table, the larger the potential maximum value (Gibbons, 1985). It is most appropriate when both nominal variables have the same number of categories. A contingency coefficient of .32 was obtained for the Flowers and Dunne-Sousa (1990) data. Note that there is a discrepancy between the Cramer's V and the contingency coefficient. In the Flowers and Dunne-Sousa case, Cramer's V is the more conservative.

Whereas the measures of association described above are those most commonly employed, a considerable number of other measures of association are available for analysis of contingency tables. These statistics all serve different functions in the analysis of the degree of association between the two categorical variables that comprise the contingency table. For further information, the reader is directed to statistical texts that emphasize contingency table analysis.

Tests For Two Related Samples

SIGN TEST. The sign test compares the differences between pairs of variables by using the sign of the difference between each pair. That is, if the second value of a pair is larger, a plus (+) is assigned; if the second value is smaller, a minus (−) is assigned; and a tie is not counted. The data pairs must have some natural relationship to each other, the data must be at least at the ordinal level of measurement, and the two variables should be mutually independent.

The data from 20 randomly selected high school band students who were measured on their preference for a band piece prior to rehearsing it and then measured again 6 weeks later just prior to the concert performance of this piece will be used to demonstrate the sign test (Asmus, 1987). The sign test will be used to determine whether the students' preference for the band work changed after the 6-week rehearsal period. The results of the analysis are presented in Table 11–19. From the table, we note that 15 students' preference actually declined while five of the students' preference increased. There were no ties. A significant difference ($p < .05$)

TABLE 11–19. Sign Test for Differences in Preference Before and After Rehearsal

Category	Students
− Differences (Preference 2 < Preference 1)	15
+ Differences (Preference 2 > Preference 1)	5
Ties	0
Total	20

2-Tailed $p < .04$

TABLE 11–20. Wilcoxon Matched-Pairs Signed Ranks Test of Price (1988) Data

	Mean Rank	Cases
− Ranks (postcourse < precourse)	13.93	14
+ Ranks (postcourse > precourse)	25.90	29
Ties (postcourse = precourse)		7
Total		50

$Z = -3.3568$ 2-Tailed $p < .0008$

TABLE 11–21. Cochran Q Test of Three Adjudicators' Success Ratings of 16 Marching Bands

	Unsuccessful	Successful
Music adjudicator	10	6
M and M Adjudicator	9	6
Percussion adjudicator	9	7

Number of Bands	Cochran Q	DF	$p <$
16	.4000	2	.8187

Abbreviations: M & M = marching and maneuvering.

between the first and second preference assessments is indicated. In other words, the students' preference for the band work did change significantly in a negative direction.

WILCOXON SIGNED RANKS TEST. The Wilcoxon signed ranks test is used to evaluate matched pairs of data from fairly small samples. The test assumes that the data are of at least the ordinal level of measurement and that the pairs are mutually independent.

Price (1988) used the Wilcoxon signed ranks test to determine if a music appreciation class affects the number of times a traditional composer is mentioned by students when "asked to list and rank their favorite composers" (p. 37). Price provides a thorough listing of these data in his Table 2. The results of the Wilcoxon signed ranks test on Price's data are presented here in Table 11–20.

The Price (1988) data analyzed with the Wilcoxon matched-pairs test produces a significant difference as indicated by the probability of $p < .0008$ for the test statistic Z. That is, there is a significant effect of the music appreciation class on the number of times formal traditional composers are mentioned by students who have completed the course. As the mean ranks in the table indicate, the students are likely to mention more formal, traditional composers after the course than before.

COCHRAN Q TEST. The Cochran Q Test is used to test the effect of a number of treatments when the effect of the treatment forms a dichotomous variable such as "success" or "failure." The data must be independent for each subject, the effects of the treatments are measured in the same manner for each treatment, and the subjects are assumed to have been randomly selected from the population. The Cochran

Q test tests the contention that all the treatments are equally as effective.

Three adjudicators' ratings of 16 marching bands participating in a contest will be used to demonstrate an application of the Cochran Q test. The bands were rated in the categories of music performance, marching and maneuvering, and percussion by an adjudicator assigned to each category. The success ratings were assigned by giving those bands with scores greater than the average in that category a success rating and those bands at or below the average in that category an unsuccessful rating. Table 11–21 presents the results of the Cochran Q test on the successful-unsuccessful data to determine if the judges rated the bands in a similar manner. As the probability figure indicates, there were no significant differences between the ways the judges rated the bands.

FRIEDMAN TEST. The Friedman test is employed in the situation where each subject ranks two or more items on some continuum. The test assumes that each subject's ranking is independent of all the other subjects, that each subject is ranking the same items, and that all subjects rank the items along the same continuum. The Friedman test evaluates the contention that the ranked items are distributed evenly across the continuum on which they were ranked.

LeBlanc, Colman, McCrary, Sherrill, and Malin (1988) presented the results of a study of the effect of tempo variation on the preferences of six age groups for traditional jazz. As part of the study, the authors presented the results of Friedman tests for each age group to determine if tempo affected the preference rating for music. Table 11–22 presents the relevant data taken from the tables and text of the research re-

TABLE 11–22. Means and Friedman Tests of Tempo Effect on Preference From LeBlanc et al. (1988)

Grade Level	Slow	Moderately Slow	Moderately Fast	Fast	Chi-square	df	p <
3	2.99	3.24	3.92	3.99	150.76	3	.01
5	2.47	2.58	3.23	3.50	186.10	3	.01
7	1.91	2.07	2.52	2.64	144.66	3	.01
9,10	2.07	2.40	2.82	2.88	164.38	3	.01
11,12	2.15	2.37	2.83	3.08	213.18	3	.01
College	2.88	3.18	3.51	3.58	91.54	3	.01

Note: The preference ratings had a possible range of 1 to 7.

port. Note that there are significant differences for each of the age groups. An inspection of the means led the authors to conclude that increasingly faster tempos brought increasingly higher preference ratings.

Independent Samples

MEDIAN TEST. The median test is conducted in situations where there are a number of samples measured on the same variable. The test does not require that the number of subjects in each sample be equal. The test does assume that each sample has been drawn at random, that the samples are independent of each other, and that the measurement scale of the variable is at least at the ordinal level. The median test is used to test the contention that all the populations from which the samples were drawn have the same median.

Consider the hypothetical case where a choral music teacher wanted to know if different forms of vocal warm-up would affect vocal performance. The teacher used three different classes: One received no warm-up (control group); another received a warm-up using staccato "ha" on a series of scales, rhythmic patterns, and arpeggios; while the final class received a warm-up on "mah-may-mee-moh-moo" on a comparable series of scales, rhythmic patterns, and arpeggios. After the warm-up, each student was tested as to vocal quality and flexibility using a performance assessment instrument the choral teacher had devised. Because the classes were intact, there was unequal sample size across the classes. The median test was applied to the vocal scores to determine whether the medians were different between the groups. As the results of this analysis indicate (Table 11–23), there was a significant difference between the medians. The table indicates that the control group had more scores below the median than any other group. The distribution of scores above and below the median was evenly split for the "mah-may . . ." warm-up group while the "ha" warm-up group had the majority of scores above the median. It could be concluded that the "ha" warm-up procedure was the most effective in this fictitious example.

MANN-WHITNEY U. The Mann-Whitney U test is used in situations similar to those of the median test, except that it is used when there are only two samples. The test is considered more powerful than the median test because it uses rankings of each sample in its calculation. There is an assumption with this statistic that the samples have been drawn at random from their populations, that the measurement scale of the variable is at least ordinal, and that the two samples are independent of each other. The Mann-Whitney

U tests the contention that the two groups have been drawn from the same population.

Flowers (1988) used the Mann-Whitney U test to determine differences between two groups of elementary education majors on their pretest-posttest differences of rated preference for four symphonic works. One of the two groups received music appreciation lessons on the symphonic works while the other group taught the music to elementary school students. The analysis performed on the posttest gain scores led Flowers to conclude that, "although both groups had increased their preference ratings, there was no significant difference between the groups in amount of gain ($z = -1.45, p = .15$)" (p. 25).

KOLMOGOROV-SMIRNOV TWO-SAMPLE TEST. The Kolmogorov-Smirnov two-sample test is used to test the contention that the scores in two independent samples are distributed in the same manner. The assumptions of this test are that the samples have been drawn at random, that the samples are mutually independent of each other, and that the data are at least at the ordinal level of measurement.

The data from a marching band contest will be used to demonstrate the Kolmogorov-Smirnov two-sample test. In the contest, bands competed in one of two divisions: Class A and Open Class. Class A bands tended to be smaller and not as advanced musically or in their presentation as the Open Class bands. The total scores five adjudicators assigned in the areas of music performance, marching and maneuvering, general effect, percussion, and auxiliary groups are used as data. The Kolmogorov-Smirnov test is applied to determine if the two distributions of total scores were the same for Class A bands as for Open Class bands. The results appear in Table 11–24 and Figure 11–11 (p. 174). A significant difference is detected between the score distributions of the Class A bands and the Open Class bands. As can be seen in Figure 11–11, Open Class bands not only had higher total scores than Class A bands, but the distribution of scores has a different shape.

KRUSKAL-WALLIS ANALYSIS OF VARIANCE. The Kruskal-Wallis ANOVA is used in the situation where there are more than two independent samples. The statistic is based upon a ranking of the entire set of data to test the contention that all of the population distributions represented by the samples are identical. The assumptions are that the samples are drawn from their respective populations at random, that the samples are mutually independent, and

TABLE 11–23. Median Test of Hypothetical Choral Data

	Control Group	Warm-up "ha"	Warm-up "mah-may . . ."
Scores greater than the median	3	11	9
Scores less than the median	15	3	9

Cases	Median	Chi-Square	DF	Significance
50	27.0	12.3303	2	.0021

TABLE 11–24. Kolmogorov-Smirnov 2-Sample Test of Marching Band Contest Scores

Band Level	n
Class A	12
Open Class	4
Total	16

K-S Z	2-Tailed p <
1.732	.005

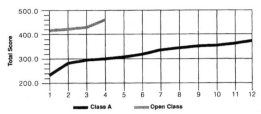

FIGURE 11–11. Distributions of Sorted Marching Band Scores.

that the variable upon which all subjects were assessed is at least at the ordinal level of measurement.

Flowers (1983), in a study of vocabulary and listening instruction on nonmusicians' descriptions of changes in music, used the Kruskal-Wallis ANOVA to test for differences between four experimental groups on pre-post verbal description gain scores. The verbal description scores were obtained by counting the number of references to elements of music made in response to changes heard in a musical excerpt. The four experimental groups included a contact control group, which received no instruction in vocabulary or listening experiences; a vocabulary group, which received instruction in music vocabulary; a listening group, which was provided with music listening experiences; and a vocabulary plus listening group, which received both vocabulary instruction and listening experiences. The Kruskal-Wallis test indicated a significant difference in the mean rankings of the gain scores for each of the four groups ($H = 17.25$, $df = 3$, $p < .001$).

DUNN'S MULTIPLE COMPARISON PROCEDURE. Following a significant Kruskal-Wallis one-way analysis of variance, Dunn's multiple-comparison procedure can be applied to determine the exact location of the mean rank differences. This allows the researcher to determine which of the populations included in the Kruskal-Wallis analysis significantly differ from each other. Flowers (1983), in the study described above, followed the significant Kruskal-Wallis analysis of variance with Dunn's multiple-comparison procedure on the four groups in her study. She found that "vocabulary plus listening produced significantly higher verbal descriptive scores than vocabulary only or contact control conditions, but not significantly different from listening only" (p. 184). Table 11–25 duplicates that provided by Flowers to support her conclusion.

TABLE 11–25. Mean Ranks of Pre-Posttest Differences Described by Flowers (1983)

Contact Control	Vocabulary Only	Listening Only	Vocabulary Plus Listening
46.44	54.37	67.50	81.69

Note: Table is duplicated from Flowers (1983). Underlines represent no differences at the .05 level. Those means not connected are significantly different.

GRAPHIC DATA ANALYSIS METHODS

For most individuals, especially those with little familiarity with statistics, graphic displays of research data provide the most easily grasped methods for understanding the data. The advent of small, yet powerful microcomputers with graphic capabilities has created a wealth of systems for the graphing of research data. Graphic methods can be as simple as a display of the number of people within a certain category through the use of bar graph or pie chart or as complex as the interaction of data through real-time display of data in multidimensional space.

Graphic methods of data analysis are expanding daily. Graphic methods no longer entail only the display of data; graphic interfaces can be used to cause the calculation of various statistics. An example of this was provided in this chapter's section on path analysis. As a whole, graphic methods help the researcher better conceptualize the research and thus allow a better understanding of the variables involved and the nature of the research study than is possible through purely numerical methods. Graphic methods have the additional benefit of utilizing less of the researcher's time in analysis of the data because of the relative ease of interpreting graphic data displays over numeric data displays, though graphic data displays do use a much greater proportion of computer time.

Throughout this chapter various forms of graphic displays have been provided to assist the reader in understanding the various concepts being discussed. This section will present some of the major graphic methods in greater detail. The methods surveyed will only skim the surface of the tremendous number of graphic analysis methods available.

Graphing Frequencies

One-Dimensional Frequency Plots The graphing of frequencies is often needed when the characteristics of a population or phenomenon are required. The graphing of frequencies can be done through the use of bar graphs or pie charts. Figure 11–12 presents a pie chart that displays the proportion of responses teachers made in the final rating of an inservice workshop experience. Note that out of the four possible categories in the rating scale, 84 percent were either

No "poor" ratings were indicated.

FIGURE 11-12. Teacher Ratings About the Quality of an In-service Workshop.

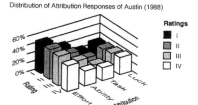

FIGURE 11-13. Proportion of Attributions for Different Division Ratings.

"excellent" or "good." The "fair" portion of the pie chart has been exploded to emphasize the 16 percent of the teachers who may not have had the level of experience that they had actually desired.

Three-Dimensional Frequency Plots An extension of the single-dimension frequency plot is the three-dimensional frequency plot. Consider the data of Austin (1988), where, in a study of elementary band students' music motivation, he provided the number of responses in the attribution categories of "Luck," "Task Difficulty," "Ability," and "Effort" for each of the recipients of four different division ratings: I, II, III, and IV. The frequency data were converted to percentages and are graphically displayed in Figure 11-13. This display is a three-dimensional bar graph where the vertical dimension represents the frequency of response and the other two dimensions represent the various categories involved. It can be seen in the figure that the most-used attribution category by the elementary students for all the division categories was "Effort." The least used was "Task Difficulty". Note, however, that there seems to be a slight increase in the use of Luck attributions with lower performance ratings.

Describing the Distribution of Interval Data

Frequency Polygon The frequency polygon displays data in line graph form with the vertical or *y*-axis representing the frequency with which the particular score occurred. The horizontal or *x*-axis of the frequency polygon is the range of interval scores for the variable under analysis. Figure 11-14 presents a frequency polygon of the scores participants in a

summer music workshop made on a 12-item knowledge test. The figure shows that the most commonly occurring score was 9 and that moving away from this score the frequency of the scores declines. If the sample size approached infinity, we would expect the frequency polygon to resemble the normal curve.

Frequency Histogram The frequency histogram is similar to the frequency polygon, but rather than having the information displayed as a line graph, a bar graph format is used. The *x*-axis remains the range of scores, and the *y*-axis is the frequency of occurrence of the particular scores. Figure 11-15 (p. 176) presents, among other information, the frequency histograms for two different sets of marching band contest scores. The sets of scores are for the same bands at the same contest in two different years. On top of each histogram, the normal curve has been plotted for the data with the same mean and representing the overall distribution of the scores. As can be seen, neither set of scores is distributed normally. Most of the scores tend to be below the mean.

Box Plots Above each frequency histogram in Figure 11-15 is a box plot that also characterizes the distribution of the respective set of marching band scores. The arrows indicate what each of the different points on the box plot represents. If the scores were normally distributed, the median line would be in the center of the box and the box would be centered on the line representing the range of scores from the minimum to the maximum. The small vertical tick mark at the extremes of the range line presents the tenth and nineti-

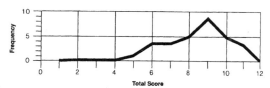

FIGURE 11-14. Frequency Polygon of Scores on a Summer Music Workshop Knowledge Test.

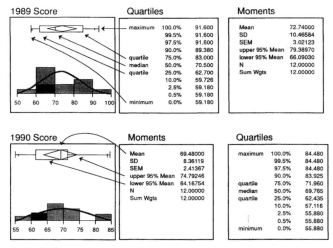

FIGURE 11–15. Frequency Histograms and Box Plots of Marching Bands' Contest Scores for Two Different Years.

eth percentiles respectively. Had the distribution been more normal, the other percentiles in the quantiles table would have been displayed. The diamond characterizes the distribution's mean and the 95 percent confidence intervals for the mean. If the distribution were normal, the median line would appear in the exact center of the diamond.

Figure 11–15 also characterizes the growing trend for graphics analysis programs to provide a wide variety of statistical information. The figure is a slightly modified form of the output from the graphics analysis package JMP (SAS, 1989). The modifications were necessary so that the arrows could be added to define the various points in the box plots.

Plots of Means

Plotting the means for various subgroups on a variable or plotting the means on a number of different variables for a particular sample is a common practice in the analysis and reporting of data. Such plots help determine particular trends inherent in the data or allow the researcher to determine relationships between the groups of variables of interest. In most cases, the vertical y-axis characterizes the value of the mean while the x-axis characterizes the particular subgroups or variables of interest.

One-Dimensional Mean Plots One of the most common forms of mean plots are those created after an analysis of variance that produced a significant interaction. The means for the various groups involved in the interaction are plotted

with the vertical y-axis representing the magnitude of the mean and the horizontal x-axis representing the grouping variable's categories. Kantorski (1986), as part of a study on the effects of accompaniment intervals and register on string instrumentalists' intonation, provided a graph of the significant register by accompaniment interaction that he obtained. Figure 11–16 is a copy of that graph. The crossed lines indicate the interaction. It can be noted that the upper register tends to be further from tempered intonation for all intervals but the unison. For the case of unison intervals, the upper register more closely approximates tempered intonation than the lower register.

LeBlanc et al. (1988, p. 156) presented the results of a study on "the effect of four levels of tempo on the self-reported preferences of six different age-groups for traditional jazz music listening examples." In their report, the authors presented a figure that plotted the preference means across all tempos for each of the age groups. The values reported by the authors were used to replicate this graph in Figure 11–17. The original graph of LeBlanc and colleagues included only the linked squares. As can be seen, the means have a decidedly curvilinear form, with the preference for traditional jazz dropping to its lowest point for the grade 7 group. This version of the graph has utilized the capabilities of the graphing program to overlay a curvilinear trend line and its associated statistics. The fit of the curved line is extremely good with these data. This is verified by the R^2 value, which indicates that 94.5 percent of the variance in the means is accounted for by the curved line. This represents an R value of .972, indicating a very substantial fit.

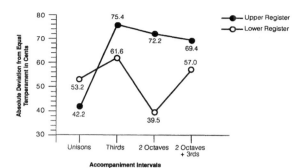

FIGURE 11–16. Plot of Two-Way ANOVA Interaction of Register and Accompaniment Intervals Duplicated from Kantorski (1986).

Two-Dimensional Mean Plots The plots of means in which there are two grouping variables of interest are often best handled by plotting the data in three-dimensional space: one dimension representing the magnitude of the means and the other two dimensions representing the two categories of interest. The data of LeBlanc et al. (1988) described above will be utilized to demonstrate this application. The effect of the grade level and tempo categories are characterized in a single graph in Figure 11–18 (p. 178). The curvilinear relationship between grade level and preference for traditional jazz noted earlier is clearly seen in this three-dimensional plot. The effect, as shown by this plot, is most pronounced for slow pieces, though there appears to be a steeper slope for the lower grades at faster tempos. The figure also indicates a tendency in all age groups for preference to rise as the tempo becomes faster. This effect is lowest for the grade 7 group, which has the overall lowest preference for traditional jazz.

Plotting Relationships

Scattergrams Scattergrams are the plotting of each individual data point by indicating the point's relative magnitude on two variables. One variable's magnitude is characterized by the vertical y-axis, and the other variable's magnitude is characterized by the horizontal x-axis. The marching band contest data for two consecutive years will be utilized to provide an example of the scattergram. Figure 11–19 (p. 178) displays the location of the juncture of each participating band's 1989 contest score with their 1990 contest score. It can be seen that the scores are distributed in a diagonal form moving from lower left to upper right. This ascending diagonal form is characteristic of variables that have a positive relationship. Variables with a negative relationship distribute the scores in a diagonal from upper left to lower right. No relationship would be indicated by a random spread of the points on the graph.

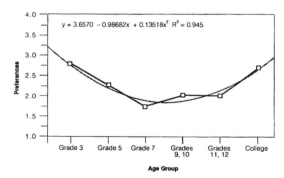

FIGURE 11–17. Plot of Jazz Preference Means from LeBlanc et al. (1988).

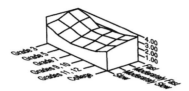

FIGURE 11–18. Three-Dimensional Plot of the Effect of Grade Level and Tempo on Means for Traditional Jazz Obtained by LeBlanc et al. (1988).

Figure 11–19 has the linear trend line plotted on the graph. The tabular information indicates that the two sets of scores have 70 percent of their variance in common. The dotted lines represent the 95 percent confidence intervals for scores predicted with the displayed regression information.

Multidimensional Graphing Multidimensional graphing is possible today in real time. This form of graphing allows items to be plotted as in a scattergram with an additional one or more dimensions added. Usually multidimensional graphing limits the plots to three-dimensional space as this is all that can be easily handled on a computer screen. Each dimension of the space represents another interval or ratio level variable. The interesting aspect of multidimensional graphing is that the data can be "spun" in space so that the relationship between the three variables can be viewed from any possible angle.

Semantic differential data collected from high school students in response to two different musical excerpts provide an excellent example of multidimensional graphing. Semantic scales are bipolar adjectives, such as beautiful-ugly, separated by a seven-point continuum. Subjects respond to an

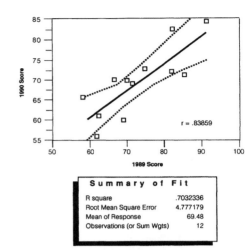

Summary of Fit	
R square	.7032336
Root Mean Square Error	4.777179
Mean of Response	69.48
Observations (or Sum Wgts)	12

FIGURE 11–19. Plot of the Marching Band Scores for Two Consecutive Years.

object or event by checking the point along the continuum that best reflects their assessment of the object or event on the bipolar adjective scale. Semantic scales typically form three groupings: activity, evaluation, and potency. In the present data, a fourth grouping reflective of preference was added. The pattern weights from a three-dimension, common factor analysis of the data with oblique rotation were plotted using a graphing program with multidimensional capabilities. The plot was rotated in space until the formulation contained in Figure 11-20 was obtained.

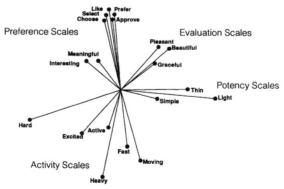

FIGURE 11–20. Three-Dimensional Plot of Four Sets of Semantic Differential Scales.

The display of Figure 11–20 was created by having lines drawn from the central point of the plot to each of the variable points within the graph. This is frequently a useful aid in identifying clusters of variables. The four groups of semantic scales are apparent in Figure 11–20. The figure reveals that the semantic scale hard-soft is across from the potency scales to which it belongs. This is because the scale should have been recorded to soft-hard; this would move it to within the cluster of potency scales. Note also that the interesting and meaningful scales cluster together slightly apart from the evaluation and preference groupings. However, these scales are in the same general region as preference and evaluation. The heavy-light scale is interesting in that it is clearly located within the region of the activity scales, but it is typically found in other studies within the potency scales.

WHEN TO USE WHAT STATISTIC

Selecting the most appropriate statistic to use in a particular situation must be tempered by theoretical and practical considerations. Theoretically, the selection of the statistic should be based on the purpose of the research as specifically described in a research question or null hypothesis. In addition, the characteristics of the data collected will reduce the number of statistical possibilities and aid greatly in the selection of the most appropriate statistic. Practically, researchers will be limited by the computing resources available and their knowledge of statistics. The hope is that the latter limitations have been lessened somewhat by this chapter as lack of knowledge is the weakest excuse for the application of inappropriate statistics.

The initial decision is to use either parametric or nonparametric statistics. Elsewhere in this chapter various facets of this issue have been discussed at length. After the calculation of descriptive statistics and, possibly, the production of frequency histograms and/or box plots, the decision can be made if the sample size is sufficient and the distribution is approximately normal. In general, if these conditions are

met, then parametric statistics should be applied. If not, nonparametric statistics should be applied.

The next decision is to determine the type of statistic that will be applied. This decision is based on the particular research question or null hypothesis that has been established to guide the research process. The choices for parametric statistics are somewhat greater than for nonparametric statistics, as can be seen in Figure 11–21.

The actual statistical procedure that is applied must be determined from both the particular null hypothesis and the type of data collected. For instance, a researcher may wish to predict from five variables, known to be normally distributed, which musical experience a student will have in high school: band, chorus, general music, orchestra. Because there is more than one predictor variable, one of two multivariate relational procedures could be applied: multiple regression or discriminant analysis. Because the dependent variable is a categorical variable that describes the group to which a person belongs, discriminant analysis would be the statistic of choice.

A flow chart describing the various categories of parametric statistics is contained in Figure 11–22 (p. 180), and a flow chart describing the various categories of nonparametric statistics is contained in Figure 11–23 (p. 180). These flow charts do not include all existing statistics, but do cover those that have been discussed in this chapter. These statistics, the authors believe, are those that have found the greatest applicability in music education.

CONCLUSION

This chapter has attempted to describe quantitative methods applicable in music education. It is hoped that, by description and example, the reader has become acquainted with the variety of available quantitative and statistical procedures that can provide significant insight into musical processes. Although they are not the entirety of available quantitative methods, the procedures described here are those

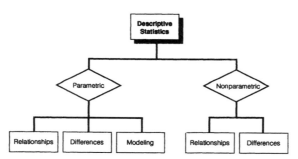

FIGURE 11–21. Flow Chart Leading to Major Type of Statistic To Be Applied.

180 • RESEARCH MODES AND TECHNIQUES

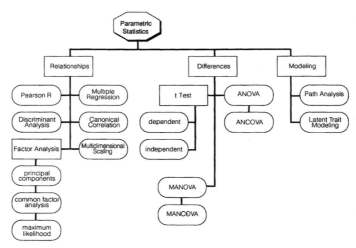

FIGURE 11–22. Flow Chart of Parametric Statistic Categories.

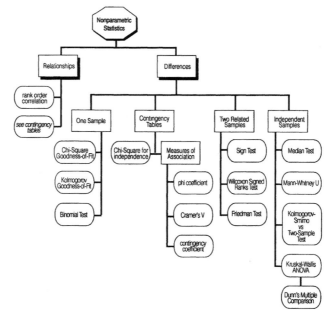

FIGURE 11–23. Flow Chart of Nonparametric Statistic Categories.

frequently applied in music education research, evaluation, and assessment or are those that, in the authors' belief, have significant potential to enhance knowledge about musical processes.

Today the reader need not be discouraged by the mathematical complexity of some of the procedures described here. Rather, if the researcher has selected the appropriate statistic, understands the assumptions that the statistic makes, and can interpret the results produced by the statistical procedure, modern computing power takes care of the mathematical details. This frees researchers from the tedium of the mathematics of the statistic and allows them to spend more time conceptualizing the research and understanding the implications of the results.

References

Asher, J. W. (1976). *Educational research and evaluation methods.* Boston: Little, Brown and Company.

Asmus, E. P. (1987). *The effects of rehearsing a musical work on the aesthetic perceptions of band students: A pilot study.* Paper presented at the Western Divisional Meeting of the Music Educators National Conference, Sacramento, April, 1987.

Asmus, E. P. (1989a). Factor analysis: A look at the technique through the data of Rainbow. *Bulletin of the Council for Research in Music Education, 101,* 1–29.

Asmus, E. P. (1989b). Computer-based modeling of music concepts for testing, evaluating, and refining theory. *Psychomusicology, 8,* 171–182.

Austin, J. R. (1988). The effect of music contest format on self-concept, motivation, achievement, and attitude of elementary band students. *Journal of Research in Music Education, 36,* 95–107.

Best, J. W. (1981). *Research in education* (4th ed.) Englewood Cliffs: Prentice-Hall.

Best, J. W., and Kahn, J. V. (1989). *Research in education* (6th ed.). Englewood Cliffs: Prentice-Hall.

Blalock, H. M. (Ed.)(1985). *Causal models in the social sciences* (2nd ed.). New York: Aldine Publishing.

Borg, W. R., and Gall, M. D. (1979). *Educational research: An introduction.* New York: Longman.

Boyle, J. D. (1974). Overview. In J. D. Boyle (Comp.), *Instructional objectives in music* (pp. 79–82). Vienna: Music Educators National Conference.

Boyle, J. D., and Radocy, R. E. (1987). *Measurement and evaluation of musical experiences.* New York: Schirmer Books.

Bruning, J. L., and Kintz, B. L. (1977). *Computational handbook of statistics* (3rd ed.) Glenview: Scott, Foresman.

Chatfield, C., and Collins, A. J. (1980). *Introduction to multivariate analysis.* London: Chapman and Hall.

Cohen, J. (1988). *Statistical power analysis for the behavioral sciences* (2nd ed.). Hillsdale: Lawrence Erlbaum Associates.

Conover, W. J. (1980). *Practical nonparametric statistics* (2nd ed.). New York: John Wiley.

Cooley, W. W. (October, 1978). Explanatory observational studies. *Educational Researcher, 7*(9), 9–15.

Cronbach, L. J. (1971). Test validation. In R. L. Thorndike (Ed.), *Educational measurement* (pp. 443–507). Washington: American Council on Education.

Cureton, E. E., and D'Agostino, R. B. (1983). *Factor analysis: An applied approach.* Hillsdale: Lawrence Erlbaum Associated.

Darrow, A., Haack, P., and Kuribayashi, F. (1987). Descriptors and preferences for Eastern and Western music by Japanese and American nonmusic majors. *Journal of Research in Music Education, 35,* 237–248.

Das, M. N., and Giri, N. C. (1986). *Design and analysis of experiments* (2nd ed.). New York: John Wiley.

Duke, R. A., and Prickett, C. A. (1987). The effect of differentially focused observation on evaluation of instruction. *Journal of Research in Music Education, 35,* 27–37.

Duncan, D. B. (1955). Multiple range and multiple F tests. *Biometrics, 11,* 1–42.

Ebel, R. L., and Frisbie, D. A. (1986). *Essentials of educational measurement* (4th ed.). Englewood Cliffs: Prentice-Hall.

Ecob, R., and Cuttance, P. (1987). An overview of structural equation modeling. In P. Cuttance, and R. Ecob (Eds.), *Structural modeling by example* (pp. 9–23). Cambridge: Cambridge University Press.

Edwards, A. L. (1968). *Experimental design in psychological research* (3rd ed.). New York: Holt, Rinehart, Winston.

Finkelstein, L. (1982). Theory and philosophy of measurement. In P. H. Sydenham (Ed.), *Handbook of measurement science* (Vol. 1). New York: John Wiley, pp. 1–30.

Flowers, P. J. (1983). The effect of instruction in vocabulary and listening on nonmusicians' descriptions of changes in music. *Journal of Research in Music Education, 31,* 179–189.

Flowers, P. J. (1988). The effects of teaching and learning experiences, tempo, and mode on undergraduates, and children's symphonic music preferences. *Journal of Research in Music Education, 36,* 19–34.

Flowers, P. J., and Dunne-Sousa, D. (1990). Pitch-pattern accuracy, tonality, and vocal range in preschool children's singing. *Journal of Research in Music Education, 38,* 102–114.

Gfeller, K., Darrow, A., and Hedden, S. K. (1990). Perceived effectiveness of mainstreaming in Iowa and Kansas schools. *Journal of Research in Music Education, 38,* 90–101.

Gibbons, J. D. (1985). *Nonparametric methods for quantitative analysis* (2nd ed.). Columbus: American Sciences Press.

Glass, G. V., and Hopkins, K. D. (1984). *Statistical methods in education and psychology.* Englewood Cliffs: Prentice-Hall.

Goodstein, R. E. (1987). An introduction to discriminant analysis. *Journal of Research in Music Education, 35,* 7–11.

Gorsuch, R. L. (1983). *Factor analysis* (2nd ed.). Hillsdale: Lawrence Erlbaum Associates.

Green, P. E., Carmone, Jr., F. J., and Smith, S. M. (1989). *Multidimensional scaling: Concepts and applications.* Boston: Allyn and Bacon.

Hair, J. F., Anderson, R. E., Tatham, R. L., and Grablowsky, B. J. (1984). *Multivariate data analysis with readings.* New York: Macmillan.

Hanneman, R. (1988). *Computer-assisted theory building: modeling dynamic social systems.* Newbury Park: Sage Publications.

Harnett, D. L. (1982). *Statistical methods* (3rd ed.). Reading: Addison-Wesley.

Harris, R. J. (1985). *A primer of multivariate statistics.* Orlando: Academic Press.

Harrison, C. S. (1990a). Relationships between grades in the components of freshman music theory and selected background variables. *Journal of Research in Music Education, 38,* 175–186.

Harrison, C. S. (1990b). Predicting music theory grades: The relative efficiency of academic ability, music experience, and musical aptitude. *Journal of Research in Music Education, 38,* 124–137.

Hays, W. L. (1988). *Statistics* (4th ed.). New York: Holt, Rinehart, and Wiston.

Hedden, S. K. (1982). Prediction of musical achievement in the elementary school. *Journal of Research in Music Education, 30,* 61–68.

Heller, G. N., and Radocy, R. E. (1983). On the significance: Addressing a basic problem in research. *Bulletin of the Council for Research in Music Education, 73,* 50–58.

Johnson, T. J., and Hess, R. J. (1970). *Tests in the arts.* St. Charles: Central Midwestern Regional Educational Laboratory.

Jöreskog, K G. (1979). Structural equation models in the social sciences: Specification, estimation and testing. In K. Jöreskog, and D. Sörbom (Eds.), *Advances in factor analysis and structural equation models* (pp. 105–127). Cambridge: Abt Books.

Jöreskog, K. G. (1982). The LISREL approach to causal model-building in the social sciences. In K. G. Jöreskog and H. Wold (Eds.), *Systems under indirect observation: Causality—structure—prediction* (pp. 81–99). Amsterdam: North-Holland Publishing.

Jöreskog, K. G., and Sörbom, D. (1989), LISREL 7.0 [Computer program]. Mooresville: Scientific Software.

Kachigan, S. K. (1986). *Statistical analysis: An interdisciplinary introduction to univariate and multivariate methods.* New York: Radius.

Kaiser, H. F., and Rice, J. (1974). Little Jiffy, Mark IV. *Educational and Psychological Measurement, 34,* 111–117.

Kantorski, V. J. (1986). String instrument intonation in upper and lower registers: The effects of accompaniment. *Journal of Research in Music Education, 34,* 200–210.

Kendall, M. J. (1988). Two instructional approaches to the development of aural and instrumental performance skills. *Journal of Research in Music Education, 36,* 205–219.

Kerlinger, F. N., and Pedhazur, E. J. (1982). *Multiple regression in behavioral research: Explanation and prediction* (2nd ed.). New York: Holt, Rinehart, and Winston.

Kirk, R. E. (1982). *Experimental design: Procedures for the behavioral sciences* (2nd ed.). Monterey: Brooks/Cole.

Kruskal, J. B., and Wish, M. (1978). *Multidimensional scaling.* Beverly Hills: Sage.

Kuhn, T. L., and Booth, G. D. (1988). The effect of melodic activity, tempo change, and audible beat on tempo perception of elementary school students. *Journal of Research in Music Education, 36,* 140–155.

Larson, R. C. (1977). Relationships between melodic error detection, melodic dictation, and melodic sightsinging. *Journal of Research in Music Education, 25,* 264–271.

LeBlanc, A., Colman, J., McCrary, J., Sherrill, C., and Malin, S. (1988). Tempo preferences of different age music listeners. *Journal of Research in Music Education, 36,* 156–168.

Lehman, P. R. (1968). *Tests and measurements in music.* Englewood Cliffs: Prentice-Hall.

Leonhard, C. (1958). Evaluation in music education. In N. B. Henry (Ed.), *Basic concepts in music education* (The fifty-seventh yearbook of the National Society for the Study of Education). Chicago: University of Chicago Press.

Li, J. C. R. (1964). *Statistical inference I.* Ann Arbor: Edwards Brothers.

Lord F., and Novick, R. L. (1968). *Statistical theories of mental test scores.* Reading: Addison-Wesley.

Lunneborg, C. E., and Abbot, R. D. (1983). *Elementary multivariate analysis for the behavioral sciences.* New York: North-Holland.

Madsen, C. K., and Madsen, C. H. (1978). *Experimental research in music.* Raleigh: Contemporary Publishing.

Madsen, C. K., and Moore, R. S. (1978). *Experimental research in music: Workbook in design and statistical tests.* Raleigh: Contemporary Publishing.

May, W. V. (1985). Musical style preferences and aural discrimination skills of primary grade school children. *Journal of Research in Music Education, 32,* 7–22.

Miller, R. (1989). An introduction to multidimensional scaling for the study of musical perception. *Bulletin of the Council for Research in Music Education, 102,* 60–73.

Moore, D. S. (1988). *Statistics: Concepts and controversies* (2nd ed.). New York: W. H. Freeman.

Moore, R. S. (1976). The effects of videotaped feedback and self-evaluation forms on teaching skills, musicianship and creativity of prospective elementary teachers. *Bulletin of the Council for Research in Music Education, 47,* 1–7.

Muirhead, R. J. (1982). *Aspects of multivariate statistical theory.* New York: John Wiley.

Nunnally, J. C. (1978). *Psychometric theory* (2nd ed.). New York: Mc-Graw-Hill.

Payne, D. A. (1982). Measurement in education. In H. E. Mitzel (Ed.), *Encyclopedia of educational research* (5th ed.; Vol. 3). New York: Free Press.

Phelps, R. P. (1986). *A guide to research in music education* (3rd ed.). Metuchen: Scarecrow Press.

Price, H. E. (1988). The effect of a music appreciation course on students' verbally expressed preferences for composers. *Journal of Research in Music Education, 36,* 35–46.

Price, H. E., and Swanson, P. (1990). Changes in musical attitudes, opinions, and knowledge of music appreciation students. *Journal of Research in Music Education, 38,* 39–48.

Puri, M. L., and Sen, P. K. (1971). Nonparametric methods in multivariate analysis. New York: John Wiley.

Radocy, R. E. (1986). On quantifying the uncountable in musical behavior. *Bulletin of the Council for Research in Music Education, 88,* 22–31.

Rainbow, E. L., and Froehlich, H. C. (1987). Research in music education. New York: Schirmer Books.

SAS Institute. (1989). *JMP: Software for statistical visualization* [Computer program]. Cary: SAS Institute.

Sax, G. (1979). *Foundations of educational research.* Englewood Cliffs: Prentice-Hall.

Scheffé, H. A. (1953). A method for judging all contrasts in the analysis of variance. *Biometrika, 40,* 87–104.

Seashore, C. E. (1936). The objective recording and analysis of musical performance. In C. E. Seashore (Ed.), *Objective analysis of musical performance* (pp. 5–11). Iowa City: The University Press.

Seashore, C. E., Lewis, D., and Saetveit, J. (1960). *Seashore measures of musical talents.* New York: Psychological Corporation. (Original publication in 1939)

Sheth, J. N. (1984). How to get the most out of multivariate methods. In J. F. Hair, R. E. Anderson, R. L. Tatham, and B. J. Grablowsky (Eds.), *Multivariate data analysis with readings* (pp. 19–29). New York: Macmillan.

Siegel, S. (1956). *Nonparametric statistics for the behavioral sciences.* New York: McGraw-Hill.

Siegel, S., and Castellan, N. J. (1988). *Nonparametric statistics for the behavioral sciences* (2nd ed.). New York: McGraw-Hill.

Simon, H. A. (1985). Spurious correlation: A causal interpretation. In H. M. Blalock (Ed.), *Causal models in the social sciences* (2nd ed., pp. 7–21). New York: Aldine Publishing.

SPSS. (1988). *SPSS^x user's guide* (3rd ed.). Chicago: SPSS.

Stanley, J. C. (1971). Reliability. In R. L. Thorndike (Ed.), *Educational measurement* (2nd ed.). Washington: American Council on Education.

Stevens, S. S. (1959). Measurement, psychophysics, and utility. In C. W. Churchman and P. Ratoosh (Eds.), *Measurement definitions and theories* (pp. 18–63). New York: John Wiley.

Stevens, S. S. (1975). *Psychophysics.* New York: John Wiley.

Tatsuoka, M. M., and Lohnes, P. R. (1988). *Multivariate analysis: Techniques for educational and psychological research* (2nd ed.). New York: Macmillan.

Whybrew, W. E. (1971). *Measurement and evaluation in music.* Dubuque: Wm. C. Brown.

Wike, E. L. (1971). *Data analysts.* Chicago: Aldine-Atherton.

Wilks, S. S. (1961). Some aspects of quantification in science. In H. Woolf (Ed.), *Quantification: A history of the measurement in the natural and social sciences (pp. 5–12).* Indianapolis: Bobbs-Merrill.

Winer, B. J. (1971). *Statistical principles in experimental design* (2nd ed.). New York: McGraw-Hill.

Winkler, R. L., and Hays, W. L. (1975). *Statistics: Probability, inference and decision* (2nd ed.). New York: Holt, Rinehart and Winston.

Wright, S. (1921). Correlation and causation. *Journal of Agricultural Research, 20,* 557–585.

Young, F. W. (1987). *Multidimensional scaling: History, theory, and applications.* Hillsdale: Lawrence Erlbaum Associates.

[10]

MEASUREMENT
AND EVALUATION
IN MUSIC

Edwin E. Gordon

The measurement and evaluation of music aptitudes is addressed in part 1, chapter 3. This chapter offers detailed information that may be put to immediate use for measuring and evaluating students' music achievement.

Understanding how to interpret test scores and manuals, how to use published tests, how to write tests, and how to weigh the comparative advantages and disadvantages of norms-referenced tests, criterion-referenced tests, and what is commonly referred to as assessment is invaluable in curriculum development. Without both measurement and evaluation, the timing of students' move to different levels of skill and content learning sequences and many other aspects of instruction becomes a matter of guesswork. One of the serious problems in music education is that many teachers rarely measure their students' achievement yet they continuously evaluate it, often using the results to then indirectly evaluate their own teaching effectiveness. I hope that my explanation of the difference between measurement and evaluation will encourage all teachers to rethink the way they examine their students' progress. **Remember, the most important use of tests is for the improvement of instruction.** The giving of grades is of far less consequence.

It should be apparent that unless a teacher has clearly stated sequential objectives and a comprehensive objective in outline form for a one-semester or one-year course of study, any test that might be used will have only limited value. For a test to have practical value, it must measure students' achievement against one or more of the sequential objectives or of the comprehensive objective in the course of study. For example, should a teacher embrace the comprehensive objective of teaching the appreciation of music without supporting that comprehensive objective with sequential objectives, the teacher will not know how to test what has supposedly been taught when it comes time to measure students' achievement, and as a consequence, a music history or music theory test will be found to be the only option.

At best, a test can measure only a sample of what a teacher has taught, which is why it would be unusual if a teacher did not need to administer more than one test to measure all sequential objectives. Teachers should not administer a published achievement test and expect it to be useful unless they first examine it to determine if what is being tested is related to at least their comprehensive objective and preferably to one or more of their sequential objectives. If the questions that are being asked in the test do not relate to what a teacher believes is important, another test should be found that is more suitable or a teacher-made should be used. Tests that most accurately reflect the specific sequential objectives in most courses are usually ones that teachers have written themselves.

All tests are measures, but not all measures are tests. A student takes a **test** and receives a score, whereas a teacher may **measure** a student's personal attitudes and physical characteristics and may or may not give the student a score. Thus, a student's test score represents measurement, which is an objective standard, but a teacher's interpretation of that test score represents evaluation, which is subjective. Be careful of the word *assessment* when it is used to analyze test scores or levels of achievement, because it means "to estimate." Unfortunately, when it is used to mean either measurement, evaluation, or both, it causes undue confusion and misdirection among educators and distorts our understanding of and attitude toward testing.

Because evaluation can be only subjective, it should be based on objective measurement. For example, a test score of 85 may be interpreted by a teacher on the basis of some predetermined standard to be worthy of a B or as an indication of satisfactory achievement. But suppose that 85 were the highest score achieved in the class. Should a score of 85 then be considered worthy of an A? And if the lowest score in the class were 80, might that suggest a different interpretation of a score of 85 than if the lowest score were 40? To answer these questions with confidence is impossible without the development and use of objective measurement techniques that support and lead to credible subjective evaluation procedures.

The words *objective* and *subjective* are used to emphasize the difference between measurement and evaluation. Nevertheless, all tests, regardless of their degree of objectivity, are subjective to some extent. For example, a multiple choice test is considered to be one of the best examples of an objective test, because its administration and scoring is completely objective. Factors that contribute to bias have no affect on the score a student receives. Nonetheless, the determination of the content of such a test may be, and often is, subjective. On the other hand, if only one teacher writes, administers, and scores an essay test, both the content of the test and the procedures for administering and scoring it are subjective.

Students' music achievement, as with their developmental music aptitude, should be measured in continuous terms at various times during the year and in summary terms at the end of a semester or year, as a way to diagnose and record academic progress. Students' stabilized music aptitude need only be measured once during a student's school career, however, because the purpose is to diagnose the student's music potential and to establish levels of expectations for the student's music achievement. Teacher-made tests, along with rating scales and standardized tests, may be used for measuring music achievement in learning sequence activities, classroom activities, and performance activities. As will be explained later, achievement tests may be either norms-referenced or criterion-referenced. Because music aptitude and music achievement are invariably confused, only standardized published tests should be used for measuring music aptitude. A music aptitude test, one that can be used with confidence, must be norms-referenced, because primary among many reasons, it does not make sense to attempt to use only one score to divide students with above-average and high music aptitude from those with below-average and low music aptitude.

THE APPLICATION OF CORRELATION TO TEST RELIABILITY AND VALIDITY

Though various types of statistics are used to interpret measurement, such as a mean, a standard deviation, and a percentile rank, the correlation coefficient is fundamental, because it can be used in a variety of ways for determining important qualities of a test. Correlation means relation. A relation between two factors may be positive or negative, or, of course, there may be no relation at all between them.

Consider test scores as factors. If two sets of scores derived from the same test administered twice to the same students, or from single administrations of two different tests, reinforce each other, they demonstrate a positive relation because they indicate that students tend to maintain their relative positions on both tests. That is, in general, students who score high on one test score high on the other, those who score average on one test score average on the other, and those who score low on one test score low on the other. When the relation is negative, high- and low-scoring students tend to reverse their positions on the tests. In general, students who score high on one test score low on the other, those who score average on one test score average on the other, and those who score low on one test score high on the other. When sets of scores do not show any relation (a zero correlation), some students may have maintained their relative positions, but the positions of most others will have changed without any clear logical explanation or pattern. In that case, there is no consistency among individual student's scores on both tests, and so students' scores on one test cannot be predicted with accuracy on the basis of their scores on the other.

For a perfect positive relation, the correlation coefficient is +1.00, and for a perfect negative relation, the correlation coefficient is -.1.00. When there are relation tendencies with discrepancies, the correlation index will range from +.01 to +.99 if it is positive (the higher the coefficient, the more positive the relation) or from -.01 to -.99 if it is negative (the higher the coefficient, the more negative the correlation). If there is no relation at all, the correlation will be 0.00. Be sure not to interpret a negative relation as a zero (0.00) correlation.

The correlation between overall music aptitude test scores and general intelligence test scores is approximately +.20, a correlation not much higher than zero. That coefficient simply suggests that, because there is only a modest positive correlation between the two factors, persons with high overall music aptitude may possess almost any degree of general intelligence and persons with low overall music aptitude may possess almost any degree of general intelligence, and, of course, vice versa.

When one interprets a correlation coefficient, however, it is important to remember that the more students differ, in both the characteristics that are being tested as well as in those that may not be, such as age and past achievement, and the greater the range of the test questions in terms of levels of difficulty, the higher one can expect the correlation coefficient to be.

Above all, it is important to understand that if a relation is found between two factors, either positive or negative, it is not necessarily true that a student's standing in relation to one factor is the cause of the student's standing in relation to the other. One or more other factors may be responsible for the relation. For example, it is known that there is a positive correlation between educational achievement and school tax assessment. That fact has led some to believe that it is the advantage of a school district's relative wealth that causes student achievement to be high. That may or may not be true. What is true, however, is that home environmental influences in terms of parental interest in a child's school progress correlates positively with both educational achievement and school tax assessment. Therefore, parental interest rather than financial advantage may be the causative factor, or the cause may be a combination of the two factors or a result of one or more unknown factors.

With regard to music, there is a known positive correlation between a student's membership in a school band and the student's overall academic achievement, and so some music educators automatically assume that if students are band members they will receive high grades in most of their school subjects. That conclusion is not necessarily warranted, however, because the cause of students' outstanding educational achievement may have more to do with the fact that they are by nature highly motivated and band may be just another activity in which they are participating. It is possible that if the students chose to pursue an activity other than band, their grade-point averages would be just as high. Negative correlations have also been reported between membership in school music ensembles and drug addiction and between membership in school music ensembles and encounters with law enforcement agencies. To draw the causative conclusion that membership in a school music ensemble will prevent students from engaging in substance abuse and from becoming involved in other unlawful pursuits may seem logical, or reasonable, but it cannot be justified simply on the basis of the correlative relations.

The primary function of a correlation coefficient in measurement is to describe test reliability and test validity. When a correlation coefficient is used to describe test reliability, it is called a reliability coefficient, and when a correlation coefficient is used to describe test validity, it is called a validity coefficient.

A test is considered to be reliable when students maintain their relative, but not necessarily their exact, score positions when the same test is administered on different days, typically during adjacent weeks, under the same administrative conditions. The magnitude of the reliability coefficient depends directly on the degree of the relation between the two sets of scores, so that the higher the positive reliability coefficient, the more reliable the test.

Different types of tests may be expected to yield different degrees of reliability. For example, because the content of a music aptitude test has less specificity than that of a music achievement test, a music aptitude test may be expected to be less reliable than a music achievement test, as is a test with many questions usually more reliable than a test with few questions. In general, a satisfactory reliability coefficient for a music achievement or music aptitude test battery (a comprehensive test that includes two or more subtests) is at least +.90 for the composite score (all subtests in the battery combined), at least +.80 for a total score (combinations of related subtests in a battery, such as two tonal subtest scores—melody and harmony—and two rhythm subtest scores—tempo and meter), and at least +.70 for each individual subtest score. That all reliability coefficients are less than perfect (+1.00) indicates that there is no test without some error of measurement. This is true for published tests as well as for teacher-made tests. There is less error of measurement with a well-designed test, however, than there is with a teacher's subjective evaluations that are not based on measurement at all.

The traditional definition of validity is considered to be as follows: "A test is valid if it measures what it purports to measure." Notwithstanding that it is the test author who determines what the test is supposed to measure, this definition may be appropriate for a test of an athlete's speed in running fifty yards, because it is obvious that such a test is measuring what it is supposed to measure, and therefore its validity need not be further investigated. Often it is difficult to prove, however, that a test measures what its author claims it measures. For example, it is not simple to prove that scores on a test of students' achievement in reading music notation, which is based on the students' ability to read a series of short phrases, is related to the students' practical achievement in reading the notation of a piece of music. Even in the unlikely event that students' scores on the test and the ratings of their skill in actually reading music literature demonstrates a perfect positive correlation, without further evidence there are no grounds for concluding that the two factors represent the same skill with any more certainty than concluding that because a perfect positive relation is found between students' height and weight, that height and weight are not different from each other.

Consider the difficulties in validating a music aptitude test. Because no one knows exactly what music aptitude is, it is impossible to prove that a music aptitude test is indeed a valid measure of music aptitude. Moreover, a simple **investigation** of correlating scores on a music aptitude test and a music achievement test that have been administered no more than a few weeks apart is not sufficient. A longitudinal **experiment**, covering years, is necessary to validate a music aptitude test **for one or more specific purposes.**

Simply claiming a test is valid rather than validating the purposes for using that test are quite different matters. For example, when it has been demonstrated that students who score high on a music aptitude test before they receive formal music instruction also score high on a validity criterion, such as a music achievement test, after at least a year of formal instruction, it can be assumed that the music aptitude test has longitudinal predictive validity. That is, it will have been demonstrated that the music aptitude test may be used for the purpose of identifying those students with the greatest potential to profit from musical instruction. Or if it has been demonstrated that students' scores on various subtests in a music aptitude test battery correlate highly after a year or more of formal instruction with corresponding validity criteria that are indicative of the students' musical strengths and weaknesses in music performance, it can be assumed that the subtests have diagnostic validity, and so the individual subtest scores may be used for the purpose of adapting music instruction to students' individual musical differences.

Normally, one can expect that there will be a higher relation between two sets of scores for the same test than between a set of scores on one test and a set of scores on another which may, for example, be serving as a validity criterion for the first. Therefore, a reliability coefficient is usually higher than a validity coefficient for a given test. The extent to which the validity coefficient of a test will be lower depends in part on the reliability of the validity criterion itself. A validity criterion with a low reliability tends to reduce the validity of the test under investigation. Also, if the test itself has low reliability, its validity will tend to be reduced even more, and the more alike to one another the students to whom the test and the validity criterion are administered are, the lower the validity of the test for that group of students. It should be clear, then, that tests may be valid for one group of students but not for another. Satisfactory validity coefficients associated with composite scores for a music aptitude or music achievement test battery generally range from +.40 to +.75, the majority being +.50. Validity coefficients for total and subtest scores, because they have fewer questions, can be expected to be lower.

Theoretically, the validity coefficient for a test can be no higher, and is usually lower, than the square root of the reliability coefficient for that test. If a test is not reliable, it cannot be valid. That is, a test with a reliability coefficient of 0.00 must have a validity coefficient of 0.00. The more reliable a test is, the more valid it **may** be. For example, a test with a reliability of +.81 could have, though it is unlikely, validity as high as +.90, but no higher, and a test with a reliability +.49 could conceivably have validity as high as +.70.

People often ask why an achievement test has any practical value if it has already been shown that a teacher can determine the comparative levels of students' music achievement in terms of a validity criterion. It is highly unlikely that a teacher's subjective evaluation of students' comparative achievement would be as reliable as an objective test, however. In fact, if the teacher's evaluations (the validity criterion) were more reliable, the test would have to be a remarkably ill-considered one. In addition, a good test is designed to examine objectively a small but representative sample of students' achievement. As a result, a valid test gives a teacher accurate information more quickly than it would take the teacher to accumulate the same information over a period of one or two semesters of instruction, and so the teacher may put test results to immediate use to improve the quality of instruction. It follows that the fundamental and most useful role of what are currently referred to as authentic assessment tools, even though their reliabilities may be less than substantial, is to serve as criteria for establishing the validity of an objective test. Given a valid (objective) test, neither the teacher's nor the students' time is used unwisely.

There are numerous ways to compute a correlation coefficient, identified by the symbol "r." The method used in the following example is comparatively simple and may be used with or without a calculator or a computer. Only after you understand how a correlation coefficient is computed should you use a computer to facilitate the computation, however.

The example shown here includes two sets of hypothetical test scores (X and Y) for ten students. As you can see, the first student received a score of 3 on the first test (X) and a score of 3 on the second test (Y), and so on for each student, with the mean (M) for each set of test scores at the bottom of each column. The third column (xd) indicates how each student's score deviates from the average X score, so that, for example, the first student's xd score is 0.0 because the student's X score did not deviate at all from the average X score. The third student's xd score was one point higher than the average X score, and that resulted in a positive (+) xd score +1.0. The sixth student's xd score was one point lower than the average X score, and that resulted in a negative (-) xd score -1.0. The fourth column (yd) indicates how each student's Y score deviates from the average Y score.

	X	Y	xd	yd	xyd	xd2	yd2
1.	3	3	0.0	—0.1	0.0	0.0	.01
2.	3	4	0.0	+0.9	0.0	0.0	.81
3.	4	5	+1.0	+1.9	+1.9	1.0	3.61
4.	4	4	+1.0	+0.9	+0.9	1.0	.81
5.	3	3	0.0	—0.1	0.0	0.0	.01
6.	2	1	—1.0	—2.1	+2.1	1.0	4.41
7.	1	2	—2.0	—1.1	+2.2	4.0	1.21
8.	3	3	0.0	—0.1	0.0	0.0	.01
9.	5	4	+2.0	+0.9	+1.8	4.0	.81
10.	2	2	—1.0	—1.1	—1.1	1.0	1.21
	M=3.0	M=3.1	Σ0.0	Σ0.0	Σ+10.0	Σ12.0	Σ12.9

$$ r = \frac{\Sigma xyd}{\sqrt{(\Sigma xd^2)(\Sigma yd^2)}} = \frac{+10.0}{\sqrt{(12.0)(12.9)}} = \frac{+10.0}{\sqrt{154.8}} = \frac{+10.0}{12.4} = +.81 $$

When negative scores are added to positive scores in a set of normally distributed scores, the theoretical result, the sum ($\sum$), is zero. In practice, however, particularly with small groups of students, the result is usually slightly higher than or slightly lower than zero.

The fifth column (xyd) represents each student's xd score multiplied by the student's yd score. (Any score multiplied by zero equals zero, a positive score multiplied by a negative score results in a negative score, and a negative score multiplied by another negative score results in a positive score.) The sixth column (xd^2) includes each student's xd score squared, and the seventh column (yd^2) includes each student's yd score squared.

If the sum for the xyd column is positive, the correlation coefficient will be positive, indicating a positive correlation between the two sets of scores, and if the sum for the xyd column is negative, the correlation coefficient will be negative, indicating a negative correlation between the two sets of scores.

The formula for computing a correlation coefficient using the figures from the example, followed by the actual computation, is given in sequential steps below the figures. A table of squares and square roots might be helpful, particularly if a calculator is not being used.

RELIABILITY

Correlation may be used for deriving various types of reliability. The three most common types of reliability coefficients are those that are associated with the coefficients of stability, equivalence, and internal consistency. A coefficient of stability, popularly referred to as test-retest reliability, describes the relation between two sets of scores from the same test administered to the same students under the same conditions from three to ten days apart. A coefficient of equivalence, popularly referred to as parallel-forms reliability, describes the relation between two sets of scores from different tests that measure the same factor administered to the same students under the same conditions from three to ten days apart. A coefficient of internal consistency, popularly referred to as split-halves or odds-evens reliability, describes the relation between two sets of scores from the same test, the test having been divided after it was administered and then scored in two parts as if there were two tests in one. In the last case, the test is usually divided into two "equal" parts on the basis of one or more of the following considerations: the number of questions; the content of the question; the type of learning, either discrimination or inference, associated with the questions; the difficulty of the questions; and the reliability and the validity of the questions. The test should not be arbitrarily split into halves or divided in terms of odd-numbered and even-numbered questions if the most realistic internal consistency is to be determined. Some test theorists recommend that an alpha coefficient, which is a theoretical average of all internal consistency coefficients that would be found if a test were split into all possible halves, be used, rather than a coefficient of internal consistency, to determine the reliability of a test.

When the test is divided into halves for scoring purposes, the coefficient of internal consistency yields a reliability estimate for a test half the length of the actual test. The more questions in a test, however, the more reliable the test is likely to be. To solve the problem and thus to obtain an appropriate estimate of the reliability of the actual full-length test, the Spearman-Brown prophecy formula is used. For example, if the correlation coefficient for the half-length test is +.60, using the formula, the corrected-for-length correlation coefficient as it relates to the actual full-length test is predicted to be +.75. That is determined by dividing two times the reliability of the half-length test by one plus the reliability of the half-length test, as shown in the formula below. (If the correlation coefficient has neither a plus nor a minus sign, it is assumed to be positive.) An adaptation of the Spearman-Brown prophecy formula may also be used for estimating the reliability of a test more than twice as long or for a test shorter than half-length.

$$\text{S-B Prophecy Formula} = \frac{2(r)}{1 + r} = \frac{2(.60)}{1 + .60} = \frac{1.20}{1.60} = .75$$

Because of the amount of time it takes to administer the same test twice or to administer two different tests, the coefficient of internal consistency is most widely used to derive test reliability in that only one test administration is necessary. As I will explain presently, when appropriate test statistics are available, a Kuder-Richardson formula may also be used to estimate the reliability of a test that is administered only once. Each type of reliability coefficient should be interpreted in accordance with what it does and does not take into account. Of the three types of reliabilities that might be reported for a given test, internal consistency usually yields the highest coefficient and equivalency the lowest, with the coefficient of stability falling somewhere between the two. Although the differences are usually not great, the coefficient of internal consistency will be highest, because it does not take into account changes in students' physical and psychological well-being from day to day, as do the coefficients of stability and equivalence. The coefficient of equivalence will be lowest, because in addition to the normal physical and psychological changes that occur in students from day to day, it, like the coefficient of internal consistency, takes into account the effect of different questions that pertain to the same subject matter. The coefficient of stability is affected only by the same kinds of changes in students' physical well-being or psychological outlook that affect the coefficient of equivalence. Students' physical and psychological changes from day to day can have a more profound affect on test scores than can differences associated with varied questions that pertain to the same subject matter.

VALIDITY

Objective validity

Correlation may also be used for determining various types of objective validity for a test. Concurrent validity, otherwise known as criterion-related validity, is the most popular; longitudinal predictive validity and diagnostic validity are the two most important types because they bear on practical needs; and congruent validity is least important. All are objective and experimentally derived, and all are usually described in terms of correlation coefficients. In general, published tests are validated objectively.

Concurrent validity describes the relation between scores on a test and a criterion (a validity criterion or criterion measure) that the test is designed to measure. For example, a test that requires students to read small samples of music notation is said to demonstrate concurrent validity if students' scores on that test correlate substantially with the teacher's ratings of their ability to read the notation of actual music. The test is administered and the teacher's ratings are collected closely within a short space of time, or, even better, concurrently. Concurrent validity is also called criterion-related validity, because of the relation of the test scores to the criterion. In the example above, the criterion is the reading of actual music notation.

Concurrent validity can be direct, as I have just described, or indirect, direct validity being, of course, the more important of the two. For example, it would be reasonable to expect that results on a music aptitude test would not show a substantial relation with results on a test of general intelligence. When students who receive high scores on one test do not receive high scores on the other, or when students who receive low scores on one test do not receive low scores on the other, that is an indication that the two tests have little in common. That the correlation between them is close to zero offers indirect evidence that the music aptitude test and the general intelligence test are not measuring the same traits, and that they are measuring what they are designed to measure. It is because indirect concurrent validity and criterion-related validity have opposite meanings that the term *criterion-related validity* often causes confusion when used in place of the term *concurrent validity*.

Congruent validity, a variation of concurrent validity, describes, for example, the relation between scores on a newly developed test and scores on an established test of the same type that has already been shown to be valid. When a substantial correlation is found between scores on the two tests, that leads the author of the new test to claim that the new test is also valid.

Longitudinal predictive validity resembles concurrent validity but differs in one very important way. For example, in concurrent validity, music aptitude test scores and criterion data are obtained within a short time span, but in longitudinal predictive validity, the music aptitude test is administered before instruction takes place and the criterion data are gathered later, in most cases years after instruction began. If there is a high positive correlation between pretraining aptitude test scores and post-training achievement criterion data, the test is said to have longitudinal predictive validity, because music aptitude test scores will have shown themselves to be good indicators of the level of students' future music achievement. Although concurrent validity might, in some cases, be acceptable for the validation of an achievement test, it is rarely acceptable for the validation of an aptitude test, because an aptitude test is designed to measure the potential to achieve, not to measure current achievement.

Unfortunately, some test authors substitute concurrent validity for longitudinal predictive validity when they are attempting to validate an aptitude test, because confirmation of longitudinal predictive validity is more expensive in time and money than is concurrent validity. Concurrent validity is a poor substitute for longitudinal predictive validity because when a test is administered at the same time that criterion data are collected, the resultant correlation coefficient cannot be interpreted to explain causation. When test authors assume that the reason students demonstrate high achievement is because they have high aptitude, these authors are assuming causation from relation. It is just as likely, however, that because students have high achievement, they score high on the music aptitude test. In either case the research may be meaningless, because both the test and the criterion data have been validated as either measures of aptitude or of achievement. When an aptitude test is administered before instruction begins and achievement data are collected only after instruction has been completed, as when conducting an investigation of the longitudinal predictive validity of a test, causation may be inferred from the relation between aptitude test scores and the achievement criteria. Only in a study of that type would it be reasonable to conclude that aptitude caused achievement. Obviously, it would be absurd to claim that achievement, which had not yet taken place, is responsible for students' high and low scores on an aptitude test.

Diagnostic validity is indicative of the relation between subtest scores and criteria that each subtest is designed to measure. For example, for a subtest to have diagnostic validity, scores on a tonal subtest should correlate highly with tonal criteria and lower with rhythm criteria. Similarly, scores on a rhythm subtest should correlate highly with rhythm criteria and lower with tonal criteria. The more specific the content of the subtest, the greater its diagnostic value should be. Depending upon the type of test, aptitude or achievement, and thus the intended use of test results, diagnostic validity may be established either longitudinally or concurrently.

Subjective validity

Subjective validity is very important in teacher-made tests and often in published tests as well. Of the three types of subjective validity— content, construct, and process—content validity seems to be most important to teachers and more so in curriculum-based achievement tests than in aptitude tests.

Whether or not objective validity has been demonstrated for a teacher-made achievement test or a published achievement test, content validity (often called face validity) is of primary importance, because in order for an achievement test to have content validity, the test questions must reflect the types of learning skills, both discrimination and inference, called for in a curriculum. Unless one or more teachers subjectively decide that questions in an achievement test reflect the subject matter associated with the sequential and comprehensive objectives in the curriculum, the test cannot be considered to possess content validity. If in the subjective opinion of teachers an achievement test is lacking in content validity, even the most impressive objective validity becomes irrelevant. Published achievement tests are usually said to have poorer content validity than teacher-made achievement tests, because a teacher-made achievement test is expressly written with the specific types of learning and the sequential and comprehensive objectives of a given curriculum in mind. A published achievement test, through necessity, is more comprehensive and thus not restricted to specific content or types of learning.

Unless an achievement test has content validity, it cannot provide pertinent information for the teacher. It cannot serve adequately as an objective aid for improving instruction and for teaching to students' individual differences. Without content validity, results from an achievement test will not indicate whether students have achieved a sequential objective in a curriculum at a level that will permit the next sequential objective to be undertaken with confidence, or whether previous sequential objectives should be reconsidered.

Construct validity, which is closely related to content validity, is a type of subjective validity that is more pertinent to aptitude tests than to achievement tests. Whereas content validity bears on information and learning skills included in test questions, construct validity deals primarily with how the questions are asked. For example, teachers must decide whether recorded musical examples that students are to listen to are satisfactorily performed, whether instruments that are used to perform the examples are acceptable, whether hearing only one instrument throughout the test is better than hearing two or more, or whether the absence of a subtest of pitch discrimination and the inclusion of a subtest of tonal memory in the test battery is acceptable.

As you have probably deduced, it is difficult to draw a sharp line between content and construct validity. Nonetheless, unless teachers are in agreement with the psychological constructs of a test as well as with the content of the test questions, they will not trust the scores that the test offers.

A last type of subjective validity is called process validity, and it has to do with the clarity of the test directions, with whether the test directions are recorded or are meant to be read aloud by the teacher or by the students themselves, with the length of the test, with the design of the answer sheet, with whether the answer sheet and the test directions complement each other, with the ease of scoring the test, with the appropriateness of the norms, and with whether the test manual includes suggestions for interpreting the test results. While some test authors pay little attention to process validity, most teachers are very concerned with it. Neither objective validity nor content or construct validity will persuade teachers to have faith in a test that they believe is confusing or inadequate.

Indirect information

When a teacher is in doubt about the subjective validity of a test, even one that the teacher has written, there are ways of obtaining preliminary objective evidence that will help to determine the validity of the test. Such evidence, although it is derived from coefficients of internal consistency, intercorrelations, test means, and score distributions, is not, of course, sufficient in itself for determining the quality of a test.

A test that has a high internal consistency demonstrates that the test questions have much in common with one another in terms of content. Although that finding is good, because it indicates that extraneous factors are not dominating the test, it does not take into account whether the specific content that is being measured is what should be measured as indicated by the goals of the test as they are stated by the title.

Intercorrelation coefficients, which are computed as correlation coefficients, should more correctly be called intracorrelation coefficients, because they are indexes of the relations among pairs of subtests in the same test battery. A relatively low intercorrelation coefficient suggests that the two subtests under consideration are measuring different content, as their test titles would seem to suggest. A relatively high intercorrelation coefficient suggests that both subtests are associated with the same content, even though they may have different titles. In that case, it would seem that one, if not both, of the subtests lacks validity.

An intercorrelation coefficient must be interpreted in conjunction with the reliability coefficient of the tests in question. It is important to note that an intercorrelation coefficient will be low if the reliability of one or both of the subtests for which it is computed is low, and so a low intercorrelation coefficient should not automatically be looked upon as preferable. Theoretically, when score distributions are normal, an intercorrelation coefficient cannot be higher, though it is usually much lower, than the square root of the product of the reliabilities of the two subtests. For example, if the reliability of one subtest is .80 and the other is .70, the product (one coefficient multiplied by the other) is .56, the square root of .56 is .75, and so the intercorrelation between the two tests is limited to a coefficient of .75. The theory is based on the same assumptions that are used for estimating the theoretical limit of the validity of a test in terms of its reliability, so that if, for example, a subtest has a reliability of .64, its validity is limited to a coefficient of .80. In general, an intercorrelation coefficient for two subtests, though lower than the reliability of either subtest, is generally found to be higher than the validity coefficient of either subtest.

Should a substantial number of students find a test too easy or too difficult, that is, should most scores fall above or below what in the teacher's opinion ought to be an average score (the mean) for the test, this would indicate that the test probably lacks validity for measuring what the test author intended it to measure. This does not necessarily suggest, however, that it would not be found to be valid for another group of students. If, on the other hand, approximately two-thirds of the students score near a theoretical mean and one-sixth score above and one-sixth score below that point, there is reason to believe that the test has validity.

A score distribution can reveal a great deal about the quality of a test. For example, consider a test that includes 60 questions. Suppose the highest score were 45. That would indicate that even the best students in the class could not answer 25 percent of the questions, presumably the most difficult questions in the test, and that as a result, because the test does not discriminate between superior and above-average students, the content validity of the test should be questioned. Suppose the lowest score were 30. That would indicate that 50 percent of the questions in the test are so easy that they were not challenging even to the poorest students. Thus, there is no way to discriminate between below-average students and poor students. Given those data, the validity of the test would again be suspect. In addition, a test with such a narrow score distribution would practically preclude the possibility of using the test results for adapting instruction to students' individual differences.

Taking guessing into account

In order to increase test validity, some test theorists recommend that scores be adjusted to compensate for answers that students have correctly guessed. This can be accomplished by penalizing students for giving an incorrect answer or by rewarding students for not trying to answer a question if they are not sure of the correct answer. When both systems are used with the same set of scores, there will be a perfect positive correlation (+1.00) between the two. Moreover, if all students answered all of the questions, scores that have been adjusted to penalize students for giving wrong answers would also yield a perfect positive correlation with the set of unadjusted scores. Only when a substantial number of questions are not answered by students will either system of adjustment have an appreciable affect, but because research has not established whether unadjusted or adjusted scores are more valid, it does not make sense to adjust scores for guessing without substantial reasons.

There are test theorists who also suggest that test questions should be weighted, that is, that more points should be awarded for answering more-difficult questions correctly, or that additional points should be awarded to above-average scores and that points should be subtracted from below-average scores on the more important subtests in a test battery. Although those systems may have some merit, an enormous amount of research is required to show that such procedures increase the validity of a test. Unless proved otherwise, the unadjusted scores should be considered to be most valid for teacher-made tests as well as for published tests.

The in-doubt option response should not be confused with a correction for guessing. It allows and encourages students not to guess if they feel they are not sure of the correct answer. They do not receive credit for not guessing, and if they do guess and mark a wrong answer, they are not penalized. The value of the in-doubt option response is that students do not waste time by guessing and so lose their concentration. The greatest factor in low test reliability is, of course, guessing, yet for whatever the reasons, it has been found in actual practice that when the in-doubt response is provided as an option, and so less guessing takes place, test reliability actually decreases, although test validity increases. Thus, I suggest that teachers give the in-doubt option response serious consideration when they are constructing their own tests and that they consider this option as a plus when it is included in a published test they are examining for its construct validity.

A test plays a formidable role in educational and psychological research. In test development, as I have explained, test scores are compared to a validity criterion to establish the validity of the test. In research, be it an experiment or an investigation, the situation is reversed. There a test is often used to determine, for example, which teaching method produces the highest level of student achievement under controlled conditions. Thus, in research, the test itself becomes a validity criterion, and it is called a criterion measure. But unless a researcher devotes a great deal of time to establishing the validity of a test that is intended for use as a criterion measure, the research results will be misleading or inaccurate. Because most researchers engage in microscopic research in an effort to prove macroscopic theories, research results are typically interpreted in terms of a theory. Thus, the most critical part of a research project is the development of a valid criterion measure, because without a valid criterion measure, even the most elegant research procedure, design, and analysis will not legitimatize the research results. Understanding how to validate a test for purposes of measurement, then, is necessary for understanding how to validate a test for purposes of research.

TEACHER-MADE TESTS

Rating scales

The most widely used type of teacher-made test for measuring music performance is the rating scale, because when it is used appropriately, it provides the best measurement of students' instrumental and vocal achievement. A rating scale may be used in the following manner: A student is asked to sing one or more major or harmonic minor tonic or dominant tonal patterns using tonal syllables. As the student is performing or later, using a recording of the students' performances, the teacher may rate the student's achievement in terms of the student's ability to sing in a singing voice, to sing with a sense of tonality, to sing with appropriate melodic direction, to sing the correct pitches in the patterns, and to sing correct tonal syllables, all depending, of course, on what the student has been taught and what the rating scale is intended to measure.

A rating scale should include at least two, preferably more, dimensions, such as measures of a student's tonal achievement and rhythm achievement, and perhaps the student's expressive achievement. Each dimension should include five criteria, all related to the overall dimension and as unrelated as possible to every other dimension included in the rating scale. The five criteria in a rhythm dimension might refer to a student's ability to follow or choose a correct tempo, to maintain a consistent tempo, to maintain a meter, to perform rhythm patterns correctly, and to make appropriate metric modulations.

The use of fewer than five criteria in a dimension tends to decrease the reliability of the dimension and hence the reliability of the overall rating scale (all dimensions combined). The use of more than five criteria, however, tends to decrease the validity of the dimension and probably the validity of the overall rating scale.

There are various ways to design a rating scale. An example of one dimension of a rating scale including five criteria is presented on the following page. The numerals that precede the criteria indicate the relative difficulty of each criterion: 1 is the easiest and 5 the most difficult to achieve in the dimension.

Measurement is accomplished, as in the example of the rating scale shown, by making all criteria in each dimension interdependent in terms of continuous (increasing) difficulty. When that is not possible, a student's achievement tends more toward evaluation, less toward measurement, and in such a case it is recommended that, when possible, each new criterion be treated as one dimension and that continuous criteria then be developed for each of those dimensions.

RATING SCALE

The student is able to imitate using tonal syllables

    5 - one familiar tonic pattern and one familiar dominant pattern in
       major or harmonic minor tonality
    4 - one familiar dominant pattern in harmonic minor tonality
    3 - one familiar dominant pattern in major tonality
    2 - one familiar tonic pattern in harmonic minor tonality
    1 - one familiar tonic pattern in major tonality

The dimensions of a rating scale incorporate continuous criteria when a rating of 2 is not awarded unless a student is capable of 1, a 3 is not awarded unless a student is capable of 2, and so on. The easiest criterion accounts for at least some achievement, and so if the student's achievement is less than that defined by 1, 0 should be given.

The difference between objective measurement and subjective evaluation for a rating scale is that in objective measurement, each dimension includes at least two, preferably more, clearly stated continuous criteria. Imprecise words—such as excellent, good, average, fair, and poor—do not represent continuous criteria, however, because they are too broad to be meaningful. To rate a student's achievement on a scale of 1 to 5 as superior to inferior offers no specific information about what the student is actually capable or incapable of, and provides the teacher with no clues about how to improve instruction.

To say that a student has or has not attained a curricular goal is simply an evaluation, not the result of any systematic measurement. Similarly, when a student's achievement is rated as good or poor, satisfactory or unsatisfactory, A or F, or 1 to 10, rather than in terms of defined criteria, the evaluation is not based on measurement. When evaluation is used in place of measurement, the reliability and, of course, the validity of the rating scale are put in doubt.

All dimensions and criteria of a rating scale should be related to an overall curricular objective. However, contradictory as it may seem, although all dimensions should be related to that objective in terms of content validity, **ideally** they should show a zero intercorrelation with one another. In practice, however, they will at best show a low to moderate positive intercorrelation, so that whether they are dimensions on a rating scale or subtests in a test battery, low intercorrelation coefficients as opposed to zero are the expected result. On the other hand, whenever the intercorrelations among dimensions on a rating scale are relatively high, it is almost certain that evaluation, not measurement, is taking place.

When a student is to be rated on a sequential objective for which research has not yet established a basis in skill or content learning sequence, such as the ability to perform with style, phrasing, tone quality, or dynamics appropriate to the music, it might be advisable to use additive criteria instead of continuous criteria for one or more dimensions in the rating scale. The number of points awarded in an additive dimension of a rating scale, however, is calculated by the number of criteria that the student has achieved, none being dependent on any other as in a continuous dimension. Although a dimension with additive criteria will yield more valid results than one based on an undefined scale of 1 to 5, a dimension with continuous criteria is preferable, because it is more useful for adapting instruction to students' carefully identified musical strengths and weaknesses.

If continuous difficulty levels of tonal patterns and rhythm patterns are not used in conjunction with a rating scale, other continuous criteria can, of course, serve just as well for measuring individual differences in music achievement. However, when tonal patterns and rhythm patterns are used as part of other criteria, so that the patterns themselves are not considered as the continuous criteria, all students should be tested on the same skills using the same content, the only difference being that students with high music aptitude might perform more-difficult patterns and students with low music aptitude might be perform less-difficult ones.

The reliability of the score for each dimension and for the composite (all dimensions combined) on a rating scale may be determined 1) when the same teacher awards ratings to the same students who were tested on the same criteria under similar conditions on two occasions, 2) when the same teacher, listening twice to recordings of the students' performances, awards two sets of ratings to the same students who were tested on the same criteria on one occasion, or 3) when different teachers award ratings to the same students who were tested on the same criteria on one occasion. In the first and second examples, provision has been made for a coefficient of stability and in the third for a coefficient of equivalence. Though the first and second approaches yield coefficients of stability, the first takes into account the stability of both the students' performances and the teachers' ratings from day to day, whereas the second takes into account only the stability of the teacher's ratings from day to day. Internal consistency is not appropriate for determining the reliability of a rating scale.

When teachers record students' performances, it is preferable that they use numbers, not names, to identify each performance. That way they guard against bias and enhance the validity of the rating, because they may listen to the performances as many times as necessary without being influenced by extra-musical factors, such as a student's attitude or attendance record. Of course, a recording makes it more difficult to rate students' instrumental and vocal technique.

When a recording is used, the teacher should listen to each performance as many times as there are dimensions on the rating scale. In that way the teacher may attend to one dimension at a time during the rating procedure. If ratings on all dimensions are awarded after only one hearing of the performance, the intercorrelations among the dimensions may be unusually high, and so the overall validity of the rating scale will be lower than it reasonably should be.

Obtaining preliminary evidence of the validity of a rating scale is a relatively simple matter. That is, when two teachers award similar ratings for each student, this suggests that the psychological constructs of the ratings are valid and thus the rating scale has construct validity. (To that extent, the coefficient of equivalence may be interpreted as evidence of congruent validity.) The intercorrelations among the dimensions might also be investigated along with reliability, because a valid rating scale demonstrates relatively low intercorrelations among the dimensions. Although the intercorrelation coefficient for any two dimensions should be lower than the reliability of either dimension, in practice, that is not always the case. Also, the higher the reliability coefficient for each of the two dimensions, the higher the intercorrelation coefficient may be expected to be between the two. Nonetheless, it follows that a valid rating scale would demonstrate a composite reliability that is greater than the reliability for any one of its dimensions.

As I have already explained, unless each dimension of a rating scale is associated with a sequential objective stated in a curriculum, the ratings will have little objective validity. This is equally true if criteria are defined in terms of quantity without quality, that is, if they are simply given numbers or value words and are not clearly stated as they relate to continuous criteria in terms of a curricular objective. Perhaps even more detrimental to the validity of a rating scale, however, is when in the name of objectivity a teacher awards ratings on the basis of the number of individual notes that a student performs correctly or determines a student's rating on the basis of whether "some," "few," "occasional," or "many" errors were made. This typically occurs in the absence of objectives and usually results in spuriously high reliability for the dimensions and in a compromise of the content validity of those dimensions.

Multiple choice tests

Except for a rating scale designed for measuring students' performance achievement, a well-designed multiple choice test is the best type of test for measuring students' music achievement as it relates to both discrimination and inference learning. If an achievement test does not test students' ability to define and summarize course content as well as to draw generalizations from the information that they have learned, it may be confidently said that the test is lacking in purpose and value. A multiple choice test, unlike a matching test, lends itself to objective analysis, which makes it more reliable and thus, more valid.

Depending upon the material that is to be tested, the availability of time and money, and the persuasion of the test author, a recording of musical examples may or may not be used in conjunction with a multiple choice music achievement test. Recordings are a necessity, however, for a music aptitude test. When a recording is used, serious consideration should be given to whether the directions for taking the test should be recorded; to whether the directions should include recorded practice exercises; to the types of instruments and voices that might be most suitable; to the length of each musical selection; to how tonality and meter will be established, if they need to be; to whether each musical selection should be heard more than once, and if so, how much silence there should be between repetitions; to how much time should be allotted for students to mark their answers; and to the design of the answer sheet in relation to the recording.

All of these considerations bear on the construct validity and the process validity of the test and are only the more important ones that will need attention when a recording is being designed. Although a recording will enhance the objectivity of a test and should contribute to the quality of a test, it can, for all intents and purposes, invalidate a test if it is not prepared appropriately.

Ideally, each multiple choice test question should include four option responses. When there are fewer option responses, the question will resemble a true-false question for which the correct answer may be more easily guessed. That is undesirable, because guessing is a prime source of low test reliability. Although reliability may be increased if there are more than four option responses, the question will then become too broad in scope, and content validity will probably be sacrificed. This is particularly the case when a given option response is "none of the above" or "all of the above," either as one of four or as a fifth option.

It is, of course, difficult and time consuming to write thoughtful option responses that are incorrect but that nevertheless serve to provide students with a useful learning experience. If a teacher is not experienced in writing test questions, the teacher should, look to an authoritative source for guidance. Note particularly that incorrect grammar in the body of a multiple choice question, particularly as it relates to each option response, produces a poor question.

For greatest validity, there should be about the same number of multiple choice questions in a test as there are minutes available for administering the test, provided that it is not a speed test or a listening test. A speed test includes more questions than an untimed test and, depending on the length of the musical examples, a listening test, recorded or not, may have more or fewer questions.

The content validity of a multiple choice test is almost assured if the questions are developed according to a taxonomy. For example, based on the curricular sequential objectives under consideration, a teacher should write an outline of the music content and skills that he or she wants to cover in the test and then write questions that correspond to each part of a taxonomy. Ideally, content should be based on tonal and rhythm content learning sequence and on skill learn sequence.

For determining the reliability of a multiple choice test, the coefficient of internal consistency is most efficient and most commonly used. When the test is split into halves for scoring purposes, each half should contain similar proportions of questions that correspond to each part of the taxonomy. After one has acquired practical experience with measurement procedures, it becomes increasingly apparent that the reliability of a multiple choice test is determined by the consistency of the students' responses, whereas the reliability of a rating scale or an essay test depends on the consistency of the teacher or teachers who award the ratings or score the test, as well as on the consistency of the students' answers or performances.

Once a multiple choice test has been given to a class on an experimental basis, one or more item analyses (a test question is referred to as an "item") should be performed to determine which questions need to be revised or eliminated before the test is put into final form. The two most important aspects of an item analysis are item difficulty and item discrimination.

The difficulty index indicates the percentage of students taking the test who answered each item correctly. The higher the difficulty level, the **easier** the item. The discrimination index is indicative of a correlation coefficient that describes the relation between students' correct and incorrect responses to a given test item and their total scores on the test except, depending upon the computation procedures used, for extremely easy or difficult items. The higher the discrimination index, the more valid the test item.

If more high-scoring students than low-scoring students answer an item correctly, that item will have a positive discrimination value and thus will increase the reliability and probably the validity of the test. If more low-scoring students than high-scoring students answer an item correctly, however, that item will have a negative discrimination value and so will decrease the reliability and probably the validity of the test. An item with zero (0.00) discrimination neither increases nor decreases the reliability or validity of a test. Some test authors routinely delete negatively discriminating items from a test. If one is convinced, however, that a negatively discriminating item is appropriately written and that it possesses content validity in terms of a sequential objective in the course curriculum, it should not be deleted merely to improve the reliability of the test.

There are various ways to calculate an item analysis, with or without a computer, and the results are essentially the same except for very easy or very difficult items. To perform an item analysis by hand, score the test and then divide the answer sheets into two groups, one group including those of the higher-scoring 50 percent of the students and the other the answer sheets of the lower-scoring 50 percent. Then examine each item individually by counting the number of students in each group who answered the item correctly. Assuming, for example, that 30 students took the test and that 15 in the higher-scoring group and 6 in the lower-scoring group answered an item correctly, the difficulty index for that item would be .70 and the discrimination index would be .60.

To derive the figure for the difficulty index, the number of students in the higher-scoring group who answered the item correctly **plus** the number of students in the lower-scoring group who answered the item correctly is divided by the total number of students who took the test: 15 plus 6, divided by 30 equals .70. For the discrimination index, the number of students in the higher-scoring group who answered the item correctly **minus** the number of students in the lower-scoring group who answered the item correctly is divided by **half** the total number of students who took the test: 15 minus 6, divided by 15 equals .60.

Other information can also be determined from an item analysis. For example, it can easily be discovered which option responses are not being used by students, and after the nature of the problem is discovered and those particular option responses have been reworded or replaced, the statistical characteristics of the item should improve. Thus, the reliability and validity of the item and the test should increase.

Knowledge of the difficulty indexes of items can also enhance the reliability of a test. When each half of a test includes items of similar difficulty levels that measure students on similar content and skills, the internal consistency (split-halves) reliability will be enhanced. Moreover, the reliability of a test increases as the range of item difficulty levels becomes broader, and particularly in a multiple choice test used for diagnostic purposes, the broader the range of item difficulties, the more valid the test will be.

Once an item analysis has been performed for a test, the reliability of that test may be directly estimated through the use of the Kuder-Richardson Formula 20, which is based on item analysis data. The formula may be used only if questions are homogeneous in content and vary in difficulty, if there are more than two option responses for each question, if only one point is awarded for a correct answer and no points are subtracted for an incorrect answer to a question, and if students are given ample time to answer all questions.

Look at the formula below: k represents the number of items in the test, p represents the percentage of students who answered a given item correctly, q represents the percentage of students who answered that item incorrectly, and SD represents the standard deviation (which will be explained presently) for the test. The formula requires that p and q be multiplied for each item and then summed for all items. That sum is then divided by the standard deviation squared, then subtracted from 1, and then multiplied by the fraction derived by dividing the number of items in the test by the number of items in the test minus 1.

$$r = \frac{k}{k\text{-}1} \left[1 - \frac{\Sigma pq}{SD^2} \right]$$

As an example, consider a test with a standard deviation of 2.0 that has 10 items. The pq values and the sum of those values are shown on the following page. The sum of the pq values (1.90) is divided by the standard deviation (2) and then squared (4). The result is .475, which when subtracted from 1, equals .525. Then the number of items in the test (10) is divided by the number of items in the test minus 1 (9), and this equals 1.11. Finally, .525 is multiplied by 1.11 to make .58, which represents the estimate of reliability as determined by the Kuder-Richardson Formula 20. Though some persons believe that the Kuder-Richardson Formula 20 somewhat underestimates the reliability of a test, in my experience it has always yielded a good approximation.

Item	p	q	pq
1	0.4	0.6	0.24
2	0.7	0.3	0.21
3	0.8	0.2	0.16
4	0.5	0.5	0.25
5	0.9	0.1	0.09
6	0.2	0.8	0.16
7	0.3	0.7	0.21
8	0.5	0.5	0.25
9	0.6	0.4	0.24
10	0.1	0.9	0.09
			1.90

Knowledge of the mean and standard deviation of a multiple choice test can be helpful for determining the quality of a test as well as for evaluating student achievement. The mean (the average score) is derived by dividing the sum of the scores of all students who took the test by the number of students who took the test.

The standard deviation indicates the extent to which the test scores vary around the mean, and it serves as a reference for determining how much higher and how much lower some scores are than others. Given a reasonably large group of students and a valid test, it may be assumed that scores will be distributed up to three standard deviations above the mean and up to three standard deviations below the mean. Such a distribution is referred to as a normal curve. Approximately 34 percent of scores will fall somewhere between the mean and one standard deviation above the mean, approximately 14 percent will fall somewhere between the first and second standard deviations above the mean, and approximately 2 percent will fall somewhere between the second and third standard deviations above the mean. The percentages are the same for scores below the mean. When the standard deviation is used as a guide, it is evident that the majority of students, approximately 68 percent, can be considered average, 28 percent can be considered above or below average, and 2 percent can be considered exceptionally good or exceptionally poor.

In the example on the following page, showing how the formula is used for computing a standard deviation (SD), the 10 scores for the X test previously used in the computation of a correlation coefficient are reproduced, as are the mean, deviations, and squared deviations of those scores. The formula is given below the data. The square root of the sum of the squared deviations divided by the number of students (N) who took the test is found to be 1.1. Given the standard deviation of 1.1 and a mean of 3.0 for the test, it may be assumed that approximately 34 percent of scores would fall between 3.0 and 4.1, 34 percent would fall between 3.0 and 1.9, 14 percent of scores would fall between 4.1 and 5.1, 14 percent would fall between 1.9 and 0.8, 2 percent would fall above 5.2, and 2 percent would fall below 0.8.

	X	xd	xd^2
1.	3	0.0	0.0
2.	3	0.0	0.0
3.	4	+1.0	1.0
4.	4	+1.0	1.0
5.	3	0.0	0.0
6.	2	−1.0	1.0
7.	1	−2.0	4.0
8.	3	0.0	0.0
9.	5	+2.0	4.0
10.	2	−1.0	1.0
	$M=\sum 3.0$	$\sum 0.0$	$\sum 12.0$

$$SD = \sqrt{\sum xd^2/N} = \sqrt{12.0/10} = \sqrt{1.2} = 1.1$$

To assess test quality, an obtained mean and standard deviation can be compared with the theoretical mean and theoretical standard deviation of a test. For example, for a multiple choice test with 48 questions, each with four option responses, the theoretical mean will be 30 and the theoretical standard deviation will be 6. The data are obtained in the following way: First, the theoretical chance score for the test must be determined. A chance score occurs when a student pattern marks or randomly marks an answer sheet, or when the student marks the same-numbered option response for each question without first understanding the question. If the test is designed as it should be, so that each of the four option responses is a correct answer an equal number of times throughout the test, the chance score can be determined by dividing the number of questions in the test by the number of option responses provided for each test question. This means that for a test with 48 questions, each having four option responses, 48 will be divided by 4 to equal 12. To derive the theoretical mean, the chance score is subtracted from the number of questions in the test (48 minus 12 equals 36). That figure is divided by 2 (36 divided by 2 equals 18). Finally, to determine the theoretical mean, that figure is added to the chance score (18 plus 12 equals 30).

To derive the theoretical standard deviation, the difference between the theoretical mean and the highest possible score obtainable on the test is divided by 3. For a test with 48 questions each having four option responses, 30 would be subtracted from 48 to equal 18, and then 18 would be divided by 3 to equal 6.

If an obtained mean and a theoretical mean are not comparable, the content of the test may be inappropriate. When an obtained mean is significantly higher than the theoretical mean, the test is probably too easy for the group of students who took the test, and when an obtained mean is significantly lower than the theoretical mean, the test is probably too difficult.

When there is great discrepancy in the obtained standard deviation and the theoretical standard deviation, it is certain that the test is inappropriate and so lacks validity for the group. However, even when the obtained and theoretical standard deviations are comparable, this is not absolute assurance that the test is appropriate. Such a finding offers only preliminary objective evidence of the content and construct validity of the test. Thus, the test results must be examined to determine that the highest obtained score is comparable to the highest possible score, and that the lowest obtained score is comparable to the chance score. Though the computation procedure is different, the concepts of a chance score, a theoretical mean, and a theoretical standard deviation are as useful for assessing the quality of a rating scale and an essay test as they are for assessing the quality of a multiple choice test.

A raw score is a simple count of the number of questions a student answers correctly on a test. A raw score alone is difficult to interpret, however. For example, if the mean of a test is 40 and the standard deviation is 7, a score of 47 is relatively easy to interpret, because it is one standard deviation above the mean. But what about a score of 42, and how does it differ from a score of 43, and is the difference between a score of 42 and 43 the same as the difference between a score of 43 and 44? To answer those questions with any degree of accuracy, percentile rank norms are needed.

A simplified way of computing percentile ranks is as follows: Consider the score distribution in table 23. The first column (RS) includes the unordered raw scores for 25 students. A frequency distribution for those raw scores, that is, the raw scores rearranged from high to low with the number of students who attained each score indicated after the slash, is found in the second column (FD). In the third column (CFD) the cumulative frequency distribution of the raw scores is shown. Beginning at the bottom of the second column, notice that one student received a score of 21 and that two students received a score of 29. By adding 1 (for one student) and 2 (for two students), it can be seen in the third column that the cumulative frequency for a raw score of 29 is 3. Because two students received a raw score of 32, the cumulative frequency for a raw score of 32 is 5 (1 plus 2 plus 2). In the fourth column (PR) the percentile rank norms for each raw score are listed. A percentile rank for a given raw score is derived by dividing each cumulative frequency by the number of students who took the test. For example, the percentile rank norm for a raw score of 32 is 20 (5 divided by 25) and the percentile rank for a raw score of 54 is 76 (19 divided by 25).

TABLE 23

COMPUTING PERCENTILE RANKS

RS	FD	CFD	PR
79	79/1	79/25	99
60	65/1	65/24	96
32	62/1	62/23	92
29	60/2	60/22	88
29	55/1	55/20	80
32	54/1	54/19	76
69	51/2	51/18	72
54	50/4	50/16	64
21	49/1	49/12	48
40	48/1	48/11	44
42	45/1	45/10	40
51	42/1	42/9	36
50	40/2	40/8	32
50	36/1	36/6	24
51	32/2	32/5	20
49	29/2	29/3	12
48	21/1	21/1	4
55			
45			
50			
62			
65			
50			
40			
36			

Percentile ranks are very simple to interpret. For example, if a student receives a percentile rank of 40, that means that the student scored as high or higher than 40 percent of the students who are being compared to one another and that 60 percent of the students scored higher.

Percentile ranks are standard scores because they have standard meaning. That is, even though the means and standard deviations may be different for two tests, a percentile rank is interpreted the same way for both tests. Because the distribution of percentile ranks is rectangular, not bell-shaped, ordinary computations cannot be undertaken with them. There is, however, another type of standard score from which sums and averages can be derived. These scores are simply referred to as standard scores. Theoretically, they are T scores.

When converted from any distribution of raw scores, standard T scores will have a mean of 50 and a standard deviation of 10. Because of their distribution, which ranges from 20 to 80, standard T scores can be added together to derive an equally weighted composite score, one in which all test scores for a semester or year, when added together, contribute equally to the final score. Standard scores are also used when subtests in a test battery, considered together, are meant to contribute equally to the composite score.

Standard T scores are cumbersome and time-consuming to compute when a computer is not available. Thus, rather than explaining all of the formulas required for computation, I have converted percentile ranks to standard T scores in the chart in table 24. Once the percentile ranks for raw scores are computed for a test, find the percentile rank (PR) in the chart that is associated with a given raw score. Then move directly across to the adjacent column (SS) to find the standard score. That is a normalized standard T score equivalent to the raw score associated with that percentile rank.

Essay tests

An essay test is not a preferred measure because it emphasizes memory, whereas a multiple choice test emphasizes recognition and the ability to generalize. Moreover, an essay test does not lend itself to quality analysis as easily as does a multiple choice test. Some teachers use essay tests because they believe that through such tests students learn to organize content and to express themselves in writing, but a term paper seems more useful for that purpose. A good multiple choice test not only teaches students to organize their thinking, it also promotes inferential thinking through exposure to a broader sample of content. Unlike an essay test, an appropriate multiple choice test provides students with a way to sum up their learning experience, and for the teacher it provides an objective measure of how well students have been taught and what they have learned. Questions in a multiple choice test may be improved through item analysis, and when they are in their final form, many of the questions may be used over again with different students from year-to-year, thus assuring reliable and valid test results. Although an essay test may be easier to compose, it is difficult and time-consuming to score. A multiple choice test, on the other hand, is difficult and time-consuming to compose, but easy to score every time that it is administered.

When an essay test, like a rating scale, is administered and scored with standard procedures, the results may be objective. I recommend that it be treated as a rating scale. Identification numbers should be substituted for students' names on test papers, and definite criteria for measuring the quality of students' answers should be established before the test papers are scored. For example, before an essay test is administered, the teacher should take the test. Using those answers as a guide, the teacher should read every student's written response to the first question before going on to the second, and so on. One point might be awarded for every statement made by a student that coincides with a part of the teacher's answer and two points might be awarded for every good answer given by the student that the teacher neglected in his or her response. Likewise, one point might be subtracted for each incorrect statement. When such a procedure is used, not only will the content validity of the test be enhanced, but the reliability and objective validity of the scores will increase.

The increase in reliability is in most part a direct result of having predetermined standards. As the score range of an essay test increases, so will the range of the composite score and thus, again, the reliability and validity of the test itself.

When an essay test is scored twice by the same teacher, with the students identified by number only, a coefficient of stability may be derived. Better still, if two teachers score the tests independently, a coefficient of equivalence, which may be interpreted as a coefficient of congruent validity, may be derived. The coefficients of stability and equivalence for an essay test, as for a rating scale, are more accurate indicators of the teacher's or teachers' reliability than of the students' reliability. Unless scoring procedures for an essay test similar to those described above are used, research indicates that it can be assumed that the reliability of the test will be too low to permit a teacher to make evaluations with confidence.

TABLE 24

SCORE CONVERSIONS

PR	SS	PR	SS
99.9	80	49	50
99.8	79	48	50
99.7	78	47	49
99.6	77	46	49
99.5	76	45	49
99.4	75	44	49
99.3	74	43	48
99.2	73	42	48
99.1	72	41	48
99	71	40	48
98	70	39	47
97	69	38	47
96	67	37	47
95	66	36	47
94	65	35	46
93	64	34	46
92	64	33	46
91	63	32	46
90	63	31	45
89	62	30	45
88	62	29	45
87	61	28	44
86	61	27	44
85	60	26	44
84	60	25	43
83	59	24	43
82	59	23	43
81	59	22	42
80	58	21	42
79	58	20	42
78	58	19	41
77	57	18	41
76	57	17	41
75	57	16	40
74	56	15	40
73	56	14	39
72	56	13	39
71	55	12	38
70	55	11	38
69	55	10	37
68	54	9	37
67	54	8	36
66	54	7	36
65	54	6	35
64	53	5	34
63	53	4	33
62	53	3	31
61	53	2	30
60	52	1	29
59	52	0.9	28
58	52	0.8	27
57	52	0.7	26
56	51	0.6	25

55	51		0.5	24
54	51		0.4	23
53	51		0.3	22
52	50		0.2	21
51	50		0.1	20
50	50			

PUBLISHED TESTS

When the word *standardized* is used to describe a test, it means that the test is designed to be administered and scored in a standard manner, and that provision is made for interpreting test results in a standard manner. Although percentile rank norms are typically provided with a published test, the use of the word *standardized* does not necessarily mean that other types of standard scores are also provided.

It is worth emphasizing that only published standardized test batteries should be used for measuring students' music aptitudes. Teacher-made music aptitude tests, often improperly referred to as music ability or talent tests, typically measure music achievement. An appropriate music aptitude test battery is designed to measure separately each of the important dimensions of students' developmental and stabilized music aptitudes. Tests of developmental music aptitude include fewer subtests in the battery than do tests of stabilized music aptitude. Each subtest score in a music aptitude test battery is used as an aid in adapting instruction to students' individual musical differences. Of course, the inclusion of more than one subtest in a battery does not necessarily mean that the battery has been validated for diagnostic purposes.

Information on the extent to which subtest scores for a music aptitude test battery have been investigated for diagnostic validity and the extent to which the composite score has been investigated for longitudinal predictive validity should be included in an accompanying test manual, which normally includes a rationale of the test battery. This is especially important to verify content and construct validity, and a test manual should also include the reliability for all subtests and other related statistical information.

The standard error of measurement (SE of M) is of special importance for both music achievement and music aptitude tests. It should be reported in a test manual, because it indicates the extent to which a student's score may be expected to fluctuate on a test. That the magnitude of all reliability coefficients are less than perfect demonstrates that there is error of measurement associated with any test score, be it derived from a teacher-made test or a published test. In a sense, the standard error of measurement relates to the reliability of a single score on a test, not to the entire test itself, but by using the standard error of measurement, a teacher can then determine the range within which a student's "true" score may be found. For example, assume that a test has a reliability of .91 and a standard deviation of 10. According to the formula below, the standard error of measurement would be 3.0, because that is the number derived from multiplying the standard deviation for the test by the square root of the remainder of 1 minus the reliability of the test. Thus, in this case, there is about one chance in three that a student's true score may differ from his or her obtained score by as much as 3.0 points, which is equal to one standard error of measurement, and there is about one chance in twenty that a student's true score may differ from his or her obtained score by as much as 6.0 points, which is equal to two standard errors of measurement.

$$\text{SE of M} = \text{SD} \sqrt{1\text{-}r} = \sqrt[10]{1\text{-}.91} = \sqrt[10]{.09} = 10(.3) = 3.0$$

Like a published standardized music aptitude test, a published standardized music achievement test is most appropriate when it is composed of a battery of subtests. Moreover, the most appropriate published standardized music achievement test is designed as a multilevel (different levels that are most appropriate for different groups of students) battery that focuses on content and skill. Different levels of tests in the battery may be administered to different groups of students according to their levels of skill development and their understanding of content. Even more important, different levels of the test may be administered to the same group of students on different occasions to measure their growth in music achievement. In the former case, when teachers can choose among the levels of a test they plan to administer to a group of students, they can match the content of the skills reflected in the test with the content and skills that they feel are important. In the latter case, when different levels of a test are administered to the same group of students, one level administered before and the other after instruction has taken place, the content and skills measured by the test can be matched with the current knowledge and skills of the students. When the same test is administered to a group of students more than once, however, the skills and content that the test is measuring become less and less appropriate for the students, and so test reliability as well as content and construct validity decline. Because it will be neither too easy nor too difficult for students, a given level of a multilevel achievement test will accord higher reliability than a single test. *The Iowa Tests of Music Literacy*, published by GIA, is a multilevel music achievement test battery.

The test manual that accompanies a published standardized music achievement battery should report several types of validity and at least concurrent (criterion-related) validity. Further, it must include the rationale of the battery as it relates to content validity, and to serve as an objective aid in the evaluation process, it should also provide percentile rank norms and relevant standard score conversions.

Another statistic is helpful in idiographically comparing a student's music aptitudes with one another, aspects of a student's music achievement with one another, and a student's music aptitude with his or her music achievement, and this is the standard error of a difference (SE of D). It is particularly useful in adapting instruction to students' individual musical differences. For example, the standard error of a difference aids a teacher in determining whether a student's scores on two subtests that represent different dimensions of music aptitude are actually different, whether a student's scores on two subtests that represent different dimensions of music achievement are actually different, and whether a student's scores on a music aptitude test when compared to his or her scores on a music achievement test are actually different.

Only under certain conditions, however, can the standard error of a difference be used. First, the scores from both tests being examined must be based on the same type of standard score scale, and second, the standard score scales must be derived from the test results of the same group of students or from highly similar groups of students. Some teacher-made music achievement tests may meet those conditions, as do some published music aptitude tests and music achievement tests, and whether specific published tests meet those conditions may be determined from the test manuals. Published test batteries, both music aptitude and music achievement, that yield standard scores for every subtest are particularly suited for comparing a student's standing in separate but corresponding dimensions of music aptitude and music achievement, because the higher the reliability coefficients and the lower the intercorrelation coefficients for the two subtest scores, total test scores, or composite scores, the greater the reliability of the standard error of a difference associated with the two tests.

The standard error of a difference is determined by computing the square root of the sum of the squared standard error of measurement of one test and the squared standard error of measurement of the other, as shown in the formula and computation on the following page. A difference between a student's score on two subtests or tests may be considered to be a real difference if it is of the same or greater magnitude than the standard error of a difference. Teachers may prefer to consider an observed difference as representative of a real difference only when it is at least the magnitude of two standard errors of a difference. A real difference between two subtest or test scores would, as in the example below, need to be 5.0 or 10.0 points, depending on the teacher's preference.

$$\text{SE of D} = \sqrt{\text{SE of M}^2 + \text{SE of M}^2} = \sqrt{4^2 + 3^2} = \sqrt{16 + 9} = \sqrt{25} = 5.0$$

CRITERION-REFERENCED TESTS AND NORMS-REFERENCED TESTS

The tests I have described thus far are called norms-referenced tests, because they are designed to yield scores that can be objectively compared and subjectively evaluated and interpreted in terms of a norm, such as a percentile rank. A criterion-referenced test, on the other hand, can be used only as an achievement test, never as an aptitude test, because it is not designed to yield norms. Rather, it incorporates a predetermined criterion in terms of a raw score (the number of questions answered correctly) that a student must attain in order to pass the test. A criterion-referenced test is actually a mastery test that tells the teacher whether a student should pass or fail, and thus, it is actually misused because it is employed as a means of evaluation rather than as a measurement tool. Mediocrity among students prevails because minimum achievement becomes the maximum. A better description of a criterion-referenced test might be that it simply reduces to criterion-referenced grading.

There are those who insist that just because a student has passed or failed a criterion-referenced test does not mean that a teacher may not examine the test results further in an attempt to derive diagnostic information. To some extent they are correct, but if the results of such a test are examined for that purpose, the test is, in a limited way, serving one of the same functions as a norms-referenced test. It would in that case make more sense to use a well-designed norms-referenced test that is intended to yield accurate measures to establish a pass-fail criterion **after** a test is scored and the test statistics have been examined and then to make use of the normative information that the test yields. A norms-referenced test, after all, can serve as a criterion-referenced test, but not the reverse.

When a student passes a criterion-referenced test, the student's score is measured against given criteria, never against the scores of other students, so that if a student attains the criterion score, the student passes. How is the criterion score determined? When it is designed properly, the criterion, ironically, must be established by a norm that is based directly or indirectly on a norms-referenced test. A criterion-referenced test or a criterion-referenced rating scale deals directly with evaluation and has no firm foundation in objective measurement. A norms-referenced test or a norms-referenced rating scale, on the other hand, deals directly with objective measurement and so provides a firm foundation for appropriate subjective evaluation.

A teacher who uses a criterion-referenced test is concerned primarily with assigning students pass-fail status or particular grades. A teacher who uses a norms-referenced test, however, will naturally be more concerned with the improvement of instruction than with grading. In addition to its diagnostic value, a well-constructed norms-referenced test provides students with a good learning experience.

If a criterion-referenced test could make provision for adapting instruction to students' individual musical differences, there would be less practical difference between a criterion-referenced test and a norms-referenced test. That is, unless ample comparative information is available for evaluating the extent of students' musical strengths and weaknesses, a teacher is limited in adapting instruction to the individual musical differences among students. A criterion of pass or fail can be determined easily from a norms-referenced test after it is scored and norms are derived, and in order for a teacher to adapt instruction to address students' musical weaknesses and enhance their musical strengths, more information than a mere pass or fail is necessary. With the results from a norms-referenced test a teacher can distinguish between a student who barely meets a criterion and one who meets the criterion with ease, or between a student who almost meets the criterion and one who does not even understand what is being asked.

Assume, for example, that students are asked to play a major scale in the keyality of E on a pass-fail criterion-referenced rating scale. It can be expected that no student will perform the scale perfectly, even when each student performs it more than once. Thus, it is difficult to determine accurately how well or poorly one must play the scale in order to pass or fail, and so the rating scale will have low reliability and validity. Moreover, after a student has been graded, little or no information is available should the teacher want to help the student improve his or her performance skill or to determine if the student should be advanced to a more complex skill or more complex content. If the teacher had used a well-defined norm-referenced rating scale with clearly stated continuous sequential criteria, however, specific aspects of the student's performance could have been measured and evaluated. As a result, regardless of whether the student passed or failed, the teacher would know the student's specific level of accomplishment, and his or her individual musical needs would be obvious. Merely to evaluate how well a student can play a major scale is one thing, but to measure a student's finger technique, intonation, bowing technique, and tone quality, for example, as the student performs a major scale is a far more practical and valid approach to evaluation.

It is possible that the practice of using a criterion-referenced test was introduced as a way to overcome the protests of some parents and students against the social prejudices and ill-conceived objectives of some teachers. Nonetheless, currently there is no published music criterion-referenced test that can be used to accurately assess individual students, although the professional philosophical literature is replete with statements advising the use of such tests, and simply to compare classes as a whole because a criterion-referenced test lacks reliability for individual students ignores the important purpose of testing.

Quasi criterion-referenced tests designed to serve as admission tests into music programs in institutions of higher learning have been used with some success. They identify, but do not discriminate among, students who are able to score above a specified criterion. Students who do not meet the criterion are not admitted to the program and those who are best among the rejected are not discriminated from the others in that group. Of course, the results of such a test are not intended to aid a teacher in teaching a student admitted to the program, nor are the results intended to aid a teacher in counseling a student if the student fails to be admitted to the program.

Given appropriate instruction, students with different levels of music aptitude will, over time, range more and more widely in terms of their music achievement, but regardless of their level of music aptitude, all students learn. However, it should be expected that students with lower music aptitudes will achieve less than will students with higher music aptitudes, and norms-referenced test results should provide a teacher with the necessary information to increase these differences among students by addressing their individual needs, thus allowing all students to achieve at a pace they find most comfortable. When criterion-referenced tests are used, however, teachers tend to reduce standards for all students, especially for those with higher music aptitudes, and, thus, the achievement level of a class overall becomes more even.

One might approve of a criterion-referenced test for a subject such as physical education, in which a student must run the fifty-yard dash in a prescribed number of seconds or accomplish a prescribed number of push-ups to pass a physical fitness task, but it does not follow that a criterion-referenced mastery test can serve equally well for measuring music achievement. In the case of the physical education test, the units of seconds are equal to the number of push-ups, in spite of the element of fatigue. The units of a music achievement test, that is, the actual test questions, can never show that kind of equivalence, however, because it is virtually impossible to write different test questions that are intended to include exactly the same content and skills. When a norms-referenced test is used for grading as well as for diagnostic purposes, it would seem that the same argument might apply. However, it is precisely because questions on a norms-referenced test cover such a broad range of skill and content, and thus are not intended to be equal units, that such a test serves so well as a basis for diagnosis as well as for evaluation.

It would be impossible to imagine what a test would be like if the content and skill level of all questions that it included were intended to be exactly the same. Even if such a boring test could be written, it would be a waste of time, because two questions that are similar (but not exactly the same) on a norms-referenced test would contribute more to the reliability and the validity of a test than would one hundred questions that were exactly the same. One question contributes as much, perhaps more, to test reliability as does the exact same question repeated one hundred times.

When test questions are not of equal units, a passing criterion score of, for example, eight of ten questions answered correctly does not make sense, because the issue then becomes which eight of the ten? Regardless of the intent of the test writer, some questions will in fact be more difficult than others, and so not all questions will cover exactly the same skills and content. If, for example, one student answers the first and second questions correctly and another student answers the ninth and tenth correctly, do both students meet the criterion of eight of ten? Not unless it can be proved that all ten questions are of equal difficulty, content and skill notwithstanding. And if so, why not include just one question in the test rather than ten? Further, if one student passes the test the first time and another student passes it after several tries, how does the teacher interpret that information when trying to differentiate between the two students?

An alternative, which would be to consider a perfect score as a criterion regardless of how many times a student attempted the test, would not be acceptable particularly to one who understands the concepts of test reliability, test validity, and error of measurement. Only rarely would any student pass the test, but if the criterion for passing the test were made too low, the reliability, and thus the validity, of the test would approach zero. For those resons, and because the reliability of a test can be expected to be higher for group measurement than for individual measurement, some educators suggest that criterion-referenced tests be used only to determine the proportion of a class that has mastered a task or to determine which classes in a school or district have mastered a task, rather than to determine which individual students have mastered a task.

EVALUATION AND GRADING

Grading, which is a type of evaluation, should be both normative and idiographic. When a student's work is evaluated normatively, the grade is based on the student's achievement as it compares with the achievement of all other students in the class, and when a student's work is evaluated idiographically, the grade is based on the student's actual achievement as it compares with the student's potential to achieve. Another way to evaluate a student idiographically is by comparing the student's past achievement with his or her current achievement.

There are students, for example, whose music achievement is low but whose music aptitude is high. If they were to receive a normative grade of A and an idiographic grade of C, they would then be better aware of the expectations the teacher and the school had of them. On the other hand, when students whose music aptitude and music achievement are both low receive a normative grade of C and an idiographic grade of A, they might be encouraged and better motivated to continue their good attitudes in class. An idiographic grade of A informs students with low music aptitude and low music achievement that a teacher is aware that they are working up to their potential and for that reason alone, they deserve to be proud.

Some teachers determine the scores necessary to receive a specific grade before a test is administered. For example, they might decide that scores from 90 to 100 equal an A; from 80 to 89, a B; from 70 to 79, a C; from 60 to 69, a D; and 59 and below, an F. This is not recommended, because as I explained earlier, if the grades are to be valid and instruction is intended to be adapted to students' individual musical differences, grades should be determined on the basis of the distributions of students' scores after a norms-referenced test has been scored.

Consider a class in which no student received an A because of a predetermined criterion. Might it not be possible that although there were A students in the class, the content of the test was inappropriate for the students or that the teacher was not doing an adequate job of teaching, or both? Typically, when mastery tests and mastery grades are used, they become methods for intimidation and punishment rather than tools to actually help students learn.

Some educators believe that normative grading causes friction between a student and teacher, and they suggest that an agency such as an unbiased board of educators be responsible for grading so that the teacher and student may interact as a team with a common goal, rather than as adversaries. Such an arrangement could have merit, but only if the student, parents, and teacher were kept informed of the results of the periodic evaluations as well as of end-of-the-term evaluations. In any case, the teacher would still need to be responsible for idiographic measurement and evaluation.

A sample student-parent report form is presented below. Space is provided for evaluating each student both normatively and idiographically on several sequential objectives and on two comprehensive objectives as they might be stated in a curriculum for each period of instruction. The comprehensive objective would include all relevant sequential objectives.

The teacher would write the titles of the sequential and comprehensive objectives in the left-hand boxes on the report form, and each student would be given a composite grade that represents the student's achievement of the comprehensive objective. Corresponding idiographic grades may be based on music aptitude or past music achievement.

	Student		Class Normative Distribution				
	Normative	Idiographic	A	B	C	D	F
Sequential Objective							
Sequential Objective							
Sequential Objective							
Sequential Objective							
Sequential Objective							
Comprehensive Objective							
Comprehensive Objective							
Composite Grade							

In order for parents and students to interpret a normative grade, the distribution of normative grades for the class should be included on the student-parent report form. For example, knowing how many A's, B's, C's, D's, and F's were given in a class would enable students and parents to interpret more precisely the value of a given grade. For most effective evaluation, each student-parent report should be discussed in a conference in which the teacher, the student, and one or both parents participate.

[11]

Talking about Music: Interviews with Disabled and Nondisabled Children

Judith A. Jellison, *The University of Texas at Austin*
Patricia J. Flowers, *The Ohio State University*

The purpose of this study was to describe, categorize, and compare data concerning music preferences, experiences, and skills obtained from interviews with 228 students labeled "disabled" (n = 73) or "nondisabled" (n = 155). A structured assessment interview was used by university student proctors to collect information from the students in four age-groups. Students identified by their respective schools as eligible for special education services constituted the group labeled "disabled." Questions developed for the interview focused on listening preferences and experiences, musical instrument preferences and performance, and singing and clapping (steady beat) performance. Following procedures consistent with naturalistic inquiry, audiotapes and transcriptions of the interviews were content-analyzed, and categories were developed from the responses. Perhaps the most notable outcome of this study is the similarity of responses between students with disabilities and their nondisabled peers. Results are discussed specific to music curriculum development, the integrated music classroom, and peer/teacher acceptance.

The past two decades have brought about increased public awareness of issues concerning the transition of individuals with disabilities into communities and schools with their nondisabled peers. This awareness, which eventually resulted in the passage of The Education for All Handicapped Children Act of 1975 (Public Law 94–142) (*Federal Register*, 1977b), brought about dramatic changes in educational policy and procedures as well as respective changes in the genre of research questions and methodological practice for professionals concerned with the well-being of individuals with disabilities.

The predominant educational philosophy inherent in the legislative mandates and educational literature throughout the 1970s and 1980s emphasized the process of "normalization"—making available to the disabled patterns and conditions of everyday life that are as close as possible to the norms and patterns of everyday society (Wolfensberger, 1972). Special education curricula and instruction were designed to assist citizens with disabilities to function ultimately as productively and independently as possible in integrated environments (Brown, Nietupski, & Hamre-Nietupski, 1976). Music therapists and music educators were encouraged to develop functional music curricula to assist students to be maximally independent in integrated home, school, and community music and nonmusic environments (Jellison, 1979, 1983). The philosophy of "normalization" continues throughout the 1990s, as evidenced by current legislation concerning civil rights for individuals with disabilities.

The regular music classroom is frequently designated on the disabled student's individual educational plan (IEP) as the integrated environment wherein disabled students can engage in "normalizing" activities and interact with nondisabled peers (Alley, 1979). Although there is a substantive research base concerning the therapeutic application of music with disabled children and young people, there is little research that is specifically concerned with the music behaviors of students with disabilities and their nondisabled peers (Jellison, 1988).

The absence of specific behavioral information concerning student performance is particularly consequential if teachers develop expectations for student performance based on the label "disabled" or "handicapped" given to the student receiving special education services. Teachers' overall expectations, for the most part, have been lower for students who are labeled as having a "handicap" or "deficiency" than are the teachers' expectations for the students' nondisabled peers (Foster, Ysseldyke, & Reese, 1975; Reynolds, Wang, & Walberg, 1987; Rolison & Medway, 1985).

In the music setting, music teachers found music objectives to be less important for students labeled "severely handicapped" than for unlabeled students and, similarly, less important for unlabeled students than for students labeled "gifted" (Jellison & Wolfe, 1987). In a study by Cassidy (1987) and an extension by Cassidy and Sims (1989), a priori knowledge of "special education" labels had a significant, positive effect on undergraduate and sixth- and seventh-grade students' ratings of a musical performance by students with disabilities. When the student's actual performance is seen to be unlike that suggested by the label, initial biases have been shown to be overcome (Reschly & Lamprecht, 1979).

A review of findings from several comparative music studies of nondisabled students and students with disabilities indicates that, on several specific music performance and perception tasks (generally related to rhythm activities), the actual performance of students with disabilities is similar, and in some cases, superior to that of their nondisabled peers (Jellison, 1988). Considering the variety of music experiences and types of social interactions that occur in the music classroom, it becomes important not only to obtain and compare data specific to music performance but also to obtain a breadth of information specific to music preferences and experiences that are not easily available using traditional research methodology.

The structured assessment interview, a data source in naturalistic inquiry, provides a useful data collection procedure that can result in obtaining information not easily available using observation or pencil-and-paper methods (Korchin & Schuldberg, 1981; Paget, 1984). The purpose of this study is to describe, categorize, and compare data concerning music preferences, experiences, and skills obtained from interviews with students labeled "disabled" and "nondisabled." Since the intent of this study was to compare behavioral responses within the generic labels "disabled" and "nondisabled," further labeling (i.e. mental retardation, learning disability, etc.) was not determined to be appropriate.

324   JELLISON–FLOWERS

METHOD

Subjects

The subjects were 228 students from four age-groups: 3–5 years (n = 26), 6–8 years n = 83), 9–11 years, (n = 91), and 12–14 years (n = 28). Seventy-three of the students were identified by their respective schools as students eligible for special education services and in the present study made up the group labeled "disabled." The remaining 155 students made up the "nondisabled" group.

Procedure

A structured assessment interview procedure was used to collect data for this paper. In a structured interview procedure, questions are decided upon in advance of the interview and are asked with the same wording and in the same order for all respondents (Maccoby & Maccoby, 1954). The structured interview form has particular advantages in that it allows for comparisons and reliability across interviewers and across time, and it assures that important topics and broad dimensions of behavior are included (Maccoby & Maccoby, 1954). All interviews were audiotaped in order to control for potential sources of error that are critical to reliability and validity (Paget, 1984).

Questions were developed that focused on music preferences, experiences, and skills. Specific questions concerned listening behaviors and interests, music performance experiences, and abilities to sing a favorite song and clap a steady beat (see Figure 1). All interviews were conducted individually and audiotaped. The interviewer was instructed to ask each question in order and to allow the student to respond to the question in his or her own words. The interviewer was not to make suggestions or model singing or clapping unless absolutely necessary.

Interviewers were university students enrolled in music methods courses at The Ohio State University, The University of Texas at Austin, and The University of

---

Questions:
1. Do you like music?
2. What do you like to do while you're listening to music?
3. What is your favorite kind of music? Why do you like this kind of music the best?
4. Is there any other kind of music that you really like?
    (If yes) What is it? Why do you like it?
5. Where do you listen to music most often?
6. Have you ever played a musical instrument?
    (If yes) Which one? Where did you get to play it?
7. Would you like to play a musical instrument?
    (If yes) Which one? Why would you choose this instrument?
8. Do you have music class at your school?
    (If yes) What is your favorite music class activity?
9. What is your favorite song? Would you sing it right now?
10. Can you clap a steady beat? Would you try to clap a steady beat right now?
11. Is there anything else you'd like to tell me about music?

Figure 1.

JRME   325

Texas at San Antonio. The inexperience of the interviewers in assessment techniques of disabled children was not considered to be a factor for concern given (a) the high level of structure for the interview, (b) the audiotaping of the responses, and (c) evidence to suggest that disabled students can perform more strongly with inexperienced examiners who develop rapport than with professionally experienced, unfamiliar examiners (Fuchs, Fuchs, Dailey, & Power, 1985).

Interviewers of disabled students in the present study were instructed to develop rapport through informal interactions (singing, games, talk, and play) with the disabled students prior to the structured interview. Although unfamiliarity of an examiner negatively affects disabled students' performance, it does not seem to be a negative factor for nondisabled students performance (Fuchs, Fuchs, Power, & Dailey, 1985). No specific instructions for the development of rapport were given for students interviewing nondisabled students.

All university interviewers were instructed to obtain information concerning the child's age, grade, and for disabled students, the disabling condition if known, prior to the interview. Audiotaping of the interview process was used to control for (a) errors that may have resulted from individual interviewer effects, (b) the extent to which the standardized procedures were actually followed, (c) clerical errors in the interviewer's written transcription of the verbal responses, (d) misunderstanding of the question by the respondent, and (e) over-prompting of responses. All interviewers provided a written transcription of verbal responses of the audiotaped interview.

RESULTS

Using procedures consistent with naturalistic inquiry, the transcriptions of the interviews were analyzed for content. Following an independent categorization of the data from nondisabled students by one of the investigators, both investigators discussed inconsistencies and refined procedures to arrive at a set of categories for the verbal data.

Categories were also determined for the singing and clapping data. If the subject named and sang his or her favorite song, the singing was analyzed for completeness, tonality (modulation), starting pitch, lowest pitch, and vocal range. More specifically, songs that were sung were assessed to be "complete" or "incomplete." Maintenance of tonality was assessed using procedures established by Flowers and Dunne-Sousa (1990): each singing example was categorized as "modulating," "somewhat modulating," "no modulation," or "indeterminable." Starting pitches were determined using a Korg AT-12 Auto Chromatic Tuner. If the subject clapped when asked to "clap a steady beat," the clapping was categorized as "2 or fewer claps," "steady beat," "steady rhythm," or "unsteady beat." A metronome was used to determine an estimate of the tempo for each response categorized as either "steady beat" or "steady rhythm."

Data from 41 subjects (18%) were used to determine reliability for agreement between written transcriptions and audiotaped versions for subjects' verbal, singing, and clapping responses. An independent reliability observer compared the written transcription of verbal responses recorded by interviewers with the audiotaped responses. Written responses were determined to be accurate (reflecting subject's verbalizations, although every word was not transcribed) or inaccurate. Reliability for accuracy of audiotape to written transcriptions for verbal responses was 100%. For those subjects who sang, tonality was determined using two categories: data from "yes" and "somewhat" were combined to constitute the "modula-

326 JELLISON–FLOWERS

tion" category, and data from "no" made up the "no modulation" category. For those subjects that clapped, categories were also combined: data from "2 or fewer claps" and "unsteady" constituted the "unsteady" category and data from "steady beat" and "steady rhythm" made up the "steady" category. Reliability for both singing modulation and steady/unsteady clapping response categories was 100%.

An additional 41 subjects were selected to determine pitch and tempo reliability. For singing, data from two independent observations were compared for starting pitch, lowest pitch, highest pitch, and range. Pitch data were compared for agreement for exact pitch, pitch within a half step, and pitch within a whole step. Overall exact pitch agreement was low (65%) although there was an overall 95% agreement within a half step and overall 99% agreement within a whole step. A Pearson Product-Moment Correlation calculated on two sets of tempo scores indicated $r = .90$.

When frequency data for respective categories derived from the subjects' responses were examined, a high degree of similarity was noted among age groupings. As a result, the data for several of the response categories that occurred most frequently across age-groups were combined for each of the two groups and are presented in Figures 2 and 3. An examination of the data for Question 4 (see Figure 1) indicated a high level of redundancy when compared with responses from Question 3: data from Question 4 are therefore not included in the final results.

Overall, greater variety was indicated for the response categories for nondisabled students although both groups indicated a similar pattern in responding with greater variety indicated for the 6–8-year-old and 9–11-year-old age groupings and less variety for the 3–5-year-old and 12–14-year-old age groupings.

Of the 228 students, ages 3–14 years, disabled or nondisabled, all but one reported "yes" to liking music. A few responses categorized as "other" for nondisabled students were qualifying responses (e.g. "Depends on the kind of music," or "Some I do and some I don't") and account for the lower percentage for this question (see Figure 2).

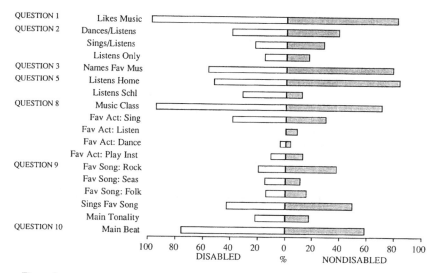

Figure 2.

Responses to Questions 2, 3, 5 and the first part of 9 (see Figure 1) indicated
listening preferences and experiences. Responses were most frequently categorized as "dance," "sing," or "listen" for both groups for the question "What do you
like to do while you're listening to music?" For Question 2, percentages for students with disabilities for dancing, singing, and listening only "while listening to
music" were 40%, 23%, and 16% respectively, and for nondisabled students, 39%,
28%, and 17% respectively (see Figure 2). Figure 2 shows that, for Question 3,
57% of the students with disabilities and 79% of nondisabled students indicated
their favorite kind of music by naming style, a particular song, or performer.
When responses for Question 5 ("Where do you listen?") were examined, 84% of
the responses from nondisabled students were in home-related categories, and
12% were in school-related categories; 53% of the responses from students with
disabilities were categorized as home-related and 32% as school-related (see
Figure 2). When students named their favorite song (Question 9), most often the
category for that song was pop/rock for both groups although seasonal songs and
folk songs were also named frequently by students (see Figure 2).

Responses to Questions 6 and 7 indicated preferences and experiences related
to music instruments. Figure 3 shows that 89% of the students with disabilities and
67% of the nondisabled students answered that they had played a musical instrument; the category of the instrument played was most frequently percussion for
both groups. A large majority of students from both groups also indicated that
they wanted to play an instrument with 75% of the students with disabilities and
70% of the nondisabled group indicating interest; instrument categories for
responses to the question "Which one?" are presented in Figure 3. When asked
"Why you would choose this instrument?" most students in all age groupings indicated that they wanted to play a particular instrument because of its sound;
responses that focused on the physical characteristics of the instruments occurred
less frequently than did sound-related responses.

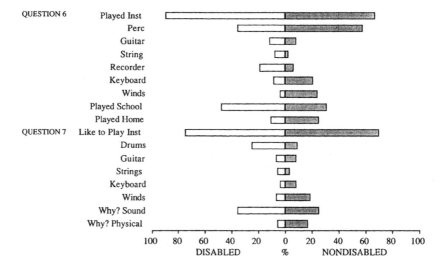

Figure 3.

Table 1

Mean Percentage of Responses of Students with Disabilities and Nondisabled Students for Singing Favorite Song and Clapping Steady Beat

| | Age-groups for Disabled (D) and Nondisabled (ND) | | | | | | | |
| | 3–5 | | 6–8 | | 9–11 | | 12–14 | |
Categories	D	ND	D	ND	D	ND	D	ND
Sings favorite song	75%	73%	30%	57%	66%	36%	0	35%
Mean starting pitch	$C\#_4$	D_4	Ab_3	$C\#_4$	$C\#_4$	C4	-	B_3
Mean lowest pitch	Bb_3	Bb_3	Ab_3	Bb_3	A_3	A_3	-	A_3
Mean highest pitch	F_4	G_4	E_4	G_4	F_4	F_4	-	E_4
Vocal range	A_4	M_6	P_5	M_6	M_6	m_6	-	A_4
Claps steady beat	75%	55%	70%	51%	87%	72%	73%	59%
Steady rhythm[a]	0	0	5%	22%	5%	11%	9%	0
Mean tempo estimate[b]	125	145	102	123	114	97	94	95

Note. Data represents responses to Questions 9 and 10 (see Figure 1).
[a]Students were asked to "Clap a steady beat," although some clapped a steady rhythm.
[b]Tempo estimates were determined using a metronome and are reported in beats per minute.

A majority of the students in both groups answered "yes" that they had music at their school (Question 8): singing was the response mentioned most frequently as a favorite music class activity (see Figure 2). After students named their favorite song (Question 9), 43% of the students with disabilities and 50% of the nondisabled students agreed to sing the song, although most students did not complete the entire song and, for the most part, did not maintain tonality throughout their singing. The tonality data presented in Figure 2 represent only those singing responses that were categorized as "no modulation."

The pitch data presented in Table 1 (starting, lowest pitch, highest pitches) are taken from pitches the students actually sang and does not necessarily represent their possible vocal ranges. Table 1 shows that most students in both groups sang within the range of a sixth (or less) and frequently started their songs around $C\#_4$, although starting pitches for the 9–11-year-old age grouping for students with disabilities were slightly lower than pitches for nondisabled students.

Figure 2 indicates that, when asked to clap a steady beat (Question 10), 76% of the students with disabilities and 59% of the nondisabled students maintained a steady beat while clapping. Some students clapped a steady rhythm (see Table 1). When steady beat and steady rhythm data are combined, percentages increase to 81% for students with disabilities and 68% for nondisabled students. The tempo of steady beat clapping was determined using a metronome while listening to the audio tape of steady beat responses. In several cases, there were too few claps by single subjects to determine precise data; therefore, tempo data should be considered to be tempo "estimates."

DISCUSSION

Perhaps the most notable outcome of this study is the similarity of responses between students with disabilities and their nondisabled peers. Although the music teacher must take into account individual differences that are important for the development of meaningful music curricula and effective teaching strategies, the label "disabled" or "handicapped" may connote more differences or even a variety of differences that are simply unimportant for day-to-day music classroom instruction and classroom routines. The recognition of similarities and specific areas of difference among the groups in the present study has implications for the development of positive social behavior of students in the integrated music classroom and implications for curriculum and instruction as well.

Issues relating to socialization and classroom social behavior have long been recognized as concerns of educators. The recognition of similarities among people is an important instructional component in preparing teachers and nondisabled students to receive students with disabilities in a positive manner into the regular classroom and subsequently to increase the quality of social interactions in these classrooms (Stainback & Stainback, 1981). Numerous studies and reviews of research show that desegregation alone, without intervention, does not result in peer or teacher acceptance or the development of appropriate academic programs for students with disabilities (Donaldson, 1980). Similarly, in the music setting, Jellison, Brooks, and Huck (1984) found that positive social interactions between nondisabled and disabled students during classroom and free time in the integrated music classroom and nondisabled students' acceptance are not a result of music classroom experiences and music instruction only but are a result of the degree to which the teacher structures small-group experiences and reinforcement for positive interactions.

When social/leisure interactions are promoted between nondisabled students and students with disabilities, similar interests can be identified with resulting increases in positive interactions in the classroom and the development of mutual respect among groups and individuals (Cole, Vandercook, & Rynders, 1989; Voeltz, 1980, 1982). Results of the present study indicate many common music interests and music preferences between students with disabilities and their nondisabled peers. Although these group data are important to help dispel possible attitudes that disabled students are musically very different from their nondisabled peers, direct application of these findings must be treated with caution. Teachers who are aware of similarities between groups of students would be further advised to conduct similar interviews with their own students. Knowledge of a specific individual's preferences and interests is vital to the development of strategies to promote positive interactions in the classroom. Since negative stereotypes persist and may even worsen without early intervention (Jellison, Brooks, & Huck, 1984), music teachers should assess interests and preferences and develop experiences for positive interactions early in the school year.

In addition to implications of this study for attitudes and behaviors in the integrated classroom, several other findings have important implications for the music curriculum and music experiences for students with disabilities. Several researchers have found that it is generally difficult for children to verbally analyze music (Hair, 1981; Flowers, 1983, 1984). In the present study, many similarities were noted between the verbal responses of the two groups; however, a higher frequency of verbal responses and a greater variety of verbal responses were noted among nondisabled students than were noted among students with disabilities. The fact that certain terminology was not used by students with disabilities does not necessarily imply a lack of knowledge. Students with disabilities may simply need more opportunities to "talk" about music with teachers, parents, and friends. Music teachers and music therapists may wish to incorporate functional music conversation into their curricula to assist students in the appropriate use of the vocabulary and terminology that they are learning in the classroom.

Dancing while listening to music was the most preferred activity for both groups. Given that the favorite music for both groups was pop/rock, it is probable that the dancing preferred was informal "social" dancing and not necessarily the type of dance/movement activities traditionally associated with the music classroom. The selection of pop/rock as a listening preference is consistent with numerous studies examining the listening preferences of school-age children (Greer, 1981; LeBlanc, 1979; LeBlanc & McCrary, 1983).

Singing was also a classroom activity highly preferred by both groups, although most students were not generally accurate singers. Findings were consistent with previous literature suggesting that children are more accurate in approximating contours (modulating or somewhat modulating) than pitches (Davidson, McKernon, & Gardner, 1981; Flowers & Dunne-Sousa, 1990). Singing accuracy may have been greater if students were asked to sing a familiar song (one sung often in the classroom) and not necessarily a "favorite" song, particularly given that the favorite was most often a pop/rock favorite. Since the singing of the pop/rock song was often inaccurate, it is possible that students do not necessarily learn the melody of pop/rock tunes but prefer them for dancing. Differences in ratings of singing accuracy between the groups should be interpreted cautiously due to possible variations in difficulty levels of the songs. Overall, older students with disabilities and nondisabled students were less willing to sing than were their younger peers.

Many of the students with disabilities in the present study had opportunities to sing with nondisabled students or to sing the same materials as their nondisabled peers in the public schools. In the review of educational research, Madden and Slavin (1983) found beneficial academic and social gains for students with mild disabilities who were placed in regular classrooms when compared to gains of their disabled peers in segregated special classrooms. Without particular instruction, public school music experiences may have positively influenced the results in the present study in that no striking differences were noted in mean starting pitches between the two groups. Also, it should be noted that students with disabilities in the present study represent a group with a wide range of abilities. When a group of individuals with a single disability classification (retardation) in a segregated setting were studied, their singing ranges and midpoints were generally found to be lower than the ranges and midpoints of their nondisabled peers of the same chronological age (Delio, 1976; Larson, 1977).

In the present study, the mean starting pitches B_3, C_4, and $C\#_4$ across the two groups and age groupings were, for the most part, consistent with results from several studies of students within this age group as reported by Welch (1979). There is no particular explanation for the slightly lower mean starting pitch for students with disabilities in the 6–8-year-old group. Interpretations of vocal range data should be made with caution since students sang a variety of songs and most often sang song fragments.

Similarities were also noted in clapping and clapping tempos. Most students in both groups were able to clap a steady beat, and a few students kept a steady rhythm. Tempos were generally similar between the two groups, with the larger difference for the 9–11-year-old group and the smaller difference for the 12–14-year-old group. Both groups showed an overall "slowing down" of clapping tempo across the age groups.

Few similarities were identified when students responded to questions concerning musical instruments. Percussion instruments were mentioned frequently as having been played by both groups although more nondisabled students had played traditional orchestral or band instruments than had students with disabilities. Guitar and recorder were mentioned more frequently by students with disabilities than by their nondisabled peers. Since data show that few students with disabilities study music outside of the music classroom and that school appears to be the primary environment for music in their lives, it is understandable that classroom instruments would be mentioned more frequently. The inclusion of recorder responses may account for the higher percentage of positive responses among students with disabilities for the question "Have you played a musical instrument?"

Most of the students wanted to play a musical instrument; drums were mentioned more frequently by students with disabilities, and wind instruments more frequently by nondisabled students. For the most part, differences relating to musical instruments appear to be the result of several factors: (a) the definition of "musical instrument"; (b) opportunities for students with disabilities to play traditional keyboard, orchestral, and band instruments; and (c) their knowledge of the names of a variety of traditional orchestral and band instruments.

Writers of several studies (Bruscia & Levinson, 1982; Furman, 1988; Steele, 1984; Staum & Flowers, 1984) and numerous informal articles in music education journals report that students with disabilities are able to read music successfully and learn to play traditional instruments. Although several students in the present study indicated that they had played traditional instruments, the percentage is much lower than is that of their nondisabled peers. Obviously, more opportunities and experiences with traditional instruments need to be made available for students with disabilities. Playing instruments is an experience that readily extends from the school to the home and community and provides, for all students, excellent opportunities for quality social and leisure activities outside the school day.

Music is perceived by society as a highly valued social and leisure activity, and this perception, in part, may account for the selection of music as a curricular subject for students. Although music may be offered in public schools, the music opportunities that are provided for a particular student may differ when that student is known to be "disabled" or "handicapped." Although a student is labeled "disabled" or "handicapped" and is receiving special education services, the present study shows that the student is not "musically disabled" to the extent that preferences, experiences, and skills are dramatically unlike those of nondisabled peers. Knowledge of similarities among students may function to encourage teachers to seek out and use similarities to structure and facilitate positive social and academic growth in their students. The differences that were most notable occurred in the areas of musical instruments and of vocabulary, where knowledge and experiences of students with disabilities have been limited. Findings of the present study suggest future research in strategies for teaching performance skills (playing traditional instruments and singing) and music vocabulary to students with disabilities and subsequent implications for quality musical and social experiences in integrated school and community environments.

REFERENCES

Alley, J. M. (1979). Music in the IEP: Therapy/education. *Journal of Music Therapy, 16*, 111–127.
Brown, L., Nietupski, V., & Hamre-Nietupski, S. (1976). Criterion of ultimate functioning. In M. A. Thomas (Ed.), *Hey, don't forget about me!* (pp. 2–15). Reston, VA: Council for Exceptional Children.

332   JELLISON–FLOWERS

Bruscia, K. E., & Levinson, S. (1982). Predictive factors in Optacon music-reading. *Journal of Visual Impairment & Blindness, 76,* 309–312.

Cassidy, J. W. (1987). The effect of "special education" labels on musicians' and nonmusicians' ratings of selected choirs. *Journal of the International Association of Music for the Handicapped, 3*(2), 25–40.

Cassidy, J. W., & Sims, W. (1989). Effects of special education labels on peers' and music educators' evaluations of a handicapped youth choir. Paper presented at the Eighth National Symposium for Research in Music Behavior, Baton Rouge, LA.

Cole, D. A., Vandercook, T., & Rynders, J. (1989). Comparison of two peer interaction programs: Children with and without severe disabilities. *American Educational Research Journal 25,* 415–439.

Davidson, L., McKernon, P., & Gardner, N.E. (1981). The acquisition of song: A developmental approach. *Documentary report of the Ann Arbor symposium: National symposium on the applications of psychology to the teaching and learning of music* (pp. 301–315). Reston, VA: MENC.

Delio, C. L. (1976). The relationship of diagnostic and social factors to the singing ranges of institutionalized mentally retarded persons. *Journal of Music Therapy, 13,* 17–28.

Donaldson, J. (1980). Changing attitudes toward handicapped persons: A review and analysis of research. *Exceptional Children, 46,* 504–514.

Federal Register (1977a). Education of Handicapped Children. Implementation of Part B of the Education of the Handicapped Act, 42 (163). Part II, Tuesday, August 23, 1977.

Federal Register (1977b). Nondiscrimination of basis of handicap. Part IV, Wednesday, May 4, 1977.

Flowers, P. J. (1983). The effect of instruction in vocabulary and listening on nonmusicians' descriptions of changes in music. *Journal of Research in Music Education, 31,* 179–190.

Flowers, P. J. (1984). Attention to elements of music and effect of instruction in vocabulary of written descriptions of music by children and undergraduates. *Psychology of Music, 12,* 17–24.

Flowers, P. J., & Dunne-Sousa, D. (1990). Pitch pattern accuracy, tonality, and vocal range in the singing of preschool children. *Journal of Research in Music Education, 38,* 102–114.

Foster, G., Ysseldyke, J., Reese, J. (1975). I wouldn't have seen it if I hadn't believed it. *Exceptional Children, 41,* 55–48.

Fuchs, D., Fuchs, L. S., Dailey, A. M., and Power, M. H. (1985). The effects of examiners' personal familiarity and professional experience on handicapped children's test performance. *Journal of Educational Research, 78,* 141–146.

Fuchs, D., Fuchs, L. S., Power, M. H., & Dailey, A. M. (1985). Bias in the assessment of handicapped children. *American Educational Research Journal, 22,* 185–198.

Furman, C. E. (Ed.). (1988). *Effectiveness of music therapy procedures: Documentation of research and clinical practice.* Washington, DC: National Association for Music Therapy.

Greer, R. D. (1981). An operant approach to motivation and affect: Ten years of research in music learning. *Documentary report of the Ann Arbor symposium: National symposium on the applications of psychology to the teaching and learning of music* (pp. 101–121). Reston, VA: MENC.

Hair, H. I. (1981). Verbal identification of music concepts. *Journal of Research in Music Education, 29,* 11–21.

Jellison, J. A. (1979) The music therapist in the education setting: Developing and implementing curriculum for the handicapped. *Journal of Music Therapy, 16,* 128–137.

Jellison, J. A. (1983) Functional value as criterion for selection and prioritization of nonmusic and music educational objectives in music therapy. *Music Therapy Perspectives, 1*(2), 17–22.

Jellison, J. A. (1988). A content analysis of music research with handicapped children and youth (1975–1986): Applications in special education. In C. K. Furman (Ed.), *Effectiveness of music therapy procedures: Documentation of research and clinical practice* (pp. 223–279). Washington, DC: National Association for Music Therapy.

Jellison, J. A., Brooks, B. H., & Huck, A. M. (1984). Structuring small groups and music reinforcement to facilitate positive interactions and acceptance of severely handicapped students in the regular music classroom. *Journal of Research in Music Education, 32,* 243–264.

Jellison, J. A., & Wolfe, D.E. (1987). Educators' ratings of selected objectives for severely handicapped or gifted students in the regular classroom. *Contributions to Music Education, 14,* 36–41.

Korchin, S. J., & Schuldberg, D. (1981). The future of clinical assessment. *American Psychologist, 36,* 1147–1158.

Larson, B. A. (1977). A comparison of singing ranges of mentally retarded and normal children with published songbooks used in singing activities. *Journal of Music Therapy, 14,* 139–143.

LeBlanc, A. (1979). Generic style music preferences of fifth-grade students. *Journal of Research in Music Education, 27,* 255–270.

LeBlanc, A., & McCrary, J. (1983). Effects of tempo and performing medium on children's music preference. *Journal of Research in Music Education, 31,* 283–294.

Maccoby, E. E., & Maccoby, N. (1954). The interview: A tool for social science. In G. Lindzey (Ed.), *Handbook of social psychology* (Vol. 1, pp. 449–487). Cambridge, MA: Addison-Wesley.

Madden, N. A., & Slavin, R. E. (1983). Mainstreaming students with mild handicaps: Academic and social outcomes. *Review of Educational Research, 53,* 519–565.

Paget, K. D. (1984). The structured assessment interview: A psychometric review. *Journal of School Psychology, 22,* 415–427.

Reschley, D. J., & Lamprecht, M. J. (1979). Expectancy effects of labels: Fact or artifact? *Exceptional Children, 46,* 55–58.

Reynolds, M. C., Wang, M. C., & Walberg, H. J. (1987). The necessary restructuring of special and regular education. *Exceptional Children, 53,* 391–398.

Rolison, M. A., & Medway, F. J. (1985). Teachers' expectations and attributions for student achievement: Effects of label, performance pattern, and special education intervention. *American Education Research Journal, 22,* 561–573.

Stainback, S., & Stainback, W. (1981). Educating nonhandicapped students about severely handicapped students: A human differences training model. *Education Unlimited,* March/April, 17–19.

Staum, M. J., & Flowers, P. J. (1984). The use of simulated training and music lessons in teaching appropriate stopping to an autistic child. *Music Therapy Perspectives, 1*(3), 14–17.

Steele, A. L. (1984). Music therapy for the learning disabled: Intervention and instruction. *Music Therapy Perspectives, 1*(3), 2–7.

Voeltz, L. M. (1980). Children's attitudes toward handicapped peers. *American Journal of Mental Deficiency, 84,* 455–464.

Voeltz, L. M. (1982). Effects of structured interaction with severely handicapped peers on children's attitudes. *American Journal of Mental Deficiency, 86,* 380–390.

Welch, G. P. (1979). Vocal range and poor pitch singing. *Psychology of Music, 7,* 13–31.

Wolfensberger, W. (1972). *The principle of normalization in human services.* Toronto: National Institute on Mental Retardation.

August 20, 1990

[12]

Demonstration and Recognition of High and Low Contrasts in Teacher Intensity

Clifford K. Madsen, Jayne M. Standley,
Jane W. Cassidy, *Florida State University*

The purpose of this study was to investigate teacher intensity, *the global attributes of enthusiasm combined with an astute sense of timing in relation to classroom management and effective subject presentation and delivery. The authors also tried to ascertain whether high and low contrasts in teacher intensity could be taught to and then demonstrated by prospective music education student teachers (n = 20) and whether other music education majors untrained in the concept of intensity could recognize these contrasts (freshmen, n = 23; seniors, n = 22; and graduate students, n = 29). Results of the study indicated that intensity as a concept could be operationally defined, easily taught to prospective student teachers, ably demonstrated, and recognized with an extremely high degree of reliability across levels of sophistication within the music education major.*

The ability of a teacher to initiate and maintain a high level of student attention has been of major concern to researchers and teacher educators for years. To prepare future teachers for productive and effective teaching, it is necessary to identify those observable, quantifiable characteristics that separate expert teachers from novices (Brandt, 1986). Berliner (1986) has suggested a number of attributes needed for high teacher effectiveness and, therefore, high teacher intensity.

When used to refer to teacher presentation of subject matter, the terms *enthusiasm, magnitude,* and *affect* are used somewhat interchangeably, suggesting that teacher behavior can be executed and observed in varying degrees. Collins (1978) developed a measurement device that operationally defined eight teacher behaviors under low, medium, and high levels of enthusiasm. Behavioral descriptors were used in a training session designed to increase enthusiasm level of preservice elementary teachers. Collins's data, in the form of observer enthusiasm ratings, showed that experimental subjects increased their display of enthusiasm after training and that control subjects changed little from pretest to posttest, indicating that it is possible to train preservice teachers to increase teacher enthusiasm. McKinney et al. (1983) used the Collins model in an experimental training session. After treatment, teachers were asked to display high, medium, or low enthusiasm in the classroom on demand. Observers of these performances correctly assigned ratings to virtually all teachers across the three categories of enthusiasm, but the level of enthusiasm had *no* effect on posttest student achievement on a social studies task.

Music teacher behaviors of eye contact, closeness to students, volume and modulation of voice, gestures, facial expressions, and pacing were first operationally defined and differentiated as high and low levels of magnitude by Yarbrough (1975). In a choral rehearsal setting, the effects of high and low magnitude on student behavior were reliably observed. Students seemed to prefer and were more attentive during high magnitude conditions, although magnitude had *no* significant effect on performance level. Sims (1986) varied teacher affect (high versus low) and student activity (active versus passive hand movements) during music listening activities with preschool children. Changes in student off-task behavior were more obvious when high affect was followed by low affect than under the opposite condition.

Preliminary investigations specifically relating to the current project included three separate experiments. Experiment 1 (Standley & Madsen, 1987) compared videotaped performances of 42 freshman music education majors under two conditions: (a) each student speaking 30 seconds before the entire group of subjects about the individual's personal goals for a music career and (b) each subject leading a familiar song with a group of six preschoolers ranging in age from 4 to 5 years. Intensity, defined as sustained control of the student/teacher interaction with efficient, accurate presentation and correction of the subject matter combined with enthusiastic affect and pacing, was evaluated on a 10-point Likert scale. Correlation analysis indicated that intensity in speaking about oneself was *not* highly related to intensity in a music teaching situation (Spearman Rank Correlation Coefficient $r_s = .43$).

Experiment 2 (Standley & Madsen, 1987) assessed teacher intensity of three groups of music education/therapy majors engaged in a music task similar to Experiment 1: teaching a new song to a group of preschoolers ages 4 to 5 years. Subjects were 15 freshmen in their first semester of study, 15 senior music education majors in their final week of campus study prior to internship in the schools, and 15 senior music therapy majors in their final week of campus study prior to internship in clinical agencies. We rated subjects on intensity using a 10-point Likert scale. Mean scores for each group were compared with a Kruskall-Wallis one-way analysis of variance (ANOVA) and revealed significant differences ($H = 18.73$, $df = 2$, $\alpha < .001$). A Dunn's Multiple Comparison procedure determined the freshmen to be significantly lower in intensity ratings ($\bar{R} = 34.1$) than either the music education ($\bar{R} = 21.4$) or the music therapy seniors ($\bar{R} = 13.6$). There was no statistical significance between the two senior groups. Results of these two studies suggested that intensity is a teaching skill that can be measured and that performance of a musical task may enhance the intensity of the teaching interaction.

Researchers in the third experiment (Madsen & Geringer, in press) focused on the relationship between demonstrated effective teaching and teacher intensity or teacher "on-task." Senior music education majors ($n = 22$) in their last week of student teaching made a videotape of their best teaching, which included both teacher and student responses. A panel of four expert teacher educators independently judged the videotapes using a 5-point Likert scale. Student teachers were evaluated on the basis of demonstrated effective teaching in relationship to student responses. Reliability among judges was $W = .86$. These same videotapes were then independently judged by two different experts trained in judging teacher "on-task" or intensity using an evaluative instrument specifically designed to assess behaviors relating to teacher intensity. These judges viewed videotaped examples of 15-second intervals and marked specific teacher behaviors. They also used a subjective rating scale to evaluate teacher intensity by assigning a rating of *low* (0) to *high* (10) at the end of each minute. Reliability for the judges was $r_s = .85$ on the more subjective rating. We then assessed the correlation between effective teaching and intensity. The Spearman Rank Correlation Coefficient was $r_s = .92$. Thus, results of the study suggested that intensity may be an important attribute of effective music teaching and warrants additional investigation.

METHOD

Our intent in this study was to ascertain whether high and low contrasts in teacher intensity could be quickly taught to and then demonstrated by prospective music education student teachers and whether subjects untrained in the concept of intensity could recognize these contrasts. Subjects were music education majors ($N = 94$) who were divided into one experimental and three control groups. The experimental group (student teachers) consisted of music education majors ($n = 20$) in their final week of on-campus preparation prior to beginning a public school internship with emphasis in general, choral, or instrumental areas. The three control groups were differentiated according to level of preparation in the music education or therapy major: freshmen ($n = 23$), seniors ($n = 22$), and graduate students ($n = 29$).

Prospective student teachers received one afternoon of training in a teaching session of 1.5 hours. Extreme contrasts in teacher intensity were modeled by the instructor across several specific musical activities (e.g., conducting the speaking of accurate rhythmic patterns or the singing of simple chord progressions or several folk songs). Student teachers then emulated these contrasts in teaching the same activities before their peers for short periods beginning with 10–15 seconds and extending to a few minutes.

The next day, we asked each subject to demonstrate high and low teacher intensity *contrasts* across 1 minute while teaching a self-selected music activity. The minute was divided into four 15-second intervals by the ringing of a bell. Differing combinations of high and low intensity had been randomly preassigned for the intervals of each minute and were known only to that subject. The presentation order of high and low intervals was counterbalanced by the experimenters and all possible orders of combinations were assigned.

At the conclusion of the first 20 demonstrations, we asked the subjects to repeat the task with each assigned high or low interval changed to the opposite concept (e.g., high-low-high-low to low-high-low-high). Again, a bell differentiated the four 15-second intervals within each minute. Both 20-minute demonstrations were videotaped, and the videotape included the sound of the bell that separated each 15-second interval. The numbers 1–4 were superimposed on the tape so that they appeared simultaneously with the auditory stimulus, providing an additional means of identifying the intervals. Equipment for this aspect of the study consisted of a VHS portable videocassette recorder (Panasonic, Model AG-2400), a color camera (Panasonic, Model WV3040K), and a character generator for superimposing numbers (Panasonic, Model WV-KB10). Videotapes were shown on two color monitors (Zenith, Model C 1382W and Panasonic, Model CTG-1911), arranged to maximize visibility for each participant.

Following the two demonstrations, the student teacher group was asked to view each 20-minute videotape and, for each 15-second interval, to mark an "H" indicating high intensity or an "L" indicating low intensity. Four intervals a minute for 20 minutes yielded a total of 80 intervals to be marked and a possible correct score of 80. At the end of the observation task, each subject was asked to give a self-rating of his or her own overall ability to achieve high intensity on a Likert-type scale from 1 to 10 (1 indicating *low intensity* and 10 indicating *high*). In addition, the prospective student teachers were asked to vote for the five people in the group they thought would be the best teachers. They were also asked to define "teacher intensity" and to state what they had learned about the particular task of contrasting high and low intensity.

Comparison of the responses ($n = 20$) on Tape 1 and Tape 2 yielded mean correct scores of 73.22 and 72.0, respectively. We computed agreement between the two observations using a Kendall Coefficient of Concordance that resulted in $W = .81$, which was statistically significant ($\chi^2 = 27.68$, $df = 17$, critical value = 27.59, $\alpha < .05$). We determined that the student teachers had adequately demonstrated high and low intensity such that it could be differentiated with accuracy across multiple observations.

Tape 1 was then shown to subjects within the three control groups who marked "H" or "L" at the end of each designated interval. Prior to the control observations, intensity was not taught, demonstrated, or defined. At the end of each four-segment minute, the videocassette recorder was placed in the pause mode for 5 seconds and control subjects gave each student teacher an overall ability to achieve high intensity rating from 1 (low) to 10 (high). At the end of the observation task, we asked the control subjects to define intensity by writing on the back of the observation form.

RESULTS

We compared observation scores and overall intensity ratings across groups and analyzed observation errors by interval and by subject. The single most important result was that intensity as a concept was operationally defined, easily taught to prospective student teachers, ably demonstrated, and easily recognized with an extremely high degree of reliability by almost all subjects in the study. The total rate of correct responses across the 15-second intervals was 82.7%. Additionally, the 20 overall intensity ratings (on a scale of 1–10) given by each subject within the control groups were compared for agreement with the Kendall Coefficient of Concordance, resulting in an extremely high reliability (W = .99) that was, of course, statistically significant (χ^2 = 55.87, df = 19, critical value = 43.82, α < .001). This result was considered extraordinary because the task involved rating a concept that was neither taught nor explained, yet agreement was almost 100% across subjects ranging from freshman level to graduate status.

The self-rating given by the student teachers who actually did the teaching task was then compared with the mean rating given by subjects within the untrained groups who had such high agreement among themselves. The Kendall Coefficient of Concordance then dropped to W = .74, which was not statistically significant (χ^2 = 28.12, df = 19, critical value = 30.14, α < .05), indicating low overall agreement. A t test comparing the student teachers versus the combined other groups yielded statistically significant results (t = 3.88, df = 38, α < .001) (see Table 1). These results show that the student teachers rated themselves an average of more than 2 points higher on a 10-point scale ($\bar{M}$ = 7.25) compared to the more objective observers ($\bar{M}$ = 4.41), who demonstrated highly consistent agreement among themselves. These findings substantiate prior research showing that self-ratings of students are both higher and less reliable when compared with those of other professionals (Greenfield, 1978).

Table 1

Analysis of High Versus Low Errors by Interval

	Beginning intervals		Changing intervals				Overall		
	Begin high	Begin low	Low to high	High to low	High to high	Low to low	Total high	Total low	Total
Intervals									
n	10	10	15	15	15	15	40	40	80
(Percentage)	(.125)	(.125)	(.187)	(.187)	(1.87)	(.187)	(.50)	(.50)	(1.00)
Errors									
n	298	80	371	147	174	232	843	459	1,302
(Percentage)	(.23)	(.06)	(.29)	(.11)	(.13)	(.18)	(.65)	(.35)	(1.00)

Total observers = 94; total intervals = 7,520; total errors = 1,302.
Error rate = .173.

We analyzed high versus low observation errors in Tape 1 by interval across all subjects ($N = 94$). Table 1 shows that almost twice as many errors occurred in recognizing high intensity (843) as in recognizing low intensity (459), with the bulk of the high errors occurring when student teachers were assigned a *change* from low to high (371) or were assigned to *begin* their demonstration with high intensity (298). This finding indicates that either acquisition or perception of high intensity is more difficult when compared to that of low intensity.

The observation errors of the student teachers were analyzed by subject, then rank ordered and compared with the rank of "best teacher votes" as awarded by the student teachers. A Spearman Rank Correlation Coefficient resulted in $r_s = .64$, which was statistically significant ($t = 3.83$, $df = 19$, critical value $= 2.861$, $\alpha < .01$). The vote for "best teacher" correlated fairly highly with the subject's ability to demonstrate high and low contrasts in intensity.

We asked all subjects to define "intensity." Rates of responses varied. The fewest number of ideas was expressed by the student teachers ($n = 20$, comments $= 37$, $M = 1.9$) followed by freshmen ($n = 23$, comments $= 62$, $M = 2.7$) and seniors ($n = 22$, comments $= 99$, $M = 4.5$), with the greatest number of ideas expressed by the graduate students ($n = 29$, comments $= 144$, $M = 4.97$). Student teachers who were trained to demonstrate intensity were most concise about its definition. Number of expressions increased and varied with the length of time in the curriculum.

Table 2 shows degree of agreement among groups in the major ideas expressed and includes 14 items that accounted for 260 of the 342 total responses. Responses included by fewer than six persons were omitted, including 39 single ideas expressed solely by 39 different persons. Eye contact and proximity (the second and third most frequent responses) were not mentioned by any of the freshman subjects, who also omitted such specific instructional techniques as pacing; short, simple instructions; good posture; and the need for making music as opposed to talking. More advanced students are evidently taught these concepts in the curriculum, and they used such concepts to describe the teaching interactions observed. These items are very similar to the list compiled by Yarbrough (1975) to define high magnitude. Although the words used to define intensity varied greatly, agreement was very high in identifying intensity as either high or low, and it was also high on the overall rating of intensity.

Although they were not of major importance to this study, results were assessed to determine differentiation across groups. Table 3 shows the means and standard deviations of correct observation scores by group. With a possible maximum score of 80, means ranged from 73.22 (student teachers) to 63.04 (freshmen). The student teachers who were trained in demonstrating intensity scored higher than those groups who were untrained. A One-Way Analysis of Variance on these scores yielded significant results between groups ($F = 5.05$, $df = 93$, $p < .001$).

We believe that effective education in any field or area has to do with (a) student selection and (b) the demonstrated effects of teaching. Obviously, if the selection issue is the most important ("teachers are born not made"), the profession must find the important variables that constitute recruitment for effective teaching (as in Experiment 1). If skills can be taught, learned, and measured, the profession still has the same problem: What are the variables necessary for effective teaching?

Table 2
Definitions of Intensity by Group

Comment	Interns	Graduates	Freshmen	Seniors	Total
Enthusiastic, excited expression	5	22	11	11	49
Eye contact	7	15	0	9	31
Proximity; movement toward group	2	15	0	8	25
Concentration; attention to students or teaching; involvement	2	6	8	7	23
Strict, precise body movement or conducting gestures	1	8	3	10	22
Voice volume, pitch, inflection; change in voice	0	9	2	10	21
Energy; effervescence; vigor; pizzazz	3	10	3	3	19
No hesitation in voice; no filler words (uh, ah)	0	8	4	2	14
Planning; knowledge; competence	2	4	3	4	13
Pacing	1	7	0	4	12
Short, simple instructions	2	5	0	3	10
Good posture; change in posture	0	4	0	4	8
Confidence	1	3	2	1	7
Little talk, lots of singing; vary techniques to increase attention; as much time in learning activities as possible	4	1	0	1	6
Totals	30	117	36	77	260

Table 3
Group Means and Standard Deviations of Observation Scores

	Interns	Seniors	Graduates	Freshmen
n	20	22	29	23
Mean score	73.22	66.27	63.56	63.04
Standard deviations	1.93	1.8	2.27	2.24

$N = 94$

Other than knowledge of subject matter, two recurring variables concern (a) demonstrated teacher *enthusiasm* (high teacher affect) in live, positive student/teacher interactions and (b) a sense of *timing* in relationship to classroom management and effective subject matter presentation and monitoring. Both of these variables require the ability to "see oneself as others do" or to "know how one is coming across." Therefore, one's social awareness seems paramount. Teacher intensity in some ways seems to blend the attributes of enthusiasm and timing in that people who are perceived as having high intensity are enthusiastic as well as effective in managing the class. It is difficult to imagine an intense teacher who does not possess both these qualities.

Because previous researchers found a strong relationship between teacher intensity and teacher effectiveness, it seems that all issues relating to teacher intensity need to be investigated. These issues include student attentiveness, subject matter acquisition, the degree of intensity associated with the subject matter itself (i.e., the activity of making music), various levels of social and peer interaction that contribute to intensity, and the general level of teacher "on-task."

Issues concerning intensity are important in both selection and training of prospective teachers, especially in relation to student achievement. The experiments described in this article indicate that teacher intensity is an attribute that can be learned and demonstrated by preservice music teachers and that almost anyone can recognize it with very high reliability. Obviously, much more research is warranted.

REFERENCES

Berliner, D. C. (1986). In pursuit of the expert pedagogue. *Educational Researcher, 15*(7), 5–13.

Brandt, R. S. (1986, October). On the expert teacher: A conversation with David Berliner. *Educational Leadership,* pp. 4–9.

Collins, M. (1978). Effect of enthusiasm training on preservice elementary teachers. *Journal of Teacher Education, 29*(1), 53–57.

Greenfield, D. G. (1978). Evaluation of music therapy practicum competencies: Comparisons of self and instructor ratings of videotapes. *Journal of Music Therapy, 15*(1), 15–20.

Madsen, C. K., & Geringer, J. M. (in press). The relationship of teacher "on-task" to intensity and effective music teaching. *Canadian Music Educator.*

McKinney, C. W., Larkins, A. G., Kazelskis, R., Ford, M. J., Allen, J. A., & Davis, J. C. (1983). Some effects of teacher enthusiasm on student achievement in fourth grade social studies. *Journal of Educational Research, 76*(4), 249–253.

Sims, W. L. (1986). The effect of high versus low teacher affect and passive versus active student activity during music listening on preschool children's attention, piece preference, time spent listening, and piece recognition. *Journal of Research in Music Education, 34,* 173–191.

Standley, J. M., & Madsen, C. K. (1987). Intensity as an attribute of effective therapist/client interaction. *Quodlibet,* Summer, 1987, 15–21.

Yarbrough, C. (1975). The effect of magnitude of conductor behavior on performance, attentiveness, and attitude of students in selected mixed choruses. *Journal of Research in Music Education, 23,* 134–146.

September 9, 1987

[13]

On "American Music for American Children": The Contribution of Charles L. Seeger

Marie McCarthy, *University of Maryland*

The distinguished music scholar Charles L. Seeger (1886–1979) viewed music education as playing a critical role in the development of American musical life. During his long career, he made an important contribution to the history, philosophy, and sociology of music education. The purpose of this study was to identify a primary aspect of Seeger's contribution by exploring one of his ongoing professional concerns— American music for American children. The study progresses from a profile of Seeger the music educator to his approach to music in American culture, his plan for revitalizing music in American education, and, finally, an appraisal of his criticisms and recommendations. Music in American education, he believed, would better serve American society if some vital connections with school music were activated or renewed. The writer identifies these as the child's own music, American vernacular music in general, other music professionals (and particularly musicologists), and the cultural-political context in which music and education function. Seeger played a significant role in introducing vernacular music into the schools, in extending the definition of American music in the curriculum, in presenting music as a cultural subject, and in assisting music educators in dealing with musical diversity in the classroom.

Charles Seeger is universally acclaimed as one of the foremost music scholars of the twentieth century. His preeminence was gained "not because he was famous for any one thing, but for the collectivity of all his contributions to the American music scene and to American society."[1] Since many of his writings are conceptually complex and semantically dense, scholars have been reluctant to explore his works and apply his ideas to issues in contemporary music scholarship.[2] Furthermore, Seeger has been viewed narrowly as a musicologist with tenuous connections to music education. An overview of the major histories of music education in the United States indicates

clearly that Seeger's legacy to and leadership in the profession is min-
imally acknowledged and totally unexplored.[3] The primary purpose
of this article is to present Charles Seeger the music educator—to
induct him, as it were, into the annals of music education history—
and to begin to explore the wealth of his contribution and legacy to
the profession. In a sense, this is a response to Seeger's biographer
when she stated: "My hope—and I think his would be, too—is that
this book will initiate more in-depth and definitive research into each
facet of Seeger's work."[4]

A comprehensive study of Seeger's contributions to music education is not possible within the scope of the present study. This initial
exploration focuses on one of the dominant themes of his career—
the relationship of music and culture as applied to American society.
Within this theme, Seeger frequently addressed "the missionary role
of educators in 'making America musical'"[5] and their responsibility
in expanding the definition of American music for American children. The motivation for choosing this topic over a host of others
from his immense corpus of literature is twofold. First, Seeger was a
primary innovator and activist in introducing vernacular music into
American public schools in the 1940s. In that capacity, he had a fundamental impact on professional practice and paved the way for subsequent efforts to broaden school music repertoire. Second, an
examination of his role in promoting music as a cultural subject in
the curriculum provides insights into the multiple dilemmas and
paradoxes music educators face today in accommodating diversity
and in linking school music with vernacular music culture.

"American Music for American Children," a Seeger article cited in
the title of this study, was published in the Novem-ber–December
1942 issue of *Music Educators Journal.*[6] It described the project on
"American Songs for American Children," which was presented earlier that year by Seeger, among others, at the national biennial conference of the Music Educators National Conference (MENC) in
Milwaukee, Wisconsin. Viewed in the context of his entire career, the
title served as a symbol for one of his ongoing professional concerns,
and the article may be explored and interpreted at a number of different levels. First, the article communicated to music teachers a new
definition of school music and promoted folk music as worthy of
inclusion in the curriculum. Second, Seeger's arrival at this perspective was the result of years of forethought and scholarship on the role
of music in culture, society, and education. Third, it provided clear
testimony of an intellectual and musical journey that Seeger had
made from an elite, nineteenth-century view of music for music's
sake to a democratic, twentieth-century view of music rooted in its
sociocultural functions. Fourth, it demonstrated his quest for a definition of American music beyond the hegemonic European one of
previous decades. Finally, his efforts to define American music for
American children offered a stimulus for a lively debate in contemporary music education as to the usefulness of such a definition. His
ideas can provide that same stimulus today as we try to answer such

questions as: Is it futile to attempt to define American music in the curriculum? Have we surpassed a discussion of such an issue? Is it a topic that is related to the contemporary debates in the multicultural education movement?

Charles Seeger the Music Educator

Seeger was raised in a bicultural environment because his father's business ventures took the family back and forth between the United States and Mexico City. In 1904, he entered Harvard University where, against the wishes of his parents, he pursued studies in music. He later wrote:

> My youthful ambitions and ideals by the time I got to Harvard were to avoid going into business. ... When I told my father that I was going to be a composer, he was horrified. He said: "But gentlemen are not musicians." ... He pointed out the impracticality of it and the argument closed.[7]

After graduating from Harvard *magna cum laude* in music in 1908, Seeger spent two and a half years in Europe. In 1912, he was hired as chairman of the Music Department at the University of California at Berkeley, and remained there until 1919. One of his appointments while at Berkeley was to a committee on music education, and "his committee service meant that he spent a few weeks each spring visiting public high schools in the California foothills."[8] In these years at Berkeley, during subsequent periods back in New York at the Institute of Musical Art (1921–33) and the New School for Social Research (1931–35), and later in Washington, D.C., as music adviser for various federal projects (1935–41), Seeger's intellectual ideas were formed. The period during which he was most involved in music education extended from 1940 to 1953, coinciding with his tenure as chief of the Music Division of the Pan American Union (PAU, now called the Organization of American States). His intense engagement with the music education profession during this period is reflected in the fact that all but one of his writings on education appeared between 1940 and 1953.[9]

Seeger conducted his scholarly inquiry from multiple vantage points. This is consonant with Gilbert Chase's view of Seeger's ideas as transcending all categorical boundaries.[10] Unlike other scholars who focused their life's work on questions that lay within the increasingly narrow confines of disciplinary terrain, Seeger, driven by an "intellectual curiosity of such enormous proportions, touched every aspect of the music world."[11] Music education thus occupied a central position in his grand scheme of intellectual inquiry. In 1947, he was publicly identified with the music education profession in his article in the *Music Educators Journal*, "Music Education and Musicology: A Musicologist Who Is Also a Music Educator Examines the Ivory Tower from the Grassroots Point of View."[12]

He served in many leadership roles. The pivotal figure in his relationship with national and international music education was Vanett

Lawler who, as Executive Secretary of MENC, also served as education consultant to PAU and worked closely with him.[13] Seeger made presentations at several music teachers' national conventions, including presentations at the Music Teachers National Association (MTNA) conventions in 1940 and 1946, and MENC's national conferences in 1942 and 1944. He was a member of the MENC Music Education Research Council (1944–48) and organized a committee on music education and musicology.[14] His aim was to nurture positive relationships between the two professional groups (music educators and musicologists). In general, he advanced thinking on the role of music in education not only in the United States but also in the various Latin American countries; he also supported music education through the key role he played in the founding of the International Society for Music Education in 1953.[15]

Of central importance to his contribution to music education were his efforts to promote American vernacular music in the public schools. In collaboration with his wife Ruth Crawford Seeger and Vanett Lawler, among others, he organized the publication of folksong materials for use in schools, directed the collection of recordings of folk music from various Latin American countries, served as consultant to several publishing houses on American folk music for children, and made presentations to teachers on the value and use of folk music in the classroom.

After 1953, the year Ruth died, his direct connections with the music education profession weakened. He moved from Washington, D.C., to California, and a new phase of his life began. Although he published little in the music education field after that, his seminal ideas on the relationship between music in society and in education continue to be relevant, insightful, and applicable to contemporary dilemmas and challenges in music education.

Music in American Culture: A Grassroots Approach

An exploration of Seeger's theory of music in culture, and in American society in particular, is a prerequisite to understanding the nature and significance of his contribution to the history, philosophy, and sociology of American music education. Perhaps the most important factor in the formation of his approach was his intense observation of and reflection on the musical values and practices of American people in communal contexts, especially during the years 1920–1940. Having a classical music education himself at Harvard University followed by an extended period of time as opera director at the Cologne Municipal Opera, Seeger had internalized the values of Western art music culture.

His intellectual curiosity led him to question the nature of value in connection with music. With his first wife Constance and their three children, Charles, John, and Peter, he set out from New York in November 1920 and traveled to North Carolina, intending to perform "good" classical music for people who were deprived of that musical experience. However, he and Constance soon realized that their definition of "good" music "did not impress their audiences, for they had their own music that they valued."[16] Seeger observed and interacted with banjo and fiddle players and gained some insights into the relationship among music, the individual, and society. He learned, as Dunaway put it, that "music transplants poorly ... especially in the name of civilization."[17] No doubt this journey into the musical life of the South impacted his future thinking about and advocacy for folk music in culture and in education.

Seeger was further directed toward the study of folk music by his student, Ruth Crawford, who later became his wife. (Charles and Constanse's marriage deteriorated during the 1920s and the couple separated. Ruth became a student of Seeger's in 1929, and they married in 1932.) She worked with Carl Sandberg on *The American Songbag* (1927) and became increasingly involved in the collection and arrangement of folk songs for publication. Although Seeger himself did little with folk music until after 1935,[18] his strong beliefs about acknowledging the music of the people were established in the 1920s. As Kerman put it, "Seeger always worked to promote music that comes from 'below,' rather than music imposed from 'above.'"[19] A striking example of this approach is evident in his work within the Composers Collective in New York (1931–35). In an interview with David Dunaway, he described his guidelines for the field workers:

> I had a whole list of things they [field workers] were to do. First, they would probably find that they could work with music in the school, but for God's sake, don't give them a songbook, don't teach [the children] songs you like, but find out what songs they like to sing, and get them to sing them. Find out what their singing games are and encourage them to sing and play them, instead of looking down on the games and forbidding them, as some of their parents had been doing.[20]

Similarly, as music adviser to Roosevelt's Resettlement Administration in Washington, D.C. (1935–41), he advocated that social workers ought "to encourage the singing and playing of songs the children knew and loved."[21] His experiences had taught him that "music must serve. That you must use the music that the people have in them already."[22] Seeger's involvement with projects that nurtured music in various social contexts during the 1920s and 1930s laid the foundation for his philosophy of vernacular music in education. He witnessed the vitality of the vernacular, and "his deep and wide social consciousness"[23] recognized and responded to the human values involved in music-making. As he put it later, "For cross-traditionally, music is above all a value system."[24]

As Seeger became more involved in various American musical genres beyond art music, he realized that the traditional concept of "folk" music was narrow and unsatisfactory. In its place, he used the term "vernacular music, which he viewed much more broadly."[25] The traditional concept of folk music, in Seeger's view, created problems in that

JRME 275

attention has tended to be directed mainly to material artifacts—structures, particular "pieces" of speech, and music—their collection, their classification, in repertorial canons, their sequestration in bodies of collectanea often as not regarded as private property by collectors and sometimes even copyrighted in the collectors' names.[26]

This approach to folk music lacked the vitality he had witnessed in the folk music practices of American people. Instead of attempting to keep folk music alive "as something quaint, antique, and precious," he wrote, "let us say 'the folk is changing—and its songs with it.'"[27] He argued that folk music was not merely composed of pieces that "stay still" while one contemplates them.[28] Rather, it was "a summary of the way of life of a culture community ... a veritable code of individual and social behavior."[29] In essence, his definitions embraced the neglected area of the social functions of music:

> In the Western world, music is talked about to a greater extent in terms of structure—concrete structures, at that—with immutable beginnings, endings, and inner construction.[30]

The desire to promote the study of music in terms of its social functions motivated Seeger to develop a theory of music in total culture. He delivered two papers on the topic at MTNA national conventions in the 1940s: "Music and Culture" (1940), and "Music and Musicology in the New World" (1946). What did he consider important to impart in a music teachers' forum? The goal of his 1940 paper was to draw teachers' attention to the fact that no longer could they focus narrowly on the structural aspects of music. As he told his listeners, "The concept of total culture is before us and constitutes a challenge which ... we must accept, apparently, whether we like it or not."[31]

He then identified basic assumptions about music that permeated Western intellectual circles, assumptions that teachers carried as products of a Western educational system. First, he discussed the assumption that music progressed from lower to higher stages, from folk to art music. "Traced by the 'advanced' culture," he said, "a fixed, one-directional evolutionary pattern led somewhat naively to itself as representing the highest stage."[32] Second, he warned teachers to "be careful to avoid the fallacy that music is a 'universal language.'"[33] He explained this by pointing out that "what music we know, we know only in the frame of our own culture, in which a certain place and function is allowed to it by custom."[34] He urged teachers to learn more about various idioms of American music culture, while acknowledging the difficulty of moving beyond their own.

> For any one of these idioms is some way like a language—one has to learn it in order to understand it and estimate its value—and sometimes even to discover it. It is not easy for a person brought up in the tradition of one music idiom to acquire understanding (and still less, ability to express himself) in the tradition of another idiom.[35]

Seeger's dialogue with music teachers on assumptions about music continued in an article published in 1941 in the *Music Educators Journal.* He brought before them assumptions that originated in Europe and that dominated American music during the previous century. These assumptions included the notions that music was a universal language, that the best music was written music, and that the basis for music education was in written techniques and in the performance of written masterpieces.[36]   Again, he addressed the functional approach to music: "While it is true that musical 'good' is inherent in music itself, it is equally true that it is to be found also in the function the music serves."[37] Returning to the MTNA forum in 1946, he presented teachers with a comprehensive approach to studying music within the context of the culture as a whole. It embraced musical traditions, methods of transmission, quantitative distribution of traditions, idioms, criteria of evaluation, development of services, and integration of traditions, idioms, and services into the culture.[38]

As Seeger's vista for viewing music in culture broadened and deepened, he began to consider the complexity of the American music scene—the multiplicity of traditions serving different functions and their interrelationships. He identified four types of music idioms— folk, primitive or tribal, art, and popular music—and was careful to point out from the beginning that the relationships among them were highly complex, unexplored, and controversial. Later in his career, he reported that

> modern scholarship sees the relationship between the four music idioms less as a one-way street between exclusive classes and more as a reciprocal two-, three-, or even four-way activity of give-and-take within the social body as a whole.[39]

In numerous writings, and particularly those written expressly for music teachers, Seeger focused on transmission of the various idioms to demonstrate their interrelationships. He described three varieties: "exclusively oral, mixed oral and written, and predominantly written."[40]   In reality, the transmission of music in the Western hemisphere was viewed in simplistic, dualistic, and dichotomous terms: oral or written modes to correspond with folk or cultivated music, respectively. This "pitted oral and written traditions against each other"[41] and created regrettable chasms among the idioms. On the surface, oral and written traditions refer innocently to the manner in which music is inherited, disseminated, and left to one's descendants. "Undoubtedly, this 'manner-in-which' molds the traditional *forms which music takes.* But the social function of the music groups ... in a culture molds the kind and range of *content* or meaning of those forms, and through this, the forms as well."[42] In other words, a focus on the manner of transmission was necessary but not sufficient for acquiring an understanding of music's social function.

Seeger proceeded to illustrate his argument by examining music in the United States. His analysis shed light on the history of music

JRME 277

in American culture and education. He defined American music
"first, as designating the music and music activity actually existing in
the United States; second, as referring to the part of this music that
expresses or characterizes the American people as distinguished
from other peoples."[43] He identified four elements that shaped the
development of music in the United States—the Native American,
the European, the African, and the music brought back by wealthy
Americans and professional music students who went to Europe during the nineteenth century "and acquired, with the psychology of the
colonist returning to the mother country, a musical attitude and taste
of distinct and peculiar character." It was in terms of this fourth element, he claimed, that American music education had grown.[44]

Because of this belief, he was critical of the course taken by music
education in the public schools during the nineteenth century.
Lowell Mason, in his opinion, spearheaded the group who "sought to
substitute, throughout the areas it can influence, not only the products but even the process of the written tradition for those of the
oral."[45] He also associated Mason with "a small vanguard of private
citizens" who "set themselves with almost religious zeal to 'make
America musical' in the exact image of contemporary Europe as they
saw it."[46] This goal underpinned music in the schools where "until
after 1900 the music education movement bogged down in the boredom and difficulty of solfège (note-reading) and of dull, genteel textbooks.[47] Meanwhile, as the American music industry grew, a "sell-
America-music" group emerged that was concerned with "the taste
preferences of the people—that is, the quality judgements of buy-
ers." One of their largest markets was the public school. However,
the materials demanded there were not necessarily what the children
wanted but, rather, what the teachers wanted. Seeger believed that
after the establishment of the Music Supervisors National Conference in 1907, change took place. The music education profession

> abandoned authoritarian leadership of the make-America-musical group for the
> more democratic opportunism of the sell-America-music group. Instead of
> offering school administrators an upper-class, intellectual, divine, quasi-
> European art, the Conference tried to find out what the administrators would
> buy and pay for in the way of music. This turned out to be the somewhat
> old-fashioned, middle-class popular music of the day. By giving them this in
> quantity and at the same time allowing the 'good music boys' to work within
> such a frame as best they could, a revitalization of music education in the
> schools took place, the magnitude and quality of whose effect upon the use of
> music in the United States can scarcely yet be estimated.[48]

In the context of folk music, Seeger saw a close relationship
between its rejection by the schools and by urban music intellectuals
and the musical immaturity of the nation. He observed, "It may be
said that one mark of a mature and vigorous people is its *ability to be
at home with itself,* to accept itself and to value itself for what it is."[49] A
major integrative force was necessary to unite the various traditions
of music that expressed or characterized the American people. To
achieve this goal, he turned to music education "as an integral part

of American music as a whole—as possibly the most effective agency
we have for the integration of American music within itself and within the culture of which it is a part."[50] He recognized the launching
of the project "American Songs for American Children" at the 1942
MENC biennial convention, as

> the most momentous single step to be taken toward the time when the United
> States will *be at home with its own music.* This step is the adherence of the music
> educators of the United States to the principle that one essential basis of music
> education in a country is the folk music of that country.[51]

Furthermore, for Seeger, to be at home with one's own music was
a necessary but not sufficient end for music education. A complementary goal was that the individual be *"at home in the world at large—
to give and take in the free intercourse of peoples without too much
regrettable loss on any side."*[52] Seeger's contribution to the understanding and development of American music in culture and education did not stop at the philosophical level. He worked arduously to
organize and disseminate folk-music materials for educational use.
From his presentations and writings, there is evident a plan for the
implementation of his theory in education.

Music in American Education: Some Vital Connections

Seeger considered music education to be a critical and influential
partner in the development of American musical life as a whole. His
writings throughout his career reflect this belief, especially those
published or delivered during 1940–53, the period in which he was
most intensively involved with music education. As critic, philosopher, and sociologist, his contributions provide insights into music
education that transcend the time period in which they were made.
His recommendations to the music education profession were based
on observations of its strengths and shortcomings. These were articulated in a statement read before the National Institute on Music
Education in Wartime, held in Chicago, November 12–14, 1942. On
one hand, he identified the many strengths of the profession's
endeavors and achievements—devoted teachers, improving teacher-training programs, an incredible number of ensembles in the
schools, the widening scope of music education from nursery to
graduate levels, increased integration with other subjects of instruction, and good working relations with many groups in public life. At
the same time, he observed a general lack of vitality and dynamism
in the structures, networks, and processes of music education—lack
of development of creative techniques in the schools, lack of utilization of oral tradition in the classroom, lack of contact with contemporary fine-art composers, "lack of use of music as a vehicle of living
thought, feeling, or whatever it is that music embodies or conveys
from one person to another, or from one group to another," and
rather poor public relations with fields such as musicology.[53]
Some vital connections[54] were missing, in Seeger's opinion—con-

JRME 279

nections that he sought to activate, nurture, and strengthen in his leadership roles in music education. The inertness he witnessed in school music could be reversed by changing the nature of the relationship between the child's and the school's music cultures, by broadening the repertoire of school music, by increased communication among all music professionals, and by considering music in its cultural-political context, both in society and in education.

Of primary importance for Seeger was making a vital connection between school music and the child's own music. Already in his work in New York in the 1930s, he advocated listening to and accepting the children's music as a base for formal music instruction. Seeger was attuned to the educational thought of his day and the child-centered, experiential approach to schooling, "for, as we all know, it is an inescapable principle of modern education that the child should first be grounded in a knowledge of his own native environment and traditions."[55] More than thirty years later, in another article published in the *Music Educators Journal,* Seeger reiterated this principle: "From a musical point of view, the prime concern in education would seem to be acquisition of competence in one's own music, the tradition inherited, cultivated, and transmitted by the members of the sociocultural continuum into which one has been born."[56] His definition of competence was focused on the practice of music: he believed that "*music is primarily in the making of it;* only secondarily in the listening to it."[57] Although Seeger believed that, in many ways, children were musically sophisticated when they entered school, he observed that few American children "possess the ability to improvise even a single line of sound that constitutes a simple melody such as they have to improvise the not entirely different single line of sound that constitutes a simple sentence."[58]

A second vital connection needed to be in place to improve the child's ability to use music as naturally as language—that is, the use of vernacular music in the classroom, presented as a living, functional means of personal and collective expression. The goal of public school music education in its first century was that of presenting music as "a good in itself." Addressing music educators in 1942, Seeger reported a change toward the presentation of music as "good for something."[59] Inherently, this change in perspective and approach created a set of challenges for music educators who were schooled in the narrow Western definition of music literacy as synonymous with reading notation and re-creating musical works.

To help teachers encounter the challenges, Seeger provided philosophical and pedagogical direction in addition to the provision of appropriate materials in the larger context of his work with Ruth Seeger, Vanett Lawler, and the Pan American Union. His first major statement to music teachers on the topic of folk music occurred on March 30, 1942, at the MENC biennial conference in Milwaukee. As part of the general session on "American Songs for American Children,"[60] Seeger addressed the future of the American folk song. A subsequent report in the *Music Educators Journal* conveyed the significance of this event:

> Music educators left the folk song session with a new insight into the importance
> of American folk song in education and the responsibilities of their profession
> in the utilization of this material.[61]

In the Foreword to *American Songs for American Children*, Seeger
stressed that in order for the United States to be at home with its own
music, music educators needed to adhere to the principle that "one
essential basis of music education in a country is the folk music of
that country."[62] To adhere to the principle, teachers needed careful
guidance, since the use of folk music in the schools was, in his opinion, "nothing short of a revolution." In fact, to have folk music handled properly would take generations of teacher training.[63]

He proceeded in subsequent writings to point out some of the
unique features of folk music and effective pedagogical strategies for
its transmission. As distinct from art music, a folk song or tune transmitted orally depended on the variation principle. No one, absolute,
authentic version existed, a fact that needed to be reflected in pedagogy where the guiding principle should be that of variation as
opposed to "repetition of the single, authentic text."[64] Seeger
believed that using this principle to guide music teaching and learning would help remedy the lack of creative activity he was critical of
in music education.

A further concern was the translation of folk music from unwritten
to written forms. He warned that "abstraction of the notes from the
style of singing and playing is one of the worst sins against proper
folklore study."[65] An alternative means of transmitting folk music
was the recording. He offered this comparison: "What print is to the
art of speech in a literate world, the record would seem to be in the
musically illiterate world."[66] Seeger continued to confirm the role of
mass media as a means of "bypassing the bottleneck of notation" of
the folk song and of learning to sing "from hearing the voices of
authentic singers."[67] The question of authenticity was as alive in the
1940s as it is today. Seeger empathized with music educators who
encountered difficulty in knowing whether they have "in hand a genuine folk song or a false one," based on the variation in quality of
materials being printed. He anticipated that the emerging field of
comparative musicology would provide leadership in this respect.[68]
First, music educators needed to reach out and draw on the resources of related fields such as musicology. This constituted a third
artery in the network of connections basic to vitalizing music in education.

In his vision for music in American culture and education, Seeger
stressed the need for a close relationship between musicologists and
music educators. Many of his writings refer to the tensions and diffi-
dent relations existing between these groups. His 1947 article, "Music
Education and Musicology," provided some historical background to
this situation. In his opinion, American musicology was steeped in

nineteenth-century values and practices and failed to provide music educators with a vital, contemporary view of music. He wrote:

> In the fight for a twentieth-century educational approach to the problem of music in the schools, music educators had to fight nineteenth-century educational practice as it existed in the conservatories of music. Not having at hand a twentieth-century musicology with which to strengthen their hand, there was evolved, as the next best weapon, a strong trend toward anti-intellectualism in music. This gave music educators freedom from bondage to outworn tradition and enabled them to forge the unique instrument they now possess.[69]

Seeger's conviction about the interdependence of these music professions did not stop at the level of criticism. He brought together members of both groups at the 1944 MENC biennial convention in St. Louis. A committee on music education and musicology was established, chaired by Seeger. It started out "as a kind of sub-committee of the Research Council."[70] Similar forums were authorized in the American Musicological Society and the MTNA.

He continued to promote increased communication between the groups, emphasizing that "the time has come when few of us can afford to tend our home garden as if it were a thing in itself, independent of the rest of the world."[71] It seems that his pleas and efforts had limited influence on building a vital connection between music educators and musicologists. Almost two decades later, Johannes Riedel, writing on the sociology of music and music education, referred to the conflict that existed between the same two groups and revisited Seeger's plea toward unity and cooperation in promoting the use of music in the life of human beings.[72] The sociological and cultural context of music, as Riedel pointed out, was the common ground for musicologists and music educators.

Another context of which Seeger was acutely aware and in which he was actively involved was the political context of music in culture and in education. During his career, he witnessed developments in American music that resulted from the two World Wars, and, later, the multicultural music movement of the 1960s and 1970s. Music served political agendas in music education programs such as American Unity through Music during World War II. These agendas did not necessarily end in the post-war years. In fact, Seeger observed increased political influence on music's development. Writing in the *Music Educators Journal* in 1972, he concluded that the task of music education "has become cultural-political on a large scale."[73]

American Music for American Children: An Epilogue

Charles Seeger's contribution to American music education is unique in several ways. Rarely do we find a major scholar from outside the profession playing as significant and active a role within the profession as Seeger chose. Each scholarly discipline, in his opinion, incorporates "a world view of its own."[74] Seeger penetrated the "world view" of music education and disturbed the equilibrium with his radical views, his sometimes harsh criticisms, his arresting ideas, and his progressive thinking. However, it is the very disturbance of the profession's "world view" that makes his contribution dynamic and worthy of exploration and continued study.

What sets him apart as a musicologist–music educator is the central role he granted music education in the development of American musical life. His appraisal of and recommendations for the profession were made in that broad sociocultural and political context. From this vantage point, he was able to identify points of tension or potential conflict in music education. Thus, he was in a position to make recommendations for empowering music students and teachers, for making music programs relevant to American sociocultural life, and for strengthening the fiber of American musical life.

Not only did Seeger observe and criticize from the outside, but he entered the forum and communicated meaningfully with music teachers and those in leadership positions. His dialogue with them embraced a broad spectrum—from the history, philosophy, and sociology of music education to repertoire and pedagogical issues. It is noteworthy that he emphasized, albeit indirectly, the importance of music education history for teachers. Seeger expressed regret that music educators were, in his opinion, ignorant of the historical forces that informed their philosophy and shaped their practices:

> So American educators have had to get along with second- and third-hand echoes of European philosophies of music. Besides being considerably distorted, these echoes are out of date. The foundations of music education in the United States are, then, strictly twentieth century upon their educational side but garbled nineteenth century on the musicological side. And worst of all, the music educators do not know it.[75]

Although some may not agree with much of his revisionist thought on the history of American music education, Seeger does provide an alternative perspective for viewing music education in the context of total American culture. He is quite critical of the course taken by Lowell Mason and his colleagues in establishing music in American education. More than one century later, armed with a different "world view," Seeger doubtless found it tempting to graft the values and paradigms of his own view onto the actions and practices of predecessors.

In an almost contradictory vein, he identified Mason and his followers with the "make-America-musical" group. The goal of their mission corresponded, in essence, with the one Seeger envisioned for American music education in his era. The difference lay in the definition of a musically educated American. In keeping with the general MENC theme of the 1940s, "Widening Horizons for Music Education," Seeger sought to expand the musical horizons and broaden the musical perspectives of teachers and students by motivating change not only in the content of music curricula but also in the processes of music transmission in school culture.

Seeger was by no means a pioneer in addressing the use of folk

JRME 283

music in education. There is abundant historical evidence that folk music, in various forms and definitions, had been used in music education for decades previously. He, however, sought to abandon former definitions that treated folk repertoire as museum pieces that could be decorated with the ornaments of Western harmony and preserved in written form. Folk music, for Seeger, was the vernacular of the people—what the people value, transmit, and change—a pulse of life in their communities. A folk song was not an esoteric piece from a distant land; rather, it was a living tradition from a local community. Thus, Seeger highlighted for teachers the importance of interfacing school music with music traditions in the surrounding communities.

Related to this concept was his innovative thinking on music as a cultural subject, with emphasis placed on its social function. Considering the fact that it is only in recent years that music educators have begun to approach music from the sociocultural perspective, Seeger's 1940 MTNA presentation "Music and Culture" was revolutionary in its paradigmatic base and its conceptual canvas, and laden with ideas whose time had not yet come. More tangible, though perhaps no less radical, to music educators' experience and world view was his definition of American music for children. No doubt the impact of World War II shaped this definition. For example, the promotion of Latin American music reached a climax during the 1940s, the intensity of which has not been equalled since that period. Although Seeger advocated all American musics for children, the focus of his promotional efforts was on Anglo-American and Latin American folk music, with minimal attention devoted to Native American or African American music. Theoretically, I believe that his thinking was catholic and inclusive; the focus of his efforts reflected the political assumptions and expectations of his time and, in a sense, the limitations of his world view.

In addition to expanding the context of school music repertoire, Seeger also sought to change the process of music transmission in the classroom. He elevated the status of oral processes and attempted to diffuse the dichotomous view of orality and literacy as being synonymous with folk and art music, respectively. The heart of the music education process, in Seeger's opinion, was "doing" music. In contemporary terms, he might be considered a proponent of the praxial philosophy of music education, advocating practice-focused, value-centered, people-oriented music teaching and learning that was socially and culturally contextualized. Music, for him, was "above all a value system," a belief that grew out of his own observations of the role of music in people's lives.

All of his recommendations were aimed at creating or renewing connections that he considered vital to American music education—connections with the child's own music; with American vernacular music in general; with other music professionals, particularly musicologists; and with the cultural-political context in which American music and education are situated. Seeger's prediction and hope that "comparative musicology" would provide music educators with a twentieth-century philosophy of music have been realized to a certain extent, reflected in the increased communications between music educators and ethnomusicologists in the last two to three decades. Each scholarly discipline, as Seeger pointed out, has its own world view. In the context of American musical life, it is necessary to be aware of, communicate with, and learn from other disciplines whose mission is also to "make America musical."

On the theme of "American Music for American Children," Seeger's legacy is rich and provocative, with many of his ideas applicable to the dilemmas and challenges of American music education today. He expanded the definition of American school music, promoted the use of vernacular music in the schools, heightened awareness of the function of music in American culture, and paved the way for dealing with musical diversity in American schools. In a sense, his attempts to define "American music for American children" illustrate that it is a dynamic concept, constantly in transition. American musical life was as diverse in the 1940s as it is today. What Seeger provided were some principles and avenues of approach to deal with diversity, regardless of the particular music cultures in question. His ideas addressed perennial questions regarding music in American culture and education. His voice lives on in the multivocal and complex dialogue of contemporary music education.

Notes

1. Ann M. Pescatello, *Charles Seeger: A Life in American Music* (Pittsburgh and London: University of Pittsburgh Press, 1992), vii.
2. Seeger's biographer, Ann Pescatello, writes that "Seeger had frequently rued the fact that people did not read his scholarly articles—or, if they did, they had no comments or criticisms to make about them." *Charles Seeger: A Life in American Music*, 274. In "Reminiscent of Charles Seeger," Mantle Hood referred to Seeger's "long list of publications too seldom read, too little comprehended." *Yearbook of the International Folk Music Council* 11 (1979), 99.
3. In Michael L. Mark and Charles L. Gary, *A History of American Music Education* (New York: Schirmer Books, 1992), the authors refer to the influence Seeger had on Vanett Lawler during her time as education consultant to the Pan American Union, stating that "her close association with Charles Seeger was fortuitous," 249.
4. Pescatello, xii.
5. Archie Green, "Charles Louis Seeger (1886–1979)," *Journal of American Folklore* 92 (October–December 1979): 397.
6. Seeger, "American Music for American Children," *Music Educators Journal* 29 (November–December 1942): 11–12.
7. Charles Seeger, dictated to Peggy Seeger Cohen, April 22, 1977, in Pescatello, 37.
8. Pescatello, 64.
9. *Ibid.*, 303.
10. Gilbert Chase, An Exagmination Round His Factification for Incami-

JRME 285

nation of Work in Progress. (Review Essay and Reminiscence)." *Yearbook of the International Folk Music Council* 11 (1979), 143.

11. Pescatello, 285.
12. *Music Educators Journal* 33 (January 1947): 10–11. The latter part of the article title is perhaps an editor's addition. Either Seeger identified himself with the profession or the editor wished him to be presented as a music educator to the professional community.
13. For a detailed study of Vanett Lawler's work with the PAU, see Christy Izdebski and Michael L. Mark, *The Bulletin of Historical Research in Music Education* 8 (January 1987): 1–32.
14. Seeger was a member of numerous MENC committees in the 1940s and early 1950s, including the American Folk Song Committee, the Committee on Creative Music Projects, the National Committee on Song Writing Project, and the editorial board of the *Music Educators Journal.*
15. For a detailed description of Seeger's contribution to international music education, see Marie McCarthy, "'Canticle to Hope': Widening Horizons in International Music Education, 1939–1953." Paper delivered at the Twenty-first Biennial World Conference of the International Society for Music Education, Tampa, FL, July 18–23, 1994 and subsequently published in the *International Journal of Music Education* 25 (1995), 38–49.
16. Pescatello, 82–83.
17. David Dunaway, *How Can I Keep from Singing: Pete Seeger,* rev. ed. (New York: Da Capo Press, 1990), 34.
18. Pescatello, 111.
19. Joseph Kerman, *Contemplating Music: Challenges from Musicology* (Cambridge, MA: Harvard University Press, 1985), 156.
20. Seeger to Dunaway, in David K. Dunaway, "Charles Seeger and Carl Sands: The Composers' Collective Years," *Ethnomusicology,* 24 (May 1980), 168.
21. Pescatello, 140.
22. Seeger to Dunaway, "Charles Seeger and Carl Sands," 168.
23. Chase, 142.
24. Seeger, "The Music Compositional Process as a Function in a Nest of Functions and in Itself a Nest of Functions," *Studies in Musicology 1935–1975* (Berkeley: University of California Press, 1977), 153. Based on a 1966 article, "The Music Process as a Function in the Context of Functions," *Yearbook, Inter-American Institute for Musical Research* (New Orleans, LA: Tulane University, 1966).
25. Bruno Nettl, "The Dual Nature of Ethnomusicology in North America," in *Comparative Musicology and Anthropology of Music,* ed. Bruno Nettl and Philip V. Bohlman (Chicago: University of Chicago Press, 1991): 268.
26. Seeger, "The Folkness of Nonfolk and the Nonfolkness of the Folk," in *Studies in Musicology,* 335. Based on a 1966 article, "The Folkness of the Nonfolk vs. the Nonfolkness of the Folk," in *Folklore and Society* (Hatboro, PA: Folklore Associates, 1966).
27. Seeger, "Folk Music in the Schools of a Highly Industrialized Society," *Journal of the International Folk Music Council* 5 (1953): 44; reprinted in *Studies in Musicology,* 330–34.
28. Seeger, "The Compositional Process," 140–41.
29. Seeger, "Folk Music in the Schools," 40.
30. "The Music Compositional Process," 140.
31. Seeger, "Music and Culture," *Proceedings of the Music Teachers National*

286   McCARTHY

Association, 35th Series (1941).

32. *Ibid.*, 112.
33. *Ibid.*, 122.
34. *Ibid.*, 115.
35. *Ibid.*, 118.
36. Seeger, "Inter-American Relations in the Field of Music: Some Basic Considerations," *Music Educators Journal* 27 (March–April 1941): 18.
37. *Ibid.*
38. Seeger, "Music and Musicology in the New World," *Proceedings of the Music Teachers National Association, 40th Series* (1946): 38–39.
39. Seeger, "Folk Music," *Collier's Encyclopedia*, vol. 10 (New York: P. F. Collier, Inc., 1965), 132.
40. Seeger, "Music and Musicology," 40.
41. Seeger, "American Music for American Children," 11.
42. Seeger, "Music and Culture," 118.
43. Seeger, "American Music for American Children," 11.
44. *Ibid.*, 12.
45. Seeger, "Folk Music in the Schools," 41.
46. Seeger, "Music and Class Structure in the United States," in *Studies in Musicology*, 225. First published in *American Quarterly*, 9 (Fall 1957): 281–94.
47. *Ibid.*, 226.
48. *Ibid.*, 230. In "American Music for American Children," Seeger identifies the "somewhat old-fashioned" popular music as that of Foster, Work, Root, Emmet, Band—on the whole, a nineteenth-century, cosmopolitan style, 12.
49. Seeger, "American Music for American Children," 11.
50. *Ibid.*
51. Seeger, Foreword to *American Songs for American Children* (Chicago: MENC, ca. 1942), 3.
52. Seeger, "American Music for American Children," 11.
53. Seeger, in "Proceedings of the National Institute on Music Education in Wartime," Chicago, November 12–14, 1942. Unpublished paper, MENC Historical Center, University of Maryland at College Park, 163–64; published subsequently in the *Music Educators Journal* 29 (January 1943): 12–14.
54. The identification of "some vital connections" results from the author's interpretation of Seeger's writings.
55. Seeger, "Inter-American Relations in the Field of Music," 65.
56. Seeger, "World Musics in American Schools: A Challenge to Be Met," *Music Educators Journal* 59 (October 1972): 107.
57. *Ibid.*, 111. Seeger had voiced this opinion throughout his career. For example, in "The Musician: Man Serves Art/The Educator: Art Serves Man," *UNESCO Courier* 6 (February 1953): 12. Reprinted in *The Australian Journal of Music Education* 30 (April 1977): 15–16.
58. Seeger, "World Musics in American Schools," 107.
59. "Proceedings of the National Institute on Music Education in Wartime," 162.
60. The project was undertaken in cooperation with the MENC American Unity Through Music Committee, with assistance from the Rockefeller Foundation. Charles and Ruth Seeger edited the music and text, and Alan Lomax wrote the explanatory notes.
61. "American Songs for American Children," *Music Educators Journal* 38 (May–June 1942): 29.

62. Seeger, Foreword to *American Songs for American Children*, 3.
63. Seeger, "Notes on Music in the Americas," *Bulletin of the Pan American Union* 79 (June 1945): 344.
64. Seeger, "Folk Music in the Schools," 334.
65. "Folk Music," in *Collier's Encyclopedia*, vol. 10 (1965), 132.
66. Seeger, "Notes on Music in the Americas," *Bulletin of the Pan American Union* 79 (June 1945): 344.
67. "Folk Music in the Schools," 334.
68. Seeger, "Music Education and Musicology," in *Music Education Source Handbook*, ed. Hazel Nohavec Morgan (Chicago: MENC, 1947), 196.
69. *Ibid.*, 197.
70. Conference Digest of the Music Educators National Conference, "Widening Horizons for Music Education," 9th Biennial Meeting, St. Louis MO, March 2–8, 1944; MENC Historical Center, College Park, MD.
71. Seeger, "Music and Musicology in the New World," 47.
72. Johannes Ridel, "The Function of Sociability in the Sociology of Music and Music Education," *Journal of Research in Music Education* 12 (Summer 1964), 158.
73. Seeger, "World Musics in American Schools," 111.
74. Seeger, "Toward a Unitary Field Theory for Musicology," in *Studies in Musicology*, 107. Originally in *Selected Reports*, vol. 1, no. 3, Institute of Ethnomusicology (Los Angeles: University of California, 1970).
75. Charles L. Seeger, "Music Education and Musicology: A Musicologist Who Is Also a Music Educator Examines the Ivory Tower from a Grassroots Point of View," *Music Educators Journal* 33 (January 1947), 11.

Submitted November 15, 1994; accepted January 23, 1995.

Part III
Pedagogy/Curriculum

[14]

METHODOLOGIES IN MUSIC EDUCATION

Peter Costanza

OHIO STATE UNIVERSITY

Timothy Russell

NAPLES PHILHARMONIC CENTER FOR THE ARTS

In music education, ways of doing things have variously been called techniques, methods, curricula, and methodologies. The assumption that they all have the same meaning is erroneous. Yet even though these terms are employed with regularity by professionals, they are not clearly defined. The following definitions, as applied to teaching and learning, define the terms as they will be used in this chapter:

Technique: a teaching activity or strategy that is used to achieve an objective

Method: "a procedure or process for obtaining an objective, as a systematic plan followed in presenting material for instruction" *(Webster's Seventh New Collegiate Dictionary,* 1963, p. 533)

Curriculum: a plan or course of study that describes what is to be taught and in what order and that may or may not include information regarding how it is to be taught

Methodology: a body of techniques, methods, and curricula that is based on a philosophical system and a foundation of research

The activities, materials, and procedures used to teach music may be based on (1) suggestions in a set of music books (perhaps the most common of occurrences), (2) an original approach to teaching music (a less common occurrence), or (3) what is known about the art and science of music, the nature of the learner, the learning environment, and the effectiveness of the experiences (the rarest of occurrences).

Music education uses the activities of singing, playing, moving to, listening to, and creating music. These activities may employ techniques that could evolve into a method, which may achieve the status of a curriculum, and, with the appropriate philosophical base and foundation of research, may ultimately result in a methodology. Thus, these terms may be considered hierarchical. They may also be considered cyclical in that new techniques, methods, and curricula may come from the research in a methodology.

Although music educators have techniques, methods, and curricula that are effective for them, they are constantly in search of the perfect methodology. Workshops abound in the latest technique and/or method of teaching music. The pitfall is when music educators incorporate into their teaching a new technique or method without ever considering "why" it is done or to be done. The ultimate danger is, as Bennett (1986) concludes, that technique or method becomes authority.

In the field of music, as with most educational disciplines, curricula and methodologies are often related and interdependent. In the broadest terms, they can be divided into those in which teacher-learner contact is a prerequisite (e.g., classroom instruction; applied music lessons) and those in which teacher-learner contact is optional (e.g., programed/computer-assisted instruction).

There is an extensive tradition of teaching techniques and methods that have been transmitted historically from one generation of teachers to the next, not always codified into an actual methodology. In the field of teacher training, there is speculation as to whether such strategies are systematically taught at the university level, or merely "caught," as young teachers often end up teaching just as they were taught. New teachers often fail to explore the best possible teaching techniques, methods, curricula, and methodologies.

This chapter is restricted to an exploration of selected research applications in the following areas: general music education (including Dalcroze, Orff, Kodály, Gordon, and general music series textbooks), choral music education, instrumental music education (including instrumental methods books, string music education, and Suzuki), and trends in music education methodologies (modeling and imitation, individualized instruction, the discovery method, and comprehensive musicianship).

GENERAL MUSIC EDUCATION

The majority of the studies in general music education have compared the effects of one technique or method with those of another in the teaching and learning of music or compared a defined technique or method with a "traditional" method. This latter treatment (the "traditional method") is not well defined and typically uses materials that have been employed by a particular individual, within a particular course, or within a particular music series.

There have been few studies that have attempted to establish the effectiveness of a well-defined methodology (e.g., Dalcroze, Orff, Kodály). These studies tend to examine one aspect or several aspects of the methodology and rarely deal with the methodology in its entirety. Studies that have attempted to compare the effectiveness of two methodologies are rare indeed.

The methodologies in general music education that are present in the classroom today can be traced to a number of individuals whose philosophy of music in the education of children incorporated the nature of music, the learner, and a particular approach to instruction. Among these individuals were Johann Pestalozzi, who contributed to the ideas of sequence, repetition, and rote; Lowell Mason, who advocated the Pestalozzian principles and their importance in the education of the child; and John Dewey, who advocated the discovery method for the solving of problems. Methodologies in use in the general musical education of children incorporate many of the principles of Pestalozzi, Mason, and Dewey, but have evolved into specific applications as advocated by such individuals as Emile Jaques-Dalcroze, Carl Orff, and Zoltan Kodály.

Emile Jaques-Dalcroze Dalcroze had Pestalozzian influences in his musical training, and his methodology reflects these influences. It began as an attempt to improve hearing in a sight-singing class by incorporating movement and evolved into the use of body movement to develop rhythmic concepts associated with pulse, meter, and rhythm (Landis and Carder, 1972).

Several comparisons of Dalcroze and traditional approaches have been examined. Crumpler (1983) examined the melodic musical growth of children in the first grade by a comparison of the Dalcroze methodology and musical activities as found in the music books of Silver Burdett Publishers (1974). Four groups of first-grade children were exposed to an experimental treatment: Two control groups taught using the Silver Burdett series and two experimental groups using the Silver Burdett series and Dalcroze eurythmics. A dependent measure of the ability to identify the direction of groups of two and five tones was administered as a pre- and posttest. Crumpler found no significance in the change in achievement scores of the control group, but she did find a significant increase in achievement in the Dalcroze/Silver Burdett series students ($p < .0001$).

The rhythmic movement and improvisation achievement of kindergarten students was examined by Joseph (1983). Contrasting the effects of three types of musical instruction (informal instruction, Dalcroze with improvisation activities, and Dalcroze excluding improvisation activities), Joseph measured randomly selected subjects from each group on their ability to recognize and respond to familiar rhythm patterns and on their ability to use rhythm patterns while performing on a set of bells. Joseph concluded that the Dalcroze methodology should be considered for inclusion in early childhood education.

Carl Orff The methodology developed by Carl Orff implements the activities of singing, saying, dancing, and playing (Shamrock, 1986). These behaviors are considered central to the methodology because Orff Schulwerk teachers believe they are a natural part of the behavior of children. Active music making begins with rhythm and is based on speech patterns. The techniques used are exploration, imitation, improvisation, and creation. Children must have experiences in exploration and imitation before any improvisation and creation take place.

Olson (1964) compared the effects on melodic sensitivity of Orff techniques and various techniques commonly used in elementary music classrooms. Groups matched on IQ, musicality, melodic memory, attitude, experiences, and socioeconomic status were provided instruction in both approaches. Although the difference in gain scores between groups was not significant, both groups did improve significantly.

A comparison of musical achievement and attitude of students taking part in Orff-inspired instruction and those in a traditional approach is reported by Siemens (1967, 1969). Her posttest-only design compared students who had participated in the Orff approach for at least 1 year (some as long as 3 years) and students who had received "traditional" music instruction in general music. Students who participated in the Orff program scored significantly higher in interest and attitude and reported greater enjoyment of part singing and rhythm activities. Munsen (1986) used an Orff approach to examine the ability of students to improvise melodically and rhythmically. She concluded that students' abilities to improvise peaked at about grade 3 and that their attitudes became increasingly negative from grades 1 through 5.

Zoltan Kodály Zoltan Kodály developed a methodology primarily to teach choral musicianship to the children of

Hungary (Landis and Carder, 1972). Using the folk music of his own country, Kodály devised a methodology that stresses the teaching of music-reading and -writing skills and includes walking, running, and marching movements to accompany the singing activities.

Studies that have compared the Kodály methodology and other approaches include those by McDaniel (1974) and Palmer (1974). McDaniel (1974) compared the Kodály methodology, as presented in the *Threshold to Music* materials (Richards, 1966), and musical activities represented in the *Making Music Your Own* music books (Landeck et al., 1968). Results showed no significant differences between the groups in posttest or mean change scores, although the non-Kodály group did have higher mean improvement scores.

Palmer (1974) investigated the effects on rhythm reading of Kodály (as presented in the *Threshold to Music* books), a learning sequence by Gordon (1971; as presented in *The Psychology of Music Teaching)*, and a version of a traditional approach that did not include instruction in rhythm reading. Students in two schools were randomly assigned to either the Kodály or the Gordon approach, and students in a third school received the traditional instruction, minus rhythm-reading activities. Palmer, using the *Musical Aptitude Profile* as a dependent measure, reported no significant difference between the Kodály and Gordon approaches, although a significant difference was found between the Kodály and Gordon approach groups and the traditional approach group. The mean improvement of the group taught using the Gordon approach was slightly higher than that of the group taught by the Kodály approach. Darazs (1966) utilized the Kodály method with high school students and found that music reading increased for students in a select group.

Gordon Learning Theory One of the recent developments in the teaching and learning of music is the learning theory of Edwin E. Gordon (1989a). This theory explains how persons gain knowledge, comprehension, or mastery when they study music. Gordon (1989b) writes:

"Music learning theory includes three categories of music learning sequence. They are 1) skill learning sequence, 2) tonal content learning sequence, which includes tonal pattern learning sequence, and 3) rhythm content learning sequence, which includes rhythm pattern learning sequence" (p. 88).

These music-learning sequences are divided into two general types: discrimination and inference. When the music-learning sequences are incorporated into their teaching, students learn not only what to learn but how to learn.

Gordon (1986, 1987) has incorporated the music-learning theory and sequences into a curriculum for both general music education and instrumental music education. Shuler (1986) investigated the effects of Gordon's music-learning sequence on music achievement, with the intent of improving music pedagogy. He found that no conclusions could be drawn regarding the effects of learning sequence activities

on music performance achievement but that some teachers may be more effective when they incorporate learning sequence activities into their instructional procedures. Stockton (1983) investigated the use of rhythm-learning sequence activities with older (nonmusic major college) students. His experimental group received a rote performance method derived from the Gordon rhythm-learning sequence, and the control group received a lecture-demonstration approach incorporating notational skills without performance. Stockton concluded that the rhythm-learning sequence was superior to the reading and listening approach presented in the lecture-demonstration. In the previously cited study, Palmer (1974) found no significant difference between groups (cf. p. 7).

The Music Learning Theory, as presented in the *Jump Right In* series for general music and instrumental music, is a curriculum that incorporates techniques and methods of sequencing. A foundation of research to verify the effectiveness of this curriculum has yet to be established.

General Music Series Textbooks Whereas music books have been used in the teaching of music to elementary and secondary school children in the United States for many years, several series of music textbooks published since 1970 differ from their predecessors. Particular note should be made of the general music series textbooks published by the Silver Burdett Publishers and by Holt, Rinehart, and Winston.

Reimer (1989) calls the series of textbooks entitled *Silver Burdett Music* (Crook et al., 1978) "my own attempt to build a comprehensive curriculum for general music classes in grades 1-8" (p. 151). The philosophy upon which the series is based is that, as Reimer writes, "music education is valuable because the art of music is valuable" (p. 148). The series is unique in that competency tests were developed to accompany the curricular materials (Colwell, 1979). Boyle and Radocy (1987) describe the tests as "very comprehensive, especially regarding perception of melody, rhythm, timbre, texture, form, tonality, and dynamics" (p. 168).

The *Silver Burdett Music* series is a curriculum in that there is a plan of study that describes what is to be taught and includes methods and techniques for achieving the objectives. It approaches a methodology in that it is a body of techniques and methods, and a curriculum that is based on a philosophical system. All that remains is for a foundation of research to verify the effectiveness of the curriculum.

The general music series textbooks *Holt Music* are based on the Generative Theory of Music Learning (Boardman, 1988a, 1988b). The basic assumptions of this theory are that (1) the basic unit is a system, of which the whole is greater than the parts, (2) symbols and symbol systems not only serve to represent our view of reality, but mold that view, and (3) the purpose of knowledge is generative—to make possible the expansion of not just one's personal grasp of existing information but the total body of possible knowledge (p. 5). This theory (philosophical system), based on the writings of Jerome Bruner, Howard Gardner, Susanne Langer, Charles Morris, and Nelson Goodman, has been incorporated into the techniques and methods as presented in the music series *Holt Music*. Until a foundation of research that verifies the effectiveness of the Holt series has been established, the *Holt Music* general music series textbooks can be called a curriculum, but not yet a methodology.

Summary

Findings from these studies in general music education are variable, at best. The studies that have compared various techniques or methods with each other or with a "traditional method" have found no differences between experimental and control groups, but have reported increases (some significant, some not) in gain scores for the experimental groups. The methodologies of Orff, Kodály, and Dalcroze have been shown to be effective in increasing musical learning. The effectiveness of one methodology over any other has not been demonstrated as controlled comparisons of methodologies have not yet appeared in the literature. The theories and philosophies of Gordon, Reimer, and Boardman, as presented in their music books, are best designated as curricula that approach methodology. They lack the foundation of research that is essential to a methodology.

In the studies reported, it appears that those techniques, methods, curricula, and methodologies that are most effective and bring about increased learning are those that the teacher knows best. The teacher's knowledge of what is to be taught and confidence about how it is being taught enhance the musical learning of students.

CHORAL MUSIC EDUCATION

An examination of the research in choral music education does little to shed light on the techniques, methods, curricula, or methodologies employed. Topics in the journal literature discuss choral compositions, analyses of compositions, stylistic characteristics, choral composers, and various aspects of literature, including its appropriateness and difficulty. The research that is reported tends to examine techniques to improve choral singing (including the teaching of music reading), aspects of the choral rehearsal, and techniques that the choral conductor uses to improve choral singing (including those that assist the choral conductor in detecting performance discrepancies).

If there is any area of choral music education that will produce intense debate, it is whether students should learn the music by sight-reading or through rote learning. Sight-reading may remain one of the weakest components in choral programs. Choral music education has followed the patterns of rote teaching established in the teaching of songs. Weyland (1955) and Hales (1961) have reported that rote learning is the predominant approach in the teaching of choral music. Daniels (1986) notes that the occasional use of rote procedures to teach music improved the ability to sight-read music. Shehan (1987) showed that a combination of rote and note presentations provided the best performance and retention of rhythm patterns among younger students.

It is surprising that sight singing or sight-reading remains one of the weakest components in the teaching of choral music in that it is one of the few areas in choral music education that has specific methods. These include movable *do*, fixed *do*, numbers and letter names, shape notes, and hand signals. Each of these will be discussed briefly, with the relevant research.

Movable *do* is the most common method used in the teaching of sight singing in the United States. With its roots in the system of Guido d'Arrezo (ca 955–1050), its primary advantage is in its tonal relationships. There are several variations on the movable *do* method, including the English or Lancashire method (advocated by John Curwen [1816–1880]), which disregarded *do* and *re* and used letter names instead of syllables (Zinar, 1983). Rainbow (1979) notes that this was a supplemental device meant to lead to notation on the staff, not replace it. Among those who have been advocates of the movable *do* method include Johann Pestalozzi, Carl Orff, Zoltan Kodály, and Fred Waring. Bonham (1977) has suggested that movable *do* is unsuitable to atonal music. Winnick (1987) disagrees and is a strong advocate of the method.

Fixed *do,* also known as the conservatory French fixed *doh,* or stationary *do,* has its roots in the European conservatories. Its advantages are that it is not affected by modulations and letter names and keys are not used. The traditional fixed *do* method does not distinguish between natural and chromatic pitches, so that the pitches C and C♯ are both called *do.* One variation of fixed *do* does include chromatic names for the flats and sharps. Advocates of fixed *do* include Emile Jaques-Dalcroze, Robert Shaw, and Robert Page.

Other techniques for the teaching of sight singing include the intervallic method, in which students are presented with the different intervals as found in popular melodies, and practice and drill is provided until the intervals are learned. Shape notes, a distinctively American method in use in the southern United States, substitutes shapes for notes and has been shown to be an effective approach to sight singing (Kyme, 1960). The use of hand signals, as advocated by Kodály, is another popular method to teach sight singing, although this is a predominantly diatonic method.

Summary

Hylton (1983) concluded from his survey of the research in choral methods that the scope of the research was narrow and fragmented. Stockton (1983) found that there are no universally accepted methods of choral teaching. The adaptations are diverse and reflect the skills and interests of the teachers. Corbin (1982) reported that the research in choral rehearsal techniques was extremely limited and was primarily based on subjective opinions, and that no one technique was better than any other. Unfortunately, little has changed since Gonzo (1973) reported that the structure of the choral curriculum has not changed in 60 years.

INSTRUMENTAL MUSIC EDUCATION

There exist in the field of music education a plethora of method books. With the exception of those traditions passed on from one generation of teachers to another, the oldest systematic materials in music education were singing books and instrumental instruction books, such as *The Modern Musick-Master,* or *The Universal Musician,* published in 1791. Many of these are curricula; others constitute genuine methodologies (e.g., Suzuki).

This section presents selected research applications related to instrumental methods books; string music education; the Suzuki methodology; developments in the areas of modeling and imitation; individualized instruction (including programed instruction and computer-assisted instruction); the discovery method; and comprehensive musicianship.

Instrumental Methods Books From the time of England's "Maidstone Movement" to the present, there has been an interest in teaching instrumental music to large numbers of students. Countless methods and method books have been developed to teach piano, as well as stringed, wind, and percussion instruments, to individuals and groups. Even though this source of teacher/student material is the largest in music education, there is, unfortunately, very little research regarding its validity or effectiveness.

Texter (1975) offered a comparative analysis of selected instrumental music books written between 1910 and 1972. She concludes that, with few exceptions, pedagogical approaches consistent with current knowledge of the music teaching-learning process are not present in contemporary instrumental method books used in music education.

Sampson (1968) investigated deficiencies in beginning band method books. He concluded that, in many respects, a majority of beginning band method books do not measure up to the aims and expectations of instrumental teachers and that little systematic study of band method books is occurring.

Kress (1981) compared *The Individualized Instructor* (Froseth 1976), which applied Piaget's theory of conservation to the conservation of music concepts, to the *First Division Band Method* (Weber, 1968), which was found to encourage conservation only indirectly. The researcher found no significant difference between the conservation of musical concepts when compared to the students' musical achievement and musical performance.

String Music Education Nelson (1983) reviewed the research findings in the teaching of strings and string performance. He notes that "string teaching and performance are among the least researched areas of music education" (p. 39). His overview of this subfield of instrumental music education includes two sections: "Suzuki Studies" and "Techniques of String Instruction."

Gillespie (1991) presents results from the research regarding techniques and methods of strings instruction that string teachers should consider. Among his implications are the following:

1. Teacher modeling with student imitation, accompanied by a minimum of verbal description, may be the best mode of instruction for very young students.
2. Starting violin students in third position rather than first position does not significantly increase students' intonational accuracy or rhythmic skills.
3. Developing students' intonational accuracy with or without finger placement markers is directly related to the overall string competence of the teacher.
4. Teachers must be careful to diagnose and train their students to correct motions in string playing that may impair intonational accuracy.
5. Delaying note-reading training does not impair the technical progress of beginning students' performance development and may help to facilitate it.
6. Suzuki pedagogy and materials may be successfully adapted for beginning heterogeneous class string teaching.

This list includes results from those research studies that could be considered to deal with techniques and methods of string music teaching. Research in curricula has not been reported in the literature, and where curricula do exist (e.g., Rolland), their effectiveness has not been established. However, in string music education, there is a methodology that meets all of the guidelines of the definition. That methodology is the one set forth by Shinichi Suzuki.

The Suzuki Methodology The Suzuki methodology is based on an interplay of the following groups of pedagogical tenets: the child's exposure to music at an early age; listening, imitation, tonalization, and modeling; sound before signs and rote learning; sequential materials; review, repetition, and mastery learning; and parental involvement (Suzuki, 1969). In specifically considering Suzuki's principles in a research context, one must distinguish between those that are curricular and those that are methodological. The Suzuki books alone are a curriculum. Teachers who merely utilize the sequentially presented repertoire pieces and do not make use of the remaining principles clearly cannot be considered to be using the Suzuki methodology.

Nelson notes that Project Super (1966–1968) evaluated the feasibility and potential effectiveness of Suzuki instruction administered by North American teachers (Wensel, 1970). An evaluation of the project revealed that (1) the Suzuki methodology could be adapted to the social and educational systems of the United States, (2) string teachers could manage the Suzuki approach with minimal training under Dr. Suzuki, and (3) the approach could be used in a variety of school systems and communities of different socioeconomic levels (Nelson, 1983, pp. 40–41).

Several projects have been undertaken to study the Suzuki methodology as well as the adaptation of Suzuki to other areas of instrumental music education. Sperti (1970) and Blaine (1976) conducted studies that applied the Suzuki principles to wind instrumental music classes. Sperti (1970) adapted three concepts of the Suzuki methodology (use of rote teaching, parental involvement in the child's home study, and implementation of a comprehensive listening program) to clarinet instruction and compared their effectiveness to that of widely accepted practices in teaching the clarinet. Achievement of the subjects in the Suzuki group was significantly superior to that of the control group in all categories of performance.

Blaine (1976) adapted the Suzuki-Kendall methodology to the teaching of trumpets and trombones, comparing it to what he called a traditional methodology. Results of the data analysis indicated that the Suzuki group achieved higher performance scores on the Whybrew *Performance Evaluation Scale* (subjective elements of musicality such as breath and control of tone and the subdivisions of technique, articulation, fingering dexterity), whereas the control group performed higher on the *Watkins-Farnum Scale* (sight-reading ability).

Although the Suzuki methodology was designed as an individual approach, Brunson (1969) investigated its application in a fourth-grade heterogeneous string class. The investigator judged the program a success on the basis of acceptable student performance, no dropouts, and positive student feedback.

Adaptations of the Suzuki methodology to the teaching of piano and other instruments have been proposed, although reports of these adaptations have not yet appeared in the research literature. Clearly, the teaching of instrumental music as presented by Shinichi Suzuki can be called a methodology. It has a philosophical base that is clearly articulated, and research studies that demonstrate its effectiveness.

TRENDS IN MUSIC EDUCATION METHODOLOGIES

As the profession of music education has expanded since the decade of the 1960s, research activities and productivity have also expanded. Much of this research has explored the techniques, methods, curricula, and methodologies in music teaching and learning. Some of this research has explored applications of techniques and methods of instruction from other areas of research associated with music education, including education and psychology. Among the research results that hold promise for application and/or adaptation to music education are those relating to the areas of modeling and imitation, individualized instruction, and the discovery method. These, as well as comprehensive musicianship, a methodology that has existed for some time in music teaching and learning, will be discussed and relevant research presented.

Modeling and Imitation   Research studies have investigated the use of modeling and/or imitation in instrumental music education. One study examined students in two groups that were taught using the same approach, with the exception that one of the groups listened to recorded models of the

music being studied. As reported by Duerkson (1972), a panel of experts judged the performance of the group that had been prepared with the aid of recorded models superior in expression, accuracy, intonation, and balance to the group prepared without the aid of recorded models. Sang (1987) examined the relationship between instrumental students' performance behavior and teachers' modeling skills, and concluded that a teacher's ability to model and the frequency of demonstrations in rehearsals have an effect on student performance level. Delzell (1989) found that the incorporation of models/discriminator foils and modeling/imitation in the classroom is effective in developing the rhythmic and melodic musical discrimination skills of beginning instrumentalists.

Research in the use of recorded models in instrumentalists' home practice has produced a variety of findings. Zurcher (1972) found that beginning brass players who used cassette-recorded models and instructions had fewer pitch and rhythm errors and developed pitch-matching skills better than those who followed traditional practice methods. Yet in contrast to these results, Anderson (1981) found that there was no significant difference in regard to pitch reading, rhythm reading, tempo accuracy, and intonational accuracy between sixth-grade clarinetists who had used tape-recorded aural models and those who had not.

Modeling and its effects on advanced wind players' musical performances have been examined in two more recent studies. Rosenthal (1984) studied the effects of four modeling conditions—guided model (verbal and aural), model only (aural), guide only (verbal explanations), and practice only—on the musical performance of advanced instrumentalists. Subjects in the "model only" group scored significantly higher than all other groups. Second in effectiveness was the guided model group, with the subjects scoring significantly higher than subjects in the guide only and practice only groups. A similar study by Rosenthal, Wilson, Evans, and Greenwalt (1988) examined five practice conditions (modeling, singing, silent analysis, free practice, and control-practice of an unrelated musical composition) and their relationship to the performance accuracy of advanced instrumentalists. Modeling and practice were most effective, while singing and silent analysis were generally no more effective than sight-reading.

Individualized Instruction   Individualized instruction may take the form of programed instruction (PI) or computer-based instruction (CBI)/computer-assisted instruction (CAI). Programed instruction may be used to replace a particular area of teacher instruction or to supplement conventional teacher and classroom instruction. Results from these studies show no significant differences between groups and that individualized instruction is an effective technique.

Shaw (1971) tested the effects of programed learning on the development of musical psychomotor skills (snare drum technique) and reported that the method developed for his study did not efficiently teach the elements of snare drum technique. Higgins (1981) investigated the feasibility of teaching beginning applied clarinet with a microcomputer.

The attitudes of the students were positive toward the program, but the lack of feedback was viewed as a drawback.

Woelflin (1961) investigated the use of a teaching machine program to teach clarinet fingerings. There were three groups in the experiment: the control group, which received all of the instruction from the teacher, and two experimental groups, which used the teaching machine. Both experimental groups had a clarinet to hold and finger while using the teaching machine, but only one group had a mouthpiece to play. All three groups received classroom instruction about embouchure and breath support. Results indicated that the three groups made equal gains in knowledge of fingerings. In a similar study, Drushler (1972) compared the use of classroom instruction and programed instruction in the teaching of fingerings and pitch notation to beginning instrumentalists. The data showed that the scores for students in the programed instruction group exceeded those of the classroom instruction group, but the differences were not significant. Puopolo (1971) found that students who used self-instructional materials, printed lesson material, and cassette tape recordings of the required lesson materials for the week scored significantly higher on the *Watkins-Farnum Performance* Scale than did students who practiced the same material for the same amount of time without using the tape-recorded materials.

Individualized instruction within an instrumental music classroom has been investigated by McCarthy (1974, 1980). In both studies a heterogeneous band class approach was compared to an individualized instructional program in which students practiced exercises on their own. The instructor provided only individual help or permission to proceed to new material. Results from the 1974 study indicated that students at the extreme ends of intelligence, musical aptitude, and personal adjustment (those with high or low levels) received the greater benefit, in terms of performance achievement, from the individualized instruction program. Findings from the 1980 study indicated that individualized instruction resulted in higher performance test scores for students with above-average academic reading skills.

Research indicates that it is logical and practical for the instrumental music educator to use technology to further the teaching and learning of music. If used properly, "instructional technology seems to lead to more effective instruction in instrumental music" (Duerkson, 1972, p. 21). Abeles, Hoffer, and Klotman (1984) write:

The question of the ability of PI and CBI to provide effective instruction seems to have been answered. Literally hundreds of studies comparing PI and CBI materials with "traditional approaches" have been conducted. . . . They indicate, in general, that automated instructional materials are equally as effective as teacher-presented instruction. (p. 224)

The Discovery Method The discovery method actively involves students in the learning process. A teacher utilizing the discovery method does not provide all the answers and directions for the student, but guides the student through leading questions and clues to discover the correct answers.

D'Aurelio (1973), investigating the effects of a teacher-dominated strategy and a teacher-guided strategy (discovery method) on the abilities of beginning instrumental music students to detect and correct pitch and rhythm errors, found no significant differences between the two strategies. However, the teacher-guided group obtained higher scores on pitch and rhythm error detection than the teacher-dominated group.

Groeling (1977) investigated the effects of the discovery approach on beginning instrumentalists. An experimental group explored sounds, beginning with nonmusical sound sources and later writing short sound compositions, explored the sounds of real instruments by family groupings, and then chose one instrument on which to specialize. Groeling found that while the experimental and control groups were equal in playing skill and musical comprehension, students in the experimental group maintained a high level of enthusiasm during the duration of the experiment (one academic year), whereas students in the control group lost interest in the lessons after 3 months, and all the students in the experimental group completed the course of instruction, while 30 percent of the control group dropped out.

Reimer (1989) writes, "Artistic decisions are those which are made to carry forward the process of exploring and discovering the expressive potentials of some materials" (p. 64). Students who have the opportunity to make artistic decisions develop a deeper sense of musical understanding and aesthetic awareness. A philosophical basis has been established for discovery learning as a methodology. All that remains is a foundation of research to verify its effectiveness.

Comprehensive Musicianship Comprehensive musicianship methodology differs from the strictly performance-oriented approach in that music concepts such as melody, harmony, style, rhythm, form, texture, and the historical context of music are studied in addition to the development of performance skills. Parker (1974) compared two methods of band instruction at the middle school level. Students in the comprehensive program received full band instruction 50 percent of the time and related musical activities (listening sessions, class electronic piano lessons, music theory lessons, fundamentals of popular music classes, and music and related area) the remaining 50 percent of the time. Students in the performance-oriented program received full band instruction 75 percent of the time, with the remaining 25 percent spent in small/large performance ensembles. Results indicated that the performance-oriented group did not perform significantly better or evaluate their experience significantly differently than students in the comprehensive program.

Comprehensive musicianship concepts were studied by Garofalo and Whaley (1979). Two groups studied the same compositions, but one group followed traditional rehearsal procedures, while the other followed a comprehensive music program developed by Garofalo. Students taught with this methodology acquired conceptual knowledge, aural skills, and performance proficiency to a significantly greater degree than students taught with the traditional approach. Whitener (1983) also compared a comprehensive music methodology to the traditional performance-oriented approach. Findings indicated that members of both groups performed equally well and, in the areas of interval, major-minor mode, and auditory-visual discrimination skills, those students who were taught through the comprehensive music methodology scored significantly higher than those students who were taught through the traditional performance-oriented approach.

Findings from these studies would support the inclusion of the comprehensive musicianship methodology in the music curriculum. Music educators tend to believe that because of the time necessary for a methodology such as this, the development of their students' performance skills would be hindered. Results from the aforementioned studies would refute this belief. One of the main goals of a music education program is to develop musical literacy. Comprehensive musicianship appears to be one way of achieving that goal.

Conclusions

There are many factors inherent in the success of any music education program. Some of these include the techniques, methods, curricula, and methodologies employed by the teacher; the students' backgrounds, previous musical experiences, and motivations; and the instructional setting. This chapter has presented selected research findings and applications of the techniques, methods, curricula, and methodologies in selected areas of music education teaching and learning.

There has been a good deal of research regarding the techniques, methods, and curricula used in the field of music education; however, because of the absence of a philosophical basis and a foundation of research for many of these techniques, methods, and curricula, there have not been many exemplary studies dealing with music education methodologies. Following are conclusions that are based on results of those research studies:

1. Findings from those research studies in general music education are variable, at best. Few differences have been reported in those studies that have compared various techniques or methods with each other or with a "traditional method." The effectiveness of one methodology over any other has not been demonstrated as controlled comparisons of methodologies have not yet appeared in the literature. The methodologies of Orff, Kodály, and Dalcroze have been shown to be effective in increasing musical learning. The theories and philosophies of Gordon (in his learning theory), Reimer (in the *Silver Burdett Music* series), and Boardman (in the *Holt Music* series), because they lack the conclusive research findings essential to demonstrate their effectiveness, are best designated as curricula that approach methodology.
2. Research studies in choral music education have focused

on selected aspects of techniques to improve choral singing (including the teaching of music reading), aspects of the choral rehearsal, and techniques that the choral conductor uses to improve choral singing (including those that assist the choral conductor in detecting performance discrepancies). The research that has been reported is so narrow in scope as to render unchanged the choral curriculum. A philosophical base and a foundation of research for methodologies in choral music education do not exist at the present time.
3. Research in instrumental music education has shown that there are very few conclusive findings regarding the validity or effectiveness of instrumental methods books, the largest source of teacher/student material in music education. The research in string music education has been limited to selected aspects of string teaching techniques and methods. The teaching of instrumental music as presented by Shinichi Suzuki, because it has a philosophical base that is clearly articulated, and research studies that demonstrate its effectiveness, can be called a methodology.
4. Comprehensive musicianship can also be considered a methodology and clearly should be incorporated into music education teaching and learning. Modeling and imitation, individualized instruction, and the discovery method hold high promise as methodologies. A foundation of research should bring that promise to realization.
5. Although much has been learned in recent years about the teaching/learning process, it would appear that, in the research literature in music education regarding methodologies, no new conclusions have been reached as profound as the one highlighted in the famed *First Grade Reading Studies*. Stauffer (1967) writes that, while these studies were conducted in different localities across the country, were directed by individuals with varying training, and explored many different approaches to the teaching of reading, "in almost every instance the experimental populations made significantly greater gains than the control populations" (p. v). Those techniques, methods, curricula, and methodologies that are most effective and bring about increased learning are those that the teacher knows best. Seemingly, in music education the teacher's knowledge of what is to be taught, and confidence about how it is to be taught, enhance the musical learning of students.

As researchers in music education formulate and shape their questions, hypotheses, and designs, it is hoped that they will find ways to investigate the effectiveness of the techniques, methods, curricula, and methodologies in music education; that they will examine the relationships and interactions between and among the techniques, methods, curricula, and methodologies and the numerous teacher, learner, and setting variables; and that their investigations will address the perspectives of those teaching, as well as those being taught, in relationship to both achievement and attitude. Most importantly, study of these variables should be conducted in a longitudinal manner. The ongoing challenge is still the identification and utilization of effective research-based methodologies.

References

Abeles, H., Hoffer, C., and Klotman, R. (1984). *Foundations of music education.* New York: Schirmer Books.

Anderson, J. (1981). Effects of tape-recorded aural models on sight-reading and performance skills. *Journal of Research in Music Education, 29*(1), 23–30.

Bennett, P. (1986). When "method" becomes authority. *Music Educators' Journal, 72*(9), 38–40.

Blaine, R. (1986). Adaptation of the Suzuki-Kendall method to the teaching of a heterogeneous brass-wind instrumental class of trumpets and trombones. Unpublished doctoral dissertation, Catholic University of America, Washington.

Boardman, E. (1988a). The generative theory of musical learning, Part 1. *General Music Today, 2*(1), 4–5, 26–30.

Boardman, E. (1988b). The generative theory of musical learning, Part 2. *General Music Today, 2*(2), 3–6, 28–32.

Bonham, G. (1977). Australian music education-traditions of the enlightenment. *The Australian Journal of Music Education, 20,* 17–21.

Boyle, D., and Radocy, R. (1987). *Measurement and evaluation of musical experiences.* New York: Schirmer Books.

Bridges, D. (1982). Fixed and movable *doh* in historical perspective. *The Australian Journal of Music Education, 30,* 11–15.

Brunson, T. R. (1969). An adaptation of the Suzuki-Kendall violin method for heterogeneous stringed instrument classes. Unpublished doctoral dissertation, University of Arizona, Tempe.

Colwell, R. (1979). *Music competency tests.* Morristown: Silver Burdett.

Corbin, L. (1982). Vocal pedagogy in the choral rehearsal: The influence of selected concepts on choral tone quality, student understanding of the singing process and student attitudes toward choir participation. Unpublished doctoral dissertation, Ohio State University, Columbus.

Crook, E., Reimer, B., and Walker, D. (1978). *Silver Burdett Music.* Morristown: Silver Burdett Company.

Crumpler, S. E. (1983). The effect of Dalcroze eurythmics on the melodic growth of first grade students. Unpublished doctoral dissertation, University of Kansas, Lawrence.

D'Aurelio, G. C. (1973). An investigation of the effects of two teaching strategies on the development of skills in detecting and correcting pitch and rhythm errors by beginning instrumental music students. Unpublished doctoral dissertation, University of Wisconsin, Madison.

Daniels, R. D. (1986). Relationships among selected factors and the sight reading ability of high school mixed choirs. *Journal of Research in Music Education, 34*(4), 279–289.

Darazs, A. (1966). The Kodály method for choral training. *American Choral Review, 8*(3), 8–12.

Delzell, J. (1989). The effects of musical discrimination training in beginning instrumental music classes. *Journal of Research in Music Education, 37*(1), 21–31.

Dickey, M. R. (1982). A comparison of the effects of verbal instruction and nonverbal teacher-student modeling on instructional effectiveness in instrumental music ensembles. Unpublished doctoral dissertation, University of Michigan, Ann Arbor.

Drushler, P. (1972). A study comparing programmed instruction with conventional teaching of instrumental fingerings and music

pitch notation for beginning students of clarinet, flute, and trumpet in a flexible scheduled curriculum. Unpublished doctoral dissertation, State University of New York, Buffalo.

Duerksen, G. (1972). *From research to the classroom no. 3: Teaching instrumental music.* Washington: Music Educators National Conference.

Froseth, J. (1976). *The individualized instructor.* Chicago: GIA Publications.

Garofalo, R. J. and Whaley, G. (1979). Comparison of the unit study and traditional approaches to teaching music through school band performance. *Journal of Research in Music Education, 27*(3), 137–142.

Gillespie, R. (1991). Research in string pedagogy for developing the playing skills of students in string classes. *Dialogue in Instrumental Music Education, 15*(1), 1–9.

Gordon, E. (1971). *The psychology of music teaching.* Englewood Cliffs: Prentice-Hall.

Gordon, E. (1986). *Jump Right In; The music curriculum.* Chicago: GIA Publications.

Gordon, E. (1987). *Jump Right In; The instrumental curriculum.* Chicago: GIA Publications.

Gordon, E. (1989a). *Learning sequences in music: Skills, content and patterns. A music learning theory.* Chicago: GIA Publications.

Gordon, E. (1989b). Music learning theory. *Proceedings of the Suncoast Music Education forum on creativity.* Tampa: University of South Florida.

Gonzo, C. (1973). Research in choral music education. *Bulletin of the Council for Research in Music Education, 35*(2), 1–9.

Green, D. R. (1973). An investigation of the effects of two modes of notating and structuring the rhythmic content of a beginning instrumental method book on the rhythmic reading ability of beginning instrumental students. Unpublished doctoral dissertation, University of Wisconsin, Madison.

Groeling, C. (1977). A comparison of two methods of teaching instrumental music to fourth grade beginners. *Bulletin of the Council for Research in Music Education, 51,* 41–44.

Hales, B. (1961). A study of music reading programs in high school choruses in the Rocky Mountain States. Unpublished doctoral dissertation, University of Oregon, Eugene.

Higgins, W. R. (1981). The feasibility of teaching beginning applied clarinet with the microcomputer. Unpublished doctoral dissertation, Pennsylvania State University, University Park.

Hylton, J. (1983). A survey of choral music education research: 1972–1981. *Bulletin of the Council for Research in Music Education, 76,* 1–29.

Jones, M. S. (1979). An investigation of the difficulty levels of selected tonal patterns as perceived aurally and performed vocally by high school students. Unpublished doctoral dissertation, University of Michigan, Ann Arbor.

Joseph, A. (1983). A Dalcroze eurhythmics approach to music learning in kindergarten through rhythmic movement, ear training, and improvisation. Unpublished doctoral dissertation, Carnegie-Mellon University, Pittsburgh.

Kress, H. (1981). An investigation of the effect upon musical achievement and musical performance of beginning band students exposed to method books reflecting Piaget's theory of conservation. Unpublished doctoral dissertation, University of Colorado, Boulder.

Kyme, G. (1960). An experiment in teaching children to read music with shape notes. *Journal of Research in Music Education, 8*(1), 3–9.

Lander, R. (1980). *The talent education school of Shinichi Suzuki: An analysis.* Hicksville: Exposition Press.

Landeck, B., Crook, E., and Youngberg, H. (1968). *Making music your own.* Morristown: Silver Burdett Company.

Landis, B., & Carder, P. (1972). *The eclectic curriculum in American music education: Contributions of Dalcroze, Kodály, and Orff.* Reston: Music Educators National Conference.

McCarthy, J. (1974). The effect of individualized instruction on the performance achievement of beginning instrumentalists. *Bulletin of the Council for Research in Music Education, 38,* 1–16.

McCarthy, J. (1980). Individualized instruction, student achievement, and dropout in an urban elementary instrumental music program. *Journal of Research in Music Education, 28*(1), 59–69.

McDaniel, M. (1974). A comparison of *Music Achievement Test* scores of fourth-grade students taught by two different methods - Kodály (Threshold to Music) and traditional (Making Music Your Own). Unpublished doctoral dissertation, Louisiana State University, Baton Rouge.

Major, J. (1982). The effect of subdivision activity on rhythmic performance skills in high school mixed choirs. *Journal of Research in Music Education, 30*(1), 31–47.

Meske, E., Pautz, M., Andress, B., and Willman, F. (1988). *Holt Music.* New York: Holt, Rinehart and Winston.

Mount, T. (1982). Pitch and rhythm error identification and its relevance in the use of choral sectional rehearsals. Unpublished doctoral dissertation, University of Southern California, Los Angeles.

Munsen, S. C. (1986). A description and analysis of an Orff-Schulwerk program of music education (improvisation). Unpublished doctoral dissertation, University of Illinois, Urbana.

Nelson, D. (1983). String teaching and performance: A review of research findings. *Bulletin of the Council of Research in Music Education, 74,* 39–46.

Olson, R. G. (1964). A comparison of two pedagogical approaches adapted to the acquisition of melodic sensitivity in sixth grade children: The Orff method and the traditional approach. Unpublished doctoral dissertation, Indiana University, Bloomington.

Palmer, M. H. (1974). The relative effectiveness of the Richards and Gordon approaches to rhythm reading for fourth grade children. Unpublished doctoral dissertation, University of Illinois, Urbana.

Parker, R. (1974). Comparative study of two methods of band instruction at the middle school level. Unpublished doctoral dissertation, Ohio State University, Columbus.

Puopolo, V. (1971). The development and experimental application of self-instructional practice materials for beginning instrumentalists. Unpublished doctoral dissertation, Michigan State University, East Lansing.

Rainbow, B. (1979). Curwen, Kodály and the future. *The Australian Journal of Music Education, 25,* 33–35.

Reimer, B. (1989). *A philosophy of music education (2nd ed.).* Englewood Cliffs: Prentice Hall.

Richards, M. (1966). *Threshold to music.* Palo Alto: Fearon Publishers.

Rosenthal, R. K. (1984). Relative effects of guided model, model only, guide only, and practice only treatments on the accuracy of advanced instrumentalists' musical performance. *Journal of Research in Music Education, 32*(4), 265–273.

Rosenthal, R. K., Wilson, M., Evans, M., and Greenwalt, L. (1988).

Effects of different practice conditions on advanced instrumentalists' performance accuracy. *Journal of Research in Music Education, 36*(4), 250–257.

Sampson, U. (1968). An identification of deficiencies in past and current method books for beginning heterogeneous wind-percussion class instrumental music instruction. Unpublished doctoral dissertation, University of Michigan, Ann Arbor.

Sang, R. (1987). A study of the relationship between instrumental music teachers' modeling skills and pupil performance behaviors. *Bulletin of the Council for Research in Music Education, 91,* 155–159.

Shamrock, M. (1986). Orff Schulwerk: An integrated foundation. *Music Educators Journal, 72*(6), 51–55.

Shaw, A. (1971). The development and evaluation of a programmed learning approach in teaching the elements of snare drum technique. Unpublished doctoral dissertation, Indiana University, Bloomington.

Shehan, P. (1987). Effects of rote versus note presentations on rhythm learning and retention. *Journal of Research in Music Education, 35*(2), 31–47.

Shuler, S. (1986). The effects of Gordon's learning sequence activities on music achievement. Unpublished doctoral dissertation, Eastman School of Music of the University of Rochester, Rochester.

Siemens, M. T. (1969). A comparison of Orff and traditional instructional methods in music. *Journal of Research in Music Education, 17*(3), 272–285.

Siemens, M. T. (1967). Current status, practices, and procedures of two instructional methods of music education of Jefferson County elementary schools. Unpublished doctoral dissertation, University of Toledo, Toledo.

Small, A. R. (1983). The effect of male and female vocal modeling on pitch matching accuracy of first grade children. *Journal of Research in Music Education, 31*(3), 227–233.

Sperti, J. (1970). Adaptation of certain aspects of the Suzuki method to the teaching of the clarinet: An experimental investigation testing the comparative effectiveness of two different pedagogical methodologies. Unpublished doctoral dissertation, New York University, New York.

Spillane, K. (1987). Breath support directives used by singing teachers: A delphi study. Unpublished doctoral dissertation, Columbia University, New York.

Stauffer, R. G. (1967). *The first grade reading studies: Findings of individual investigations.* Newark: International Reading Association.

Stegall, J. R. (1978). Shape notes and choral singing. *The Choral Journal, 24*(2), 5–10.

Sterling, P. (1985). The effects of accompanying harmonic content on vocal pitch accuracy of a melody. *Psychology of Music, 13*(2), 72–80.

Stockton, J. (1983). An experimental study of two approaches to the development of aural meter discrimination among students in a college introductory class. Unpublished doctoral dissertation, Temple University, Philadelphia.

Suzuki, S. (1969). *Nurtured by love.* Jericho: Exposition Press.

Texter, M. E. (1975). A historical analytical investigation of the beginning band method book. Unpublished doctoral dissertation, Ohio State University, Columbus.

Weber, F. (1968). *First division band method.* Rockville Center: Belwin, Incorporated.

Webster's Seventh New Collegiate Dictionary. Springfield: G. & C. Merriam and Company, 1963.

Wensel, V. (1970). *Project Super 1966-1968.* Eastman School of Music.

Weyland, R. (1955). The effects of a workshop on certain fourth-grade teachers' skills in teaching music reading. Unpublished doctoral dissertation, University of California, Berkeley.

Whitener, W. T. (1983). Comparison of two approaches to teaching beginning band. *Journal of Research in Music Education, 31*(1), 5–13.

Winnick, W. (1987) Hybrid methods in sight-singing. *The Choral Journal, 28*(1), 24–30.

Woelflin, L. (1961). An experimental study on the teaching of clarinet fingerings with teaching machines. Unpublished doctoral dissertation, Southern Illinois University, Carbondale.

Zinar, R. (1983). John Curwen: Teaching the tonic sol-fa method 1816-1880. *Music Educators' Journal, 70*(9), 46–47.

Zurcher, Z. (1972). The effect of model-supportive practice on beginning brass instrumentalists. Unpublished doctoral dissertation, Columbia University, New York.

[15]

Music for Children and Young People

David Forrest

The title of this contribution comes from the extensive collection of music by the Russian composer and educator Dmitri Kabalevsky (1904–1987) entitled *Piano Music for Children and Young People*. It directly relates to the work of Doreen Bridges who has devoted so much of her energies and intellect to the enlightened cause of music for children as willing performers and participants, discerning and discriminating listeners and audience members. Throughout her life she has maintained her active passion regarding the place of the piano within the musical experience.

I aim to provide an exploration of music for children and young people from a framework proposed by I. B. Aliev (1970). My intention is to illustrate this through the music and writings of Kabalevsky and particularly the works he wrote for children. For this purpose I will take Aliev's relatively stark definition of children's music as 'music intended for children to listen to and perform. The best children's music is distinguished by a concrete subject, lively poetic content, picturesque imagery, and simple and clear form' (1970, p. 35).

Aliev (1970) in the *Great Soviet Encyclopedia* identified a series of categories of music for children. He limited his discussion to: works written to be performed by children; songs and instrumental works written for children's broadcasts, for plays performed in children's theatres, and for children's films; works based on subjects drawn from the life of children but performed by professional musicians, and not specifically designed for an audience of children; and music for educational purposes. Kabalevsky undoubtedly contributed to each of these categories.

In many ways Kabalevsky's writings were determined by his place and time, and the political and social structures in which he lived and worked. From a present day perspective however, it is clear that his ideas have a universal application.

Background

Music for children as performers and listeners has been richly served by Russian composers throughout the nineteenth and twentieth centuries. Amongst the nineteenth century composers who contributed to the body of works for children are Glinka, Grechaninov, Ippolitov-Ivanov, Liadov, Myaskovsky, Tcherepnin, Reboikov, and Tchaikovsky. Some of the twentieth century Soviet composers who have written for children include Dunayevsky, Gedike, Gliere, Gnesina, Krasev, Khatchaturian, Prokofiev, Shchedrin, Shebalin, and Shostakovich. Russian composers from the nineteenth and twentieth centuries have made significant contributions to the literature on music that uses the subject of children or childhood from both a pedagogical and performance perspective.

Over his life, Kabalevsky published more than 250 works including large-scale compositions (principally the operas, cantatas, symphonies and concertos) as well as the sets of songs and piano pieces. Of his total output approximately half of the works were written for children or use the resources of children. The majority of Kabalevsky's works for children fall into two main groups: 80 song collections and 153 separate compositions for solo piano. The following sections provide a consideration of the categories provided by Aliev in relation to Kabalevsky and his response to children's music.

Music to be performed by children and young people

The music Kabalevsky composed to be performed by children (and young people) is divided into two sections: the instrumental music and the piano music. Table 1 presents the instrumental music written for children.

180

Table 1: Instrumental music for children and young people

Year of comp.	Name of work
1948	Violin Concerto 'Youth' in C major Op. 48
1949	Cello Concerto No. 1 'Youth' in G minor Op. 49
1952	Piano Concerto No. 3 'Youth' in D major Op. 50
1961	Major-Minor Studies for cello solo Op. 68
1963	Rhapsody for Piano and Orchestra, 'School Years' Op. 75
1965	Twenty Easy Pieces for violin and piano Op. 80
1977–78	Prague Concerto for Piano and String Orchestra Op. 99

The three 'youth' concertos (Opp. 48, 49 and 50) provide a major contribution to the concerto literature. They were written immediately following the 1948 Decree by the Central Committee on Music, and were seen as his response to the edict. The decree had a significant impact on the direction, work and output of Soviet composers for the next decade. The Rhapsody Op. 75 and Prague Concerto Op. 99 are small yet effusively brilliant works written for piano competitions. These works sit comfortably alongside the other works in this genre. Kabalevsky (1975) in his note on the Piano Concerto Op. 50 stated that 'by introducing the 'Our Native Land' song into my concerto I wanted the young musicians and listeners to realise that the music deals with their own lives – with the Soviet Land, its people, its children and youth' (p. 2).

Kabalevsky wrote piano music for children throughout his life. His first piano works for children were published in 1927. Between 1972 and 1987 he assembled the twelve volume collection of *Piano Music for Children and Young People* from his total published output. The collection was published in Moscow by Sovetsky Kompozitor under the composer's supervision. Significantly for any composer each of the works has remained available in the current published catalogues under a range of imprints. The works in the collection are listed in Table 2.

Table 2: Piano Music for Children and Young People

Year of composition/revision	Name of work
1927/1968	In the Pioneer Camp Op. 3/86
1930, 1933	Two Sonatinas Op. 13
1931/68	From Pioneer Life Op. 14
1937	Thirty Children's Pieces Op. 27
1939/69	Three Rondos from the Opera 'Colas Breugnon' Op. 30
1943	Twenty-Four Easy Pieces Op. 39
1944	Easy Variations Op. 40
1952	Easy Variations on Folk Themes Op. 51
1958	Four Rondos Op. 60
1958–59	Preludes and Fugues Op. 61

182

1964	Spring Games and Dances Op. 81
1967	Recitative and Rondo Op. 84
1966,1968, 1969	Variations on Folk Themes Op. 87
1971	Six Pieces Op. 88
1971	Lyric Tunes Op. 91
1972	Thirty-Five Easy Pieces Op. 89

Rita McAllister (1975) stated that 'the significance of his works for young performers, which he regards not as a hack task but as a field of primary importance, is universally acknowledged; his earlier works for the young were in many respects models for subsequent children's music by Prokofiev, Shostakovich, and others' (p. 1135). Nicholas Slonimsky (1992) stated that 'Kabalevsky's music represents a paradigm of the Russian school of composition during the Soviet period' (p. 875). Punctuated throughout his compositional life are the larger instrumental, choral and orchestral and concert works (including the symphonies, concertos, sonatas, operas and cantatas). It should be emphasised that the works for children were not written in isolation from his other compositions, but occupied an ongoing and integral place within his compositional processes.

Works for broadcasts, theatre and film
Kabalevsky wrote a large number of compositions for radio broadcast, theatre and film. All of his works were performed, recorded and broadcast. Prominent

musicians, orchestras and choirs premiered each of his works. It should be noted that he held the position of Chief of the Board of Feature Broadcasting, All-Union Radio Committee – the body that determined what works would be performed and therefore also the works that would be recorded and broadcast. Although he chaired this committee for a relatively short time, he continued to exert influence on the work of this committee. The main works that fall under the category for broadcasts, theatre and film are listed in Table 3.

Table 3: Works for broadcasts, theatre and film

Year of comp.	Name of work
1931	*Galician Zhakeria* (*The Galician Jacquerie*) Op. 15 a radio work for soloists, choir and orchestra
1935	*The Merry Tailor* (incidental music), Puppet Theatre, Moscow
1940	*Komedianti* (*Comedians*) Op. 25 (incidental music)
1940	*Golden Childhood* incidental music, radio production
1940	*Parad molodosti* (*Parade of Youth*) Op. 31 presentation for children's chorus and orchestra
1941	*The City of Masters* incidental music (Central Children's Theatre)
1946	*Her First Year at School* film music
1957	*Pesnya utra, vesni i mira* (*Song of Morning, Spring and Peace*) Op. 57 cantata for children's chorus and orchestra

184

1958	*Leninitsï* (*Lenin's Lads and Lassies*) Op. 63 cantata for children, youth, adult choir and orchestra
1958	*V skazochnom lesu* (*In a fairytale forest*) Op. 62 musical scenes for children, narrator, choir and piano
1965	*O rodnoy zemle* (*About Native Land*) Op. 82 cantata for children's choir and orchestra
1970	*Pis'mo v XXX bek* (*Letter to the 30th Century*) Op. 93 oratorio
1975	*Friendship Songs* (Leipzig Cantata) Op. 97 for soloists and women's and children's choruses

One of the great developments of the early years of the Soviet Union was the establishment of the Central Children's Theatre. This institution, through the initiatives of Natalia Satz, saw the development of a large number of composers and their contribution of works for children. It was for this theatre that Prokofiev wrote his *Peter and the Wolf* Op. 67 (1936). Kabalesvky made some important contributions of incidental music to theatre and film. Many of these works were extracted and appeared in a range of versions. One of his most lasting compositions that remains in the concert and recorded repertoire is the *Comedians* suite for small symphony orchestra Op. 25 (1940).

Works drawn from the lives of children

The titled larger works that draw on the lives and experiences of children and young people are included in Table 4.

Table 4: Works drawn from the lives of children

Year of comp.	Name of work
1932	*Mstislav the Valiant* incidental music
1940	*Golden Childhood* incidental music and radio production
1946	*Her First Year at School* incidental music
1955	*Restless Youth* film music

To this list is added the large quantity of songs and piano music that draw on the experiences of children as the subject matter. An example is the set of Preludes and Fugues Op. 61 for piano where the six preludes and fugues are identified programmatically as A Summer Morning on the Lawn, Becoming a Young Pioneer, An Evening Song Beyond the River, At the Young Pioneer Camp, The Story of a Hero, and A Feast of Labour. Similarly, Kabalevsky (1983) stated that *In the Pioneer Camp* 'its six items are unified by a common program (a day at a Young Pioneer Camp)' (p. 2).

Larger works that require the resources of children

Kabalevsky drew on the resources of children in a wide range of his works. Table 5 lists the larger compositions (including the cantatas, oratorios, opera and Requiem) that use the resources of children.

186

Table 5: Larger works that require the resources of children

Year of comp.	Name of work
1931	*Galician Zhakeria* (*The Galician Jacquerie*) Op. 15 a radio work for soloists, choir and orchestra
1941	*Parad molodosti* (*Parade of Youth*) Op. 31 presentation for children's chorus and orchestra
1947	*Sem'ya Tarasa* (*Taras' Family*) Op. 47 opera
1957	*Pesnya utra, vesnï i mira* (*Song of Morning, Spring and Peace*) Op. 57 (cantata) for children's chorus and orchestra
1957	*Vesna poyot* (*Spring Sings*) Op. 58 operetta
1958	*Leninitsï* (*Lenin's Lads and Lassies*) Op. 63 cantata for children, youth, adult choir and orchestra
1958	*V skazochnom lesu* (*In a fairytale forest*) Op. 62 musical scenes for children, narrator, choir and piano
1962	*Requiem* Op. 72 'To those who fell in the battle with fascism' for soloists, mixed chorus, children's chorus and orchestra
1965	*O rodnoy zemle* (*About Native Land*) Op. 82 cantata for children's choir and orchestra
1967	*Sestrï* (*The Sisters*) Op. 83 opera

1972	*Pismo v XXX bek (Letter to the 30th Century)* Op. 93 oratorio
1974	*ISME Fanfares* (orchestra) Op. 96
1975	*Friendship Songs* (Leipzig Cantata) Op. 97 for soloists and women's and children's choruses

From this collection the only orchestral work is the *ISME Fanfares* written to be played by young performers of the country hosting the conference of the International Society for Music Education. It was first performed at the 1974 ISME conference in Perth, Australia.

Educative works for young performers

The educative works of Kabalevsky form one of the largest single groups of compositions. Principally these works come under the group of *Piano Music for Children and Young People* (12 volumes), however there are also instrumental works for violin and cello as identified in Table 1. Although Kabalevsky did not organise his works into a sequential pedagogical experience, the larger collections provide a developmental progression of technical and musical materials for the young performer.

In approaching music for children Kabalevsky adopted the model of what he called the 'three whales'. The name is taken from a legend where the world was supported on the backs of three great whales. The whales in music he said were the song, the dance, and the march. Kabalevsky's education philosophy was centred on the understanding by children of the characteristics and components of the song, the dance, and the march. He believed that if children could distinguish between these three forms or genres then they could enter the larger world of music. *About the Three Whales and Many Other Things: A book about music* explores the three genres for children and in doing so makes an important contribution to the music education literature.

MUSICAL DIMENSIONS

188

It is evident the audience for *About the Three Whales* is children. It was not the teachers (who would guide the children), or academics (who might construct programs around the ideas). It is directed to children to enable them to enter and appreciate the world of music.

This book is meant not only for those children who are studying music, play musical instruments and are therefore familiar with musical notation, but also for those who do not know it at all and who cannot read music. That is why I am not going to use any examples of musical notation in the book, even though music is its main subject. (pp. 9–10)

About the Three Whales is divided into two parts: 'About the three whales' and 'About many other things'. The first part focuses on an exposition of the song, the dance and the march. He said:

And so it is not surprising that these simplest musical forms have reached us as repositories of genuine musical treasures, representing as many national musical languages as there can be found in the world, as many thoughts and feelings as the human mind and the human heart can hold. (p. 19)

He pursues a discussion on 'Where the song will lead us', 'Where the dance will lead us', and 'Where the march will lead us'. The first part of the book concludes with 'The three whales come together' in which he discusses various combinations of the genres in a range of music and then concludes with a discussion of opera (with his focus on Bizet's *Carmen*, Rimsky-Korsakov's *The Tale of the Invisible Town of Kitezh and the Maiden Fevronia* and Shostakovich's *Lady Macbeth of Mtsensk)*. The issue that he continually returned to and reinforced throughout the book was limiting your acquaintance with music to the song, the dance and the march, is like peeping into a beautiful garden through the gate without stepping inside to explore and enjoy it and to understand why so many people wish to get into this garden and why they talk about it with such delight. (p. 19)

The 'many other things' of the second part is organised around the questions: Can music depict things? Can we see music and hear paintings? Can music and literature live without each other? Should we always imagine something when listening to music? Here he guides the students to the great artistic and literary works of Russian (and Soviet) history. He refers to writers including Tolstoy, Marshak and Mayaskovsky, and the artists Repin, Grekov, Aivazovsky and Levitan. He places the discussion against music and considers how meaning is conveyed in the art forms. He established the link between music and the other arts, as well as the link between 'music and life' (Kabalevsky, 1988, p. 22).

Composition for children

Kabalevsky's compositions for children and his writings shared a common philosophy. In many of his addresses and interviews he repeated such comments as:

When somebody asked the writer Maxim Gorki, 'How should books for children be written?' he replied, 'The same as for adults, only better!' This reply can equally well be applied to music for children. (1988, p. 120)

He later extended the much quoted statement by saying:

Maxim Gorki was right when he said that the way to write for children was as for adults, only better. In my opinion, however, it should be added that in order to write well for children one also needs to be *able* to write for adults. (1988, p. 148)

MUSICAL DIMENSIONS

190

Kabalevsky (1976) reinforced that when he referred to music he was talking about 'the great art of music and not music simplified specially for children' (p. 123). He clearly acknowledged that the composer of music for children must write in a considered manner, but must also be able to write for adults. He believed that composers must be able to direct their skills to different levels of performance and understanding. Elaborating on writing for children, he argued:

> it is not enough to be a composer to write such music. You have to be at the same time a composer, an educationalist [academic] and a teacher. Only this way can good results be achieved. The composer will ensure that the music is good and lively, the educationalist will ensure that it is educationally reasonable. As for the teacher, he must not lose sight of the fact that music, like any art, helps children to see the world and nurtures their education by developing not only their artistic tastes and their creative imagination, but also their love of life, mankind, of nature and their country. (Kabalevsky, 1988, p. 120)

His insistence on the importance of basing a system of music education on what he saw as the inherent nature of music is perhaps best expressed in the following statement:

> In my many years of teaching music to school children of various ages, I have attempted to arrive at a concept of teaching arising from and relying on the music itself, a concept that would naturally and organically relate music as an art to music as a school subject, and that would just as naturally relate school music lessons to real life. I have attempted to find the sort of principles, methods and approaches that could help to attract the children, interest them in music, and bring this beautiful art, with its immeasurable potential for spiritual enrichment, close to them. (Kabalevsky, 1988, p. 21)

The song, dance and the march gave Kabalevsky a means of conveying his educational beliefs to children. The three genres became for Kabalevsky the bridge upon which he was able to access the world of children, and in turn give children access to the world of music. Kabalevsky and Aliev were in agreement about what constitutes music for children. Probably more than any other Russian Soviet composer Kabalevsky devoted a considerable amount of effort to his work for children. The music he wrote and his rationale could provide a good framework for a larger study of music that is now appropriately described as 'music for children'.

References

Aliev, I. B. (1970). Children's Music. In A. M. Prokhorov (Ed.), *Great Soviet Encyclopedia* (3rd ed.). (Vol. 8). New York: Macmillan, Inc.

Kabalevsky, D. B. (1972). *Pro treh kitov i pro mnogoe drugoe.* (*About the Three Whales and Many Other Things: A book about music*). (2nd ed.). Moscow: Detskayar Literatura.

Kabalevsky, D. B. (1974/2004). *ISME Fanfares.* Perth: ISME.

Kabalevsky, D. B. (1975). Concerto No. 3 for piano and orchestra Op. 50. *Piano Music for Children and Young People.* (Vol. 11). Moscow: Sovetsky Kompozitor.

Kabalevsky, D. (1976). Music in General Schools. In F. Callaway (Ed.), *Challenges in Music Education.* Perth: University of Western Australia.

Kabalevsky, D. B. (1983). In the Pioneer Camp Op. 3/86, From Pioneer Life Op. 14. *Piano Music for Children and Young People.* (Vol. 1). Moscow: Sovetsky Kompozitor.

Kabalevsky, D. (1988). *Music and Education: A Composer Writes About Musical Education.* London: J. Kingsley in association with UNESCO.

McAllister, R. (1980). Kabalevsky, Dmitry Borisovich. In S. Sadie (Ed.), *The New Grove Dictionary of Music and Musicians* (Vol. 9). London: Macmillan.

Slonimsky, N. (Ed.). (1992). *Baker's Biographical Dictionary of Musicians.* (8th ed.). New York: Schirmer Books.

[16]

Teacher-Artist Partnership in Teaching Cantonese Opera in Hong Kong Schools: Student Transformation

Bo Wah Leung
Eddie C. K. Leung

The Hong Kong Institute of Education

Citation: Leung, B. W., & Leung, E. C. K. (2010). Teacher-artist partnership in teaching Cantonese opera in Hong Kong schools: Student transformation. *International Journal of Education & the Arts*, *11*(5). Retrieved [date] from http://www.ijea.org/v11n5/.

Abstract

This study aims to examine how and why students transform in terms of learning motivation in learning the Cantonese opera with a teacher-artist partnership approach in Hong Kong schools. An artist and seven teachers from four schools collaborated to teach the genre for eight weeks. Students' learning motivation changes in Cantonese opera was measured by a set of pre- and post-learning questionnaires. Qualitative data were drawn from class observations and focus group interviews with teachers and students. Results indicate that students' motivation in learning the genre has been changed. The statistical analysis suggests that, while primary students had significantly increased their motivation in learning Cantonese opera, the secondary students' motivation had not increased. Attributions include age differences, self-consciousness, intrinsic value and socio-cultural impact. However, the partnership was found to be an appropriate and effective approach in teaching the ethnic genre for its "role supplementation" between the teacher and the artist.

IJEA Vol. 11 No. 5 - http://www.ijea.org/v11n5/   2

Background

Promoting the Chinese identity in schools through arts learning has been encouraged by the Hong Kong government since the 1990s. Facing the music curriculum reform that began in 2003 (Curriculum Development Institute, 2003), teaching Cantonese opera has been one of the major initiatives because it is a regional Chinese art form that serves as a good platform for learning Chinese culture in Hong Kong.

Nevertheless, including Chinese genres in the school music curriculum has always been a difficult task in Hong Kong schools. According to a survey implemented by the Curriculum Development Institute (1998) of the Education Department, music teachers rarely taught Chinese music, including Cantonese opera, in schools. In addition, the younger generation might find it outdated and old-fashioned and would thus not be keen in learning. In general, Cantonese opera, like other traditional Chinese cultural arts, has been marginalized in the field of arts and culture in the Hong Kong community.

In the international realm, teaching traditional ethnic and multicultural music has been a common practice. Teaching traditional ethnic music is considered to be an effective method of cultural transmission (Clark, 2005; Sheridan & Byrne, 2008). However, there is a dilemma in which Hong Kong students prefer Western art and popular music to traditional Chinese music (Ho & Law, 2006). In the USA, for example, which is regarded as a multicultural country that accepts and encourages the teaching and learning of multicultural music, only 0.23% of the program in a four-year music education undergraduate program in the USA consisted of non-Western music, while more than 92% of the music taught in this program is Western art music (Wang & Humphreys, 2009).

Based on the current circumstance, this paper reports part of a study examining the impact of employing a teacher-artist partnership in teaching Cantonese opera in Hong Kong schools. The paper focuses on the possible motivational transformation of students and explore how and why the students change their motivation levels toward learning the indigenous genre. An in-depth understanding of students' attributions on how they perceive learning Chinese traditional music generated from this study may provide implications on resolving the current dilemma.

Cantonese opera

Cantonese opera has been popular in the Guangdong (Canton) Province since the Qing Dynasty (1644-1911). It is one of more than 350 regional opera genres in China (Zoeng, 1982) using Cantonese (the dialect used in Guangdong Province) as the language of singing and dialogues. There are two main functions of Cantonese opera: ritual (e.g., celebrating the birth of Chinese gods) and entertainment (Yee, 1998). Since Hong Kong was originally part of Guangdong Province, Cantonese opera was very popular in this region in the early 20th century. Many famous actors and actresses performed in Hong Kong during the 1950s and 1960s. However, since the introduction of Western pop music and movies in the 1970s, Cantonese opera began to experience a decline in popularity in Hong Kong (Chan, 1991). This has resulted in the declining interest to appreciate and learn the genre among the young generation in recent decades.

Nature of teacher-artist partnership

Partnership between the teacher and the artist is established when arts teachers find themselves incapable and lacking the confidence to produce authentic artistic experiences for their students. Professional artists are thus invited to collaborate with the teachers in schools to work with students in art making and experience. According to Gradel (2001), teaching artists can be involved in different levels and activities ranging from performing and exhibiting, interacting with audience, creating context for learners to participate, working in residency in classrooms, engaging with schools and teachers to plan instruction and assessment, and to develop programs. In order to achieve an effective level of teacher development, programs should be created with long-term follow-up which generate situations that encourage collegiality, foster agreement among participants on the goals of the program, acknowledge participants' beliefs and practices, and make use of outside facilitators such as the participating artists (Richardson, 2003).

Theoretical Frameworks

This study employs the cultural-historical theory of learning as a theoretical framework. Cultural influences have been regarded to be critical in affecting the content and course of human development and learning. According to Oers (2009), "individual developmental courses may differ enormously depending on the system in which they are positioned" (p. 4). Rogoff (2003) argued that human development is comprehended in the light of cultural practices.

In the field of music education, Butler et al. (2007) proposed a conceptual model featuring issues of teaching multicultural music in the classroom using five primary categories: teacher, student, content, instruction, and context. Among all, students' age, gender, cultural values, cultural identity, cultural style, musical experiences and preferences, beliefs, and expectations are critical in learning effectiveness. Specifically, students' age, gender and ethnic group identity are critical in affecting the development of their musical preferences (LeBlanc, 1987).

Other variables including learning style preference and racial identity may affect their learning of ethnic music.

The frameworks aforementioned reflect that elements related to students' culture and cultural values, such as cultural identity, cultural context, cultural beliefs and expectation remain a critical attribution to their musical preferences and their learning motivation. Based on these frameworks, this article will explore possible student transformation of learning the Cantonese opera under the partnership with attention on students' cultural identities, cultural beliefs, expectations and their surrounding cultural contexts.

Student transformation

Student transformation with different innovations has been fertile in various disciplines. For instance, in the field of English composition, Alexander (2009) suggested that complex computer games may contribute to student transformation in literacy. In science education, while using flow charting as a planning tool, students would transform to define problems in a more holistic way, and demonstrate more insightful and integrated approaches to their use of tools (Norton, et al., 2007). And Chen (1999) argued that the Physical Education curriculum was not improving because negative social changes had denied students' access to necessary social capital for successful learning, and thus called for a transformation in students rather than reproduction of knowledge.

Studies on student transformation as a result of teacher-artist partnership are rather limited. One study was undertaken on the issue of students' vocational choices. Abeles (2004) examined the vocational choices of fourth grade students from 11 elementary schools in the US which participated in three different partnerships between the schools and orchestral groups and compared the result with students from four other schools that did not participate in any partnership. Results indicated that there were significant differences between students from partnership schools and students from the non-partnership ones. The former selected music vocation more frequently than the latter. It was attributed to the fact that the students from partnership schools were more familiar with instrumental music through their direct encounter and experiences with the orchestral groups. The partnership between schools and the orchestral groups was regarded to be an effective way of elevating students' interest in instrumental music through direct contact with musicians. The employment of school-artist partnership as a positive intervention in promoting student motivation in music learning seems to be rather effective. From the existing literature it is worthwhile to seek similar effects by collaborating professional artists of indigenous genres with teachers in teaching the genre.

Aims and Objectives

The ultimate goal of the partnership, like other educational devices, is to improve the quality of students' learning. However, student transformation in partnership approach is rarely studied. Targeting the issue of lack of learning motivation and interest toward traditional ethnic music, the aim of this study was to examine how and why students changed their learning motivation after learning the genre in a partnership approach between the music teacher and an artist in teaching Cantonese opera in class. The objectives of the study were to determine if students would change their motivation in learning Cantonese opera after the program, and to identify the reasons behind such changes if any. The findings would be significant for teachers to reconsider how to employ and design a teacher-artist partnership approach to motivate students in learning the genre. Implications will be drawn for the purpose of enhancing the process of teaching ethnic music with such an approach for other regions or countries.

Method

This study employed a mixed approach of both qualitative and quantitative methods. A pre- and post-activity questionnaire survey was employed to study the motivation changes of students after they had undertaken eight weeks of the program employing the teacher-artist partnership method. Paired sample t-tests were used to measure the possible changes in motivation. However, the statistics could not provide in-depth understanding of how and why students were motivated to learn. In order to understand the attributions of the questionnaire findings, a number of semi-structured focus group interviews with students as well as observation of video recordings of class teaching were implemented.

Participants

Two primary and two secondary schools were invited to participate in this study. The sample group consisted of 696 students, broken down into 354 primary and 342 secondary students from the schools involved in the study. The schools were considered to be convenient samples as they volunteered to be subjects in the study. They received the endorsement of their principals and parents to participate in the study. Five primary and two secondary music teachers from the schools participated in the project. All the teachers were females, with a minimum teaching experience of three years.

Mr. Wong, a Cantonese opera practitioner and tutor, was invited to participate as the artist of the project. Mr. Wong had been a full-time tutor teaching Cantonese opera singing for more than 10 years before he established his own studio. Before being involved in teaching, he was a stage performer of Cantonese opera in Hong Kong for several years. In addition, he taught

Cantonese opera singing in the Hong Kong Academy for Performing Arts, which offered certificate programs for nurturing professional artists of the genre. He was often invited by individual organizations, including textbook publishers and tertiary institutions, to offer workshops on Cantonese opera singing. Thus, he is considered to be both a Cantonese opera artist/performer and an experienced tutor in this subject.

Procedures

The project was financially sponsored by a local non-government organization which promoted Cantonese opera. The recruitment of participating schools was open. Consequently two primary and two secondary schools had applied to participate in the project. The participating teachers were first invited to participate in four teacher workshops in order to develop their basic skills and knowledge. Afterwards, they designed their teaching plans with the assistance of Mr. Wong before partnership teaching for eight weeks. After teaching, a series of focus group interviews with students and teachers and a questionnaire survey were conducted.

Teaching in Partnership

Before teaching, the artist liaised with the teachers in designing the teaching contents and method. In this process, the researchers left the autonomy to the teachers and the artist in making decisions concerning the teaching including timing, content, and methods.

The artist then visited the four participating schools and collaborated with the teachers in class teaching within eight weeks. A research assistant was hired to visit and videotape each and every class during the teaching period. The videotaping of class teaching and interviews were permitted by the school principals. The first author visited each school twice and observed all the video recordings for analysis.

Questionnaire Survey

A set of pre- and post-activity questionnaires were developed to measure the possible changes in motivation on learning Cantonese opera before and after the implementation of the eight-week teaching. The questionnaire comprised six motivational constructs based on the Self-efficacy theory (Bandura, 1995, 1997) and the Expectancy-value Theory (Wigfield & Eccles, 2000). These constructs included: 1) expectancy, 2) intrinsic value, 3) attainment value, 4) utility value, 5) perceived cost, and 6) self-efficacy. Expectancy refers to the subject's task-specific beliefs and ability beliefs. Intrinsic value refers to the enjoyment of doing the specific task, while attainment value is defined as the importance of doing well in a specific domain by a subjective judgment of an individual. Utility value is regarded as how the individuals can benefit from participating and learning the specific domain in the future. Perceived cost refers to the perceived loss that the individuals will bear, including time and effort spent if one is engaged in the domain learning.

Different questions were derived to investigate the feedback in each measure. Students were requested to report their level of motivation in a series of five-point semantic differential scales. To ensure that the students could understand the questions, the questionnaires were written in Chinese which was the mother-tongue of the students. In order to maintain high level of reliability, the questionnaire was piloted by 5 primary and 4 secondary students before implementation. Minor revisions in wording were made before sending to all schools for the survey. The questionnaires were collected and data were compiled and analyzed. The SPSS 17.0 software was employed to analyze the raw data. Mean scores and their standard deviations were calculated and compared by a series of paired sample t-tests to measure the possible motivational differences of students before and after learning.

Observation

In order to maintain a naturalistic setting of the class, an unobtrusive observation (Angrosino, 2008) was employed as one of the data collection methods in this study. The research assistant, who was to take video recordings, was introduced to the students by the teachers and attended each and every class so that the students were familiar with her. Her strategy of video recording was to first observe the general situation of teaching and learning, and to focus on specific issues related to student motivation in learning the Cantonese opera. She might use the zooming device of the video camera to focus on individual students for closer observation with higher level of specificity on motivation. These strategies were employed in order to preserve a naturalistic setting of the classroom as far as possible.

The first author reviewed all the video recordings of each and every class and made observation notes, which were given to the research assistant for validating the data so that the categorization of issues will be validated through a researcher triangulation (Denzin, 1970). The objectivity was also maintained by repeated reviews of the video recordings by the second author.

The researchers aimed to observe to what extent the students were motivated in learning the Cantonese opera during the class. Attention was paid to the student behaviors reflecting their learning motivation and their reaction on the delivery of teaching by the teacher and the artist. The observation data is considered to underpin the findings of the questionnaire survey by providing qualitative evidence. Observation data was analyzed once they were collected. A coding process was done after reviewing each piece of video recording.

Interviews with Teachers and Students

After the collaborative teaching and the questionnaire surveys, groups of four to five voluntary students from each school were invited to attend a series of semi-structured interviews in focus groups conducted by the first author. In addition, the secondary teachers were interviewed individually while the primary teachers were interviewed in groups. The conversations were tape recorded and transcribed. The semi-structured format of the interview was employed because it "allows the researcher to respond to the situation at hand, to the emerging worldview of the respondent, and to new ideas on the topic" (Merriam, 1998, p. 74).

The main aim of the interviews was to seek in-depth reasons that might impact on transformation of the students that could not be observed (Patton, 1990). The content of the interviews included students' respective perceptions on learning the Cantonese opera, as well as how and why they enjoyed learning the genre. Students were also asked to provide their views on the partnership teaching in schools and their learning experience of Cantonese opera. The teachers were asked to provide an account of their musical background and their expectation on their students' learning of the genre. Analysis of the interviews was done by a content analysis encoding and decoding the categories aforementioned.

Results

Reliability of the Questionnaire

Reliability analysis was done on both the Pretest and Posttest data. The inter-item reliability (Cronbach's Alpha) coefficients for the six scales are presented in Table 1. All scales had alpha reliability coefficients of between 0.765 to 0.936 with p-value less than 0.01. It shows that the scales were highly reliable and the questionnaire was appropriate to measure students' self-efficacy and motivation in Cantonese Opera. It is observed that the reliability coefficients for Posttest data are generally higher than the corresponding values for Pretest data. These increases across various scales indicate that the students changed, to a varying extent, their perception of Cantonese Opera after teaching.

Table 1. Reliability of Scales of Questionnaire

Pre-post Scales	*Pretest Alphas*	*Posttest Alphas*
Expectancy of task-specific and ability beliefs	0.893	0.904
Attainment value	0.844	0.862
Intrinsic value	0.896	0.897
Utility value	0.894	0.936
Perceived cost	0.882	0.885
Self-efficacy	0.765	0.772

Motivation Changes after Eight Weeks of Teaching

A total of 146 Primary 4 (year 4, aged 9-10), 208 Primary 6 (year 6, aged 11-12), 141 Secondary 2 (year 8, aged 13-14), and 201 Secondary 3 (year 9, aged 14-15) students participated in the questionnaire survey. Table 2 shows the mean scores of their self-reported motivation in the six constructs.

Table 2. Results of paired sample t-tests on the motivation measures of both primary and secondary students

	Primary students (n=354)				Secondary students (n=342)			
	Mean	Mean difference	t	p	Mean	Mean difference	T	p
Expectancy		.300	3.438	0.001***		.071	1.012	0.312
Pre-test	2.781				2.651			
Post-test	3.081				2.721			
Intrinsic Value		.548	5.803	0.000***		-.141	-	0.065
Pre-test	2.558				2.854		1.848	
Post-test	3.106				2.714			
Attainment Value	2.972	.242	2.723	0.007**	2.814	.085	1.229	0.220
Pre-test	3.214				2.899			
Post-test								
Utility Value		.151	1.673	0.095		-.025	-.355	0.723
Pre-test	2.946				2.651			
Post-test	3.097				2.626			
Perceived Cost	2.573	.304	5.066	0.000***	2.516	.156	2.709	0.007**
Pre-test	2.877				2.673			
Post-test								
Self-efficacy		.300	3.599	0.000***		-.044	-.603	0.547
Pre-test	2.650				2.647			
Post-test	2.949				2.603			

*p<.05   **p<.01   ***p<.001

As shown in Table 2, there are a number of observations that can be made on both groups (primary and secondary) after eight weeks of learning:

1. Primary students had significantly increased their expectations, while the secondary students had no significant changes;
2. Primary students had significantly increased their intrinsic values, while the secondary students had no significant changes;
3. Primary students had significantly increased their attainment values, while the secondary students had no significant changes;
4. Both primary and secondary students had no significant changes on their utility values;

IJEA Vol. 11 No. 5 - http://www.ijea.org/v11n5/   10

5.   Both primary and secondary students had significantly changed their perceptions of difficulty (cost) in learning Cantonese opera (they thought that learning was not so difficult as they had originally thought); and

6.   Primary students had significantly increased their self-efficacy, while the secondary students had no changes.

Class Observations

The main goal of class observation was to seek evidence of students' motivation in learning Cantonese opera. Three vignettes were selected from the video recordings to reflect the students' motivation in primary and secondary school settings.

Vignette 1

In a secondary 3 (aged 14-15) class, the artist taught the class to sing a selected excerpt. He started by inviting the class to sing with the teacher playing the melody on the piano as an accompaniment. The artist was counting the tempo of the excerpt using hand signs, while singing with the students with his verbal encouragement and reminders. The students appeared to be shy and hesitant to sing. Their voices were very low in terms of both volume and pitch. Most students were looking at the sheet music without singing, while many boys even bowed down their heads. Most of them appeared to be unconfident in singing the excerpt.

Vignette 2

The same excerpt taught in the secondary 3 class was used in teaching a primary 4 (aged 9-10) class. The teacher played an audio recording of the excerpt for the students with lyrics provided. One of the boys sang with the recording with high concentration. Although the excerpt was sung by a female character, the boy seemed to ignore this issue and was enjoying his singing.

Vignette 3

After listening, the same primary class was invited to sing the excerpt together and the artist used the violin to accompany the class singing. The music score with lyrics was projected on a screen so that every student could see the lyrics and sing together. All the students appeared to be concentrating on singing and their voices demonstrated a special vocal style used in Cantonese opera which included glissando-like melodic lines.

There were apparent differences in the levels of participation between the primary and secondary classes described above. In the secondary class, students appeared to be hesitant to sing, and most of them tried to hide their faces while singing. The vocal sound was weak and in a rather low voice, which was considered to be inappropriate in the authentic style. A common scene found in the secondary classroom was that students were listening passively to the teacher and the artist (see Figure 1). In contrast, the primary students appeared to be much more confident in singing the genre. They showed their enjoyment through the sufficient volume of singing and imitation of the appropriate singing style. In another scene, primary students were taught to learn about a specific movement employed in Cantonese opera. Those students neither showed shyness nor hesitance in learning the movement (see Figure 2).

Figure 1. Teacher-artist partnership in a secondary classroom

IJEA Vol. 11 No. 5 - http://www.ijea.org/v11n5/   12

Figure 2. Primary students learning a specific movement used in Cantonese Opera

Interviews with Teachers and Students

This section describes the results of analyzing the qualitative data from the interviews with teachers and students in the next section. The data covers the teachers' musical background, teachers' expectation on students' learning, teachers' view on learning the Cantonese opera, and students' perception of their learning of Cantonese opera under the partnership. The transcript quotes were given identification codes for reference. For example, (F/T/Pri/1) indicates a female (F) teacher (T) teaching in a primary (Pri) school and the number indicates the identity of that teacher. (M/S/Sec/2) indicates a male (M) student (S) in a secondary (Sec) school who was student number 2 in the focus group interview.

Teachers' Musical Background.

Most of the participating teachers started out by learning Western art music. All of them admitted that Cantonese opera was new to them. They admitted being familiar with the genre when they were very young during the times when their parents or grandparents listened to the radio or watched television:

I started to learn the piano since primary 5, and I entered the College of Education and started on the clarinet as my second instrument. I learnt the oboe and piano, too. I took a Master's program in Music when I was teaching, and that's all of my learning in music. [Have you learnt about Chinese music?] Very limited. (F/T/Sec/2).

One of the teachers, however, admitted that she had changed, to a certain extent, her perception and attitude toward Cantonese opera. She started to accept this genre due to an understanding of the genre:

I think I have learnt something [about Cantonese opera]. I have listened to it more frequently, but I am still not very fond of it. I still like Western music more. But since I know more, my appraising capability has been uplifted. I don't resist the genre as before. I can finish appraising the whole opera. I would convince myself that I am a music teacher and there is no reason that I should not know about it. (F/T/Sec/1)

The quotation from this teacher suggests that changing an attitude on musical preferences can be difficult. However, the key to the change of attitude was the cognitive development of the teachers on the genre. When the teacher has developed a higher level of understanding of the genre, her competence on understanding would be enhanced, which might lead to a positive change.

Teachers' Expectations

Both secondary teachers admitted that they had very modest expectations on students' attitudes toward Cantonese opera:

Actually my expectation is very low – I just hope that my students would not hate Cantonese opera (F/T/Sec/2)

I hope my students would possess a positive attitude toward Cantonese opera. I don't ask for a very keen attitude, but at least they don't resist [to appraise the genre], and could increase their knowledge about it. (F/T/Sec/1)

Teachers' View on Students' Perception toward Cantonese Opera

According to the teachers, the students' disinterest in learning Cantonese opera was due to different reasons, including the intrinsic value of Cantonese opera, unfamiliarity with the genre, a mindset that the genre represented something outdated and old-fashioned, and other physical and psychological reasons:

I think they would say that it [the Cantonese opera] is something very boring. Our position is to make them not to feel boredom and resistance… Thus, we taught a little in every aspect – we worried that teaching too much might make them feel bored. (F/T/Pri/1)

The children think Cantonese opera is unpleasant – it is due to the fact that they have gotten used to the Western harmony. They thought the sound is not harmonized, and that it is unpleasant… But if we start to teach the children not only Western music but also Chinese music at a very early stage, I think they would minimize their level of resistance because of this early encounter with Chinese music. (F/T/Pri/3)

The students would think that it [the Cantonese opera] is old-fashioned. It is important to change their mindset… It is always the elderly people who sing Cantonese opera; this makes them think that singing Cantonese opera belongs to the older generation. For instance, when I asked them if they had seen that before, they said that they would change the channel immediately if they find it on the TV. (F/T/Sec/2)

Mr. Wong [the artist] started to teach with me in April when the project began. He was very busy at that time thus he stopped for a while, until late May he came back for our lessons. They [the students] said, "Hurray, no Cantonese opera class!" At the beginning they didn't like to sing and I understood later, those boys in secondary 3 were in their period of voice change, and those girls were too shy to commit in singing. (F/T/Sec/2)

Interviews with Students

Students' Thoughts about Cantonese Opera

Primary students were found to be too shy to provide detailed and elaborative answers on their perceptions. However, most of them appeared to have a positive mindset in learning the genre:

I think Cantonese opera is very interesting. (F/S/Pri/2)
I'd like to do and to know [about the genre]. (F/S/Pri/3)
Those stories are very attractive. After learning the story, I hope to learn it [singing]. (F/S/Pri/1)
I think [the story] is very good, very creative. (F/S/Pri/4)

Because the others would think that it is old-fashioned, so we can be outstanding [when we learn the Cantonese opera]. (M/S/Pri/5)

Some primary students expressed that they appreciated the Chinese culture found in the Cantonese opera: "But I think… it [Cantonese opera] can reflect our Chinese culture… it is very meaningful." (F/S/Pri/5). Learning the Chinese musical genre may prompt the students to learn about the Chinese culture.

Secondary students were more elaborative on this issue. Some of them felt that the genre could be interesting: "Before learning, I thought it was the hobby of the elderly – for time killing. But after learning, I think some were quite interesting since we can learn something about Chinese history and language" (F/S/Sec/1). Learning the Chinese musical genre seemed to be an alternative way for these students in understanding more about Chinese history and language, which are offered in all schools in Hong Kong.

Furthermore, some students admitted that they were not familiar with the genre, which was a reason for their uninterested manner. In addition, the special nature of the genre, such as the usage of high pitches was another issue that they were not familiar with and did not understand: "Because I have not encountered Cantonese opera, I don't quite like it; it is very noisy and sounds like screaming." (M/S/Sec/3)

> We didn't learn about it since we were very young. Suddenly, we have to learn it and to change the voice, it would be difficult for us to get used to it. For instance, we learnt to sing in the Western opera style, and now we are asked to sing in this style. It would be difficult for us to adapt. (F/S/Sec/2)

One of the secondary students related this issue to her future career:

> Because I am not very keen on it, I won't learn it wholeheartedly. You want me to learn? It's ok. But if you want me to learn it with much effort, or make it as my future career, I won't do it. (F/S/Sec/3)

One of the secondary students admitted that she didn't understand the meaning of the lyrics due to the usage of ancient Chinese language employed in the traditional Cantonese opera libretto:

> Yes, but… some of the wordings… I couldn't understand some of the wordings…it seems too difficult for me… I just don't understand, no matter how good it is… it is most important to understand what they were singing [in order to like it]. (F/S/Sec/2)

And it was echoed by a primary student: "my grandpa brought me to the Cantonese opera… it seems very boring… they [the actors and actresses] spoke in different ways… I don't understand, I just have to read the subtitles so that I can understand." (M/S/Pri/7)

In addition, some secondary students thought that the genre seems to be "old fashioned" and "superstitious": "These are those things happening long time ago… there are superstitious things related to the Cantonese opera, you know…such as… 'baai sun' [worship gods]… we just don't like those things." (F/S/Sec/6)

Students' Thoughts About Including Cantonese Opera in the Music Curriculum

When students were asked to elaborate on the issue of including Cantonese opera in the school music curriculum, they tended to think that the Western culture seemed to be more valued by the schools and the community, which served as a major constraint for students to learn about Chinese culture:

> With the examination system of Hong Kong and the students' expectations, all are expecting the teachers to be experts in Western music. Chinese music is not so valued. You can see so many people learning the piano and the violin but few learning the Zheng. Therefore, I think it is normal to see a [music] teacher who doesn't know Chinese instruments; but a bit weird if he or she doesn't play a Western instrument. After all, this is Hong Kong. We expect the teachers could do these. (M/S/Sec/1)

> In the Hong Kong curriculum, it is compulsory to teach the recorder in primary schools, and singing… Most of them are English songs… and Western music history. We normally have Western music first and then Chinese music. She [the music teacher] has tried to balance these, and now Cantonese opera also. It seems that it [the Cantonese opera] was taught in a superficial level. (F/S/Sec/2)

When the primary students were asked if Cantonese opera should be included in the school curriculum, all the students responded positively. When they were asked if they thought that the female singing voice in the Cantonese opera style was too high and weird, they said, "No, it was really pleasant," while others nodded in agreement. They added that they would love to have more time learning it and they would like to try to wear the costumes for performance. Two primary students even proposed some concrete methods to teach the genre:

I suggest that when learning, let them [students] understand the story first but don't tell them this is about Cantonese opera. Just tell them it is a story, don't tell them 'it is a story from the Cantonese opera'. Otherwise their response would not be good. But if you say 'just tell you a story', then they will say 'Good, we can have stories in the music lessons.' (F/S/Pri/4)

Or we can say 'do you know the story of "Princess Cheung Ping"? Do you know this story?' The students must talk about this with their peers. And then, you can say, "now I am going to tell you another similar story." Afterwards, you finally say "this is a story from the Cantonese opera". I think it would make a difference. (F/S/Pri/3)

Students' Perception on the Partnership

Students were asked about their perceptions on the collaboration between the teacher and the artist. It is reported by the students that some teachers were not confident and competent enough to teach Cantonese opera even though they had attended the workshops. Thus, they had to rely on the assistance of the artist:

Miss C [the teacher] said that she was incompetent in Cantonese opera. Therefore, she just stayed at the back of the music room. She would only ask us if we could remember the content taught in the last lesson... only these kinds of questions... Actually she didn't teach anything... Miss C got much information... because she found them on the Web, and she has the Powerpoint... And I think listening a bit is not enough. Miss C valued our singing, and listening to the original melody, teaching music history... But when teaching Cantonese opera, her focus was on the instruments, and there was insufficient listening materials and other relevant information. (F/S/Sec/2)

One of the primary students reflected that the artist made a difference in introducing the genre in a special way: "Originally I didn't like it too much... it was very complicated. However, once Mr. Wong brought us many instruments and music and we sang and I found it very funny." (M/S/Pri/7)

For secondary students, whether or not the lesson was "boring" was regarded to be very important in motivating students to learn: "Mr. Wong [the artist] sometimes taught in a boring way. I felt it even though I was interested [in the genre]... if teachers teach in a boring way, I would rather learn by searching for information on the Web." (F/S/Sec/2)

Positive opinions focused on the mutual supplementation of the strengths and weaknesses of both parties were also reported:

> It would be possibly better to have one more teacher [in the class]. As our music teacher recognized that she was not strong in teaching Cantonese opera, if we have one more teacher, we can be helped. (M/S/Sec/1)

> It would be better to be taught by two teachers… can be supplemented… sometimes if something is missing, [the other teacher] can supplement the missing parts. (F/S/Sec/3)

> Mr. Wong had the performing experience. He can tell us how to give a signal… the advantage [to have him] was that, say for example, after explaining that we did not thoroughly understand, he would demonstrate for us… he can really teach us and make us understand. (F/S/Sec/5)

> [If students are taught by the music teacher only,] no way. Our music teacher understands us more. That's ok. But she can facilitate while the invited teacher [the artist] is teaching. That means her position is to facilitate, and the invited teacher can teach more. Our teacher can only manage the classroom, or maybe she can provide some more explanation. She is familiar with us and understands our thoughts. (F/S/Sec/2)

> He [the artist] often demonstrated to us, but he wouldn't ask us to come out and do it. Generally it was Ms. K [the teacher] who said, "How about if someone comes out to do it?" then we would do it. He wouldn't ask us… that is, he just did it by himself and we looked at him. If we understand, then he won't supplement. (F/S/Sec/3)

> Our music teacher was not as strong as Mr. Wong in Cantonese opera. Therefore, a good way is to have our teacher teaching with her method but Mr. Wong can supplement. (F/S/Pri/7)

> I think the difference between our teacher and Mr. Wong is that our teacher is better in teaching, and I would understand more from her, just like her teaching of doh, re, mi, fa; Mr. Wong does not seems to know how to teach. (F/S/Pri/5)

The responses from the primary students were straightforward. Some of the primary students found that they could learn more easily with two teachers:

It is good to have two teachers in class. For example, the music teacher's explanation was clear, which makes it easy for us to understand. Mr. Wong also explained some, which can make us understand more. (F/S/Pri/2)

I think if there are two teachers, they can teach half of the class. If there is only one teacher, she cannot take care of the whole class, and she may not know she is wrong…It might be troublesome when she finds out she was wrong and had to make amendments. (F/S/Pri/6)

However, some students thought that two teachers in the same classroom might create confusion:

Sometimes, when they [both teacher and artist] taught different things, I became confused. Sometimes, one of them might say, singing needs to be an octave higher… They say it in different ways… I could be confused. (F/S/Pri/5)

Discussion

The aim of this study was to examine how and why students changed their learning motivation after learning the genre in a partnership approach. The findings from the questionnaire survey indicate that there are differences between primary and secondary students with regard to their perceptions and motivational changes in learning the genre. Primary students have significantly uplifted their motivation toward learning Cantonese opera in terms of intrinsic value, attainment value, expectancy, self-efficacy, and perceived cost. In other words, they feel that learning Cantonese opera is more interesting and more important, but is not as difficult as they have thought before participating in the project. In addition, after the program, they become more confident in learning the genre and expected that they could learn successfully. This finding reflects a very positive learning motivation among primary students and, to a certain extent, the success of the partnership approach.

Secondary students have shown very limited significant changes in their motivations. The only significant change is that they think Cantonese opera is not as difficult as they have thought before participating in the program. However, after learning through the partnership, they have not changed other motivational constructs toward learning the genre. They remain rather uninterested in perceiving the genre as before; and they have not shown an increased level of expectancy in learning Cantonese opera. They do not think learning the genre is important in their lives and they do not expect that they could learn the genre very well. In addition, the mean scores ranging from 2.516 to 2.899 in a five-point scale reflect that they tend to possess a negative perception toward learning Cantonese opera.

IJEA Vol. 11 No. 5 - http://www.ijea.org/v11n5/   20

Age Difference

Apparently, the differences of motivational changes between the primary and secondary students are related to their different ages, which affect their self-consciousness, and level of intrinsic values toward the genre.

Self-Consciousness

The first attribution for the differences between the primary and secondary students' motivation changes is considered to be the self-consciousness derived from the age difference. Teenagers normally possess a higher level of self-consciousness than younger ages. Self-consciousness implies a "self" to be discovered and the possibility that people can sustain a "sense of self" across time and place (Warin & Muldoon, 2009). One of the attributions of self-consciousness is regarded to be shyness (Lund, 2008). According to the interview evidence, the adolescents in secondary schools found singing Cantonese opera weird as it is not a common activity in their peer groups. Singing the Cantonese opera with such a high voice is also considered to be different from what they perceive to be normal in other genres such as Canto-pop music. Thus singing the Cantonese opera involves a high level of shyness for those adolescents. In contrast, primary students have lower level of self-consciousness which enables them to enjoy singing and learning the genre. This is evident from the video recording that most of the primary students sing in a high voice in an active and positive manner.

Intrinsic Value

As observed in the classroom and from the interviews, many primary students were interested in learning the genre due to different reasons. They liked the Chinese stories which were mainly traditional folklores. For the primary students, Cantonese opera was an exotic genre which raised their curiosity for learning. According to the interviews, some primary students like the genre because it reflects the Chinese culture and tradition. Based on the video clip, the primary students appear to enjoy the genre and they can follow the audio recording to sing in an active and positive manner. All these reflect that most of the primary students possess a rather positive perception toward the Cantonese opera.

Utility Value

Secondary students were not totally negative toward the Cantonese opera as some of them found it interesting. However, they tend to think more about the utility value of learning the genre. As they are older than those primary students, they may have to consider more about their academic study and future career after leaving school. Some secondary students like it because they can learn about Chinese history and language in an alternative and more interesting way; while some others dislike it because they think learning the genre would hardly be related to their future career. In this aspect, the primary students do not have such concern.

Socio-cultural Identity

One of the extrinsic factors affecting the students' motivation toward learning the genre is the socio-cultural identity. It was found in the interviews that many students admitted that the Cantonese opera had an "old-fashioned" outlook and it belonged to the elderly. Cantonese opera comprised a major source of entertainment for the Hong Kong people before the emergence of modern amusements such as the television. The elderly people therefore had a history of appreciating and understanding the genre. The fact that most of the Cantonese opera audiences consisted of the elderly has had an impact on secondary students' cultural perceptions of the genre. The teenagers feel that this genre is only for the elderly but not for the younger ones. Those adolescents who are interested in that genre might be viewed as "abnormal" or "old-fashioned" and be excluded from their peers and social groups. In addition, secondary students have a broader range of entertainment choices nowadays. They need not consider an "old-fashioned" Chinese art as a hobby.

Another issue raised by the students is the "superstitious" outlook of Cantonese opera. Traditionally, the authentic performance context of Cantonese opera was related to worshipping Chinese gods (Chan, 1991). In the early 20th century, Cantonese opera troupes were mainly hired to perform by different towns in Southern China in religious events such as worship ceremonies for Chinese gods' birthdays and celebrating Chinese New Year. This kind of performance is known as "ritual performance for the deities as a charitable and pious deed" (Chan, 1991, p. 2). Until modern day Hong Kong, this tradition has been continuing. As Hong Kong people, the ritual performances of Cantonese opera are commonly seen in different districts. Therefore it is understandable to see that the students are responsive to the ritual phenomenon of the genre. They may believe that enjoying and pursuing Cantonese opera may bring them a superstitious image.

The Hong Kong teenagers seem to be "cultural outsiders" (Behnam, 2003) where Cantonese opera is concerned. They do not possess a strong cultural identity as "Chinese citizens" but only as "Hong Kong people". As a result, they may regard Cantonese opera to be an exotic musical genre rather than a traditional heritage from their motherland. In addition, the superstitious image of the genre might have developed a negative perception in these Hong Kong students' mind. These issues are considered to be a hindrance to the secondary students, who are in their adolescent stage, to understand and accept the Cantonese opera as a kind of Chinese cultural art.

IJEA Vol. 11 No. 5 - http://www.ijea.org/v11n5/   22

Partnership Impact

Despite the differences shown above, both primary and secondary students possess a similar view of the partnership approach of teaching. They have identified the role differentiation of the teacher and the artist during teaching. The music teacher tends to be capable in classroom management and pedagogy, such as how to keep the learning pace and maintain learning interest, while the artist focuses on performance practices through demonstration and provision of in-depth subject knowledge on the genre. Based on the differentiation, the teacher and the artist have formulated a relationship of mutual supplementation. For instance, when the teacher is unsure about the correct and authentic performance practice and rationale, she tends to ask for help from the artist. On the other hand, when the artist relies on his own demonstration and talks about the subject matter, the teacher may ask the students to respond and engage in the practice, which would deepen the students' level of understanding. This strategy of learning by doing is commonly used by teachers but always ignored by the artist who has no formal pedagogical training.

The mutual supplementation between the teacher and the artist is seen as a positive reinforcement in motivating students to learn. It can be imagined that the teacher teaching the genre alone may only rely on passive listening and knowledge transfer though lecturing. As a result, learning will be passive and limited to mainly cognitive but not skill-based learning. Students will merely know about the genre with superficial facts and may have limited listening experience. In contrast, if the artist is hired to teach the class by himself, students may learn the genre by practice with pertinent knowledge. However, since the artist is not trained in professional pedagogy, he may not be competent in engaging students to learn by employing relevant and effective teaching methods. The partnership of the teacher and the artist is therefore regarded to be a better way of fully utilizing the competencies of both parties in teaching a genre which has been proven to raise difficulties in engaging students' interests.

Conclusion and Implications

This study aims to examine a partnership approach through collaboration between music teachers and artists in teaching Cantonese opera in class within the Hong Kong context. The study also aims to evaluate and examine students' transformation after being involved in a teacher-artist partnership teaching program. The findings indicate different motivational changes of primary and secondary students in terms of learning the genre through the partnership approach. While primary students tend to accept Cantonese opera as a component of their music curriculum, the secondary students tend to remain unchanged in their learning motivation as shown through their largely negative perceptions.

The attributions of the phenomenon, based on the qualitative data, include students' age difference, intrinsic value toward the genre, and socio-cultural identity. In particular, attributions of secondary students' negative feedback are related to the age difference and socio-cultural identity of the adolescents. Students' self identity as Chinese citizens needs to be addressed by the teachers when teaching the ethnic genre.

Given that the teachers' personal attitudes have an impact on students' motivation, the professional development of teachers must therefore be further developed. Before the partnership teaching, the participating teachers were involved in a total of 12 hours of teacher workshops. This was considered to be insufficient for outsiders to obtain a basic knowledge of the genre in terms of skills, cognition, and attitude. As suggested by the literature (e.g., Morrow, 2003; Richardson, 2003), the continuous and long-term professional development of teachers is absolutely necessary to uplift the subject knowledge and increase the teachers' level of commitment in teaching this artistic discipline. In addition, according to Upitis et al. (1999), there are three levels of teacher transformation. As observed in this study, most of the teachers have only achieved a low level of transformation (i.e., necessary conditions which include taking personal risks to learn about the Cantonese opera and connection with their prior experiences of music learning). Due to the limited time of the workshops and preparations for teaching, they have not developed a higher level of transformation, such as sustained learning of the genre and teacher-initiated curriculum design and changes. In the long run, it is implied that school teachers in Hong Kong should aim at a sustained partnership and continuous professional development so that they can continue to proceed to a higher level of teacher transformation. The Cantonese opera as a cultural heritage should be much valued by teachers and then transmitted to their students. The traditional ethnic music can be a musical and cultural icon of the school music program (Clark, 2005).

To encourage secondary students to overcome their self-consciousness, it is the main direction for teachers to maintain the intrinsic motivation of learning Cantonese opera by employing a safe environment in which the teacher is the first person who demonstrates how he/she enjoys and pursues the genre by singing, understanding, and teaching the genre.

Finally, cultivating students' cultural values and identities should be the top priority of music teachers' agenda. Since primary students tend to accept the cultural genre more than the secondary students, it is suggested that indigenous music should be introduced to the students in earlier ages. Facing the future, music teachers should seriously consider how to involve their students in Chinese traditional genres in order to enhance their cultural values and identities.

Acknowledgements

The authors would like to express their gratitude to the Hong Kong Cantonese Opera Development Fund and the Cosmopolitan Lion Club for sponsoring the research project.

References

Abeles, H. (2004). The effects of three orchestra/school partnerships on students' interest in instrumental music instruction. *Journal of Research in Music Education, 52*(3), 248-263.

Alexander, J. (2009). Gaming, student literacies, and the composition classroom: Some possibilities for transformation. *College composition and communication, 61*(1), 35-63.

Angrosino, M. V. (2008). Recontextualizing observation: Ethnography, pedagogy, and the prospects for a progressive political agenda. In N. K. Denzin & Y. S. Lincoln (Eds.), *Collecting and interpreting qualitative materials* (3rd ed.) (pp. 161-183). Los Angeles: Sage Pub.

Bandura, A. (1995). *Self-efficacy in changing society.* Cambridge: Cambridge University Press.

Bandura, A. (1997). *Self-efficacy: The exercise of control.* New York: W. H. Freeman.

Butler, A., Lind, V. R., & McKoy, C. L. (2007). Equity and access in music education: conceptualizing culture as barriers to and supports for music learning. *Music Education Research, 9*(2), 241-253.

Chan, S. Y. (1991). *Improvisation in a ritual context: The music of Cantonese opera.* Hong Kong: The Chinese University Press.

Chen, A. (1999). The impact of social change on inner-city high school physical education: An analysis of a teacher's experiential account. *Journal of Teaching in Physical Education, 18*(3), 312-335.

Clark, S. (2005). Mariachi music as a symbol of Mexican culture in the United States. *International Journal of Music Education, 23*, 227-237.

Curriculum Development Institute. (1998) *Secondary music curriculum (Form 1-3): A report of questionnaire survey.* Hong Kong: Author.

Denzin, N. K. (1970). *The research act in sociology: A theoretical introduction to sociological method.* London: Butterworth Group.

Gradel, M. F. (2001). *Creating capacity: A framework for providing professional development opportunities for teaching artists*. Retrieved May 5, 2009, from The John F. Kennedy Center for the Performing Arts, Washington, DC, http://www.kennedy-center.org/education/partners/creating_capacity_autumn_2001.pdf

Ho, W., & Law, W. (2006). Challenges to globalisation, localisation and Sinophilia in music education: A comparative study of Hong Kong, Shanghai and Taipei. *British Journal of Music Education, 23*(2), 217-237.

LeBlanc, A. (1987) The development of music preference in children. In J. C. Peery, I. W. Peery & T. W. Draper (Eds), *Music and child development* (pp. 137-157). New York: Springer-Verlag.

Lund, I. (2008). 'I just sit there': shyness as an emotional and behavioural problem in school. *Journal of Research in Special Education Needs, 8*(2), 78-87.

Merriam, S. B. (1998). *Qualitative research and case study applications in education* (2nd ed.). San Francisco: Jossey-Bass Pub.

Morrow, L. M. (2003). Make professional development a priority. *Reading Today, 21*(1), 6-9.

Norton, S. J., McRobbie, C. J., & Ginns, I. S. (2007). Problem solving in a middle school robotics design classroom. *Research in Science Education, 37*(3), 261-277.

Oers, B. v. (2009). Learning and learning theory from a cultural-historical point of view. In B. v. Oers, S. Wardekker, E. Elbers, & R. v. Der Veer (Eds.), *The transformation of learning: Advances in cultural-historical activity theory* (pp. 3-12). Cambridge: Cambridge University Press.

Patton, M. Q. (1990). *Qualitative evaluation and research methods* (2nd ed.). Newbury Park, Calif.: Sage.

Richardson, V. (2003). The dilemmas of professional development. *Phi Delta Kappan, 84*(5), 401-405.

Upitis, R., Smithrim, K., & Soren, B. (1999). When teachers become musicians and artists: teacher transformation and professional development. *Music Education Research, 1*(1), 23-35.

Wang, J. & Humphreys, J. T. (2009). Multicultural and popular music content in an American music teacher education program. *International Journal of Music Education, 27,* 19-36.

Warin, J. & Muldoon, J. (2009). Wanting to be 'known': redefining self-awareness through an understanding of self-narration processes in educational transitions. *British Educational Research Journal, 35*(2), 289. Retrieved May 31, 2009, from ProQuest Education Journals database. (Document ID: 1719229711).

Wigfield, A., & Eccles, J. S. (2000). Expectancy-value theory of achievement motivation. *Contemporary Educational Psychology, 25*(1), 68-81.

Yee, R. W. (1998). Yueju (Cantonese Opera) in Hong Kong. In P. Tsao (Ed.), *Tradition and change in the performance of Chinese music, Part II* (pp. 33-52). Singapore: Harwood Academic Pub.

Zoeng, G. (1982). *Zung gwok hei kuk ngae soet (The art of Chinese opera).* Tianjin: Bak Fa Press.

About the Authors

Dr. Bo Wah Leung is Associate Professor of Music in the Hong Kong Institute of Education. He is the Coordinator of Music Specialization of the Master of Education program. His areas of research include creativity in music teaching and learning, motivation in learning music and teaching Cantonese Opera in schools. He is one of the founding Co-Editors of the *Asia-Pacific Journal for Arts Education* and on the Editorial Boards of three international journals in music education. He was the Chair of the Music in School and Teacher Education Commission under the International Society for Music Education in 2006-08.

Dr. Eddie C. K. Leung is the Associate Head of the Department of Mathematics and Information Technology, Hong Kong Institute of Education. He has extensive teaching experience at both secondary and university levels. His research interest includes application of statistics, cognitive and affective aspects of mathematics education, and teacher education. Dr. Leung has been the principal/sole investigator for numerous research and development projects supported by competitive grants. He has published numerous books and journal articles in various fields of education.

[17]

Musical Connections[*]

Mary Palmer

'With rings on her fingers
and bells on her toes,
She shall have music
wherever she goes'.

These words from a traditional nursery rhyme may seem quaint in today's multimedia, high tech world in which it seems children would rather watch than do, and would rather dress like than sound like the stars. Yet music has an almost universal appeal and the potential to 'grab' young learners. Therefore, it can be an effective instructional and motivational alternative; implementing a music-infused curriculum can enhance students' academic achievement. Indeed, there is much evidence to support the notion that music helps children learn and, equally important, helps children want to learn.

Psychologist Howard Gardner's theory of multiple intelligences has been a significant influence on education theory and practice. Musical intelligence is one of the eight discrete intelligences that Gardner identified (Gardner, 1983, 1999). According to Armstrong (1994), the greatest contribution of multiple intelligence theory is the suggestion that teachers must expand their repertoire of techniques, tools, and strategies beyond the typical linguistic and logical ones predominant in US classrooms. When linguistic and logical/mathematical skills are the only measures of school success, the human potential of lll any students is left untapped. Hackett and Lindeman (2001) assert that music stimulates and enhances learning in every subject, and that students in schools with art-rich curricula excel in all subjects. For example, students in the New York City-based Learning To Read through the Arts program have made substantial and long-lasting gains in achievement, and also display improved attitudes toward learning in general (Collett, 1991). Likewise, the Ashley River Creative Arts Elementary Magnet School (Charleston County, South Carolina), an ethnically diverse school, places the arts at the core of its curriculum, and students earn high scores on standardized achievement tests (Shuler, 1991). Music and the other arts contribute not only to demonstrated academic achievement, but also to academic satisfaction.

Incorporation of music into the elementary curriculum can be approached in a myriad of ways. This chapter will explore three of these: Brain Breaks, Esprit de Corps, and Curriculum

---

[*]   This essay was originally published in Patricia A. Crawford and Kathleen Glascott Burriss (eds) *It's elementary!:Special Topics in Elementary Education*, Olney, MD : Association for Childhood Education International, 2002.

Enhancement. In each case, the use of music may be incorporated discretely or used within an integrated framework.

Brain Breaks

Music provides a change of pace in the classroom. With music, children can move; play musical instruments (even homemade ones or objects from the environment that can create 'found sounds'); sing; create their own lyrics, tunes, or accompaniments; or listen with a purpose.

Current research suggests that we can help the brain function more efficiently through various activities, including:

- Changing what we are doing as frequently as every seven minutes (an occasional musical activity can 'freshen' the children's brains)
- Standing (the children might stand to sing a song, do a movement, or perform a dance)
- Laughing ('silly' songs, musical jokes, or vocal sound play can make us all laugh)
- Having social interactions with others (music brings us together).

Thoughtful selection and use of music and music materials will help create a brain-friendly classroom environment. Music can be used to introduce a lesson, enliven the content of a lesson, or just provide a 'break' from seatwork. When teachers treat the 'brain break' as another opportunity for learning, children get a '2 for 1' value in learning.

Esprit de Corps

Music can help to bring people together and create a sense of belonging. Children get acquainted using various 'name game' songs and chants. For instance, the 'Cookie Jar' chant can be taught to the whole class and then be played by children in small groups. This song allows children to get acquainted with one another and gives them a sense of responsibility for participating in the chant. The experience can be varied by encouraging children to experiment with different vocal qualities (speaking, whispering, shouting, singing), expressive qualities (loud/soft; staccato/legato), and pitch changes (high/low) as they play, sing, and chant.

It is also helpful to develop a repertoire of songs to sing with the class. For example, teachers may wish to memorize 10 or 12 high-quality songs that are fun to sing and that advance the curriculum. Folk songs from around the world are good choices for this. These songs can be introduced during transition times, such as when students are lining up to go to lunch or the bus. They also can *be* integrated whenever a change of pace is needed in the classroom, such as when a break is needed from doing math problems. These are great times to pull out your 'hip pocket songs' and sing! These shared experiences will help to not only ease transitions, but also build a sense of community in the classroom.

Hearing a certain piece of music often invokes specific images, feelings, and events. Create some memories for your students by introducing them to great instrumental music. Select several pieces

of classical instrumental music. Help the children identify the instruments, the style, and the expressive qualities. Selections such as *The Nutcracker Suite* by Tchaikovsky or *The Carnival of Animals* by Saint-Saens have varied sections and provide opportunity for a lot of learning. Don't be afraid to try jazz or ragtime or music of another culture. The goal is to extend children's exposure to a wide variety of great *music*. As children listen over time, they will hear more and more in the music.

This deepening of listening skill will transfer to other experiences with music. In fact, practice with attentive listening will enhance children's attention to other learning as well.

Curriculum Enhancement

Choosing music and musical experiences to enhance children's music development while strengthening the total curriculum is an important goal. Music of high quality that will contribute to a lifetime of music appreciation is readily available and can be used for curricular enhancement. In language arts, for example, music can be used to accompany literature, set the tone for a story, or as a tool to support skill development (see Figure 1). Similarly, music can be used to support and enrich the social studies curriculum in numerous ways. Music can effectively convey the sense and feel of an era. Thus, the study of history *is* greatly enlivened through the incorporation of songs and dances popular during distinct time periods. Cultural appreciation is nurtured, deepened, and made more exciting through a study of people and their music (see Figure 2).

Conclusion

Music is a powerful catalyst for making lasting connections. Frequently neglected and too often relegated to the mussic teacher alone, music has the potential to enhance any classroom. Through the incorporation of song and dance, elementary teachers have the opportunity to enhance curricula, nurture a warm and joyful sense of community, and support the development of children's musical intelligence and other thinking skills. With all this, students of the 21st century may benefit immeasurably from the classroom teacher who does indeed 'have music wherever she goes'.

References

Armstrong, T. (1994). *Multiple intelligences in the classroom.* Alexandria, VA: Association for Supervision and Curriculum Development.

Collett, M.J. (1991). Read between the lines: Music as a basis for learning. *Music Educators Journal,* 78(3), pp. 42–25.

Gardner, H. (1983). *Frames of mind: The* theory *of multiple intelligences.* New York: Basic Books.

Gardner, H. (1999). *Intelligence reframed: Multiple intelligences for the 21st century.* New York: Basic Books.

Hackett, P., & Lindeman, C.A. (2001). *The musical classroom: Backgrounds, models, rind skills for elementary teaching.* Upper Saddle River, NJ: Prentice Hall.

Shuler, S.C. (1991). Music, at-risk students, and the missing piece. *Music Educators Journal*, 78(3), pp. 21–29.

Music Materials cited are from *The Music Connection*, 2001, published by Silver, Burdett, Ginn. All songs are recorded on the CDs that accompany the textbook.

'One Two Three Alary' – Grade 2, page 30

'Going on a Picnic' – Kindergarten, page 80

'Five Little Frogs' – Grade 1, page 174

'Sweet Betsy from Pike' – Grade 4, page 166

'Che Che Koolay' – Grade 2, page 167

Beethoven: Minuet in G – Grade 2, page 60 (photos of children in period costumes).

'My Cat Is Fat' was composed by the author.

Children's Books Cited

Berenstain, J., & Berenstain, S. (1978). *The spooky old tree*. New York: Random House.

Martin, B. (1988). *Listen to the mill*. New York: Henry Holt.

Rylant, C. (1992). *When I was young in the mountains*. New York: Dutton.

Wood, A. (1984). *The napping house. Orlando*, FL: Harcourt Brace Jovanovich.

LANGUAGE ARTS CONNECTIONS

Shared reading
- Create charts or sentence strips of song lyrics. Ask children to read the lyrics. Once children are familiar with a song, mix up the sentence strips and ask the children to put them in the original order.

Discover rhyming words in a song; create new pairs of rhyming words
- Invite children to 'fill in the blanks' with rhyming words as you sing 'Oh, My Cat Is Fat'. For instance, you sing 'Oh, my cat is fat. She likes playing with a ___'. (bat; rat) 'Oh, my elephant is pink. He likes playing in the ___'. (sink; ink)
- In 'One Two Three Alary', children can use their own names to create new pairs of rhyming words. For instance, 'One Two Three *Alary*, my first name is *Ben;* If you are a bit *contrary,* close your eyes and count to *ten'.*

Practice verb conjugations in a question/answer song
- In the song 'Going on a Picnic', children respond to questions such as 'Did you *bring* the (hot dogs)?' with answers 'Yes, I *brought* the (hot dogs)'. When you change the song lyrics to 'Going on a shopping trip with my Mom today ... ,' children can practice different verbs ('Did you *go* to Walgreen's?' 'Yes, I *went* to Walgreen's'.). With the change in lyrics, children also gain practice in categorizing objects, events, etc. (Where would you go on a shopping trip? What would you see on a field trip to the symphony?)

Identify and dramatize the mood of a song
- The song 'Five Little Frogs' has an upbeat, happy mood as the five frogs enjoy a day at the frog pond. Children will enjoy playing with facial expressions to show the frog's moods. As children dramatize the frogs jumping off the log into the pond, they will gain practice with number concepts (one-to-one ratio; subtraction.)

Create sound effects to enhance a story
- For the familiar nursery story of *The Three Bears,* you might assign a large drum sound for the Papa Bear, a tambourine for the Mama Bear, and a triangle for the Baby Bear. Each time a particular character appears in the story, that sound effect is played. Other sound effects may be added according to the content of the story. For instance, a vibraslap may represent the breaking chair; a guiro may represent the sleeping 'guest'.
- In *The Napping House* by Audrey and Don Wood (1984), the sleeping characters are introduced one by one. A surprise visitor (the wakeful flea) then comes to awaken the nappers. Assign instruments to represent each character. Children begin to play their instruments when their assigned characters are introduced in the story; once a character is introduced, children will continue to play their instrument. How they play their instrument (for example, soft/loud; slow /fast) will vary according to whether the character is sleeping or awake. (Some instrument possibilities: snoring granny = guiro or notched rhythm sticks; child = bell tree; dog = maracas; etc.)
- Invite children to create sound effects on instruments or with 'found sounds' (using objects in the environment) to enhance the reading of stories that you are reading in class.

Use instrumental sounds to create a 'soundscape' to enhance the mood of a story)
- A 'soundscape' is a rather continuous background accompaniment that enhances a story. Experiment with instrumental sounds to create the effect of a rainstorm. Read *Listen to the Rain* by Bill Martin and John Archumbalt (1988) and experiment with the sounds of different types of rainstorms. Shaking a piece of sheet metal (make sure that it has smooth edges!) and beating a drum will enhance the effect of the 'hurly, burly' rainstorm, while light taps on a bell chime will suggest the 'singing rain'.

Enhance the oral reading of a story with background music
- First, identify the mood, culture, or time period of a story. Then, select instrumental music to match. Music that changes as the events of the story proceed will provide further enhancement of the reading experience.
- You might like to start with a folktale from a particular era or culture and play music of that time or place to accompany your reading. For instance, to accompany Cynthia Rylant's *When I Was Young in the Mountains* (1992), you may select a piece of Southern folk music played on the dulcimer and a fiddle.
- Elton John's 'Funeral for a Friend' adds depth to the reading of *The Spooky Old Tree* by Jan and Stan Berenstain (1978).

Figure 1

SOCIAL STUDIES CONNECTIONS

Enliven history through song and dance
- The spirit of our forebears is captured in the song 'Sweet Betsy From Pike'. Guide children to recognize the humor and the 'stick to it' spirit of the '49ers through this re-telling of Sweet Betsy's travels from Pike County, Missouri, to California. In un-packing the song content, children will be able to create a map of Betsy and Ike's trip. They can determine how long the trip must have taken in the mid-19th century, as compared to today (using cars, planes, trains).
- You might re-create a 'barn' party typical of those that the pioneers enjoyed. Invite children to join in the 'play parties' (e.g., 'Skip to My Lou') and square dances of early America.

Connect with cultural groups
- 'Che Che Koolay', a call and response (follow the leader) song from Ghana, provides an introduction to an important musical form in Africa. Many children's recordings (see reference list) include authentic African instruments, such as drums, thumb piano, and shakers, to accompany the singing. Children will enjoy hearing and playing these instruments from Africa.

Create the 'feel' of an era
- Show children a picture of people attending a formal 'ball' during the 18th century. Invite them to imagine what it would feel like to wear those clothes. Encourage them to 'try out' the clothes as they listen to 18th century dance music. Play 'Minuet in G' by Beethoven. Guide children, wearing their imaginary 18th century ball clothes, to step elegantly with the beat of the music as they listen.

Figure 2

[18]

Arts Education and the Curriculum: Joining the Mainstream

Arts educators today find themselves in a frustrating position. On the one hand, they see widely published reports affirming that the arts are an essential component of a balanced education. Such testimonials support the value of arts education and suggest that the future of the arts should be bright. On the other hand, arts educators still find themselves fighting an often desperate battle for survival, facing administrators and school board members who do not see the essential nature of the arts. The frustration felt by arts supporters stems only in part from their battle for survival because such struggles have long been a way of life. Even more frustrating is the unabated continuance of the battle, in spite of the support of experts. Arts educators must examine the reasons for this troubling paradox and develop a long-range strategy that will help advance their profession.

Recent public expressions of support for the arts have come in a variety of forms. Most of the published reports and commentaries on education and educational reform have mentioned the arts at the least, and some—such as those developed by the College Entrance Examination Board, the Carnegie Foundation, and the National Commission on Excellence—have outlined quite eloquently the importance of the arts and the need to provide additional arts instruction in the public schools.[1] Polls of parents indicate

The key to becoming a partner in the new order lies in achieving a curricular status equivalent to that of subjects held sacred by the American public.

that they believe the arts are an essential part of their children's school experience.[2] Even Secretary of Education William Bennett, hardly noted for his progressive views on education, voiced support for the arts in a recent speech to a meeting of the National Association of Schools of Music:

> Arts education is weakened by failure to understand its serious place in the education of our children. . . . Not only do the arts contain an important part of what it means to be human, the arts also give coherence, depth, and resonance to other academic subjects. One of the primary tasks of our schools should be to train our young people to know, love, and respond to the products of the human spirit in music, dance, drama, and the visual arts.[3]

Unfortunately, the arts cannot live by rhetoric alone. When school boards develop their budgets, the arts are still listed with extracurricular activities in terms of funding priorities. Hence, when the total school budget shrinks, the arts take a disproportionate share of any cuts.

Arts educators cannot afford to wait passively for the funding problems of education to be vanquished because they will not disappear in the foreseeable future. Significant increases in inflation-adjusted funding for public education are unlikely, in spite of political rhetoric to the contrary, because the real income of American citizens continues to decline.[4] Realistically, arts professionals can consider themselves to be successful if they share equally in budget reductions,

Design for Arts Education

rather than bearing the brunt of those reduc- tions. If current trends continue, any fund- ing increases that do emerge will probably be applied to increasing faculty salaries, to developing accountability mechanisms, and possibly to lengthening the school year, rather than to the expansion of school arts programs. In short, the new educational order will be a lean one. The key to becom- ing a partner in, rather than a casualty of, that new order lies in achieving a curricular status equivalent to that of those subjects held sacred by the American public, such as mathematics and English. Clearly, the cur- rent, less elevated status of the arts cannot be changed overnight. The process of raising the arts from an extracurricular to a curricu- lar status will be a long one.

Curricular *Is* As Curricular *Does*

The first task faced by arts educators who want their subjects to achieve curricular status is to identify the reasons the arts are so widely considered to be extracurricular. Part of the explanation lies in the American tradi- tion of pragmatism, which caused us to re- place Latin grammar schools with programs that focused on preparing future employee- citizens. While enlightened parents laud the importance of the arts in enriching leisure time and providing sensitivity to the aes- thetic elements of life, few adults would pre- fer that their children elect the challenging and relatively unremunerative arts over more lucrative professions. To the extent that cur- ricular priorities are linked to vocational aspiration, this fact necessarily limits sup- port for the arts.

Blaming the woes of the arts entirely on societal priorities, however, is too conven- ient. The arts have been given sufficient op- portunities to establish themselves in the general curriculum, at least in the areas of music and visual art. Most American public school graduates participated in elementary art and music classes. The arts have been given a chance to be curricular and have been unsuccessful in maintaining that status. Furthermore, to blame society for the status of the arts is to give up hope, for arts sup- porters are unlikely to alter American prag- matism through their own efforts, even if it were desirable to do so. Instead, they must identify the causes for the decline of arts education that are within their control and

work for change before that decline has pro- gressed so far as to be irreversible.

Arts educators cannot change the state of A DARK the economy, and they cannot change the AREA pragmatic orientation of American society. They *can*, however, change ignorance. The very nature of education is to shed light where there has been darkness, and aesthetic sensitivity is a dark area for many American citizens. Citizens who serve on school boards and in school administrative posts make day- to-day decisions regarding which school pro- grams do and do not receive priority. If those citizens were arts supporters, arts pro- grams would receive fair consideration. Un- fortunately, however, arts educators who present proposals to school boards and ad- ministrators for improving, or even merely preserving, arts programs often come away frustrated. The persons entrusted with lead- ing our schools often suffer from the same ignorance and insensitivity to the arts that plague the rest of our population. Paul Leh- man, past president of the Music Educators National Conference, has reflected on the source of this ignorance and has come to a disturbing conclusion:

> The main reason many school administrators fail to demand strong school music programs is that they themselves did not experience chal- lenging, rewarding, high-quality music pro- grams in school. And the main reason the pub- lic allows them to do so is that many citizens were similarly deprived.[5]

Current arts professionals are paying the price for the failure of their predecessors. Arts education has benefited from the ef- forts of many dedicated, talented, and in- spiring professionals who have strived for and achieved excellence, but they apparently have not constituted a sufficient majority to overcome scars left by those who were less effective. Arts educators must determine which category of educator they represent. Even the most gifted teacher may be hin- dered by the heavy baggage of past practice.

In the process of self-analysis and, ultimately, change, arts supporters must adopt a long-term view. Japan has outpaced America in the economic arena recently primarily because, while American busi- nesses have planned for the next quarterly report, Japanese corporations such as Sony and Mitsubishi have planned for the next decade. American arts education may have

Design for Arts Education

suffered from the same shortsightedness as American business. Artists too often have lived from one public performance to the next, failing in the process to plant the seeds for support of the fine arts by the next generation of American citizens. Arts educators must confess to at least one of two failings—either they have not known *how* to sell students on the importance of the arts, or, if they did know how, they have failed to *do* it. Either failure, if allowed to continue, will ultimately prove fatal.

SURVIVAL AT STAKE

Arts educators face a dual challenge. They must earn curricular status, then convince the public that the arts deserve that status. The issue at stake is survival, and the goal is an environment that will help talented arts educators and students to flourish instead of causing them to burn out in despair. Arts educators can no longer take perverse pleasure in being "different," a difference that has led to the decline of the arts, and instead must become active participants in the mainstream of education. Once they have made a case for curricular status, they must demand their rightful place at the core of the curriculum.

The Arts Curriculum

Curricular subjects have a curriculum. Arts educators cannot achieve curricular status without a curriculum. These obvious facts are too often ignored by arts educators, who attempt to pass off a list of course offerings as a curriculum. Such feeble attempts at curricular credibility deserve the skepticism they inevitably receive from school administrators.

Frank Hodsell, chairman of the National Endowment for the Arts, has identified the development of sequential arts curricula as an essential component of the quest for curricular status.[6] Recent attempts toward structure in the visual arts, such as discipline-based art education,[7] provide models around which true curricula can be built. Sophisticated curricular models, such as the Manhattanville Music Curriculum Program[8] and Edwin Gordon's Music Learning Theory,[9] are also available to music educators. No matter what instructional models they adopt, fine arts departments and faculty must make educational decisions and program revisions as part of an ongoing process that follows accepted educational practices. They must

- develop a departmental philosophy that is compatible with the district philosophy;
- develop broad goals based on that philosophy;
- develop terminal objectives (i.e., what students should learn by the time they leave the program) based on the broad goals;
- design course offerings—including course objectives—that will best help students achieve the terminal objectives;
- plan daily activities and objectives to reach the course objectives;
- assess the effectiveness of the program and make improvements where necessary.

Arts educators must start with a defensible philosophy and make every education decision based on this philosophy. Arts curricula must address the needs of the general as well as the exceptionally talented student and of both the future consumer and the future artist. If arts educators follow this process—identifying why the arts are important in public education, then designing appropriate curricula—they can provide others with a strong justification for arts programs. If they continue to accept existing curricula and rationalize what they are doing, they will never provide a case sufficiently compelling to ensure curricular status for their programs.

Curricular Content

A curricular teacher uses the highest-quality materials available to achieve his or her goals and objectives. Arts educators, on the other hand, have often responded to budgetary pressures by selecting course content primarily on the basis of its entertainment value, a practice that they rationalize as "attitude education." Entertainment is certainly one outcome of every well-designed performance or show, but when teachers resort to pure entertainment, they abdicate their role as arts educators and embrace extracurricular status.

It is unlikely that a steady diet of 1950s rock medleys will lead students to Mozart. The attainment of sophisticated levels of understanding requires a long climb, but too many arts educators never get on the ladder. Instead, they choose the treadmill of superficial popular culture. What reasonable adult would respect an English program that

Design for Arts Education

taught students using only comic books? Why, then, should arts educators expect parents to view as curricular a drama program that focuses solely on musical comedy, an instrumental music program that teaches only marches, or a visual arts program that produces only ashtrays and vases? Substituting entertainment for content does a disservice to students and, ultimately, to the arts. Arts educators must develop positive attitudes toward the fine arts, but their failure to muster firm support for the arts among school boards and administrators suggests that the entertainment approach has failed to produce the desired results. They have sacrificed content and gained nothing.

KNOW THE WORK   Arts educators must replace "the arts are fun" with "the arts are curricular," then make their high-quality artwork enjoyable through high-quality teaching. One essential component of such teaching is a thorough knowledge of the artwork. Arts educators may appreciate an art object, know the meaning of all the words in a dialogue, or be able to wave their arms in the appropriate time signature, but they will not necessarily be effective in presenting the art to their students, even if the students are technically capable of performing or reproducing it. When arts educators do present high-quality literature, they too often do so before they are adequately prepared to "sell" the literature. When the work fails to stimulate the students' interest, the educators conclude that the students are not interested in high-quality art and resort to the superficial.

Instead of abandoning standards of content, arts educators must strive to realize them through careful preparation. They must consider each work within the context of the historical and stylistic period in which it was created. They must identify the elements that make the work expressive and that lend it tension and release, and prepare ways to communicate those elements to their students. Arts educators must also be aware of their own limitations. Even great professional conductors will generally prepare only one unfamiliar piece of music per concert. If arts educators cannot adequately present three challenging artworks, then they should attempt only two and fill out the rest of the lesson or program with art that they and their students will more easily understand. Teachers do no service to their art when they

present it in such a way that students form a negative opinion of that art.

Curricular Scheduling

Curricular teachers plan their programs so that their objectives can be met during regular class time, with a reasonable amount of individual homework. They limit the number of intrusions that their programs make into other classes and the outside lives of their students. Music and drama teachers must preserve the status of their curricular courses by curbing their outside rehearsal and performance time.

Work that takes place primarily outside the school day is, by definition, "extracurricular." Therefore, if members of a school music ensemble or drama cast and crew are spending five hours per week in rehearsals during the school day and fifteen hours per week in rehearsals and performances after school, the class may be considered to be more extracurricular than curricular. If arts educators limit themselves as much as possible to the regular school day, administrators will find it easier to view their occasional concerts, plays, and festivals as unusual events, necessary because parent audiences are only available during evenings and weekends. If the *majority* of music and drama programs take place outside of school time, administrators will continue to perceive those subjects as extracurricular.

Curricular Public Presentations

Curricular teachers balance concept and application in their classes. No self-respecting mathematics teacher would have his or her students perform computations by rote imitation or spend an entire semester merely talking about the theory of mathematics. If a parent determined that his or her child was learning to compute without understanding what he or she was doing, the parent would justifiably cease to support the school mathematics program. Fortunately, no curricular program is this narrow in scope. Arts educators, however, seem to have developed just such a limited public image. Large ensemble performances, school musicals, and art exhibits are often the only results of arts programs that the public ever sees; thus, many citizens have concluded that the sole purpose of public school arts pro-

Design for Arts Education

grams is to train performers. That image must be changed.

A BROADER VIEW Assuming that their students are learning a variety of useful lifelong skills, arts educators must constantly convey that fact to their administrators and the community. One way to do this is for performances and exhibits to project a broader view of arts programs. Printed concert programs can include a synopsis of the semester's content, including a list of goals, objectives, and activities. *All* of the top achievers in a class should receive recognition: the best performers, such as soloists with the top festival ratings and winners of medals for artwork; the hardest workers, such as those with the best practice records, the most constructive hours in the art studio, or the fastest memorization of lines; and those who earn the best scores on written tests. One student who has developed an understanding of each work can write the program notes, and another could introduce the work on the concert program or at the exhibit, explaining its important technical elements. Students might demonstrate rhythm patterns, alternative interpretations of dramatic lines, or basic drawing techniques. During intermission, a few creative drama students could present a scene extracted from the drama being presented as it might have been conceived if written by other playwrights. If prepared and timed carefully, such a format is interesting and involving for an audience. More important, the public will begin to understand the breadth of the fine arts curriculum.

Curricular Assessment

It is axiomatic in today's environment of tight budgets that priority is given first to what is tested, then to what is required, and finally to what the school administration, school board, and parents value. Perhaps less obvious is the extent to which these three are interrelated. At least once every few years, students take district-wide achievement tests in their curricular subjects, and the results are used to guide program improvement. If the test results show that students' scores in a particular content area are declining or are below national norms, parents are upset; if the scores have improved or are above national norms, parents are supportive.

Arts educators often complain that their programs are evaluated by their communities solely on the basis of festival ratings or blue ribbons in arts competitions. Such a situation is generally not the fault of the community but is rather the fault of the educators. If such criteria are the only objective evidence of achievement that the educators have provided, it is natural for members of the community to base their opinion on that evidence. DEMONSTRABLE PROGRESS

Assessment in the arts is a sticky problem that unfortunately has not been completely solved. Nevertheless, arts educators must not allow the largely subjective nature of aesthetic education to blind them to the existence of program outcomes that they can identify and measure. They must find the means to demonstrate their progress from year to year and, conversely, to demonstrate the damage that is done when arts instruction is cut back.

Two types of objective measures are available to arts educators. Criterion-referenced tests, which measure the extent to which students have attained objectives outlined in a particular curriculum, are relatively easy to develop when those objectives are expressed in terms of measurable behaviors. The alternative to developing a local test is to use a published standardized achievement test, when one that is appropriate to a particular arts curriculum exists. Standardized tests are usually easier to select and administer, and they provide the additional advantage of permitting comparison with national norms. Music teachers can use any of several commercially available standardized tests, such as the *Iowa Tests of Music Literacy*[10] or the *Music Achievement Tests*,[11] to gather evidence of the benefits of music instruction. Some progress has also been made in developing criterion-based scales of music performance.[12] Participants in Arts PROPEL, a cooperative five-year arts assessment project funded by the Rockefeller Foundation, are attempting to develop appropriate assessment devices for all the arts.[13] Whichever approach to assessment arts educators choose, they must publicize and use the results to improve both the effectiveness and the status of their programs. If arts educators wish to be treated as though they make a positive difference, they must provide concrete evidence of this.

Design for Arts Education

Curricular Grading

Curricular teachers evaluate a student's effort and progress in relation to the objectives of the course and assign a grade based on the student's work. Arts educators should have objectives that students achieve in differing degrees, and their students' grades should reflect those differences. The temptation to give every student an "A" or to grade solely on attendance and "attitude"—the latter quality usually reflecting little more than the extent to which a student gets along with a teacher—must be avoided.

DETAILED
REPORTS
Parents appreciate receiving detailed grade reports that show how their child has performed in a variety of areas. The typical computerized report card printout does not serve this purpose well. One effective alternative is to design an easy-to-use checklist format that reflects the curriculum of each arts course, including a space for general comments at the bottom of the page. Many computerized grade-book programs facilitate such a detailed approach. Sending home a content-specific report, even if this is done only once per year, demonstrates to parents that arts courses involve broad content and that the teacher understands each student as an individual. In fact, the use of such reports is one means by which arts educators can "out-curricular" the curricular subjects because many teachers still assign a single letter grade for the work of an entire semester or year.

Curricular Inclusiveness

A curricular teacher acts as though his or her subject is essential for every student. A curricular teacher helps struggling students solve their learning problems, rather than counseling them into other pursuits. *To behave as though the arts are different and are just for the exceptionally talented is to admit that the arts are not basic.* Too many inexperienced singers have been misclassified as tone deaf and discarded; too many shy students have failed drama auditions and been denied roles in school productions; and too many students with underdeveloped motor or perceptual skills have been allowed to flounder in visual arts classes. By washing their hands of responsibility to those students, arts educators have sent the wrong message about their discipline. Arts edu-

cators must help every student to achieve his or her artistic potential, regardless of talent.

There are other, often more subtle, ways by which educators exclude potential students from arts programs. The most glaring of these is by not reaching them in the first place. When arts teachers recruit, they often attempt to identify the most talented students and focus their attention exclusively on that fortunate few. Such an approach will not produce a general population that is educated in the arts.

Other students are often discouraged from enrollment in arts programs by limited course options. Secondary school music offerings consist predominantly, and often exclusively, of performing groups, which appeal primarily to students with a continuing commitment to music and often intimidate those with only a casual interest in the subject. School drama programs often consist only of annual musicals, for which students are chosen by audition. Arts educators must do their best to involve every student in arts study by offering courses designed to meet a variety of interests and needs.

Another way in which educators exclude students is by making unreasonable demands of their time. Drama and music teachers often abuse the commitment of their students by requiring them to attend numerous rehearsals and performances outside the regular school day. Students with jobs and those who need time to do homework may find themselves playing at Friday night basketball games followed by Saturday competitions—performances that necessitate attendance at extra rehearsals. Similarly, drama students may find themselves at school late every night preparing for the annual musical. Many students who have a sincere interest in the arts either cannot or will not place arts activities at the center of their lives, and arts educators must respect that attitude.

RESPECT
STUDENTS'
TIME

The arts cannot afford to be exclusive. Arts educators must strike a better balance between learning and application and must value the welfare of each student more than public relations. That student will become a part of the voting public after graduation.

Curricular Spokesmanship

Curricular teachers can devote their complete attention to teaching their subject,

Design for Arts Education

rather than having to defend the importance of that subject. Unfortunately, until the public shares the conviction that the arts are essential, arts educators cannot afford to follow this path. Neither can they afford to become vocal in support of arts education only when their programs are threatened. Arts educators must cultivate long-term success on a daily basis. They must articulate convincingly the importance of arts instruction for their students. They must share the results of research that show the positive effects of arts instruction on the brain, on the quality of life in a school, and on achievement in other subjects, all the while fostering the sensitivity to expressive detail that will make the aesthetic benefits of arts instruction obvious. By the time students become school board members or administrators, they must be arts supporters rather than detractors.

METHOD AND REASON — If teachers are to become effective arts advocates, institutions entrusted with the task of training future arts educators must adopt an increased role in teaching the *whys* of arts education. The focus in such programs is too often placed exclusively on the *hows*, and little attention is paid to why the arts have been included in school curricula. University teacher trainers usually rationalize this oversight by complaining that their methods classes are pressed for time, contending that undergraduates are unable to comprehend aesthetic theory, and parroting the traditional view that philosophy is the realm of graduate programs. Such excuses are not only unsatisfactory, they are also dangerous. If undergraduate arts majors are unable to comprehend the reasons for arts in the schools, how can they explain their programs to school boards? How can school board members, with limited backgrounds in the arts, be expected to understand the importance of arts curricula? In fact, lacking a clear philosophy of arts education, how can young teachers be expected to develop a curriculum at all? Method without reason is meaningless and mechanical, and programs rooted in such method are doomed to dissolution. Teachers who understand the importance of their subject have a reservoir of conviction on which to draw in time of need and a sense of mission that drives them on to inspire their students. The preparers of arts educators must provide their students with that

knowledge, or they doom their profession to failure.

Even the most persuasive arguments amount to little when the classroom audience is small. The inclusive approach advocated above—in which as many students as possible are recruited and then given opportunities to achieve and succeed regardless of their ability or the single-mindedness of their interest in arts work—is essential if the message is to reach tomorrow's leaders.

Guilt by Association

The process of achieving curricular status for the arts will be long and difficult, but the very survival of arts programs depends upon the success of arts educators in attaining this goal. They must examine curricular practice and apply it to the arts. They are fortunate that curricular models are available in the form of curricular colleagues.

Revival meeting preachers, in an attempt to get the members of their audience to think critically about their actions, often ask, "If being Christian were to be made a crime, would there be enough evidence to convict you?" The question arts educators should be asking themselves requires only slight paraphrasing: If being curricular were to be made a crime, would there be enough evidence to convict the arts? Currently, one could hope, at best, for a split decision. Arts educators must set about building a case that will put them away for life—a long life.

Notes

1. Paul R. Lehman, *Music in Today's Schools: Rationale and Commentary* (Reston, VA: Music Educators National Conference, 1987), 6.
2. Lee Hansen, "The Silent Debate," *California School Boards* (September 1987), 15–17.
3. William Bennett, "Civilization's Debt to Music Educators," *Soundpost* 3, no. 3 (Spring 1987), 3–5.
4. Charlotte Saikowski, "Growth in Living Standard Slows for the American Middle Class," *Christian Science Monitor*, 8 January 1986.
5. Paul Lehman, "Looking Ahead: Achieving the MENC Goals," *Music Educators Journal* 73, no. 8 (April 1987), 31.
6. Frank Hodsell, "Hodsell on the Arts in Education," *Soundpost* 2, no. 1 (Fall 1985), 10.
7. Elliot W. Eisner, *The Role of Discipline-Based Art Education in America's Schools* (Los Angeles: The Getty Center for Education in the Arts, 1986).
8. Ronald B. Thomas, *Manhattanville Music Curriculum Program: Final Report* (Wash-

Design for Arts Education

ington, DC: United States Office of Education, 1970).

9. Edwin E. Gordon, *Learning Sequences in Music: Skill, Content, and Patterns* (Chicago: G.I.A. Publications, 1984).

10. Edwin E. Gordon, *Iowa Tests of Music Literacy* (Iowa City: University of Iowa, Bureau of Educational Research and Service, 1970).

11. Richard Colwell, *Music Achievement Tests* (Chicago: Follett Educational Corporation, 1969).

12. J. M. Cooksey, "Developing an Objective Approach to Evaluating Music Performance." In R. Colwell, ed., *Symposium in Music Edu-*

cation (Urbana, IL: University of Illinois, 1983), 197–229.

13. The Arts PROPEL Project, Harvard Project Zero, 326 Longfellow Hall, The Harvard Graduate School of Education, 13 Appian Way, Cambridge, MA 02138.

Scott C. Shuler wrote this article while serving as coordinator of music education and associate professor at California State University. He is currently a music consultant for the Division of Curriculum and Professional Development of the State of Connecticut Department of Education in Hartford.

[19]

Computer-Based Technology and Music Teaching and Learning

PETER R. WEBSTER

The computer revolution in music education won't begin until we rethink what we want education to be. Only then can we clarify our goals and bring them into focus. Only then can we know how to use the computer. Only then can we know what we want in educational software. At the very least we must have software that is genuinely interactive and genuinely individualized. There are hundreds of ways to misuse computers in education and only a few ways to use them properly.

P. R. Lehman,
The Class of 2001: Coping with the Computer Bandwagon

In a publication written some 16 years ago designed to warn against the computer "bandwagon" that might affect adults in 2001, Paul Lehman's words continue to warrant consideration. Intelligent use of music technology to assist music teaching and learning is of major concern in the 21st century. If the dollars that will be spent on hardware and software for music education in this decade are to be considered a wise investment, we need the best information possible on how to use these resources for maximum effectiveness.

Most will agree that music technology today is not a passing fad but an established part of the educational scene. Since the publication of the first Handbook in 1992 and the chapter on technology by Higgins (1992), substantial changes have occurred in computer hardware, software, and Internet growth and accessibility. These changes have resulted in more affordable and powerful resources than in any other time in our history. Still, the question remains: What do we really know about the effectiveness of music technology?

This chapter will attempt to provide a perspective on this question by summarizing the major writings published

from 1990 to fall 2000. The chapter begins with an introductory section that deals with matters of definition and focus; a summary of forces that shape our current educational climate for music technology is also included. The remainder of the chapter is divided into four parts. The background section does not place emphasis on original, empirical work, but does create perspective for the empirical work. It begins with a summary of research reviews both in and outside of music. A sampling of advocacy positions for music technology follows, with writings on curriculum development and technology standards. This section ends with a profile of writings that are cautious about and critical of technology.

The core studies section includes the bulk of the summarized research. It is organized by sections devoted to music listening, performing, and composition. A special topics section includes brief summaries of the role of the researcher as programmer, use of technology in assessment, and gender and music technology. The conclusion includes recommendations for future research.

Introduction

What is music technology? Most modern dictionaries provide definitions of "technology" that center on the use of applied science for the improvement of a particular domain, such as industry, agriculture, or the arts (Agnes, 1999, p. 1470). Given this and what we know about the nature of music, one possible definition for music technology might be: *inventions that help humans produce, enhance, and better understand the art of sound organized to express feeling.* Such a focus on inventiveness in service to music as art helps to place music technology historically and purposefully. Music technology is more than designing a hardware solution to a music performance problem, more than learning how to use a music notation program. It is more than designing a multimedia presentation for a music history class or using an intelligent accompaniment program to help learn a new work. It is all these things, plus a way of engaging with music in an effort to improve the musical experience while always respecting the integrity of the art.

It is often said that technology is not the point of what musicians do as much as the means to make the musical experience better. This is a useful perspective, particularly in the context of abuses of technology in music making and teaching. It is also true that technology has always played a major role in the development of music of all types and in all cultures. Certainly the importance of technology in framing the musical experience in certain kinds of contemporary concert music inspired by electronic music studios and in the continued development of popular music styles such as the many varieties of rock music (Jones, 1992) must be noted. In these styles, both the inspiration and production of the music is so closely connected to technological resources that the distinction of technology as only "tool" becomes more difficult.

Regardless of one's view of the centrality of technology as part of the music experience, there is no denying that children today do not know a world without computers, electronic keyboards, MP3 files and players, compact discs, the Internet, and other digital music devices and formats. Additionally, they will come to know new music technology that none of us can completely understand today.

Chapter Limitations

As with other chapters in this Handbook, it was not possible to include all studies on this topic discovered during database searches. Over 150 citations in music alone were identified and reviewed carefully, but only 98 appear here. In all categories, I had to make hard decisions about which studies to feature. Judgment about quality was the most important criterion, but this was tempered with a desire to represent interesting designs and new directions of research.

Because of space concerns, I have included no summary of the utilitarian role of technology in the capture of data for general research analysis. It should be clear to all that advances in technology make capture of critical information about music experience especially effective and that such a review might well be valuable in another context. For this Handbook, only work that featured music technology as the point of analysis or as a compelling force in design was included.

Readers of the technology chapter in the first Handbook will note a decision to limit research reported here to computer-based technology, including music software and computer hardware peripherals related to music teaching and learning. There is no mention of instructional television, teaching machines that are not computer-based, stand-alone audiotape, slides, or motion pictures. This decision is based in part on space limitations but, more important, on the climate today in schools, which is dominated by computer-related technology.

Finally, I do not include the many recent developments in distance learning and the many technological developments in internet-based support for instruction and collaboration. This is included in a separate chapter by Fred Rees in part II (chap. 16).

Forces That Shape the Technological Climate in Music Teaching and Learning

In the last 10 years, three major forces have shaped the development of technology in schools and have dramatically affected the variables for research. The first is the rapid technical development of hardware and software, aided by commercial research and a strong economy worldwide. The second is the ubiquity of computer-based technology and changes in expertise among students and those that teach them. A final force are the changes in how we teach, fueled by our understanding of how students learn best.

Technological Development. A close reading of the writings that are summarized here reveals several aspects of change in computer-based technology. (Comprehensive texts such as the one by Williams and Webster [1999] provide detailed descriptions of these developments, including definitions of terms.) At the start of the new century, personal computers for less than $1000 can record, edit, print, and play back music at a level acceptable for professionals. These machines have unprecedented levels of computing power, as evidenced by processor speed, memory, and connectivity. Stand-alone and internet-based software programs are now commonly available, providing significant music experiences for listening, performance, improvisation, and composition. This software makes liberal use of multimedia such as digital audio and video, graphics, and MIDI. The relative ease of software development for most teachers and researchers without advanced programming skills has aided significantly in the development of content-rich interactive software that can be delivered locally or remotely from the internet. Advances in the digital representation, compression, and delivery of analog sound have resulted in a new and lasting respect for the power of computer-based technology to aid in teaching (Mark, 1994).

Availability and Integration. A second major force that shapes our educational climate is the dramatic growth in technology availability and integration. In terms of internet access, over 63% of United States public classrooms in 1999 were connected to the internet. This figure is expected to grow dramatically in the coming years as efforts to wire the entire school population continue. Teachers are far more computer savvy than 10 years ago. *Education Week*'s online edition (*Technology Counts: 1999 National Survey of Teachers' Use of Digital Content*, 2000) reported the following based on a return rate of 1,407 questionnaires from a stratified sample of 15,000 classroom teachers at the elementary school level and English, math, science, and social studies teachers at the middle and high school levels:

- Schools have an average of one computer for every 5.7 students, a dramatic rise from 1997 when the ratio was closer to one computer for 27 students
- 97% of teachers surveyed use a computer at home and/or at school for professional activities
- 53% use software for classroom instruction and 61% use the internet in their teaching
- 77% use software as supplementary work, while 17% use it as a primary focus, a small 6% use it as "quiet" or "bonus" time activity. Similar results were noted for internet use

Although the survey revealed that teachers continue to have difficulty finding appropriate software and internet sites for their work and continue to be frustrated with lack of resources and the monetary expense, these figures show a continual improvement in the presence and use of technology in teachers' professional work when compared to data from past years. As might be expected, the teachers surveyed expressed the wish for more time to develop experience and education themselves in the use of technology—especially the ability to discern what digital content would be best for students and then how best to use it.

Credible data on the availability of technology in music instruction in K–12 settings is beginning to emerge. The most thorough study of any one state's music teachers was completed by Reese and Rimington (2000). A systematic, random-sampling procedure was used to create an accessible sample of 493 schools in Illinois that represented a balance according to size, location, and level of instruction. Three mailings and follow-up telephone calls yielded a total return rate of 65%. Seventy-six percent of respondents indicated using a computer at school and nearly half of the sample indicated that there was a computer in the music area. Surprisingly, only 16% reported that the music area had computers linked to the internet, although nearly half of the music teachers reported that they had personal access to the internet at home. The work also revealed that one-third of the music teachers and their students use specifically music or multimedia software.

Hess (1999) questioned high school seniors ($n = 156$) as they auditioned for entrance into college to study music. He found that nearly all students felt they were computer literate to some degree and the vast majority reported having a computer at home and had access to the internet. Just under 40% indicated that they had used music software, primarily notation and sequencing titles. Both the work of Hess and Reese and Rimington also demonstrate the need to improve the manner in which we teach music technology on the college level if students are to understand its breadth and potential.

Taylor and Deal completed a pilot survey of music teachers in three states (1999) and extended this work to a national sample ($n = 991$) from all regions of the United States (2000). Over 85% of the teachers reporting in the national survey indicated that computers were within or close to the music area. An equal percentage indicated that computer technology can be used with many or some types of music instruction, but a majority of teachers (61%) have yet to integrate such technology into their teaching. Of those that did not integrate, the vast majority stated that they would like to do so and nearly all said that they would like to learn more about technology.

Such data provide some evidence of the availability and integration of technology in general and of music technology specifically into K–12 teaching. Conclusions from such work demonstrate that more work needs to be done to prepare teachers of music to use technology wisely in schools and that the current teacher population needs more in-service work in order to use the resources already in place. Clearly the availability and integration of music technology is moving forward and is influential in the design and interpretation of research reported here.

Teaching Philosophy. The final force that underscores much of the more contemporary research on music technology is the interest in constructionism as a basis for learning. Although not really new to educational theory, with roots that can be traced to Piaget and Dewey, constructionistic thinking has been given focus in writings on school reform (Gardner, 1991; Papert, 1993). The basic goal of constructionism is to place emphasis on creativity and to motivate learning through activity. Learning is seen as more effective when approached as *situated in activity* rather than received passively. In their introduction to an edited volume on constructionism in practice, Kafai and Resnick said:

> Constructionism differs from other learning theories along several dimensions. Whereas most theories describe knowledge acquisition in purely cognitive terms, constructionism sees an important role for affect. It argues that learners are

Critical Essays in Music Education

most likely to become intellectually engaged when they are working on *personally meaningful* (authors' italics) activities and projects. (Kafai & Resnick, 1996, p. 2)

At the heart of these ideas is the shift away from thinking about education as being centered solely in the mind of the teacher and more as a partnership between teaching and student, with the teacher as the major architect of learning. Project-centered learning is celebrated with students working to solve problems. Affect is seen as part of and as an aid in the learning experience. It is argued that if children learn this way, facts are learned in a situated context that helps to make clear why the facts are important in the first place. The teacher assumes more the role of a "guide on the side" as opposed to a "sage on the stage." This approach is particularly appropriate for the integration of computer-based technology in music and is the logic behind those studies that use simulation (Magnusson, 1996), hypermedia,[1] and internet-based resources as a focus for investigation.

Background Writings

Reviews

For a complete picture of the historical development of music technology and of the research prior to the studies summarized here, the reviews by Higgins (1992), Peters (1992), Berz and Bowman (1994, 1995), Walls (1997), and Williams and Webster (1999) are recommended. The chapter by Higgins and the 1994 Berz and Bowman monograph chronicle the early work on music technology research. Higgins summarized well the classic problems with research on music technology, including poor design, Hawthorne effects, inadequate treatment, and the confounds that the changing nature of technology bring. More important, he argued for a change from simplistic studies that pit music technology itself against traditional instruction to a more complex design that considers context and individual differences in students (Higgins, 1992, p. 491). The 1994 Berz and Bowman monograph provides a detailed review of selected studies completed before 1994 and summarizes by pointing to the relative neutral to positive findings or experimental work overall. They point to research generally showing positive attitudes toward music technology by students and that technology's support for improving performance skills such as error detection and rhythmic accuracy is promising.

The 1995 Berz and Bowman article and the text by Williams and Webster are good sources for historical developments in hardware and software in terms of computer-aided instruction. Berz and Bowman defined four research cycles, the last of which was called "emerging" technolo-

gies, beginning in 1989 (1995, pp. 18–20). Hypermedia tradition is summarized and related to the development of the World Wide Web. Developments in artificial intelligence and virtual reality are included. Throughout the Williams and Webster text, the authors provide historical overviews and timelines for computer-assisted instruction, music notation and sequencing, multimedia, and other topics.

Nonmusic Research Literature

Music education researchers interested in studying music technology cannot afford to ignore the rich data on technology and education in other disciplines. It is impossible to adequately summarize this literature here, but mention of a few recent studies will help place the music literature in perspective and offer clues to how to approach the general literature. The *Journal of Educational Computing Research* has published work since 1985 and is an excellent source for major trends in the literature. Several new journals have emerged in recent years, including the *Journal of Interactive Learning Research, Interactive Learning Environments,* the *Journal of Educational Multimedia and Hypermedia,* and the *Journal of Learning Sciences.* Studies of importance also have appeared in the standard education and psychology literature.

Reviews. Kozma (1991) reviewed research on learning with media in part as a reaction to a pointed article by Clark (1983), which argued that media had no real effect on learning and that we should place a moratorium on such research. Kozma reviewed over a hundred studies dealing with books, television, computers, and multimedia. He concluded:

The process of learning with computers is influenced by the ability of the medium to dynamically represent formal constructs and instantiate procedural relationships under the learner's control. These are used by some learners to construct, structure, and modify mental models; other students can rely on prior knowledge and processes, and use of computers is unnecessary. (1991, p. 205)

Kozma further concluded that the medium of computers is an excellent way to examine the cognitive processes of learning.

Several meta-analytic studies on the efficacy of traditional computer-assisted instruction (CAI) are reported in the nonmusic literature. Fletcher-Finn and Gravall (1995) completed a meta-analysis of 120 studies selected from 355 published from 1987–1992 and identified through ERIC searches. Studies were selected on the basis of availability, methodological strength, experimental design, and the research setting (must have been in a classroom content).

Course content included mathematics, reading/writing, science/medicine, arts, and education. The results were consistent with other meta-studies, showing a small but positive gain for all course content groupings. The average effect size was .24, which is equivalent to raising students' scores from the 50th to the 60th percentile. Interestingly, the greatest gain was with preschool/kindergarten, with an effect size of .55. The authors suggested that the small, positive effect size might be explained by superior CAI materials and not to the computer usage itself.

A similar meta-study was completed two years later by Christmann and Lucking (1991) examining junior and senior academic achievement. A thousand studies were examined and 27 experimental studies chosen that had at least 20 students in each group. Results showed an average effect size of .21. Music was one of the content disciplines studied (an investigation of seventh-grade music achievement), with an effect size of .23. The authors noted a varying rate of success for CAI among content disciplines, with English being the lowest and science the highest. They also suggested study of CAI embedded in teaching environments that have characteristics shown to have strong effect sizes of their own, such as cooperative learning, instructional time, home support, higher-order questions, and individualized instruction.

This recommendation of expanding the focus of such studies was taken a step further in work by Schacter and Fagnano (1999), which summarized the results of 12 meta-analyses representing different disciplines. The effect sizes reported by these studies ranged from .25 to .57. Their plea, however, was for further research to focus not on traditional CAI that used drill and practice but to examine work using more recent theories of learning (sociocultural theories, constructivist theories, and cognitive science) that use project-based, interactive and internet-based and multimedia strategies. Mayer (1997) is an example of an educational researcher who has done extensive work with multimedia teaching in science. His work and those of his colleagues demonstrate that multimedia-supported activities (animation with text) do increase ability of science students to understand cause and effect and to creatively transfer learning to other settings.

The unbridled enthusiasm that one senses in the general educational literature for the benefits associated with recent hypermedia forms (stand-alone and Web-based) is brought into perspective by an excellent review article by Dillon and Gabbard (1998). This study is highly recommended as a model for researchers interested in writing a review paper. The authors examined research cited in ERIC and PsycLIT from 1990 to 1996, which used measured results from learning outcomes that showed changes in behavior or task performance. Of the 111 studies that made the first cut, only 30 were retained. Studies eliminated were judged to have poor controls for student ability or inade-

quate descriptions of treatment. The authors divided the studies into three themes: comprehension of presented material, learner control over presentation of material, and individual differences in learning style. Studies in each section were carefully described and summarized. The authors concluded that: (1) hypermedia may be best in tasks that require rapid searching and data comparison, (2) increased learner control over access is useful for students with higher ability and more difficult for those with lower ability, and (3) learner ability and willingness to explore may be a factor in the success of hypermedia software (p. 345). A general observation was that the quality of empirical evidence for hypermedia technology for improving learning is poor and that further theoretical and empirical research is vital.

Study of Thinking. There is interest in the general literature in the link between technology and teaching thinking. Herrington and Oliver (1999) described qualitative work that "investigated students' thinking as they used an interactive multimedia program based on the situated learning approach" (pp. 4–5). The subjects were preservice math teachers and the focus was on assessment. Media employed included video clips of both assessment in action and student and teacher interviews, together with text. A complex task was presented to four groups of two students each, which involved the response to a hypothetical letter of complaint about math assessment from a parent and a follow-up memo from the principal to the teaching teams asking them to fix the problem. The subsequent use of the multimedia program by the four groups of two teachers to solve this problem was videotaped and the discussions and media use was transcribed and coded for analysis. The work provided a useful description of how to code such interchanges in order to verify the presence of higher order thinking. Characteristics are keyed to the external literature on thinking. Types of talk were analyzed and results showed substantial amounts of higher-order thinking.

Two other studies on thinking are worth noting. Clements (1995) reviewed studies that evaluated how computers enhanced creative thinking. He evaluated studies of creative thinking and production in writing and computer programming (Logo computer language), pointing to the general conclusion that thinking in such disciplines is greatly enhanced—especially if the technology use is embedded into constructionist contexts. In a more specific research effort, Liu (1998) examined experimentally whether engaging elementary school students in hypermedia authoring improved creative thinking skills as measured by the figural portion of the *Torrance Tests of Creative Thinking*. One group of fourth-grade students used the multimedia program *HyperStudio* individually to create stacks on plants and oceans. Another group worked in teams of four to create collaborative projects on the same topics.

Results showed that both groups significantly increased their creative thinking scores and that the collaborative group created more creative projects as judged by experts. Students who were evaluated as having low and moderate ability of a scholastic aptitude test showed greatest gains.

Conceptual Positions in Music

We now consider thoughtful writings in music that help form a background for systematic study. There is a lack of meaningful writing in this regard. Indeed, a philosophy of music education that embraces and celebrates music technology is an intriguing idea whose time has yet to come. What we do have are some position papers on the role of computer technology in music education. A few of these are summarized here briefly, as a way to stress the importance of this kind of thinking for researchers and practitioners.

Shifts in How We Conceptualize Teaching. Several experts have suggested that technology helps us rethink the way we teach music. In addition to assistance with skill development, technology can simulate music experiences in order to broaden the art form for a wide range of people and offers an entirely new medium for performance. For example, Brown (1999) imagined digital media as more than just tools for learning. It is common to think of a computer and its related music peripherals and software as simply convenient tools for support of the musical experience. Brown believed it is more than that. He argued that digital media can become an instrument for music expression and, perhaps surprisingly for some, a medium of musical thought. For Brown, technology and humanity are not a dualism. If digital media are considered only as tools, this dualism is maintained. Instead, he insisted that "coming to a humane conception of technology requires acknowledgment that being technological is a human trait, not an independent force" (1999, p. 11). Brown thought of digital media as an instrumental medium not only because it is capable of transmitting musical ideas but because of the way musicians use it and relate to it. The notion of control, as in computer as tool, "is replaced by one of partnership where computers are conceived as instruments; controlling and utilizing are replaced by a notion of engaging" (p. 12). Such an idea of engagement for students has a fundamental effect on the way to think about teaching with music technology and, in turn, effects our research agenda.

On a more pragmatic level, Lord (1993) wrote about technology's role in rethinking how we teach aural skills. He reminded us of the objectivist model of aural training as fact and skill. Such approaches assume transfer, value rigidity of thought, and isolate musical elements from context. Running counter to this are ideas associated with con-

structivist philosophy (as noted earlier in this chapter). Lord suggested that experiments in intelligent tutors and expert systems in music theory are closer to the constructivist philosophy but have their own inherent problems. Both drill and practice and intelligent tutors work within the same confines of a teacher-directed world; because of this, Lord imagined a need for a paradigm shift in the way we teach aural skills on the college level. He prescribed a focus on the music technology workstation (computer and MIDI keyboard) with music sequencing software as a basic setting for teaching aural skills and musicianship. He said: "What if we thought of a music workstation less as a task manager and more as a phenomenarium—a learning environment in which all aspects of the musical world are available to study, to manipulate, and to use creatively, at least in simulated form?" (1993, p. 112). Lord pointed to this setting as ideal for a constructionist philosophy that encourages music context, musical questioning, focus on sound, and creative thinking as ways to teach aural skills.

Hoffmann (1991), reflecting on his teaching at the New England Conservatory, also commented on the way we teach college music theory. Hoffman presents an argument for technology helping in forming a closer bond between composer, performer, and listener by allowing more people to become familiar with the process of music making. He also described his work with cooperative learning at the conservatory and the role that technology has helped him teach more musically the aspects of harmony that are important to musical understanding. The advantages of cooperative learning are described, as well as the disadvantages.

Music Thinking. Another theme that emerges in the literature is music thinking. Moore (1989), Webster (1990), and Upitis (1992) have all presented strong cases for using technology to stimulate thinking skills in music and to motivate students to think creatively in sound. MacGregor (1992) went further by suggesting the need for better learning theory to guide design of music composition software for young children. MacGregor pointed to the need for composition software for young children that allowed the user to have control over learning sessions, contain age-appropriate language or symbol systems, stress qualitative rather than quantitative aspects of music, and provide an alternate method for notation. Interestingly, most of these requirements have been met in recent software programs designed to encourage composition for young children (Nelson, 1998).

Other approaches to thinking embrace different starting points. For instance, some work has been done on music and artificial intelligence. Smith and Smith (1993) contributed some preliminary work from a compositional perspective and Schaffer (1990, 1991) has done so from music theory. Such work is complicated and may well bear fruit in future efforts to design more sensitive software for music experiences.

Music Performance.   Although there has been some indication that research on the effectiveness of technology for performance education is continuing in the form of experiments with acoustical analysis and pitch following software, there has not been a large interest in research among the applied faculties in higher education. Tomita and Barber (1996) have speculated on the use of computer-controlled player pianos such as the Yamaha Disklavier and the Bosendorfer SE as an important aid to piano instruction. They report on preliminary experiments at the University of Leeds in the United Kingdom using such technology. In general, such technology has been used more often in cognition research and has been considered more of an oddity in applied work.

Curriculum Contributions.   A number of published works are aimed at offering comment on curriculum integration. All of these writings are anecdotal, placing emphasis on "why," "what," and "how to" and focusing less on empirical evidence for technology's effectiveness. They are included here in the background section of the chapter because they contain clues for the construction of a conceptual base for research. For example, Jaeschke's dissertation (1996) offered strategies for incorporating technology into schools that meet the music portion of National Standards for Arts Education. Inspired by the Manhattanville Music Curriculum Project, he provided creative-based curriculum sequences that he field-tested.

Forest (1995) provided a description of how she integrated technology into an urban elementary school setting where 90% of the children qualify for free-lunch programs. She profiled the role technology played in teaching complex music ideas by describing interactive MIDI software that supports music reading and composition. The author reported an improvement in overall academic test scores, but the link to the technology use specifically awaits more systematic investigation. Similar writings were contributed by Chamberlin, Clark, and Svengalis (1993) for keyboard programs in middle schools, Nelson (1991) for general music curricula in middle schools using Gordon's learning music theory as a base, and Rogers (1997) and Busen-Smith (1999) for secondary schools in the United Kingdom. The Nelson and Busen-Smith articles are especially useful because they have some theoretical grounding, offered quite specific details on content, and provided some data on effectiveness.

Reese (1998) offered an excellent guide to designing curricula in schools by stressing the "systems approach" to hardware and software choice. This approach urges teachers to think of the choice of computer hardware and software as an integrated set of decisions based on teaching

philosophy and context. Kassner (2000) provided perspective on the use of music technology in classrooms in which only one computer can be used. The article explained how the computer can become a significant aid for total instruction and not marginalized as an "extra."

Finally, researchers should read carefully the recent development of technology curriculum standards, especially work by Music Educators National Conference (MENC) (*Opportunity-to-learn standards for music technology,* 1999). This document provides technology guidelines for preschool to high school regarding curriculum and scheduling, staffing and equipment, and materials and software. Deal and Taylor (1997) provided a useful standards model for the development of technology for higher education and the Technology Institute for Music Education (TI:ME) (http://www.ti-me.org) provides certification standards for music teachers who use technology in teaching.

Cautions and Criticisms

The majority of the literature that has been described so far has provided strong advocacy positions for music technology in the schools. A solid preparation for conducting research on this topic, however, should include a careful reading of those who offer words of caution and criticism. Both the music and general literatures contain such work.

Music Literature.   Austin (1993) reminded us of the natural continuum that forms between technophobes (often viewed as traditionalists) and technocentrists (often viewed as radicals). He pointed to the problems created by those who fall on either end of the continuum as they either ignore technology completely or imagine technology as a panacea for the ills of education. Austin cited research, similar to the status studies by Reese and Rimington and Taylor and Deal, that demonstrated the gap between available technology in schools and teachers that are prepared to use it. This is not a criticism of the effectiveness of technology, necessarily, but is a concern for planning and may be a good topic for systematic work.

Austin wondered if technology really saves time. Technology does make a number of routine tasks faster, but other tasks rush in and our time is consumed in a way that makes us all work harder. The time problem was also raised as part of an informal survey of independent, private music teachers by Hermanson and Kerfoot (1994). The survey was supportive of the integration of technology experiences into private lessons, but one negative finding was the time needed to set up such experiences and deal with the technical "bugs."

Austin also cited some classic problems with research in music technology that are noted, too, in the nonmusic literature:

The body of research that has examined the effects of technology on student attitudes and achievement is still experiencing growing pains. Not enough effort has been made to rule out rival hypotheses (e.g., Hawthorne effect, experimenter bias), test for long-term vs. short-term outcomes, explore the way in which technology might interact with learner or instructional context characteristics, or interpret any benefits ascribed to technology in terms of system costs. My hunch is that technology does reap rewards, but for whom? In what contexts? For how long? And at what price? (Austin, 1993, pp. 8–9)

Argersinger (1993), writing in the *Jazz Educators Journal,* warned about the "ease" of music notation and sequencing programs leading to abuses of the "cut and paste" feature that creates less than sophisticated music. He also pointed to the problems that digital audio sampling creates in the use of other artist's musical ideas or sounds. This particular concern was reinforced more recently by the legal battles between the Websites designed to facilitate the distribution of music in the form of MP3 files and the Recording Artists Institute of America, which represents the vast majority of recording companies (Reece, 1998). Argersinger also raised a concern about music technology adversely affecting the development of music-literacy by instantly rendering a score in a manner such that students are discouraged from developing inner hearing.

Caputo (1993–1994) offered an important view of music technology in the schools from a feminist perspective. She wondered if technology "is neutral, in that it remains outside the bounds of cultural politics, or are there consequences that are intimately linked to gender issues embedded in the application of technologies in the classroom" (p. 86). She takes exception to the idea that all students might profit equally from technology, pointing to the fact that not all students are the same. She feels that the rational, linear kind of thinking that often is celebrated in music technology is not the only way of knowing. The assertion is made that female students are socialized to pursue more relational, analogic ways of knowing and must operate differently when using technology. This sets them up for failure when compared to boys who, presumably, find linear and rational approaches more to their liking. She also warns the reader to be aware of hidden biases in software that might affect gender construction.

Finally, Folkestad (1996) raised a classic problem in the minds of many music educators, spoken and sometimes not: fear and alienation regarding the new technology and also of the young people who have acquired its possibilities (p. 26). He suggested that this is especially true for compositional activities with technology when the traditional role of performer is usurped:

> This conflict, involved in the meeting with music technology, and in which some teachers have found it hard to

decide whether it should be regarded as a threat or a possibility, implies that earlier concepts and views of musical phenomena have to be reconsidered and redefined. . . . Accordingly, when some music teachers express misgivings regarding whether children will still learn how to play an instrument properly, this might rather be a defense of their own competence, values and position, all of which are seen as questioned by the new ways of creating and relating to music. (1996, p. 27)

Nonmusic Literature. In the last 10 years, a number of writers have cautioned against the wholesale acceptance of technology in the schools. Postman's writings (1992, 1995) contained strong objections to the role technology has played in defining our culture. Writing from a reasoned, philosophical perspective, he worried about technology's potential to marginalize human and social values. Individuality itself, he maintained, is threatened by widespread use of technology. He wrote:

> I am not arguing against using computers in school. I am arguing against our sleepwalking attitudes toward it, against allowing it to distract us from more important things, against making a god of it. (Postman, 1995, p. 44)

This sentiment is present in other writings critical of technology in the schools. Stoll (1999), in his most readable volume *High Tech Heretic,* took a similar position, adding a number of concerns about the use of technology as entertainment as opposed to real learning. His writing is not cynical but skeptical, and offered a number of excellent arguments about technology integration that should be read by all researchers and those developing theory. From a practical perspective, especially interesting are his chapters on the abuses of *PowerPoint* as a presentation aid and the wisdom of donating old, unworkable computers to schools.

Perhaps the most comprehensive description of problems facing technology in the schools comes from the writings of Jane Healy. In her early book, *Endangered Minds* (Healy, 1990), she questioned the role of computers in schools in terms of thinking skills. She raised concerns about what we really know about the brain's improvement through typical computer use. But it was her most recent book, *Failure to Connect* (1998), which presented the most complete treatment of the subject. The volume is rich with personal descriptions of her visits to schools; she blended these descriptions with references to the professional literature. Topics covered in the book include problems with computer cost and adequate planning, disconnections between computer use and curriculum intent, blind acceptance of technology as the savior of educational problems, health concerns, and the inability of educators and researchers to show real evidence of improvement in learning. She also wondered about the concept of including technology in schools in order to better prepare students for the workplace; in this context, she suggested that possibly we have lost touch with what education is about (1998, p. 106).

The book is full of implications for research. Her treatment of what "information" really is about and how it can be used for real student learning is admirable. For example, her distinction between procedural, conceptual, and strategic knowledge in a domain and its relationship to technology support is informative (1998, p. 140). She also profiled the questions surrounding hypermedia and the "bricolage" approach that encourages exploration as opposed to linear teaching (p. 149). Her treatment of the role computers play in the development of creative thinking is also noteworthy:

> The fullest development of human intelligence includes the ability to use one's mind in creative ways. In fact, this particular facet of mind is doubtless the one that will enable our children to stay in charge of their ever-"smarter" digital servants. Whether and how early computer experiences expand or contract creativity is one of the most important issues in today's research agenda. (1998, p. 163)

Healy profiled both horrific and exemplary uses of technology in the schools—offering a reasonable balance between the clear abuses and the real gains that technology can provide. Like most of the general literature that is critical of technology in the schools, Healy's concerns are less about the presence of the technology and its ultimate potential, and more about the application of such research in an educational enterprise that is bereft of philosophy, theory, research, enlightened practice, and just plain common sense.

Core Studies

This section includes summaries of empirical work in music teaching and learning since 1990 that addresses music technology directly. It is organized by type of music experience studied and further divided by appropriate subcategories.

Music Listening/Skills Development: K–12

Eight studies were identified in this category and four are reviewed here; all use experimental designs. McCord (1993) reported on the effects of computer-assisted instruction on development of music fundamentals understanding in middle school instrumental students. She created her own *HyperCard* interactive program with MIDI support in order to teach note name identification, key and time signatures, rhythmic counting, and identification of sym-

bols and scales. All 178 students in the instrumental program from three middle schools participated in individual exposure to the software for 45–50 minutes during class time. Prior to analysis, students were grouped into a low-, middle-, or high-level group according to their instrumental performance ability. Results showed significant gains in each group's ability on written tests of music fundamentals. Direct comparison to a control group with no computer instruction was not part of the design.

Arms (1997) investigated meter and rhythm discrimination with 136 fourth- through sixth-grade children in general music classrooms. Computer experiences in the treatment group consisted of exposure to commercial composition software and some work with drill and practice programs for approximately 20 minutes for 18 days. The control group did not use this software, but did participate in movement, game, and classroom instrument experiences. Both groups were presented the same 10-minute scripted lesson on rhythm and meter discrimination. Results showed no advantage for the experimental classes on a standardized measure of achievement, pretest to posttest. Careful examination of both the nature of dependent variables measured and the kind of experimental treatment brings into some question what was really being studied.

Goodson (1992) documented the development and trial of an interactive hypermedia program for basic music listening. Her study involved 128 sixth-grade students. Using a four-group comparison model that included groups with no contact, traditional instruction, computer instruction in small groups, and computer instruction with one large group, she found interactive hypermedia instruction required less instructional time in order to achieve equal or higher scores on a 22-item music listening test.

In a well designed study of the effect of (1) hypermedia use, (2) cognitive style (field dependence/independence), and (3) gender on both short- and long-term retention of factual information, Bush (2000) investigated 84 sixth- and seventh-grade students after individually completing either a 40-minute session with two specially designed *HyperCard* stacks or a group expository lesson on the same subject. The subject matter was a lesson on the steel bands of Trinidad. Hypermedia content included text, audio, digital photographs, and movies. To form the groups, Bush administered a measure of field dependence/independence (FD/FI) to computer-experienced boys and girls in a "middle income" neighborhood in western Canada. Four groupings were created (Gender × Style) and students from each were randomly assigned to form a balanced experimental and control grouping. Pretest data showed equivalency for content knowledge. The dependent variable was a 20-question, multiple-choice test that was evaluated for validity and reliability. This posttest was given once at the end of the experiment and again after a 6-week time period.

Results indicated statistically significant differences with both posttests for treatment in favor of the control group (expository lecture) and for FI students. There were no differences for gender. The results for cognitive style, which showed FI students doing well in both conditions but FD doing less well in computer-based groups, reinforced past research. The gender result demonstrated that, despite evidence that male/female attitudes may differ for technology (see the special topics section of this chapter), real achievement as measured by the test does not. The result for the main effect of treatment was a surprise in light of other studies on multimedia in music instruction. Bush speculated that the nature of the multiple-choice test might not be a good predictor of what was learned in multimedia work. He also wondered if the expository lecture was better at preparing the students for multiple-choice assessment. Another possibility might be the short time for software use in an unstructured environment has no real effect on factual recall.

In this category, the only study with high school students was reported by Prasso (1997). She investigated the effect of computer-based song writing on student ability to sight-sing. Her theory was that the use of computer composition software to write melodies might provide a level of intrinsic motivation and instant aural/visual feedback that would increase achievement in sight-singing. Sixty high school students from a New York City school formed both the experimental and control groups. Random assignment was not possible, but sight-singing pretests were used to determine some degree of equivalency. Students created three melodies over a 45-day period and sang these melodies as part of choral warm-ups. The control group wrote melodies out with paper and pencil with no computer assistance; experimental students working in a lab wrote melodies with a computer and MIDI technology. Results of a reliable and valid posttest of sight-singing performance assessment showed statistically significant gains for the experimental group.

Music Listening/Skills Development: College

The majority of work in music listening/skills development has occurred with college-age students. Eighteen studies were identified and eight are noted here. The studies are divided into work with nonmusic major students, often in the context of courses devoted to music fundamentals or appreciation, and work with music majors.

Nonmajors: Music Fundamentals. Two studies have focused on elementary education majors' preparation to teach music as part of their future general classroom teaching. Lin (1994) studied the effect of 4 weeks of hypermedia instruction of various kinds on student achievement on an aural music instrument identification task with 45 stu-

dents. The types of hypermedia tested included computer-controlled laser videodisc, computer-controlled CD audio, and directed versus open-ended styles of content presentation. Results showed no difference in dependent variable testing of instrument identification with all groups doing well. Descriptive data on student attitude compiled showed significant preferences for hypermedia formats as opposed to a control group, with definite preferences for laser-disc technology and the open-ended style of presentation. Additional descriptive data was obtained by observation and posttreatment interviews.

In an extensive two-part investigation, Parrish (1997) investigated the use of computer-aided instruction to teach music fundamentals as part of nonmajor fundamentals classes. Both experiments were designed to evaluate the use of music technology outside of regular class time to teach music fundamentals (basic music notation, metric organization, scales, key signatures, intervals, and musical terms). Both studies used experimental and control groups, used multiple instructors, and were conducted over a 15-week college semester (100–150 minutes per week of class contact). Experiment 1 ($n = 148$) was designed to evaluate the custom software group (treatment) against the use of a commercial drill and practice program (control). Experiment 2 ($n = 95$) evaluated the custom software against a no-computer group that received in-class instruction on music fundamentals. The custom software was developed carefully using content analyses of several textbooks on music fundamentals designed for these types of classes. The software used folk song materials much like that which teachers would eventually use in the classroom in order to define and demonstrate the music theory. Interactive techniques were used that blended drill and practice with context-based examples using the folk songs. Mastery tests were included in the software for students to self-assess their knowledge. The software was made available for outside class use to the treatment groups of both experiments and instructors answered questions in class but did no significant teaching of theory content. Posttest scores in each experiment showed no significant difference between the students' scores on a music fundamentals test, demonstrating that out-of-class work with the custom software was as effective as in class teaching of music fundamentals. Each instructor in experimental treatment groups was able to spend significant time on other, less routine music topics. The work also demonstrated the importance of the instructor because posttest scores varied (significantly in Experiment 1) by class.

Nonmajors: Music Appreciation. Placek (1992) reported results of a study that evaluated the effect of a custom-designed, interactive computer program that controlled an audio CD. The program provided text and spoken audio information about music history and music style characteristics in different periods of music history (e.g., Baroque, Classical, Romantic). The program provided listening examples from prerecorded excerpts and allowed the student to take a quiz for mastery in identification of music style periods from audio clips. Results were posted after each quiz and students were encouraged to use the program again and again. Three intact classes of college students were used, one designated as control ($n = 12$) and the other two as the experimental groups ($n = 28$) that were given access to the software. The dependent variable was a written test of style identification. Pretest and posttest data were used in a design that used the pretest as a covariate. Results showed significant difference in posttest means in favor of the experimental treatment.

Duitman (1993) designed somewhat similar research, but used commercially available, interactive CD-ROM software that was intended to encourage exploration of masterworks in a nonsequential manner. These resources typically provide a full digital audio recording of a masterwork, such as Beethoven's Ninth Symphony, and include links to portions of the recording for random audition. Supplemental material typically includes text and images that explain the work in detail, including information about the performance ensemble. Historical background information is included and a game is added at the end to test understanding. Buitman formed two groups and randomly assigned students to each. The control group had no contact with the commercial software, but the experimental group was encouraged to use the software to prepare a final essay project. The dependent variable was a multiple-choice test on course content and did not relate directly to material on the commercial CDs. As a result, both groups showed significant gains from pretests but showed no significant difference between groups. Final project essays that might well have shown significant difference between groups because of their direct connection to software use were not considered part of the data analysis. The mismatch between the nature of the linear tasks required by the posttest and the nonlinear nature of the treatment experience is a typical problem in this kind of research.

Finally, a study of learning style[2] and mode of instruction (CD-ROM tutorial and expository teaching methods) and their effects on an achievement test of aural identification of musical properties and cognitive knowledge was completed by Bauer (1994). This well-designed work represented a different slant on music technology integration because it did not investigate one approach versus another but, rather, the effect of one type of instruction on other variables. Bauer was interested in the identification of what learning style characteristics contributed to achievement on the CD-ROM experience and on an expository teaching experience. Learning style was evaluated by the use of the *Productivity Environment Preference Survey* (PEPS) that

yields scores on 20 subscales. The CD-ROM program used was a commercial one similar to the masterworks software described earlier. In this case, the Strauss tone poem *Till Eulenspiegel* was used. Subjects ($n = 120$) were randomly selected from a pool of 775 students across all 4 years in college. Average age was 21.1 years and there were 45 males and 75 females. Students were assigned randomly to four groups, using a classic Solomon design. Results of pretest analysis showed no significant differences between groups and no effects for use of pretesting were found. Groups were then combined into two for resulting analysis. Subjects in each group were pretested, then administered the PEPS, and then either given a 1-hour expository lesson on the Strauss work (group teaching) or were given 1 hour to explore the software (individual sessions). Both groups were given an outline of the major objectives before the 1-hour period. This was done to give focus to both learning experiences. A posttest was administered to each group. Material for the pretests and posttests was drawn directly from the objectives of the teaching and answers to the questions were clearly contained in both the expository group teaching and in the CD-ROM software.

Multiple regression procedures were used by regressing the subscale scores on PEPS against first the achievement scores for the expository group and then for the CD-ROM group. No significant scores were found for the expository group, with only 11% of the variance in the achievement scores found by the PEPS set. Bauer reasoned that this may be the case because students can adapt their learning styles to traditional lectures. They have had a great deal of practice with lecture formats and can learn effectively if the lecture contains a variety of media and presentational styles. Evidence from the multiple regression for the CD-ROM group was strikingly different. The subscales of Late Morning, Evening/Morning, Afternoon, and Tactile Preferences had positive, significant relationships to the achievement scores, and the subscales of Kinesthetic Preferences and Needs Mobility resulted in negative correlation. Over 31% of the variance in achievement scores for the CD-ROM group was explained. Bauer provides logical explanations for these findings, given the nature of the computer learning and its availability at differing times during the day. Bauer's work is important because it moves the nature of research on music technology to empirical issues about individual learning and not about what is best for groups.

Music Majors.   As older literature reviews document (Berz & Bowman, 1994; Higgins, 1992), studies on music theory and aural skills dominated college-level music technology research in the 1970s and 1980s. This last decade has seen a shift to a richer blend of topics, including music history and education, as well as general studies and performance. A review of the papers accepted for presentation at the national meeting of the Association for Technology in Music Instruction (ATMI) (http://www.music.org/atmi) over the last 20 years revealed this trend. Hughes (1991), for example, studied the ability of college music history students to aurally identify core repertoire in music with the aid of hypermedia instruction. Students from an undergraduate music literature class were assigned randomly to a control and an experimental group ($n = 17$ in each group) and given a pretreatment questionnaire to determine equivalency of background and knowledge. Control and experimental group students experienced the usual instruction in class, which included repeated listening to works. Experimental subjects were given the additional opportunity outside of class time to use a specially designed *HyperCard* stack with CD-ROM support that contained guided listening for the literature studied in class. Results of posttests on the ability to identify composer, title, and movement or sections of pieces showed significantly higher scores for the experimental group. It is not clear if the significant difference was because of a novelty effect or if the results indicated a real positive influence from the technology.

In a work similar in design to Bauer's with nonmajors, Fortney (1995) examined the effect of music instruction with an interactive audio CD-ROM on the music achievement of music education majors with different learning styles. Fortney used the *Gregorc Style Delineator* (GSD) scale that places subjects into one of four categories of learner and placed 48 music education majors into the four groupings. He found no different in achievement test scores at the end of an individual, 90-minute period of exploration of a commercial CD-ROM program devoted to Stravinsky's *Rite of Spring*. Unlike Bauer, Fortney recorded behavioral data on the way each of the students used the program. Information about the number of times each subject deviated from the program sequence, time spent on individual sections of the program, and the number of supplemental cards (e.g., glossary visits, playing of extra musical examples) was recorded and compared to learning styles. The Abstract and Concrete Random learning styles used significantly more supplemental cards. This idea of a content analysis of how the hypermedia program was used is a good model for further research.

The final research summarized in this category carries on the traditional CAI model in music theory[3] that was so evident in past years. Ozeas (1992) studied the effect of computer-assisted drill and practice on internal identification and sight-singing performance. Students ($n = 58$) in a solfège class were randomly assigned to either a control or experimental group. The control group met for the entire semester, three times per week with an instructor. The experimental group met for 2 days per week, with the 3rd day devoted to work with the drill and practice program. Placement test data at the start of the semester showed no

difference between groups. Ozeas reported midterm grades on a progress test to be significantly different in favor of the control group, but that final test grades showed no significant difference. A separate investigation of those students with low placement test scores demonstrated that they did much better when they were able to meet three times per week with an instructor. Continued analysis of how different types of students react to and achieve with this kind of teaching support is needed.

Performance: K–College

The second major division of core studies in music pertains to music performance. Twenty-nine studies were identified since 1990, a major increase in this category from previous years. Thirteen of these works are noted here, divided into subcategories by performance medium.

Instrumental Performance. Orman (1998) reported results of a project to evaluate the effect of a multimedia program on beginning saxophonists' achievement and attitude. Experimental and control groups were formed from sixth-grade students ($n = 44$) in four middle schools. She developed an interactive computer program of 11 chapters covering topics such as instrument history, care, assembly, posture, hand position, and tonguing. Each chapter had an introduction and a summary section that highlighted the main concepts and was narrated by a cartoon character consistently in each chapter. Content was based on a number of topics in beginning saxophone books and verified by experts. Students were encouraged to interact with the program by using the computer mouse to solve problems and use their own saxophone for certain tasks. The program was designed to keep track of student progress and allow reentry at the point of departure if a student decided to stop after a short time. Orman designed her work to support short periods of instruction by having students in the experimental group complete sections of 8–15 minutes with the computer in a nearby room, then return to regular band class. Students completed the program in 15–17 days. Results on posttests of both written knowledge and video-recorded ability to apply understanding favored the experimental group significantly. Data also demonstrated strong, positive attitudes for the computer-assisted instruction.

Malave (1990) experimented with young instrumentalists as well but with beginning clarinetist tone quality. He used computer equipment to render a graphic representation of a model tone quality in terms of spectrum, intensity of partials, wave form, and envelope. Students were encouraged to emulate the model tone using the visual prompts as aids. Students who had reached a defined level of performance ability were assigned randomly to control and experimental groups of 15 junior high students each. Experimental subjects received exposure to the graphic system during a 30-minute private lesson. Control students received similar lessons but had no computer exposure. The time period lasted for 10 weeks, after which independent judges rated the students' tone quality. Pretests were administered as well and gain scores between pretest and posttest data showed no significant difference in ratings; however, ninth-grade students showed the most gain and an acoustical analysis of their resultant tone quality showed close matches to the model.

This use of technology in the studio is likely to gain more acceptance as studio instructors become more aware of technology and the equipment becomes more available. One current example of a studio teacher well known for his use of graphic analysis of music performers is Richard Miller at the Oberlin Conservatory. More information can be found at Miller's Website (http://www.oberlin.edu/con/divinfo/voice/obsvac) and his work is published in various journals of singing (e.g., Miller & Franco, 1994).

Surprisingly, only one major study was identified in the domain of jazz that used technology as a major focus. Fern (1995) completed descriptive work that evaluated the effectiveness of an interactive computer program focused on jazz improvisation. The program combined basic aural and theoretical elements of jazz improvisation and used CD-ROM and MIDI technologies. Transcription skill was stressed along with approaches to individual practice. Students who used the program were college student volunteers with varying levels of jazz experience. Results, expressed in questionnaire and interview data, demonstrated positive attitudes toward the program and suggested improved attention to human feedback.

Two qualitative studies in instrumental performance are worth mention. Simms (1997) studied the effect of a computer game on the motivation of four beginning piano students. She supplied a rich description of the use of an interactive music computer game designed to help the user with note identification and note-playing. Simms collected data from personal observations and interviews with students, parents, and teachers. The period of observation was 5 weeks with the game and 4 weeks following. Using a theory of personal investment designed by Maehr and Braskamp, she provided profiles of each student's background, use of the game, and results after the game was used. She reported that students enjoyed the game if they were successful but found they avoided more difficult levels. Some indicators of motivation continued after the game's use, but the effect was not uniform. This research is noteworthy for its use of quantitative data to explore the complex dynamic between teacher and student needs with technology as part of the mix.

Kim (1996) completed an interesting case study of three intermediate violin students and their use of computer-based, historical, and theoretical information about music

they were studying in their lessons. She determined that the computer work motivated students to seek more information about music studied in lessons and that there was evidence that the students used the supplementary information effectively in their applied study. This work is important because it is philosophically grounded in the spirit of comprehensive music instruction and the emerging national emphasis on this that is demonstrated by the National Standards in the Arts.

Vocal Performance.   Simpson (1996) investigated pitch accuracy among high school choral students and its possible improvement with technology-assisted visual and aural feedback. The subjects were 69 students in an urban, multiethnic high school, divided evenly into three groups. The first group received teacher-guided instruction in a small group in addition to the regular choral rehearsal. The second group received visual/aural feedback on pitch as part of the choral rehearsal. The third group received both the small-group instruction and the technology help. Comparison between posttests demonstrated no significant difference, but the second group, which received just the technology treatment, did improve from posttest scores.

Interested in the effect of hypermedia instruction on the understanding of vocal anatomy, Ester has completed a number of studies using his custom-designed *HyperCard* stacks with graphics and animation. The work reviewed here (Ester, 1997) used 52 undergraduate music majors, divided evenly by gender. Students were divided into three groups, one with no technology but with a lecture, a second with exposure to just the special stacks, and the third with both the lecture and the stacks. Each group received a study sheet. Students using the hypermedia were allowed to explore the software freely. Subsequent analysis of use data showed no difference in overall time spent by all three groups. Results showed that, when controlling for academic achievement and pretest results, students in the hypermedia groups did significantly better on a test of vocal anatomy. Interestingly, Ester reports that the group that had only the hypermedia scored the highest. If vocal anatomy is deemed important in the education of singers and teachers do not have significant time to spend on class or studio instruction on this topic, this research indicates that a hypermedia instruction module might work well.

In a descriptive investigation using quasi-qualitative techniques, Repp (1999) wondered how students and teacher might adapt to the use of three different technologies as part of applied voice instruction: autoaccompaniment software in rehearsal and performance; internet as a tool for augmenting lesson material and communication; and the measurement of acoustic phenomena as part of the lesson instruction. Data were drawn from six students who received eight 45-minute voice lessons and included weekly logs, observations, and survey questions. What is interesting about this study was the inclusion of the teacher's perspective of the technology's effectiveness as well as the students.

Repp reported that the internet materials as part of the lesson yielded mixed results. Inclusion of the computer's display of internet information was awkward to use as part of a live lesson. Better results were noted as an outside resource, but pages were not accessed extensively. As a communication tool, the internet worked well when all parties used it routinely. The spectral analysis technology allowed students to see wave patterns of their own voice, but Repp concluded that the results were questionable in terms of real effect on improving singing. Three features of the automatic accompaniment software (*Smartmusic*) were used: the accompaniment capabilities, the tuner, and the warm-up feature. Instructor reaction to all three parts was quite favorable. Student reaction was positive toward the accompaniment software and less enthusiastic toward the spectral work; however, the range of opinion was on the positive side for all. In general, students enjoyed having access to the technology outside of the lesson time more than inside. This preference for out-of-class access is worth investigating further.

Accompaniment Support. Repp's work with accompaniment is a good introduction to this next subcategory. *Smartmusic* (originally known as *Vivace*) personal computer software is designed to evaluate a solo performer's acoustic signal, judge quickly where the performer is in the score, and produce the accompaniment for MIDI software interpretation in fast enough time to be sensitive to the soloist's tempo changes. Three studies are worth noting in addition to Repp's descriptive work.

Tseng (1996) described its use with flute students using a cross-participant, case study approach. Her results supported the notion that the software helps music learning, intonation, and performance preparation. Ouren (1998) also used this software, but with middle school wind performers. Using pre- and postinterviews and independent assessments of performance achievement, he studied eight students' progress over a 6-week period. No control group was employed. Performance evaluations showed improvement for seven of the eight students, especially in rhythm and interpretation/musicianship. Interview data indicated positive reactions to the technology.

Sheldon and her colleagues (1999) have contributed the most controlled work to date with this technology. They examined differences

in performance quality ratings between instrumentalists who prepared solo music selections in three different conditions (with no accompaniment, with live accompaniment, and with intelligent digital accompaniment) and gave subsequent performances in two different conditions (without accompaniment and within the prescribed accompaniment mode). (1999, p. 253)

Instrumental undergraduate music education majors (volunteers) were subjects. They were asked to play a secondary instrument that: (1) they did not normally use in a performance ensemble, (2) was not part of the family of instruments that constituted their major, and (3) they had studied only for a semester in a methods course. The researchers reasoned that the participants would be able to conform to random assignment needs (balancing for instrument type and solo music) while still having playing ability similar to a target population that might benefit the most from this type of software. Three groups of 15 were created and students were asked to prepare a solo comparable to a typical level found in junior high school. Groups were limited to a 6-week preparation period, similar to the time frame often found in school conditions. Those in the no accompaniment group (NA) were asked to practice the solo with no accompaniment for 1.5 hours per week; those in the live accompaniment group (LA) were asked to work for the same time with a live accompanist; and the digital group with technology (DA) was asked to do the same thing but with the computer simulation. Knowledge of how to use the equipment by the DA group was ensured (including the many options possible with the software) and practice time was assumed to have been completed as requested. At the end of the practice period, soloists performed the solo without accompaniment and then again with the prescribed accompaniment mode. Performances were tape-recorded in a high-quality sound studio.

Five impartial and experienced judges rated the performances according to established procedures. Six performance subscales were used: tone quality, intonation, rhythm, technique, interpretation, and articulation. Inter-judge reliability ranged from .75 to .81. Main effects for group difference and performance difference were not found; however, there was a main effect for subscales with the highest ratings achieved for rhythm and articulation. Interesting interaction effects between subscales, groups, and performance conditions are worth evaluating carefully for clues to further research. For example, the subscales for the second performance generally paralleled the first performance except for the NA group for subscales of tone quality, intonation and interpretation. Certain individual means were of interest, including the low score for interpretation in the DA group during the second performance and the very high rating for rhythm in the DA group in the same performance. The researchers discuss implications extensively in the article.

Error Detection and Score Study. Three dissertations are noted here. Two have addressed error detection and a third studied score knowledge. All systems were developed to be used as supplements to college conducting courses.

Jones (1991) developed a computer-assisted error detection system that used random-access audio and printed music score examples. The system allowed errors to be embedded in the score and the task for 11 subjects was to detect the errors. Statistical analyses showed significant growth during the teaching period with the largest gains occurring by the fifth session. Gruner (1993) used an experimental design with 24 students. He designed a computer-assisted instruction program that taught error detection skills in synthesized, multivoiced experts from traditional school band music. Each group studied conducting, but the experimental group used the computer program. Gains from pretest to posttest results on a measure of error detection based on taped examples of real band music demonstrated a significant difference in favor of the experimental group.

Hudson (1996) tested the effectiveness of a computer-assisted program designed to teach score study skills using model work from the music literature. Conducting students at four universities were used, creating two groups of 22 students in both an experimental and control group. A pretest was given to all students that evaluated their previous knowledge of a work for band. The experimental group experienced the computer program for six sessions over a 3-week period in addition to classroom conducting experience. The control group experienced no computer-assisted instruction. Posttests showed significant gains for the experimental group.

Composition: K–12

The last category of core studies is the newest, emerging largely in the last 10 years. All of the nine works cited in this category have a common theme: the investigation of composition using music technology as a major component not only for data capture or as a medium but also as a focus of the research itself. Studies in this category include work on compositional strategy and creative thinking in which the technology is central to the research questions and design.

Strategy. Some of the most extensive and rich work done on computer-based, compositional thinking was reported by Folkestad and his associates (Folkestad, Hargreaves, & Lindström, 1998). This study is also available as a published dissertation (Folkestad, 1996). The purpose was to document the process of creation for 129 pieces by 14-, 15-, and 16-year-olds over a 3-year period in Sweden. MIDI files (887 in all) were collected during the process of

composition and interviews and observations of participants were recorded. Students with no previous compositional experience worked after school, once a week. Interviews with the students were conducted after the completion of a composition in order to understand how each student worked and what the thought processes were. The interviews were done at the computer workstation (computer with standard sequencing software and keyboard synthesizer) and access to previous versions of the compositions was possible. Unit of analysis was the group of compositions and not the 14 students, so many strategies were noted across subjects.

From the data, a typology for compositional strategies emerged. Two principal types were labeled "horizontal" and "vertical." Horizontal composers worked at the start with a conception of the piece from beginning to end. Further divisions of this approach included how the composer used the keyboard or the computer. Horizontal composers tended to complete one line at a time. Some composers worked exclusively on the computer and others would opt to use an acoustic instrument, such as a guitar, to work out ideas first before entering them into the computer. Vertical composers worked on bits of the whole at a time with one part completed before moving on the next vertical space. Some vertical composers had an idea of the whole "orchestra" ahead of time and defined each line of the vertical space from the start. Others worked this out as they composed bits of the work. This research is useful because it resulted in a model that other researchers can use to investigate different-aged children, differences caused by past experience, or with different media. Folkestad's dissertation is published with a CD recording of sample compositions so that others can hear the subtleties of the typology.

Where Folkestad examined several students and their many compositions using a traditional sequencing program and a MIDI keyboard, Stauffer (in press) reported work with one child on a limited number of projects and used a graphics-based program with a drawing metaphor. The *Making Music* software allows users to create musical gestures using the mouse as a drawing device. Tools are provided that allow the user to manipulate the graphic representations musically, including alterations in all the usual ways a composer works. After describing her role as a consultant in the development of the software, Stauffer described the composition processes of one 8-year-old child, Meg, as she manipulated the software to compose. The description tells a rich story of how Meg developed a musical style by exploring and developing fluency with sound over time. Different types of exploring and developing are described. In telling the story, Stauffer integrates previous research in composition and creative thinking as examples of Meg's behavior. Several passages of the descriptions of

Meg's work relate to the emerging typology of Folkestad. Stauffer concluded her qualitative investigation by noting:

> the media with which children compose, such as the software program used in this project, may further enable their composing by allowing children to both see and hear their work as they create it as well by extending their options (e.g., via "tools" available in the software) for composing. (p. 26 in draft)

Younker (1997) used technology in an imaginative way to offer a platform for composition that allowed for the analysis of thought processes and strategies of different-aged children. Nine students, ranging in age from 8 to 14, were asked to compose using a standard software sequencer with a computer and MIDI keyboard much like the one used by Folkestad. Younker asked children to work with the software for seven, 1-hour sessions. The first two sessions were done in groups during which time the technology was learned and aspects of music discussed. This was followed by five sessions done individually with the researcher to capture data and a final session where compositions were shared with the group. Students were asked to think aloud while composing at the computer and respond to questions in an unstructured fashion. Data revealed differences in thought processes and strategies that could serve as the basis for a developmental model. The technology allowed for a standard environment to judge compositional behavior.

MacInnis (1996) contributed a qualitative study of three high school students, working in an autoethnographic approach that used composing with computers and journaling. Rather than organizing her results by traditional concepts of music elements, MacInnis allowed the student's interaction with the technology to define 38 different exemplars of music experience. The MIDI data that emerged from the traditional sequencer allowed students to openly perform, create, and listen without reference to traditional music theory. Personal constructions of musical experience were stressed.

Ladányi (1995) also used a qualitative case study approach to examine the compositional thought processes of four high school students from a suburban high school. Observations and intensive interviews formed the basis for the study. A computer and MIDI keyboard was used, together with a music notation program. Audio from the keyboard was routed into the video camera to allow the researcher to evaluate the video and audio more clearly. Evaluation of both open- and close-ended tasks revealed very different compositional styles. One of her major findings was that there may well be four classifications of novice composers at this level: archetypal—possessing the "gift" of imaginative ideas, but without much experience and knowledge; style emulator—strongly influenced by popular genres with few original ideas of their own; technician—students who seem to concentrate on surface details without connecting to deeper musical meaning; and super composer—students with the "gift" and with past training and experience to achieve a high level of attainment. Ladányi observed that the technology allowed a balance between structure and freedom and allowed each student to construct their own effective learning with only modest teacher/researcher intervention.

On the other end of the age scale, Phillips and Pierson (1997) described the compositional explorations of two students, one 5-year-old and another severely handicapped 12-year-old with limited communication skills. The authors described observations of compositional tasks using a computer program with iconic representation of sound[4] rather than traditional notation. They argued that software of any type can be "powerful" or "empowering." Powerful software can do lower-level thinking skills quite quickly and accurately, but empowering software can visually represent patterns and relationships in clear ways, allowing higher-level thinking.[5] The icon-based software used in this work allowed the students to move small pictures that represented fragments of sound around on the screen to create melodies. This environment solves the problem of high memory loads for specific patterns that younger students must maintain in order to compose longer works. The two descriptions provided in this article are actually taken from a longer account of 21 subjects who used this program effectively (Pierson, 1996). Phillips and Pierson reported that a typical strategy in composing using this interface was: trial and error, listening, making value judgments, and editing. This was similar to one of the approaches noted by Folkestad. The authors concluded their work by pointing to scaffolding approaches in teaching that allow students to master a higher-level task if the lower-level obstacles are removed initially.

Creative Thinking Approaches.   Much of the work summarized above is more naturalistic in nature, not beginning with a defined theoretical structure but letting the strategies define theory. Other research using technology to examine composition begins with the intent to compositional behavior using the creativity literature (and other literatures) as a foundation. Hickey has completed studies evaluating creative thinking ability. Process and product data were compared from a creative thinking perspective with 21 fourth- and fifth-grade subjects (Hickey, 1995). MIDI data were unobtrusively captured from a custom *HyperCard* stack that controlled a keyboard synthesizer and was designed to encourage compositional thinking. The program guided the subjects through a variety of possibilities organized around five musical elements: melody, rhythm, texture, timbre, and dynamics. The MIDI data created by the custom program was cleverly collected for both the process and product data analysis. Final compositions were evaluated by a panel of judges using consensual assessment techniques. Compositions rated in the high third and low third were then evaluated descriptively and quantitatively.

Hickey used this same custom program to explore two subjects in detail (Hickey, 1997). In this work, she was interested in the subjects' moments of most creative output in relation to a theory of interaction between reward and task conditions. Because the technology records experimentation with musical materials unobtrusively, Hickey was able to capture and compare compositional thinking products when the subjects were exploring and developing ideas (presumably not under pressure for a final, evaluated product) and under more demanding conditions for a final product. She provided background information on both students, placing the resulting data in context. The comparison of musical content under both conditions revealed qualitatively different descriptions, with the less pressured situation resulting in far more creative content based on the established notions of divergence and convergence. The relationships between these conditions of task structure and creative music making await much more systematic work, but the use of technology to reveal these subtleties is worth mentioning.

Daignault (1996) examined children's computer-mediated strategies in relation to craftsmanship and creative thinking. Twenty-five subjects ranging in age from 10 to 11 were asked to (1) record three to eight improvisations into a typical sequencer program; (2) select the one they preferred; and (3) develop the selection further using graphic, "piano-roll" notation. The main data came by observing carefully the development process using a video camera trained on the computer screen. Interestingly, this use of a video camera for data collection was greatly improved by Seddon and O'Neill (Seddon & O'Neill, 2000), who reported use of a special video card in a computer that recorded student behavior directly to videotape.

Using techniques similar to Hickey, Daignault asked judges to consensually assess the final developed compositions for craftsmanship and creativity and the top- and bottom-rated compositions served as an indicator of which process data to evaluate carefully. Analyses of process data for high and low craftsmanship and creativity led to conclusions about compositional thinking.

Emmons (1998) used a qualitative case study approach to observe six seventh-grade students' work with a traditional music sequencer in the development of compositions within a general music class situation. This work is unique because of its situated context. Results suggested a nonlinear process that embraced concept formation, preservation, and revision.

Special Topics

This final section briefly summarizes selected work that falls outside of the core studies of traditional music experience. Each topic represents an important trend in the literature.

Researcher as Programmer

There is a clear trend for researchers in music to rely less on technical expertise from outside the discipline and to develop more of their own software technology. Much of this is the result of better authoring tools as was noted in the Background section of this chapter. Many of the studies described in the Core Studies section feature custom-built software for the capture of data. A few other published accounts of software development are worth noting.

Lipscomb has documented the development of multimedia course materials (1994) and noted certain problems in developing cross-platform software in music (1998). Wood (1998) reported on the development of two interactive composition programs development for children's compositional thinking similar to studies reported by Phillips and Pierson (1997). Kozzin and Jacobson, two music theory professors, have developed interactive guides for music history to accompany the Norton masterworks series (Wittlick, 1996).

Readers interested in the trend toward the development of software by music educators also should note the work summarized in the chapter on internet developments by Fred Rees in part II of this Handbook. Briefly noted here is the excellent work done by Reese and Hickey on the development of internet-based resources for the exchange of compositions created by students (Reese & Hickey, 1999). The sites described encourage communication between students, teacher education candidates, composers, and music education professors. The potential for systematic research on music composition and its assessment using these tools is an exciting prospect.

Computers and Music Assessment

Technology-assisted assessment continues to be of interest to music educators and researchers. Venn (1990) developed and evaluated a computer-based interactive measure of common objectives in elementary general music using a personal computer and audio CD-ROM. After reviews of published music tests, state music curricula guides, and basal textbooks, he chose four musical elements for content inclusion: melody, rhythm, texture, and tonality. Tasks were devised that evaluated the child's ability to indicate a change in the element, identify compositional devices related to the element, and identify a place in a musical selection where a change in an element occurred. The software recorded the results. Test-retest reliability for 30 students was .79 for the total measure.

In a much larger project, Peters (1993) reported on the results of an investigation sponsored by the National Endowment of the Arts and the U.S. Department of Education. The project was aimed at the development of hardware and software that could evaluate pitch matching ability and tonal memory of students using acoustical signals and without the use of MIDI keyboard technology as the method for evaluation. Goals of the work included: (1) the creation of a computer-testing station to judge performance of pitch and rhythm, (2) the collection of data for testing purposes, (3) the profiling of student performance, and (4) the creation of tutorial software. All goals were achieved using commercial products and custom software. The technology was successfully field-tested in six public school sites of different types.

Pearlman (1993) summarized efforts to computerize the Graduate Record Exam (GRE) in music using commercial multimedia authoring software. It was field-tested twice in 1992 and the results indicated that more work was necessary before it could be adopted commercially by the Educational Testing Service. The report did indicate that the scoring algorithm was workable but that further funded research was necessary to make it acceptable. Since that time, the general ability portion of the GRE has been developed for computer-based administration.

Meeuwsen and his colleagues have developed a computerized assessment of rhythm performance (Meeuwsen, Flohr, & Fink, 1998). The *Rhythmic Performance Test—Revised* (RPT-R) is computer-generated and is in two parts. The first part asked children to tap along using a computer key with five different versions of a folk tune, synchronizing their tapping with the basic pulse. Tempi for the five versions ranged from 110 beats per minute to 150. The computer recorded the deviations of the tapping in milliseconds. Part II provided 20 varying rhythm patterns that were to be auditioned, remembered, and played back by tapping a computer key. Pilot testing of the measure was promising, with good reliability and factor-analytic verification of the two-part division of skill.

Finally, Webster and Hickey (in press) reported on the computerization and first trial of Webster's Measures of Creative Thinking in Music-II. The measure was designed to evaluate the creative thinking of children aged 6 to 10 using quasi-improvisatory tasks with informal instruments. A version of the measure was adapted (Hickey as programmer) to be self-administered by a computer using a set of MIDI drum pads, a MIDI keyboard, and foot pedal. MIDI data representing creative responses were recorded by the computer for subsequent analysis by judges.

Music Technology and Gender

Questions surrounding music technology and gender in school-aged children are not well studied. There is a predominate view that computers, especially computer gaming, is significantly favored by males (Healy, 1998, p. 161). There is evidence that shows that high school males use computers more often for class work than females (Schofield, 1995) and that, by the time students reach college, attitudes toward computers and instructional technology is much more favorable for males then females (Collis et al., 1996, p. 108). Interestingly, I could find no studies that specifically address gender issues in music technology in the United States.

There are two significant studies in the United Kingdom and one related investigation in Sweden that are worth careful reading. Comber, Hargreaves, and Colley (1993) and Colley, Comber, and Hargreaves (1997) reported the results of a two-stage, funded project to investigate gender and educational computing in the humanities. Surveys from students and teachers in schools surrounding the Leicestershire district in England were summarized in the first study. Students ranged in age from 11 to 18 with the total number of students being at least 280, although the exact number is not clear from the report. The survey revealed that older males were more confident than females in their use of music technology but that younger males and females were more balanced. The data also suggested that, for both males and females, there is the attitude though that males are more able in music technology, even though the reality may well be different. The sample data did show that attitudes toward simpler forms of music technology such as electronic keyboards were balanced between genders and that all felt that music technology helped them do better in music achievement. Older girls did show some drop in interest in music technology. The qualitative data that emerged from both the interviews with students and teachers indicated a belief that males naturally gravitated toward music technology. Interviews with teachers indicated no conscious effort to encourage female students to participate more actively in music technology activities. Most teachers agree that there is nothing to indicate any innate advantages for males over females and that differences in attitudes and behavior are likely to be cultural and likely changeable with proper school experiences.

The second study used the same assessment techniques and added a focus on the effects of school type. The sample was much larger ($n = 1115$) and was drawn from 11 schools in Leicestershire, Birmingham, and Coventry. Many of the same findings were noted. One new finding was that younger students in single-sex schools were more positively disposed to music technology than older students; however, the difference was less pronounced in coeducational schools. One conclusion of the researchers is that a single-sex school might be a more nurturing environment for females as they gain more confidence in music technology usage.

The Swedish work (Folkestad, Lindström, Hargreaves, Colley, & Comber, 1996) used similar methodology but sampled two Swedish schools, one urban and one rural. A younger age group, ages 12–13 ($n = 92$) and an older age group, ages 15–16 ($n = 141$) were used. The results showed that females use computers less than males except for music making. Creative use of the computer was seen by the Swedish students as more like a *music* activity and less like a *computer* activity. This suggested that further research in the context of how computers are used in music technology might be useful. Clearly, more focused research—especially in the United States—on gender and music technology is needed.

Conclusion

There is much to be excited about in the work described above. There is also much work to do. In studying the background of music technology research, it is clear that we have continuing growth in the availability of powerful resources, but we also need to help in-service teachers find the time to learn about these resources and to offer effective models of integration. Teacher education programs need to continue to be redesigned to include ample experiences with music technology. Clearly, older types of drill and practice CAI are now being blended with exploratory, hypermedia experiences. The data shows that when traditional CAI is matched with lower-level assessment techniques, a small and positive gain in learning is achieved.

The data also show that we have not yet learned how to evaluate the exploratory experiences, nor really know how to integrate these approaches conceptually into our music teaching. This is true not only for general instruction but also certainly for music as well. The articles by Brown and Lord are thoughtful writings that speak to how we might engineer the power of the technology.

There is much reason to move cautiously with our claims about music technology. The writings of Healy and Stoll need to be widely read and debated, as should the results of reviews such as those of Dillon and Gabbard. Not all of the cautions and concerns raised by these writers apply to music, but many do. Perhaps the most important concern is that both our research and practice integrate technology with a strong theory of instruction behind the reasons for doing so. That, together with a plan for thoughtful reflection on the results and how they will be assessed for individual students, will take us a long way.

Specific Directions

In music listening and skills development, there is continued evidence that traditional CAI works relatively well when students have a clear idea of the tasks. But teachers and researchers should also look for ways to integrate and assess the hypermedia content that Bush writes about. The evaluation of this type of exploratory software needs to be done carefully and with an eye toward variables such as cognitive style and gender. These two variable sets seem most valuable to pursue in new research efforts. It also seems evident that we need more sensitive and thoughtful dependent variables to really assess this kind of software. The possibility that existed in the work by Duitman to review the essay assignment as a measure of technology success is an example of what might be done.

The point made by Parrish about technology instruction effectively teaching knowledge and skills in such a way as to free the teacher to concentrate on other kinds of instruction is a very compelling concept for future research. The difficult challenge is in finding the balance between what can be done effectively by technology and what can be reinforced and explored by a live teacher. This probably varies from context to context.

In much of the research reported here, student attitude toward the use of hypermedia software was nearly always positive. The importance of this cannot be overlooked, for it goes beyond an explanation based on just the novelty effect. It makes sense that students naturally enjoy exploring ideas, solving interesting tasks, and applying lower-level skills to solve problems, but an important question is whether this enjoyment is directly connected to music experience. We need to find ways to more systematically evaluate this by watching specifically how students use the technology. A combination of qualitative and quantitative study is necessary to do this well. The work by Bauer and Fortney is important in this regard.

It was most gratifying to see the growth in technology studies in performance. Nevertheless, more work needs to be done by applied faculty around the country who teach in university settings and in private studios. Orman's research design, which integrated small amounts of focused exploration in the context of a band rehearsal, was a nice model for additional research. Part of the success of this work and that of Bauer was that students understood what was to be learned through the use of technology and also were encouraged to explore in the ways they wished.

Work on the effectiveness of intelligent accompaniment software seems promising. Sheldon and her colleagues designed a complex and clever investigation of this software that revealed a number of clues for further work. More research, such as that reported by Repp, is needed by studio teachers who might use this technology in their classroom. Similarly, research on error detection with technology in conducting settings is compelling. Here is a clear example of the way in which research can inform practice.

The qualitative work by Simms and Kim are good models for performance research. I was especially intrigued by Kim's evaluation of how historical and theoretical knowledge was integrated into the studio by way of technology and how this appeared to enrich performance study. This is an excellent line of inquiry that has a firm conceptual base in today's educational climate.

Work in composition with technology has clearly captured the imaginations of many. Folkestad's work is critical for developing a theoretical framework for understanding how students tend to naturally approach composition tasks. Such work provides a solid foundation for continued work but also presents wonderful models for new researchers. Hickey's work with evaluating creativity in composition is equally impressive and should continue to inspire studies about music learning. Stauffer's qualitative evidence raises a number of fascinating questions about how children make decisions.

In all of this work, the computer serves not only as a convenient recording medium but also as a powerful tool for allowing children to show evidence of their cognitive processing. The distinction made by Phillips and Pierson between "powerful" and "empowering" speaks to the fascinating debate about lower versus higher levels of thinking and about how to teach competence in a discipline in an age of such powerful technology. As Turkle reminded us:

> Children use the computer in their process of world and identity construction. They use it for the development of fundamental conceptual categories, as a medium for practice of mastery, and as a malleable material for helping forge their sense of themselves. The computer is a particularly rich and varied tool for servicing so wide a range of purposes. It enters into children's process of becoming and into the development of their personalities and ways of looking at the world. It finds many points of attachment with the process of growing up. Children in a computer culture are touched by technology in ways that set them apart from the generations that have come before. (Turkle, 1984, p. 165)

The Bottom Line

So, is music technology effective and is it worth the trouble? On balance and on a very basic level, the answer to this question is yes. Does music technology hold the key for solving all our music teaching problems? Of course not. Are there abuses in its use? Absolutely. Does it always improve learning? No, much depends on the context—especially the teacher and its use instructionally. Is it worth the trouble to keep studying its role in music teaching and learning? Unconditionally, yes.

Perhaps the question about music technology's effectiveness is posed too simplistically. Because of the definition of music technology stated here, because of the ubiquity of technology in today's culture and in the entire history of music as art, because of the basic human nature of teachers as seekers of new ways to explain difficult ideas, the question is not *if* technology is effective as much as *how* can we make technology *more* effective. Stated in another way, asking if technology is really effective is somewhat like asking if a pencil or a pen is really effective in teaching music. The answer depends in large part on other variables. Certainly music technology costs more than pencils or pens and, because of this, its use must be studied carefully. But apart from the money, the development and study of technology as a means of teaching music helps make our theories, research, curricula, teaching strategies, and our entire professional development much stronger. To take full advantage of technology in teaching, we are invited to go to the core of what music is and determine best how to teach what we find. At the end of the day, that is the point of it all.

NOTES

Note: I would like to offer a special word of thanks to Sam Reese, William Bauer, and David B. Williams, who offered significant help in the preparation of this chapter.

1. "Hypermedia" is a term referring to software that chunks information of all media types into nodes that can be selected dynamically (McKnight, Dillon, & Richardson, 1991).

2. "Learning style" is not generally considered synonymous with "cognitive style," which was used in the Bush study. Learning style is thought to be a broader construct that includes cognitive style, affective and physiological phenomena, whereas cognitive style refers to modes of perceiving, remembering, and thinking.

3. Additional efforts to evaluate the integration of music technology into traditional music theory and aural skills curricula in higher education continues at campuses like the University of Delaware (Arenson, 1995), University of Kentucky (Lord, 1993), Indiana University, and the New England Conservatory. Published studies of effectiveness at these institutions await completion.

4. This use of movable icons that represent sound is similar in nature to the "Tune Blocks" first used by Bamberger in the 1970s to explore musical thinking. A modern version (Bamberger, 2000) has recently been published in the form of a textbook with accompanying software. Research with this new resource is highly recommended as a way to extend this line of inquiry.

5. This approach is celebrated in the work of Papert (1993) and is not without controversy. The argument centers on whether the teaching of the lower-level knowledge is ultimately necessary for real success. This is a rich area for research in music.

REFERENCES

Agnes, M. (Ed.). (1999). *Webster's new world college dictionary* (4th ed.). New York: Macmillan.

Arenson, M. A. (1995). *Computer lessons for written harmony.* Newark, DE: University of Delaware. (ERIC Document Reproduction Service No. ED416824)

Argersinger, C. (1993). Side-effects of technology on music and musicians. *Jazz Educators Journal, 26*(1), 33.

Arms, L. (1997). *The effects of computer-assisted keyboard instruction on meter discrimination and rhythm discrimination of general music education students in the elementary school.* Unpublished doctoral dissertation, Tennessee State University, Memphis.

Austin, J. (1993). Technocentrism and technophobia: Finding a middleground for music educators in the next millennium. In D. Sebald (Ed.), *Technological directions in music education* (pp. 1–10). San Antonio, TX: IMR Press.

Bamberger, J. (2000). *Developing musical intuitions: A project-based introduction to making and understanding music.* New York: Oxford University Press.

Bauer, W. (1994). *The relationships among elements of learning style, mode of instruction, and achievement of college music appreciation students.* Unpublished doctoral dissertation, Kent State University, Kent, Ohio.

Berz, W. L., & Bowman, J. (1994). *Applications of research in music technology.* Reston, VA: Music Educators National Conference.

Berz, W. L., & Bowman, J. (1995). An historical perspective on research cycles in music computer-based technology. *Bulletin of the Council for Research in Music Education, 126*, 15–28.

Brown, A. (1999). Music, media and making: humanizing digital media in music education. *International Journal of Music Education, 33*, 10–17.

Busen-Smith, M. (1999). Developing strategies for delivering music technology in secondary PGCE courses. *British Journal of Music Education, 16*(2), 197–213.

Bush, J. E. (2000). The effects of a hypermedia program, cognitive style, and gender on middle school students' music achievement. *Contributions to Music Education, 27*(1), 9–26.

Caputo, V. (1993–94). Add technology and stir: Music, gender, and technology in today's music classrooms. *Quarterly Journal of Music Teaching and Learning, 4–5*(4–1), 85–90.

Chamberlin, L. L., Clark, R. W., & Svengalis, J. N. (1993). Success with keyboards in middle school. *Music Educators Journal, 79*(9), 31–36.

Christmann, E., & Lucking, R. (1991). Microcomputer-based computer-assisted instruction within differing subject areas: A statistical deduction. *Journal of Educational Computing Research, 16*(3), 281–296.

Clark, R. (1983). Reconsidering research on learning from media. *Review of Educational Research, 53*, 445–459.

Clements, D. (1995). Teaching creativity with computers. *Educational Psychology Review, 7*(2), 141–161.

Colley, A., Comber, C., & Hargreaves, D. (1997). IT and music education: What happens to boys and girls in coeducational and single sex schools. *British Journal of Music Education, 14*(2), 119–127.

Collis, B., Knezek, G., Lai, K., Miyashita, J., Pelgrum, W., Plomp, T., & Sakamoto, T. (1996). Reflections. In G. Knezek (Ed.), *Children and computers in school* (pp. 105–130). Mahwah, NJ: Lawrence Erlbaum.

Comber, C., Hargreaves, D. J., & Colley, A. (1993). Girls, boys and technology in music education. *British Journal of Music Education, 10*(2), 123–134.

Daignault, L. (1996). *A study of children's creative musical thinking within the context of a computer-supported improvisational approach to composition.* Unpublished doctoral dissertation, Northwestern University, Evanston, Illinois.

Deal, J. J., & Taylor, J. A. (1997). Technology standards for college music degrees. *Music Educators Journal, 84*(July), 17–23.

Dillon, A., & Gabbard, R. (1998). Hypermedia as an educational technology: A review of the quantitative research literature on learner comprehension, control, and style. *Review of Educational Research, 68*(3), 322–349.

Duitman, H. E. (1993). *Using hypermedia to enrich the learning experience of college students in a music appreciation course.* Unpublished doctoral dissertation, Ohio State University, Columbus.

Emmons, S. (1998). *Analysis of musical creativity in middle school students through composition using computer-assisted instruction: A multiple case study.* Unpublished doctoral dissertation, University of Rochester, Eastman School of Music, New York.

Ester, D. P. (1997). Teaching vocal anatomy and function via HyperCard Technology. *Contributions to Music Education, 24*(1), 91–99.

Fern, J. L. (1995). *The effectiveness of a computer-based courseware program for teaching jazz improvisation.* Unpublished doctoral dissertation, University of Southern California, Los Angeles.

Fletcher-Flinn, C., & Gravall, B. (1995). The efficacy of computer assisted instruction (CAI): A meta-analysis. *Journal of Educational Computing Research, 12*(3), 219–242.

Folkestad, G. (1996). *Computer based creative music making: Young people's music in the digital age.* Göteborg, Sweden: Acta Universitatis Gothoburgensis.

Folkestad, G., Hargreaves, D., & Lindström, B. (1998). Compositional strategies in computer-based music-making. *British Journal of Music Education, 15*(1), 83–97.

Folkestad, G., Lindström, B., Hargreaves, D., Colley, A., & Comber, C. (1996). *Gender, computers and music technology experience and attitudes.* Goteborg: Department of Education and Educational Research, Goteborg University.

Forest, J. (1995). Music technology helps students succeed. *Music Educators Journal, 81*(5), 35–48.

Fortney, P. M. (1995). Learning style and music instruction via an interactive audio CD-ROM: An exploratory study. *Contributions to Music Education, 22*, 77–97.

Gardner, H. (1991). *The unschooled mind: How children think and how schools should teach.* New York: Basic Books.

Goodson, C. A. (1992). *Intelligent music listening: An interactive hypermedia program for basic music listening skills.* Unpublished doctoral dissertation, University of Utah, Salt Lake City.

Gruner, G. L. (1993). *The design and evaluation of a computer-assisted error detection skills development program for beginning conductors utilizing synethetic sound sources.* Unpublished doctoral dissertation, Ball State University, Muncie, Indiana.

Healy, J. (1990). *Endangered minds: Why our children don't think.* New York: Simon & Schuster.

Healy, J. M. (1998). *Failure to connect: How computers affect our children's minds, for better or worse.* New York: Simon & Schuster.

Hermanson, C. D., & Kerfoot, J. (1994). Technology assisted teaching: Is it getting results? *American Music Teacher, 43*(6), 20–23.

Herrington, J., & Oliver, R. (1999). Using situated learning and multimedia to investigate higher-order thinking. *Journal of Interactive Learning Research, 10*(1), 3–24.

Hess, G. (1999). The computer literacy of prospective music students: A survey. In S. Lipscomb (Ed.), *Sixth International Conference on Technological Directions in Music Learning* (pp. 96–99). San Antonio, TX: IMR Press.

Hickey, M. (1995). *Qualitative and quantitative relationships between children's creative musical thinking processes and products.* Unpublished doctoral dissertation, Northwestern University, Evanston, Illinois.

Hickey, M. (1997). The computer as a tool in creative music making. *Research Studies in Music Education, 8*(July), 56–70.

Higgins, W. (1992). Technology. In R. Colwell (Ed.), *Handbook of research on music teaching and learning* (pp. 480–497). New York: Schirmer Books.

Hoffmann, J. A. (1991). Computer-aided collaborative music instruction. *Harvard Educational Review, 31*(3), 270–278.

Hudson, M. E. (1996). *The development and evaluation of a computer-assisted music instruction program as an aid to score study for the undergraduate wind band conducting student.* Unpublished doctoral dissertation, University of Florida, Gainesville.

Hughes, T. H. (1991). *A hypermedia listening station for the college music literature class.* Unpublished doctoral dissertation, University of Arizona, Tucson.

Jaeschke, F. G. (1996). *Creating music using electronic music technology: Curriculum materials and strategies for educators.* Unpublished doctoral dissertation, Columbia University Teachers College, New York.

Jones, D. L. (1991). *Design and trial of a computer-assisted system supplying practice in error detection for preservice instrumental music educators.* Unpublished doctoral dissertation, University of Georgia, Athens.

Jones, S. (1992). *Rock formation: Music, technology, and mass communication.* Newbury Park, CA: Sage Publications.

Kafai, Y., & Resnick, M. (Eds.). (1996). *Constructionism in pracice: designing, thinking, and learning in a digital world.* Mahwah, NJ: Lawrence Erlbaum.

Kassner, K. (2000). One computer can deliver whole-class instruction. *Music Educators Journal, 86*(6), 34–40.

Kim, S. (1996). *An exploratory study to incorporate supplementary computer-assisted historical and theoretical studies into applied music instruction.* Unpublished doctoral dissertation, Columbia University Teachers College, New York.

Kozma, R. (1991). Learning with media. *Review of Educational Research, 61*(2), 179–211.

Lehman, P. R. (1985). *The class of 2001: Coping with the computer bandwagon.* Reston, VA: Music Educators National Conference.

Ladányi, K. (1995). *Processes of musical composition facilitated by digital music equipment.* Unpublished doctoral dissertation, University of Illinois at Urbana-Champaign.

Lin, S. (1994). *Investigation of the effect of teacher-developed computer-based music instruction on elementary education majors.* Unpublished doctoral dissertation, University of Illinois at Urbana-Champaign.

Lipscomb, S. (1994). Advances in music technology: The effect of multimedia on musical learning and musicological investigation. In D. Sebald (Ed.), *Technological directions in music education* (pp. 77–96). San Antonio, TX: IMR Press.

Lipscomb, S. (1998). The trials and tribulations of developing cross-platform multimedia applications in music education. In S. Lipscomb (Ed.), *Fifth International Conference on Technological Directions in Music Education* (pp. 45–49). San Antonio, TX: IMR Press.

Liu, M. (1998). The effect of hypermedia authoring on elementary school students' creative thinking. *Journal of Educational Computing and Research, 19*(1), 27–51.

Lord, C. H. (1993). Harnessing technology to open the mind: Beyond drill and practice for aural skills. *Journal of Music Theory Pedagogy, 7,* 105–117.

MacGregor, R. C. (1992). Learning theories and the design of music compositional software for the young learner. *International Journal of Music Education, 20,* 18–26.

MacInnis, P. (1996). *Experiencing and understanding a computer-based music curriculum: A teacher's story.* Unpublished doctoral dissertation, University of Toronto, Canada.

Magnusson, S. J. (1996). Complexities of learning with computer-based tools: a case of inquiry about sound and music in elementary school. *Journal of Science Education and Technology, 5*(4), 297–309.

Malave, J. E. (1990). *A computer-assisted aural-visual approach to improve beginning students' clarinet tone quality.* Unpublished doctoral dissertation, University of Texas at Austin.

Mark, D. (1994). Digital revolution as a challenge to music education. *ISME Yearbook,* 75–83.

Mayer, R. (1997). Multimedia learning: Are we asking the right questions? *Educational Psychologist, 32*(1), 1–19.

McCord, K. (1993). Teaching music fundamentals through technology in middle school music classes. In K. Walls (Ed.), *Third International Conference on Technological Directions in Music Education* (pp. 68–71). San Antonio, TX: IMR Press.

McKnight, C., Dillon, A., & Richardson, J. (1991). *Hypertext in context.* Cambridge, UK: Cambridge University Press.

Meeuwsen, H., Flohr, J., & Fink, R. (1998). Computerized assessment of synchronization and the imitation and timing of rhythm patterns. In S. Lipscomb (Ed.), *Fifth International Conference on Technological Directions in Music Education* (pp. 93–95). San Antonio, TX: IMR Press.

Miller, R., & Franco, C. (1994). Spectral components of five cardinal vowels in the soprano singing voice considered by means of the sequential vowel diagonal. *The NATS Journal, 50,* 5–7.

Moore, B. (1989). Musical thinking and technology. In E. Boardman (Ed.), *Dimensions of musical thinking* (pp. 111–117). Reston, VA: Music Educators National Conference.

Nelson, B. J. (1991). The development of a middle school general music curriculum: A synthesis of computer-assisted instruction and music learning theory. *Southeastern Journal of Music Education, 3,* 141–148.

Nelson, G. (1998). Who can be a composer: New paradigms for teaching creative process in music. In S. Lipscomb (Ed.), *Fifth International Conference on Technological Directions in Music Learning* (pp. 61–66). San Antonio, TX: IMR Press.

Opportunity-to-learn standards for music technology. (1999). Reston, VA: MENC, The National Association for Music Education.

Orman, E. K. (1998). Effect of interactive multimedia computing on young saxophonists' achievement. *Journal of Research in Music Education, 46*(1), 62–74.

Ouren, R. W. (1998). *The influence of the Vivace accompaniment technology on selected middle school instrumental students.* Unpublished doctoral dissertation, University of Minnesota, Minneapolis.

Ozeas, N. L. (1992). *The effect of the use of a computer assisted drill program on the aural skill development of students in beginning solfège.* Unpublished doctoral dissertation, University of Pittsburgh, Pennsylvania.

Papert, S. (1993). *The children's machine: Rethinking school in the age of the computer.* New York: Basic Books.

Parrish, R. T. (1997). Development and testing of a computer-assisted instructional program to teach music to adult non-musicians. *Journal of Research in Music Education, 45*(1), 90–102.

Pearlman, M. (1993). *An application of multimedia software to standardized testing in music.* (Report No. ET-RR-93-36). Princeton, NJ: Educational Testing Service. (ERIC Document Reproduction Service No. ED385601)

Peters, G. D. (1992). Music software and emerging technology. *Music Educators Journal, 79*(3), 22–25, 63.

Peters, G. D. (1993). Computer-based music skills assessment project: A portal to artistic innovation. *Bulletin of the Council for Research in Music Education, 117,* 38–45.

Phillips, R., & Pierson, A. (1997). Cognitive loads and the empowering effect of music composition software. *Journal of Computer Assisted Learning, 13*(2), 74–84.

Pierson, A. (1996). *The development of the use of micro-electonics in music education in schools.* Unpublished doctoral thesis, University of Nottingham, England.

Placek, R. W. (1992). Design and trial of a computer-controlled programme of music appreciation. In H. Lees (Ed.), *Music education: Sharing musics of the world, proceedings of the 20th World Conference of the International Society for Music Education* (pp. 145–152). Seoul, Korea.

Postman, N. (1992). *Technopoly: The surrender of culture to technology.* New York: Knopf.

Postman, N. (1995). *The end of education.* New York: Knopf.

Prasso, N. M. (1997). *An examination of the effect of writing melodies, using a computer-based song-writing program, on high school students' individual learning of sight-singing skills.* Unpublished doctoral dissertation, Columbia University Teachers College, New York.

Reece, D. (1998). The Billboard report: Industry grapples with MP3 dilemma. *Billboard, 110,* 1.

Reese, S., & Hickey, M. (1999). Internet-based music composition and music teacher education. *Journal of Music Teacher Education, 25–32.*

Reese, S., & Rimington, J. (2000). Music technology in Illinois public schools. *Update, 18*(2), 27–32.

Repp, R. (1999). The feasibility of technology saturation for intermediate students of applied voice. In S. Lipscomb (Ed.), *Sixth International Conference on Technological Directions in Music Education* (pp. 16–21). San Antonio, TX: IMR Press.

Rogers, K. (1997). Resourcing music technology in secondary schools. *British Journal of Music Education, 36*(2), 129–136.

Schacter, J., & Fagnano, C. (1999). Does computer technology improve student learning and achievement? How, when, and under what conditions? *Journal of Educational Computing and Research, 20*(4), 329–343.

Schaffer, J. W. (1990). Intelligent tutoring systems: New Realms in CAI? *Music Theory Spectrum, 12*(2), 224–235.

Schaffer, J. W. (1991). A harmony-based heuristic model for use in an intelligent tutoring system. *Journal of music theory pedagogy, 5*(1), 25–46.

Schofield, J. (1995). *Computers and classroom culture.* Cambridge, UK: Cambridge University Press.

Seddon, F., & O'Neill, S. (2000). Influence of formal instrumental music tuition (FIMT) on adolescent self-confidence and engagement in computer-based composition. In C. Woods, G. Luck, R. Brochard, F. Seddon, & J. Sloboda (Eds.), *Sixth International Conference on Music Perception and Cognition* (CD-ROM). Keele, UK: Keele University.

Sheldon, D., Reese, S., & Grashel, J. (1999). The effects of live accompaniment, intelligent digital accompaniment, and no accompaniment on musician's performance quality. *Journal of Research in Music Education, 47*(3), 251–265.

Simms, B. (1997). *The effects of an educational computer game on motivation to learn basic musical skills: A qualitative study.* Unpublished doctoral dissertation, University of Northern Colorado, Greeley.

Simpson, E. H. (1996). *The effects of technology-assisted visual/aural feedback upon pitch accuracy of senior high school choral singing.* Unpublished doctoral dissertation, University of Hartford, Connecticut.

Smith, B., & Smith, W. (1993). Uncovering cognitive processes in music composition: Educational and computational approaches. In M. Smith, A. Smaill, & G. A. Wiggins (Eds.), *Music education: An artificial intelligence approach conference* (pp. 56–76). Edinburgh, Scotland: Springer-Verlag.

Stauffer, S. (in press). Composing with computers: Meg makes music. *Bulletin of the Council for Research in Music Education.*

Stoll, C. (1999). *High tech heretic: Why computers don't belong in the classroom and other reflections by a computer contrarian.* New York: Doubleday.

Taylor, J., & Deal, J. (1999). Integrating technology into the K–12 music curriculum: A pilot survey of music teachers. In S. Lipscomb (Ed.), *Sixth International Technological Conference on Directions in Music Learning* (pp. 23–27). San Antonio, TX: IMR Press.

Taylor, J., & Deal, J. (2000). *Integrating technology into the K–12 music curriculum: A national survey of music teachers.* Retrieved from http://otto.cmr.fsu.edu/~deal_j/Survey _files/v3_document.htm

Technology Counts: 1999 national survey of teachers' use of digital content. (2000). Retrieved from http://www.edweek.org/sreports/tc/99/articles/survey.htm

Tomita, Y., & Barber, G. (1996). New technology and piano study in hgher education: Getting the most out of computer-controlled player pianos. *British Journal of Music Education, 13*(2), 135–141.

Tseng, S. (1996). *Solo accompaniments in instrumental music education: The impact of the computer-controlled Vivance on flute student practice.* Unpublished doctoral dissertation, University of Illinois at Urbana-Champaign.

Turkle, S. (1984). *The second self.* New York: Simon & Schuster.

Upitis, R. (1992). Motivating through technology: Lasting effect or passing fancy? *American Music Teacher, 41*(6), 30–33.

Venn, M. (1990). *An investigation of the applicability of recent advances in computer technology to the development of a computer-based, random-access audio test of common criterion-referenced objectives in elementary music.* Unpublished doctoral dissertation, University of Illinois at Urbana-Champaign.

Walls, K. (1997). Music performance and learning: The impact of digital technology. *Psychomusicology, 16*(1–2), 68–76.

Webster, P., & Hickey, M. (in press). MIDI-Based Adaptation and Continued Validation of the *Measures of Creative Thinking in Music* (MCTM). In M. Campbell (Ed.), *Conference in Honor of Marilyn Zimmerman.* Urbana: University of Illinois.

Webster, P. R. (1990). Creative thinking, technology, and music education. *Design for Arts in Education, 91*(5), 35–41.

Williams, D., & Webster, P. (1999). *Experiencing music technology* (2nd ed.). New York: Schirmer Books.

Wittlick, G. (1996). Review of *The Norton CD-ROM masterworks: Interactive music guides for history, analysis, and appreciation, Vol 1. Journal of Music Theory Pedagogy, 10,* 189–206.

Wood, R. (1998). Using authoring software to observe children's musical compositions. In S. Lipscomb (Ed.), *Fifth International Conference on Technological Directions in Music Education* (pp. 72–76). San Antonio, TX: IMR Press.

Younker, B. (1997). *Thought processes and strategies of eight, eleven, and fourteen year old students while engaged in music composition.* Unpublished doctoral dissertation, Northwestern University, Evanston, Illinois.

Part IV
Assessment and Evaluation

[20]
Measuring Musical Aptitude and Ability

J. David Boyle and Rudolf E. Radocy

The measurement and prediction of musical ability is a time-honored topic in the psychology of music. A clear indication of what a prospective music student is likely to achieve has considerable practical significance for the student, parents, and music educators. Measuring musical aptitude and ability requires deciding what is important in light of the test user's conception of aptitude and ability. This chapter addresses that issue and reviews a few representative tests.

WHAT MIGHT BE TESTED?

"Aptitude" means potential or capacity for achievement (Lehman, 1968, p. 8). Radocy and Boyle (1979, p. 263) define aptitude as including the result of genetic endowment and maturation plus whatever musical skills may develop without formal musical education. Aptitude is a broader term than "capacity" and narrower than "ability." It usually excludes specific musical achievement. In principle, anything that one believes may predict future musical success, however one defines "success," is potential material for a music aptitude test, provided that the test does not require formal musical knowledge.

Since music is an aural art, a musician logically should be able to discriminate between sounds that vary in subtle ways. While ability to hear with great acuity per se apparently is of no musical advantage (Sherbon, 1975), aural discrimination of pitch, loudness, timbre, and duration is potentially fruitful as aptitude test material. Under optimal listening conditions, people can distinguish rather small pitch differences; in one study (Zwicker, Flottorp, & Stevens, 1957), listeners could detect frequency changes in a slowly resolving tone of as little as 0.5 percent. However, the just noticeable difference for pitch is not an unchanging value; it varies with frequency, intensity, duration, and rate of change (Roederer, 1975). Discrimination of rather small loudness differences is possible, but Western music has developed in such a way that the general artistic demand for a really wide dynamic range and subtle loudness differences is restricted (Patterson, 1974; Radocy & Boyle, 1979, p. 36). Timbre is highly multidimensional; people can compare tones for degrees of similarity in a global way (Grey, 1977). Differences in duration can be discriminated readily. The importance of paired comparisons of sensory properties is a subjective judgement for the investigator of musical aptitude.

Tonal memory, which also requires aural discrimination, is perhaps a more "musical" task than comparing individual sounds. Farnsworth (1969, p. 208) claims that test makers agree that "musical memory" requires careful attention. Tonal memory can mean rather specific recall for a sequence of pitches and/or durations, or it can mean a general recall of a melodic contour or form to the extent necessary for musical recognition. Curiously, specific tonal details may be less important than overall contour for recognition of familiar melodies (Dowling & Fujitani, 1971).

When exact recall of a tonal sequence is of concern, it is worth noting that research suggests that tonal melodies are easier to recall than atonal melodies (Long, 1976/1975). Ability to recall a certain tone from a prior sequence depends in part on the time interval before recall, position in the sequence, and the sequence length (Williams, 1975).

Naturally, in an aptitude test one would not expect melodic dictation or comparing an aural stimulus with printed notation because dictation and music reading are specific achievements. It is quite possible to make "same–different" comparisons between paired tonal sequences, or to indicate which of a set of short sequences matches a standard or which tone in a sequence is changed.

Musical form is based on patterns of unity, achieved through repetition, and variety. Identifying form depends on recognizing whether particular musical material is new, has been heard before, or is some alteration of what was heard before (Radocy, 1980, p. 100). While labeling specific musical forms and long-term identification of sections (as in sonata form) àre achievement laden, aptitude measures could include contrasting paired examples that vary in their degrees of similarity. Differences could be rhythmic, as in altering a theme via augmentation or diminution, or melodic, as in retrograde or inversion. Research suggests that trained musicians are somewhat more sensitive to melodic than to rhythmic change, but that will vary greatly with individual listeners (Radocy, 1982). An effective contrasting technique is presenting a musical pattern followed by a pattern that is more ornate, but if mentally stripped of the ornamentation is either the same as or different from the initial pattern. This "imagery" technique is used in the *Musical Aptitude Profile* (Gordon, 1965), which we shall discuss shortly.

All the possibilities for assessing musical aptitude discussed thus far are essentially aural comparisons involving detecting some deviation from an initial standard. Audition skills logically *are* related to musical success, but musical ability, in a larger sense, is probably an interaction of audition, physical coordination, intelligence, and experience (Radocy & Boyle, 1979, p. 272).

So-called "nonmusical" or "extramusical" variables may bear strong relationships to eventual musical achievement, especially in specific instructional settings. Multiple regression analysis, an extension of correlation, can show the relationship of several predictors to a criterion variable. Using a criterion variable of apparent musical "talent" and "awareness," as rated by teachers of 291 students in a university laboratory school, Rainbow (1965) identified as significant predictors tonal memory, academic intelligence, musical achievement, interest in music, and socioeconomic background; academic achievement and socioeconomic background were significant while "musical" variables such as pitch discrimination, rhythm, and musical training were not. Particular combinations of significant and nonsignificant predictors varied among elementary, junior high, and senior high levels, but at least one "nonmusical" or "extramusical" variable was significant at each level. In a more recent study, Hedden (1982) used a music achievement test, presumably more reliable than teacher ratings, as a criterion variable. For 144 fifth- and sixth-grade students, the best single predictor variable was academic achievement; adding an attitude toward music or a musical self-concept measure modestly increased prediction power. A musical background measure as well as gender added nothing significant to the overall prediction ability.

Opinions differ regarding the relationship of intelligence to musical aptitude; some correlational studies (e.g., Gordon, 1968) suggest only a slight relationship. However, correlation techniques may show a spuriously low relation due to lack of reliability either of the aptitude or the intelligence measure. Sergeant and Thatcher (1974) conducted three experiments employing various measures of intellectual and musical abilities and analyzed their data via the statistical technique of analysis of variance. They concluded that all highly intelligent people are not necessarily musical, but all highly musical people are apparently highly intelligent. It is not surprising that academic intelligence in one form or another would be related to musical achievement, and therefore would be one indicator of musical aptitude, especially in a school setting. From a practical standpoint, one probably should consider intelligent children as potential musicians, particularly if they appear to have any musical interests.

"Intelligence" often refers to some sort of academic or linguistic ability, and such ability probably is assumed by most literature relating intellectual and musical abilities or aptitudes. In what may prove to be a highly influential book, Gardner (1983) presents a multiple intelligence theory, based on biological, neurological, clinical, and behavioral evidence, which encompasses separate linguistic, logical-mathematical, spatial, bodily kinesthetic, personal, *and musical* intelligences. While debate regarding the generality versus specificity of intelligence or musical ability is not new, theorizing a musical intelligence that is of equivalent stature to other forms of intelligence is new, and there may be future implications for those who wish to test musical aptitude. Certainly, more knowledge of musical development and anomalies therein are necessary.

Physical coordination obviously is relevant to playing certain instruments, but motor skill assessment is beyond the scope of this text.

What should a musical aptitude test test? That is a judgment based on what the test maker considers important. Aural skills frequently are tested, as the reviews of tests below indicate. Since success in school settings is linked to "nonmusical" variables, especially intelligence, an assessment of musical aptitude may include other variables.

REPRESENTATIVE EXAMPLES

There are or have been many tests of musical aptitude, as one might expect. According to Lehman (1968, p. 5), interest in creating musical aptitude tests grew between the two world wars and waned thereafter until the late 1960s. The tests selected for discussion here are representative of the approaches aptitude test constructors have taken, and, at least at the time of this writing, they are available commercially.

Seashore

The most widely known published standardized musical aptitude test battery may be the *Seashore Measures of Musical Talents* (Seashore et al., 1960). The Seashore battery is the oldest standardized music test available (it originally appeared in 1919); it has been researched and used extensively; it was a landmark work of a pioneering American music psychologist, and its validity is impeccable, mixed, or nonexistent, depending on the user's philosophy. A detailed discussion is justified here because of the battery's exemplary nature, positively and negatively.

The plurals "measures" and "talents" represent more than semantic nit-picking. Carl Seashore (1938) believed in a "theory of specifics," that is, musical ability is a set of loosely related basic sensory discrimination skills. One does not combine parts of the battery to obtain a total score; rather, one obtains a profile. Seashore further believed that a person's aural skills had a genetically determined capacity; battery scores would not change over time except to the extent that misunderstood directions and test-taking experience might affect the results. For Seashore, his tests were valid in and of themselves as measures of sensory skills important for musicians.

The present battery contains six sections: Pitch, Loudness, Rhythm, Time, Timbre, and Tonal Memory. The original 1919 version lacked a rhythm section; it was added in 1925. The original version also contained a consonance test, which was eliminated during an extensive 1939 revision. The basic task in each section is aural discrimination.

The pitch test requires the subject to indicate whether the second of 50 paired tones is higher or lower than the first tone, a standard of 500 Hz. The items become progressively more difficult; the frequency difference ranges from 17 to 2 Hz, which is about 59 to 9 cents (1 cent = 1/1200 of an octave, 100 cents = 1 semitone).

Fifty paired tones are judged regarding whether the second 440 Hz tone is stronger or weaker than the first in Seashore's loudness test. Decibel differences range from 4 to 0.5. As in the pitch test, the tones are "pure" tones, produced by an audio oscillator.

Pure tone patterns comprise the rhythm test. The subject listens to 30 paired patterns and indicates whether each pair's tones are the same or different. Patterns are five, six, or seven 500 Hz tones long; meters include $\frac{2}{4}$, $\frac{3}{4}$, and $\frac{4}{4}$.

The time test requires indicating whether the second 440 Hz tone is longer or shorter than the first in each of 50 pairs. The standard tone is 0.8 sec. The comparison tone varies from the standard by from 0.30 to 0.05 sec.

Complex tones (mixtures of frequencies) built on 180 Hz are used in Seashore's timbre test. For the 50 pairs, the subject indicates whether the two tones are the same or different. Differences are attained by varying the relative intensities of the third and fourth partials.

Sequences of electronic organ tones, grouped in 10 pairs each of three, four, or five tones, comprise the tonal memory test. One tone differs between the members of each pair; the smallest difference is a whole step. The subject's task is to identify the number of the tone that differs.

The tests' raw scores may be converted to percentiles in accordance with tables of norms for grades 4–16. The machine-scorable answer sheet provides space for drawing a "profile curve" that connects a subject's percentile location for each of the six tests.

The test manual claims reliabilities ranging from .55 to .85 for different sections at different grade levels. Lehman (1968, p. 40) reports that the pitch and tonal memory sections have been generally the most reliable while the timbre test is the weakest.

The Seashore battery's validity is open to question in accordance with one's views of musical aptitude and ability. There is little question regarding measurement of the particular skills; someone who scores well on the pitch test probably *is* good at making rapid minute pitch comparisons. Most validity studies were conducted with the 1919 version. Farnsworth (1969, p. 197) indicates that Seashore scores have more value for predicting success in music classes (e.g., harmony) of a tonal nature than they do for academic music classes (e.g., music history). This would be expected, due to the battery's content. Manor (1950) found a modest relation between the 1939 pitch and tonal memory tests and fourth-grade instrumental music success. Seashore's claim that the scores could be raised only as an artifact of testing is not valid. Subjects can improve their scores via relevant training procedures; for example, Wyatt (1945) showed average gains of 49 percent among adult musicians and 26 percent among nonmusicians.

Reliability and hence validity of a test requiring fine auditory discriminations will be influenced by the quality of recording and playback equipment and by listening conditions. Good listening conditions are crucial for Seashore administration; ideally, the battery should probably be administered via high quality head-phones. Sound pressure level in a free reverberant field, such as most classroom test administration situations, will vary around the room, so the sound sensation experienced by a listener varies with where he or she is seated (Plomp & Steeneken, 1973). Sergeant (1973) documented significant differences in pure tone pitch discrimination scores, among musically skilled subjects, which depended on whether the test was administered under customary group-testing conditions, individually in a sound at-tenuation booth, or via headphones. Accuracy was greatest with headphones, least in the group condition.

Four of the six tests use dichotomous items. A completely random guess will have a fifty–fifty chance of being correct; consequently, the chance score is equal to half of the number of items.

Other criticisms of the battery include the lack of item numbers on the recording (answer columns are identified) and the "monster movie" voice that labels the columns and says things such as "Ready, . . . now, . . . for . . . the . . . PITCH . . . test!"

As a test of specific aural discrimination skills, Seashore's bat-tery may be very appropriate. The person who earns a high score on all sections under good listening conditions likely will be an excellent auditory discriminator. The test user must decide whether such information is essential for his or her purposes. There certainly are musical tasks that require detecting subtle differences in tonal properties. Yet music is far more than "iso-lated" skills. To the extent that ability in those "isolated" skills is a valid indicator of musical ability as conceived by the test user, the Seashore battery is valid.

Wing

The *Standardised Tests of Musical Intelligence* (Wing, 1961) are in stark contrast to the Seashore battery. Wing, an eminent British music psychologist, believed in, and in an early factor analytic study (Wing, 1941), found a *general* factor of musical ability that should pervade all areas of musical learning. One legitimately can speak of the Wing *test* because there is a total score. The test may be considered more "musical" than Seashore because the stimuli are piano tones and are short melodies or chords. There are seven subtests.

Chord analysis is required in the first test, although some of the "chords" are two-tone simultaneous intervals. The subject indicates how many tones are presented in each of 20 stimuli. The answer sheet allows for up to six tones; no stimulus in fact contains more than four. "Hearing out" the number of tones in a simultaneous sound is not an easy task for an untrained ear; while intervals and chords generally do not merge into one sound, many people would have difficulty distinguishing beyond the fact that more than one sound is present.

The second test requires listening to paired chords for movement of one tone. The subject indicates whether the two chords remain the same, whether one tone moves down, or whether one tone moves up. The answer sheet requires only checking symbols for "up," "down," or "same."

Melodic alteration is the basis for the third test. Thirty paired melodies in which the second melody has one altered tone are presented; the subject indicates the number of the altered tone. Melodies range from 3 to 10 tones. The instructions invite the subject to write "S" for same if there is no alteration but in fact there are no unaltered melodies or places on the answer sheet to write "S." There are only dots corresponding to each tone.

The fourth test requires an evaluation of 14 paired performances regarding rhythmic accent. The subject indicates whether the "A" version or "B" version is "better" regarding the location of the "accentuated (more strongly played) notes" or if the two versions are the same, as three items are.

Another preference task comprises the fifth test; this time the subject must judge whether either version is "better" regarding appropriate harmonization or whether they are the same, as three are. The subject is told that the second version "Sometimes . . . has different notes below the tune (the notes played by the left hand may be different)." There are 14 items.

For test six the subject is told "Sometimes the louder and quieter portions are in different places when the tune is played the second time." The subject again indicates for 14 pairs whether they are the same, as three are, or, if they are different, whether version "A" or "B" is "better." The test basically requires judging the propriety of crescendo and diminuendo locations.

Phrasing sensitivity is tested in the last section. Fourteen paired melodies are judged for sameness (three are played the same) or, if different, for which version is "better." Pauses, legato, and staccato are employed. The subject is told "Sometimes the second playing has the notes differently grouped (different groups of notes may be played with short sharp strokes, or so that they follow on smoothly, etc.). The general effect may be compared to punctuation—that is, the use of commas, etc., in ordinary writing."

Wing claims a split-halves reliability of .90 for the entire test. He cautions that reliability will vary with testing conditions and subjects. Wing believes that the test is valid because test scores relate well to grades earned by children in musical training, as indicated by various studies. Much of Wing's own validity work is reported in an article (Wing, 1954) based on an earlier test version.

The tape frequently is a serious problem with administering the Wing test because (a) the technical quality is weak,* (b) the "same" performances were played twice rather than re-recorded, and (c) for American children, the characteristic British accent requires some acclimation.

The person who believes in a general factor of musical ability and a certain degree of "musicality" as characterizing the musically apt student may find the Wing test useful. The judgment of rhythmic accent, harmony, intensity, and phrasing may require a certain musical achievement, but conceivably a person can have developed the necessary sensitivity through immersion in Western musical culture.

Bentley

The *Measures of Musical Abilities* (Bentley, 1966a), another British test, are based on the author's assumption that (a) the phrase or figure is music's most elemental form, (b) detailed recall of pitch and duration information is necessary for apprehension of melody (this may be questioned; see "what might be tested," above), (c) good intonation (except for fixed pitch instruments) requires discriminating tones less than a semitone apart, and (d)

---

*It is possible, when listening with headphones, to hear birds occasionally chirping in the background.

awareness of chords is necessary for evaluating one's contribution to an ensemble. The battery, intended mainly for children ages 7 to 12, consequently contains tests of pitch discrimination, tonal memory, chord analysis, and rhythm memory. A total score is possible. The test manual is rather sparse, but Bentley's (1966b) text, in a way, functions as a complete manual.

Bentley's pitch test is similar to Seashore's except that there is a "same" option (two pairs are comprised of identical tones) and the differences range from about 100 to 12 cents. There are 20 pairs of audio oscillator tones.

The second test, labeled "Tunes," requires another Seashore-like task: The subject listens to 10 paired organ melodies and indicates which tone has been altered.

A chord analysis test, similar to Wing's (again, some "chords" really are two-tone simultaneous intervals) is third. Organ tones are used for the 20 stimuli.

In the final test, involving rhythm memory, the subject indicates which beat in the second pair contains a difference from the first pair, or if both versions are the same, as are two of the 10 pairs.

Reliability is .84 by the test–retest method, and validity, as correlation with aural skill examination grades, is .94, according to Bentley. In a study with American junior high students, Young (1973) found a composite reliability of .83 and respective reliabilities for pitch discrimination, tonal memory, chord analysis, and rhythm memory of .65, .83, .74, and .61. Correlations of Bentley scores with Gordon *Musical Aptitude Profile* scores, a potential indicator of concurrent validity, varied from .26, between chord analysis and Gordon's musical sensitivity, to .58, between composite Bentley and Gordon scores. Bentley claims that the tests measure basic judgments which are a part of music making and therefore identify children who are likely to profit from formal music instruction.

As with Wing's test, the Bentley scores are grouped into the top 10 percent, the next 20 percent, the middle 40 percent, the next 20 percent, and the bottom 10 percent for norming purposes. Bentley argues (as does Wing) that finer discriminations are unnecessary; some may disagree.

For younger children, the test has the advantage of being relatively brief; perhaps it is too easy for older children. A person who wants an easy-to-use musical aptitude measure that combines some psychoacoustic and more "musical" tasks may be interested in Bentley's test.

Gordon MAP

Edwin Gordon (1965), a contemporary American music educator, created one of the most comprehensive measures of musical aptitude, the *Musical Aptitude Profile.* The test manual is extremely thorough; there are norms for grades 4 through 12, various combinations thereof, and musically select students. The manual includes extensive reliability and validity information and a detailed history of *MAP* development. The test has had con- siderable follow-up research, as examination of the *Journal of Research in Music Education* from the mid 1960s through mid 1970s indicates. The concepts of sensitivity to musical alteration and embellishment as well as preference underlie the battery. While the test taker must make many "musical" judgments, they are global enough that musical training is not necessary. It is enough to note similarity and difference or express a preference without giving details.

The *MAP* contains three major divisions: Tonal Imagery, Rhythm Imagery, and Musical Sensitivity. Tonal Imagery has subdivisions of Melody and Harmony. Tempo and Meter are subdivisions of Rhythm Imagery. Musical Sensitivity includes sub- divisions of Phrasing, Balance, and Style. Scores are determined for the entire battery, each major division, and each subdivision. Orchestral string instruments produce the stimuli.

The Melody subtest requires indicating whether the second member of each of 40 pairs is an embellishment of the first or is basically a different phrase. The subject must decide whether removal of the added tones (paired phrases are of equivalent length) would leave a phrase like the first or different from it. The phrases include major and minor keys, mixed meter, various tempi, and syncopation. Gordon stresses that the meter remains unchanged within each pair; any rhythmic alterations are in melodic rhythm.

The Harmony subtest of the Tonal Imagery section also asks the subject for a same or different judgment in 40 items. Each item pair contains a melody line performed on violin, and a lower harmony line performed on cello. The task is to indicate whether the second lower line is the same as or different from the first lower line; the upper line always remains the same.

In the 40-pair Tempo subtest, played on violin, the subject is supposed to respond "different" if the second member has an ending in which the tempo increases or decreases. If tempo does not change, the subject should respond "same." When something is the "same," the second member is a re-recording of the first member's performance.

The Meter subtest requires another same or different judgment for 40 pairs; differences occur due to meter changes. The number of tones in paired examples remains the same. Changes in melodic rhythm occur only as necessitated by meter changes. Violin again is the performance medium.

The same selection is played twice in each of the 30 Phrasing items; violin and cello are performance media. The test taker indicates which version is "better."

The Musical Sensitivity section ends with violin performances of 30 items each in the Balance and Style subtests. Again, it is a matter of musical preference, presumably based on musical acculturation. The Balance test requires judging whether the first or second member of each pair has the "better" ending. In the Style test, the paired excerpts differ in tempo; the subject indicates preference for the first or second version.

Gordon reports numerous reliability figures. The entire *MAP* has a reliability ranging from a low of .90 for the fourth grade to a high of .96 for the eleventh grade. The respective lows and highs for the major sections are Tonal Imagery, .80 (fourth grade) and .92 (eleventh grade); Rhythm Imagery, .82 (fourth grade) and .91 (eleventh grade); Musical Sensitivity, .84 (fourth grade) and .90 (ninth and tenth grades). The lowest subtest reliability is .66, for fourth grade on the Harmony, Meter, Balance, and Style sections. Reliability estimates were computed via the split-halves procedure.

Validity, treated extensively in the manual, is based on correlations with teacher estimates of "musical talent," musical performance, and music achievement scores. Gordon also offers theoretical reasons for constructing the battery as he did.

All *MAP* items require a dichotomous decision: Something is the same or it is not; one or the other version is "better." The answer sheet, however, provides a "don't know" option. The taped instructions include an admonishment to avoid guessing. This presumably reduces the chance score and enhances reliability; in practice, of course, all guesses are not random (see Chapter 5).

Length of administration is one potential difficulty in some school situations. The manual recommends administering each major section on separate days. Each major section requires 50 minutes. Because of fatigue, it usually would be unwise to administer the entire battery in one day to any age group. Yet administration over three successive days may cause undue disruption in school situations where students must be excused from some academic activity. The test administrator could elect to administer only selected *MAP* portions, but then one is sacrificing aspects that the test author considers important. Scores and norms are available for all *MAP* divisions and subdivisions.

Few published music tests are more thorough than Gordon's *Musical Aptitude Profile*. The person who has the time to study the manual and administer the test, and who believes that musical aptitude is indicated by sensitivity to ornamentation and judgments that agree with customary practice in Western musical culture probably will find the *MAP* highly useful.

Gordon PMMA

The Seashore, Wing, and Gordon *MAP* measures basically are intended for grades 4–12; they could be used with adults. Bentley's battery provides norms for children as young as age 7. Gordon's (1979) *Primary Measures of Music Audiation* are for children in kindergarten through third grade. Gordon believes that musical aptitude does not "stabilize" until fourth grade, so a test of "immediate impressions" and "intuitive responses" is necessary. The controversial term "audiation" refers to recalling or creating musical sound without its physical presence. When one actually listens to music, one makes comparisons by "audiating" music heard previously. The *PMMA* are structured to require the child to react to immediate auditory impressions in accordance with his or her "audiation" abilities, which presumably depend on a combination of innate capacities and early informal musical experience. As a child normally has experienced music in some form since infancy, the basis for audiation exists; any new musical experience is similar or dissimilar to earlier experiences.

PMMA include a Tonal and a Rhythm test, each of which has 40 items. The Tonal test contains electronically synthesized tones of equal duration. The Rhythm test's electronically synthesized tones remain at one frequency. Tempo beats, at a low dynamic level, are included with the Rhythm stimuli. The basic task is a "same-different" comparison. Tonal items that differ do so because one or more tones change between the first and second members of an item pair; sequence length is from two to five tones. Differing rhythm items differ in meter or grouping of tones within one meter. Five seconds separate items; "first" and "second" are spoken to identify each pair member.

To simplify the response process, Gordon uses a pictographic scale and symbolic item identification. Each item is identified by a drawing of a common object with which most children would be familiar; objects include a spoon, car, sailboat, hat, and so on. The child answers by circling two smiling faces if the excerpts are the same, or circling one frowning and one smiling face if the excerpts are different.

Split-halves and test-retest reliability coefficients are reported in the manual for grades K–3. Respective composite split-halves reliabilities are .90, .92, .92, and .90; the respective test–retest reliabilities, which one normally would expect to be lower because of changes in the children between testing times, are .74, .75, .76, and .73. The lowest section reliability is a test–retest reliability of .60 for the Rhythm test at the kindergarten level.

Validity is claimed in the form of content validity, because of what Gordon believes to be "audiation's" nature, concurrent validity, because *PMMA* correlate low with academic achievement and intelligence tests and therefore presumably measure musical factors rather than general academic factors, and "congruent" (really also concurrent) validity, because of correlations of fourth grade students' *PMMA* scores with *MAP* scores. The content of the *PMMA*, in fact, requires immediate comparison of a short tonal sequence or rhythm pattern with a potential imitation. The ease with which a child can do this may be an outgrowth of "audiation." Low correlations with academic achievement and intelligence indeed do indicate that the test is measuring *something* else, and modest to high correlation with *MAP* probably would be expected.

As with the *MAP*, Gordon's *PMMA* manual provides a detailed rationale and presentation of technical information. Detailed percentile norms are available. The test appears well conceived and, even if one questions the concept of "audiation" (Gordon also discusses "keyality" as something different from tonality), the test does assess primary children's abilities to hear differences in short tonal and rhythmic patterns. The *PMMA* undoubtedly need further research, but they presently are a viable test for the person interested in children's aural discriminations of brief musical excerpts.

Gordon IMMA

Gordon's (1982) *Intermediate Measures of Music Audiation* are an advanced version of the *PMMA*. They are intended to discriminate among children who would obtain high (i.e., above the 80th percentile) *PMMA* composite or subtest scores. The *IMMA* are intended for grades 1–4 rather than K–3. The *IMMA* content is constructed to be more advanced than that of Gordon's *PMMA* but less advanced than that of his *MAP*.

The *IMMA* include a Tonal and a Rhythm test; each contains 40 items. The test taker indicates whether sets of paired tonal or rhythmic phrases are the same or different. The items are similar to *PMMA* items, but they are more difficult due to increased use of minor mode for tonal items, and, for both item types, the dispersion through the test section of six "very difficult questions."

Percentile rank norms are provided for each section and for the total *IMMA*. Gordon also provides section and total criterion scores for identifying in each grade children with "exceptionally high overall music aptitude." Split-halves and test–retest reliabilities are reported in the manual. Tonal section reliabilities range from .72 (fourth grade, split-halves method) to .88 (first-grade, test–retest method). Rhythm section reliabilities range from .70 (first and fourth grades, split-halves method) to .84 (same grades, test–retest method). The range of composite reliabilities is from .76 (fourth grade, test–retest) to .91 (first and second grades, test–retest). Validity is claimed on the basis of correlations with the *PMMA*, *MAP*, and teacher ratings on a five-point scale.

Strengths and weaknesses noted for the *PMMA* apply to the *IMMA*. The necessity for the pictographic scale becomes rather questionable for fourth graders, as indeed it may be for any child with the ability to recognize and order numbers.

Other Tests

Many tests have appeared and passed into history. In general, they no longer are available, although contact with the publisher or university testing centers might be fruitful. A listing of some tests appears in an appendix to this book.

"Promotional" tests occasionally appear, often with the cooperation of instrument manufacturers or music stores. They usually lack standardization; the lack of norms may leave the test administrator puzzled as to what the scores mean. Items generally are "easy" because differences between sounds are so obvious. Such tests are intended to recruit music students and should not be taken seriously as a means of assessing musical aptitude.

SUMMARY: WHICH TEST TO USE

There is no one criterion for selecting a measure of musical aptitude. Colwell (1970, pp. 26–42) discusses four criteria for selecting an appropriate test for a particular purpose. Two criteria are reliability and validity. Another criterion is *usability*, which refers to test administration and scoring. One must consider the time the test requires, necessary equipment and seating arrangements, cost, ease of scoring, applicability of the norms, and relation of the test to other aspects of evaluation. A fourth criterion is *usefulness*, which, for Colwell, refers to how well the test differentiates among those who take it. While an argument can be made for criterion-referenced achievement tests, aptitude testing implies selection or at least relative ordering of individuals.

The basic decision is a matter of whether a test will provide information that the user believes is important in evaluating aptitude. If one is particularly concerned with small differences in auditory signals, perhaps Seashore is appropriate. If one considers comparisons of alternate performance versions for some degree of similarity or adherence to cultural expectancy important, the Gordon *MAP* is a well-documented measure. If no published test is satisfactory because of one's philosophy or definition of aptitude, one must construct one's own measure. In many instances a test user really is interested in a student's ability to succeed in the context of formal music instruction with its requisite social and disciplinary aspects. The judicious blending of information about a student's intelligence, interests, resourcefulness, and self-discipline should be employed when a decision about a musical future is to be made, regardless of any aptitude test score.

Study Questions

1. State your own definition of musical aptitude.

2. Make a list of five or more observable behaviors that a person with a high degree of musical aptitude, in accordance with your definition, should be able to demonstrate proficiently.

3. Which one of the tests discussed in this chapter is the most satisfactory in accordance with your definition? Which is the least satisfactory? Why?

4. How should a measure of musical aptitude be validated in accordance with your definition? Why?

5. Examine your list of observable behaviors and indicate whether each is more nearly musical aptitude, musical achievement, or "nonmusical," and why.

REFERENCES

Bentley, A. *Measures of musical abilities.* London: George A. Harrap, 1966a.

Bentley, A. *Musical ability in children and its measurement.* New York: October House, 1966b.

Colwell, R. *The evaluation of music teaching and learning.* Englewood Cliffs, N.J.: Prentice-Hall, 1970.

Dowling, W.J., & Fujitani, D. S. Contour, interval, and pitch recognition in memory for short melodies. *Journal of the Acoustical Society of America,* 1971, *49,* 524–531.

Farnsworth, P. R. *The social psychology of music* (2nd ed.). Ames: Iowa State University Press, 1969.

Gardner, H. Frames of mind: The theory of multiple intelligences. New York: Basic Books, 1983.

Gordon, E. E. *Musical aptitude profile.* Boston: Houghton Mifflin, 1965.

Gordon, E. E. A study of the efficiency of general intelligence and musical aptitude tests in predicting achievement in music. *Council for Research in Music Education,* 1968, *13,* 40–45.

Gordon, E. E. *Primary measures of music audiation.* Chicago: G.I.A. Publications, 1979.

Gordon, E. E. *Intermediate measures of music audiation.* Chicago: G.I.A. Publications, 1982.

Grey, J. M. Multidimensional perceptual scaling of musical timbres. *Journal of the Acoustical Society of America,* 1977, *61,* 1270–1277.

Hedden, S. K. Prediction of music achievement in the elementary school. *Journal of Research in Music Education,* 1982, *30,* 61–68.

Lehman, P. R. *Tests and measurements in music.* Englewood Cliffs, N.J.: Prentice-Hall, 1968.

Long, P. A. Pitch recognition in short melodies (Doctoral dissertation, Florida State University, 1975). *Dissertation Abstracts International,* 1976, *36,* 4840A–4841A.

Manor, H. C. A study in prognosis. *Journal of Educational Psychology,* 1950, *41,* 31–50.

Patterson, B. Musical dynamics. *Scientific American,* 1974, *231*(5), 78–95.

Plomp, R., & Steenekén, H. J. M. Place dependence of timbre in reverberant sound fields. *Acustica,* 1973, *28,* 50–59.

Radocy, R. E. The perception of melody, harmony, rhythm, and form. In D. A. Hodges (Ed.), *Handbook of music psychology.* Lawrence, Kans.: National Association for Music Therapy, 1980.

Radocy, R. E. Magnitude estimation of melodic dissimilarity. *Psychology of Music,* 1982, *10*(1), 28–32.

Radocy, R. E., & Boyle, J. D. *Psychological foundations of musical behavior.* Springfield, Ill.: Charles C Thomas, 1979.

Rainbow, E. L. A pilot study to investigate the constructs of musical aptitude. *Journal of Research in Music Education*, 1965, *13*, 3–14.

Roederer, J. G. *Introduction to the physics and psychophysics of music* (2nd ed.). New York: Springer-Verlag, 1975.

Seashore, C. E. *Psychology of music.* New York: McGraw-Hill, 1938.

Seashore, C. E., Lewis, L., & Saetveit, J. G. *Seashore measures of musical talents.* New York: The Psychological Corporation, 1960.

Sergeant, D. Measurement of pitch discrimination. *Journal of Research in Music Education*, 1973, *21*, 3–19.

Sergeant, D., & Thatcher, G. Intelligence, social status, and musical abilities. *Psychology of Music*, 1974, *2*(2), 32–57.

Sherbon, J. W. The association of hearing acuity, displacusis, and discrimination with musical performances. *Journal of Research in Music Education*, 1975, *23*, 249–257.

Williams, D. B. Short-term retention of pitch sequence. *Journal of Research in Music Education*, 1975, *26*, 57–60.

Wing, H. D. A factorial study of musical tests. *British Journal of Psychology*, 1941, *31*, 341–355.

Wing, H. D. Some applications of test results to education in music. *British Journal of Educational Psychology*, 1954, *24*, 161–170.

Wing, H. D. *Standardised tests of musical intelligence.* The Mere, England: National Foundation for Educational Research, 1961.

Wyatt, R. F. Improvability of pitch discrimination. *Psychological Monographs*, 1945, *58*(2, Whole No. 267).

Young, W. T. The Bentley "measures of musical abilities": A congruent validity report. *Journal of Research in Music Education*, 1973, *21*, 74–79.

Zwicker, E., Flottorp, G., & Stevens, S. S. Critical band width in loudness summation. *Journal of the Acoustical Society of America*, 1957, *29*, 548–557.

[21]

Teaching Problem Solving in Practice

By James L. Byo

Musicians practice to build endurance, flexibility, and dexterity. They practice to *maintain* good performance, to sight-read better, to memorize, and simply, to enjoy music making. There are other motivations for practice, but one, more than others, is a catalyst for consequential change in musical development—practicing to solve performance problems.

This article examines problem solving in instrumental music practice and is based on the notion that too many students, too much of the time, look and feel inadequate when they attempt to problem solve. Consider, for example, two practice scenarios. Student 1 finds the music in measure 12 awkward, and every time he reaches the measure, he slows down or stops. He should drill this measure—and *only* this measure—but left to his own devices, he ignores the problem and moves on; or he starts from the beginning, even though he can play the first eleven measures flawlessly; or he drills the measure by playing it over and over—six times incorrectly, the last time correctly. Then he moves on, convinced that he is doing the right thing. He identified a problem, and he repeated the section until he got it right—but six times wrong and one time right is not the kind of repetition that will make him successful.

James L. Byo is professor of music education at Louisiana State University in Baton Rouge, LA. He can be reached at jbyo@lsu.edu.

Student 2, on the other hand, recognizes measure 12 as a "work place" because a pattern has developed; every time he plays this measure, he hesitates, stops, or thinks "it just doesn't sound good." He knows that by devoting extra time to measure 12, he may not get through the entire lesson or etude during this practice session—but that's acceptable. The student slows down and finds an errorless starting tempo. With a metro-nome, he plays the work place twice in a row with no mistakes, ignoring the slur and the crescendo. Before increasing speed, he plays the measure with expression and no mistakes twice in a row. Next, he increases the metronome four beats per minute and plays the measure with expression and without mistakes twice in a row. When he inches the metronome up another four beats per minute, he has trouble playing the measure correctly, so he reduces the difficulty by isolating the two problematic notes within the measure. He plays them very slowly, thinking about his finger movement. He rehearses the movement silently until he feels ready to play the entire measure with the metronome twice in a row without errors. Finally, he puts the measure back into the music, playing it with the measures that precede and follow it. He plays this larger section twice without errors, marking this tempo in his music.

The Accomplished Practicer

Music teachers who try to envision students solving performance problems as described above are doing what expert teachers do when they plan for instruction. Expert teachers ask, "What do I want my students to look like as accomplished learners?"[1] Expressed differently, they ask, "What do I want my students to know and do when they take the test?" Music teachers might ask, "What do I want my students to look like as accomplished practicers?" In this case, the "test" is a home practice session six weeks from now. After six weeks of instruction, will a student left to his or her own devices choose to problem solve, and if so, what will the problem-solving process entail? Expert teachers ask these questions _before_

Figure 1. Work Place Practice Protocol

❑ **Level 1. Choose a "work place" (a section of music that makes you hesitate or stop, or just doesn't sound right).** Professional musicians do it. Why shouldn't you?

❑ **Level 2. Slow down! Find a mistake-free tempo.** You'll probably have to slow down more than you think.

❑ **Level 3. Set the metronome.** The metronome is the "truth machine."

❑ **Level 4. Play the work place two times in a row mistake free.** The optimal number of times depends on the nature of the challenge, but twice in a row is a great place to start.

❑ **Level 5. Play the work place expressively two times in a row mistake free.** Including the expressive elements is a new level of difficulty. The goal is to play or sing beautifully _always_, not just as the audition nears.

❑ **Level 6. Inch forward.** Increase difficulty in small steps. While you might feel like leaping forward, remember that it takes a concerted effort to change your thinking. You are teaching your mind and body. Don't be in a hurry. Give it a chance!

❑ **Level 7. Leap back.** Sometimes you have to decrease the level of difficulty to jump-start correct repetition.

❑ **Level 8. Put the work place back into the music.** This can be a new level of difficulty.

❑ **Level 9. Record the final successful tempo.** Document the tempo for tomorrow. Practicing on consecutive days is always a good idea.

instruction begins. They work hard to develop a clear answer, even if it involves some struggle in revising and refining ideas that are initially incomplete or unclear. Finally, they set out to make it happen with their students.

> _Music teachers might ask, "What do I want my students to look like as accomplished practicers?"_

On the surface, the guidance on problem solving in practice that many music teachers offer their students looks much like the approach of

Student 2. They urge students to isolate and simplify difficult passages, caution students about incorrect repetition, and demonstrate proven practice techniques in the hope that students will choose good problem-solving strategies when practicing at home. This approach is clearly well intentioned, but it lacks an overarching structure and precise definition. Further, it focuses on what the teacher does (urge, advise, demonstrate) rather than what the student does in terms of practice. It leaves to chance how the student will practice away from the lesson.

The Work Place Practice Protocol shown in figure 1 is one example of an overarching structure in problem solving that can be adapted for use by students of any age or maturity. It provides a starting point, an ending point, and a sequence of in-between steps that address common questions. When does one set the metronome? _After_ a mistake-free tempo has been found. When does one play expressively? _Before_ the inching forward process begins. Students need to know that this structure can and should be applied to difficult passages in all music, not just to the particular piece being studied.

> *If problem solving in practice is important, then it must be a planned part of the lesson.*

Students benefit from being taught precise meanings of the words "isolate and simplify," "slow down," and "repetition." "Isolate" is a process that extends far beyond the admonition, "Take a small section of the music and work on it." Teachers should define "isolate" in specific, what-to-do terms. By defining "slow down" as slow enough for errorless performance and by defining repetition as repeating a section *correctly* before increasing the level of difficulty in incremental steps, teachers set the stage for students to reap maximum gain from these techniques. But defining is one thing; getting students to do these techniques is another. By working on the techniques during the lesson, teachers can teach students to value efficient problem solving as a practice priority.

Teaching Problem Solving in Practice

Teaching problem solving in practice begins with answering the question, "What do I want my students to look like as accomplished practicers?" A teacher need not adopt or even agree with the approach to practice explained in this article. Herein lies the beauty of the question; answers may vary.

Teaching problem-solving skills involves an initial heavy investment of lesson or rehearsal time—perhaps as much as half of the total time in

the early stages! Strategies should include advising, urging, and demonstrating, but the focus should be on student decision-making in practice with students demonstrating the practice techniques. If problem solving in practice is important, then it must be a planned part of the lesson. Students must show that they are able to problem solve in the presence of the teacher. If they are unable to do so, there is little reason to expect them to problem solve away from the lesson. Subsequent monitoring and testing of student practice is less time intensive but no less important because it helps carry a well-defined "practice" theme across all lessons and rehearsals and connects lesson or rehearsal activities with home activities. A short-term decrease in repertoire covered is minor when compared with the potential for long-term gain!

A program of assessment can facilitate the teaching of problem solving in practice in a number of ways. The tasks and assignments with assessments shown in figures 2 through 7 structure opportunities for students to practice practicing. The experiences teach students that certain approaches to practice have predictably positive results, which create feelings of accomplishment. The assessments provide information about how students are doing with the instruction and experiences provided. This information helps the teacher determine pertinent corrective instruction. Testing problem solving in practice encourages students to view both problem solving and the *process* of problem solving as priorities.

The tasks and assignments in the figures feature problem-solving opportunities that are increasingly

Figure 2. Practice Protocol: Lesson Task

Level 1. Choosing Work Places During the Lesson

1. Play the assigned piece.
2. Identify a work place.
3. The teacher will evaluate your choice of work place and the amount of isolated material.
4. The teacher will use this opportunity to discuss your choice of work place and its length.

Grading

Novice: Your response is not that of an accomplished practicer.
Developing: Your response is that of an accomplished practicer at times.
Distinguished: Your response is that of an accomplished practicer.

Figure 3. Practice Protocol: Ensemble or Lesson Assignment

Level 1. Choosing Work Places at Home

1. On practice day 1, tape record yourself as you practice the assigned piece.
2. Ask yourself, "Where do I make mistakes? Where does it sound wrong? Where do I stop and start again? Where do I hesitate?"
3. On your music, neatly circle two of these work places.
4. Rewind the tape to the beginning of the first work place.
5. Label the tape with your name.

Grading

5 points: Tape submitted on time, rewound, and labeled. Choice of work place and amount of isolated material are appropriate.
3 points: Tape submitted on time, rewound, and labeled. Choice of work place and/or amount of isolated material are deficient.
0 points: Tape not submitted.

Figure 4. Practice Protocol: Ensemble or Lesson Assignment

Level 2. Finding a Mistake-Free Tempo

1. One time this week, tape record yourself as you practice the assigned piece.
2. Choose a work place.
3. Find a tempo at which you can play the work place mistake free.
4. Play the work place twice in a row without mistakes. Ask yourself, "Am I playing the notes correctly? Am I playing the rhythms correctly?" If you make a mistake, practice until you can play it twice in a row without mistakes.
5. Find this tempo on your metronome and write the number on your music.
6. Rewind the tape to the beginning of the work place.
7. Label the tape with your name.

Grading

5 points: Tape submitted on time, rewound, and labeled. Choice of work place and amount of isolated material are appropriate. Work place was played two times in a row without mistakes. Metronome tempo is written on the music.

3 points: Tape submitted on time, rewound, and labeled. One or more of the following is deficient: choice of work place, amount of isolated material, errorless tempo, or documentation of tempo.

0 points: Tape not submitted.

Figure 5. Practice Protocol: Ensemble or Lesson Assignment

Level 6. Inching Forward

1. One time this week, tape record yourself as you practice one solo piece.
2. Choose a work place.
3. Find a tempo at which you can play the work place mistake free.
4. Play the work place twice in a row without mistakes. If you make a mistake, practice until you can play it twice in a row without mistakes.
5. If you ignored the expressive elements, put them back in now, and play it twice in a row without mistakes.
6. Inch forward in four beat per minute increments and repeat the above steps until you reach a tempo of twelve beats per minute faster than your original tempo or the optimal tempo for this piece, whichever comes first.
7. Find this tempo on your metronome and write the number on your music.
8. Rewind the tape to the beginning of the practice piece.
9. Label the tape with your name.

Grading

5 points: Tape submitted on time, rewound, and labeled. Choice of work place and amount of isolated material are appropriate. Work place was played expressively twice in a row without mistake. Process was followed to an increase of twelve beats per minute or to the optimal tempo. Metronome tempo is written on the music.

3 points: Tape submitted on time, rewound, and labeled. One or more of the following was deficient: choice of work place, amount of isolated material, errorless tempo, expressive performance, repetition at increased tempos, or documentation of final tempo.

0 points: Tape not submitted.

more advanced. They break down the practice protocol of figure 1 into its various steps with each task focusing on a single step of the protocol. Some tasks are designed for private instruction, others for the ensemble experience. Some are intended for use during the lesson or rehearsal, others for students to "take home" experiences begun in the lesson or rehearsal for continued study.

Figure 2 shows a task that provides opportunity for novices to practice choosing work places during the lesson in the presence of the teacher. Figure 3 presents an assignment that similarly challenges the student in choosing a work place, but in the home setting, where the student audiotapes his or her practice for a record of what happens when the teacher is not present. Figure 4 is a more advanced assignment because it assumes the student is able to choose an appropriate work place. The objective is to find a mistake-free tempo. The assignment in figure 5 covers the "inching forward" step of the practice protocol. The lesson or rehearsal task shown in figure 6 involves a simple yes/no evaluation form. Students go in a predetermined order to a practice room where audio- or videotape equipment records each practice performance. One student waits "on deck" outside the testing room ready to enter immediately following the previous student. When students are taught to exit and enter the rehearsal set unobtrusively, testing can occur with minimal distraction.[2] Figure 7 is a paper-and-pencil test that asks the student to list the problem-solving steps. To be independent in using the process, students must know the steps in the correct order.

Grading criteria are provided, allowing students to know from the beginning what is expected. For the sake of illustration, various grading options are provided, though teachers may have their own preferences for grading. It is also important to note that while this article addresses practice focused on targeting and mastering difficult passages, the problem-solving process is applicable with minor variation to other skill-development areas, such as embouchure, hand position, air support, and tonguing.

Figure 6. Practice Protocol: Ensemble or Lesson Assignment

Level 7. Lesson/Rehearsal Practice Challenge

You will be presented with a work place you have not seen before. You will practice it for four minutes, and then your teacher will evaluate you based on the following questions. Did you

1. find an errorless slow starting tempo on the metronome?	Yes No
2. play the work place two times in a row with out mistakes?	Yes No
3. play the work place *expressively* two times in a row without mistakes if you initially ignored expressive elements?	Yes No N/A
4. inch forward in four beat per minute increments and repeat the above steps until time was up or you reached the optimal tempo?	Yes No
5. decrease level of difficulty, if necessary?	Yes No N/A
6. write the final tempo on the music?	Yes No

Figure 7. Practice Protocol: Ensemble or Lesson Assignment

List the Work Place Practice Steps in order.

Conclusion

The path to solving a performance problem need not be mysterious. Students need not feel inadequate when they attempt to problem solve in practice. There are paths that lead students to experience tangible progress in the short and long terms as well as more frequent feelings of accomplishment. One such path is suggested in this article. It entails asking what an accomplished practicer is, devoting significant lesson or rehearsal time to teaching students how to problem solve, and developing a program of assessment—even a very modest one—to enhance instruction.

Notes

1. Robert A. Duke, "Intelligent Assessment in General Music: What Children Should Know and (Be Able to) Do," *General Music Today* 13, no. 1 (1999): 12.
2. James L. Byo, "Designing Substantive Playing Tests—A Model," *Music Educators Journal* 88, no. 2 (2001): 39–44. ∎

[22]

Assessment's Potential in Music Education

RICHARD COLWELL

An entire section of the first *Handbook of Research on Music Teaching and Learning* was devoted to assessment. Those authors successfully summarized the history of assessment in music with chapters on assessment in five areas: teaching, creativity, program, general, and attitude. This chapter is an update on a few of the issues raised in the first *Handbook*.

In the 1990s, assessment is one of the more important issues in education. The priority of education in the United States has risen, and now education outweighs almost all other social issues—immigration, the homeless, welfare, national defense, and even foreign policy. Evaluation's importance is portrayed by its use in the struggle for power over the curriculum. Arts advocates welcome positive assessments, some of which are relatively marginal in value. The high public interest and greatly expanded funding for education, preschool through college, has brought to the playing field two assessment issues, standards and accountability. The definition of a standard is a description of how well or at what level a student is expected to perform, and accountability is the avenue for ascertaining that value for resources expended is attained. A few individuals have questioned whether assessment as the single means of establishing value is appropriate (Broadfoot, 2000). High-stakes evaluation has become the subject of educational and political debates, often so emotional as to complicate the resolution of the accompanying assessment issues. The U.S. Office for Civil Rights has entered the fray, publishing in December 2000 *The Use of Tests When Making High-Stakes Decisions for Students*. John Fremer (2000) suggests that the level of public debate about testing needs to be raised, as there is "so much uninformed and wrong-headed commentary." Good assessments provide data on the extent of success and failure but only hint at causes. Assessment, of course, has always been part of teaching and learning; what is new is its uses. One type of assessment, program evaluation, has become a major discipline that provides data on programs as diverse as welfare, the military, and education. In education, assessment is used to portray the success of society in enabling all students to attain high standards in multiple areas, with the additional role of determining the value of funding for administration, programs, and facilities—these in addition to its continued role in aiding teaching and learning.

The focus of the chapter is a description of selected recent developments in assessment in education and in music teaching and learning. It is written for the individual who already has a basic grasp of the principles of assessment. Not much space is devoted to such important admonitions as the following:

1. There must be a direct match between the curriculum and what the student is expected to know and do in the assessment. (Note: a major section is devoted to research in taxonomies, which is intended to assure a close relationship between the curriculum and any assessment.)
2. On-demand assessments should address important outcomes, not trivial items selected for ease of measurement.
3. Allowing students to answer three out of five question is inappropriate on high-stakes tests. All questions should be important; all questions must be answered to determine minimal competency.

The statement that what is tested is what is taught (often used pejoratively) does not indicate a fault of the assessment system; it arises when teachers and curriculum writers are insecure about the importance and priority of the goals of instruction. Assessors have a range of excellent devices to provide data on a variety of educational procedures and products, but in the hands of the inept one or more of these tools can be counterproductive to attaining the goals of schooling.

Overview

A number of issues cloud discussions about assessment. *High-stakes assessment* is the focus of wrangling about the value and use of assessments in education. The definition of *high-stakes* is not firm; it generally refers to situations where the assessment determines whether a student passes a grade level, graduates from secondary or tertiary school, is licensed to teach, or is denied renewal of licensure of accreditation based upon an assessment. An audition or interview can be high-stakes (for example, failure to qualify for the Boston Marathon), the height of the stake depending upon the importance placed on the task by the individual or the culture. Concern intensifies when a single assessment is used in these high-stakes events, although the definition of single assessment is also controversial. Does a battery of tests that encompasses many competencies constitute a single assessment? When one has several opportunities to pass an assessment, is this a "single assessment"? There are few, if any, high-stakes assessments in the pre-K–12 school music program, although selection for the madrigals may seem high-stakes to the auditioning singers. Arts advocates champion music as a basic subject without realizing that basic subjects are those subjects of sufficient importance to society that a high-stakes test may be required. Language arts and mathematical competence are the most common high-stakes subjects. High-stakes testing is a component of the standards movement, with most states developing such assessment in conjunction with their standards. The literature and discussion of high-stakes assessment are useful to music educators to the extent that improvements in its use aid development of better measures in music.

Evaluation and *assessment* are used interchangeably in this chapter. *Measurement* has traditionally referred to a single test, a test being the smallest unit in education. Individuals are measured in terms of height or weight but not in terms of personal characteristics. *Evaluation* is distinguished by the making of judgments based on the data derived from measurements and other procedures, while *assessment* refers to a considerable body of data that has the potential to diagnose and provide clues to causes. Assessment is then used to improve or judge instruction or do both.

Little distinction is made in this chapter between achievement and ability; the term *aptitude* is today seldom used in education and is not used here. *Achievement* customarily refers to short-term learning, *ability* to more long-term outcomes. No priority is assigned to the relative importance of facts, knowledge, concepts, principles, understandings, creativity, critical thinking, metacognition, strategic knowledge, procedural knowledge, performance, and other worthwhile outcomes. Each outcome is appropriate at times. Also, no priority is assigned to types of assessments: auditions, rubrics, portfolios, videos, observations, demonstrations, exhibitions, fill-in-the-blanks, performances, interviews, essays, classroom discussion, research papers, and multiple-choice tests; each is situationally appropriate depending upon the task to be assessed and how instruction has been conducted.

Authentic assessment as a descriptor is avoided, as it is seldom related to assessment in music education. Almost all assessment in music is authentic. The more important concern is transfer of what has been learned. Critical reflection and self-assessment are also not addressed despite their presence in the educational literature. Self-assessment, especially of skills, is more complex than most realize; its importance is instructional. Reflection is also important. Experiencing music, however, is more important than talking *about* music, and an emphasis on reflection as an assessment technique could influence the objectives of instruction, an influence that should be avoided.

Rubrics is another hazy term; it refers to a tool for evaluation of performance in the areas of teaching, composing, conducting, improvising, singing, and playing. Such rubrics have seldom been subjected to the rigor required in assessment, and their misuse is potentially damaging to the assessment profession. They are most useful on items about which there is general consensus as to what constitutes excellence.

Organization

Eight areas have been selected as topics for the chapter. First, "Dependent Variables in Research" and "Recently Published Tests" describe the published research that relates to assessment since the publication of the first *Handbook* in 1992. Second, "Unpublished Measures" describes unpublished instruments that were systematically developed. Third is a brief discussion of the criteria for a rubric to be used as an assessment device and the rubric's limitations. Fourth, there is a brief description of the potential of program evaluation in music. Fifth, the various types of validity are defined; sixth, recent developments in educational taxonomies are outlined. Here the intent is to emphasize the importance of connecting instructional objectives and procedures with assessment. Seventh and eighth are the chapter's two concluding sections, one on the potential of technology in assessment, the other on what the future of assessment *may* be should the current reform movement result in systemic change in education. As the extent of change in education or in the music program is hypothetical, the future of assessment can be based only on current premises.

Assessment in Music Education

To achieve high standards for everyone requires an extensive assessment program to chart progress and to facilitate learning in a multitude of areas: facts, skills, understandings, self-esteem, metacognition, and interest in continuing to learn. Past assessment measures have not provided satisfactory answers; if those measures had been adequate, education would not be so impoverished, with many of the traditional assessment measures completely inadequate for any high-stakes evaluation. Educators and others have criticized assessment devices and procedures for not being valid, for being poorly connected to the competencies expected of students, and for failing to provide data needed for change. Assessment, however, is not an exact science; there will always be a certain amount of error, providing an opportunity not only for the politicization of assessment but also, more important, for the voicing of many viewpoints and interpretations.

It is difficult to suggest just how important assessment is to music education in the 21st century, as music education is not connected to education in the same manner as mathematics, language arts, science, or even social studies. Music education is not one of the subjects criticized for its lack of effectiveness; music's public issue has been an inadequate amount of instructional time due to its low priority in the eyes of most educational administrators, at the local and/or state level. Program evaluation is hampered by the existence of two (or more) independent music programs: required music education and elective music education, each with variations. Variations of required music programs include integrated course work, enhancement of other subjects, and recreation. Elective music—band, orchestra, choir, guitar, group piano, advanced placement theory, and more—is focused on skill development, and these experiences, traditionally defined, have few common outcomes. With such diversity, development of assessments of student competency in music has been impeded due to multiple *satisfactory* outcomes. It is likely, although not certain, that music would command higher priority on the school's resources if a music assessment were high-stakes—and high-stakes at every grade level. Any judgment about the importance of assessment must wrestle with the initial question of whether the purpose of assessment is aiding progress toward achieving "standards" or toward accountability, an important difference. The accountability movement currently appears to have more support than the standards movement. Use of assessment to improve instruction remains relevant.

Music educators may decide that their outcomes are not high-stakes and take a lower road toward assessment, but if so there will still be a need to rethink the role of assessment and music's relationship to basic subjects. Further, new curricula, new ways of teaching, new priorities require new forms of assessment. Ratings at contests and festivals and student satisfaction have been the primary assessment indicators in music; these do not reveal current program strengths and weaknesses and provide only partial answers in any assessment endeavor.

Evidence from learning psychology reveals that assessment properly conducted makes a major difference in student learning and, when incorrectly used, a corresponding negative effect. The current hype, however, has not produced much action in music education in the United States, Canada, or Great Britain. To many music educators, assessment is so much a part of instruction—especially in achieving goals in performance—that they do not believe more is needed. Other music educators believe that any assessment is inappropriate as either too quantitative or too mechanical. The literature commonly divides assessment by its purpose, summative assessment indicating degree of worth of the finished product, formative assessment indicating only feedback obtained in the process of moving toward the final goal or outcome. Assessment when embedded in music instruction is formative evaluation because its primary purpose is to improve the performance and, one would hope, the learning. Despite the desire of arts advocacy groups to have "hard" data on music learning, there has been little interest in summative evaluation of learning in required music instruction and only slightly more interest in outcomes of elective music experiences. The expensive 1997 arts assessment by NAEP (National Assessment of Educational Progress) had little effect on teaching priorities, and few teachers can relate the results or describe their programs in relation to these national outcomes. Pockets of interested officials, such as SCASS (State Collaborative on Assessment and Student Standards), are pondering arts assessment issues, but any connection with extant programs is unknown. FairTest, a nonprofit organization based in Cambridge, Massachusetts, is a national player in criticizing tests and how they are used. It looks for issues of equity in the instruments. Educational Testing Service, however, has promoted the use of evaluation devices for half a century and tends to be the natural target for barbs from FairTest. FairTest is not against all assessment (although its publications give that impression), tending to approve of portfolio assessments without addressing their equity or validity. The public generally accepts the idea of assessment as a source of data on teaching and learning, aware of its importance in describing outcomes in science and medicine. Licensing tests are accepted as routine, ranging from a license to operate a motor vehicle to a license to operate in a hospital whether with knives, machines, or on-the-couch questions. The testing of teachers prior to awarding a license has become accepted practice in 41 states, and the public currently supports an assessment to determine whether students deserve to graduate or even pass from one grade to another.

Dependent Variables in Research

With assessment in music consisting mainly of formative evaluation, a primary resource to identify devices used to assess outcomes is the body of research in the field. All research has independent and dependent variables (although those two sometimes hide under different names). The discussion that follows is a result of scrutinizing the 1990–2000 issues of the major relevant publications in the field: *Psychology of Music, Psychomusicology, Journal of Research in Music Education*, the *Bulletin of the Council for Research in Music Education, Research Studies in Music Education, Music Education Research*, the *British Journal of Music Education*, and *Dissertation Abstracts International*. The studies cited were selected to indicate *types* of assessment used, with no judgment of their appropriateness. Many of the studies have serious flaws in the research design or in the interpretation of results and would not be cited in a chapter on research.

Continuous Response Digital Interface

The paucity of use of valid and reliable measures as dependent variables is surprising, as is the frequent use of observation or description, these latter procedures unaccompanied by a description of their systematic development. A Continuous Response Digital Interface (CRDI) developed at Florida State University was the dependent measure in a large number of studies (Blocker, Greenwood, & Shellahamer, 1997; Brittin, 1996; Brittin & Duke, 1997; Brittin & Sheldon, 1995; Byrnes, 1997; Davis, 1998; DeNardo & Kantorski, 1995, 1998; W. Fredrickson, 1994, 1995, 1997, 1999; Geringer, 1995; Gregory, 1994; Johnson, 1996; Lychner, 1998; Madsen, 1997a, 1997b, 1998; Madsen, Brittin, & Capprella-Sheldon, 1993; Rentz, 1992; Sheldon, 1994; Sheldon & Gregory, 1997; Siebenaler, 1997; Skadsem, 1997). Initially this device was used only to report on one dimension of a subject's response to musical stimuli; by the end of the decade the device was sufficiently more sophisticated so that it could provide a reading on two responses. The reading is displayed on a dial, connected to a computer. The connection with the computer provides multiple readings per second and thus provides data that are reliable. The validity of the data remains unknown. The premise for its use is that there is a match between aesthetic response, the dial reading, and the place in the score at which the reading was taken. Should *reflection* be necessary to respond, the CRDI would mea-

sure an important *preaesthetic* point. The chief developer of the CRDI reports that the same information is obtained that one obtains from a paper-and-pencil test, a finding that is supportive of its concurrent validity (Madsen, 1997a, p. 64). A current criticism of assessments throughout education is that they are not authentic; that the evaluation is not "real-world" but an artificial, multiple-choice assessment. Authenticity is not a major issue in music research, as nearly every dependent variable involves some type of music performance. Assessment critics would fault the CRDI because manipulating a dial is artificial to the same extent as a multiple-choice test is. In defense of its partial authenticity, the CRDI has been used with recordings of accepted great music similar to the requirement of many multiple-choice tests.

Along with authentic assessment, reflection is promoted as an assessment tool. Requiring students to describe musical meaning and understanding is troublesome. Students with equal understanding are not equally verbal. Even the terms *higher* and *lower* are confusing to young music students (Hair, 1997); thus attempts to measure student reflections when the experience entails far more complex musical concepts calls into question the potential of student verbalization as an important assessment tool.

Observation

The most common dependent variable in the research studies examined was simple observation of student and teacher performance, either live or videotaped. No observation schedule provided data on its validity or reliability, whether a Likert scale or a professional description of the observation was used. A common study was one that modeled the observation form used in earlier studies by Madsen and Yarbrough, but no statements were made that concerned the rigor of the form's development or the adaptation (Elkholm, 2000). An encouraging trend is an increase in the number of points on the Likert scales used, often 7 or 9; Yarbrough's observation of teaching videos used 10 criteria (Effective Teaching Response Form, [Yarbrough & Henley, 1999]). Curiously, no criteria for excellence in teaching exist. To avoid establishing criteria, Goolsby (1996) identified three levels of teaching: student teachers, first-year teachers, and experienced teachers, rough categories if teaching excellence is the research criterion.

The misconceptions about the validity of many of the dependent variables indicate the present naïveté of much music education research. The use of observation as a valid assessment tool is one of the most flagrant flaws. Observation is an extremely crude method of determining the extent of learning in music, as a little serious thought will reveal. Yet teachers are often evaluated solely on the basis of observation, a process that does not reveal their teaching capabilities and gives only minimal evidence of student learning that occurs as a result of the teaching intervention. A student performance, live or recorded, is perhaps a better assessment device, but any single performance provides only an approximation of musicianship, musical understanding, attitude toward learning music, knowledge of and about music, or ability to discriminate. A seminal article on the weaknesses of observation in music (Froelich, 1995) pointed up that observer agreement and precision of agreement reveal little about the validity and reliability of assessing the behavior of the teacher. Froelich argues that valid observations require: (1) that they be derived from a specific instructional theory; (2) that, once collected, they are examined within the context of that theory; and (3) accuracy, which depends upon not only the construct of interest to the researcher but also on the participants' agreement that what was observed reflected their own interpretation of the behavior under study (p. 188). Froelich's arguments begin to address the complexities of observing teaching and learning and the minimal requirements for generalizability, transfer, and assumption of task and attribute relationship. As in all research and evaluation, estimation of error is important, and without well-designed investigative procedures predicting the amount of error is extremely difficult.

Other Measures

On the few occasions where the semantic differential was used as an assessment measure, there was a consistent lack of the expected rigor, that is, of establishing the viability of the semantic differential, and a statement of the extent to which the three constructs that are the usual outcomes—evaluation, potency, and activity—related to the research question.

Music education researchers did use a few dependent measures from outside the field to assess basic knowledge, personality, or teacher competencies; those that were used were rarely employed more than once during the past decade. Thoe measures emphasized an affective component—Gregorc's *Style Delineator*, Eysenck's tests, and the Dunn, Dunn, and Price *Learning Indicator*. The competence devices used more than once included the *Wechsler PreSchool Test*, the *Developing Cognitive Abilities Test*, the *Watkins-Farnum Performance Scale*, the Ohio and Australian proficiency examination, the Asmus attitude scale (unpublished), and Gordon's *Primary Measures of Music Audiation*.

Summary

Inspection of the dependent variables in published research and doctoral dissertations reveals little change from past practice, that is, teacher/researcher/panel of judges deter-

mining treatment effect. Interjudge reliability is generally high except in judging musical compositions. This interjudge reliability is a correlation among judges, not between judge and dependent variable. Limited use was made of researcher-constructed instruments, only one of which was examined for reliability except as noted in "Recently Published Tests," later in this chapter. Researchers appeared to believe there was no need to determine reliability or validity of interviews, observations, and especially Likert scales.

Recently Published Tests

Edwin Gordon's Readiness Test

Only one new test was published during the past decade—Edwin Gordon's *Harmonic Improvisation Readiness Record* and *Rhythm Improvisation Readiness Record* (1998)—which is actually two tests, as the scores of the two parts are not combined. As the title suggests, this readiness test was not developed as an achievement test but more as a needs-assessment measure. Its use to measure improvisational competence has not been established, nor does the author suggest this as a use. These tests are important as they continue to emphasize Gordon's primary contribution to music education, which is the centrality of the *mental conception* of music, an ability he has termed audiation. One wonders why there has not been more emphasis placed on teaching audiation in music classrooms, as this competency is essential to attaining many of the goals of the complete musician. It may be that teachers relate audiation only to creating and improvising and believe, as Gordon states in the test manual, "neither improvisation nor creativity . . . can be taught" (p. 8). The test results are of interest, as the scores for students in third-grade general music do not differ significantly from those of high school students in selective ensembles. One of the author's explanations for the lack of difference is that little instructional effort has been exerted to attain the needed competencies.

Gordon describes three ways one can improvise (possible dependent variables): One may perform a variation of a melody, without giving attention to the underlying existent or implied harmony (p. 8); a melody may be performed over a series of harmonic patterns (harmonic progressions); and harmonic patterns may be improvised to an old or new melody (p. 9).

Technical Considerations. The manual has numerous typographical errors, making it difficult to be confident of any critique. The sample size used to establish the norms is more than 15,000 students, Grades 3–12 (p. 48); the Ns for Grades 3–6, 7–8, and 9–12 are not provided. The number of students by grade level is established, however, based on a study conducted in Gilbert, South Carolina (pp. 58–

59), where the total N was 918. In a second study, a clever strategy to establish validity was to have 95 fourth- and fifth-grade students in a parochial school listen to six recorded unfamiliar songs, performed twice, and ask the students to "sing a response that sounded like the song but was not an imitation of the song."

Gordon concludes that the harmony and rhythm tests are independent and that the rhythm test is more basic (p. 76). He asserts that students with scores of 22 and above are "ready." As a score of 20 can be obtained by chance (40 items with response of "same" or "not same"), additional research is necessary. Researchers interested in test development should study Tables 7 and 8 (pp. 52–53), Item Difficulty and Item Discrimination for Grades 3–12, as both indices are nearly the same for all 86 items for Grades 3–6, 7–8, and 9–12, one of the most impressive examples of item stability for any test battery.

Nonstandard Published Measures

One test published only on the computer, John Flohr's *Contemporary Rhythm Skills Assessment* (2000), is computer-administered. It is designed to assess steady beat and rhythm pattern competence of students ages 4–12. It can be accurate to a millisecond. Part 1 consists of a folk song played at five different tempi; the task is to supply the beat. In part 2, the testee must listen to and repeat 20 rhythm patterns by tapping on the computer's space bar. A critique is not possible due to the fact that the results from students of nine different age groups, 4–12, are combined, making the data difficult to interpret.

James Froseth and Molly Weaver published *Music Teacher Self-Assessment* (1996), but this is not an assessment tool. Its purpose is to train teachers in observation techniques. The authors made no attempt to establish any validity or reliability for the observation scales or to argue that the observations are focused on important teaching ventures. It is also not based on any observational research. The use of the word *assessment* in the title is misleading.

Unpublished Measures

Instrumental Music Assessment

Gary McPherson (1995) developed a five-part assessment for instrumental music as his doctoral dissertation and has since continued its development. McPherson's work is important because he addresses concerns of teachers—practice, technique, and improvisation. His test is appropriate for Australian music education, where there is more emphasis on aural skills, musicology, theory, listening, appraising music, and composing, a much broader program than found in instrumental music instruction in the United

States. The current tentative movement toward teaching more *music* in the rehearsal indicates the importance of a careful review of McPherson's assessment research. His contribution is more a think piece to the literature in assessment than a rigorously developed assessment instrument. McPherson's concern was instructional; the tests were his way of attempting to identify strategies that students use in performing. In a search for learning strategies, McPherson provides an excellent description of the process of learning to play an instrument, enabling the reader to make a decision on the content- and criterion-related validity of the assessment measures. McPherson's term is *convergent* validity. Test reliability is not addressed; data on the reliability of the judges are provided, but this reliability number is not informative about the tests themselves, their coverage, length, and other qualities that would be important should the test be considered as a high-stakes measure. McPherson's primary concern was assessment of the student's musical memory and ability to play by ear. His sample consisted of 101 clarinet and trumpet students who lived in New South Wales, Australia, and were preparing to take the Australian Music Examinations Board (AMEB), which assesses a student's ability to perform a repertoire of rehearsal music. As his interest was in high school students, he divided his sample into students 12–15 years of age and those 15–18. (Often test developers seek a disparate group, as reliability may be enhanced when students vary.) McPherson used the *Watkins-Farnum Performance Scale* as a measure of sight-reading and data from the 12-point rating scale of performance from the AMEB test. He then created three additional measures, one assessing the ability to perform from memory, one the ability to play by ear, and a third to improvise. McPherson established pitch, rhythm, and phrasing as the criteria and asked three judges to rate the performance on a 6-point scale: no attempt, very poor, fair, good, reasonably accurate, and no errors.

Playing by ear was defined as the ability to perform a melody shortly after hearing it, perform a piece held in long-term memory that was learned aurally, and transpose a piece learned under one of the two methods. It was necessary for McPherson to identify two well-known songs for which his subjects had never seen the notation.

McPherson constructed a two-part test, the first part requiring the students to play "Happy Birthday" in two keys, F and G, and "For He's a Jolly Good Fellow" in F and C. Part 2 consisted of four short melodies played by the same instrument as that of the student. The melodies were played four times, with a one-measure rest between each playing. After each melody, the subject was asked to play the melody twice in the original key and twice in the transposed key. The evaluation was, again, on a 6-point scale for both renditions.

The third test, on ability to improvise, consisted of

seven items. Items 1 and 2 required the student to formulate an answering phrase to a four-measure musical question. Item 3 required a rhythmic improvisation to a melody that used only the durations of a given rhythm pattern. Items 4 and 5 provided an opening phrase for an improvisation. In Item 6, students were given a recorded piano accompaniment and asked to improvise a melody. Item 7 was a free improvisation in any style.

Having an instrumental music test available other than the Watkins-Farnum may encourage teaching the competencies McPherson investigated. McPherson's interpretation of his results suggests that the study of piano is important; beginning instruction at a young age helps, as well as the more obviously important mental rehearsal and envisioning how one would perform a song or improvisation on one's instrument. The requirement for judges makes the test inconvenient to administer.

Cognitive-Affective Measure

Lee Bartel (1992) aided the research community by providing research data on the robustness of the semantic differential to provide a measure of cognitive and affective responses to music. His tool was appropriately named the Cognitive-Affective Response Test; it consisted of 18 semantic differential scales, 9 for each dimension. His premise is that meaning in music can be assessed using the ideas of Charles Osgood (1957) in measuring meaning in language. Bartel emphasized the importance of minimizing the *evaluative* component of the semantic differential (while retaining the cognitive and affective components) when listening to music—should meaning have a relationship to the evaluation component it would be a separate construct.

Bartel's research results indicate that careful selection of the adjectives is required before the semantic differential can be trusted as an assessment measure. If one is constructing a semantic tool (questionnaire, Likert-type scale, etc.), pilot studies are necessary. Reliability and validity are critical and must be reported. Bartel's task was to identify adjectives meaningful both to the music and to the cognitive and affective dimensions of linguistics. Bartel drew upon the philosophical position of Peter Kivy (1984), who had provided a tripartite framework of adjectives to describe music. Bartel's task was to use different musical styles (he began with classical and gospel) that loaded on his two constructs of *cognitive* and *affective* when subjected to factor analysis, as his goal was to construct a test that provided a single score of meaning. The test has not been published; this is unfortunate, as it and a study by Robert Miller (1979) are seminal works in multidimensional scaling and should be related to responses from the CRDI.

Computerized Adaptive Technology

In view of the widespread reliance on observation and professional judgment for the assessment of objectives in music, it is not surprising that little attention has been paid to capitalizing on advances in the field of measurement. Walter Vispoel (1992), an educational psychologist, applied computerized adaptive technology (CAT) to extant music aptitude tests, using item response theory (IRT). With IRT (CAT) the computer selects the next appropriate question based on the correctness of the last response. The difficulty level of the questions in the computer's item data bank must be known or estimated, as the task of the computer is to advance the competent student quickly to more demanding items (it selects easier items when a response is incorrect). Testing is begun with a question of average difficulty, and the computer takes over until the desired reliability criterion is met. The use of a computer adaptive test is particularly appealing for situations where students must listen acutely, and fatigue is an issue in obtaining reliable and valid scores. Vispoel's use of only 30 college students means that the results are tentative and considerable additional research is needed. He used the tonal memory section of Seashore's *Measures of Musical Talents*, and the musical memory subtest from the second edition of the Drake *Musical Aptitude Tests*, finding that 9 items were as reliable as 30; he estimated concurrent validity based upon student self-reports on measures used by Drake a half-century ago. As neither the Seashore nor the Drake is currently in use, Vispoel's research teases us to identify important outcomes and to construct IRT measures that cover a broad range of outcomes, including mastery, diagnostic, and grade-specific tools.

Auditory Skills and Other Efforts

Louise Buttsworth, Gerald Fogarty, and Peter Rorkle (1993) developed a test for tertiary students to replace individual auditions, using as the criterion a battery of tests given at the end of one semester of aural training. Fourteen tests were constructed, all dealing with auditory skills, most with low reliability. Their work, too complex to be summarized, is an excellent example of the difficulty of constructing even a skills assessment.

One doctoral student (McCurry, 1998) constructed a test battery based on the Voluntary National Standards to document the value of using hand chimes in fourth- and fifth-grade general music. She used 80 students divided into four groups: choral, instrumental, general music, and hand chime. Her dependent variable, a measure of achievement on the nine standards, is of interest, as it illustrates the perspective of a classroom teacher on appropriate tasks at this grade level.

Other research that involved test construction, this less rigorous, includes doctoral dissertations by Diane Hardy, The Construction and Validation of an Original Sight-Playing Test for Elementary Piano Students (1995); Claude Masear, The Development and Field Test of a Model for Evaluating Elementary String Programs (1999); Henry Mikle, The Development of an Individual Sight-Reading Inventory (1999); and Hong Wei, Development of a Melodic Achievement Test for Fourth Grades Taught by a Specific Music Learning Methodology (1995). There has been little interest in reestablishing the validity of extant tests, the one exception being a doctoral dissertation by Charles Norris (1998), who explored the relationship of the aural tonal memory section of aptitude tests to a student's ability to vocally reproduce short tonal patterns. With a (small) sample of 210 students across eight grade levels (5–12) he found a stable relationship and a correlation of .66 with the Seashore measures.

Building on her doctoral dissertation, Sheila Scott (2000) experimented with 7 students to determine if it was possible to obtain a measure of a student's understanding of the characteristics of melody through oral explanations that she called think alouds and whether the student's understanding matched 1980s learning outcomes (Biggs & Collis, 1982). Scott found the task extremely time-consuming; to create the test materials, she wrote 26 melodies that portrayed 13 different characteristics of melody. Students responded inconsistently, ranging from understanding Level 2 to Level 5 on her test. Understanding at Level 5 did not indicate understanding at Levels 1–4, raising validity and sequencing issues.

A Published but Unavailable Test

The major assessment effort of the decade was the music portion of the NAEP that assessed students in Grade 8 (Persky, Sandene, & Askew, 1998). The contribution of this assessment (other than elevating the status of music among school subjects) was the construction and scoring of open-response tasks. Students were asked to perform, to improvise, and to create, providing a comparison of student achievement on these tasks with the 1970 national assessment. The new assessment raised as many questions as it answered; for example, the final report says that no consistent pattern was found between frequency of instruction and student scores (p. 145).

Rubrics

Development and Definition

Because rubrics have become almost a separate assessment technique, a definition and a short discussion of them seem appropriate. As used for assessment, a rubric is generally a well-defined rule, guide, or standard. Teachers of composition often offer carefully worded rubrics as their sole assessment device for a classroom experience, the scoring of which is enormously time-consuming and subjective (Hickey, 1999). Rubrics are often associated with authentic assessment devices but in fact lead to standardization of responses rather than to divergent and original thought. However, rubrics can clarify performance objectives, as the student is able to understand in rather precise terms what is expected. Rubrics are highly effective in focusing student effort (narrowing it) and serve well as external motivation. The greatest use of rubrics has been in language arts, and it is clear that students can and will "write to the rubric." The appropriate research process in rubric development is to have a panel of judges evaluate a large number of musical compositions, place these in four or five categories according to worth, and then formulate rubrics that best describe the compositional attributes that distinguish each group. Once adequate research has been completed, additional student compositions can be evaluated against these rubrics.

The intent of those who believe in rubrics is to obtain a single score, often for use in high-stakes assessment. Unless the rubric becomes as detailed as a checklist, it is difficult to imagine a rubric providing feedback that would be helpful. Thomas Newkirk (2000) believes that the use of rubrics indicates a resurgence of "mechanized instruction" in writing (p. 41). He argues (in the case of English composition) that rubrics conceal or mystify the process of writing when process may be one of the objectives. Linda Mabry (1999) in an excellent treatment of rubrics and their effect on teaching argues that rubrics overwhelm the writing curriculum and that writing to the rubric is more powerful than teaching to the test. The use of rubrics has not only standardized scoring but also standardized writing. Rubric construction in music has not had any rigorous scrutiny and at present is usually an inappropriate evaluation measure. Acceptance in assessment has been based on the power of the descriptions and whether these descriptions appear to differentiate quality in products and tasks.

Use in Portfolios

Our understanding of rubrics in portfolios stems from research in language arts. Aschbacher (1999) conducted an extensive project with establishing rubrics for middle school language arts, beginning with six descriptor scales: type of assignment, type of content knowledge used, type of student response, type of choice students were given, grading dimensions used, and types of feedback provided, plus five 4-point evaluative scales: cognitive demands of the task, clarity of grading, alignment of the task with learning goals, alignment of grading criteria with learning goals, and overall task quality. The alignment between grading with rubrics and student learning was .65, not high. Teachers not only volunteered but also were paid to be interviewed and to allow the investigator to look at student work. Even experienced teachers have had insufficient preparation to use rubrics. The relationship between overall rating and grading clarity was .14, with goals/task .16 and with goals/grading .24 at the elementary school level, slightly higher for middle school. Teachers had difficulty articulating their goals for the students and had only a vague notion of the criteria they used in grading student work. Seldom were students given assignments that were both coherent and intellectually challenging, and one-third or less of the reading comprehension, draft writing, and project assignments provided any intellectual rigor. No assessment method can be successful unless there is excellent instruction.

Program Evaluation

Importance of Program Evaluation

Few examples can be found of program evaluation in music. Indeed, in the entire area of teacher education little attention is given to program evaluation. Why then is it the subject of discussion here? The answer lies in the fact that if music is to be considered as an equal subject, educators and the public will focus on the adequacy of the *program,* not the test scores of individual students enrolled in the program or the competence of ensembles. The few evaluators who have assessed music "programs" have assessed ad hoc activities such as those of composers in the schools, opera organizations, and interested groups, and activities sponsored by orchestras. Constance Gee's (1994) evaluation of the artist in the classroom accurately portrays a valid assessment of a partial program. Program evaluators, often advocates, have seldom looked at typical school programs and, when they have, have neglected to give consideration to the goals of the program.

At present, program evaluation is the dominant form of assessment in all areas affected by the federal government (and what area is today not affected by the federal government?). The Government Performance and Results Act of 1993 called for the use of performance measurement in virtually all federal agencies by the year 2000. This act has provided a major impetus to assessment of the large-scale social (and other) programs funded by the federal government (Richardson, 1992). Assessments have been conducted, for example, of programs designed to reduce smoking and alcohol use among adolescents, programs to eliminate drug usage, and programs to educate school-age children about sexually transmitted diseases. Other programs evaluated are those that concern toxic waste, catastrophic illness, air safety, deterring insider trading, terrorism, health care costs, nuclear hazards, AIDS, industry competitiveness, the trade imbalance, the social underclass, and employment for welfare mothers. There are also program assessments of those after-school and extended-day programs that receive federal money.

Music education needs to establish its place in the nation's educational priorities, but it lacks quantitative data necessary for comparison purposes or for use by efficiency experts. Government leaders use program evaluation to make decisions, especially when the data match their beliefs. Resources are allocated on the basis of program evaluations. Program evaluations are conducted for a variety of purposes: to back up beliefs, monitor public opinion, obtain a sense of what occurs in a program, show the program's importance, and affect the power structure. Arts advocates appear to have a better sense of the potential use of program evaluation data than do music teachers. Advocates sense that the reform movement is a power struggle over the curriculum, and in that struggle data from program evaluation are important, especially when standards are used for program justification. The federal government has actively supported the standards movement and has initiated program assessment on the effectiveness of curricula in most basic subjects.

Philosophies of Program Evaluation

Several differing evaluation philosophies exist, arising from the varying possible political colors of program assessment. The sheer quantity of material—citing one point of view or the other—makes fair treatment of program assessment nearly impossible. Most people in the field agree that the text by Shadish, Cook, and Leviton (1991) is the basic source. This volume, titled *Foundations of Program Evaluation: Theories of Practice,* consists of the ideas of seven leading program evaluators, followed by a critique of the strengths and weaknesses of each. Each of these seven, plus others in the field, has named his own assessment technique, making it necessary for any discussant to wade through differences among adaptive, realistic, discrepancy, cost-benefit, utilitarian, connoisseurial, planned variation cross-validation, justice, pluralistic, program theory, goal-free, and many more program evaluation models.

Purpose

In defining the purpose of evaluation, Ernest R. House (1994) cites Michael Scriven, determining the merit or worth of something according to a set of criteria, with those criteria often (but not always) explicated and justified (p. 14). House suggests that the work of evaluation consists of collecting data, including relevant values and standards, resolving inconsistencies in the values, clarifying misunderstandings and misrepresentations, rectifying false facts and assumptions, distinguishing between wants and needs, identifying all relevant dimensions of merit, finding appropriate measures for these dimensions, weighting the dimensions, validating the standards, and arriving at an evaluative conclusion which requires a synthesis of all these considerations. (p. 86)

Program evaluation, although only one facet of evaluation, encompasses all these aspects of evaluation.

Programs and policies can be simultaneously good and bad, depending upon how the evaluation is conducted and the side effects incurred. The questions asked by the evaluator about the program and its policies would include: what are the uses, the foci, the audience, the training, what data must be collected, and so on. *Good* and *bad* are relative terms. The individuals involved in any single evaluation project will have different interests and will approach education with fairly clear but differing ideas about what are valid education and music education programs. Because these differences exist, clear statements of program purpose are required, as well as the ability on the part of the evaluator to understand the reasoning of those affected by the evaluation. Often the resources to fund program evaluation in education are inadequate for the length of time required for educational interventions to have any effect; thus the history of program evaluation in education appears to show that (most) interventions do not have a lasting effect on learning. Among the many types of program evaluation, two are distinctive. The first, associated with Scriven (1993, 1997), requires that the evaluator provide his or her interpretation of the data and make a judgment of the program's worth. Judgments and recommendations often require hard choices, and this type of evaluation brings evaluators close to or into the political arena of education. A second school of thought would have an external evaluator gather data, then put that data in the hands of the program manager for the stakeholders to interpret (Stake, 1991, 2000). Often this approach involves negotiating among all involved in the assessment to arrive at the meaning of the data and decisions to be made. This approach avoids, for the external evaluator, both the "summative" decision and the task of interpreting raw and derived scores, as well as establishing the significance of any differences.

Focus

Cronbach (1995) took issue with the general experimental model for gathering program evaluation data when he suggested that the primary purpose of an evaluator was to be a program *improver* (p. 27). He put the emphasis on formative rather than summative evaluation, suggesting that the primary purpose of evaluation might be to ascertain whether students can paraphrase, generate examples, use models, solve problems, identify the critical properties in a concept, give reasons why things are done, and as a final step synthesize complex arguments in favor of or against a relationship or concept. Cronbach's stance is that philosophical and conceptual beliefs are more powerful than lists of significant and nonsignificant differences; thus theories can be more successful in changing behaviors than lists of consequences for failure to change. Cronbach's thinking often does not satisfy the politician who wants to know why things are as they are—is there profiling, ineffective staffing, or incompetent teaching? To answer these questions the "hard" approach to assessment is needed. Often, however, the focus is not on whether success has been achieved but on providing documentation that there is equal participation and a proper allocation of resources. Equity concerns are addressed by gender, age, socioeconomic class, and race to ensure that no one group of individuals is disadvantaged due to, for example, physical handicaps, language, place of residence, or political affiliation.

Social Context

An important concept in program evaluation, especially that conducted through case studies and qualitative means, is putting all data into an appropriate context. Diversity issues prompt this concern, but other prompts stem from the recognition that there are major differences not only among individuals but also among classrooms, schools, and communities. In light of these differences, the question is raised as to whether all students and all teachers can or should be assessed through use of a single standard. Consideration of the social context allows educational outcomes to differ and still be equal. With the acceptance of different outcomes, the results of evaluation may need to be interpreted *relative* to floating standards. The support for relativity comes from constructivist philosophy. Humans can construct what is meant by *competent* and by *the good life*; as the goals of education are something society creates, society is free to construct various definitions of success.

Context influences outcomes. For the evaluator, established programs and their context increase the difficulty of conducting a meaningful assessment. If the school's band program has consistently won blue ribbons at marching band, jazz, and concert contests and festivals, ascertaining that the program does not meet the school's educational goals would require extremely compelling data. Even average programs are contextually influenced for evaluators of any persuasion. The constructivist would suggest that society values excellence arrived at through cooperative learning; thus the goals attained by the band are as valid as any goal the school's administration might propose. The connection between evaluation and the politics of education is most obvious in the assessment of long-established programs and those *perceived* by the public to be successful.

With knowledge of how the music program fits into the social, political, educational, and organizational context, a realistic look at its range of effects in each of the contexts is possible. The qualitative approach to program evaluation has advantages here: The evaluator can devote sufficient time on-site to become familiar with the local situation and its biases, traditions, and values, where liberal and conservative views are most likely to surface.

Another viable approach to program evaluation is to involve a limited number of external evaluators, perhaps only one, and to train the stakeholders to conduct a self-evaluation. Shadish and Cook (2000) suggest that communities differ in the way they construct reality, contributing to differences in how they perceive an evaluation, methods of observation, validations, reporting formats, and strategies for evaluation use (p. 45). Because of these differences, assessment training in self-evaluation situations is necessary; few teachers have had any systematic instruction in any form of evaluation. Robert Stake (1997) would like the stakeholders to discover for themselves what changes they wish to make—he believes if teachers have conducted or helped conduct the assessment, their personal investment will contribute to the possibility that the results will be used. Similar arguments are made by Fetterman (2001), who champions *empowerment evaluation,* where through the evaluation process the stakeholders are enabled (empowered) to make necessary changes and to defend the validity of current practices. How well a teacher or student should perform is a concept that is "constructed" by a school system or a teacher; thus multiple stakeholders must be involved in constructing or reconstructing the definition of acceptable performance if constructive use is to be made of the data collected.

Quantitative Versus Qualitative

During the 1990s and the first decade of the 21st century, program evaluation literature abounded with discussions about quantitative and qualitative assessment and the extent to which the two could be combined in a single assessment (House, 1994; Reichardt & Rallis, 1994; M. L. Smith, 1994). There are important differences between the two techniques, but these differences should not affect the actual evaluation. It appears that those empowered to make changes usually require *quantitative* data—there is a need to know the number of students who were successful as a result of an after-school program compared to the number of successful students who missed the offering.

Success can have any number of important *qualitative* definitions, but they are usually not relevant to the need of school board members focused on costs, the number of students who do not graduate, the number of music students who fail, or even the number of students who have quit smoking as a result of a requirement in the after-school program. Quantitative data report the success or lack of success of a program in the simplest terms, a summative evaluation. Summative evaluations are used in comparing schools, states, and various remedial or gifted programs. A rich description, no matter how deep, of a student's experience in the school or in a classroom is seldom sufficiently generalizable or definitive to warrant school board action. Rich descriptions are more useful in formative evaluation, an evaluation that aids in changing classroom practices and classroom methods.

The methodology to be used in any assessment depends upon the subject matter and what it is that one wants to know. Until the content to be assessed is known, discussions about whether one should use quantitative or qualitative methodology in an assessment are not productive. The *problem* is the deciding factor. Teachers generally are not concerned with issues related to summative evaluation—it was not teachers who inspired the reform movement in education and its attendant content and performance standards. Teachers did not demand graduation examinations and, historically, have not requested information on how their class compares with other classes in the state or nation.

Currently evaluations in music that supposedly address program concerns through employment of qualitative data outnumber those that employ quantitative data, but those with quantitative data appear to be the more influential assessments in support of music programs. These data are not based on *musical outcomes;* data on higher academic tests scores, graduation rates, college acceptances, fewer delinquency incidents, better work habits, and such are the data that resonate with school administrators, school boards, and music activists. Qualitative data are more compelling on *instructional issues,* quantitative data on policy questions about the *value* of the program. A few qualitative assessments do not actually evaluate but are important instructional tools.

A major objection to the quantitative approach is that it reminds individuals of the pass-fail examination and all its related anxiety. The criticism of the quantitative evaluation involves the difficulty in teasing out the causes for any improvement or deficiencies from a summative score. The reference is usually to the "black box," meaning that administering a standardized test like the PRAXIS II examination provides a pass-fail based on the "cut-score" established by the state department of education, but the score provides little information to the candidate or his or her school on how to build upon successes or correct any

Critical Essays in Music Education

weaknesses. The black box is the test that reveals nothing about what *caused* the score, whereas qualitative techniques are designed to observe frequently and in enough depth to identify probable causes of program weaknesses. It is not clear that observation, no matter how skillful, can assess many of the competencies required to be a successful teacher, but program evaluation is designed to look at programs, *not* individuals.

A Model

The current model for program evaluation in the arts is John Harland's *Arts Education in Secondary Schools: Effects and Effectiveness* (2000). A number of concerns in Great Britain prompted this study, among which were the following: There were fewer advisory services from local school districts, a decline in the arts content of initial training courses for primary teachers, a relaxation in the curriculum requirements to allow more time on literacy and numeracy, a worry that out-of-school programs were being boosted to replace in-school programs, and the promotion of the arts for their contribution toward combating social exclusion (p. 3). Harland's charge was to document the range of effects and outcomes attributable to school-based arts education, to examine the relationship between these effects and the key factors and processes associated with arts provision in schools, to illuminate good practice in schools' provision of high-quality education experiences in the arts, and to study the extent to which high levels of institutional involvement in the arts correlate with the qualities known to be associated with successful school improvement and school effectiveness. A survey of pupils in their junior year was conducted with interviews of employers and employees. The questions centered on objectives comparable to those in the United States; critical discrimination, aesthetic judgment, techniques, and skills at the key stage that was the end of required instruction, furthering of thinking skills, and the capacity to use the arts in their social, artistic, and cultural contexts and to prepare for a cultural life. Students in Great Britain ranked music as the least favorite subject with the highest proportion of responses that the curriculum had no impact on their abilities or attitudes. The curriculum and the school were not as persuasive as the teacher, a conclusion that indicates the importance of selection and education of all teachers involved with music.

Validity

Three Traditional Types

Validity has long been the sine qua non of research and evaluation. The term has been so misused that its meaning

and even importance are subject to confusion. One can discuss validity only in relational terms; whereas a general statement that *results* were invalid might be quite appropriate. To establish validity, the gathering, interpreting, and reporting of data should be valid *in relation to* a concept or idea of importance. Traditionally, evaluators focused efforts to establish validity on one of three areas: content, criterion-related, or construct. *Content validity* indicates a match between the assessment techniques and the content of a course or program. High-stakes tests have been delayed in several states to ensure that the students have been taught the content that appears on the high-stakes examination. Students often recall an experience when there was little match between the content of classroom discussions and the final examination and when a legitimate complaint was lodged about the content validity of a test, especially tests that influenced the final grade in the course. *Criterion-related validity* matches the results of an assessment with an accepted measure of competence in the same domain. There should be a relationship between a medical student's passing "the boards" (a battery of tests) and his or her ability to diagnose standard illnesses. Criterion-referenced assessments are also expected to predict future performance. Some assessors separate predictive validity from validity established by a match between test results and current task competency. *Construct validity* has long been considered the most important validity check for many assessments in formal schooling. A construct is a trait or ability (like personality) that is difficult to assess directly. Observations should have construct validity. Musicality is a construct, a construct recognizable under special conditions but one whose fuzzy definition presents assessment problems. Musicality is currently assessed through an audition, through an improvisational or compositional task, by requiring one to distinguish a musical from a nonmusical event—seemingly different abilities.

More Recent Types

Other descriptors of validity better convey the value of an assessment, and additional types of validity are of concern. A common type is *consequential validity*, where one asks what are the consequences to students who succeed or fail on the assessment or the consequences to the school. The consequences of failing a high-stakes assessment can be greater than the consequences of passing it, although both scenarios have consequences.

Predictive validity has been teased out of criterion-related validity in many assessments due to the importance of admissions tests in many fields. For example, the question is regularly asked as to how well the SAT score predicts one's success in college.

Systemic validity is a concern in schools where it was decided to not just make minor revisions in a course but be bold and make systemic changes in how students are educated. Reducing the number of electives and increasing graduation requirements to 4 years of math, science, language arts, and social science is a systemic change in the philosophy of secondary education. The change from junior high to middle school was a systemic change. Multiple-intelligence schools see themselves as involved in systemic changes. Assessment of these changes requires systemic validity. The 1997 NAEP in music with its emphasis on creating and improvising along with a test of sight-reading ability could be judged on its systemic validity—to what extent did this new assessment capture a major change in the priority of objectives in the music curriculum?

The relationships between assessment and task in these types of validity are important because inferences on the meaning of the assessment results depend upon the strength of these validity relationships. If one were to find little relationship between the instruction in the high school band rehearsal and the tasks of the 1997 NAEP, a lack of instructional validity would be indicated. NAEP could have strong consequential validity should graduation from high school for these band members depend upon their NAEP scores. Strength and type of validity is a judgment call.

A Taxonomy of Objectives

The Cognitive Domain

In the mid-1950s, Benjamin J. Bloom published his taxonomy in the cognitive domain (1956). It was a carefully worked out delineation of the many aspects of cognition, the ways in which the various aspects related to one another, and a hierarchical ordering of the development of cognition through its various aspects. Book 1 of *Taxonomy of Educational Objectives, Cognitive Domain,* opened up to educators a way of establishing clear objectives, sequencing these objectives, and assessing the extent to which the objectives were attained. Although the taxonomy was ordered from simple to complex, Bloom did not suggest that his sequence should necessarily be followed in instruction; teachers were expected to be simultaneously using several levels of the taxonomy. A striking feature of the taxonomy was that it consisted of multiple-choice and open-ended questions that looked, walked, and quacked like an assessment tool. Bloom's taxonomy demonstrated the importance of connecting the objectives of cognitive development with assessment and the necessity for the objectives to be clear and specific. Tremendous insights were gained by applying Bloom's taxonomy to a musical experience and constructing a task for each of the taxonomy categories. Such an exercise could serve as a check on the breadth and appropriateness of goal levels within one ac-

ademic grade. The taxonomy was frustrating to music educators, as there was no accommodation for tasks that involved perceptual skills and knowledge. (Bloom's colleagues later constructed a taxonomy of the affective domain [Krathwohl, Bloom, & Masia, 1964, the second domain of learning], and independent researchers, especially Anita Harrow [1972] and Elizabeth Simpson [1966], constructed a taxonomy in the psychomotor domain, the third hypothesized dimension of learning. Krathwohl's major levels were receiving [attending], responding, valuing, organizing, and characterization by a value or value concept, while Simpson's levels were perception, set, guided response, mechanism, and complete overt response.)

A Holistic Approach

Recently, influenced by the ideas of Howard Gardner and Bennett Reimer, education (including music education) has been moving toward a greater emphasis on cognition and broader definitions of learning. This new emphasis has given rise to the need for a new taxonomy, one that would reflect the new knowledge about learning. In 1998 A. Dean Hauenstein published *A Conceptual Framework for Educational Objectives: A Holistic Approach to Traditional Taxonomies,* which was an effort to update taxonomies in the three domains, Bloom's cognitive, D. Krathwohl's affective, and Simpson's psychomotor. In addition to making suggestions that allowed for constructivist thought, Hauenstein posits that the 63 categories contained in the three taxonomies were too many for teachers to use in curriculum planning. He revised the three taxonomies and added a fourth "behavioral domain" taxonomy with five levels: acquisition, assimilation, adaptation, performance, and aspiration (containing 15 subcategories), for a total of 20 categories, rather than the 63 in the Bloom/Krathwohl/Simpson configuration. Hauenstein's revised categories are applicable to research, assessment, and thoughtful curriculum planning. The revised basic categories for the cognitive domain are conceptualization, comprehension, application, and synthesis; for psychomotor: perception, simulation, and conformation (short-term goals) and production and mastery (long-term goals). Psychomotor learning depends on the interrelationship of cognition and affect.

Hauenstein's retention of the affective domain (to the consternation of the pure cognitivists) is helpful to arts curriculum planning. He asserts that the affective domain is "equal to, if not more important than, the cognitive domain" (p. 59). The development of feelings, values, and beliefs and the development of lifelong interests, values, and appreciations such as for arts and music are crucial to the outcomes of education—knowledgeable, acculturated, and competent individuals (p. 60). The revised categories for the affective domain are: receiving, responding, valuing, believing, and behaving. These are organized similarly to the categories established by Krathwohl, as both have three subcategories for the first three categories and two each for believing and behaving. Believing and behaving replace Krathwohl's organization and characterization by value or value complex.

Other updates in the cognitive and psychomotor taxonomies better account for recent thinking about learning. The author was careful to ensure that the taxonomy was applicable and inclusive, that the categories were mutually exclusive, and that there were consistent "principles of order" for the categories (p. 31).

The purpose of this taxonomy is "for curriculum writers: no attempt is made to provide information on how to write objectives or measure achievement" (p. 123). The premise is that assessment takes its cue from the curriculum and that a profitable place to begin is with the taxonomies of the curriculum. The emphasis is on learning as a whole person. All three taxonomies are essential, with the fourth for curriculum research, and use of them makes education more organized. In the cognitive domain, conceptualization, comprehension, and application are short-term goals, evaluation and synthesis long-term. Taxonomies focus on objectives that enable students to explore, refine, or change prevailing dispositions, values, and beliefs as they form their own concepts. Education is dependent on the degree to which prescriptions and information/content are included in the curriculum for instruction. Space prohibits giving examples in music even for the 20 categories. Readers might wish to review the examples in my 1970 *Evaluation of Music Teaching and Learning* and write assessment exercises for the four Hauenstein taxonomies.

A Revision of Bloom's Taxonomy

A second new taxonomy appeared in 2001, written by a task force that included Krathwohl (*A Taxonomy for Learning, Teaching, and Assessing: A Revision of Bloom's Taxonomy of Educational Objectives,* edited by Lorin W. Anderson and David Krathwohl). It is an update of only the cognitive taxonomy and is two-dimensional: cognitive processes and knowledge. The revised cognitive processes are remembering, understanding, applying, analyzing, evaluating, and creating, premised on the assumption that these processes are linear in complexity. Knowledge consists of the factual, conceptual, procedural, and metacognitive, also arranged linearly, proceeding from concrete to abstract. The authors posit that use of the taxonomy provides a better understanding of objectives and of what is important in education (p. 6) and that a taxonomy helps one to plan, to select and design assessment instruments and procedures, and to thereby ensure that objectives, instruction, and assessment are consistent.

The alignment of objectives and assessment is basic to high-quality instruction. The different types of objectives that result not only from new knowledge but also from state and federal frameworks require different instructional approaches.

Another reason for revision is that Ralph Tyler's behaviors became confused with behaviorism, requiring that the word *behavior* be replaced with *cognitive processes* (Anderson & Krathwohl, 2001, p. 14).

The Marzano Taxonomy

A third new taxonomy of educational objectives, this one formulated by Robert J. Marzano (*Designing a New Taxonomy of Education Objectives* [2001]), reflects the philosophical shift to cognition and recognizes the role of new knowledge about how learning occurs. Marzano's taxonomy is a new guide to understanding cognitive development and a new way of appraising the appropriateness of objectives, curriculum, and assessment in education. It is a marked departure from the Bloom taxonomy and the two revisions, particularly in that it combines the cognitive and psychomotor domains. The foundation level of the taxonomy of educational objectives is knowledge, which is attained through three systems: a cognitive system, a metacognitive system, and a self-system. There is no allowance for an affective domain; emotion is subsumed under Level 6, Self-System. A further complication for music educators is the lack of clarity that concerns a possible perceptual domain. Reimer (1996) suggests that perception is a type of cognition, but this explanation only partially answers the question of how the attainment of perceptual skills fits into the music curriculum. Marzano concludes that *information* cannot be executed, an understandable argument if, and only if, perception is not considered. When musicians hear an unknown piece of music and mentally classify it to obtain deeper meaning, they are actually executing one type of information; their minds process the information and a response to the music so perceived occurs. Another concern of music educators will be the emphasis the cognitive approach places on verbalizing, for example, verbalizing about the music and the musical experience. A large part of the musical experience defies verbal description; one is reminded of Martha Graham's comment to the effect that "if I could describe it, I would not have to dance it."

For the researcher in music education this taxonomy offers a guide to exploring many aspects of the musical learning process that have not yet been considered. And although at first glance the taxonomy may seem beyond any practical application for the music teacher in the classroom, the taxonomy is in reality an excellent tool for *thinking* about the learning process, *planning* learning sequences, *recognizing* various kinds of learning not previously considered, and *helping* to ensure that assessment gets to the heart of the learnings the teacher deems of primary importance. The practicing music teacher may find the taxonomy initially formidable but with some small effort will be able to see the ways in which it opens up the nature and the facts of learning in a way that is applicable to the teacher's goals.

Levels. Knowledge consists of information, mental procedures, and psychomotor procedures; to obtain this knowledge it is necessary to consider the three systems: cognitive, metacognitive, and self. There are six levels to the taxonomy, four of them cognitive, plus the levels of *metacognition* and *self*, which are intact levels.

Level 1: Knowledge Retrieval
Level 2: Comprehension
Level 3: Analysis
Level 4: Knowledge Utilization
Level 5: Metacognition
Level 6: Self

The levels are not organized by complexity, as was the earlier Bloom and the two revised taxonomies; rather, they are based on how an individual processes the stimuli received. Although there are subcomponents to the systems of metacognition and self, there is no order to these subcomponents. There is, however, an implied order to the cognition system, beginning with Level 1 and advancing to Level 4. The numbering of the levels is confusing, as the first step in learning is to engage the *self*-system, followed by the *metacognition* system. The *cognitive* system is the last one to be engaged. This taxonomy, like the Anderson and Krathwohl, is a work-in-progress, with Marzano allowing that not every subcomponent of the six levels may be essential to all subjects.

Marzano's Taxonomy Applied to Music. In view of the uniqueness of music and the importance of perception in music, this taxonomy is not entirely satisfactory, because audiation, a subcompetence of perception, does not fit neatly into it. Music educators believe that a student should perceive chord changes, melodic motifs, and the extent to which performers are in tune with one another. If the student is a performer, the ability to sing chord tones or to play in tune can be observed, but performance is not essential to derive meaning from music. Music educators believe that there are degrees of perceptual ability; due to talent or learning, some individuals have a "Harry Begian ear," where the smallest deviation is perceived, while others are apparently satisfied with gross approximations of the tonality.

Subcomponents. Each of the six levels of the taxonomy has three subcomponents: information, mental procedures, and psychomotor procedures.

Information (sometimes called declarative knowledge) consists of (1) details and (2) organizing ideas. *Details* consist of vocabulary, facts, time sequences, cause/effect sequences, and episodes. Music vocabulary and facts are familiar to all of us. Less is done in music with the other components of information detail. A time sequence requires identifying important events that occur between two dates, such as 1792 and 1795, Haydn's period in London, when he wrote the *London* Symphonies. (We'll ignore 1792–1794, when he returned briefly to Vienna and took Beethoven as a pupil.) Cause/event sequences would require understanding the relationship between the valve for brass instruments and the change in brass music. An episode could be the riot created by the premier of Stravinsky's *Le Sacre du Printemps*. Details are not limited to information retrieval and Level 1 of the taxonomy. *Organizing ideas* consist of principles and generalizations. Principles can be either correlational, a change in one factor resulting in a change in another factor, or cause- and effect, where one factor *causes* a change in the other.

Mental Procedures (sometimes called procedural knowledge) consist of (1) processes and (2) skills. *Mental processes* could be organized into a simple hierarchy, as some are more complex than others. If all students were assigned to improvise on a theme or to compose a piece, the varying products could be assigned to a rough hierarchy, but an exact hierarchy is unlikely, as the improvisations would have different strengths. *Mental skills* consist of tactics, algorithms, and simple rules. Following a single rule would be the simplest mental process; the skills should be included in any rough hierarchy of mental processes.

Psychomotor Procedures consist of (1) processes, (2) skills, and (3) the same mental procedures. *Psychomotor processes* consist of complex combination procedures, such as performing one's part accurately and musically in a concert. *Psychomotor skills* are simple combination procedures and foundational procedures. A simple combination procedure would be double-tonguing, while a foundational procedure would be exhaling correctly.

For Bloom, knowledge was "little more than the remembering of the idea or phenomenon" (1956, pp. 28–29). Bloom's nine levels of knowledge were clear, but there was no provision for the mental operation that accompanied the behavior at each level. Marzano's argument is that there must be a process for retrieving and using the knowledge acquired. His stages indicate how the cognitive, metacognitive, and self-systems act upon the various knowledges. Declarative knowledge remains basic to learning, the taxonomy placing the emphasis on how vocabulary, facts, and criteria are used. To use knowledge requires attention to three kinds of memory: sensory memory, where we learn, briefly, from our senses; long-term memory which is the basis for knowing and understanding; and working memory, the memory used when focusing on a task.

Application to Assessment: Level 6, Self.   Although much of the emphasis in the music classroom is on the cognitive requirements, the new taxonomy allows one to inspect the entire learning sequence. *Level 6: Self* is the first consideration. Bloom's taxonomy did not consider the self system.

Level 6: Self consists of examining importance, examining efficacy, examining emotional response, and examining motivation. Examining student motivation reveals a summary of the student's beliefs about importance, efficacy, and emotion. These differ in relative weight and combine to produce motivation.

The self-system of thinking addresses the question of whether to engage in the learning, how much energy to expend, what will be attended to, and to what extent this effort will satisfy a basic need. Personal goals are important in the self-system, as goals have to be at the personal level before one learns. Students may join music ensembles to have or be with friends, rather than to learn. The self-system begins to address the major questions of the purpose of life and to what extent the individual will need to change his or her environment to attain new goals. Bandura, Maslow, Buber, and other educational psychologists stress the importance of the student's investment in his or her own education.

In the self-system, the process is the same across the three domains of information, mental procedures, and psychomotor procedures. (Examples in this chapter are given only for the self and metacognition levels, as these are apt to be the most unfamiliar to the teacher.)

Self-system: Examining importance. The student decides what specific information is important:

Information
• *Details.* How important is it for me to know the events that surrounded the beginning of opera? Why do I believe this and how logical is my thinking?
• *Organizing ideas.* How important is it to me to know the principles of bowing? Why would I need to know the principles; how valid is my thinking about this?

Mental procedures
• *Skills.* How important is it to audiate? Why is it important? How logical has my thinking been in establishing this importance?
• *Processes.* How important is the ability to compose? Why is composing important to me? How logical have I been in deriving this importance?

Psychomotor procedures
• *Skills.* How important is it to me to practice double-tonguing? Why would I want to double-tongue? How logical have I been in making this decision?
• *Process.* How important is it for me to be able to perform my part well in the chorus concert? Why do I want to be proficient? How valid is my thinking at ascertaining the importance of practicing with all the other things I have to do?

Self-system: Examining efficacy. The student must have the will (motivation) to change from not knowing to knowing. To what extent do I believe that I can improve my understanding or competence relative to this week's goals of the music class? (Determining efficacy likely does not generalize to all of the goals of the music experience.) Do I have the resources, the ability, the power to change my situation or the situation at school? What are the veridical or logical aspects that might demonstrate to me that I can accomplish the goals?

Information
• *Details.* How much can I increase my understanding of the conditions that surrounded the origin of the opera? What is my reasoning?
• *Organizing ideas.* How much can I improve my knowledge of the principles of bowing in different genres? Have I been logical and realistic in my reasoning?

Mental procedures
• *Skills.* To what extent will I be able to improve my ability to audiate? What is my reasoning and how logical is it that I can actually improve?
• *Processes.* To what extent will I be able to improve my skill at composing? How likely is it that this is possible?

Psychomotor procedures
• *Skills.* How much can I improve my double-tonguing and be able to perform the way I want to? How reasonable is this goal?
• *Processes.* How close can I come to getting everything right in next week's choral concert? How logical is my reasoning?

Self-system: Examining emotional response. Negative emotions dampen a student's motivation. Emotions, though we have limited control over them, can be powerful motivators. Many charismatic leaders appeal essentially to a person's emotions; patriotism and respect for the motherland are emotion-based reasons for action. Marzano suggests that the flow from emotion to cognition is stronger than the flow from cognition to emotion. The emotional response differs from other categories, as the objective is to understand the *pattern* of one's thinking. There is no basis for determining that one pattern is better than another or that change is in order.

Information
- *Details.* How do I feel about paying for music that I was able to get free from Napster? Why do I feel this way? How logical is this reaction? (What emotions do I have about the need to sell grapefruit in order for the school orchestra to have new music?)
- *Organizing ideas.* What feelings do I have about the time spent warming up in choral rehearsals? How did I arrive at this feeling about warming up?

Mental procedures
- *Skills.* Why do I get so upset when we are expected to audiate? Is this feeling logical? How and when did it begin?
- *Processes.* Why do I become so emotional about the music I compose? Why do I not want anything to be changed? How logical am I? What is my reasoning?

Psychomotor procedures
- *Skills.* Why do I believe that I can triple-tongue at MM = 142? Is this logical or just a feeling? What logic or reasoning did I use to believe I could improve that much?
- *Processes.* Why am I so emotional and sad after the final choral concert of the year? What reason do I have for making this so important yet so sad? Am I logical in behaving as I do?

Self-system: Examining motivation. Assessing the strength of motivation is identical to assessing the three components of the self-system of thinking. Students review their reaction to the importance of goals, to what extent they have the resources to meet the goals, and any emotional reaction that can interfere with accomplishment of these goals. The importance of the goal to the individual is usually the strongest motivator. It is useful, however, to have students reflect upon and write responses to the information, mental procedures, and psychomotor procedures involved in motivation even when the material draws solely from past reflections. (Space will not be taken here for examples, as motivation is a summary step.)

Application to Assessment: Level 5, Metacognition. Taxonomy level 5: Metacognition follows Level 6. It prepares the student to learn and assess the depth of interest and capacity for learning. Metacognition moves beyond cognition and consists of four categories: goal setting, process monitoring, monitoring clarity, and monitoring accuracy. Metacognition is a way of determining the functioning of the other types of thought. If there is a hierarchy, goal setting is the most important accompanied by three monitoring strategies.

Metacognition: Goal setting. For knowledge to occur,

there must be a clear objective, a rough but thoughtful time line to accomplish that goal, and a knowledge of the resources required to meet that goal. There must be a clear picture of what the final product will look like and the relationship of any experiences to that product. Just practicing is not enough; one has to have an objective for any practice or drill. Where the student is involved in self-systems and in metacognition, the role of the teacher is changed.

Information
- *Details.* What is a goal that you might have relating to the Voluntary National Standards? What would you have to do to accomplish this goal?
- *Organizing ideas.* What goal would you suggest for yourself to improve your musical creativity? How might you accomplish that goal?

Mental procedures
- *Skills.* What goal might you set for your ability to audiate? What instruction and practice plan will enable you to reach that goal?
- *Processes.* Based upon your current competence, what goal do you have to learn to improvise in the genre of country and western music? What does your plan to accomplish this goal look like?

Psychomotor procedures
- *Skills.* State a terminal and intermediate goal that you have to improve your vocal high register. What resources will be required for you to meet these goals?
- *Processes.* What are your goals for this week to improve your musical understanding of the music we are singing in chorus? What are the procedures for improving understanding and how long would that process take?

Metacognition: Process monitoring. The function of this stage of monitoring is to assess the effectiveness of the algorithms, tactics, or rules used in a task. The taxonomy does not include monitoring the information stage, as the monitoring is to be authentic, that is, monitored in actual minutes required to accomplish a task. Thus the concern for the mental imagery of classifying a piece of music; little time elapses, and some classifying becomes almost automatic. Information such as vocabulary, facts, and causal sequences can be remembered and recalled but not acted upon. In ignoring perception to some extent, this definition indicates that much of the thrust of cognitive-based education could be *about* music, not *of* music. The mental and psychomotor skills that involve performance are unquestionably musical goals; there can be a question, however, about the importance in a music class of the extensive verbalization and reflection.

The student is to think about what he or she is doing *while* doing it. In some subjects, a verbal protocol is possible as it is in some music activities, but there are other situations where the opportunity to respond must be contrived, conducted after the experience.

Mental procedures
- *Skills.* To what extent were you able to hear every pitch mentally before you sang it?
- *Processes.* To what extent were you able to envision your composition before you performed it and how well were you able to interpret and perform your composition?

Psychomotor procedures
- *Skills.* Demonstrate a proper vocal warm-up. How effective were you at becoming more relaxed in your upper torso and getting the vocal cords to respond?
- *Processes.* As the student conductor of the orchestra, describe your musical thoughts into the tape recorder as you conduct. Comment on your effectiveness from your perception. I shall also stop you occasionally and ask you to orally evaluate your effectiveness at that point.

Metacognition: Monitoring clarity. The monitoring process is designed to assess any ambiguity in the goal or in how well the goal is to be attained. Often students do not understand all of the subgoals required in learning a piece of music and that more is required than getting the notes and rhythms correct. Clarity assists in establishing a disposition for learning the required tasks.

Information
- *Details.* Identify those sections of the test about which you were confused. What do you think caused your confusion on those sections? Are they related in some way?
- *Organizing ideas.* What concepts about appropriate breathing don't you understand? Be specific about the places in the music where you have inadequate breath support, where your breath support does not support the tone, and where your tone lacks a center due to your breathing.

Mental procedures
- *Skills.* Identify the places in the music where the score was confusing. What do you think caused this confusion?
- *Processes.* Identify the places in the score where the orchestra was unable to follow you. What is it about the music, the performers, or the situation that confused you?

Psychomotor procedures
- *Skills.* Identify those places in today's bowing exercises where you lost concentration. What do you think caused your inattention?
- *Processes.* Identify where in today's concert you missed the bowing pattern and became confused and played in the rests. What caused this confusion? Were you at letter B? With a downbow?

Metacognition: Monitoring accuracy. Accuracy is important in all subjects but none more so than music where the notes, rhythm, intonation, articulation, diction, and so forth must be precise. The student is to self-monitor to verify his or her own accuracy.

Information
- *Details.* How do you know that your explanation of Bach and Handel being the culmination of the Baroque period is an accurate explanation? What evidence do you have?
- *Organizing ideas.* What evidence do you have that you followed the compositional practices that were prevalent during the Classical period? What evidence do you have to verify that your composition authentically matches music of the Classical period?

Mental procedures
- *Skills.* Identify those parts of today's sight-reading exercise where you were able to audiate your part. How can you check your accuracy in audiating?
- *Processes.* Identify those computer programs that you used to help you arrange the music in the style of Ravel. What evidence do you have that your use of the programs provided a valid representation?

Cognitive System Processes. The four levels of the cognitive system detail the most familiar objectives, although some of the expected knowledge will require time-consuming assessments.

Level 1: Knowledge retrieval. Knowledge retrieval is defined as the ability to move knowledge from one's long-term memory to working memory. The level of knowledge is not sophisticated, consisting of facts and the simple structure of the topic. Questions about the style or genre of a piece of music satisfy Level 1.

Level 2: Comprehension. This level is comparable to comprehension in the Bloom taxonomy, except it does not include Bloom's extrapolation level. Synthesis in the new taxonomy matches Bloom's "interpretation." Comprehension is the process of preparing the major components of knowledge for inclusion in long-term memory. Knowledge specific to an experience may not be retained if it is not generalizable. The two stages of comprehension are synthesis and representation.

Level 3: Analysis. The basis for conducting an analysis is generation of new knowledge or new understanding. There are five types of analysis: matching, classifying, error analysis, generalization, and specification. For Marzano, analysis is comparable to Piaget's accommodation (1971), rather than assimilation or the idea of restructuring (which follows accretion and tuning), a system of Rumelhart and Norman (1981).

Level 4: Knowledge utilization. Level 4 is more advanced, if not more complex, than the other levels of cognition in the new taxonomy. The general categories are: decision making, problem solving, experimental inquiry, and investigation.

Assessment Strategies with the Marzano Taxonomy. As indicated by the length of the task descriptions, if music education programs were to be based upon this learning process, the assessments would need to parallel the objectives, follow the format suggested, and be embedded in the instruction.

Although retrieval of information is critical, as demonstrated in knowledge utilization, the most efficient way to assess a student's recall competence is through open-ended questions, multiple-choice, and on-demand type items.

Music notation could be used in matching, classifying, and demonstrating that the student understood the symbols of literacy. This assessment measure would satisfy a portion of Level 2: Comprehension and two of the methods of Level 3: Analysis, those of matching and classification.

Essays and oral reports are appropriate for all of the levels of the taxonomy except retrieval of information. Traditional sampling would constitute such a major source of variance that one could not determine the student's depth of knowledge of facts, definitions, time sequences, episodes, and cause/effect sequences; hence, new assessment formats are required.

Observation by teacher, peers, or outsiders is an inefficient and inaccurate assessment tool, because the observer brings too much baggage to the scene. Observing a student perform provides limited evidence of the range of the student's performing ability and even less of his or her comprehensive musical knowledge and skills. Observation provides partial information on a student's comprehension at one particular time and may provide partial information on the student's ability to retrieve information. In the best situations, the measurement error is great.

Performance tasks provide the opportunity to assess not only the student's cognitive competence but the metacognition and self levels when the performance task is substantive and on material worth knowing. A library assignment to conduct research and write a paper on an artist would not be very informative in assessing any of the nine Voluntary National Standards or one's basic musicianship. Administering one on-demand performance task will seldom produce adequate information. Even a complex task, if performed only once, is subject to substantial measurement error, less than that for the onetime high-stakes multiple-choice examination but of concern with any high-stakes assessment.

Assessment to improve (formative) must consist of frequent performance tasks, each scheduled to provide im-

mediate feedback to the student and an opportunity to demonstrate that corrective action has been taken.

New Devices

The emphasis in this chapter is on assessment issues that will arise with new instructional modes and the appropriateness of both embedded and external assessments. The new knowledge about both thinking and learning, coupled with advances in technology, allows psychologists and educators to create truly diagnostic and adaptive systems in the areas of ability, learning, development, and achievement.

Some of these advances have resulted from new statistical techniques or new uses of old techniques that increase assessment efficiency or that better interpret the data. No effort is made here to explain the mathematical or statistical background of these techniques; the reader needs to seek statistical understanding elsewhere.

Processing and Strategy Skills

Snow and Lohman (1993) in editors Norman Frederiksen, Robert Mislevy, and Isaac Bejar's *Test Theory for a New Generation of Text* (1993) identify stimulus encoding, feature comparison, rule induction, rule application, and response justification as examples of processing skills that can now be identified in ability test performance. Most of these processes are assessed through the multicomponent latent trait approach that can arrange the factors being assessed to provide a powerful means of gathering data relevant to how and in what sequence certain concepts are understood. Most statistical techniques, however, contain assumptions that are less easily met in the real world than in the statistical laboratories where these programs are devised. Music educators need to know their students and their subject well in ascertaining whether the statistical assumptions apply to their teaching situation. With reasonable course requirements or electives in graduate programs for teachers, a new frontier in music education is possible. Should this new interest occur, it will represent a major change in the profession compared to past lack of serious interest in assessment. Student variations in self-regulation with respect to speed, accuracy, and sequence are three of the assumptions of computer testing about which little data are available on tasks in music. Widespread use of computer testing in music must await such data. The computer programs make assumptions about the problem-solving strategy being used, a strategy not dependent upon skill but on how one processes information, how one learns from responding to other test items, and whether one recognizes the characteristics of the test items. The research of Ippel and Beem (1987) and Kyllonen, Lohman, and Woltz (1984) is based on a computer-administered test that systematically manipulates strategy choices and strategy shifts based on student response. At issue in most of these computer-generated tests is an understanding of why an individual has difficulty with a particular item, as that understanding must be programmed into the machine. If this is a problem for language arts teachers, as it is, it will be a greater problem for music. The item analysis currently available from music achievement tests is spotty, and little analysis exists as to the effect of preceding and follow-up questions.

In aural perception, simple intervals, timbres, and patterns often have high difficulty indices, due perhaps to student expectation or experience, factors that have not been systematically investigated for even one style or genre of music. Cognitive psychologists believe that cognitive analyses can lead to computerized item generation that is more valid than items written by humans. If this process becomes a reality, the concerted effort of both humans and computers will be required to devise tests that can explain (measure) the "Aha!" in musical understanding that escapes verbalization. A major advantage of the computer is that it can alter the assumption about the test taker's basic ability and adjust accordingly, where humans have to assume that a single ability continuum underlies the various tasks to be solved. The computer can also accommodate additional distractors or sources of variation as they are identified during the test administration. Test theory depends upon the degree of focus or concentration required by a specific item and also must account for learning and responses that become automatic during the test taking. Some individuals use multiple strategies to solve problems, thus requiring computer programs based upon fluid reasoning to respond to students who grasp quickly the conceptual basis for the test. Cognitive psychology is gaining a better understanding of how various individuals learn; music educators may find this attention to learning unprecedented, but if they cooperate with educational psychologists, throughout the required trial-and-error process, music education assessment can arrive at a position to take advantage of "the possible."

Lohman (1988) suggests that our understanding of spatial ability tests has been superficial and that spatial abilities also involve multiple strategies, some of which are not at all "spatial." Research with spatial ability testing is pertinent to music education when arguments are made that experiences with music improve students' spatial and temporal-spatial abilities. In other areas also, questions are being raised as better descriptions are created about what occurs as students learn to perceive, memorize, reason, and solve problems. These descriptions are especially relevant to the use of portfolios where convergent and discrimina-

tion validity of contrasting portfolio scores can be established by computers through use of a set of structural equations and LISREL.

Reasoning and Understanding

Such advances have allowed educators such as Ann L. Brown and John C. Campione (1986) to conduct research on student reasoning and on transfer that has led to accepted principles in the field of education. Their ideas on the self-regulatory functions of planning, monitoring one's own progress, questioning, checking, and correcting errors are based upon research that used student responses. The promotion of teaching for understanding through semantic networks, schemata, scripts, prototypes, images, and mental models is also based upon recent advances in assessment that have provided a view of the acquisition and structure of knowledge different from that derived using data from multiple-choice tests only. The use of elaboration, chunking, connecting, restructuring, and similar basic ideas in connectionism arises from analyses of achievement, mainly in mathematics and science but increasingly applied to other basic subjects. Whether these instructional ideas apply to music education will depend upon the application of cognitive psychology and its assessment techniques to priority issues in the music curriculum. Accepting these methodologies without such assessment research is unwarranted. Some information on these techniques can be gained from interviews and teach-back procedures that should provide data on chunk size and some strategies on restructuring and elaboration. These mental processes are what humans use to reason, recall, reflect, and solve problems. Thus music educators must be cautious in suggesting that current curricular practices are efficient in aiding students in these various thinking and understanding strategies. Previous learning is critical in the research conducted in test development in other subjects, and music educators have little experience in collecting substantive data about previous learning. Mislevy (1993) argues that standard test theory failed to consider just how people know what they know and do what they do and the ways in which they increase these capacities. His ideas are supported by Snow and Lohman (1993), from whom I quote at some length:

Cognitive psychology is now teaching us that to understand a particular individual's performance on a particular task, one must delve more deeply into its constituents—the configurations of knowledge, skill, understanding, belief, and attitude that underline particular responses. A richer, denser, more sensitive description is especially needed if tests are to be designed for diagnosis and classification in guiding instruction, rather than for summary selection and evaluation purposes only. This would seem to require test theories that use multivariate categorical as well as interval scale indicators and that apply to time series, not just to single-point assessments. The design of test items, the methods by which they are organized into tests, and the rules by which scores are assigned to responses must be guided by the purposes of testing. Modern theories of cognition and learning have described new, potentially useful constructs for measurement. One of the more important challenges for a new test theory and design, then, is to explore the measurement properties of these new scores. (p. 13)

Research on New Assessments

Computers. Much of the research on new assessment procedures is based upon a general probability model and a Bayesian approach to estimating the parameters of the student and of the content to be assessed (Mislevy, Almond, Yan, & Steinberg, 2000). Shum's (1994) evidentiary reasoning derived from his Portal Project is a fundamental construct as investigators manage belief about a student's knowledge and skill (even that which is not observable) based upon what students say and can do. Content evidence is obtained in the context of a task that allows the computer to construct individualized tests, adding new tasks to each student's item pool and measuring different students with different items. The investigator builds the task model by describing the important features of a task (these must be known with certainty) along with the specifications for the work environment, the tools that the testee may use, the work products, stimulus materials, and any interactions between the testee and the task.

The model describes the mixture of tasks that go into an operational assessment, either a fixed or a dynamic task, and the model is built based upon probability consistent with knowledge about the underlying problem and the data collection process. The "unobservables" are obtained from responses to a given task from a large number of examinees. The test is continually updated, new items added, and the estimate of general proficiency changed by the Monte Carlo Markov Chain of estimation procedures. This technique has been applied to present tests that include the Graduate Record Examination and the ASVAB, in which the computer constructs an individual examination at the student's level. The ERGO computer program (Noetic Systems, 1991) provides probabilities for each student on as many as five skills. Multiple skill testing in one test is possible only when, in the initial test design, there is a coherent design for all of the skills.

At the heart of the development of computer-assisted assessment are the new psychometric models of learning where the purpose of assessment is not to establish the presence or absence of specific behaviors but to infer the nature of students' understandings of particular phenom-

ena. There is little interest in the computer's ability to score isolated bits of knowledge; the goal is to develop programs that provide a model of understanding by individual students. The task is to design a set of questions that will expose different levels of understanding of a concept based on student response to several related questions, questions selected to reveal inconsistencies as well as consistencies in thinking. Computer-assisted assessments are not designed to replace current assessment measures that are appropriate to assess student learning of a body of factual material necessary in music and for which a well-designed multiple-choice format can reveal deep comprehension (Carroll, 1993).

Terminology and Concepts

Schemas. Cognitive psychologists who conduct research in learning suggest that schemas are one way to reflect the nature of the domain, the instruction, and the learner's knowledge about that domain. Schemas, however, are poorly defined in the literature; they are really just a collection of information organized like a story with a theme and characters. Individuals, based on their own experiences, use different schemas to solve the same problems. Individuals differ not only in the depth of each schema but also in their ability to search for the best schemas to solve new problems. With complex problems, individuals link several extant schemas, thus requiring a healthy long-term memory to solve substantive issues. The linking of schemas reveals the common elements that everyone uses in problem solving and is the value of schema theory (Marshall, 1993). (In computerized testing, each item contributes to the estimate of the contents of the schema and/or to its connecting links.) The data that can be provided to assessors is the extent to which students have acquired the schemas taught for problem solving, not whether students can produce the correct answer. Chomsky (1968) differentiated between competence and performance, competence being the knowledge of language and performance being the ability to use language. This distinction is followed by those who employ research in learning and assessment. Assessors are interested in the schema constructs (strategies, knowledge structure, and related components) as an indicator of competence and an indicator of the individual differences that are the student's span of abstract or general reasoning.

Latent Trait. Latent trait models are the psychometric standard for measuring ability, with the latent trait a mathematical model of the probability that an examinee passes a specific item, the Bayes probability mentioned earlier. The model is not based on the linear model of classical test theory but is sensitive to the nonlinear relationship of the probability of solving an item to the individual's actual ability. The relationship of item solving to actual ability (Rasch latent trait model) is an S-shaped curve in which the probability of .50 is reached when ability equals item difficulty. Verification of this model is often based on scores from the paper-folding spatial ability test that has become familiar to music educators as the dependent variable in the research of Shaw and Rauscher (1993). Test and item reliability are not based on the variance among student responses as is reliability in classical test theory but can be estimated through probability for each student.

Item Response Theory. This theory is loosely related to latent trait theory (although some would argue that it is philosophically at the other end of the continuum) in that it demonstrates the relationship of ability to performance in a nonlinear learning situation. The change in probability between any two abilities depends upon their relative location on the item response curve. An assumption is that there is more information when high-ability students do well on a difficult item and when low-ability students perform well on items appropriate for their ability. Pre- and posttests based on IRT must be designed to measure the same construct if gain scores are of interest; otherwise change score data are difficult to interpret. This change, however, is not measured on the same scale for individuals of different ability levels, thus providing a spurious negative relationship between change score and pretest score. Item response theory applies to dichotomously scored items although it probably can be used with more complicated responses; further research is needed. Despite accounting for individual differences, IRT assumes that there is a "characteristic" curve for each item that represents ability on that item. What IRT does best is assign a single, unidimensional continuum scale value to the examinee.

Behavioral Scaling. Behavioral scaling is a technique used to establish construct validity and is often not related to issues of generalizability or external validity. Scaling can be applied only to well-constructed tests, of adequate length and reliability. The assumption is that the task being measured is unidimensional and that a series of tasks of varying levels of difficulty can be constructed to measure this single construct. Reading skill, for example, is considered to be based on a single construct. Music educators Robert Miller (1979) and Lee Bartel (1992) separately investigated the potential of scaling, but their primary interest was in establishing the presence of constructs and not in developing classroom tests. There is inadequate research at present to indicate the extent to which this technique will be useful.

Another type of behavior scaling is used to establish anchor points on large-scale tests. The anchor points are verbal descriptions of a level of competence designed to be parametric descriptions that are both clear and objective.

(Anchor points for the test developer need not be describable to the public, but the test developer must have a thorough acquaintance with the characteristics of the task, scale, or domain, in order to report any results or to use the results in further test development.) Anchor points were used to describe results of the music portion of the 1997 NAEP, but the data used to establish these were not provided.

Summary

The use of computers in assessment holds considerable potential should music educators devote some of their resources to gaining more information about what learning is important, the extent of current student competency, and the importance of the situation. Knowing how to interpret error remains one of the difficulties in several of the strategies used in computer-adapted testing. The assessment strategies being developed rely on a relationship between instruction, learning, and testing. The research results in fields such as mathematics indicate that deep understanding of complex subject matter is not easily attained and seldom present in today's students. To attain any such goal will require the systemic change in education emphasized in educational literature. That change could be a narrowing of the curriculum to allow for the needed time, a greatly extended school day or year, or the development of more effective teaching strategies than are known at present. A greater integration of subject matter is also an option, but one that has been fraught with outcomes of misunderstanding, wrong information, and a lack of constructs for further learning. Concepts that appear to be related in the classroom seldom have the same strong relationships in the real world. The solution to this problem, some argue, is to enable students to recognize that the goals of instruction and ordinary experience are the same; others argue that the schools need to change what today passes for ordinary experience. One cannot assess complex ideas without stimuli that build a framework equal in complexity to that of the ideas involved; in essay assessments, for example, a detailed question would be necessary to elicit the extent of a student's understanding. Subjects and connections that appear to be logical on the surface often are not learned in the same way, and students may use different schemas to solve problems in different subjects. Such issues require considerable more research before the premise that it is easy to integrate music into the teaming efforts of middle school teachers can be accepted.

Portfolios

The idea of a portfolio to better capture evidence of student learning appears in almost all contemporary educational literature. Assessment professionals recommend multiple measures to reduce the error that exists in any assessment, including scorer error in arriving at a composite score for a portfolio. The advantage of a portfolio in determining student competence is that it can contain evidence from multiple indicators; the portfolio is not the assessment tool, but it *contains* the results of valid and reliable assessments and enough information about the student and instructional goals to allow for interpretation of these materials. The rise of the portfolio challenged the testing establishment, with the result that Educational Testing Service, CRESST, and other large organizations have devoted major resources during the past decade to improving the portfolio and to investigating how it might be used in their programs (Gitomer & Dusch, 1994; Jones & Chittenden, 1995). The initial efforts to employ portfolios as assessment tools in state assessment plans such as those in Vermont, Kentucky, and California were too ambitious; the users did not understand the difficulties of scoring a group of items that were far from homogenous. Portfolios suffer from low reliability and questionable standards-based validity.

The California Learning Assessment System (CLAS) was modeled after the most current constructivist ideas in education, subjected to intense scrutiny by the public, and eventually vetoed by the governor, but not until extensive research had been conducted. CLAS was to be involved in making high-stakes decisions, those decisions requiring not only several types of validity but respectable (high) reliability for the indicators upon which these decisions are based. Percentiles are commonly used by the state or the school district to report assessment data to the public, as being in the upper half of a class is not only understandable but a reasonable generalization. American business leaders like to know that *all* high school graduates are competent but still need to know which students would make the "best" employees. Individuals opposed to assessment have effectively used the lack of stability in percentile scores on these state and national tests to attack their use. The argument, based upon test reliability, is impressive, usually computed at the 50th percentile, which allows portrayal of the most severe cases. (Large numbers of students are grouped in the middle, which means that a small change in a score can make a rather large difference in a student's rank or percentile standing among the total group of students being compared.) There is always error in teacher judgments, in observation, in classroom tests, in contest ratings, and in performances (an error that is greater in qualitative assessments). The user of assessment data of any kind needs to know the amount of this error, but reducing error is seldom the primary consideration in qualitative assessment. Could a student who has made noticeable progress over the course of a year actually obtain a lower percentile rank in the second year? According to Ro-

gosa (1999), if a test had a reliability of .8, the probability of this occurring is .229 (20% of the time). A test needs to have a reliability of .9 to reduce this error to .133 and .95 to further reduce the error to .053. (These figures should be retained by the reader to assist in interpreting research results where the author reports a "satisfactory" reliability of .71!) Is it difficult to improve the reliability of assessments? Yes. To increase the reliability from .90 to .95 requires doubling the length of the test.

Portfolio scoring of the CLAS (Webb & Schlackman, 2000) enabled scorers to determine general competence, but the results were not adequate to justify inferences about individual student performance (p. 66). Portfolio data did, however, allow teachers and students to learn how the quality of student work related to California's dimensions of learning (dimensions of learning are similar to standards). Scoring of portfolios does not allow for comparisons or for obtaining a ranking or percentile, as portfolios contain both differing items and items produced under differing conditions for each student. The CLAS portfolios were in many respects models. They were not limited to exhibitions but contained multiple-choice test scores, performance tasks, and on-demand questions that were curricular embedded. Curriculum-embedded tasks in portfolios must provide evidence of the critical concepts of the discipline, as embedded tasks most often relate to the objectives mandated or expected by the community and state. On-demand tasks in a portfolio are more likely to reflect the priorities of the teacher and the school system.

Reliability of scoring of major portfolio items is improved when a larger number of competence levels is used. The American Council on the Training of Foreign Languages (1989) (Aschbaker, 1999) established 10 levels: novice-low, novice-mid, novice-high; intermediate-low, intermediate-mid, and intermediate-high; advanced, advanced-plus, superior, and distinguished. Ten levels in music are desirable. Though the often-recommended 3 levels are inadequate, some states are recommending only a 2-level (pass-fail), which invites serious assessment problems that extend beyond reliability, affecting student morale and beliefs. It is not unusual to find portfolio research that employs 3 or 4 levels and the investigator reporting reliability based on agreement and agreement within 1 level. With 3 levels, it should be obvious that chance will be a major factor in establishing "agreement" within 1 level!

The portfolio is not a simplistic and straightforward method of documenting student learning; a portfolio is to help students develop concepts, theories, strategies, practices, and beliefs that are consistent with the ways of knowing, arguing, and exploring. In music, material in a portfolio needs to conform to practices in learning, knowing, criticizing, discriminating, and exploring. Portfolios add additional ways of knowing but are not intended to replace extant methods. It is expected that students (as well as teachers) will be able to see changes in their understanding of music through the systematic and progressive change in conceptual structures displayed by the projects in the portfolio. Projects, therefore, cannot be randomly selected. Each student approaches his or her portfolio having a theory of how he or she comes to understand, a theory based upon the crucial concepts learned in and out of school. The teacher's task is to identify this theory and move that student toward theories that represent "best practices" in music. If this is done, the portfolio will eventually demonstrate to the student (he or she will discover) that the projects in the portfolio actually portray one or more ways of knowing and standards and practices in the field.

The projects in a portfolio might include demonstrations of competence in practiced performance ability, the ability to sight-read, to improvise, to compose, to write a reflective essay, to discuss the contributions of Stravinsky, and more, depending upon the extent of the instructional use of various frameworks and standards. An adjustment has to be made for each task to account for individual differences, as even the best student is not likely to be "best" in meeting each of the objectives currently espoused for music education. Thus instability—or lack of reliability—results not only from changes in the rater but also from the difficulty of establishing clear standards for the variety of tasks. It is not unusual for a rating to be based upon the student's improvement and/or the student's competence in relationship to his or her past competence and hypothesized ability. This basis is valuable but affects reliability. (Reliability can of course be improved when the most trivial tasks find their way into the portfolio as raters agree more easily on a level of competence in trivia.)

The New Standards Project

The New Standards Project, a partnership of 19 states and six urban school districts, has developed methods of assessment that are intended to function not as an "external" test but as integral elements within the system, thus increasing validity and reliability. The project recognizes that time requirements obviate the need to integrate assessment. The project's model for assessing understanding is derived from the military, where assessment practices effectively determine individual competence on problem solving, understanding, and ability to think. The success of the military is due to the clarity of their instructional goals and the acceptance that *every* soldier given a map and a compass and dropped into the middle of nowhere must be able to determine not only location but also the direction to the nearest mess hall. If public education is serious about all students reaching high standards, those standards and the

projects that demonstrate knowledge and understanding of those standards must be equally clear. The New Standards Project found that teacher scoring of portfolios ranged from a reliability of .28 to .60, too low for most uses (Resnick, 1996). To raise the reliability, the project found it necessary to have multiple-choice or other on-demand items in the portfolio that provided evidence that the work in the portfolio was the student's own. Even with this stability, raising the reliability to a range of from .6 to .75 required constructing a clear course syllabus, setting the questions, describing the criteria for different grades, and establishing a grading sample. L. Resnick avers that a much more explicit theory of situated cognition is needed before performance assessment, the kind of assessment upon which portfolios are based, can progress (1996, p. 17).

Portfolio Validity

Student performance is sensitive to the assessment format (the context in which students are asked to perform, the type of task, and the conditions under which they assemble their portfolios). Portfolios, although authentic in one sense, differ from other authentic measures. For example, two-thirds of the students who were classified as capable on the basis of their portfolios were deemed not competent on the basis of a direct writing prompt, also an authentic measure. Observing students in the laboratory does not predict competent performance on a laboratory simulation. A number of researchers (Dunbar, Koretz, & Hoover [1991]; Linn, Burton, De Stefano, & Hansen [1995]; Shavelson, Baxter, & Gao [1993]; Shavelson, Baxter, & Pine [1991]; and Shavelson, Mayberry, Li, & Webb [1990]) have established that 15 to 19 tasks are needed in a portfolio for *each* objective if a portfolio is to serve as an assessment with a reliability of .80. The inclusion of one musical composition would reveal little about a student's musical understanding or about any of the reasons for asking the student to compose. In Vermont the average classroom teacher spent an additional 17 hours a month just managing the portfolios, leading 90% of the reporting principals to conclude that portfolios were helpful but probably too burdensome (p. 29).

Myford and Mislevy (1995) report that if AP Studio Art were viewed only as portfolio assessment, it would be nothing short of depressing (p. 13). What is learned from a portfolio in visual arts is an opportunity to assess not only skills and knowledge but also what students and judges value. The value component is more a social phenomenon than one in measurement (p. 13). The portfolio's greatest value is not in assessment but in improving learning, which, of course, is a major purpose of assessment when not used for accountability.

The Future

The lack of interest in assessment in music education may stem from music's low priority in the school, or, just as likely, it may be that the public is satisfied with the current status of music education. Another explanation is that the public is unconcerned about the music education *curriculum* and believes that any proposed outcomes will be positive but unimportant. The efforts of arts advocacy groups indicate that the public is uninformed about the music program and the student competencies it fosters. This lack of knowledge of outcomes is difficult to explain, as the music program is often highly visible in the community. The important outcomes may be the obvious ones. Advocates of music education programs seldom, if ever, suggest improving or changing the program; the effort is totally on rallying the public to *support* music education in the schools. This support apparently does not include allocating additional instructional time, reducing the student-teacher ratio, increasing the music knowledge/skill base of the classroom teacher, or encouraging school boards and school administrators to place a higher priority on a quality music program. Rather, support means providing instruments for students or contributing to the fund-raising efforts required to maintain the current program. The objectives of the advocates do not easily fit into any of the taxonomies.

Without external pressure to demonstrate what students should know and be able to do on accepted objectives, little internal change will occur. This status quo situation is both positive and negative. The positive side is that music education comes to the reform table without any of the negative reports and baggage that accompany the basic subjects. Music education has no history of misusing multiple-choice and true-false tests; the primary assessment has been "evaluation" by friendly audiences. These evaluations have not been used diagnostically, needs assessment has not been conducted, and assessment data have not been used to justify the requests for resources. Teachers have not "taught to the test," and there are no national norms or competence standards. Parents do not expect grades in music, and if grades are given their meaning is obscure. Instrumental music may report student competence through chair placements that are then listed on the concert program, but few would accept this indicator as a measure of success of the music program, only that of the individual student. Music education has few leaders who champion any role for assessment. Charles Leonhard wrote a seminal article on evaluation in *Basic Concepts of Music Education* (1958), a book that initiated major changes in music education, but his chapter was ignored and Leonhard is remembered for other significant contributions but not for this effort.

Basic Music and Performance Programs

Music education can profit from the current interest in assessment only if the profession realizes that there are at least two distinct programs in the schools—a basic program and a performance program. These are so distinct that both the instructional and the assessment concepts differ, often substantially. Additional programs or variations on the programs may exist in various school systems, but both the performance and the basic program have a legitimate claim on curriculum resources. The basic or required program is a cognitive program (Phillips, 1995) and relates most closely to the educational reform movement. A third program, one focused on "instrumental" or nonmusical objectives, is not discussed in this chapter, despite its potential importance. Instrumental objectives include development of skills for lifelong learning and leisure activities, such skills as cooperation, responsibility, prioritizing, and numerous other worthwhile outcomes.

Although the two established music programs differ in significant ways, they are mutually supportive. Basic music that includes the required music program provides competencies that enhance the performance program; performance in turn can enhance understanding of some of the goals of the basic program. Mediocrity occurs when the priorities of the two programs are not observed and too much "overlap" is attempted. A school system may wish to support only a performance program *or* a basic program, and where this situation exists the difficulty of achieving challenging goals will be great. It is not realistic to accept goals when the resources to accomplish these goals do not exist. Music is a large and wonderful field, too broad for even the professional to feel competent in performance, musicology, composition, and music in general education.

Assessment and Educational Reform

The thrust of this chapter has been on assessment strategies for basic music, for music programs that match some of the programs in other basic subjects. Currently there are marked philosophical differences between the cognitivists and the situativists (Greeno, Collins, & Resnick, 1996), whether educational experiences are to be structured according to what we know about learning from the world of psychology and educational psychology or all learning is situated in a particular location, a particular time, and the sociocultural background of students and teachers. Eventually there will likely be some compromise; these substantive differences need not currently concern the music educator. Systemic reform in education is emphasizing learning strategies and issues of transfer rather than performance. Doing well on a standardized test is a performance, and although external assessment of performance is accepted by most educators, the current gathering and use of assessment data is for its potential in improving the learning process. Students who believe the purpose of education is to enable them to perform tend to select easy tasks they can do well; students who believe that education is for learning accept setbacks when they recognize that they are developing strategies, skills, and knowledges that move them toward worthwhile objectives. Education for these individuals is analogous to running a confidence course: If the course is too easy, it fails to build any lasting confidence. Confidence courses involve problem solving: The individual forms hypotheses of the best route and the best order of tasks and draws upon his or her extant knowledge and skills. With a cognitivist orientation, students will want to sing individually as well as offer individual reflections on a number of classroom experiences. The older behavioristic orientation adhered to outdated theories of motivation that emphasized the negative consequences of failure rather than what is now believed about motivation. There will never be adequate instructional time for the expected content and character of assessment unless the teacher changes his or her instructional procedures to include recording on a regular basis each student's competence in accordance with standards *and* that individual student's improvement. Even when embedded in instruction, such an assessment process will seem formidable to the teacher who is pressed for instructional time. The reform movement advocates that assessment be individualized to the extent possible, to record how well each student is learning in relationship to his or her sociocultural background as well as his or her competency on grade-level standards. Although the most extreme cognitivists or situativists (Anderson, Reder, & Simon, 1996) are fearful of the standards movement, all recognize the philosophical importance of educating all students to high standards. Standards require the assessing of students, individually and collectively, on developmentally appropriate grade-level goals. The assessment, however, is not for accountability but to assist the teacher and student in identifying what is yet to be accomplished. Teachers currently control grade-level objectives in the basic music program and can drastically reduce their goals to a manageable level. State and district curricula merely suggest. Textbooks for basic music, school district music curriculum guides, and state and national frameworks are not appropriate sources for establishing content validity of future assessments, as their suggestions for content do not take into account the resources available.

The instructional and assessment strategies recommended for the basic subjects are applicable to a basic music program that is focused on understanding music listened to in and out of class. Understanding music would enable a graduate of the program to listen to music with heightened aural abilities and knowledge of what is occurring in the music, to attend concerts, to be discriminating, and to use music in his or her daily life. The emphasis on cognition and problem solving means that students learn to identify musical problems, talk about musical issues, argue about the qualities of music, establish criteria for excellence in musical performance and in musical works, and be open to all quality music and musical experiences. The questions included in the Marzano taxonomy suggest the knowledge and skill that will be needed. The unsolved question is one of transfer. The expectation is that an understanding of the principles of music composition and performance will be an enabler for transfer. The ideas of Vygotsky imply that only if these principles are derived from the situation and the interaction with the music, individually and collectively, will transfer to different music in different situations be achieved (Brown & Farrar, 1985). New teachers in all subjects must think hard about these educational ideas and strategies and how they apply to their subject matter content, as educators are making these teaching suggestions based on face validity; they make sense in light of what we know today and in light of past failures. (Without past assessment, we do not know what aspects of the basic music program have failed; the only evidence is from the performance program.)

The basic music program will have to use all types of measurement devices. Low-level knowledge is required in sequential programs before high-level knowledge and its concomitant understandings can be attained at a level that makes transfer possible. Multiple-choice, single-answer, and matching tests will be part of instruction; equally necessary will be assessment of singing and perceptual skills—on a regular basis and recorded. Contemporary philosophy rejects the idea that instruction ceases for assessment and that all students take the same test at the same time. Individualized assessment requires more time, but if the skill or knowledge is worth teaching, it is worth each student's attaining that competence. Matching pitch and singing an arpeggio in tune is a low-level but necessary ability in most music programs. This low-level skill, however, must make sense to the student, or he or she will not be actively involved in the learning. Performance programs often involve passive learning; students seldom object to a class where little thinking is required. They are told what and how to perform, what to practice for the next lesson, and how well the lesson should be performed—a luxurious escape from the arduousness of active learning. Passive learning is less likely to transfer, thus making understandable the lack of transfer in many performance programs. A performance program will profit from tracking—not tracking by race, gender, or socioeconomic status but by competence. When all students have an equal chance to study, practice, and learn, tracking does not discriminate; it is not elitist. Excellent performance programs exist in all types of schools, from Phillips Exeter to Eisenhower High School.

The basic program can emphasize instruction where the historical and cultural factors of the community not only influence learning but also are indicators of the student's initial knowledge and the skills that are needed to participate in a community of practice. These classrooms emphasize the socially negotiated meaning to experiences (Eisenhart, Finkel, & Marion, 1996). The instruction is characterized by not only open demonstrations of perceptual abilities but also discussions about music that allow the teacher to identify misunderstanding, skipped sequences, and lack of competencies that will interfere with future learning. In traditional "general" music classes students do not develop the needed skills or knowledges and there is no provision for remedial work, resulting in an American population of musical illiterates.

Revising and correcting the traditional general music program will result in students' becoming engaged in learning in fundamentally new ways. The model would be the music critic; that is, the focus would be on hearing and understanding music. It is this discipline, not the discipline of the high school chorus, that provides the content and ways of "knowing" desired for all students. To assume that all students can learn music requires a new way of thinking on the part of both students and teachers. A large number of students (and adults) reject learning in music on the basis of lack of ability because the model presented to them has been an incorrect model. Self-assessment of knowledge in the constructive classroom is not only possible but also necessary. Self- and teacher assessments need not meet the same standards as published tests when they are frequent and used primarily to improve. Shepherd, in her hypothetical vision of the future, suggests that it is *possible* for teachers thinking systematically over time to develop highly accurate assessments of student learning (2001). The italics in the original indicate that this will not be easy even for the teacher with a small classroom.

The music critic is the suggested model as the emphasis is on understanding relationships—to other performance, to other musics, and to other times. This type of learning seldom occurs in a performance program, as it requires time for listening, researching, comparing, contrasting, and, most of all, discussing the *important* features of the music. The broader range of assessment tools required will likely also require attention to long-term musical and factual knowledge. It will necessitate students' recognizing and singing melodies, motives, unifying rhythmic patterns, and more. If this sounds ambitious, it is, but these competencies are only a few that involve higher order thinking and are prerequisite to problem solving. Identifying an incorrect note is a trivial event in problem solving and leads to more trivial problem solving (Leper, Drake, &

O'Donnell-Johnson, 1997). With younger children more informal assessments will be needed, but these can be observation-based individual performances and responses and even the retelling of the stories in and of music.

Research by Camp (1992) indicates that students can articulate and apply critical criteria if given practice in doing so. This practice is necessary with portfolios, where the advantage is in analyzing past work. Portfolio scholars have found that it might be necessary to maintain two portfolios, instructional and performance, a near-impossibility in most music-teaching situations. Shepherd indicates that whether portfolios can be productively used for these two purposes is highly controversial even in basic subjects (2001). She indicates that the use of rubrics, which often accompany portfolios, is likely inappropriate in classrooms with young children. Rubrics are objectionable to others because of their resemblance to positivistic modes of assessment (Wile & Tierney, 1996). Other future assessment concerns center on the prescriptive nature of the scoring in using rubrics (Wolf & Reardon, 1996). A major need is research on rubric development. Their current use in teacher evaluation is unwarranted. Assessments should occur in the classroom as a normal part of instruction to take advantage of the social situation advocated by Vygotsky and to make assessment seem a part of learning. This description of assessment is not so different from current teacher efforts but demands new procedures and instruments. Assessments should not just judge competence as correct or incorrect, in-tune or out-of-tune, as might be expected in a performance program, but should also aid students in learning to distinguish quality of ideas, whether remarks are clear and accurate, whether previous knowledge is used in formulating a comment or reflection, and whether reference is made to standards. Assessment must also show the importance of *thinking* that occurs in reacting to musical experiences.

Assessment is ineffective whenever students do not have a clear understanding of the criteria by which their work will be assessed (Frederiksen & Collins, 1989). When required to become involved with self- and peer assessment, students become extremely interested in the criteria for excellence (Klenowski, 1995).

A Final Word

The suggestions for systemically changing education brought on by education's response to the reform movement are an idealization; research and experience are needed to determine their potential, including that for assessment. Teachers with successful music programs should not assume that these futuristic suggestions will automatically help their programs. Research has provided us with few cues, and those few are not based on current philosophies of education. Changing the culture of the music classroom to meet the new frameworks will change music education as it is currently practiced. Teachers cannot continue to randomly add and subtract experiences and objectives, as teaching for musical understanding requires focus on fewer objectives, fewer musical selections, and fewer types of music. The effort to develop assessment tools and dependent measures for research will occupy music educators for the next decade as not only the reliability and validity of even embedded measures need to be ascertained but also the requirements and substance of tools for program evaluation. Research in assessment needs to verify that NAEP has indeed established a working framework for the profession and to ascertain what are the alternatives. The teacher's rewards lie in positive feedback and the knowledge that one's efforts are worthwhile. More than a few of the ideas about the "mindful" school will require teachers to reflect on not only their own musical beliefs but also what they believe is possible for students to know and understand and what knowledge will be available to students on demand when performing, hearing, thinking about, and discussing music, in and out of school.

REFERENCES

Anderson, J. R., Reder, L. M., & Simon, H. A. (1996). Situated learning and education. *Educational Researcher, 25,* 5–11.

Anderson, L. W., & Krathwohl, D. (Eds.). (2001). *A taxonomy for learning, teaching, and assessing: A revision of Bloom's taxonomy of educational objectives.* New York: Longman.

Aschbacher, P. (1999). Developing indicators of classroom practice to monitor and support school reform. (CSE Tech. Rep. No. 513). Los Angeles: UCLA CRESST.

Bartel, L. (1992). The development of the cognitive-affective response test-music. *Psychomusicology, 11*(1), 15–26.

Biggs, J. B., & Collis, K. F. (1982). *Evaluating the quality of learning: The SOLO taxonomy.* New York: Academic Press.

Blocker, L., Greenwood, R., & Shellahamer, B. (1997). Teaching behaviors of middle school and high school band directors in the rehearsal setting. *Journal of Research in Music Education, 45*(3), 457–469.

Bloom, B. J. (Ed.). (1956). *Taxonomy of educational objectives: Book 1. Cognitive domain.* New York: Longman.

Brittin, R. V., & Sheldon, D. A. (1995). Comparing continuous versus static measurements in music listeners' preferences: Comparing response modes. *Journal of Research in Music Education, 43,* 36–45.

Brittin, R. (1996). Listeners' preference for music of other cultures: Comparing response modes. *Journal of Research in Music Education, 44*(4), 328–340.

Brittin, R., & Duke, R. (1997). Continuous versus summative evaluations of musical intensity: A comparison of two methods for measuring overall effect. *Journal of Research in Music Education, 45*(2), 245–258.

Broadfoot, P. (2000). Preface. In A. Filer (Ed.), *Assessment: Social practice and social product.* London: Routledge Falmer.

Brown, A. L., & Campione, J. C. (1986). Psychological theory and the study of learning disabilities. *American Psychologist, 41,* 1059–1068.

Brown, A. L., & Farrar, R. A. (1985). Diagnosing zones of proximal development. In J. Weartsch (Ed.), *Culture, communication and cognition: Vygotskian perspectives* (pp. 273–305). Cambridge: Cambridge University Press.

Brynes, S. R. (1997). Different age and mentally handicapped listeners' response to Western art selections. *Journal of Research in Music Education, 44,* 569–579.

Buttsworth, L., Fogarty, G., & Rorke, P. (1993). Predicting aural performance in a tertiary music training programme. *Psychology of Music, 21*(2), 114–126.

Camp, R. (1992). Portfolio reflections in middle and secondary school classrooms. In K. B. Yancey (Ed.), *Portfolios in the writing classroom* (pp. 61–79). Urbana, IL: National Council Teachers of English.

Cantu, N. (2000). *The use of tests when making high-stake decisions for students: A resource guide for educators and policy makers.* Washington, DC: U.S. Department of Education, Office of Civil Rights.

Carroll, J. B. (1993). *Human cognitive abilities.* New York: Cambridge University Press.

Chelimsky, E. (1992). Expanding evaluation capabilities in the General Accounting Office. In C. Wye & R. Sonnichsen (Eds.), *New directions for program evaluation: Vol. 5.* San Francisco: Jossey-Bass.

Chomsky, N. (1968). *Language and mind.* New York: Harcourt Brace Jovanovich.

Colwell, R. (1970). *The evaluation of music teaching and learning.* Englewood Cliffs, NJ: Prentice Hall.

Cronbach, L. (1995). Emerging roles of evaluation in science education reform. In R. O'Sullivan (Ed.), *New directions for program evaluation: Vol. 65* (pp. 19–29). San Francisco: Jossey-Bass.

Davis, A. P. (1998). Performance achievement and analysis of teaching during choral rehearsals, *Journal of Research in Music Education, 46*(1), 496–509.

DeNardo, G., & Kantorski, V. (1995). A continuous response assessment of children's music cognition. *Bulletin of the Council for Research in Music Education, 126,* 42–52.

DeNardo, G. F., & Kantorski, V. J. (1998). A comparison of listeners' musical cognition using a continuous response assessment. *Journal of Research in Music Education, 46*(2), 320–331.

Dunbar, S. B., Koretz, D. M., & Hoover, H. D. (1991). Quality control in the development and use of performance assessment. *Applied Measures in Education, 4,* 298–303.

Eisenhart, M., Finkel, E., & Marion, S. F. (1996). Creating the conditions for scientific literacy: A re-examination. *American Educational Research Journal, 33,* 261–295.

Ekholm, E. (2000) The effect of singing mode and seating arrangement on choral blend and overall choral sound. *Journal of Research in Music Education, 48*(2), 123–135.

Fetterman, D. (2001). *Foundations of empowerment evaluation.* Thousand Oaks, CA: Sage.

Flohr, J. (2000). *A contemporary rhythm skills assessment.* Champaign, IL: Electronic Courseware Systems.

Frederiksen, J. R., & Collins, A. (1989). A systems approach to educational testing. *Educational Researcher, 18,* 27–32.

Frederiksen, N., Mislevy, R., & Bejar, I. (Eds.). (1993). *Test theory for a new generation of tests.* Hillsdale, NJ: Erlbaum.

Fredrickson, W. (1994). Band musicians' performance and eye contact as influenced by loss of a visual and/or aural stimulus. *Journal of Research in Music Education, 42*(4), 306–317.

Fredrickson, W. (1995). A comparison of perceived musical tension and aesthetic response. *Psychology of Music, 23*(1), 81–87.

Fredrickson, W. (1997). Elementary, middle, and high school student perceptions of tension in music. *Journal of Research in Music Education, 45*(4), 626–635.

Fredrickson, W. (1999). Effect of musical performance on perception of tension in Gustav Holt's First Suite in E-flat. *Journal of Research in Music Education, 47*(1), 44–52.

Fremer, J. (2000, December). A message from your president. *Newsletter,* National Council on Measurement in Education.

Froelich, H. (1995). Measurement dependability in the systematic observation of music instruction: A review, some questions, and possibilities for a (new?) approach. *Psychomusicology, 14,* 182–196.

Froseth, J., & Weaver, M. (1996). *Music teacher self-assessment.* Chicago: GIA.

Gee, C. (1994). Artists in the classrooms: The impact and consequences of the National Endowment for the Arts' artist resident program on K–12 arts education, parts 1 and 2. *Arts Education Policy Review, 95*(3), 14–29, (4), 8–31.

Geringer, J. (1995). Continuous loudness judgments of dynamics in recorded music excerpts. *Journal of Research in Music Education, 43*(1), 22–35.

Gitomer, D., & Duschl, R. (1995). *Moving toward a portfolio culture in science education* (Document 94-07). Princeton, NJ: Center for Performance Assessment.

Goolsby, T. W. (1996). Time use in instrumental rehearsals: A comparison of experienced, novice, and student teachers. *Journal of Research in Music Education, 44*(4), 286–303.

Gordon, E. (1998). *Harmonic improvisation readiness record and rhythm improvisation readiness record.* Chicago: GIA.

Greeno, J. G., Collins, A. M., & Resnick, L. B. (1996). Cognition and learning. In D. C. Berliner & R. C. Calfee (Eds.), *Handbook of educational psychology* (pp. 15–46). New York: Macmillan.

Gregory, D. (1994). Analysis of listening preferences of high school and college musicians. *Journal of Research in Music Education, 42,* 331–342.

Hair, H. (1997). Divergent research in children's musical development, *Psychomusicology, 16,* 26–39.

Hardy, D. (1995). *The construction and validation of an original sight-playing test for elementary piano students.* Unpublished doctoral dissertation, University of Oklahoma, Norman.

Harland, J., Kinder, K., Lord, P., Stoff, A., Schagen, I., & Haynes, J. (with Cusworth, L., White, R., & Paola, R.).

(2000). *Arts education in secondary schools: Effects and effectiveness.* Slough, UK: National Foundation for Education Research,

Harrow, A. (1972). *A taxonomy of the psychomotor domain.* New York: Longman.

Hauenstein, A. D. (1998). *A conceptual framework for educational objectives: A holistic approach to traditional taxonomies.* Lanham, MD: University Press of America.

Hickey, M. (1999, January). Assessment rubrics for music composition. *Music Educators Journal, 85*(4), 26–33.

House, E. R. (1994). Integrating the quantitative and qualitative. In C. Reichard & S. Rallis (Eds.), *New directions for program evaluation: Vol. 61. The qualitative–quantitative debate: New perspectives* (pp. 13–22). San Francisco: Jossey-Bass.

House, E. R. (1995a). Principled evaluation: A critique of the AEA guiding principles. In W. Shadish, D. Newman, M. A. Scheirer, & C. Wye (Eds.), *New directions for program evaluation: Vol. 66. Guiding principles for evaluators* (27–34). San Francisco: Jossey-Bass.

House, E. R. (1995b). Putting things together coherently: Logic and justice. In D. Fournier (Ed.), *New directions for program evaluation: Vol. 68. Reasoning in evaluation: Inferential links and leaps* (33–48). San Francisco: Jossey-Bass.

Ippel, M. J., & Beem, L. A. (1987). A theory of antagonistic strategies. In E. DeCorte, H. Lodewijks, R. Parmentier, & P. Span (Eds.), *Learning and instruction: European research in an international context* (Vol. 1, pp. 111–121). Oxford: Pergamon Press.

Johnson, C. (1996). Musicians' and nonmusicians' assessment of perceived rubato in musical performance. *Journal of Research in Music Education, 44*(1), 84–96.

Jones, J., & Chittenden, E. (1995). *Teachers' perceptions of rating an early literacy portfolio* (Document 95-01). Princeton, NJ: Center for Performance Assessment.

Kivy, P. (1984). *Sound and semblance: Reflections on musical representation.* Princeton, NJ: Princeton University Press.

Klenowski, V. (1995). Student self-evaluation process in student-centered teaching and learning contexts of Australia and England. *Assessment in Education, 2,* 145–163.

Krathwohl, D., Bloom, B., & Masia, B. (1964). *Taxonomy of educational objectives: The classification of educational objectives handbook II: Affective domain.* New York: Longman.

Kyllonen, P. C., Lohman, D. F., & Woltz, D. J. (1984). Componential modeling of alternative strategies for performing spatial tasks. *Journal of Educational Psychology, 76,* 1325–1345.

Leonhard, C. (1958). Evaluation in music education. In N. Henry (Ed.), *Basic concepts of music education* [57th Yearbook of the National Society for the Study of Education], part 1. Chicago: University of Chicago Press.

Leper, M. R., Drake, M. F., & O'Donnell-Johnson, T. (1997). Scaffolding techniques of expert human tutors. In K. Hogan & M. Pressley (Eds.), *Scaffolding student learning: Instructional approaches and issues* (pp. 108–144). Cambridge: Brookline Books.

Linn, R. L., Burton, E., DeStefano, L., & Hanson, M. (1995). Generalizability of new standards project 1993 pilot study tasks in mathematics (CSE Tech. Rep. 392). Los Angeles: UCLA CRESST.

Lohman, D. F. (1988). Spatial abilities as traits, processes, and knowledge. In R. J. Sternberg (Ed.), *Advances in the psychology of human intelligence* (Vol. 4, pp. 181–248). Hillsdale, NJ: Erlbaum.

Lychner, J. (1998). An empirical study concerning terminology relating to aesthetic response to music. *Journal of Research in Music Education, 46*(2), 303–319.

Mabry, L. (1999, May). Writing to the rubric: Lingering effects of traditional standardized testing on direct writing assessment. *Phi Delta Kappan, 80*(9), 673–679.

Madsen, C. (1997a). Emotional response to music. *Psychomusicology, 16*, 59–67.

Madsen, C. (1997b). Focus of attention and aesthetic response. *Journal of Research in Music Education, 45*(1), 80–89.

Madsen, C. (1998). Emotion versus tension in Haydn's Symphony no. 104 as measured by the two-dimensional continuous response digital interface. *Journal of Research in Music Education, 46*(4), 546–554.

Madsen, C., Brittin, R., & Capprella-Sheldon, D. (1993). An empirical investigation of the aesthetic response to music. *Journal of Research in Music Education, 41*, 57–69.

Madsen, C., Geringer, J., & Fredrickson, W. (1997). Focus of attention to musical elements in Haydn's Symphony # 104. *Bulletin of the Council for Research in Music Education, 133*, 57–63.

Marshall, S. (1993). Assessing schema knowledge. In N. Frederiksen, R. Mislevy, & I. Bejar (Eds.), *Test theory for a new generation of tests* (pp. 155–180). Hillsdale, NJ: Erlbaum.

Marzano, R. J. (2001). *Designing a new taxonomy of educational objectives.* Thousand Oaks, CA: Corwin.

Masear, C. (1999). *The development and field test of a model for evaluating elementary string programs.* Unpublished doctoral dissertation, Teachers College, Columbia University, New York City.

McCurry, M. (1998). *Hand-chime performance as a means of meeting selected standards in the national standards of music education.* Unpublished doctoral dissertation, University of Georgia, Athens.

McPherson, G. (1995). The assessment of musical performance: Development and validation of five new measures. *Psychology of Music, 23*(2), 142–161.

Mikle, H. (1999). *The development of an individual sight reading inventory.* Unpublished doctoral dissertation, University of Minnesota, Minneapolis.

Miller, R. (1979). *An analysis of musical perception through multidimensional scaling.* Unpublished doctoral dissertation, University of Illinois at Urbana-Champaign.

Mislevy, R. (1993). Introduction. In N. Fredrickson, R. Mislevy, & I. Bejar (Eds.), *Test theory for a new generation of tests* (pp. ix–xii). Hillsdale, NJ: Erlbaum.

Mislevy, R., Almond, R., Yan, D., & Steinberg, L. (2000) *Bayes Nets in educational assessment: Where do the numbers come from?* Los Angeles: Center for the Study of Evaluation.

Myford, C., & Mislevy, R. (1995). Monitoring and improving

a portfolio assessment system (Document 94-05). Princeton, NJ: Center for Performance Assessment.

Newkirk, T. (2000). A manual for rubrics. *Education Week, 20*(2), 41.

Norris, C. (1998). *The relationship of tonal memory tests of recognition and tonal memory tests of reproduction.* Unpublished doctoral dissertation, University of Illinois at Urbana-Champaign.

Osgood, C., Suci, G., & Tannenbaum, P. (1957). *The measurement of meaning.* Urbana: University of Illinois Press.

Persky, H., Sandene, B. & Askew, J. (1998). *The NAEP 1997 arts report card.* Washington, DC: U.S. Department of Education.

Phillips, D. C. (1995). The good, the bad, and the ugly: The many faces of constructivism. *Educational Researcher, 24*, 5–12.

Piaget, J. (1971). *Genetic epistemology* (E. Duckworth, Trans.). New York: Norton.

Rauscher, F., Shaw, G., & Ky, K. (1993). Music and spatial task performance. *Nature, 365*, 611.

Reichardt, C., & Rallis, S. (1994). The relationship between qualitative and quantitative traditions. In C. Reichardt & S. Rallis (Eds.), *New directions for program evaluation: Vol. 61. The qualitative-quantitative debate: New perspectives* (5–12). San Francisco: Jossey-Bass.

Reimer, B. (1996). *Musical roles and musical minds: Beyond the theory of multiple intelligences.* Evanston, IL: Northwestern University Press.

Rentz, E. (1992). Musicians' and nonmusicians' aural perception of orchestral instrument families. *Journal of Research in Music Education, 40*(3), 185–192.

Resnick, L. (1996). Performance puzzles: Issues in measuring capabilities and certifying accomplishments (CSE Tech. Rep. 415). Los Angeles: UCLA CRESST.

Richardson, E. (1992). The value of evaluation in evaluation in the federal government: Changes, trends, and opportunities. In C. Wye & R. Sonnichsen (Eds.), *New directions for program evaluation: Vol. 55* (pp. 15–20). San Francisco: Jossey-Bass.

Rogosa, D. (1999). *Accuracy of Year 1, Year 2 comparisons using individual percentile rank scores: Classical test theory calculations.* Los Angeles: UCLA CRESST.

Rumelhart, D. E., & Norman, D. A. (1981). Accretion, tuning and restructuring: Three modes of learning. In J. W. Colton & R. Kaltzky (Eds.), *Semantic factors in cognition* (pp. 37–53). Hillsdale, NJ: Erlbaum.

Scott, S. (2000). An application of the SOLO taxonomy to classify the strategies used by grade 5 students to solve selected music-reading tasks. *Contributions to Music Education, 27*(2), 37–57.

Scriven, M. (1993). *New directions for program evaluation: Vol. 58. Hard won lessons in program evaluation.* San Francisco: Jossey-Bass.

Scriven, M. (1997). Truth and objectivity in evaluation. In E. Chelimsky & W. Shadish, *Evaluation for the 21st century: A handbook* (pp. 477–500). Thousand Oaks, CA: Sage.

Shadish, W., & Cook, T. (2000). As cited by M. Patton in

Overview: Language matters, in R. Hopson (Ed.), *New directions in evaluation: Vol. 86. How and why language matters* (pp. 5–16). San Francisco: Jossey-Bass

Shadish, W., Cook, T., & Leviton, L. (1991). *Foundations of program evaluation: Theories of practice.* Newbury Park, CA: Sage.

Shavelson, R. J., Baxter, G. P., & Gao, X. (1993). Sampling variability of performance assessments. *Journal of Educational Measurement, 30,* 215–232.

Shavelson, R. J., Baxter, G. P., & Pine, J. (1991). Performance assessment in science. *Applied Measurement in Education, 4,* 347–362.

Shavelson, R. J., Mayberry, P. W., Li, W.-C., & Webb, N. M. (1990). Generalizability of job performance measurements: Marine Corps riflemen. *Military Psychology, 2,* 129–144.

Sheldon, D. (1994). Effects of tempo, musical experience, and listening modes on tempo modulation perception. *Journal of Research in Music Education, 42*(2), 190–202.

Sheldon, D., & Gregory, D. (1997). Perception of tempo modulation by listeners of different levels of educational experience. *Journal of Research in Music Education, 45*(3), 367–379.

Shepherd, L. (2001). The role of classroom assessment in teaching and learning. In V. Richardson (Ed.), *Handbook of research on teaching* (4th ed.). Washington, DC: American Educational Research Association.

Shum, D. A. (1994). *The evidential foundational of probabilistic reasoning.* New York: Wiley.

Siebenaler, D. J. (1997). Analysis of teacher–student interactions in the piano lessons of adults and children. *Journal of Research in Music Education, 45*(1), 6–20.

Simpson, E. (1966). *The classification of educational objectives, psychomotor domain.* (OE 5-85-104). Washington, DC: U.S. Department of Health, Education and Welfare.

Skadsem, J. A. (1997). Effect of conductor verbalization, dynamic markings, conductor gesture, and choir dynamic level on singers' dynamic responses. *Journal of Research in Music Education, 45*(4), 509–520.

Smith, M. L. (1994). Qualitative plus/versus quantitative: The last word. In C. Reichardt & S. Rallis (Eds.), *New directions for program evaluation: Vol. 61. Approaches in evaluation studies* (pp. 37–44). San Francisco: Jossey-Bass.

Smith, N. (1992). Aspects of investigative inquiry. In N. Smith (Ed.), *New directions for program evaluation: Vol. 56. Varities of investigative evaluation* (pp. 3–14). San Francisco: Jossey-Bass.

Smith, N. (1995). The influence of societal games on the methodology of evaluative inquiry. In D. Fournier (Ed.), *New directions for program evaluation: Vol. 68. Reasoning in evaluation: Inferential links and leaps* (pp. 5–14). San Francisco: Jossey-Bass.

Snow, R. E., & Lohman, D. F. (1993). Cognitive psychology, new test design, and new test theory: An introduction. In N. Frederiksen, R. Mislevy & I. Bejar (Eds.), *Test theory for a new generation of tests* (pp. 37–44). Hillsdale, NJ: Erlbaum.

Stake, R. E. (1991). Responsive evaluation and qualitative methods. In W. R. Shadish, T. D. Cook, & L. C. Leviton (Eds.), *Foundations of program evaluation: Theories of practice* (270–314). Newbury Park, CA: Sage.

Stake, R. E. (1997). Advocacy in evaluation: A necessary evil. In E. Chelimsky & W. R. Skadish (Eds.), *Evaluation for the 21st century* (pp. 470–478). London: Sage.

Stake, R. E. (2000). A modest commitment to the promotion of democracy. In K. E. Ryan & L. DeStefano, *New directions for program evaluation: Vol. 85. Evaluation as a democratic process: Promoting inclusion, dialogue, and deliberation* (pp. 97–106). San Francisco: Jossey-Bass.

Vispoel, W. (1992).Improving the measurement of tonal memory with computerized adaptive tests. *Psychomusicology, 11*(1), 27–43.

Webb, N., & Schlackman, J. (2000). *The dependability and interchangeability of assessment methods in science* (CSE Tech. Rep. 515). Los Angeles: UCLA CRESST.

Wei, H. (1995). *Development of a melodic achievement test for fourth grades taught by a specific music learning methodology.* Unpublished doctoral dissertation, University of Illinois, Urbana.

Weiss, C. H. (1998). *Evaluation* (2nd ed.). Upper Saddle River, NJ: Prentice Hall.

Wile, J. M., & Tierney, R. J. (1996). Tensions in assessment: The battle over portfolios, curriculum, and control. In R. Calfee & P. Perfumo (Eds.), *Writing portfolios in the classroom: Policy and practice, promise, and peril* (pp. 203–215). Mahwah, NJ: Erlbaum.

Wolf, D. P., & Reardon, S. F. (1996). Access to excellence through new forms of student assessment. In J. B. Baron & D. P. Wolf (Eds.), *Performance-based student assessment: Challenges and possibilities* (pp. 1–31). Chicago: University of Chicago Press.

Yarbrough, C., & Henley, P. (1999). The effect of observation focus on evaluations of choral rehearsal excerpts. *Journal of Research in Music Education, 47*(4), 308–318.

[23]

Measuring Musical Talent

Robert A. Cutietta

If you remember from Chapter 1, aptitude is the term used to describe your child's *potential* for becoming musical. Aptitude is what most people call talent. You would think it would be pretty straightforward to tell if individuals have aptitude. Simply listen to them play their instrument and, if they play well, they are talented; if they don't, they are not. End of story.

Unfortunately, it is a bit more complex than that. First, not everyone lives up to his potential. Second, something may be keeping a child from showing his potential. For example, a child may be a wonderfully talented pianist, but if she sprained a finger the day before her playing test, she would not score up to her potential. More subtle examples would be a child who was asked to perform when he was not feeling well, was distracted or upset, or simply was not used to the piano being played.

The same is true in a variety of settings. How can you spot a child with high musical potential if the child is too young to play an instrument? What if a child with high musical potential comes from a family that could not provide the opportunities to learn to play an instrument? What if the child is trying to play an instrument for which she is not well suited? All these situations would hinder the ability to identify musical talent in a child.

You may be wondering if it is important to actually measure a person's musical potential. You are not alone. Testing is a very controversial topic in music education and I will make no attempt to try to solve that controversy here.

Still, some schools do give formal music aptitude tests and many others use informal methods to identify aptitude. As a parent, know-

Measuring Musical Talent

ing what these tests can and cannot determine will help you. I am not including the addresses for purchasing these tests because they are not intended for use by nontrained personnel. Instead, I offer these descriptions to help you understand the process if your child's aptitude is tested.

Why test?

The primary reason to test for musical aptitude is to identify a child who has outstanding potential so that it can be properly nurtured. Some schools test for this and place students in a gifted and talented program based on their musical, not academic, talent. The second reason is to identify children who have low potential—they will need extra attention to help them along. For the vast majority of children in the middle, I am not sure testing has much usefulness. From a teacher, parent, or student standpoint, it would not seem to help much to know you are average. In fact, it can be detrimental to a child's motivation and drive to know that he or she is average. Still, there is no way to determine who is above or below average without also identifying all the kids in the middle.

How to Use the Results of an Aptitude Test

There are many tests available that will measure musical aptitude. Regardless of the test used, you must remember that it is only one piece of the whole puzzle. No test can predict who will become a great musician because aptitude is only one ingredient. Becoming a good musician takes a combination of effort, the proper opportunities, intelligence, interest, and personality.

The primary reason to test for musical aptitude is to identify a child who has outstanding potential so that it can be properly nurtured.

Raising Musical Kids

This multifaceted foundation for musical skill is supported in the research literature and by common sense. Every study I have read that looks at good musicians finds that aptitude is just one ingredient.[1] Talk to accomplished musicians and they will tell you about people they have known who seem to have more musical aptitude than they do, but never became good musicians because they were not self-motivated or interested enough to practice.

Once you have the results of the aptitude test and other indicators, what you choose to do with these results varies. If your child shows high potential, you will probably want to provide every possible musical experience. However, I would hope you would do this even for a child of average ability. One thing that should never be done is to use a test to exclude a child from receiving music instruction. Every child has some degree of ability. A test can sometimes identify the child who will need extra help and experiences to reach her potential.

Many teachers feel that they do not need a test to tell if someone has musical aptitude. They can just "see" it when working privately with a student. All children are attracted to what they are good at. Therefore, a child with high musical aptitude will be drawn to playing instruments, singing, or dancing.

Still, tests can be very valuable, especially in school settings. Public school music teachers often meet with several hundred students each week. There is no possible way for them to identify the aptitude of all their students without the aid of a test. The danger is that some potentially talented child could get lost in the cracks. Therefore, tests can be a real aid to both teachers and parents.

Norms
Just about all musical aptitude tests are based on norms. To establish norms, a test is given to many students from a variety of settings and backgrounds. From these scores, it is determined what is average (and therefore what is above and below average). Usually there are different norms for different ages and different norms for boys and girls.

A test that is based on norms is called a standardized test. Every standardized test produces a variety of scores (a raw score, a t score, a stanine score, a percentile rank score). Perhaps the easiest score to interpret is a percentile rank. This score simply tells you what percentage of children scored below your child's score. So a percentile rank score of 65 says that 65 percent of the students scored lower. When interpreting these scores, it is important to remember that most people who take the test will be in the average range. Because

Measuring Musical Talent

there are so many people in the middle, a small difference in the score of the test could result in a large difference in percentile.

For example, consider a marathon. After the race has been under way for some time, three distinct groups will emerge: a small group way out in front, a large group in the middle, and another small group far behind. If you are in the middle group, you will have people all around you. If you run a little faster, you will pass several people, thus having more people behind you. This is like moving up in a percentile rank. But if you are in the front group, there are fewer people to pass. If you run a little faster, you will probably pass no one and so your percentile rank will not change. In other words, if you increase your speed while in the average range, you will have an increase in percentile rank because you have passed a certain percentage of the other runners. If you increase your speed exactly the same amount while running with the faster (and thus smaller) group, you might have little or no change in percentile rank because you pass fewer people.

The same is true with standardized tests. One or two answers, either right or wrong, will affect percentile rank substantially if that rank is in the average range, but may not do much if your child's score is already high or low. Therefore, I suggest concentrating on the following rule of thumb. Consider just about anything between the 35th and 65th percentile as average. Use the 65th to 80th percentile as above average. Above the 80th percentile is outstanding.

Available Tests

Several tests are commercially available. The ones described here are the most popular and will most likely be those you may encounter as a parent. For more detail on these tests, other tests, or any of the issues involved with musical testing, I direct you to the book *Measurement and Evaluation of Musical Experiences* by Boyle and Radocy.[2]

Seashore Measures of Musical Talents—as idyllic as its name implies, this test has nothing whatsoever to do with an actual seashore. Instead it is named after the test's creator, Carl Seashore. This is the oldest available test and has six sections: pitch, loudness, rhythm, time, timbre, and tonal memory. In each section the child listens to pairs of example and has to determine whether they are the same or different. This is intended for grades 4 through 12.

The *Musical Aptitude Profile* is a test intended for grades 4 through 12. This test, created by researcher Edwin Gordon, is probably the most popular test of aptitude in use today. It has three major divisions: tonal imagery, rhythm imagery, and musical sensitivity. The first two sections require the student to hear two pairs of musical phrases and determine whether they are the same or different. The last section plays short sections of music and asks the student if the second was better, the same, or worse than the first. The "correct" answer in each section was determined by trained musicians agreeing on which was better.

Offshoots of the Musical Aptitude Profile, also created by Edwin Gordon, are the *Primary Measures of Musical Audiation*, which is intended for children in kindergarten through grade 3, the *Intermediate Measures of Music Audiation*, intended to help discriminate children who do well on the primary version (above the 80th percentile), and *Audie*, a test for children ages six month to five years.

In addition to these standardized tests, there are many instrument manufacturer tests for teachers to use. One of the most popular is the Selmer test, which is marketed by the Selmer Instrument Company. These tests are very popular because they are readily available, inexpensive, and provide the music teacher with practical information. They are designed to test students' potential in music and also to help determine which instrument will be best for them. Naturally, the instrument manufacturers want every child to end up with an instrument, so it is pretty hard to score poorly on one of these tests. Still, many teachers find the results to be helpful.

Many music stores advertise that they will give a free piano lesson with a test that predicts your child's potential. These are the same types of tests as those designed for use in school, but are geared toward private lessons. They probably have some worth, but I doubt that these tests would show anybody as less than slightly above average. It would not be a great marketing technique for a music store to tell a parent "Your son's musical potential is below average. Can I interest you in renting a piano and purchasing six months worth of lessons?"

Creating a good test of a child's musical potential is difficult and time consuming. Still, many teachers devise such tests, often with surprisingly good results. Your child's teacher may have a variety of tests to help in determining your child's potential. These often involve having your child echo rhythmic clapping or echo sing a short phrase. Often teachers ask the child to attempt to play an instrument so they can check things like body and finger size as it relates to the instrument.

～ 42 ～

Measuring Musical Talent

Such tests can be quite accurate. But they depend on the observation and experience of the teacher. As I noted earlier, an experienced music teacher can often assess a student's potential. These little tests allow them to observe your child and make a determination. Although not scientific, they are often surprisingly accurate, but can be quite off the mark as well.

In these tests, as in all tests, it is important to remember that no one test will determine your child's musical potential. Take all the information available to you, add some common sense regarding your child, and trust your gut reaction. This combination will produce the best possible results.

[24]

The Power of the National Standards for Music Education

Paul. R. Lehman

One of the things I learned early in my term as president of MENC that it is very difficult to draw valid generalizations about anything pertaining to music education. The nation is so large and music education involves so many people in so many settings that any generalization is bound to be based on a relatively small sampling of cases. But having offered that disclaimer, I won't allow it to deter me from drawing several generalizations.

I believe that the response to the National Standards for Music Education from the nation's music educators – including teachers of performance – has, in general, been very positive. When we published the first draft of the Standards and invited comments, the most common response was, in effect, "It's about time. We've needed something like this, and now we finally have it."

But it's difficult to explain such a complex undertaking so that the details are immediately clear to everyone. I recall especially the response of a high school choir director who said that she agreed that all of these outcomes were important and that her students should learn these skills but, she said, she simply didn't have time within her schedule to teach "all of this". She went on to explain that when she came to her current job six years ago, she inherited a choir of thirty members. She then developed a large concert choir, an advanced choir, a madrigal group, and a show choir. Her students presented a musical every year. She had an active program of small ensembles. She spent her lunch hours giving private lessons and section rehearsals. She was busy from 8:00 a.m. to 5:00 p.m. every day and most evenings, and she couldn't possibly do anything more.

She was right, no doubt, that she needed more time. Many music teachers do. But her response reflected a basic misunderstanding that I suspect is shared by many readers of the Standards. She thought that the Standards represented a set of learnings that were to be superimposed on her present curriculum. She assumed that they were another layer of skills to be taught in addition to everything she was presently teaching. In fact, the Standards are intended to provide a basic framework for all music teaching that is applicable in every setting, regardless of how much or how little time the teacher has.

Although most teachers seemed to welcome the Standards, I know that there are teachers who see them as largely irrelevant to what they do. I'm thinking, for example, of the band director who believes, "My mission is to develop the best band possible in this school. That involves teaching the kids to play with a good tone, in tune, and in rhythm. It involves giving them the technique to play the notes and the musicianship to interpret the music effectively. Never mind the historical and cultural context or relationships with the other arts. Never mind analysis. Those things are nice, but they're not central to my goals."

I suspect that this group is composed of two subgroups. One subgroup is amenable to persuasion in the face of convincing arguments. The other subgroup is unwilling to broaden its perspective no matter what anyone says. How many people belong in each of these groups and subgroups? No one can say.

Regardless of how teachers have responded to the Standards, the response from the leadership of the various music educators' organizations has been almost unanimously positive. For example, at an annual convention of the American School Band Directors Association, I was given an opportunity to explain why band directors should support the Standards and develop Standards-based programs. I was also invited to present a session on the Standards at an annual Newly Published Music Workshop sponsored by the U.S. Navy Band, and I know that many music education leaders in the standards movement have spoken at similar meetings.

I believe that one of the most impressive demonstrations of support came at the National Music Education Summit sponsored by MENC in September 1994. That meeting brought together some seventy representatives of diverse music organizations to explore how their organizations could work together to implement the Music Standards. These people demonstrated a clear sense of mission and a unanimous view that it was in the best interests of each of their organizations to support the Standards and to seek their implementation in every school district across the nation.

Let's look for a moment at some of the implications of the Standards for the music educator. Some teachers look at the Standards and say, "Everything I do is here. This is all very familiar." They're right, of course. The Standards were designed to reflect the best practices of our profession. Most teachers can teach to the Standards immediately because there's nothing in them that's totally new. But other teachers look at them and find many learnings that they have never taught and perhaps never learned. That can be very intimidating. After all, we can't teach things that we can't do ourselves.

Still, everything called for in the Standards is being taught by good teachers across the nation. What we need are means for those teachers to share their skills and experience with their colleagues who want to learn. We have many avenues to provide those in-service experiences, even though most of the funds for professional development have been short-sightedly eliminated from the *Goals 2000: Educate America Act* by Congress. We have a wide variety of professional meetings organized by all of our professional associations. We have numerous and diverse professional publications. We have large numbers of workshops presented by colleges and universities, especially in summer. We need to find ways to utilize these channels more effectively and to expand them so that professional development opportunities are readily accessible to all music educators.

Exactly what is there in the Standards that causes concern among some teachers? Standards 1 and 2 deal with singing and playing instruments. That's what we do best. That's what we have traditionally emphasized. There's nothing at all that's troublesome here.

Standard 3 concerns improvisation. This has been emphasized almost exclusively in jazz groups and to some extent in elementary and middle-school general music programs. But especially at the earlier levels, we tend to teach improvisation superficially and unsystematically. Our instruction often resembles aural finger painting, in which we accept uncritically whatever the student does and call it creative. We need ways to teach the skills of improvisation more rigorously.

Standard 4 calls for teaching composition. We do this in high school classes labelled Composition and, again, we do it superficially in elementary and middle-school general music programs. But, as in the case of improvisation, we should find ways to bring more rigor and higher expectations to our teaching of composition. We also need to teach both composition and improvisation in more diverse settings.

Standard 5 deals with reading and notation. This is something else that we have traditionally done well. Teachers tend to be comfortable with this standard. Again, there's nothing new here.

Standard 6 concerns listening to, analysing, and describing music. Many of our colleagues emphasize these skills and teach them very effectively. Others devote less effort to these matters.

Standard 7 deals with evaluation. Our attention to this topic is very uneven. It is probably fair to say that in most instances evaluation is treated in an incidental manner and is not emphasized in a systematic and rigorous way.

Standard 8 stresses relationships between music and other disciplines. Although some music teachers do this well, as a profession, we need considerable help with this topic.

Standard 9 deals with the historical and cultural context of music. Again, some teachers do this well, but many of us need help.

Throughout the Standards there is an explicit call for teaching a broader repertoire. There is an emphasis not only on Western art music but also on Western music from outside the art music tradition, including jazz, pop, and folk music, and there is an emphasis on music from the various cultures and ethnic groups throughout the world. It's unrealistic to expect that teachers can quickly expand their repertoires to include knowledge of a broad sampling of all these types of music, but it is possible for teachers to learn some representative exemplary works from the various genres and to expand their personal repertoires gradually on a continuing basis.

The Music Standards specify that "every course in music, including performance courses, should provide instruction in creating, performing, listening to, and analysing music, in addition to focusing on its specific subject matter."[1] This is an idea from the Comprehensive Musicianship Project of twenty-five years ago, to which the faculty of Northwestern University contributed significantly. It's still a good idea, though it will require a broader perspective than some of us have taken in the past.

Teachers have asked, "Should every student electing a music course at the high school level be expected to meet all of the standards for grades 9-12?" The answer is "not necessarily." At the high school level the standards are designed for students who have completed relevant course work. A student electing orchestra, for example, should be expected to do especially well with respect to standards 2 and 5. The level of expectation with respect to the other standards will depend on the emphasis placed by the director on the skills called for in those standards. One would expect that a student who elects any course in music would do better on all of the standards than a student who elects no music, but every student will do better on

---

[1]   Consortium of National Arts Education Associations, *National Standards for Arts Education: What Every Young American Should Know and Be Able to Do in the Arts* (Reston, VA: Music Educators National Conference, 1994), 42.

some standards than on others, depending on the subject matter emphasized in the course(s) elected.

The critical issues in this discussion are these: Why are standards important to music teachers? Why should music teachers support the Standards? Why should they implement Standards-based programs? Here are some of the major reasons in my view:

1. *Standards will benefit students.* They'll benefit students because they can help to ensure that every young American has access to a comprehensive, balanced, and sequential program of music instruction in school. If we can sell the Standards to the public and muster the resources to implement them, every future citizen will have a better life because of music and the other arts. Music programs exist to bring joy, beauty, and satisfaction into the lives of people: to enhance the quality of life.

2. *Standards can focus our efforts.* Standards make it possible to bring every aspect of education into alignment. Now that we have achieved a national consensus on standards specifying what every student should know and be able to do, we can use those standards as a basis for developing curriculum, reforming teacher education, assessing learning, and improving every other aspect of education. Standards provide a basis for rationalizing the entire educational process and making it consistent in a way that has never before been possible.

3. *Standards clarify our expectations.* That's important because, if we can't state clearly what it is we want our students to learn, then we can't be taken seriously by school administrators or by parents. And if students don't know what it is that we want them to learn, they may never learn it, and we can't blame them. Someone once said that if students understand what teachers want them to learn, that's half the battle. Schools have standards already; the problem is that too many schools don't say what they are. The standards are set by default and by individual teachers. So no one is held accountable. Whatever the student does, we find some excuse to accept it. As a result, these de facto standards are so low that we would be embarrassed to state them publicly.

4. *Standards bring equity to our expectations.* Every year one-fifth of the nation's students move to new schools. Their new teachers have no idea what they can do, especially in music, because curricula are so different among districts and states. Teachers can't assume anything. Further, some schools currently have high expectations for students and some have low expectations. Is that fair? It's morally inexcusable and it's socially devastating to expect less of some students just because they come from a certain area of town or a certain socioeconomic background. Basic fairness demands greater equity in our expectations, and standards make that possible. If we expect students to learn, they will, and if we don't, they won't.

5. *Standards move music beyond entertainment.* The Standards give us credibility in claiming that our programs, like those in the other basic disciplines, are based on teaching specific skills and knowledge. They strengthen our argument that music is not simply an activity. It is not merely something to be engaged in as a respite from the serious business of education. It is not primarily entertainment. There is indeed an important body of skills and knowledge to be taught and learned.

6. *Standards give us a basis for claiming needed resources.* If we want students to know and be able to do specific things, then we will need specific minimal levels of time, materials, equipment, and support. With standards we can argue for the resources we need to do our jobs. MENC's Opportunity-to-Learn (OTL) Standards specify what music educators need with respect to curriculum and scheduling, staffing, materials, equipment, and facilities to implement the Standards.[2] The development of OTL standards was originally an important part of the *Goals 2000: Educate America Act*, but, unfortunately, OTL standards became a political casualty and have disappeared for the moment. That doesn't matter much to teachers of math and English because they usually have the time and other resources they need. But OTL standards remain important to music teachers because too often what we have is far short of what we need.

7. *Standards give us a basis for insisting on qualified teachers.* Having standards enables us to bypass the argument about whether music should be taught by classroom teachers or specialists. If the outcomes we seek are vague, imprecise, and undemanding, then it doesn't matter. Anyone can teach music. We don't need music specialists. But if we want to teach specific skills and knowledge as outlined in challenging standards, then we need teachers who possess those skills and that knowledge. If a teacher can teach students to read music and to sing in tune, in rhythm, and with a good tone quality, then it doesn't matter whether the teacher is labelled a music specialist or a classroom teacher. Most teachers who can do those things will be music specialists, but what counts is the result. However, if a school district expects classroom teachers to teach to the Music Standards, then it has to ensure that the classroom teachers it hires possess the necessary skills and can achieve the necessary results.

8. *Standards give us a basis for assessing music learning.* The standards movement has changed the educational landscape utterly and completely. I believe that the standards movement has set the stage for an assessment movement, and I believe that assessment may become the defining issue in music education for the next decade. Developing standards and defining clear objectives that flow naturally from standards make assessment possible where it was often not possible before. But standards do more than make assessment possible. They make it necessary. Standards have brought assessment to the center of the

---

[2]   Music Educators National Conference, *Opportunity-to-Learn Standards for Music Instruction, Grades PreK–12* (Reston, VA: MENC, 1994)

stage and have made it a high-priority, high-visibility issue. Standards and assessment inescapably go hand in hand. We cannot have standards with out assessment.

9. *Standards give music a place at the curricular table*. If we want to play in the game of education reform, we have to play by the rules. Today, increasingly, the rules require standards. Where would we be in the struggle for time in the curriculum if every discipline except music had standards? At the very least, our standards should earn for music a place at the table in the major forums where education reform is discussed. The Standards further strengthen our position because they represent a broad national consensus. They were developed not by music educators alone but through a massive consensus-building process involving representatives of every group with an interest in the arts or in education. These are not MENC's standards; they are America's standards. They give us a banner around which to rally our supporters and a basis for claiming a fair share of the school curriculum.

10. *Standards provide a vision*. Perhaps the most compelling reason for adopting standards is that a school is more likely to be effective if it has a clear vision of what it seeks to achieve than if it doesn't. I believe this is a commonsense notion that will be accepted by most Americans once it is explained to them.

In implementing the Standards through performance, the task that lies ahead is threefold. We should seek to persuade our colleagues to (1) broaden their teaching emphases to include aspects of performing, creating, and analysing music in every music class, (2) broaden the repertoire they teach to include Western art music, Western music from outside the art music tradition, and representative music from the various cultures and ethnic groups of the world, and (3) implement Standards-based programs.

Some of our colleagues will probably pay little attention to the Standards, but I think there is considerable risk involved in that attitude. We cannot expect to exist in isolation from what is happening elsewhere in education. We must understand the process that is taking place around us and participate in it effectively if music education is to survive and flourish in the twenty-first century. If we offer high-quality, Standards-based programs and if we develop good assessment procedures, our programs will almost certainly be less vulnerable to cutbacks or elimination than if we don't.

I have tremendous confidence in the nation's music teachers. I believe that as a group they are well-qualified, committed to their students, and dedicated to their arts. I believe that they are willing to change if and when a strong case for change is presented. The opportunity available in the coming years is historic in its dimensions. Standards will not solve all of the problems facing music education, but they can be a powerful weapon in our arsenal as we seek the support we need to preserve and enhance our programs for the sake of the young people of America.

[25]

The Development and Validation of a Measurement Tool for Assessing Students' Ability to Keep a Steady Beat

Glenn E. Nierman
University of Nebraska—Lincoln

Abstract

The purpose of this study was to develop a valid and reliable way to assess nine-through fourteen-year-old students' ability to maintain a steady tempo of regular pulses given at different tempos in a group setting. One hundred and sixty-seven fifth- and sixth-grade students were asked to count six sounded tones silently and to continue counting at the same tempo established by the six tones during a subsequent period of silence until they heard a major chord sounded. Then they were to mark on their answer sheet the number that had been reached in their silent counting when the chord was sounded. After adjustments, a second version of the Steady Beat Exercise (SBE) was found to be internally consistent ($\alpha = 0.7532$) and item analysis revealed all items indices were within an acceptable range. Criterion-related validity was assessed by correlating teacher ratings with SBE scores using the point-biserial technique.

Choosing the right instrument for beginning instrumental music study is an important decision faced by young students and their parents. Information about students' musical aptitude, timbre preferences, eye-hand coordination, etc. could help students, parents, and teachers to reach a decision about which instrument to play that could result in fewer dropouts from the instrumental music program, and ultimately, a lifetime of enjoyable musical encounters for students. Several years ago, the *Student Musical Instrument Compatibility Test (SMICT)* (Nierman and Pearson, in progress) was designed to provide relevant information for this important decision[1]. The tasks (subtests) included in the SMICT consisted of the assessment of (a) the ability to keep a steady beat, (b) tone color preferences, (c) musical aptitude, and (d) eye-hand coordination. In this study we focused on the development and validation of a tool to assess students' ability to keep a steady beat (or described another way, "to audiate" a steady beat at different tempos), a component which has been identified in the literature as a key component of success in instrumental study.

Assessing rhythmic ability has been a topic of interest to authors of standardized music aptitude and achievement tests since Carl Seashore devised his *Measures of Musical Talent* in 1919. The rhythmic aspect of particular concern for this study was how to assess

---

1 The author gratefully acknowledges the work of Bruce Pearson, co-researcher and developer of the SMICT.

students' ability to keep a steady beat or pulse. Although this aspect of rhythmic ability has received far less attention from researchers than other temporal areas, some studies investigating this area were found. Gordon and Martin (1993–94), for example, used keyboards to determine that one-third to one-half of the subjects (ages 12 to 14) were unable to play consistently in time. Some, such as Parncutt (1994) and Fraisse (1982), looked theoretically at the matter of pulse salience. Others (Geringer, Madsen, and Duke, 1993–94; Geringer, Duke, and Madsen, 1992; and Duke, Geringer, and Madsen, 1991) examined the perception of beat note within varying contexts such as tempo changes. Thackray's (1969) steady beat exercise asked students to join in tapping the pulse at various tempos and then to continue tapping for an additional eight pulses at exactly the same speed (22). This task, however, is very time-consuming, requiring students to be assessed individually. John Flohr (2003) had a similar idea in mind for assessing steady beat. Flohr's (2006) *Rhythm Performance Test Revised (RPT-R)* is a standardized, norm-referenced instrument that measures rhythmic performance to the nearest millisecond. The RPT assesses skills across two domains: (1) matching the steady beat of recorded examples and (2) listening to and repeating rhythm patterns.

The purpose of this study was to develop a valid and reliable way to assess nine-through fourteen-year-old students' ability to maintain a steady tempo of regular pulses given at different tempos in a group setting.

Procedure

The researcher-designed Steady Beat Exercise (SBE) was constructed and validated to determine how well students' inner pulse or sense of a steady beat has developed. There were two administrations of the SBE, a pilot study followed by the primary study. Subjects for the pilot study were 82 fifth grade students, 10–11 years of age, from a suburban school district in the Midwest. Subjects for the primary study were 167 fifth- and sixth-grade students, ages 10–12, again from a suburban school district in the Midwest.

The pilot study was revised for the present study. The total time for administration of the revised 12–item SBE was seven minutes, forty-two seconds. The SBE items were written using Finale™ notation software, which allowed the metronomic markings to be specified exactly, and were then realized for recording on a cassette tape using a Yamaha DX100 synthesizer.

We determined the number of test items and the range of individual test item parameters using the following rationale. Based on research by Geringer, Madsen, and Duke (1993–94), we varied the metronome markings (MM) by twelve beats within a range of MM = 60–120, reasoning that anything less than a difference of twelve may not be perceived by students as significantly different. This resulted in six possible tempos: 60, 72, 84, 96, 108, and 120. It was decided to list beat numbers (BN) 7–16 on the answer sheet, but place the sounded chord only on beats 9–14. This produced a range of six possible beat numbers (9, 10, 11, 12, 13, and 14) on which the chord could be sounded. Placing the sounded chord on beat 7 or 8 would have been too easy and would have perhaps hindered discrimination power. Similarly, placing the chord on beats 15 or 16 at slow tempi was found to be too difficult for children in this age group. To utilize all of the possible MM/BN combinations for the pilot test, thirty-six test items (six MMs times six BNs) were constructed. These items began in beats (beats 9 through 14) on which the major chord was sounded were represented in the revised item pool. An examination of this table showed that all of the beats on which the major chord was sounded were represented twice within the twelve-item pool, but no items at MM = 108 were represented. An examination of the pilot data showed that all MM = 108 items not selected were in the last half of the test, suggesting that fatigue might have been a factor in poor reliability coefficients for these items. Pilot item 34 (MM = 108) was then selected to replace an item in the table of specifications so that this tempo group would be represented. These changes resulted in the twelve-item version of the SBE which had an acceptable reliability coefficient (α = 0.7921). Each of the six beats on which the major chord was sounded represented twice, and each of the six tempo groupings represented at least once (MM = 60—1 item; MM = 72—2 items; MM = 84—3 items; MM = 96—3 items; MM = 108—1 item; and MM = 120—1 item).

The mean of the revised twelve-item SBE given to 167 subjects was 7.907 (SD = 2.869), with an overall reliability coefficient of α = 0.7532. The difficulty and discrimination indices for each item are shown in Table 1.

A criterion-related validity coefficient was obtained by using teacher ratings of students' abilities to keep a steady beat according to a format used by Colwell (1969) in designing the *Music Achievement Tests* (23–24). Teachers in each of the nine classes were asked to list the three students who they thought would score highest and the three students who they thought would score lowest on the SBE. This process imposes an artificial dichotomy upon a truly continuous variable. To eliminate any possible contamination, teachers were not furnished SBE test scores. The results of the biserial technique used to correlate the dichotomous variable (e.g., high/low achievers) with the continuous dependent variable (SBE scores) are shown in Table 2.

Table 1. Item Analysis of SBE (Second Administration)

Item Number (MM/Beat)	Difficulty	Discrimination
1 (84/9)	.705	.333
2 (96/13)	.513	.433
3 (60/11)	.777	.278
4 (120/12)	.534	.441
5 (84/13)	.746	.336
6 (72/24)	.632	.248
7 (96/9)	.762	.519
8 (108/10)	.705	.490
9 (84/11)	.720	.452
10 (108/12)	.570	.472
11 (72/10)	.813	.357
12 (96/14)	.430	.303

the middle range of both MM and BN and then alternated from fast tempo/most delay of sounded chord to slow tempo/least delay of sounded chord until all possible combinations of MM/BN were utilized.

The directions for the revised SBE were modified based on item analysis of the pilot study and observations of those administering the pilot study. The revised directions are noted below:

> In this exercise we are interested in determining how well your inner pulse (P) or sense of a steady beat has developed. For each item you will hear a series of six tones sounded at different speeds—sometimes fast, [P1: sound six beats at MM = 120] sometimes slow [P2: sound six beats at MM = 60]. Count each of these six tones beginning with the number "1" silently to yourself as they are sounded [P3: sound six beats at MM = 96 with whispered counts 1–6]. Continue counting to yourself at the same speed using the numbers (7–8–9–10, etc.) during the period of silence following the tones until you hear a chord that sounds like this: [sound chord alone]. The number you reached in your silent counting when the chord is sounded is the answer we are seeking.

Results

In addition to face validity, construct validity and criterion-related validity were considered relevant to the measure's development. Internal reliability, examined by computing coefficient alpha, and item analysis (computing difficulty and discrimination indices) were further examined in the primary study ($N = 167$).

The construct validity of the SBE, defined as the degree to which the ability to keep a steady beat is a unique aspect or dimension of rhythmic ability, was examined through a review of the literature. Thackray's (1969) study of the relationship between rhythmic perception and rhythmic performance was particularly relevant to construct validity considerations. He concluded in his analysis of his combined rhythmic performance batteries that although there was "...considerable evidence for a substantial factor of 'general rhythmic ability' running through the tests" (34), "the general low correlations between the [rhythmic perception] tests suggest a fairly high degree of specificity, which supports the hypothesis that rhythmic ability is complex and many-sided" (18).

It was considered desirable to assess students' ability to maintain a steady tempo of regular pulses given at different tempi using less time and fewer test items. Therefore, using information from face validity reviews by a panel of experts, from item analysis, and from SPSS Reliability Analysis–Scale (Alpha) of the pilot study, the SBE was revised for a second administration.

The revision of the SBE began by making adjustments in the directions based on the review of the panel of experts and resulted in the changes previously noted in the Procedure section of this report. Then, using the SPSS Reliability Analysis–Scale (Alpha), various SBE items with the most damaging effects to coefficient alpha were discarded. This resulted in the elimination all but twelve of the original thirty-six items. With attention to keeping items with acceptable difficulty and discriminating indices, a table of specifications was then created to ascertain that all six tempo groups (MM = 60, 72, 84, 96, 108, and 120) and all six

Table 2. Correlations of Teacher Ratings (High/Low)
with SBE Scores (Second Administration)

Class (n)	r
1 (20)	.705
2 (23)	.580
3 (22)	.830
4 (22)	.742
5 (22)	.532
6 (26)	.424
7 (29)	.274

Discussion

The purpose of this study was to develop a valid and reliable way to assess nine-through fourteen-year-old students' ability to maintain a steady tempo of regular pulses given at different tempos. The essence of the discussion, then, should focus on the validity and reliability of the instrument.

The information supplied from item analysis statistics can provide useful guidelines for construction and interpretation of the data-gathering instrument. Colwell (1970) offers the following guidelines for the difficulty value:

...there should be no question that everyone answers correctly and no question that everyone misses; all those taking the test should be able to correctly answer some of the items, but no one should be able to make a perfect score. Test makers often strive for a range of difficulty from 0.20 to 0.80, with most of the items from 0.40 to 0.70 (65).

Item discrimination may be misleading and requires careful scrutiny of the questions themselves. Colwell interprets this value as follows: "The higher the item discrimination, the more fair the measurement. With the previous exceptions, item discrimination should be above 0.20" (Colwell, 1970, 66).

With these criteria in mind, an examination of Table 1 shows that in terms of the difficulty index, the SBE items are all within the acceptable ranges indicated by Colwell, although there were two students who got a perfect score on the exercise. Likewise, all of the discrimination values are acceptable in terms of the criteria given by Colwell. The highest discrimination value was only 0.519, however.

In the interpretation and evaluation of a reliability coefficient, it should be remembered that factors such as length, objectivity, heterogeneity of the group, clarity and conciseness of directions and test items, conditions of administration, independence of items, order of items, and scope contribute in varying degrees to the reliability of a test (Lehman, 1968, 14). However, in criteria discussed by Nunnally (1978, 245), the SBE correlation coefficient ($\alpha = 0.7532$) would seem to be acceptable for measuring an area where a wide range of abilities exist.

Just as SBE reliability was found to be acceptable, so the validity of the SBE was found to be suitable for assessment of student's ability to keep a steady beat. Face and construct validity were probed as part of the pilot study, and appropriate revisions were made before the second administration of the exercise. Of particular interest are the point biserial correlations between teacher rankings and SBE scores from the revised version of the exercise found in Table 2. The majority of the correlations are moderately high, i.e., the correlation is equal to or greater than 0.50. However, one of the correlations (0.274 for class 7) showed a very low correlation between teacher rankings and SBE scores. Perhaps the teacher rankings for class 7 were made more difficult by the fact that several students new to the district were enrolled in that class.

In conclusion, the twelve-item version of the SBE was found to have an acceptable reliability coefficient, verifying the internal consistency of the test. Construct validity was supported by a review of the literature, which confirmed that the ability to keep a steady beat is a unique aspect or dimension of rhythmic ability; and criterion-related validity was shown by the correlations between SBE scores and teacher ratings of ability to keep a steady beat. It seems plausible, then, that the SBE is a valid and reliable tool that could assist music educators and researchers in assessing students' ability to maintain a steady tempo of regular pulses given at different tempos.

References

Colwell, R. 1968–70. *Music achievement test manuals.* Chicago: Follett Educational Corporation.

Duke, R., J. Geringer, and C. Madsen. 1991. Performance of perceived beat in relation to age and music training. *Journal of Research in Music Education, 39*(1):35–45.

Flohr, J. 2006. *Rhythm performance test-revised.* Champaign, IL: Electronic Courseware Systems.

Fraisse, P. 1982. Rhythm and tempo. In D. Deutsch, ed., *The psychology of music,* 149–177. Orlando, FL: Academic Press, Inc.

Geringer, J., Duke, R., and Madsen, C. 1992. Musicians' perception of beat note: Regions of beat change in modulating tempos. *Bulletin of the Council of Research in Music Education, 114,* 21–33.

Geringer, J., Madsen, C., and Duke, R. 1993–94. Perception of beat change in modulating tempos. *Bulletin of the Council of Research in Music Education, 119,* 49–57.

Gordon, A., and Martin, P. 1993–94. A study of the rhythmic skills of musically unsophisticated secondary school students when playing the electronic keyboard with a drum machine. *Bulletin of the Council of Research in Music Education, 119,* 59–64.

Parncutt, R. 1994. A perceptual model of pulse salience and metrical accent in musical rhythms. *Music Perception: An Interdisciplinary Journal, 11,* 409–464.

Nierman, G., and Pearson, B. *Student Musical Instrument Compatibility Test (SMICT).* In progress.

Thackray, R. 1969. *An investigation into rhythmic abilities.* London: Novello and Company Limited.

Part V
Multicultural and World Music

[26]

Teaching About and Through Native American Musics: An Excursion into the Cultural Politics of Music Education

Bryan Burton and Peter Dunbar-Hall

Abstract

Expectations that comprehensive music education includes all types of music have led to a situation in which musical diversity has become standard in music classrooms. Concomitant with these expectations is the requirement that the cultural contexts of music are also studied. These developments in music education have produced, however, a situation in which the ways music is taught may be at odds with the cultural contexts of the music in question. This disjuncture between expectation and practice is highlighted here in discussion of teaching through and about the musics of Native Americans. In that their musical characteristics and lyrical messages raise issues of post-colonialism, analysis of the position of these musics in music education acts as a form of post-colonial critique of music education, and is used to raise issues which relate to the teaching of music as a cultural artefact with political and social implications.

Educating Native Americans. Those three words encapsulate a 500 year-old battle for power to define what education is – the power to set its goals, define its policies, and enforce its practices – and second, the power to define who native people are and who they are not. European and American colonial governments, operating through denominations of the Christian Church, first defined 'education' for Native Americans as the cleansing, uplifting and thoroughly aggressive and penetrating force that would Christianise, civilise and individualise a heathen, barbaric and tribal world (Tsianina Lomawaima, 1995, p. 331).

In her analysis of the systemic education of Native Americans, Muskogee-Creek researcher Tsianina Lomawaima raises a number of issues which underpin the present discussion – definition and control of pedagogy, implications of the value of indigenous ways of knowing, and post-colonial critique of education. While Tsianina Lomawaima's comments refer to the education of Native Americans, the present article applies the issues she raises to music education as a means of discussing disjuncture between the broad aims of education, the expectations placed on music educators, and the day to day teaching methods of music classrooms. To give the discussion a focus, the music of Native Americans, as it appears in north American music education, is used. In addition to using a post-colonial artefact to investigate educational handling of post-colonialism, this provides a means by which indigenous voices can be heard in an educational arena. The site of the discussion is culture, and a position is adopted which resonates with that of Mitchell (2000) - that disputes engendered by culture are symptomatic of the current world situation, that we are in a period of "culture wars – those battles, rooted in ideology, religion, class difference, the social construction of racial, ethnic and gender difference, and so on that mark contemporary society" (Mitchell, 2000, p. 4). Through its focus on culture, and the ways this influences music teaching and learning, the present discussion can be classified in general terms as belonging to debates about multiculturalism in music classrooms; post-colonialism is subsequently categorised as a sub-discipline of that wider field of research, one which implicates politics as an aspect of music education.

Before outlining the arguments raised in this article, it is important to clarify the use of the term 'post-colonial' in relation to music education. Like 'post-feminism', 'post-modernism' and 'post-structuralism', 'post-colonialism' is used across many fields with many implications. Here it is used to define that movement in education that proactively seeks to focus attention on the critique of knowledge construction to expose ways in which what is taught in schools induces students into ways of thinking which are culturally derived. It implies that through omission of consideration of other ways of thinking that current methods of instruction define official ways of knowing. These official ways of knowing are Eurocentric, and thus perpetuate colonialist positions, marginalise indigenous ways of knowing, and ultimately negate the basic premise of education as equitable. In that they ignore pedagogic factors inherent to different types of music, and that these pedagogic factors may assist in the development of understanding of a music, the continuation of these 'official' ways of knowing can hinder comprehensive understanding of music. A post-colonial critique of music education seeks to uncover contradictions between the cultural sources and uses of music, and the strategies through which music is taught. At the same time, through its intention to teach music "in terms of itself" (Hood, 1971, p. v), music education which seeks to be post-colonial in nature uses the teaching of indigenous musics to redress the cultural stereotyping of indigenous peoples through musical representation in multiple forms of media, especially popular media including film, literature, popular music, television, and radio, to raise awareness of social issues relevant to indigenous lives, and through experience of the symbolic nature of music to reaffirm the potential of music education to develop symbolic competence in students.

Already a number of issues problematic to music education have been signalled in these definitions of the terms of reference of this article. Perhaps the best way to summarise the contradiction between current ways of teaching, and a futurist, post-colonial pedagogy, is to place two statements about the concept of universalism as an underlying ideology of arts education alongside each other. The (American) Consortium of National Arts Education Associations (CNAEA) presents arts education as a cultural levelling process when it states that:

> Arts education standards . . . insist . . . that students learn about the diverse cultural and historical heritages of the arts. The focus of these Standards is on the global and universal, not the local and the particular (CNAEA, 1994, p. 10),

while Ashcroft, Griffiths and Tiffin (1995, p. 55) remind us that universalism furthers the implicit power of European thinking:

> The concept of universalism is one of particular interest to post-colonial writers because it is this notion of a unitary and homogeneous human nature which marginalises and excludes the distinctive characteristics, the difference, of post-colonial societies. . . The myth of universality is thus a primary strategy of imperial control (which) has a pernicious effect in the kind of colonialist criticism which denigrates the post-colonial text on the basis of an assumption that 'European' equals 'universal.'

How does this apply to the teaching of Native American musics? Despite syllabus and educational policy statements which mandate cultural sensitivity, acknowledge music's cultural perspectives, and expect that students develop competency in culture (CNAEA, 1994, passim), analysis of the musical aesthetics of Native American cultures as "local and particular" peoples (if such a Western concept as musical aesthetics can be applied in this case) shows music which may be at odds with the underlying premises of music education as represented by the Consortium of National Arts Education Associations. These issues are discussed here through reference to the following areas: attempts by researchers since the 1970s to encourage not only the inclusion of Native American musics in the curriculum, but to deconstruct the strategies through which this is done; some brief analytical comments on contemporary Native American music practices, particularly with reference to music as post-colonial artefact; and investigation of how teaching through and about Native American musics introduces levels of post-colonial discourse to classrooms.

Native American Musics in Music Education

In American arts education, competency in 'culture' is positioned by the Consortium of National Arts Education Associations as something which "students should know and be able to do" (CNAEA, 1994, passim). As in many other countries, in the teaching of music this relies on diversity of musical content, and requires that teachers lead students to an "understanding of music in relation to history and culture" (CNAEA, 1994, p. 29). Among the types of music mentioned in explanation of these ideas, music of Native Americans is specifically cited:

> The culture of the United States is a rich mix of people and perspectives, drawn from many cultures, traditions, and backgrounds . . . The cultural diversity of America is a vast resource for arts education, and should be used to help students understand themselves and others. . . the polyrhythmic choreography of Native American dancing (is) more than simply cultural artefact; (it is) part of the world's treasure house of expression and understanding (CNAEA, 1994, pp. 13-14).

To teach this music automatically brings post-colonial discourse into the music classroom, as musically and textually this music results from and states opinions about the past and present status of indigenous peoples in colonised settings. Through the information required to explain it, traditional music from the past raises issues of the history and cosmology of Native Americans; contemporary music by Native Americans expresses political opinion, analyses historical events from the perspective of the present, and depicts the current situations of Native Americans. As with the music of indigenous peoples in other post-colonial settings, in contemporary songs the voices of formerly subaltern peoples are heard – both literally and figuratively.

Teaching about and through these musics poses problems. The first is the disjuncture between teaching content and teaching method. Since the 1970s the inclusion of diverse musics as the content of music education classes has been accepted. However, while the music of Native Americans might be studied in classrooms, attention to how this is done in a culturally sensitive manner is rarely raised in music education literature. A small number of authors has discussed the pedagogic and philosophical problems of this situation. In an article in *Music Educators Journal* in 1970, Cherokee-Quapaw musician and educator Louis Ballard listed characteristics of Native American music which differ from Western tonal music and therefore require their own teaching and learning strategies. He notes that in Native American societies, music is learnt by ear or rote and in traditional music is not notated. In these settings, music: must be learnt as scriptless oral language; has distinctive characteristics of the tribal culture from which it arises; always serves a purpose and never exists alone. He points out that tunings differ from those of Western tonal music, and that how people sing is as meaningful as what they sing (Ballard, 1970, pp. 40-42). All of these challenge ways in which Western, notated music is usually taught, and how received music education methods function. Two decades later Campbell (1989) focused her discussion of song acquisition among Native Americans on learning which acknowledges the spiritual dimensions of music, and on recognition that music relies on ongoing creativity. Sarrazin (1995) noted the links between music and actions or behaviour, music's functional nature, that music for isolated listening does not exist, that music is primarily vocal, and perhaps the greatest threat to notions of music derived or implied from Western music, that "the idea of a composer as we know it does not exist" (Sazzarin, 1995, pp. 34-35). Boyea (1999a) investigates Native American senses of time to show how understanding of these are essential to comprehension of Native American music. Like Campbell, she discusses the spiritual and symbolic nature of Native American music. In another article, she questions the motives for inclusion of Native American music in the curriculum:

> In the curriculum, Native American music is often seen as an element . . . aimed at laying foundations for effective community in a diverse society, a kind of cultural bridge, and a part of multicultural education. . . . not everyone agrees on what such a curriculum should be . . . (Boyea, 1999b, p. 105).

In a subsequent article (Boyea, 2000, p. 22), she calls for music teaching which "makes the invisible visible" and which teaches from and towards the "deeply, potent (and) meaningful" nature of Native American music.

Some solutions to these pedagogic problems have been proposed. Schupman (1992) provides lesson materials for the performance of a Plains Indian dance, and to encourage understanding of aspects of a recorded performance of its accompanying song. In a series of conference papers and publications, Burton (incl. 1993, 1994, 1996, 1998, 2000) demonstrates how performance, listening which leads to cultural understanding, and contextualisation of music through reference to Native American ways of thinking about and using music can be incorporated into music teaching and learning. Speaking from a Navajo-Ute perspective, Nakai

(Nakai & Demars, 1996) provides ways of understanding one specific repertoire of Native American music through activities for teaching and learning the Native American flute. Most recently, Shelemay (2001) includes a Comanche lullaby in her overview of music in diverse cultural settings to demonstrate the complexities of Native American music which has specific uses, but which has different meanings for different performers and listeners. She also includes the music of a Shoshone Pow-wow as an example of music in Native American political life.

Native American Musics: Some Explanatory Notes

In recent years country, folk, rap, reggae and 'classical' sounds have been melded with the traditional sounds of Native American music. While some researchers consider this to be symptomatic of a breakdown in traditional cultural and musical values, others see it as the adaptation of new media and forms of expression as a means of transmitting traditional information to new audiences, both indigenous and non-indigenous. These stylistic developments of Native American musics are all suitable topics through which music teaching and learning can proceed. The uses of instruments, presence of native languages in lyrics, traditional melodic and rhythmic structures, and cultural functions of music also yield potential issues for study.

While Native American traditional instruments such as rattles and drums occur on many recordings by contemporary indigenous musicians (eg. Red Road Ensemble, Red Thunder, Walela, XIT), R Carlos Nakai's recordings of the Native American flute provide demonstrations of this instrument in combination with the instruments of Western popular music and of how problems of intonation are negotiated when disparate tuning systems meet; this is particularly salient when traditional 'flute songs' provide the melodic material of Nakai's jazz. Through these recordings and Nakai's publication of traditional Native American flute repertoire (Nakai & Demars, 1996) study of the construction, uses, and repertoires of instruments can be accessed. In some cases the use of traditional instruments is linked to other symbolic statements in performance. When XIT use Native American drums, perform in Indian dress in front of the American Indian Movement flag, utilise material culture (such as Native design blankets) on stage, and sing songs such as 'Coming of the whiteman', race-related messages and statements of position are clearly implied.

In their writings on Native American music, some authors (notably Campbell, Boyea and Sazzarin) emphasise its spiritual characteristics. XIT's *'Nihaa shil hozho'*, a courting song, uses symbolism which is recognisably Native American;

> I call you sunflower,

> You're the flower that happiness grows . . .

reminiscent of Navajo poetry, the ritual connecting of elements of nature to the human spirit, and establishing that elusive balance within the circle of life that Navajo call *hozho* (beauty). Among many Native Americans, there is strong belief that music is all surrounding and exists in all living things – natural occurrences, such as wind, a storm, or sunlight, can reveal songs to people who 'catch' them to share with others. This traditional belief is what the group Songcatcher alludes to in their name. Here, differences between Native American relationships of music and its creator, or medium, and those in other music systems provide another level at which thinking about music becomes a pedagogical issue. Melodies used by this group follow the collapsible melodic contour characteristic of Plains-style Native American music, beginning in an upper register and gradually descending to repetitions of the final pitch. In their songs racial tension is given as a cause for the loss of spiritual balance. Their songs, rely on levels of spiritualism, express the idea that traditional values persist, and that it is possible to re-establish balance with the universe, to "walk in beauty . . . dream in colour". This group also utilise the Native American tradition of using music to teach history, ideas of racial harmony, cultural values, and spirituality.

In addition to teaching aspects of Native American cosmology, contemporary Native American music can be aligned with trends in the wider world of popular music. In 'NDN Kars', a 1980s hit song by Keith Secola and his Wild Band of Indians, fusion of Native American sounds with world beat and tribal dance characteristics in a style known generically as 'alterNative' can be heard. Again, combinations of a Native American language (Lakota) and English, the Native American flute, and collapsible melody can be observed. This song is a powerful commentary on contemporary Native American life, addressing issues of poverty, alcoholism, political activism, racism, and the values placed in spiritualism. Secola, an Anishinabe Native American, lists Bob Dylan, Neil Young and Woody Guthrie as influences on his songs, as well as Native Americans Peter Lafarge, Buffy St Marie, and Floyd Red Crow Westerman. He has also benefited from the mentoring of Jerry Garcia, David Bowie, Mickey Hart, Nirvana and U2. Other Native American musicians whose songs belong in both indigenous and wider contexts include the Oneida musician Joanne Shenandoah, who protests about the Gulf War in 'This baby of mine', and Cree singer/songwriter, Buffy Sainte-Marie. While some of Sainte-Marie's songs, such as 'Now the buffalo's gone', refer to issues specific to Native American concerns, her 'Universal soldier' is an anti-war song, and 'Cod'ine' discusses drug dependence.

Post-colonial Applications of Native American Musics in Music Education

As these comments on contemporary Native American music practices demonstrate, this music includes more than traditional sounds. As with many other indigenous peoples in post-colonial countries, traditional sounds are integrated into contemporary forms of music. This can clearly be heard in the music of Australian Aboriginal performers such as Yothu Yindi; in New Zealand, in contemporary Maori songs by Moana and the Moahunters; in recordings by the Papuan musician, Telek; and in the work of the Innu duo, Kashtin. Like the songs of contemporary Native American musicians, the songs of these musicians include high levels of social and political comment. Reference to contemporary Native American musics in this way acts beyond simply the teaching of Native American musics as a specific music system and introduces global practices among indigenous musicians in which music acts as a medium of post-colonial comment. As Burton (1994) and Zimmerman, Zimmerman and Bruguier (2000) note, the infrastructure of electronic technologies is crucial in this context as a site for the exposition of musico-political opinion. In addition, in countries where teachers lack the confidence to teach music systems which might not have been studied as part of their pre-service training, or where the ethical and religious implications of traditional musics are poorly understood, teaching through and about contemporary indigenous music presents music educators with a solution to a problem of inclusion. This is borne out by Dunbar-Hall and Wemyss (2000), who point out in their analysis of the position of popular music in music education, that for Australian music educators, teaching indigenous music through recordings of Australian Aboriginal and Torres Strait Islander rock groups, rather than through these peoples' little known traditional musics, alleviates problems arising from the expectation that Australian indigenous musics will be included in the music curriculum.

An important objective of post-colonial activity is the intention of colonised peoples to contradict received images of them, and to challenge perceptions of indigenous peoples as examples of 'museum cultures'. In a museum exhibit view of a culture, a culture is set in a traditional past, is usually stereotypically constructed (Tsianina Lomawaima mentions perceptions of Native Americans as "heathen, barbaric and tribal"), and is limited to cultural cliches reproduced and replicated in forms of popular media. The use of a limited number of musical effects (such as a "'tom-tom' rhythmic drumming figure of equal beats, the first of every four beats being accented", Gorbman, 2000, p. 235) in films since the earliest days of sound films through to the 1990s series of *Pochahontas* films, has implied a strereotypical, limited cultural representation of Native Americans in popular culture. This has been reinforced in popular songs (eg, the 1959 Johnny Preston hit, 'Running Bear'), and by personalities such as 'the Indian' member of Village People. Teaching of the range of musics from Native American cultures, experiences of singing and dancing, knowledge of instruments their uses and developments over time, and realisation of the ongoing developmental nature of these cultures, evident in the relatively recent development of intertribal pow-wow songs (Taylor, 1995; Browner, 2000) and the recordings of contemporary Native American popular musicians, teach that Native

American cultures are varied and developmental, that they respond like all cultures to ideas and actions, and that they provide a means of comprehending culture as a force in human life.

A final way in which Native American music in the classroom raises issues of post-colonialism is through the lyrics of songs. Two issues arise here: the topics of songs, and the languages used in lyrics. If expectations that the cultural perspectives of music are studied are to be met, the lyrics of songs automatically require awareness of economic, political, and sociological aspects of indigenous life in America. Songs which refer to the treatment of Native Americans in the past (Floyd Red Crow Westerman's 'Custer died for your sins'), to the environmental concerns of Native Americans (Joanne Shenandoah's 'Mother Earth speaks'), to statements of social and cultural conflict (Songcathcer's 'Getaway car'), to indigenous land rights (Red Thunder's '*Makoce wakan* [Sacred ground]'), to loss of native language (Buffy Sainte-Marie's 'My people 'tis of thy people you're dying'), and to the strength of Native American belief systems (Sharon Burch's 'Yazzie girl') all raise issues of Native American life. When in the 1960s Buffy Sainte-Marie sang in 'My country 'tis of thy people you're dying':

> Now that the longhouses breed superstition
>
> You forced us to send our toddlers away
>
> To your schools where they're taught to despise their traditions
>
> Forbid them their languages, then further say
>
> That American history really began when Columbus
>
> Set sail out of Europe . . .,

in addition to employing post-colonial strategies of subverting nationalistic anthems (cf. 'My country 'tis of thee') and correcting historical fallacy, she also drew attention to ways in which the use of native languages was forbidden. The use of Native American languages in the lyrics of contemporary songs is not only a way in which formerly subaltern voices are performed and heard, but a means of teaching the role of language as a context in which culture is maintained.

Conclusion

It would be difficult not to introduce levels of post-colonialism into classrooms in teaching through and about Native American musics, as these musics express post-colonialism in may ways. Musically, their mixtures of traditional indigenous and contemporary sounds define a basic cultural practice of colonised peoples – the symbolic integration of and tensions between continuing tradition and the present. Uses of music to reclaim cultural signifiers, such as language, and to counter received stereotypical images of Native Americans resonate with post-colonial arts practices internationally; issues of the colonised past and its present outcomes provide the topics of songs. Continuing belief in the power of music not only to state Native American positions, but to reference levels of symbolism, imply a music aesthetic which may be at odds with that of other, mainstream musics. As some authors have noted, musical differences require pedagogic ones. Alterity is clear; despite the intentions of universalist arts education, musically, the local and particular cannot be avoided.

While socio-cultural aspects of Native American musics can be demonstrated, it is important to be wary of essentialising Native Americans and their musics. As reference to songs by Buffy Sainte-Marie (above) shows, these musics belong in the many wider contexts of contemporary music and address issues beyond those specifically drawn from Native American experience. Similarly, the study of Native American musics can be seen as part of broader moves within academe in general. For example in anthropology (Deloria, 1969; Biolsi & Zimmerman, 1997), cultural studies (Smith & Ward, 2000), education (Tsianina Lomawaima, 1995; Smolkin & Suina, 1999) and history (Brown, 1970 ; Fixico, 1997), 'rethinking' (Fixico, 1997) the position of Native Americans is now a definable thread of discourse. Part of this "new era (which has) challenged scholars to reconsider carefully previous views and interpretations" (Fixico, 1997, p 3) is attention accorded to the voices of Native Americans through indigenous recollection (Ahenakew et al, 1995; Gonzalez et al 1997), film (the 1990 *Dances with Wolves*), political statement (Alfred, 1999) and autobiography (Mankiller, 1993). In this broader perspective:

> We have begun to study women, immigrants, workers, slaves, lesbians and gays, children, Native Americans, African, Asian and Hispanic Americans, Eastern and Southern European Americans, and indeed Northern and Western European Americans as well, for what we're talking about is not simply ethnicity or gender but *power* . . . (Levine, 1996, p. 146)

Levine's analysis of the study of culture as power related reminds us that the way something is studied becomes the way that thing is conceptualised and known. Native American musics in music classrooms have the potential to teach much about Native Americans, about culture as an aspect of human life, and about the intricacies and ambiguities of cultural representation. Acceptance of these musics, and clarity about the implications of the study of them, is however only the initial step in the ongoing development of music education as an equitable enterprise. The issue of culturally appropriate pedagogy remains the challenge for music educators. Wilson (1997, p. 101), writing about the position of Native American oral traditions in the field of American history, indicates a corresponding situation in the relationships between teaching content, teachers, and teaching method. Her comments are applicable to music education as much as to any other field:

> Since its inception, the area of American Indian history has been dominated by non-Indian historians who use non-Indian sources to create non-Indian interpretations about American Indians . . . very few have attempted to find out how native people would interpret, analyse, and question the written documents they confront, nor have they asked if the native people they are studying have their own versions or stories of their past that might be pertinent . . .

Recordings

The Best of Buffy Sainte-Marie. Buffy Sainte-Marie. Vanguard 3/4-2.
Dreaming in Color. Songcatcher. A&M Records 31454-0247-2.
Fingermonkey. Keith Secola and His Wild Band of Indians. Akina Records ARCD001.
Kashtin – Akua Tuta. Kashtin. Columbia CK80209.
Kokopelli's Café. R. Carlos Nakai. Canyon Records CR-7013.
Makoce Wakan. Red Thunder. Thunder Records 3-7916-2-HI.
Music for the Native Americans. Robbie Robertson and the Red Road Ensemble. Capitol CDP 7243 8 28295 2 2.
Once in a Red Moon. Joanne Shenandoah. Canyon Records CR5-48.
Plight of the Redman. XIT. Sounds of American Records SOAR 101-CD.
Serious Tam. Telek. Origin OR055.
Tahi. Moana and the Moahunters. Festival D30787.
This Land is Your Mother/Custer Died for Your Sins. Floyd Red Crow Westerman.
Touch the Sweet Earth. Sharon Burch. Canyon Records CR-535.
Tribal Voice. Yothu Yindi. Mushroom D30602.
Walela. Walela. Mercury 314 536 049-2.

References

Ahenakew, F., Gardipy, B., & Lafond, B. (Eds.), (1995). *Voices of the First Nations*. Toronto: McGaw Hill Ryerson.

Research Studies in Music Education   63

Alfred, T. (1999). *Peace, power, righteousness: An Indigenous manifesto*. Oxford: Oxford University Press.

Ashcroft, B., Griffiths, G., & Tiffin, H. (Eds.), (1995). *The post-colonial studies reader*. London: Routledge.

Ballard, L. (1970). Putting American Indian music in the classroom. *Music Educators Journal, 56*(7), 38-44.

Biolsi, T., & Zimmerman, L. (Eds.), (1997). *Indians and anthropologists: Vine Deloria Jr and the critique of anthropology*. Tucson: University of Arizona Press.

Boyea, A. (1999a). Encountering complexity: native musics in the curriculum. *Philosophy of Music Education Review, 7*(1), 31-48.

Boyea, A. (1999b). Native American music and curriculum: controversies and cultural issues. *Philosophy of Music Education Review, 7*(2), 105-117.

Boyea, A. (2000). Teaching Native American music with story for multicultural ends. *Philosophy of Music Education Review, 8*(1), 14-23.

Brown, D. (1970). *Bury my heart at wounded knee: an Indian history of the American west*. London: Barrie & Jenkins.

Browner, T. (2000). Making and singing pow-wow songs: text, form and the significance of culture-based analysis. *Ethnomusicology, 44* (2), 214-233.

Burton, B. (1993). *Moving within the circle: contemporary Native American music and dance*. Danbury (CT): World Music Press.

Burton, B. (1994). Preservation, destruction or evolution? The impact of music technology upon Native American musics. In H. Lees (Ed.), *Proceedings of the 21ˢᵗ World Conference of the International Society for Music Education* (pp. 41-45). Auckland: International Socierty for Music Education.

Burton, B. (1996). Native peoples of North America. In W. Anderson& P. Shehan Campbell (Eds.), *Multicultural perspectives in music education* (pp. 11-40). Reston (VA): Music Educators National Conference.

Burton, B. (1998). *Voices of the wind: Native American flute songs*. Danbury (CT): World Music Press.

Burton, B. (2000). Lullabies and childrens' game songs of the native peoples of North America. In M. Taylor & B. Gregory (Eds.), *Proceedings of the ISME 2000 World Conference, Edmonton, Canada*, (pp. 76-85). Edmonton: International Sopciety for Music Education

Campbell, P. (1989). Music learning and song acquisition among Native Americans. *International Journal of Music Education, 14*, 24-31.

Consortium of National Arts Education Associations, (1994). *National Standards for Arts Education: What Every Young American Should Know and Be Able To Do in the Arts*. Reston (VA): Music Educators National Conference.

Deloria, V. (1969). *Custer died for you sins*. New York: Macmillan.

Dunbar-Hall, P., & Wemyss, K. (2000). The effects of the study of popular music on music education. *International Journal of Music Education, 36*, 23-34.

Fixico, D. (Ed.), (1997). *Rethinking American Indian history*. Albuquerque: University of New Mexico Press.

Gonzalez, A., Houston, M., & Chen, V. (Eds.), (1997). *Our voices: essays in culture, ethnicity and communication*. Los Angeles: Roxbury Publishing.

Gorbman, C. (2000). Scoring the Indian: music in the liberal western. In G. Born & D. Hesmondalgh (Eds.), *Western music and its others: difference, representation and appropriation in musi c* (pp. 234-253). Los Angeles: University of California Press.

Hood, M. (1971). *The ethnomusicologist*. New York: McGraw-Hill.

Levine, L. (1996). *The opening of the American mind: canons, culture and history*. Boston: Beaconsfield Press.

Mankiller, W. (1993) *Mankiller: a chief and her people*. New York: St Martin's Press.

Mitchell, D. (2000). *Cultural geography: a critical introduction*. Oxford: Blackwell.

Nakai, R., & Demars, J. (1996). *The art of the Native American flute*. Phoenix (AZ): Canyon Records.

Sarrazin, N. (1995). Exploiting aesthetics: focus on Native Americans. *Music Educators Journal, 81*(4), 33-36.

Schupman, E. (1992). Lessons on Native American music. *Music Educators Journal, 78*(9), 33.

Shelemay, K. (2001). *Soundscapes: exploring music in a changing world*. New York: Norton.

Smith, C. & Ward, G. (Eds.), (2000). *Indigenous cultures in an interconnected world*. Vancouver: UBC Press.

Smolkin, L. & Suina, J. (1999). Cross-cultural partnerships: acknowledging the 'equal other' in the rural/urban American Indian teacher education program. *Teaching and Teacher Education, 15*, 571-590.

Taylor, D. (1995). Powwows evolving from traditional to high-tech. In F. Ahenakew, B. Gardipy, & B. Lafond, (Eds.), *Voices of the first nations* (pp. 162-164). Toronto: McGaw Hill Ryerson.

Tsianina Lomawaima, K. (1995). Educating Native Americans. In J. Banks & C. Banks (Eds.), *Handbook of research on multicultural education* (pp. 331-347). New York: Macmillan.

Wilson, A. (1997). Power of the spoken word: native oral traditions in American Indian history. In D. Fixico, (Ed.), *Rethinking American Indian history* (pp. 101-116). Albuquerque: University of New Mexico Press.

Zimmerman, L., Zimmerman, K., & Bruguier, L. (2000). Cyberspace smoke signals: new technologies and Native American ethnicity. In C. Smith & G. Ward (Eds.), *Indigenous cultures in an interconnected world* (pp. 69-88). Vancouver: University of British Columbia Press.

About the Authors

Dr Bryan Burton, Professor of Music Education at West Chester University of Pennsylvania (USA), has written numerous books and articles on Native American music and culture and world music education. He has presented papers and workshops on these topics for music education organizations on five continents.

Dr Peter Dunbar-Hall is Chair of the Music Education Unit of Sydney Conservatorium of Music (University of Sydney). He is widely published on areas of the philosophy of music education, Australian cultural history, Balinese music, and Australian indigenous studies.

[27]

Unsafe suppositions? Cutting across cultures on questions of music's transmission

PATRICIA SHEHAN CAMPBELL, *University of Washington, USA (Email: pcamp@u.washington.edu)*

ABSTRACT   *The study of transmission, the delivery and acquisition (or teaching and learning) of music, is a cross-cultural phenomenon that is of increasing interest and importance to music teachers who strive for a broadly conceived template of pedagogical considerations that transcend cultural boundaries. The potential for idiographic studies of transmission is considered along with an approach that encompasses cross-cultural comparisons (if not universals) of transmission. A spectrum of formal and informal processes by which culture is acquired and learned is outlined at the outset. These issues serve to frame an examination of cross-cultural components of musical learning in the cases of children's songs, Balinese gamelan, Bulgarian traditional music and Filipino kulintang. Comparisons of transmission principles are briefly noted, including the aural-oral techniques of demonstration and imitation; the visual-kinaesthetic network; the spectrum of holistic to analytical reception of skills and knowledge; the necessity of eye-hand coordination and the perception of gestural patterns for instrumentalists; and the role of the expert or more experienced musician. Recommendations point to the development of further studies of music's transmission in various cultural circumstances, with the intention of determining the likelihood of pan-human principles of teaching and learning.*

Some of us have thought that song-learning and rhythm-getting were pretty much all the same everywhere, that with a singer, her song, and an eager, open and receptive learner, transmission would take place without much variance from one setting and circumstance to the next. Teaching, learning, transmission, and acquisition as it was, and as it ever will be, is an aural endeavor. This was the singular way of operation prior to our formal training as Western art musicians and prior to knowledge of 'the notation code'. Our observation-and-imitation process was ingrained in us long before our years of musical training, followed by pedagogical training, and finally of experience teaching young people, and even others who now teach.

216   *P. S. Campbell*

Questions of music's transmission became a fixation for me in *Lessons from the World* (1991). Still, as we probe more deeply into studies of musical cultures, they call all the louder for our attention. We wonder collectively: is the transmission of music a human phenomenon whose variance is minimal, with barely noticeable turns and twists? Or is it possible that transmission/teaching and learning/acquisition varies greatly from culture to culture, shaped by local circumstances? Is to learn notation, to read and write music through notation, to pass on music that is perfectly preserved (well, at least partially preserved) in symbols a Western high art cultural behavior? What then of the transmission of 'low-brow' music? Or folk, traditional, popular music, and music of children?

These questions emanate from experiences in the continuing study of musical traditions different from that of teachers' first 'home-and-family' musical culture, and from the aim of their collective lens on the nature of the teaching-learning process. I raise them as a learner (a student of Pakistani qawwali one year, the gaitas of Venezuela another year, and currently the kulintang of the Philippines), and also because of my wish to engage in culturally appropriate means of teaching selected dimensions of the musical culture. We are inspired as well by others who have examined transmission processes in near and distant musical cultures, and we are drawn to the words and writings of visionaries who stimulate our own thoughts on the subject. John Blacking long understood that as musicians '[o]ur concern must be with the process rather than the product. That is, how do people make sense of music? What is traditional? And what are traditional ways of making sense of the world, and making sense of music?' (1981). It is not surprising that Blacking should be concerned with process, however, given that 22 months of his fieldwork and a lifetime of analysis of children's music culture was spent in search of not only the social and cultural meaning of the songs, but also the means by which they acquired song, rhythms, and instrumental melodies (1967). Bruno Nettl called for the study of music transmission as a key to understanding music, musical culture, and culture (1983) and noted increasing interest by scholars in the ways in which societies teach their musical systems (1992b). A gradual pursuit of process, of questions of musical transmission and acquisition, has developed among ethnomusicologists, including a spin-off scholarly group engaged in 'cognitive ethnomusicology', and their parallel interest group of educators who call their field 'comparative music education'. The study of process has brought some to the brink of the question that inspires this paper: is it 'safe', or fair, to suppose (and to describe and assume) the learning of music as having cross-cultural commonalities? Or is there reason to safeguard against supposing and assuming music's transmission as a universal phenomenon? While I have avoided the term 'universal' in descriptions here, I have also found myself wondering why.

The Frame

Two framing issues are worthy of consideration prior to the tales of transmission which are cross-culturally considered and compared. They are (i) the idiographic study of transmission versus an approach that envelops cross-cultural comparisons, and their inherent praise for and fear of universal principles, and (ii) the spectrum of formal and informal processes by which culture is acquired and learned. These issues, defined and described at the outset, may be useful in understanding the examples of music's transmission described later, and in making sense of it as music education practitioners and researchers.

Praise For and Fear of Universals

In recent years, research in the humanities and some of the social sciences has evolved a solemn insistence on the placing of context within the consideration of practical and theoretical questions. In post-modern fashion, a more careful scrutiny is also given by educationists to the particular places of music-making, music teaching, and music learning; and a more receptive ear than ever before is now given to individual musicians, teachers, and students and their cultural circumstances. The current fashion among ethnomusicologists is to study individual musicians in all of their vast array of contexts, allowing each one to be considered as emblematic of only themselves, their background and training, and their political agenda. Currently, there is little in the field by way of ethnological examination of individual musicians for their shared traits, or of comparisons of ethnographic-based studies for their salient and shared features, for context has now become everything. Comparisons between singers, fiddlers, drummers, pipers, and dancers for what and how they learn have become barely a whisper, as the study of the individual and her circumstance has become a central endeavor (Danielson, 1997; Diamond, 2001).

Some of us advocate idiographic studies, biographies of great men and women, and oral histories of 'the lesser ones' and 'the ordinary' in the population. One such excursion into the particulars of individual children was my own romp into the lives of children in the *Songs in Their Heads* project (1998). While drawing individual profiles of children, I raised issues that are relevant to children in general, 'cross-child' principles triggered by the thoughts and behaviors of children as individuals. It seems to follow, too, that as in the case of individual children, one might also consider individual musical cultures as launches to more general, cross-cultural questions about how we learn. Research in music education has long been about seeking out common features, but given the trend in recent scholarship to consider only individuals, it may be useful to be reminded to aim for the wide-angled view. In studying music transmission, if we can accept that we are biologically wired in similar ways across cultures, it seems reasonable for us to examine the nature of music as it is learned and taught in an array of formal and informal settings, and to note the similarities as well as the distinctions across learners in many contexts. Certainly, there are cognitive musical templates to ponder, and templates of music transmission and pedagogy to examine, in striving to understand both the particulars as well as the traits that relate one music's transmission system to the next.

Acquired and Learned Culture

In examining cross-cultural traits of transmission, it is useful to review the explanations some have already given of types of learning that encompass formal and informal processes, and discrete subsets of these processes. There is what I have categorised (1998) as enculturative (natural and without formal instruction), partly guided (guided by informal and non-consecutive directives), and highly structured (transmission as it happens in schools). Through any of these means, the psychic structure of a group in a society is passed from one generation to the next, from the most natural and least formal to the codified, sequential system that occurs in institutionalised settings. Estelle Jorgensen (1997) posed five 'ways' of musical learning, from most to least formal: (i) schooling (institution-oriented and teacher-directed instruction); (ii) training (musical forms of apprenticeship and private study with a teacher); (iii) eduction (growth-oriented arranged educational experiences such as the Suzuki program); (iv) socialisation (the process by which a group shares its beliefs and values in a learner-constructed and usually life-long learning experience); and (v) enculturation (a life-long multidisciplinary approach which honors the reciprocity of culture-specific music and the interaction of music and culture).

E. T. Hall's postulation of acquired and learned culture is an exceptional perspective, as it considers the non-conscious process by which understanding emerges as preliminary to, but also coincidental with learning (1992). He established acquisition as similar to 'implicit learning', a process by which people come into contact with knowledge outside their conscious awareness. The basic foundations of language and communication, including definitive points of culture such as daily rhythms, gender roles, self-identity, kinesthetics (body language), proxemics (the social distance between people in conversation), and regional accents are 'learned but not taught'. Acquired culture is so fundamental, so automatic and outside of people's awareness that most do not even think of it as 'culture'. Cultural patterns are rarely seen as learned, either, for they appear always to have been there, 'in the air' and permeating the manner and style of our being. As for learned culture, Hall designates three types: formal learning (the serious business of learning in institutionalised settings), technical learning (the exactness and precision of learning systems within or beyond schooling, such as instrumental training by private instructors in private studios), and informal learning (the non-linear and cooperative learning that is controlled by the social group rather than an individual).

These concepts of learning can be seen as a continuum of processes relevant to a study of the transmission of music. In studying the manner in which cultures transmit, receive, preserve, and invent music, it is useful to have in mind these typologies of music transmission and learning processes by which comparisons can be made. Techniques by which music is acquired, taught and learned within the cultures of children, Balinese gamelan, Bulgarian gaida-playing, and Filipino kulintang will be briefly noted and discussed.

Children's Transmission of Their Musical Culture

Children constitute their own over-arching, all-encompassing folk group, in that they share common traditions in language, values, and behaviors. They are a 'big culture' (Slobin, 1993), united by experiences of their brief lives and the knowledge they have acquired and stored within them, yet they also can be seen as separate subcultures, or 'little cultures' determined by age and stage of their intellectual, social, and emotional growth. Children are known to express themselves in somewhat spontaneous ways: inventing but also preserving expressions that have been standard for generations. Despite the prediction of Peter and Iona Opie in their classic work, *The Singing Game* (1985), the 'final flowering of children's music' and their abandonment of their collective musical lore is not yet in sight. Children's processes for sharing their music, for passing it on to other children, seem to be replete with demonstration-and-imitation techniques, oral-aural strategies, an awareness but under-emphasis in phrases as a means of structuring transmission, and an immediate sense of the importance of self- and peer-corrections of errors.

Their songs, rhythmic rhymes, and spontaneous musical utterances are drawn from the influences of their environment, including the repertoire of their siblings, friends, and the media, and the natural flow of the transmission and learning process appears to be more holistic than atomistic in style.

Where young girls gather, particularly those from about the age of 6–9 years old, there are intriguing musical demonstrations of intimate friendships in the making. As they sing, chant and clap rhyming verses they know, softly and with little facial expression, they seem almost in a daze, staring ahead at their moving hands that clap their partner's hands. Many of the hand-clapping verses are not new, but are in fact variants that can be found in earlier collections (Abramson, 1969; Withers, 1948). The rituals of movement patterns, literary conceits, introductory and preparatory phrases and 'tag' endings, cross-rhythms between melody and rhythmic gestures, and text topics are common to such songs sung by children in many contexts, and the transmission and learning styles are equally standard. In a recent field experience, I asked the girls to repeat some of the words for me so that I could be sure to take them down correctly. They stopped, hesitated, and then one girl said, 'sure. But we have to sing it because it's not a talking song. And we start from the beginning, not in the middle, so listen for what you need to get.' Their comments were clear indication of two important transmission issues: (i) the manner in which the text is supported and thoroughly connected to the melody, and (ii) the perception of a song as performed holistically rather than in a separate and disjunct phrase-by-phrase manner.

Eve Harwood's conversation with one child is telling of the process by which children learn songs (1999). In response to the question, 'What is your favorite way to learn a song', the 9-year-old girl responded: 'Well, I guess my favorite is hearing the song over and over like on the radio, when they play it every once in a while and you start learning the words as you go along, 'cause then nobody's trying to tell you what to learn and you can learn the parts you really want to learn and stuff. You can just pick up whatever you hear and stuff'. This immersion process, learning by repeated listening to the entirety of the piece, was further supported through the findings of a study led by Rita Klinger (Klinger, Campbell & Goolsby, 1998), in which 8-year-old children, taught songs by 'immersion' and 'phrase-by-(small)phrase', performed songs with fewer errors when they were taught by immersion, holistically, sung to them (and gradually with them, as they joined in) from start to finish.

Harwood's conversation with this 9-year-old girl continued, as she asked the question, 'Is it easier when a teacher teaches you a song?'. The girl responded, 'Well, sometimes I don't like it when my music teacher teaches us songs 'cause it's usually forever till we learn the songs. She sings it and you sing a line back and she sings and you sing back ... and it bugs me 'cause I want to sing the whole song at once, 'specially if I already know the song'. This is the standard school process of learning a song, the 'I-sing-you-sing' phrase-by-phrase method. I listened to a musically inventive 11-year-old girl who did not require this 'break-down', chunking method, and who changed her renditions of the phrase with every singing occasion (1998). The teacher sang the phrase, but the girl had her own plan, apparently, moving intentionally further from the melody with each successive opportunity to pour out variants that would harmonise with her classmates' melody.

Another fascination of children's song repertoire is that they may not necessarily transmit or learn musically simple songs before more complex songs. John Blacking observed the order of song-learning by Venda children as 'out of sequence' when compared to a curricular plan suggested by Kodàly. In his attempt to come to terms with an evolutionary process by which children learned songs, he examined their songs in accordance with the Hindemith method. He was surprised by his discovery that 'Children didn't necessarily sing three-tone songs before they sang four-tone songs. In fact, one of the most popular songs they sang was a six-tone song' (1984). In his explanation of the music transmission process of the Venda children, he noted the holistic and autogenic manner of their music-making as fully integrated within their play and social interactions (1967).

Children learn their songs by listening, applying oral and aural strategies and visual-kinesthetic strategies as they proceed. Several observations from the field confirm this (Campbell, 1998). After a long discourse by 6-year-old George on the coordination of his breathing for playing harmonicas and whistles, which was really quite intricately detailed to the finest minutiae of 'how-to', his response to my query of his manner of learning was: 'I just figured it out'. He later added: 'I figure it out. I listen and figure it out'. A 9-year-old drummer, Manuel, explained how he learns to play: 'My teacher uses my drum. I watch him play. I stand on the other side of the drum from him, and right after he plays, I play. We just go back and forth.' Alan, a 10-year-old who enjoys playing his keyboard, disclosed that the key to getting a song is 'to sing it in my mind, not out loud, but my inside-singing is my guide to playing.' He claimed that he was able to memorise his songs, too, 'by singing along with them, inside'. No doubt, children are listening to the sounds within them and those that surround them, and find demonstration and imitation as not only an aural but also a visual and kinesthetic experience.

Because children, particularly young girls, strive to develop a repertoire of standard and peer-approved songs, they will discourage personalisation of these songs and may fire sharp criticisms to those who side-sweep or alter the appropriate texts, pitches, rhythms, and nuances. They care that their songs are performed correctly, and correctness means faithful adherence to the existing tradition. They encourage their friends to sing, and will clap if a song is 'well done'. They will also mimic a lifeless rendering of a song, or turn teacher to those who do not perform well, directing them to 'watch me' as they step up the tempo, and sing with greater clarity and energy.

Children are a culture all their own, if not multiple subcultures, and their music 'au naturel' is worthy of study not only for its musical and textual content but for the means they use to pursue the transmission and acquisition of a repertoire they value. They have acquired culture and learned culture, musically speaking, and their transmission spans the spectrum of enculturative and informal to fairly technical. When they 'get serious' about preserving their traditions, their transmission may even take on the trappings of some of the more structured learning of formal education as they imitate some of the techniques they have seen their teachers utilise.

Balinese Gamelan, Learned Holistically

In Bali, where few gamelan players are professional musicians, most merchants, farmers, tourist workers, and their families consider gamelan performance to be an important community activity. Nearly all the men can play the instruments; generally their sons listen and wait their turn at performances, and many of the young girls learn the traditional dances.

In his 1954 essay, *Children and Music in Bali*, Colin McPhee painted an evocative portrait of the method by which Balinese gamelan music is learned:

> The teacher does not seem to teach, certainly not from our standpoint. He is merely the transmitter; he simply makes concrete the musical idea which is to be handed on, sets the example before the pupils and leaves the rest to them ... . No allowance is made for the youth of the musicians; it never occurs to the teacher to employ any method other than the one he is accustomed to use when teaching adult groups. He explains nothing, since for him, there is nothing to explain. (pp. 232–33)

Almost a half-century later, Michael Bakan reported that this means of transmission continues (in *Music of Death and New Creation*, 1999). The oral/aural tradition is known as *maguru panggul*, literally 'teaching with the mallet', as the xylophones, gongs, and drums require hammers or mallets to sound. No music notation is employed in the transmission process, and the effectiveness of teaching is almost exclusively dependent on a holistic demonstration-and-imitation mode of transmitting musical knowledge from teacher to student.

Beleganjur gamelan, the subject of Bakan's study, is one of 20 regional styles in Bali, featuring an ensemble of metal or bronze xylophones, gongs, and two double-headed drums called *kendang*. Bakan described his one-to-one lessons on the kendang, noting that the drum teacher's performance demonstration of the drum part to be learned is the only 'score' available to the student. He recalled that his teacher would play a lengthy section of the piece for him in complete form and at full speed. The music was not segmented into phrases or otherwise simplified into short patterns, and he explained how he had kept his focus on the mallet's constant movement to the drumhead, so that what he heard he could also see. He was expected to add the kinesthetic dimension to the aural and visual modes in play as quickly as possible, jumping in to play along with the teacher as best he could. His task as a student of the kendang drum was to emulate the physical manner and expression of the teacher's visual performance.

Not only Bakan, but also Benjamin Brinner (1995) and Michael Tenzer (1991) discuss the process by which gamelan musicians bypass notation and instead learn kinesthetic gestures that they transform into the act of musical performance. They learn a movement vocabulary that emerges prior to the precision of individual pitches, timbres, and durations falling into place, fitting the specific elements into place after a general sense of the piece is known. Over repeated occasions to play while listening, their attempts at reproducing what they have heard becomes gradually more attuned to the finished product, when the exactness of the piece is known and performed.

Demonstration and imitation give way to the student's greater technical awareness and thoughtful performance that is stylistically appropriate and musically expressive. The teacher's feedback is rare, with little in the way of verbal statements. Students of the gamelan must learn self-reliance, self-motivation, and self-evaluation. Moreover, they must develop their own critical ear, coming to terms with what they have performed as matching or not the performance of their teachers. The teaching is holistic and anti-analytical, as students learn in apprenticeship fashion to attend to any little musical nuance, change in playing motions, or slight nod of the head as signs of their progress.

The making of a gamelan musician requires technical knowledge that is learned through a linked system of listening, watching, and doing. In its holistic sense, the process of learning kendang drumming (or other gamelan instruments) is not unlike children's ways of giving and getting songs, as there is no attempt to break a musical work into discrete and manageable segments but rather a start-to-finish progression. The relationship between the gamelan teacher and his student is a Vygotskyan, expert-to-novice, association again not unlike children; whoever within the gamelan culture has experience and expertise may be designated as teacher to those with lesser (or little or no) experience. This teacher is ever-present in the learning process, and yet maintains a low verbal profile. The transmission of Balinese music has a structure of sorts, but it is not of the sequential sort found in formal learning. Rather, the repeated performance by the teacher introduces, surrounds, and soon permeates the student's being, motivating and compelling his partial and gradually more complete reproduction of the music he is experiencing. It is a technical learning that ensues, since the teacher's ultimate expectation of the student is for a precise performance.

Bulgarian Music, Learned but not Taught

From southeastern Asia to southeastern Europe, there are sophisticated musical traditions that require no notation in their transmission and preservation. In Bulgaria, among rural and urban populations, professional and amateur musicians, and men and women, there are rich musical expressions for solo and ensemble voices and instruments, many of which were once 'learned but not taught' through an informal process far beyond the venue of schools. The learning of songs and instrumental tunes is a partly a social process, as young people grow into music as an integral component of their heritage. It is also the means for maintaining societal values and the roles one learns to play and pass through in the course of living as a Bulgarian.

Women are the song-keepers in Bulgaria, while instrumentalists are traditionally male. My observations of, and interviews with women in Macedonia in the middle 1980s (a region in southwestern Bulgaria and also an independent nation across the border and south of Serbia) and with elderly Macedonian women living in the USA, offered an image of Bulgarian girls learning songs at the knees of their mothers, grandmothers, aunts, and older sisters (Shehan, 1987). The girls and women spoke of the natural presence of singing at home in the kitchen, working in the yard, or at *sedyanka* gatherings where women sewed, talked, and sang together. They recalled singing as a constant activity, with no one individual isolated to star status. Even young girls, barely school age, are learning the repertoire of songs through constant exposure and encouragement to sing. They typically learn to hum the melody, then memorise the words, and finally arrive at a complete performance with emphasis on melodic style and vocal expression.

For an understanding of the transmission of Bulgarian instrumental music, the work of Timothy Rice is a rich resource (1994). Rice's principal informant in *May It Fill Your Soul* is Kostadin Varimezov, a player of *gaida* (bagpipe), who began his musical journey while playing a *pishtalka* (a double-reed pipe of straw with six fingerholes) as a boy while herding pigs, graduating to an *ovcharska svirka* (shepherd's flute) later. As to the learning process of those instruments, which were seen more as playthings by adults, Kostadin said 'No music was taught. I played it for other kids while another kid banged on some wood' (p. 44). Children imitated adults with these musical 'playthings', and were expected to play it out of earshot. Kostadin recalled sitting together with an older boy, a more advanced player, in the fields where they 'noodled' on the pipe and flute for hours in a type of Vygotskian 'peer learning' process (p. 45). He was learning melodic phrases as gestures of the fingers and hand that twisted and turned, and in this way was coming to terms with key patterns that he could later call upon in his performance of a piece.

Kostadin's principal instrument became the gaida, and his early years on the shepherd's flute were not wasted, nor was his listening to other players. He had acquired a basic motoric sense necessary for playing a wind instrument, plenty of basic tunes of the repertoire, and some sense of the style of the music. The transfer from flute to gaida bagpipe was possible, and for Kostadin it was a most successful one. He sought out gaida players at weddings and festivals, and learned also from friends who played, taking on the role of a part-time (or even full-time) apprentice with players who knew what he wanted to know. Without a doubt, Kostadin had come a great musical distance from his early beginnings on straw pipe to the powerful wail of a Bulgarian bagpipe, and it is the casual learning process, the 'noodling', the chance opportunities to listen and thus to pick up new tunes and techniques from one musician or another, that shakes a Western art musician's expectations of a more formal transmission and learning system to match a sophisticated musical tradition.

The women singers of Bulgaria illustrate the process of socialisation by which a group shares its values and in a co-operative, partly guided manner, passes its repertoire to its members. For gaida players and other instrumentalists, learning begins in non-linear fashion and in natural settings, but progresses to a kind of technical learning with one or more expert players who can teach by demonstration techniques and tunes. The techniques of demonstration and imitation come into play in the case of singers and instrumentalists, while aspiring gaida players become engaged in the use of visual-kines-thetic strategies and the development of melodic and kinetic gestures that favor a holistic rather than an analytical route to learning.

Filipino Kulintang, Recontextualised

Returning to southeastern Asia, I wish to develop here a brief personal narrative of my experience in learning to play the *kulintang*, the ultimate national musical symbol of the Philippines. As James Clifford sought understanding as a dialectic of experience and interpretation (1988), I hope to take this personal research also to the possibilities for understanding a traditional music transmission system through my experience of entering into it as an outsider. In this way, the study of a pedagogical method might be seen as a negotiation between a teacher steeped in the tradition and her student, myself, whose own pre-understandings and Western analytical manner required compromised efforts on the part of both teacher and student.

'Kulintang' is both the name of an ensemble as it is also a single instrument, which appears as an oblong wooden box-like instrument that is elevated by chairs or benches at either end, with the player on a chair in the center and just behind the box. There are cords strung within the box on which rest bronze kettle-shaped gongs, each with its own raised middle area (called embossed gongs). Each gong is about the size of a kitchen cooking pot, from about 5 to 7 inches across the top, and there are eight in all. There are two long, light wood 'mallets' so thin as to be bendable, each wrapped in yarn and cloth at the striking end. An entire kulintang ensemble includes also three to four hanging gongs and a single-headed barrel drum, but it is this rack of gongs that is the main feature of the ensemble. It plays the melody percussively, and the tuning is like no other instrument in Southeast Asia, and far from the equal-tempered tuning of the West. Despite my acquaintance through performance with other southeastern Asian musics, including Thai mahori and Khmer mohori ensembles, I was unprepared for the tuning of the kulintang.

My goal was to learn to play kulintang in less than a year, well enough to join with a university ensemble, and for the purpose of thinking through and understanding this music as a tradition which American school children might learn to play. Of course, I wanted to learn from Felicia Ramon in a manner that would be in keeping with the oral tradition, and fully expected that I would need to listen carefully, to play by memory, to let the transcriptions go, and to truly release myself from the reading process.

The first lesson was nothing short of a revelation for me. As a teacher of musicianship at the university, and with experience in learning other musical forms by ear (including

Karnatic mridangam, Venezuelan cuatro, Celtic harp, and instruments of both Javanese and Balinese gamelans), I did not expect to struggle. Felicia drew up a chair on the other side of the kulintang, faced me, and then played the whole *bilalag* (standard Filipino musical form), and then played it again. I watched her as she played the piece in what was for her a backwards position, so that it would appear forward and correct for me. I was flustered: I couldn't sing the melody, as the instrument sounded out of tune. I couldn't figure out where the pitches were coming from because her hands were moving too fast. I found myself grasping for patterns she was playing, and not really finding where they started or where they were going. I was disheartened and feared that I might need to drop my kulintang plan before I began. While Felicia's expectation was that I would come in to join her on a phrase or two that began to sound and look familiar, I felt locked down and immobile.

She stopped and asked whether I wanted the piece broken down, 'small phrases, maybe?' I asked, 'Was that traditional? She responded, 'No, but I could do it for you.' My sense was that if I could still learn it without notation, then maybe we would still be following the traditional transmission process. I knew I was bargaining with myself, and re-defining the traditional Filipino mode of transmission to suit my own inadequacies. We began a phrase-by-phrase imitation method that was to last through the entirety of my study with Felicia. I watched her play backwards, and began to follow her every movement of the mallet. I trying singing as she played, with solfege, and then without it (because the 1s and 5s of the kulintang did not match my sols and mis). Yet even my singing on 'loo' was distracting me, as my attempt to sing what was essentially in the cracks of the western piano was proving impossible. Although we were in a basement studio in Seattle on a chill November day, I was sweaty with apprehension and frustration.

'Could I write?', I wanted to know. 'Sure, you can, some students do', she claimed. 'Will any system do?' I asked, and she nodded, curious as to what I would come up with. We continued, she compromising by playing the entire piece several times, then playing double phrases with me following in my attempts to play them back. Then she would give me time to scratch out a notation of stick rhythms, a combination of pitch numbers and solfege syllables, and comments on which phrase happened when. I watched her mallets like a hawk, and then tried to follow the same visual pattern. On dropping out my singing, I found that my focus was increasingly visual and immediately kinesthetic; sometimes I would even follow on my side in imitation of her playing motions as she gave a phrase or segment to me. When I would err in a phrase, she would come back in, playing the appropriate gongs just opposite me. The more I gave way to the visual and the kinesthetic, and the more we came into a groove of this transmission process we were evolving, the better it was getting for me. I stumbled when she asked for cumulative playing, however, going back to the starting phrases and playing up to the point we had learned. It took time to connect the phrases, to understand that one phrase was proceeded by or followed with another.

But I 'got' the *bilalag*, and I could play it in ensemble with her on drum and several others on the hanging gongs, punctuating away. I compared myself to my 10-year-old, who was learning a Schumann piece a week on piano (although not without its bumps and halts), while it took me four lessons in 4 weeks to learn a 64-measure bilalag piece. My notation was helpful to me despite the seeming interference one might expect from labelling as 're' a pitch that was far closer to 'mi-flat'. I 'played' from my notation at home on a paper kulintang, just $8\frac{1}{2} \times 11$-inch sheets of paper taped together across the dining room table. I tried the piece on kitchen pots and pie pans, too, tapping them with the rubber tips of pencils. I knew that the practice I needed was about the eye–hand coordination in order to strengthen my kinesthetic memory, and that the sound, the different tuning, would come later, gradually. The negotiated method and experimental practices had worked, however, and I was now able to play the piece from start to finish, thanks to the flexibility of my teacher in blending her method with my need. Most amazing to me is that I now find myself singing the bilalag melody in Western tuning and (with conscious effort) closer to the tuning of the Filipino tradition as well.

As in the case of the music of children, the Balinese gamelan, and of Bulgarian singers and gaida players, the transmission of Filipino kulintang music is traditionally an oral/aural process where demonstration and imitation are prominently featured. The lessons took place in a university studio, and thus what is learned through informal and only partly guided means on the island of Mindinao in the Phillipines was functioning within a formal, institutionalised setting just down the hall from the violin and viola studios. Yet the structure of the lessons was not rigidly set, and a few sessions of non-linear operations were necessary in exploring the boundary at which two people, teacher and student, could meet and give-and-take the essence of the musical tradition. The visual-kinesthetic channels of information were critical to my learning of the piece, as I watched the teacher and played immediately after her.

Again in this illustration, it appears that learning music requires repeated listening and continued efforts to execute in practice what one has been taught.

Safe Suppositions of a Preliminary Sort

In striving to untangle complex questions raised about music's transmission across cultures, we cannot do justice in answering them 'dead-on' and straightaway, for the subject requires more than these brief excursions to sort out the complexities. Nonetheless, this whirlwind tour may serve to highlight ideas that require our further investigations. We may concede that it would be foolhardy and certainly premature to accept the view that music's transmission (teaching, acquisition, and learning) is all the same, just as we find it unacceptable anymore to call music 'the universal language of all cultures'. Yet we would do well to note several phenomena at play in the transmission process as 'cross-cultural operations', surfacing repeatedly in quite varied contexts: the aural–oral techniques of demonstration and imitation; the visual-kinesthetic network; the spectrum of holistic to analytical reception of skills and knowledge to be acquired; the necessity of eye–hand co-ordination and the perception of gestural patterns for instrumentalists; and the role of the expert (from a master of the tradition to a peer whose knowledge is only slightly greater than the learner). These components of the learning act could be the start of a template of music transmission and pedagogy. Through ethnographic and observational studies produced by ourselves, as students of music, as music teachers and educationists, we might begin to piece together the larger realm of how people make sense of music: how they offer music to their young, how the young themselves preserve their valued music, and even how cultural meaning and beliefs are reflected in the manner of music's transmission. It seems to me that this is an important quest ahead of us, and that, as 'thinkers and doers' of music transmission in our daily practice, we might be among the most likely members of the scholarly community to pursue this quest, with expert eyes and ears to be able to detect and asses the key components of transmission. Even as John Blacking claimed that his study of Venda music led him to a deeper understanding of his own music (1973), perhaps we would understand teaching and learning better with the knowledge of how others do it.

What would be the gains of knowing the high incidence of certain pedagogical practices, across different cultures? Our teaching hats fit snugly on our heads, it seems

226   *P. S. Campbell*

that we should want to know as much in the way of transmission techniques as is available to us. It would seem that it is not enough to apply only those teaching practices that were employed by our teachers on us as students, or that we were taught to know in our methods courses, even in the event that we may believe that we have come to craft our own personally effective method. A broadly conceived template of pedagogical considerations may stretch us in ways we need to be stretched; it may suggest techniques we have forgotten (or never knew); it may bring strong possibilities for learning music that are unfamiliar to our students, and to us. It may also provide strategies for working with students whose learning styles are unlike our own, who may come from communities far different from ours; and it may help us to eliminate misconceptions about how music is learned and taught. Perhaps of overriding importance is that it may bring confidence to us in the knowledge that we are not alone in fashioning the act of giving and receiving music, but are connected in cross-cultural and even pan-human ways.

In my view, that would indeed be a very safe supposition.

REFERENCES

ABRAMSON, R.D. (1969) *Jump-rope Rhymes: A Dictionary*. American Folklore Society Bibliographical and Special Series, vol. 20 (Austin, University of Texas Press).

BAKAN, M.B. (1999) *Music of Death and New Creation* (Chicago, University of Chicago Press).

BLACKING, J. (1967/1995) *Venda Children's Songs: An Ethnomusicological Analysis* (Chicago, University of Chicago Press).

BLACKING, J. (1973) *How Musical Is Man?* (Seattle, University of Washington Press).

BLACKING, J. (1981) Transcript of keynote presentation, International Folk Music Council, Oman, in: *Special Collections: The Blacking Papers* (Perth, University of Western Australia).

BLACKING, J. (1984) Transcript of address to the Manchester (U.K.) Council of Music Teachers, in: *Special Collections: The Blacking Papers* (Perth, University of Western Australia).

BRINNER, B. (1995) *Knowing Music, Making Music: Javanese Gamelan and the Theory of Musical Competence and Interaction* (Chicago, University of Chicago Press).

CAMPBELL, P.S. (1991) *Lessons from the World* (New York, Schirmer Books).

CAMPBELL, P.S (1998) *Songs in Their Heads* (New York, Oxford University Press).

CLIFFORD, J. (1988) On ethnographic authority, in: *The Predicament of Culture: Twentieth-Century Ethnography, Literature, and Art* (Cambridge, Harvard University Press).

DANIELSON, V. (1997) *Um Kulthum: The Voice of Egypt* (Chicago, University of Chicago Press).

DIAMOND, B. (2001) *Canadian Musical Pathways Project* (Toronto, York University).

HALL, E.T. (1992) Improvisation as an acquired, multilevel process, *Ethnomusicology*, 36, pp. 223–245.

HARWOOD, E. (1998) Go on girl! Improvisation in African-American girls' singing games, in: B. NETTL (Ed.) *In the Course of Performance* (Chicago, University of Chicago Press).

JORGENSEN, E. (1997) *In Search of Music Education* (Urbana, IL, University of Illinois Press).

KLINGER, R., CAMPBELL, P. & GOOLSBY, T. (1998) Approaches to children's song acquisition: immersion and phrase-by-phrase. *Journal of Research in Music Education*, 46, pp. 24–34.

McPHEE, C. (1954/1970) Children and music in Bali, in: J. BELO (Ed.) *Traditional Balinese Culture* (New York, Columbia University Press).

NETTL, B. (1983) *The Study of Ethnomusicology*. (Urbana, Univeristy of Illinois Press).

NETTL, B. (1992a) Ethnomusicology and the teaching of world music, in: *Music Education: Sharing the Musics of the World* (Proceedings from the International Society for Music Education, Seoul, Korea) (Christchurch, NZ: The Printery).

NETTL, B. (1992b) Recent directions in ethnomusicology, in: H. MYERS (Ed.) *Ethnomusicology: An Introduction* (New York, W. W. Norton & Company).

OPIE, I. & OPIE, P. (1985) *The Singing Game* (Oxford, Oxford University Press).

RICE, T. (1994) *May It Fill the Soul* (Chicago, University of Chicago Press).

SHEHAN, P.K. (1987) Balkan women as preservers of traditional music and culture, in: E. KOSKOFF (Ed.) *Women and Music in Cross-Cultural Perspective* (New York, Greenwood Press).

SLOBIN, M. (1993) *Subcultural sounds: Micromusics of the West* (Hanover, NH., University Press of New England for Wesleyan University Press).

TENZER, M. (1991) *Balinese Music* (Berkeley and Singapore, Periplus Editions).

WITHERS, C. (1948) *A Rocket in My Pocket* (New York, Henry Holt).

[28]

MULTICULTURAL MUSIC EDUCATION IN A PLURALISTIC SOCIETY

Joyce Jordan
UNIVERSITY OF MIAMI

American educators have initiated many programs in recent years in an effort to deal with such issues as billingual/bicultural education, racial awareness, and multicultural education. American schools, by design, are places in which young people are provided opportunities to attain knowledge and skill. Not by design they also have become centers for social change and the preservation of values. When ideals are postulated or differences arise, the aftershocks or disagreements almost always manifest themselves in the schools. Schools either covertly or overtly are pressured to meet the challenges, counteract injustices, or attempt to balance the forces between extremism and mediocrity. One such movement receiving attention from nearly all strata of society today is multiculturalism.

Music education has been a part of this movement. This chapter will focus on a broad range of research studies related to multicultural music education—studies that reflect historical, philosophical, and practical issues that impact on music education in elementary and secondary schools as well as on teacher-training programs. Long before social movements forced these issues, interest in musics of various world cultures could be found in music instruction. Anderson (1974) traces this interest back to the early years of the progressive education movement.

HISTORICAL BACKGROUND

In 1916, Satis Coleman, a piano teacher at the Lincoln School of Teachers College, Columbia University, developed classes in creative music. She believed that music study should begin with the sounds of instruments. Children were encouraged to collect or construct a variety of percussion, wind, and string instruments and compose and perform their music. Among the instruments mentioned were panpipes, ocarinas, Swiss bells, Chinese gongs, aerophones, and chordophones. Coleman's (1927) *Creative Music in the Home* contained, among other information, instructions for making instruments from India, Polynesia, Africa, and China. In 1924, this growing interest in nonwestern musics was reflected in a songbook series for public schools called *The Music Hour* (McConathy, 1927–1941).

This interest of American educators in the music of other cultures may have been fostered by two international conferences held by the Music Supervisors National Conference (MSNC) in Lausanne, Switzerland, the first in 1929 and the second in 1931. In the decade of the 1930s, textbooks published by C. C. Birchard and Company, Ginn and Company, and Silver Burdett and Company continued to include songs and pictures relating to various dimensions of cultural life in foreign countries. In 1937 a three-year investigation of young children's capacity for musical expression and creativity in a natural setting was begun. Instruments mostly of eastern origin were utilized in the project. The project, supported by the Pillsbury Foundation, resulted in a publication by Moorhead and Pond (1941).

In 1939, attention focused on hemispheric unity among peoples of North and South America. A music division of the Pan-American Union, the Music Educators National Conference (MENC), and other organizations initiated intercultural exchanges among musicians and educators in the United States and Latin American countries. Encouraged by individuals such as James Mursell, teachers began to familiarize themselves with the music found in both Americas.

In 1948, the United Nations Educational, Scientific, and Cultural Organization (UNESCO) laid the groundwork for the establishment of the International Music Council, which became operational in 1949. In the 1960s, attention was directed to the study of foreign musics, and colleges and universities began to offer courses in ethnomusicology. Foreign musics were discussed at conferences on music education at Yale University in 1963 and at Tanglewood in 1967, both promoting musics of all periods, styles, forms, and cultures in curricular development. As a result of this renewed emphasis on music of other cultures by professionals in music education and the blossoming field of ethnomusicology, textbook publishers employed consultants on musics from foreign countries and increased the use of authentic versions of both vocal and instrumental music examples. In addition, several research studies resulted in which elementary or secondary students were introduced to the music of various cultures—May and Hood (1962), Larson and Anderson (1966), May (1967), and Anderson (1970).

Moore (1977) discusses three events reflective of upheavals in the social structure that gave impetus to multicultural awareness: the Civil Rights Movement of the mid-1950s and early 1960s, the Civil Rights Act of 1964, and the college student activism that led to the student activism in education during the mid to late 1960s and early 1970s. "The concerns of minority students for the inclusion of studies that reflected their culture (Black, Chicano, and Native American studies) and accurately represented their ancestors as well as themselves filtered downward to the elementary and secondary levels to become the ground for multicultural education in its beginning stages of implementation throughout the United States" (Moore, 1977, p. 71).

The humanistic philosophy so prevalent during this period influenced education by advocating the development of the individual's total potential, including the intellectual, physical, and affective domains. The hope was that generating positive images of minorities within the classroom setting would carry over into larger societal interaction. Federal legislation provided the needed funding, and wide-scale reforms began.

The impact of humanistic education had a strong effect on music education. Music instruction, performance driven or not, was advocated for all children. Educators felt strongly that exposure to various world cultures was a viable vehicle for instilling pride in the broadening tapestry of ethnic America.

The impetus for a truly multicultural curriculum came in 1972 with the enactment of Public Law 92-318, Title IX, established by the 92nd Congress of the United States (Montague, 1988). The law promotes multicultural education in that it recognizes

the heterogeneous composition of the Nation and the fact that in a multiethnic society a greater understanding of the contributions of one's own heritage and those of one's fellow citizens can contribute to a more harmonious, patriotic, and committed populace, and in recognition of the principle that all persons in the educational institutions of the Nation should have an opportunity to learn about the . . . nature of their own cultural heritage, and to study the contributions of the cultural heritages of other ethnic groups of the nation [Sec. 901]. (quoted in Montague, 1988, p. 3)

This pronouncement prompted many states to enact specific legislation to implement multicultural education. A survey taken in 1973 by the National Project of Ethnic America indicated that 33 of the 40 states responding had published materials related to multicultural mandates; 26 had formal policy statements; 13 had specific laws on the books; and four had passed bilingual laws.

Montague (1988) updated the status of legislative activity in the 1980s with responses from all 50 states plus the District of Columbia. Her study reported "twenty-one states with legislation affecting multicultural/bicultural education, five states with related legislation affecting multicultural education, nine states with policies affecting multicultural education, and twelve states plus The District of Columbia with a law affecting bilingual education" (p. 176). Among those 21 states with legislation, both instructional materials and teacher certification were addressed. The 14 states with either related legislation or policies affecting multicultural education have publications that encourage multicultural education, publications of resource materials, or programs operating at local levels.

Montague found that although laws do tend to foster compliance on some level, her data do not support a law's being the main reason for multicultural music education programs in higher education. In addition, many laws are addressed to elementary and secondary education rather than higher education. In only five instances do the laws address teacher certification, which indirectly impacts higher education and, according to the results of her study, was one of the reasons for involvement by universities. The second and most frequent reason was the individual faculty member's own training or personal background. Professors and administrators promoting multiculturalism had received training in college classes or workshops, had some close experience with another culture, or were themselves of an ethnic background.

SEARCH FOR A PHILOSOPHICAL BASE

Two common misconceptions regarding multiethnic diversity and musical expression, are (1) that music is a universal language, and (2) that America is a cultural melting pot. Concerning the first, despite a general acceptance of the existence of a multiplicity of musical languages, until recent years, and continuing to the present in our music institutions and schools, many professionals have tended to perpetuate the validity of only one musical tradition—western art music. As our scholarship has broadened, we now know that music can also create divisions among peoples. Often, this is true because a people's music is inseparable from the people themselves and accepting or rejecting a culture's music is, in fact, acceptance or rejection of the individuals within that culture. Elliott (1989) believes that the profession's preoccupation with the aesthetic aspects of nonwestern music has led educators to overlook the fact that music in any culture is first and foremost a human practice. The aesthetic perspective, by definition, tends to exclude nonformal considerations such as the technical and social aspects that impact profoundly on the processes of music making and music listening within the culture. In music education practice, music is often separated from its context of use and production so the listener can experience it in some "pure" form.

The second notion, that America is a cultural melting pot, which glorified the eradication of ethnic differences, never truly materialized. Music is not necessarily a harmonious thread to unite peoples. But because it is a major means of distinguishing, identifying, and expressing differences across cultures, it is a window to the minds that created it (Elliott, 1989).

This brings us to an alternative view, that of cultural pluralism. John Dewey, an avid proponent of pluralism, viewed public education as a system plagued by numerous dualisms, many of which we recognize as the philosophical targets of the last 50 years: academic versus artistic study, process versus product, specialized music versus comprehensive musicianship, music for the talented versus music for every child, fine arts versus practical arts, cognitive versus affective domain. Steinecker (1976, p. 13) quotes from Dewey's writings: "Men still want the crutch of dogma, of beliefs fixed by authority, to relieve them of the trouble of thinking and the responsibility of directing their activity by a thought."

Much of this conflict stems from an increasingly pluralistic society. Leonard Meyer postulates:

Our sense of crisis stems largely from the pluralism of our society; but this unease is related to the expectation that society should, in fact, be linear and nonpluralistic. Pluralism does not produce conflict unless the expectation is for unity. Once one recognizes pluralism as the dominant fact of our society, the ability to live with and understand and appreciate the divergent ideologies is not necessarily a source of unease. (quoted in Steinecker, 1976, p. 7)

The advancement of cultural pluralism allows many different groups to maintain their cultural heritage or to assimilate other cultural traits, as they will. Such is the basis of a democracy. Differences among groups become a national resource and the emerging common culture a mosaic of subsidiary cultures.

Palmer (1975) considered the philosophical and practical problems of including the world's musics in public school curricula. His investigation sought to probe the question of why music and music education were on a plane of such global dimensions, and to explore the problems relative to broadening the pedagogical base to a world perspective.

In his search for a philosophical base, Palmer enumerated four categories of philosophical ideation:

1. The "global village" concept, introduced by Marshall McLuhan, recognized the impact on music in each culture of technology in travel and communications media. The notion of western cultural superiority began to diminish as scholars and musicians began to realize that other music cultures were valid and artistic expressions of human needs and aspirations not unlike those of the

west. Intercultural study was a natural consequence of this realization.

2. The western ideal of aesthetic value as a closed system warranted fresh inquiries since many music cultures in the world value functional, ritualistic, or religious ends either in place of, or in addition to, aesthetic values. The search for musical significance began to be intertwined with an emerging sociological view of music.

3. As indigenous music became endangered in the last two hundred years through western colonialism, missionary ventures, and more recently, urbanization and scientific technology, acculturation dominated where change was rapid. Many music traditions, whether covertly or overtly, were in danger of extinction. Countermovements advocated principally by musicians, scholars, and educators emerged. Two important organizations fostering global exchanges were The International Society for Music Education and the International Institute for Comparative Music Studies and Documentation. In addition, the rise of social turmoil in the United States in the 1960s focused increased attention on ethnic minorities. Intercultural education was viewed as a viable means of promoting cultural identity and fostering racial and ethnic equality. If through education the values of music in various world traditions could be viewed objectively, this experience might advance a deeper understanding of one's own culture.

4. Academic scholarship and increased ethnomusicological fieldwork resulted in the awareness that while the end products of various music systems were different, the process of music making retained more similarities than differences. Universals emerged, not on the grounds of music as a "universal language," but on psychophysiological grounds of aesthetic response. "Music in this circumstance is accepted for its own intrinsic values and as a unique human endeavor to be beheld and contemplated for its own sake" (Palmer, 1975, p. 122).

Palmer offers implications for a pedagogical framework for music education. Without adequate preparation to understand the structural nature of various world musics and their value systems, inaccurate pictures of the culture itself can result. Moreover, the power of music to evoke peace and understanding between peoples often exists only within a specific cultural setting; therefore, music taught under such a guise is a highly questionable means-ends philosophical conception of music education. To utilize music to achieve cultural identity is perhaps too narrow a basis for inclusion of such musics in the curriculum. However, given the cultural pluralism of today's schools, the music educator must recognize that many different musics are worthy of inclusion in music education programs, with the major goal being a truly world perspective rather than a vantage point from which to establish any one musical tradition as "superior." If students can be brought to the realization that all traditions of music reflect in some way a full range of human emotions, then the potential for a beneficial exploration of various musical systems has some validity.

MULTICULTURAL MUSIC
EDUCATION—PRACTICAL PROBLEMS

Given the premise that a pluralistic view of music is philosophically sound, certain practical problems emerge in the implementation of a world music curriculum. Palmer (1975) summarizes problem areas as they relate to the learner, the teacher, and the educational institution.

The primary problems related to the learner involve musical capacity; in essence, a musicianship that allows an individual to practice one or more musical systems as either a performer or a listener is questionable. The music education profession is based on the premise that all children have a right to music education. The assumption that all students, regardless of talent, have the capacity to achieve a functional level of proficiency within their own culture's musical system remains a dichotomy. The commercial world invests large amounts of capital on the premise that the listener is somehow affected by the musical medium. Reports from both the Yale Seminar and the Tanglewood Symposium reaffirm that all possess sufficient musicality to warrant music instruction. However, the music education profession continues to be performance oriented, with selectivity based primarily on perceived "talent." School music requirements are by no means consistent and universal. What then is the implication for a world music curriculum within the context of mass public education?

Another issue involves the question of multimusicality. Can one's capacity to interpret an indigenous musical system be expanded to include other musical systems? The results of some early studies tend to affirm that "restraints on the musicality of peoples are culture bound rather than intrinsic limitations of the human intellect and musical capacity" (Palmer, 1975, p. 142).

In 1962, May and Hood (1962) experimented with teaching Javanese songs to a first- and a fifth-grade class of elementary-age children. While the older children demonstrated more delay than the younger group in grasping the nonequal-tempered system, with practice, both groups were able to grasp the scalar subtleties of *pelog* and *slendro* Javanese tuning systems. May (in Palmer, 1975) reported similar findings in working with Australian children using music of the Australian aboriginal peoples, and in a later replication with American children (in Palmer, 1975) obtained similar findings. No recent studies were found that sought to address the issues of multimusicality or capacity of young children to function within cultures other than their own.

The second problem related to the learner involves the emotional-attitudinal mind-set of the student, necessary not only for the motivation to master a foreign musical system but also to foster responsiveness at beginning levels of understanding. Although no research exists specific to the issue of foreign musics, research results reported by Rokeach (1960) tend to reinforce the proposition that conceptual and perceptual processes have strong correlations. The willingness of a subject to be open or closed to new ideas may be related to personality development in early childhood. Es

tablishing an openness to various world cultures may need to occur with the very young. Although the work by Rokeach was based on experiments with serial music and has little significance to the question under discussion here, it does open up an aspect of potential research pertinent for educators, especially with early childhood issues surfacing in so many areas.

Lomax (1968) discussed several factors within the cultural fabric that act to inhibit one from transcending one's own cultural base. The Indian Council for Cultural Relations, convening in Delhi, India, in 1964, was particularly significant in light of problems of cultural transcendency. Peter Crossley-Holland, a participant of the conference, enumerated three specific problems encountered in listening to music of another culture:

1. There is a natural tendency to judge music by one's own criteria, which frequently are not appropriate for the music being perceived.
2. There is a lack of background information on aesthetic factors, logic, and convention, which assist in focusing attention in the proper way.
3. The presence of nonmusical factors—such as mind wandering, expectations of a work prior to hearing it, assumption of superiority or inferiority—all cause distraction from focusing on the sound of the music (in Palmer, 1975, p. 151).

Thus, while students in elementary and secondary schools may be capable of engaging in musical activities within their own culture and even expanding to additional musical systems, personal and cultural factors may create obstacles to this end. The notion that the younger the child, the fewer conditioned barriers there are is not validated by research but certainly holds a glimmer of hope for those who espouse enrichment through exposure to cultures other than our own.

Problems related to the teacher are, in many ways, similar to those encountered by students. Issues involved in a music education program that incorporates world musics are (1) teacher preparation, (2) authenticity of performers, (3) methods and materials, (4) feasibility and practicality, (5) selection of specific musical traditions, and (6) other miscellaneous considerations. Many of these issues discussed by Palmer (1975) were revisited in discussions held at the Wesleyan Symposium in 1984. In a summary report entitled *Becoming Human Through Music* (1985), symposium participants reiterated the importance of viewing the music of nonwestern cultures within their own social structures and realizing that in most cultures music is interrelated with dance, drama, ritual, and visual elements. Many questioned whether music teachers confronting a folk song found in a book isolated from its cultural context would have the background to do this. Music teachers expressed openly their skepticism respecting adequate training, performance skills, and cultural competence.

Montague (1988) investigated teacher training in multi

cultural music education in selected universities and colleges. Her review of literature is notable and covers a broad range of issues. She reports that a number of multicultural teacher-training conferences in the 1970s were prompted by passage of Title IV of the 1964 Civil Rights Act. Publications from these conferences indicated that preservice education in the area of multicultural training was far from ideal. A comprehensive project, reported in four volumes, was undertaken in 1980 by the Commission on Multicultural Education of the American Association of Colleges for Teacher Education. Volume one discussed implementation of multicultural education, preservice and inservice teacher-training programs, models for training activities, and the importance of interpersonal skills training for personal cultural orientation necessary to affect educational practice. Volume two was a collection of case studies that provided alternative strategies for implementing programs in various settings. Volume three was an annotated bibliography of resources and reference materials for use in preservice, inservice, and graduate classes. Volume four presented guidelines for planning and evaluating programs based on National Council for Accreditation of Teacher Education (NCATE) standards. Other publications devoted to the training of educators were produced by Webb (1979), Moody (1979), and Moody and Vergon (1979). Two additional sources devoting large portions of their publications to teacher preparation are *Multicultural Education and Ethnic Studies in the United States: An Annotated Bibliography of Selected ERIC Documents* (1976), by Gollnick, and Baker (1983), *Planning and Organizing for Multicultural Instruction*. Finally, a dissertation by Johnson (1980) explores preservice teacher perceptions of a lecture series provided by the School of Education at the University of Michigan. These references deal with multicultural education and not multicultural music education, but they do provide an important base for teacher preparation since many issues of teacher training are in some ways unaffected by specific content areas and many of the ideas related to methodology lend themselves to the area of music.

Reports related specifically to music and multicultural issues began to appear in the late 1970s and 1980s. Duncan (1977), in a survey of junior high school general music teachers, recommended that teachers be given training to develop in-depth cultural, sociological, and psychological understanding of the disadvantaged student. A similar recommendation resulted from a study by Jones (1985) in an investigation with teachers in rural settings.

One of the first dissertations specifically on the preparation of music teachers was conducted in North Carolina public schools and dealt with performance practices of black gospel music. The study yielded some interesting results. The 1980 study by Gilchrist, as summarized by Montague (1988), reported that (1) public school students were perceived by teachers to be enthusiastic about the study and performance of black gospel music, (2) black gospel music was perceived by teachers to be less significant than other music forms, (3) teachers did not feel adequately prepared to teach black gospel music, (4) teachers did not receive training in preservice programs to teach black gospel music, and

(5) teachers were generally unable to recognize distinctions between traditional and more contemporary forms of black gospel music.

Another dissertation related to preservice training is by Stephens (1984). The study examined the effect of a course that integrated Afro-American music into a musical setting. Seventy-eight undergraduates received training in the form of lectures, films, listening activities, readings, and discussion. Results showed some effect on the degree of preference for Afro-American music, a strong effect on the degree of acceptance of this music, and mixed effects on the subjects by race.

Additional dissertations that stress the need for adequate teacher training but are primarily concerned with the development or the analysis of resource materials are by Anderson (1970), Moore (1977), Horton (1979), and Britt (1980).

The most relevant information regarding preservice undergraduate training for teachers is a study by Montague (1988) identifying courses and/or course content related to multicultural music education in select universities and colleges. Information was obtained through a questionnaire with a follow-up interview requested. Of 31 professors contacted, interviews were obtained with 22 music educators and eight ethnomusicologists. Information from these interviews provided descriptions for 40 courses. The investigation gathered data from eight universities in the West, 11 in the Midwest, four in the South, two in the East, and two in the islands. Courses mandated for undergraduate music education programs rather than elective offerings were given priority since the former were considered to have the most long-lasting effect on multicultural goals within the profession.

Of the 40 courses described, five were special multicultural music education courses required for undergraduate music education students and taught by a music educator; 20 were music education methods courses with a multicultural component, required for music education students and taught by a music educator; seven courses were elective for undergraduate or graduate music education students and taught by a music educator; and eight were world music or ethnomusicology courses required or elective for undergraduate or graduate music education students. Because the investigation concerned required preservice courses within music education departments, courses in the first and second categories were sought after more diligently than those in categories three and four, which accounts somewhat for the lower numbers in the latter; in reality, many more courses could have been cited in categories three and four.

While category one courses focused primarily on nonwestern musics and presumably involved more in-depth study, many more courses were found in category two. Montague speculates that it is easier to incorporate a unit into an existing course than to introduce an additional course within already overcrowded curricula. Although the incorporation of multicultural materials into a methods course is far from ideal, it does provide some information to students and can serve to increase awareness of the need for further study at a later time. Courses in categories three and four were in no way minimized by Montague. Elective courses were considered to be an immediate way to move toward required courses, and courses in category four were viewed as the most desirable situation where two departments, music education and ethnomusicology, work together to prepare students. Many of the music educators interviewed believed that multicultural education could not be accomplished without first being addressed in higher education at the preservice level of instruction. The ethnomusicologists agreed, but in general saw competence as the most essential need, stating that without the proper experience with varied musics, essential listening and/or performance skills, and knowledge of musical terms in contexts beyond western traditions, students would be reluctant to introduce music of other cultures in public school settings. In addition, ethnomusicologists felt that collaboration between departments must be initiated before advancement in multicultural education could be fully realized on a scale broad enough to make a difference.

CURRICULUM DEVELOPMENT

The largest number of studies relating to multicultural music education fall into the category of curricular issues or development of resource materials for general use for either a particular age group or a specific population.

Palmer (1975), in determining realistic projections for the incorporation of world musics into the elementary and secondary music curricula, discussed three areas of concern—materials, methodology, and students. He viewed the availability of specific materials as essential for implementation. Three proposals were outlined to address what he felt were major problem areas.

The first proposal addresses the problem of great diversity of pitch phenomena of various music systems. He suggested the development of an electronic instrument capable of producing various scale structures and tunings not possible for the equal-tempered piano or other classroom instruments. Palmer envisioned the project to be carried out by a team of individuals qualified in electronics design and implementation, musical theory, and acoustics; scholars in various world music traditions; and a knowledgeable music educator to validate the pedagogy. Today's technology has produced such an instrument, but its widespread use in conjunction with the study of world musics in schools has not occurred.

The second proposal called for source books about various world music traditions designed especially for use in elementary schools. Most essential are textbooks including authentic examples of world music as a normal part of music instruction, supplementary books that concentrate on specific cultures or genres within a culture, and storybooks related to various aspects of nonwestern cultural traditions. The increase in availability of such sources, many of which include accompanying tapes to ensure more authentic aural examples, is indeed notable. An increasing number of children's books with themes related to other cultures are available in public libraries and catalogs.

The third proposal suggested the establishment of an extensive data bank cross-referenced for various kinds of information and materials for music specialists. The data bank should be designed for easy retrieval, utilize a system for ongoing expansion, indicate level of difficulty or age appropriateness, and be inexpensive. The need for such a system still exists.

With regard to methodology, two approaches have dominated curricular formats in the studies reviewed. One approach organizes instruction around universal musical concepts, and the other emphasizes performance. To give the reader some perspective on the nature of curricular studies, several are briefly reviewed here. However, they are not organized around these two basic approaches, although both are reflected in the studies discussed. Rather, the studies are grouped according to higher education curricula, K–12 curricula, and curricula developed as a result of urban issues, and there are a few studies focusing on curricula in an international context.

Higher Education Curricula

Studies targeted for adult or undergraduate multicultural experience are sparse. Butcher (1970) developed materials for a course in African music as part of a project at Howard University. Schmid (1971) developed a curriculum for use in undergraduate music education, providing a syllabus for the course and a select bibliography, discography, and film list. The first three chapters discuss, respectively, the rationale for the study, the need for it, and projections of educational models pertaining to tribal, Oriental, and folk music of nonwestern cultures. The remaining chapters address orientation for the study, the music of tribal cultures. the music of Oriental cultures, European folk music, and folk music in the Americas.

Levine and Standifer (1981) produced *From Jumpstreet: Television and the Humanities,* a series of 13 half-hour television programs for preservice and inservice training that focus primarily on the black musical heritage from its African beginnings to its influences in modern American music. Another publication designed particularly for teacher training was a manual by Rodriguez and Sherman (1983) in which the music of three culture groups is explored—black Americans, American Indians, and Hispanic Americans. Detailed background on the uses of music in each culture and general information on musical performance are included along with specific classroom activities.

Three other studies present a somewhat different emphasis. Gartin (1981) assessed the intercultural perspectives provided in music appreciation textbooks used in the five-college consortium of western Massachusetts. Mumford (1984) developed an instrument to measure the attitudes of prospective music educators toward black popular music and its use in the classroom. He concluded that direct contact with ethnic and popular music was superior to lectures and readings in effecting positive attitudinal change. Stephens (1984) used the Mumford Afro-American Popular Music Attitude

Scale to measure possible effects of the integration of Afro-American popular music into the undergraduate curriculum. Treatment consisted of lectures, films, listening, readings, and discussion. The results indicated that the degree to which a subject preferred Afro-American popular music was slightly affected, and that the degree of acceptance of this music was strongly affected.

Elementary and Secondary Music Curricula

A number of studies were found that specifically sought to synthesize and organize various musics for use in schools across a wide spectrum of ages. Heidsiek (1966) undertook to collect authentic music of the Luiseño Indians of Southern California and relate it to a program of music education for schools in the area. Fifteen songs found in the Southwest Museum, Los Angeles, were transferred to tape, transcribed into standard notation, and organized into eight study units of Luiseño music for use by teachers. Each unit is a body of information and music related to a ceremony or other social activity. Each unit consists of background information, related mythology, dance directions, and descriptions of instruments, implements, and costumes.

Freebern's study (1969) was designed as a guide and resource for incorporating the cultures of India, China, Japan, and Oceania into the classroom. Information on each culture includes historical and geographical data; references to the art, architecture, drama, and literature; and a list of resource materials such as recordings and films to augment the musical study of these cultures.

Anderson (1970) explored the teaching of two non-western musics—Javanese and Indian—in American elementary schools. Included were basic historical backgrounds for each of the cultures; descriptions of various types of vocal and instrumental forms; and activities designed for use with children, such as singing, the playing of instruments, listening to prepared tape recordings, and viewing slides and films.

A similar study for junior high school general music classes was conducted by Okimoto (1974). Using the structural and taxonomic base of the Hawaii Music Program as a framework in which basic musical concepts were introduced and reinforced, Okimoto selected additional music of the three largest immigrant cultures in Hawaii—the Chinese, Japanese, and Filipino cultures. The use of nonwestern music was not treated as the sole basis of study or even as a separate unit, but rather as one aspect of the wide range of material available expressing the universal existence of basic musical concepts.

Behnke (1975) collected musical material and cultural and bicultural resources for the study of Mexican and Mexican-American music, including the history and style characteristics of Mexican Indian music, folk music, art music of both the Spanish colonial period and the twentieth century, and Chicano rock music. Music and materials were organized into units with emphasis on the cultural-social setting, the elements of musical structure, and style characteristics.

Gamble (1978) designed a curriculum that emphasized the principles of the spiral curricular model using the music of Java and Bali as content. Concepts of pitch, rhythm, form, dynamics, and timbre were identified and reinforced at four different levels of increasing complexity, from kindergarten to eighth grade. Musical behaviors were described for each level for each concept and constructed in such a way that students must achieve the objectives for one level before proceeding to the next level. Suggested activities were included to accomplish the desired objectives. Students were expected to perform, create, listen, move, notate, interpret, and evaluate each of the levels. The curriculum employed the music and cultural traditions of Java and Bali as an example of how to incorporate a specific type of ethnic music in a conceptually based approach. Lists of source materials, covering recordings, songs, gamelan compositions, and films, were included.

Harpole (1980) gathered data about Hispanic vocal and instrumental music of the southwestern United States in order to design curricular units for use at the middle school level (grades 6 through 9). The term "Hispanic" referred specifically to all types of music in the Southwest that evidence the Spanish language and cultural background. Two major types of Hispanic music were chosen for unit development—the mariachi ensemble and its accompanying song type, the *son*, and the *corrido* ballad form. One set (of two units) represented Mariachi music; the second set (also two units) was devoted to the *corrido*. Each set includes an introduction to the topic utilizing a cassette tape containing both narration and musical examples, supportive materials including teaching instructions and suggestions, transcripts of the tape in both English and Spanish, maps, and vocabulary sheets. Each introductory unit is designed to be used by classroom teachers with minimal music background as well as music specialists. The second unit involves the student directly in musical activities incorporating singing and playing of instruments and composition.

Shehan (1981) sought to determine the effectiveness of two different methods of introducing gamelan music of Indonesia to groups of sixth-grade students. The heuristic method emphasized the performance of gamelan compositions by the students singing and playing instruments. The didactic method was more traditional in format, in that students discussed musical style and culture of Indonesia as presented by the teacher through lectures, films, slides, and so on. Results suggested that involving students actively with the vocal and instrumental performance of gamelan music not only improved cognitive skills but increased preference for the music under study.

Even though the Anderson, Harpole, and Shehan studies suggested that actively involving students in making music as opposed to learning about music of other cultures resulted in positive responses from students, it is not an argument that necessarily validates the teaching of world musics. The value of active involvement is well established irrespective of the content under study. Inferior performances of music by students with little skill or the performance of Indonesian scales on diatonic instruments points out the limitations of school settings. On the other hand, there is nothing to indicate that these limitations cause irreparable harm. Students as well as teachers enjoy and can benefit from the variety of "new" musics.

The Gamble and Okimoto studies focused on the use of ethnic musics as an alternative to more traditional musics in educational settings in the learning of musical concepts. Credence for multicultural music is enhanced by any approach that can verify that students are accomplishing basic musical goals.

Although these studies indicate that students can benefit from the study of ethnic musics, curricular oriented studies simply do not provide the research base to satisfy the enormous philosophical and practical issues mentioned earlier.

Multicultural Studies Related to Urban Issues

Many dissertations and funded studies that relate to multicultural music education curricula are reflective of the 1972 mandate by the government's passage of Public Law 92-318 discussed above under "Historical Background." Many of the studies in the mid to late 1970s take on a decided "urban" character, attempting to identify problems, introduce an innovative curriculum within the cultural context of the school's urban ethnicity background, and investigate attitude changes as a result of multicultural initiatives.

Reyes-Schramm (1975) investigated *The Role of Music in the Interaction of Black Americans and Hispanos in New York City's East Harlem*. The data base for the investigation was the music performed by live musicians, whether they were formally structured, informally structured, or contextually structured groups. A study by Lampkins (1976) investigated the history of the Lakeside School of Music and its role in fostering understanding and the teaching of Afro-American music. A similar study by Whitworth (1977) exposed students in predominantly black inner-city Chicago high schools to music units based on cultural and historical contributions of blacks. Results showed improvement in both achievement and attendance for students exposed to the experimental curriculum.

The purpose of a study by Diaz-Cruz (1979) was to investigate and describe the music programs and their relationship to the bilingual-bicultural programs of a Chicago high school and elementary feeder schools. An ethnographic study by Merrill-Mirsky (1988) investigated the musical play of children from four major ethnic groups in Los Angeles elementary schoolyards—Euro-American, Afro-American, Latino, and Southeast Asian. A total of 342 variants of 117 items was collected over a period of five years, including hand clapping and ring games, jump rope chants, and cheers. The repertoire represents games that have been passed from generation to generation through oral tradition, as well as games of recent creation, recycled within local communities and transmitted from area to area.

An underlying assumption of these curricular studies seems to be that focusing on a minority's indigenous culture can mitigate the inequities that are responsible for the prob-

lems of that minority in the home, community, and school. There is an inherent danger in advocating an ethnocentric curriculum to replace established curricula in an effort to raise the self-esteem and academic achievement of children from ethnic or minority backgrounds. To imply that the only way to reach self-determination is through one's own heritage (history, art, music, and so forth) intimates that self-identity is preserved by divorcing oneself from a common culture, that is, the American culture. Such extremism is notably different from the cultural pluralism that recognizes diversity as an organizing principle of American society, acknowledges the racism and discrimination of the past and present, and advocates the notion that our common culture is defined by immigrants, native Americans, and Africans and their descendants; and that American music, art, literature, language, food, customs, all reflect the commingling of diverse cultures. Such an extremist approach would seem to be closing the minds of children, isolating them from any hope of an enriched cultural life, and narrowing the path that lies ahead of them.

International Studies

Multicultural issues in music education have been studied by researchers from other countries. Nakazawa (1988) investigated the lack of interest shown by Japanese youth toward their own traditional music. Nakazawa (1) investigated music education in Japan and found that a conscious effort was made to subordinate Japanese traditional musics to western classical music; (2) surveyed the attitudes of Japanese parents living in the United States and found that they feared the loss of Japanese identity in their children; and (3) compared the music preferences of youth in Japan with those of youth in the states and found that children exposed to the most intercultural interaction showed increased interest in both ethnic musics and traditional Japanese music. Similarly, in an effort to involve Korean schools in the preservation of Korean traditional music by making it the core of the school music curriculum, Lee (1988) conducted a study that compared the use of Korean-based materials and western-based materials in two senior high schools in Seoul. Not surprisingly, Lee found that instruction in traditional Korean music idioms contributed significantly to the development of students' perception of Korean music.

Ekwueme (1988), recognizing the lack of indigenous music in Nigerian primary schools, developed a curriculum utilizing folk music and materials through which students were sensitized to musical elements, improvisation strategies, local musical materials, and the expressive aspects of their own indigenous music. The study provided a basis for teacher training and a curriculum consistent with Nigerian cultural values.

These studies indicate that even within cultures other than American culture, there is evidence that students do not relate to their own traditional musics. Elliott (1989) suggests that to achieve the goals we have set for multicultural authenticity we must decipher objectively the various curricular models that have emerged over the past several decades. He introduces the work of Richard Pratte, entitled *Pluralism in Education* (1979), which details six different curriculum models; Elliott adapts these for the study of music.

The first model focuses on the major musical styles of western art music. Because it is concerned with development of "taste," the goal is to break down students' affiliations with popular and/or subculture musics, especially the affiliations of minority students. The second curricular model, while it includes some ethnic and subculture musics (e.g., gospel, rock, Mexican, African, baroque) sees them only as inspiration for new music composed in accepted styles and forms; in this way, values of minorities are accepted as a source for their potential contribution to a stronger, hybrid society. The third curricular model views cultural heritage as an impediment to progress, proposing that only "now" music has the power to draw all to a national identify. Value is placed on everything that is contemporary, with musical values pivoting on political and economic whim. Self-expression is validated through such musics as fusion, punk, commercial, electronic, and aleatoric. The *explicit* goal shared by these three curricular models supports the inculcation of majority values; the *implicit* goal promotes the unification of a culture (melting pot theory) and the elimination of cultural diversity.

In contrast to these three models, the last three curricula share a common concern for the preservation of cultural diversity. In the fourth model the core repertoire is selected from within the largest minority group of a local community. Although this model seems "multicultural" because it permits alternative musics, it actually serves to insulate the population from the broad scope of world musics' enrichment.

The fifth model distinguishes itself from the fourth (1) by incorporating musics on the basis of regional and/or national boundaries of culture, ethnicity, religion, function, or race; (2) by organizing the curriculum itself conceptually by the musical elements, processes, roles, and behaviors accepted by majority value; and (3) by introducing musics in much the same way as they are learned and taught in their original cultures. While Elliott views this model as the one that comes closest to achieving the criteria for multicultural music education, he believes it has two basic weaknesses. First, it is biased at the outset by the "aesthetic" perspective inherent in the notion of teaching within a conceptual framework, a perspective that judges all musics within a standard set by the ideal the "aesthetic" represents. Second, it tends to be limited to the styles available in the contemporary musical life of the host culture, with only those styles being selected that have some relativity to the students in that setting.

The sixth model discussed by Elliott, and the one that he feels has the most potential for multicultural music education practice, is called dynamic multiculturalism. The model preserves the integrity of past musical traditions yet is open to unfamiliar values, procedures, and behaviors necessary to understand the music of a variety of cultures. This approach allows students to develop ideas about music without the didactic preservation of unconscious prejudice, be it academic or social.

The combination of the widest possible range of world musics and a world view of musical concepts separates the dynamic curriculum model from all the rest. Thus, in addition to developing students' abilities to discriminate and appreciate the differences and similarities among musical cultures, a dynamic curriculum has the potential to achieve two fundamental 'expressive objectives' or ways of being musical: 'bimusicality' at least, and 'multimusicality' at most. (Elliott, 1989, p. 18)

Miscellaneous Resource Guides

A number of published materials are available for use with varying age groups and settings. Two issues of the *Music Educators Journal* (October 1972; May 1983) were devoted to the topic of world musics and multicultural music education. Standifer and Reeder (1972) published the *Source Book of African and Afro-American Materials for Music Educators,* which combined the concepts of comprehensive musicianship and multicultural music education. A more recent MENC publication by Anderson and Campbell (1989) provides detailed information on utilizing the musics of various nonwestern cultures in elementary and secondary general music. In both of these collections the focus for multicultural insistence lies within the musical elements, and direct contact with the music is suggested as the catalyst for openness toward the music itself.

In 1983, the Seattle School District published a series of booklets under the title *Selected Multicultural Instructional Materials.* The booklets list and describe major U.S. holidays and events and American ethnic minority and majority individuals and their achievements, including those of the Chinese, Korean, Vietnamese, Hawaiian, Mexican, Japanese, and American Indian ethnic groups. Although most of the booklets do not focus on music specifically, they offer guidance in all subject areas in achieving the stated goals and objectives.

One curriculum guide that specifically includes music was developed by the Los Angeles Unified School District. Entitled *Incorporating Multicultural Education into the Curriculum* (1981), it focuses on the aspects of cultural similarities and differences and is designed to develop acceptance of individual and group heritage. There are nine sections, each related to a specific culture. Each section contains activities pertaining to interdisciplinary goals and to specific goals and objectives in art, reading, health, physical education, music, language arts, and social sciences for grades 4–8. Cultural groups include blacks, European Americans, Hispanics, American Indians and Eskimos, and Asian Americans and Pacific Islanders.

Ethnomusicological Studies

Another group of studies related to multicultural music education is primarily ethnomusicological. These studies provide more in-depth information about specific cultures, which can serve as resource material for teaching purposes. Many such dissertations can be found in the references to this chapter. Only continued collaboration between the ethnomusicologist and the music educator can assist in the realization of the goal of multicultural authenticity.

SOME ISSUES FOR THE FUTURE

The research discussed illustrates a movement that was labeled as "multicultural" and that has emerged slowly and, to a great extent, as a reaction to other more dynamic expressions of ethnomusicological or sociological happenings. Despite the recognition by the Yale Seminar, the Tanglewood Symposium, school textbooks, and MENC and ISME publications, the inclusion on nonwestern musics in elementary and secondary curricula is far from global.

If philosophy has provided at least a glimmer of a theoretical pathway, there still remain a number of practical problems. Both preservice and inservice training for teachers have been inadequate. A host of related problems is identified by Schwadron (1984): "the availability of native instruments, informants and performers; issues of authenticity and compromise; tuning and scalar differences; national and political attitudes; place in the shrinking K–12 curriculum; teacher preparation; and, not the least, the musical maturity of children" (p. 94).

Research has provided much information regarding the background of various music cultures and curricular sources. Materials alone will not solve the problems of teacher competency. It is doubtful that even traditional programs are meeting the goals set by the profession given the present constraints in time, facilities, staff, and administrative support. Justification for additional multicultural goals must be found in rationales that go beyond availability of content materials.

Research has yet to answer the questions regarding the effects of cross-cultural exposure on musical perception, the developmental readiness of various ages for the study of world musics, the effectiveness of various approaches, and the question of bimusical and multimusical capacity. With this notion of bimusicality and multimusicality, we return full circle to ideas discussed earlier by Palmer (1975). The reality of bimusicality and/or multimusicality needs to be revisited in the 1990s by researchers sensitive to both sides of the issues, who are familiar with the performance and discrimination abilities of students throughout the age spectrum.

A more immediate need is that of addressing the fundamental issues relevant to both philosophy and practice. Schwadron continues:

Put simply, we are not agreed on matters of values or directions of study. In the U.S. there still is some confusion between liberal outcomes and socio-ethnic goals which identify more readily with such movements as affirmative action, equality of opportunity, and other concerns for minority rights. The idealistic hope is that by searching out value systems in music cultures throughout the world, music education will assume an inclusively valuable humanistic role—one that is alert to cultural differences and commonalities while nurturing

aesthetic self-realization from a rich field of musical potential. (Schwadron, 1984, p. 94)

This focus on "value" is not inconsistent with writings from the dawn of the multicultural movement. Dolce (1973) discussed several ideas plaguing the multicultural movement in the early 1970s. The Board of Directors of the American Association of Colleges for Teacher Education issued statements as early as 1972 that differed significantly from "model American archetype" and the ideal of assimilation represented by the "melting pot theory." Dolce marveled then, that for such a revolutionary idea, there was little hostility evidenced toward proponents of multiculturalism. He believed that the word itself carried a number of interpretations that actually masked conflicts among value systems. In addition, for many the changes implied were either of such superficiality that change was inevitable or so radical that it could never be accomplished.

Three types of multicultural advocates emerged throughout the 1970s, each with their own value statement. The first perceived the movement as a utilitarian vehicle for achieving larger ends, that is, to increase the leverage and power of minority ethnic groups. The second saw the movement as an opportunity for something new, a spark for innovative approaches and novel content. The third envisioned multiculturalism as near the top of a hierarchical scale of values; hence, compliance implied a willingness to reevaluate one's most basic ideas and behaviors.

Dolce (1973) outlined several characteristics of multicultural education, which still seem viable today:

1. Multiculturalism is a reflection of a value system which emphasizes acceptance of behavior differences deriving from differing cultural systems and an active support of the right of such differences to exist. . . . Advocates often wrongly assume that all share basic cultural values.

2. The concept of multiculturalism transcends matters of race. A one-to-one correlation between race and culture is simply not supported by the evidence.

3. Multiculturalism is not simply a new methodology which can be grafted onto an educational program. The concept of multiculturalism in education is based upon a different view of society than that which appears to exist. . . . A single course on multicultural education in such a setting is an attempt to capture the appearance without the substance.

4. A multicultural state of affairs is not one which is devoid of tensions. All differing cultures are not complementary. The interaction of such cultures will tend to create new tensions and possibly increase existing tensions.

5. Based upon mutual respect among different cultures, multiculturalism is not a euphemism for disadvantaged. Cultures are neither inherently superior nor inferior to each other. (pp. 282–283)

In 1979, the Commission on Multicultural Education of the American Association of Colleges for Teacher Education issued a statement that acknowledged that cultural diversity should be preserved and extended, not just tolerated. The statement defines multicultural education as (1) sets of courses or skills involved in coping successfully with a culturally diverse society; and (2) a general approach to education that seeks to organize schooling around both the fact and the value of cultural pluralism (Rodriguez, 1979).

Is it possible that in an age where even the global market of fashion has sensed the urgency of multicultural awareness, we in education will follow rather than lead in issues that shape the future? Rodriguez (1979) cautioned the profession a decade ago. "Only a well-conceived, sensitive, thorough, and continuous program of multicultural education can create the broadly based ethnic literacy necessary for the future of our nation" (p. 14).

References

Akpabot, S. E. (1974). Functional music of the Ibibio people of Nigeria. Unpublished doctoral dissertation, University of Pennsylvania, Philadelphia.

Al Faruqi, L. I. (1974). The nature of the musical art of Islamic culture: A theoretical and empirical study of Arabian music. Unpublished doctoral dissertation, Syracuse University, Syracuse.

Anderson, W. M., Jr. (1970). A theoretical and practical inquiry into the teaching of music from Java and India in American elementary schools. Unpublished doctoral dissertation, University of Michigan, Ann Arbor.

Anderson, W. M. Jr. (1974, Autumn). World music in American education. *Contributions to Music Education.* 23–42.

Anderson, W. M., Jr., and Campbell, P. S. (1989). *Multicultural perspectives in music education.* Reston: Music Educators National Conference.

Multicultural, nonsexist teaching strategies reference (K–6). (1980). Cedar Falls: Area Education Agency 7. (ERIC Document Reproduction Service No. ED 241967)

Bahree, P. (1986). *Asia in the European classroom: The CDCC's teachers bursaries scheme.* Council for Cultural Cooperation, Strasbourg.

Baker, G. (1983). *Planning and organizing for multicultural instruction.* Reading: Addison-Wesley Publishing Company.

Becker, J. M. O. (1972). Traditional music in modern Java. Unpublished doctoral dissertation, University of Michigan, Ann Arbor.

Becoming human through music. (1985). *The Wesleyan Symposium on the Perspectives of Social Anthropology in the Teaching and Learning of Music.* Reston: Music Educators National Conference.

Behnke, M. K. (1975). Resources and suggested organizational procedures for courses in Mexican and Mexican-American music. Unpublished doctoral dissertation, University of Colorado, Boulder.

Benary, B. L. (1973). Within the Karnatic tradition. Unpublished doctoral dissertation, Wesleyan University, Middletown.

Berliner, P. F. (1974). The soul of Mbira: An ethnography of the Mbira among the Shona people of Rhodesia. Unpublished doctoral dissertation, Wesleyan University, Middletown.

Blum, R. S. (1972). Musics in contact: The cultivation of oral repertoires in Meshed, Iran. Unpublished doctoral dissertation, University of Illinois, Urbana.

Bragg, D. A. (1971). The teaching of music concepts in the elementary schools of Puerto Rico. Unpublished doctoral dissertation, Florida State University, Tallahassee.

Britt, M. R. (1980). The assimilation of Afro-American music Idioms into the music education curriculum. Unpublished doctoral dissertation, Stanford University, Stanford.

Buckner, R. T. (1980). A history of music education in the black community of Kansas City, Kansas, 1905–1954. *Journal of Research in Music Education, 30,* 91–106.

Burman-Hall, L. C. (1974). Southern American folk fiddling: Context and style. Unpublished doctoral dissertation, Princeton University, Princeton.

Butcher, V. (1970) *Development of materials for a one-year course in African music for the general undergraduate student.* (Research project No. 6-1179, Final Report). Washington: U.S. Department of Health, Education, and Welfare, Bureau of Research.

Carriuolo, R. E. (1974). Materials for the study of Italian folk music. Unpublished doctoral dissertation, Wesleyan University, Middletown.

Chen, L. (1983). Development of a Chinese music listening program. Unpublished doctoral dissertation, Columbia University Teachers College, New York.

Chi, C. Y. (1975). The influence of Chinese music on Korean music. Unpublished doctoral dissertation, University of Northern Colorado, Greeley.

Cho, G. J. (1975) Some non-Chinese elements in the ancient Japanese music: An analytical-comparative study. Unpublished doctoral dissertation, Northwestern University, Evanston.

Coleman, S. N. (1927). *Creative music in the home.* New York: The John Day Company.

Diaz Cruz, H. (1979). A descriptive study of the music programs in Roberto Clemente High School and selected feeder schools as they relate to bilingual-bicultural education. Unpublished doctoral dissertation, University of Illinois, Urbana.

Dolce, C. J. (1973). Multicultural education—some issues. *Journal of Teacher Education, 24,* 282–285.

Duncan, R. A. (1977, March). *Teacher perceived problems in general music in inner city junior high schools with implications for teacher education.* Research report presented to the North Carolina and Southwestern Division Conference, Music Educators National Conference, Kansas City.

Ekwueme, L. U. (1988). Nigerian indigenous music as a basis for developing creative music instruction for Nigerian primary schools and suggestive guidelines for implementation. Unpublished doctoral dissertation, Columbia University Teachers College, New York.

Elliott, D. J. (1989). Key concepts in multicultural music education. *International Journal of Music Education, 13,* 11–18.

Ferguson, D. L. (1988). A study of Cantonese opera: Musical source materials, historical development, contemporary social organization and adaptive strategies. Unpublished doctoral dissertation, University of Washington, Seattle.

Franklin, J. C. (1976). Relationship between teacher viewpoints towards a culturally oriented music program and black pupils' achievement and viewpoints towards the program. Unpublished doctoral dissertation, Purdue University, West Lafayette.

Freebern, C. L. (1969). The music of India, China, and Oceania: A source book for teachers. Unpublished doctoral dissertation, University of Arizona, Tucson.

Frissell, S. (1985). A historical study of the implications of black music and its relationship to the selected aspects of social, cultural, and educational experiences of black Americans: 1955–1980. Unpublished doctoral dissertation, Loyala University, Chicago.

Gamble, S. (1978). A spiral curriculum utilizing the music of Java and Bali as a model for teaching ethnic music from kindergarten through grade eight. Unpublished doctoral dissertation, Pennsylvania State University, University Park.

Gartin, B. A. H. (1981). Intercultural perspectives in music appreciation: A survey of five college textbooks. Unpublished doctoral dissertation, University of Massachusetts, Amherst.

Gilchrist, C. H. (1980). An assessment of the preparation of North Carolina public school music teachers in performance practices of black gospel music: Implications for curriculum revisions in higher education. Unpublished doctoral dissertation, University of North Carolina, Greensboro.

Giles, M. M. (1977). A synthesis of American Indian music as derived from culture: Examination of style, performance practices, and aesthetic for music education. Unpublished doctoral dissertation, University of Oklahoma, Norman.

Gollnick, D. (1976). *Multicultural education and ethnic studies in the United States: An analysis and annotated bibliography of selected ERIC documents.* Washington: Ethnic Heritage Center for Teacher Education of the American Association of Colleges for Teacher Education.

Hallman, C. L., Capaz, A., and Capaz, D. (1983). *Value orientations of Vietnamese culture.* Office of Bilingual Education and Minority Languages Affairs, Washington: (ERIC Document Reproduction Service No. ED 269533)

Harpole, P. W. (1980). Curricular applications of Hispanic music in the southwestern United States. Unpublished doctoral dissertation, University of California, Los Angeles.

Harrell, M. L. (1974). The music of the gamelan degung of West Java. Unpublished doctoral dissertation, University of California, Los Angeles.

Hartenberger, J. R. (1974). Mrdangam manual: A guidebook of South Indian rhythm for Western musicians. I. Rhythmic theory. II. Analysis of Mrdangam lessons. III. Mrdangam lessons in Mrdangam notation. Unpublished doctoral dissertation, Wesleyan University, Middletown.

Haughton, H. S. (1984). Social and cultural reproduction in the (music) curriculum guideline process in Ontario education: Ethnic minorities and cultural exclusion. Unpublished doctoral dissertation, University of Toronto, Toronto.

Heidsiek, R. G. (1966). Music of the Luiseño Indians of Southern California—a study of music in Indian culture with relation to a program in music education. Unpublished doctoral dissertation, University of California, Los Angeles.

Hendon, W. S. (Ed.). (1980). *The arts and urban development: Critical comment and discussion.* (Monograph Series in Public and International Affairs No. 12), University of Akron: Center for Urban Studies.

Heth, C. A. W. (1975). The stomp dance music of the Oklahoma Cherokee: A study of contemporary practice with special reference to the Illinois district council ground (Vols. I & II). Unpublished doctoral dissertation, University of California, Los Angeles.

Hicks, C. E., Standifer, J. A., and Warrick L. C., (Eds.). (1983). *Methods and perspectives in urban music education.* Lanham: University Press of America.

Horton, C. D. (1979). Indigenous music of Sierra Leone: An analysis or resources and educational implication. Unpublished doctoral dissertation, University of California, Los Angeles.

Hughes, S. E. (1987). A compilation of Afro-American and Puerto Rican music materials for use in the New York City public schools. Unpublished doctoral dissertation, Columbia University Teachers College, New York.

Incorporating multicultural education into the curriculum. Grades four through eight. (1981). (Publication No. GC-89-1981). Los Angeles: Los Angeles Unified School District, Office of Instruction. (ERIC Document Reproduction Service No. ED 231 905)

Isaku, P. M. (1973). An introduction to Japanese folk music. Unpublished doctoral dissertation, Wesleyan University, Middletown.

Johnson, J. T. Jr. (1988). Enculturation in a formal setting: A study of programs and prospects in Afro-American music education. Unpublished doctoral dissertation, University of Pittsburgh, Pittsburgh.

Johnson, M. L. R. (1980). An exploration of preservice teacher perception on the effectiveness of multicultural lecture series. Unpublished doctoral dissertation, University of Michigan, Ann Arbor.

Jones, B. J. (1985). Preservice programs for teaching in a rural environment: Survey and recommendations. Summary of results and recommendations. Ann Arbor. (ERIC Document Reproduction Service No. ED 26 1826)

Jones, L. J. (1977). The Isawiya of Tunisia and their music. Unpublished doctoral dissertation, University of Washington, Seattle.

Keene, J. A. (1982). *A history of music education in the United States.* Hanover: University Press of New England.

Klein, G. and King, E. W. (1984). *Resources for teaching about antiracism and multiethnic education: Recent outstanding materials from Britain selected especially for American teachers.* Washington: National Institute of Education. (ERIC Document Reproduction Service No. ED 260 160)

Knight, R. C. (1973). Mandinka Jaliya: Professional music of the Gambia (Vols. I & II). Unpublished doctoral dissertation, University of California, Los Angeles.

Lampkins, E. H. (1976). The understanding and teaching of Afro-American music. Unpublished doctoral dissertation, University of Pittsburgh, Pittsburgh.

Larson, P., and Anderson, W. (1966, December). Sources for teaching nonwestern music. *The School Music News, 30,* 27–31.

Lau, C. A. (1971). An inquiry into the traditional music of Tahiti and its pedagogy. Unpublished doctoral dissertation, University of Oregon, Eugene.

Lee, H. (1988). The development and trial of resource materials focusing on traditional Korean music idioms for a senior high school general music course in Korea. Unpublished doctoral dissertation, University of Michigan, Ann Arbor.

Levine, T., and Standifer, J. (1981). *From jumpstreet: Television and the humanities. A workshop on multicultural education in secondary schools.* Washington: WETA-TV. (ERIC Document Reproduction Service No. ED 220 388)

Lomax, A. (1968). *Folk song style and culture.* Washington: American Association for the Advancement of Science.

Lundin, J., and Smith, T. (Eds.). (1982). *Visual and performing arts framework for California public schools: Kindergarten through grade twelve.* Sacramento: California State Department of Education. (ERIC Document Reproduction Service No. ED 231 708)

May, E. (1967, December). An experiment with Australian aboriginal music. *Music Educators Journal, 54,* 47–50.

May, E., and Hood, M. (1962, April–May). Javanese music for American children. *Music Educators Journal, 48,* 38–41.

Mbabi-Katana, S. (1972). Proposed music curriculum for first eight years of schooling in Uganda. Unpublished doctoral dissertation, Northwestern University, Evanston.

McConathy, O. (Ed.). (1927–1941). *The music hour.* New York: Silver Burdett and Company.

McKeller, D. A. (1987). Sociomusicology: The next horizon for music education. *International Society for Music Education Yearbook,* Vol. II, 173–179.

Menez, H. Q. (1986–87). Aoyu and the skyworld: The Philippine folk epic and multicultural education. *Amerasia Journal, 13*(1), 35–49.

Merrill-Mirsky, C. (1988). Eeny, meeny pepsadeeny: Ethnicity and gender in children's musical play. Unpublished doctoral dissertation, University of California, Los Angeles.

Montague, M. J. (1988). An investigation of teacher training in multicultural music education in selected universities and colleges. Unpublished doctoral dissertation, University of Michigan.

Moody, C. D. (Ed.). (1979). *Cross cultural communication in the schools.* Ann Arbor: Program for Educational Opportunity, University of Michigan.

Moody, C. D., and Vergon, C. B. (Eds.). (1979). *Approaches for achieving a multicultural curriculum.* Ann Arbor: Program for Educational Opportunity, University of Michigan.

Moore, M. C. (1977). Multicultural music education: An analysis of Afro-American and native American folk songs in selected elementary music textbooks for the periods 1928–1955 and 1965–1975. Unpublished doctoral dissertation, University of Michigan, Ann Arbor.

Moorhead, G. E., and Pond, D. (1941). *Music of young children.* Santa Barbara: Pillsbury Foundation Studies.

Mumford, J. E. (1984). The effect on the attitudes of music education majors of direct experiences with Afro-American popular music ensembles—A case study. Unpublished doctoral dissertation, Indiana University, Bloomington.

Nakazawa, N. (1988). School music, environment, and music preferences: A comparison of Japanese students living in Japan and Japanese students living in the United States. Unpublished doctoral dissertation, Columbia University Teachers College, New York.

Nelson, E. J. (1981). Black American folk song: An analytical study with implications for music education. Unpublished doctoral dissertation, Stanford University, Stanford.

Nyberg, J. L. (1974). An examination of vessel flutes from prehistoric cultures of Ecuador. Unpublished doctoral dissertation, University of Minnesota, Minneapolis.

Okimoto, R. I. (1974). Folk music of the dominant immigrant cultures of Hawaii as resource for junior high school general music. Unpublished doctoral dissertation, George Peabody College for Teachers, Nashville.

Olsen, D. A. (1973). Music and shamanism of the Winikina-Warao Indians: Songs for curing and other theurgy (Vols. I & II). Unpublished doctoral dissertation, University of California, Los Angeles.

Ornstein, R. S. (1971). Gamelan Gong Kebjar—the development of a Balinese musical tradition. Unpublished doctoral dissertation, University of California, Los Angeles.

Palmer, A. J. (1975). World musics in elementary and secondary music education: A critical analysis. Unpublished doctoral dissertation, University of California, Los Angeles.

Pinkston, A. A. (1975). Lined hymns, spirituals, and the associated lifestyle of rural black people in the United States. Unpublished doctoral dissertation, University of Miami, Coral Gables.

Portland Public Schools. (1986–87). *A statistical portrait of the multicultural/multiethnic student population in Portland Public Schools.* Portland: Management Information Services.

Pratte, R. (1979). *Pluralism in education: Conflict, clarity and commitment.* Springfield: Charles C Thomas.

Reid, J. L. (1977). The Komagaku repertory of Japanese gagaku (court music): A study of contemporary performance practice. Unpublished doctoral dissertation, University of California, Los Angeles.

Reyes-Schramm, A. The role of music in the interaction of black Americans and Hispanos in New York City's East Harlem. Unpublished doctoral dissertation, Columbia University, New York.

Riddle, R. W. (1976). Chinatown's music: A history and ethnography of music and music-drama in San Francisco's Chinese community. Unpublished doctoral dissertation, University of Illinois, Urbana.

Ringer, A. L. (1971). Kodály and education: A musicological note. *College Music Symposium, 11,* 60–65.

Rodriguez, Fred. (1979). *Accreditation and teacher education: a multicultural perspective.* (ERIC Document Reproduction Service No. ED 177 253)

Rodriguez, F., and Sherman, A. (1983). *Cultural pluralism and the arts. A multicultural perspective for teacher trainers in art and music.* Lawrence: Kansas University, School of Education. (ERIC Document Reproduction Service No. ED 232795)

Rokeach, M. (1960). *The open and closed mind.* New York: Basic Books.

Rosenfelt, D. S. (Ed.). (1982). *Cross-cultural perspectives in the curriculum: Resources for change.* California State University, Long Beach: Office of the Chancellor.

Schmid, W. R. (1971). Introduction to tribal, oriental, and folk music: A rationale for undergraduate music education curricula. Unpublished doctoral dissertation, University of Rochester, Eastman School of Music, Rochester.

Schwadron, A. A. (1984). World musics in education. *International Society for Music Education, 11,* 92–98.

Selected multicultural instructional materials. (1983). Seattle School District 1, Washington, Office of the State Superintendent of Public Instruction, Olympia. (ERIC Document Reproduction Service No. ED 240 217)

Shamrock, M. E. (1988). Applications and adaptations of Orff-Schulwerk in Japan, Taiwan and Thailand. Unpublished doctoral dissertation, University of California, Los Angeles.

Shehan, P. K. (1981). The effect of didactic and heuristic instruction on the preference, achievement, and attentiveness of sixth grade students for Indonesian gamelan music. Unpublished doctoral dissertation, Kent State University, Kent.

Shumway, L. V. (1974). Kibigaku: An analysis of a modern Japanese ritual dance. Unpublished doctoral dissertation, University of Washington, Seattle.

Simon, R. L. (1975). Bhakti ritual music in South India: A study of the Bhajana in its cultural matrix. Unpublished doctoral dissertation, University of California, Los Angeles.

Small, C. (1977). *Music, society, education: A radical examination of the prophetic function of music in Western, Eastern and African cultures with its impact on society and its use in education.* London: J. Calder.

Smith, E. P. (1976). Assessments of the cultural elements by generic areas of teaching competence in multi-cultural settings and their socio-demographic correlates. Unpublished doctoral dissertation, University of Houston, Houston.

Standifer, J. A. (1990). Comprehensive musicianship: A multicultural perspective—looking back to the future. *The Quarterly, 1*(3), 10–19.

Standifer, J. A., and Reeder, B. (1972) *Source book of African and Afro-American materials for music educators.* Reston: Music Educators National Conference.

Starks, G. L., Jr. (1973). Black music in the Sea Islands of South Carolina: Its cultural context-continuity and change. Unpublished doctoral dissertation, Wesleyan University, Middletown.

Steinecker, J. L. (1976). *John Dewey's empirical pluralism: Implications for music education.* Unpublished doctoral dissertation, Temple University, Philadelphia.

Stephens, R. W. (1984). The effects of a course of study on Afro-American popular music in the undergraduate curriculum. Unpublished doctoral dissertation, Indiana University, Bloomington.

Swadener, E. B. (1986, April 16–20). *Implementation of education that is multicultural in early childhood settings: A case study of two day care programs.* Paper presented at the 67th annual meeting of the American Educational Research Association, San Francisco.

Tellstrom, T. (1976). *Music in American education: Past and present.* New York: Holt, Rinehart, and Winston.

Tewara, L. G. (1974). Folk music of India: Uttar Pradesh. Unpublished doctoral dissertation, Wesleyan University, Middletown.

Washington Office of the State Superintendent of Public Instruction. (1983). *Guidelines for multicultural Education.* Olympia: Office of Equity Education.

Washington Office of the State Superintendent of Public Instruction. (1983). *Selected multicultural instructional materials.* Olympia: Seattle School District.

Webb, L. (1979). *Implementing multicultural curriculum: A handbook.* Ann Arbor: Program for Educational Opportunity, University of Michigan.

Whitworth, L. E. (1977). Determination of attitude change toward high school general music resulting from instruction in curricular units incorporating cultural and historical contributions of blacks. Unpublished doctoral dissertation, Northern Illinois University, DeKalb.

Wisconsin State Department of Public Instruction. (1979). *Asian and Pacific American education: Directions for the 1980s.* Madison: Bureau for Food and Nutrition Services.

[29]

A Case for Multiculturalism in the General Music Classroom

Marvelene C. Moore

Music educators generally agree on the importance and value of a multicultural approach to music instruction in the general music classroom. However, there is a tendency to support this approach to curriculum and instruction by giving merely 'lip service' to its inclusion. All too often music curricula reflect a dominance of Western classical music and a small percentage of music that proports to represent other cultures. In many instances, this music is composed in the style of the music culture and upon close examination is found not to be authentic to the culture. The degree to which Western classical music occupies a place in the music curriculum, of course, depends on the country and the community in which the school resides, determined by the activism of parents and community leaders who may exert some influence on curriculum design. When ultimately faced with the challenge of altering or designing a music curriculum that is truly multicultural in philosophy and practice, teachers may approach the process by asking the following questions: 1) What is multicultural music education? 2) Why should I make time for teaching music of ethnic cultures when students lack exposure and experience with Western classical music? And 3) How does one construct curricula that maintain high standards of performance, instruction and learning?[1] In this article, the writer will attempt to address these concerns, provide responses to the queries and offer suggestions for creating a curriculum that embodies a multicultural approach to teaching music.

What is Multicultural Music Education?

Multicultural music education in its broadest sense refers to an approach to teaching and learning that incorporates the music of various cultures and ethnic groups along with the study of the history, customs, and social issues. Patricia Shehan Campbell, in an article published in the *American Music Teacher* defines multicultural music education as 'the study of music from groups distinguished by race or ethnic origin, age, class, gender, religion, life style and exceptionality.'[2] Terese Volk goes a step further in defining multiculturalism in music as 'the ability to function competently in several cultures…and includes the possibility of reforming an educational system to embrace students from a variety of cultures.'[3] Indeed Mary Reed goes even further and takes the position that diversity (inclusive of multicultural music instruction) is 'an 'obligation' to teach music in a variety of ways, in a variety of settings, to a variety of students.'[4]

In the United States, the move towards teaching from a multicultural perspective can be traced back to John Dewey, professor of philosophy at Columbia University in 1916. In a paper presented at the National Education Association, Dewey declared that 'No matter how loudly anyone proclaims his Americanism, if he assumes that any one strain, any one component culture, no matter how early settled it was in our territory, or how effective it has proven in its own land, is to furnish a pattern to which all other strains and cultures are to conform, he is a traitor to an American Nationalism … Our unity cannot lie a homogeneous thing … it must be a unity created by drawing out and compassing into a harmonious whole the best, the most characteristic, which each contributing race and people has to offer.'[5] This spotlight on unity through diversity in every facet of the American society, including education, was continued through the Civil Rights movement of the 1950s and 1960s. In music education within the United States, the focus moved closer to becoming a reality at the Tanglewood Symposium where music educators included in their Declaration the importance of including current music and avant-garde music, American folk music, and the music of ethnic cultures. The result was emphasis on representation of diverse cultures in music education in instructional materials and in practice. The most recent pronouncement in the United States on the importance of multicultural music appeared in the MENC National Standards for Arts Education. In Standard #9: 'Understanding music in relation to history and culture' and in the achievement competencies that relate to this standard, students are expected to a) identify by genre or style aural examples of music from various historical periods and cultures; b) describe in simple terms how elements of music are used in music examples from various cultures of the world; c) identify various uses of music in their daily experiences and describe characteristics that make certain music suitable for each use; d) identify and describe roles of musicians in various music settings and cultures; e) demonstrate audience behavior appropriate for the context and style of music performed.[6] It can be concluded then that multicultural music education is an approach to instruction that incorporates diverse music cultures as an **integral** part of music learning and performance that is not driven by focus on a particular culture or period, but promotes inclusion of music from many cultures along with that of the Western classical art music.

Why Multicultural Music?

As we consider why multicultural music is important in education/music education, perhaps a look back at the role of the arts (music) in society would be beneficial. Harold Williams, former president and chief executive officer of the J. Paul Getty Trust in the United States, believed that the arts are basic and central to human communication and understanding. He advanced the ideas that the arts are how we talk to each other and that they are unquestionably the language of civilization, past and present, through which we express our anxieties, our hungers, our hopes and our discoveries.[7] Former United States assembly woman Maureen Ogden of New Jersey supported Williams' position and held to the conviction that when comparing two similar schools, one with a strong arts (music) curriculum and one without, you will soon discover that there are non-artistic benefits that make the school arts curricula a higher performance environment.[8] Since music and the related arts have been documented as having profound effects on student learning, it seems logical that a curriculum rich in music from diverse cultures would yield greater benefits. It can be central to experiencing a range of music styles and genres and contribute to understanding cultural heritage. Consequently, when considering a plausible reason for creating a multicultural music curriculum, two categories of benefits emerge: musical benefits and social gains. Musical benefits may include: 1) broadening students' exposure to musical sounds; 2) providing opportunities for different types of musical performances; 3) offering experiences in creating music representing various cultural styles; 4) learning about a variety of musical types from one's own culture; 5) providing opportunities for examining music through traditional and non-traditional analytical techniques; and 6) learning music in the manner in which it is taught in a culture. The social and personal gains may encompass: 1) acquiring a greater understanding of one's self and culture; 2) reaffirming one's self-worth; 3) confirming that experiences in one's culture are of value in a multicultural society; 4) learning about culture through a multidisciplinary approach; 5) expanding one's knowledge of languages through the study of texts; 6) aiding in eradication of biases of cultural groups; and 7) developing skills for successful living in a diverse society.[9]

It is possible that students may not respond initially in a positive way to music that is unfamiliar to them. However, with repeated exposure and active participation in the music, they will gradually acquire a greater appreciation and possibly a preference for the once unfamiliar music. In a study on children's preferences, Demorest and Schultz found that students' proclivity for World Music increased with greater exposure, experience, and manipulation with the music.[10] The challenge for the music teacher is to present the music in the most positive way, regardless of personal preferences or biases of the music and individuals from the cultural groups.

How Can Multicultural Music be Taught?

In preparation for teaching multicultural music the teacher must approach instruction with respect for the music and sensitivity to the people of the culture. Music instruction must be accompanied by accuracy, integrity, authenticity, and attention to issues related to the group. Before and during instruction, the teacher should conduct an in-depth 1) examination of the culture and 2) analysis of the music.

An examination of the culture will require a study of customs, traditions, religion and cultural values of the people. A study of the history, geographical location, foods, dress, children's games, stories, and celebrations will enhance the examination. If the teacher feels uncomfortable in addressing some of these areas it may become necessary to locate and invite native people from the community into the classroom to provide first hand information about the culture. The teachers should be aware of the tendency to expose students to too many cultures within a limited period of time. Focusing on a few cultures at a time is the most preferred procedure for successful instruction. The cultures may be selected from those represented in the school and the community or minority groups within the country and/or world music cultures that are completely foreign to the students.

A thorough analysis of the music from the cultures to be studied is a 'must' for successful music teaching. Rhythmic and melodic features, form and harmonies (if they exist), should be examined for their uniqueness as well as similarities to all music. An investigation of authentic, real, true melodies should be a priority. Often this is a difficult task to achieve because of the limitation of Western notation in representing pitch, rhythm and timbre of non-Western music. It becomes necessary then to listen extensively! In addition to CDs and DVDs, the internet has made music of all genres and cultures more accessible to people of all nations. Therefore, authentic versions of music have been made easier to acquire. Instruments that characterize the culture should also be authentically represented in the music classroom. It is understandable that teachers may not possess the instruments, but should make an effort to acquire visuals of instruments and listening examples that will support music learning. Here again, the internet can be a useful tool for exposing students to many types of instruments through YouTube and other websites.

MUSICAL DIMENSIONS

240

In summary, the importance of inclusion of multicultural music in the general music classroom cannot be overstated. Through exposure to music from cultural groups students will 1) acquire new musical experiences, 2) actively participate in different ways of making music, 3) develop understanding of indigenous music groups, 4) acquire an appreciation for diversity, and 5) develop a tolerance and respect for people of other cultures. If we are successful in achieving these goals, we will convey to our students, the school and the community that our society is not merely a 'melting pot.' Rather, it is a mosaic that requires the music, representative of many, to make the picture complete.

Notes

1   Marvelene Moore, 'Multicultural Music: The Connection to Music Learning and Performance,' *Tennessee Musician* 58, no.2, Winter 2005: 42–44.
2   Patricia Shehan Campbell, 'Music Instruction: Marked and Molded by Multiculturalism,' *American Music Teacher*, June/July 1993: 15.
3   Terese M. Volk, *Music, Education, and Multiculturalism: Foundations and Principles* New York: Oxford University Press, 1998, 196.
4   Mary Theresa Reed, 'Some thoughts on Diversity in Music Education...It Is More than Multiculturalism,' *Illinois Music Educator* 65, no. 1 Fall 2004: 70–71.
5   John Dewey, 'Nationalizing Education,' *Addresses and Proceedings of the National Education Association* 54, 1916: 184–185.
6   Moore, p. 43.
7   Harold Williams, The Language of Civilization: The Vital Role of the Arts in Education, *National Conference of State Legislators*, 1992: 1–7.
8   Ibid, p. 5.
9   Moore, p. 42.
10   Steven M. Demorest, and Sara J.M. Schultz, Children's Preference for Authentic versus Arranged Versions of World Music Recordings, *Journal of Research in Music Education* 52, no. 4 Winter 2004: 310.

[30]

WHAT PROSPECTIVE MUSIC TEACHERS NEED TO KNOW ABOUT BLACK MUSIC

ROSITA M. SANDS

The need for addressing the issues of multiculturalism and diversity in American schools has been debated and finally, it appears, formally acknowledged. It is a fact that the populations of America's schools are characterized by diverse cultures and ethnic groups, and this diversity will increase as we enter the twenty-first century. In a 1990 text on the topic of multicultural education, the changing population of America's schools is described in the following manner:

> Students who will make up our future schools will represent much greater diversity than is currently seen. . . . [C]hildren will be inexorably more Asian-American, more Hispanic (but not more Cuban-American), more African-American, and less white. By the end of this century, over 30 percent of the school population will be composed of students of color. (Gollnick and Chinn 1990, 2)

The implications for education are significant in terms of curriculum and instruction, the school's culture and environment, and in particular, the need to train and prepare teachers to teach from a culturally pluralistic perspective.

This paper deals with black music in the context of multiculturalism by addressing the role that knowledge of black music plays in multicultural music education and in teacher education programs that prepare students to teach from a multicultural perspective. It specifically addresses

ROSITA M. SANDS is professor of music and Coordinator of the Music Education Program in the College of Fine Arts at the University of Massachusetts, Lowell. Her publications include "Multicultural Music Teacher Education" (*Journal of Music Teacher Education* 2, no. 2) and "A Survey of Unpublished Materials Focusing on the Pedagogy of Afro-American Music" (*Black Music Research Journal* 8). Her current research activities treat the integration of music of diverse cultures in music education curricula and programs.

the need for inclusion of information about black music, a body of music that is traditionally under-represented in the curricula and materials employed in music education teacher-training programs. It addresses the reasons why prospective music teachers need to know about this body of music, what types of knowledge and experiences they need to have, and how they should go about acquiring this knowledge.

The need for multiculturalism has, in fact, already been acknowledged by the music education profession. Standards issued by national and state accreditation agencies now routinely include reference to the need for preparing students to teach from a broadened cultural perspective. The National Association of Schools of Music (NASM), the official accreditation agency for programs in music in higher education, addresses this issue in its standards for all baccalaureate degree curricula by stating that "students must have opportunities through performance and academic studies to work with music of diverse cultural sources, historical periods, and media" (NASM 1995, 73). Specifically in reference to the preparation of music education majors, the NASM states that "teachers should be prepared to relate their understanding of musical styles, the literature of diverse cultural sources, and the music of various historical periods" (84).

Perhaps the most significant recent development in education concerning multicultural music education is the development of national standards for arts education, a project undertaken to identify educational goals in the areas of art, dance, music, and visual arts as part of the "Goals 2000: Educate America Act." The standards were written by four arts education organizations, including the Music Educators National Conference (MENC), this country's foremost music education association. The resulting document of this project, titled *National Standards for Arts Education: What Every Young American Should Know and Be Able to Do in the Arts*, includes a strong affirmation of the need to provide an arts education that is representative of diverse cultural sources in the K–12 school curriculum. This is addressed specifically in the document by the following statement:

> The cultural diversity of America is a vast resource for arts education and should be used to help students understand themselves and others. The visual, traditional, and performing arts provide a variety of lenses for examining the cultures and artistic contributions of our nation and others around the world. Students should learn that each art form has its own characteristics and makes its distinctive contributions, that each has its own history and heroes. . . . Subject matter from diverse historical periods, styles, forms, and cultures should be used to develop basic knowledge and skills in the various arts disciplines. (*National Standards for Arts Education* 1994, 13–14)

All of the directives cited above should lead to changes in the way that prospective music teachers are being trained. No longer should such training employ performance and study materials that almost exclusively reflect European classical or Western art music. Prospective music teachers need the opportunity to study and perform music that is representative of a variety of cultures. They need opportunities to interact with and utilize these musics in their pedagogy and methodology courses. A commitment to preparing students from a multicultural perspective will undoubtedly require significant changes in the music education curricula typically found in colleges and universities throughout the country.

What Teachers Need to Know about Black Music

When working with students who may have limited knowledge of the scope of black music and who are acquainted primarily with only the popular styles of the music, it is absolutely critical to present the music in its full spectrum, as a broad repertoire comprising many styles, idioms, and genres. Prospective music teachers need to understand that black music is the music of a variety of cultures, including that of Africa, and any paradigm employed to examine the music must allow it to be understood as a body of musical expressions with fundamental and defining characteristics that are linked to and emanate from the music and culture of Africa. Students, and particularly prospective teachers, must be given an opportunity to explore the evolution of black music from these African roots to its various historical and contemporary manifestations found in the United States, the Caribbean, Latin America, and all other areas where peoples of African descent formed new cultures. Students also must be presented with the sociological, political, religious, and psychological aspects of the music that are essential to a complete understanding of the music and culture.

For each specific area of black music that is studied, students need to be introduced to the particular functions the music serves as well as the accompanying genres and styles of music that developed as a result of these functions. This is one of the more effective pedagogical means of illustrating the extra-musical components of the music. Although many examples of sociological, political, religious, and/or psychological functions are served by various types of black music, only two examples will be cited here. One example derives from Latin-American and Caribbean music-cultures. In the context of these new environments, with new European religions being forced upon them, African peoples created new religious forms by extracting from Catholicism, for example, those aspects of ritual and spirituality that were psychologically and emotion-

ally appealing and socially and culturally significant to them. This resulted in the new syncretic religious/musical forms of Kumina in Jamaica,
candomblé in Brazil, and santería in Cuba. These religious art-forms represent examples of musical forms that can be studied as a means of
understanding religious, sociological, and psychological aspects of black
music.

Calypso is a traditional folk music form of the Caribbean with lyrics
replete with social commentary, criticism, and political satire. This can be
used effectively to demonstrate how sociological and political concepts
are frequently expressed through black music. Students need to understand the power that this music holds within the respective Caribbean
cultures, so much power, in fact, that calypso was at one time banned
from radio broadcasts on the island of Grenada due to the music's harsh
criticism and mockery of the ruling government there. An understanding
of the purpose and function of music in black cultures and its salient relationship to the sociology and politics of the people—its creators and its
audience—is critical to the understanding of black music.

Those learning about black music need to be aware of the distinctive
characteristics of the musics that form the body of black music and of the
definitive traits, commonalities, or idioms that link these disparate
musics. They need to know that black music is not defined by any one
style of music but rather represents a body of musical styles, genres, attitudes, approaches, and processes of making music that are related to each
other because of the common heritage, shared characteristics, and cultural and social milieus shared by its creators.

It is important also to understand the creative concepts involved in
"black music" as representing both a product and a process. As a product, black music represents a body of music with definitive characteristics; but within this body of music a process is also delineated—a way of
making music that is characteristic of a particular style and a musical
process involving the manipulation of various elements of music which,
in fact, can be applied even to styles or genres of music that are not black
in origin. For example, black church singers and musicians took
European hymns and applied a process to them that included distinctive
performance practices as well as melodic and rhythmic inflections that
were distinctively black. These traits include call-and-response textures,
a predilection for syncopated rhythms and rhythmic complexity, a modified approach to pitch involving the use of blue notes, and both melodic
and textual improvisation. These processes, rooted in African sensibilities
and approaches to making music, originated in direct response and relationship to the people's aesthetic values and to the particular functions or

roles that the music served in black culture. These processes, in fact, resulted in new products—new forms and styles of music.

Ragtime is another example of this musical evolution. As a product, it is a combination of improvised and composed music, characterized by syncopated rhythms in a manner involving two distinct functions for the left hand and right hand in rag piano-playing. This process of creating ragtime piano music represents a characteristic style that can be applied to any musical composition. That is, "ragging" a piece of music would mean to play it in a syncopated manner with a bass line or left-hand style that enunciated the chords in a percussive rhythmic manner. According to Eileen Southern (1983, 309), this process of piano playing associated with ragtime music is rooted specifically in the dance-music practices of black people during the time of slavery.

> The style of piano-rag music—called "jig piano" by some—was a natural outgrowth of dance-music practices among black folk. . . . In piano-rag music, the left hand took over the task of stomping and patting while the right hand performed syncopated melodies, using motives reminiscent of fiddle and banjo tunes.

An understanding of the connection that exists between musical characteristics and the role and function that the music serves in black culture is critical for mastery of the study of this music.

For the prospective music teacher it is important to explore the music's historical background; to be aware of the characteristics and functions of the various styles and genres, both religious and secular; to know the names of important historical and contemporary artists and composers representative of the various musical styles; to be aware of representative, exemplary works; to have an understanding of the continued progression and evolution of the music into new styles; and to understand the influence of black music on American popular music styles. Additionally, teachers must present the music with integrity, utilizing an approach that is based on a sensitivity to and respect for the total significance and meaning of the music within black culture and an understanding and appreciation of the particular functions or purposes that the music serves within the culture.

Music teachers also need to develop appropriate analytical skills for examining this music. In most cases, methods borrowed from the field of ethnomusicology will be most successful, combining musicological analysis with an examination of the music in relation to cultural, social, conceptual, and contextual concerns. In reference to analysis of the music, students need to have an opportunity to explore the different approaches to sound and sound production that exist in music that does not emanate from a purely European or Western orientation, including the distinctive treatments of pitch, harmony, rhythm, timbre, and essentially, all of the constituent elements of music. An example of such an approach from African-American music is the melodic and harmonic use of blue notes—the employment of intervals that are smaller than the whole step and half-step increments used in the Western scale, most commonly on the 3rd, 5th, or 7th scale degrees. Other examples of such approaches are the preference for rhythmic complexity evidenced by the frequent use of syncopation and polyrhythms in the music of West Africa; the tradition-al music of cowbells, goat skin drums, and whistles that accompanies the Junkanoo celebration in the Bahamas; and the music of many Caribbean and Latin-American music-cultures. Children's game songs, chants, and jump-rope rhymes that emanate from black-music cultures present addi-tional illustrations of distinctive traits or treatments of musical elements; syncopation, rhythmic complexity, mixed meters, heavy reliance on body rhythms and movement, and/or use of blue notes in melodies can be found in examples of children's game songs from Africa, the United States, and the Caribbean. These musical sources, which provide excel-lent examples of musical idioms and characteristics that can be found in the music of the larger cultures, are appropriate and particularly relevant for use by teachers at elementary and middle-school levels of music edu-cation.

In general, prospective teachers of music must learn in their analysis and evaluation of black music to employ values or standards that specif-ically emanate from the respective cultures, like cultural norms, cultural aesthetics, and preferences for certain music practices. They must be care-ful not to ascribe Western values or standards to what they hear and to understand that aesthetic values and cultural norms vary among the world's peoples. An objective understanding of these differences in val-ues and standards is critical to students' understanding. In addition, stu-dents must be provided with knowledge of appropriate performance and stylistic considerations in black music—the idiomatic treatments of rhythm, melody, pitch, and timbre in various styles of the music and, of equal importance, the role of movement.

With consideration given to the reality of time constraints and the gen-erally over-extended nature of teacher education curricula and programs, prospective teachers must be introduced to the existing research in the field and to the works of scholars who have made significant contribu-tions to our understanding of individual styles of black music and to the music as a whole. Such research is critical for an appreciable comprehen-sion of black music and is of even greater import to understanding the theory that substantiates the translation of these musics and musical materials into pedagogical formats such as lesson plans, units of study, or other types of curriculum materials. Music teachers should be aware of the scholarship contained in Eileen Southern's *The Music of Black Americans* (1983), the most authoritative, comprehensive history of the music in existence today.

Other sources that are particularly useful in helping prospective teachers identify materials for study, analysis, or performance include de Lerma's "A Concordance of Scores and Recordings of Music by Black Composers" (1984) and "Black Composers in Europe: A Works List" (1990); Murphy's "Films for the Black Music Researcher" (1987); and Hughes's "A Compilation of Afro-American and Puerto Rican Music Materials for Use in the New York City Public Schools" (1987).

Following are general considerations and guidelines for the appropriate use of black musics in the classroom.

- Always pay strict attention to accuracy of rhythms in the performance of black music, particularly with examples where rhythm is an important or prominent feature.

- Be careful not to stereotype the music and/or culture by leaving students with the impression that the examples used in class are the only types or styles of music within the particular culture. Be sure to point out that many different styles and types of music exist within these cultures.

- Present the cultural context for the music. Like traditional, folk, or ethnic music in other cultures, these musical styles and genres exist as the result of specific functional uses in black culture. Be sure to inform students of these functions and allow the opportunity for drawing parallels to similar functions and music within their own culture or within contemporary American society. Impress upon students the importance and significance of the roles that music may serve within the particular cultures.

- Let the students see and hear the music being performed. This is particularly important in the study of black music where movement is an important part of most musical performances. Students need the opportunity to observe the idiomatic treatment of movement—the essential role that movement and dance play in the music of most black cultures and the distinctive uses of the body. Viewing live performances also provides an important opportunity for students to observe the manner in which the music is received by the audience in black cultures and to discuss the distinctive trait of "communal participation," a characteristic that has been identified in most examples of black music cross-culturally. Use video examples if live performances are unavailable.

- Remember to integrate the music in the curriculum and program. Black music should not be presented only during the month of February or only when dealing with a multicultural unit. Remember that black music is composed of the same basic elements as any type of music and, therefore, can be selected to illustrate aspects of rhythm, melodic contour, form, and any of the many uses of musical examples in the classroom at a variety of levels. This "common elements" approach to multicultural music education is one that is espoused in many writings on the topic. Scott Joplin's ragtime compositions can be utilized in the classroom as examples of rondo form, alongside or in place of European classical examples of this form. The works of African-American composers who write in traditional classical music forms can also be used in the classroom for formal analysis purposes, illustrating a variety of musical forms and techniques typically studied in theory or literature classes. Vocal music from black music traditions can be used to illustrate different types of vocal timbre or the distinctive use of vocal inflections like those found in the worksongs, blues, spirituals, and gospel music of the African-American music culture. In fact, examples from black music might be the most effective examples of particular musical features such as syncopation, improvisation, or polyrhythms. In units addressing composers and/or musicians, teachers must avoid the misguided tendency of including only the names of European classical artists and make a conscious effort to include artists who represent genres or styles often overlooked, such as folk, jazz, ragtime, gospel, calypso, or that of other black music artists whose names and works appropriately belong in such units of study. In discussions of various functions of music or types of musical celebrations, teachers should be sure to incorporate discussions of Trinidad's Carnival, Brazil's Carnaval, the Bahamian Junkanoo, and Bermuda's Gombay celebrations as examples of some of the more exciting and vital cultural and artistic celebrations in existence in the world today.

- Remember that in clapping to or maintaining the beat, the accent for African and African-derived musics is usually on the weak beats, or the 2 and the 4 of $\frac{4}{4}$ time. Occasionally, one might hear or witness musical examples where the emphasis or accent is placed evenly throughout the measure.

- If movement such as rocking or swaying to the beat is added to vocal performances, this must be done in an appropriate manner with all students swaying in the same direction and to the same beat.

- Attempt to teach the music as authentically and accurately as possible without altering rhythms, melodies, or text. The standard or goal of authenticity is determined by the degree to which replications or performances of the music conform to or incorporate the aesthetic qualities and defining characteristics of the music. For example, when attempting to teach the music for performance purposes, teachers must resist the tendency to simplify rhythms, to add accompaniments to music that is traditionally performed unaccompanied, or to change the lyrics or alter the vernacular or speech patterns of black music-cultures. Instead, teachers should choose examples that are appropriate for use in school settings and are appropriate to the age, developmental, and skill levels of their students.

Sources of Information

The best and most appropriate means of providing the prospective music teacher with an understanding of black music in conjunction with information regarding method and the appropriate use of the music in the classroom is unarguably through the music teacher education program, either in undergraduate or graduate level courses focusing on methodology, pedagogy, or materials. For students who do not have the opportunity to engage in such study prior to beginning their careers in music education, workshops and summer study opportunities provide the best means of increasing their knowledge of this music. While courses or workshops focusing specifically on the pedagogy of black music or on the music of other specific cultures might be difficult to locate, courses addressing multicultural music education are becoming more available, particularly as summer study offerings. The content of such courses usually includes the subject of African-American music and, occasionally, the music of Africa, providing students with some experience and information relevant to the subject but certainly not a comprehensive treatment of the subject.

Music education majors also should be encouraged to enroll in history or genre courses focusing on black music in order to gain an appreciation and understanding of the subject. Such courses, however, typically do not include a pedagogical focus and would not alone provide all information needed to prepare students to teach this music effectively. It is clear that colleges and universities must include opportunities in their teacher-training program for preparing students to teach the music of particular cultures, particularly in light of the new national standards for music education and the increasing focus on the need for a multicultural music curriculum.

The prospective teacher of music must be aware of existing materials that can serve as resources for the teacher. These materials exist in the form of books and audio-visual media of an ethnomusicological nature, focusing on various styles and genres of black music, as well as materials specifically designed for classroom use, for particular grade levels, and for particular types of courses. It is indeed fortunate for music educators that such materials have become available in significantly increasing numbers over the past decade or so and that the quality of these materials is generally high today.

My own dissertation, "An Annotated Bibliography of Published and Unpublished Sources Focusing on the Pedagogy of Afro-American Music," is a document that directs teachers to a number of resources, including other dissertations and theses that present pedagogical discussions and teaching materials relative to various styles and genres of African-American music (Sands 1983). The sources identified and described in this dissertation include such features as lesson plans, descriptions of listening and creative activities, syllabi and curriculum development, and/or resource materials in the form of bibliographies, discographies, and annotated lists of repertoire.

Some other dissertations that present pedagogical discussions include "A Study of Recommended Techniques and Materials for Teaching Jazz Style to the Junior High School Student" (Hale 1988), "Enculturation in a Formal Setting: A Study of Problems and Prospects in Afro-American Music Education" (Johnson 1988), "Strategies for Teaching African-American Music in the Elementary Music Class" (Ellis 1990), "A Conceptual Model for Analyzing Rhythmic Structure in African-American Popular Music" (Sykes 1992), and "Five Wind/Band Works of Hale Smith and Their Implications for a Multicultural Curriculum" (Davis 1994).

Over the past ten years or so, MENC has responded to the multicultural imperative in music education by devoting entire issues of its *Music Educators Journal* to discussion of the topic; by co-sponsoring the 1984 "Wesleyan Symposium on the Perspectives of Social Anthropology in the Teaching and Learning of Music"; by co-sponsoring a 1990 symposium on "Multicultural Approaches in Music Education" with the Society for General Music, the Smithsonian Institution's Office of Folklife Programs, and the Society for Ethnomusicology; and by developing and distributing materials specifically for the teaching of the music of diverse cultures. MENC has recently initiated a "Music in Cultural Context" series of articles addressing the music of a variety of cultures in its *Music Educators Journal*. As part of this series, the May 1995 issue presents a discussion of the music of the Yoruba people of Nigeria, and the July 1995 issue includes a discussion of the gospel music tradition of African-American culture (Campbell 1995a and 1995b). Both articles provide selected resources for teaching the music in addition to sample lesson plans for analyzing and performing the music.

The *MENC Professional Resources Catalog 1995–1996* of MENC-sponsored publications lists some materials specifically addressing the teaching of black music. Among them are the book *Teaching Music with a Multicultural Approach* (Anderson 1991), which includes lesson plans and resource lists of materials for teaching the music of African Americans; the video "Teaching the Music of African Americans," which shows the sessions presented at the 1990 Symposium; and "Bringing Multicultural Music to Children," a videotape of past MENC sessions that include lessons incorporating chants and music from Africa, Jamaica, and the United States. A textbook, a teacher's guide, and audio and video materials focusing on the music of Huddie Ledbetter (Leadbelly) and Woody Guthrie are also included. Another important work published by MENC is *Multicultural Perspectives in Music Education*, a collection of lesson plans and descriptive analyses of the music of a variety of cultures, including African-American, Caribbean, and sub-Sahara African cultures (Anderson and Campbell 1989).

Clearly, the most promising and exciting collection of materials can be found in catalogs outside music education itself. Students must be introduced to companies such as World Music Press, Multicultural Media, and Media for the Arts; these are excellent resources for a broad selection of cultural materials, including those specifically addressing the music of black cultures (see Appendix). An examination of a recent issue of the catalogs of these companies resulted in the identification of audio-visual materials on the topics of blues, gospel, spirituals, zydeco, jazz, African rhythms and instruments, soul music, ragtime, salsa, calypso, reggae, and samba. They also list videos profiling the lives and presenting the music of such artists as Nigerian musician Sunny Ade, Blind Tom, John Coltrane, Elizabeth Cotten, Billie Holiday, Mississippi John Hurt, Scott Joplin, the group Ladysmith Black Mambazo of South Africa, and Charlie Parker. These lists are not inclusive but represent a sampling of the types of materials that are included as resources in these catalogs and are an example of the materials available today to assist teachers in the study and presentation of this music.

Finally, prospective teachers themselves must take the opportunity for formal and informal field experience and research by observing and participating, as appropriate, in performances of the music as often as possible. This will be of invaluable assistance in learning the sometimes subtle nuances involved in the performance of the music and will ultimately assist in the accurate and appropriate method of presenting the music. In addition to attending actual performances, prospective teachers should listen to authentic recordings of the music and utilize community resources to gain first-hand experience in the musical culture. The method borrowed from ethnomusicology, involving interviews of native participants as well as actual performers, can be an invaluable means of learning about the music itself and the role it plays in black culture.

The profession of music teacher education and the faculty and administrators who design and deliver teacher-training curricula and courses have the preeminent responsibility for ensuring that future teachers are prepared to teach and present a multicultural music curriculum. Such preparation must include examination of black music and must provide prospective teachers with the knowledge and skills necessary for effectively presenting this music and integrating it in their curricula and programs.

One essential factor must be stressed. Before teachers can willingly include black music in their curricula and give it an integral role in their music programs, at all levels and in all areas, they must first value this music. They must consider it worthy of study and worthy of having a place in their educational programs. Those responsible for the training of our future teachers have the task of providing an educational environment where black music is studied alongside other musics and where students have the opportunity to study the music objectively and determine its inherent values. Without an acknowledgement of black music's rightful place in the curriculum by both teacher-trainers and prospective teachers, the music will continue to be under-represented. The challenge to do this and do it well represents one of the most important goals in the field of contemporary music education.

REFERENCES

Anderson, William M., ed. 1991. *Teaching music with a multicultural approach.* Reston, Va.: Music Educators National Conference.

Anderson, William M., and Patricia Shehan Campbell, eds. 1989. *Multicultural perspectives in music education.* Reston, Va.: Music Educators National Conference.

Campbell, Patricia Shehan. 1995a. Christopher Waterman on Yoruba music of Africa. *Music Educators Journal* 81, no. 6:35–43.

———. 1995b. Mellonee Burnim on African American music. *Music Educators Journal* 82, no. 1:41–48.

Davis, Mark. 1994. Five wind/band works of Hale Smith and their implications for a multicultural curriculum. Ed.D. diss., Washington University.

De Lerma, Dominique-René. 1984. A concordance of scores and recordings of music by black composers. *Black Music Research Journal* [4]:60–140.

———. 1990. Black composers in Europe: A works list. *Black Music Research Journal* 10, no. 2:275–334.

Ellis, Brenda A. 1990. Strategies for teaching African-American music in the elementary music class. Ed.D. diss., Columbia University, Teachers College.

Gollnick, Donna M., and Philip C. Chinn. 1990. *Multicultural education in a pluralistic society.* 3rd ed. Columbus, Ohio: Merrill.

Hale, Darlene J. 1988. A study of recommended techniques and materials for teaching jazz style to the junior high school student. M.A. thesis, California State University, Fullerton.

Hughes, Stacy E. 1987. A compilation of Afro-American and Puerto Rican music materials for use in the New York City Public Schools. Ed.D. diss., Columbia University, Teachers College.

Johnson, James T., Jr. 1988. Enculturation in a formal setting: A study of problems and prospects in Afro-American music education. Ph.D. diss., University of Pittsburgh.

Murphy, Paula. 1987. Films for the black music researcher. *Black Music Research Journal* 7:45–64.

Music Educators National Conference. 1995. *MENC professional resources catalog 1995–1996.* Reston, Va.: Music Educators National Conference.

National Association of Schools of Music. 1995. *1995–1996 handbook.* Reston, Va.: National Association of Schools of Music.

National standards for arts education: What every young American should know and be able to do in the arts. 1994. Reston, Va.: Music Educators National Conference.

Sands, Rosita M. 1983. An annotated bibliography of published and unpublished sources focusing on the pedagogy of Afro-American music. Ed.D. diss., Columbia University, Teachers College.

Southern, Eileen. 1983. *The music of black Americans.* 2nd ed. New York: W. W. Norton.

Sykes, Charles E. 1992. A conceptual model for analyzing rhythmic structure in African-American popular music. D.Mus.Ed. diss., Indiana University.

APPENDIX

Addresses of Selected Companies That Publish Materials for
Multicultural Education

Media for the Arts
360 Thames
Newport, RI 02840
(401) 846-6580

Multicultural Media
31 Hebert Road
Montpelier, VT 05602
(800) 550-9675
(802) 223-1284

World Music Press
P. O. Box 2565
Danbury, CT 06813-2565
(203) 748-1131

[31]

The History and Development of Multicultural Music Education as Evidenced in the *Music Educators Journal*, 1967–1992

Terese M. Volk, *Kent State University*

In 1967, secretary-general of ISME Egon Kraus challenged music educators to become multicultural in their perspective, a challenge spurred on by the Tanglewood Symposium. Music educators in the United States have long been interested in the musics of other cultures. Often they have learned about these musics and how to implement them in the classroom through the pages of the Music Educators Journal *(MEJ). The MEJ has covered multicultural perspectives in music through its articles, special issues, book reviews, and reports from MENC conferences and symposia. A study of the MEJ from 1967 to 1992 revealed the growth of multicultural music education. During the 1970s, a greater depth of interest in, and knowledge about, world musics developed. Throughout the 1980s, this initial interest grew steadily into a need for methods and materials for the implementation of multicultural music studies in the classroom, as did the need for teacher training in these musics. A formal declaration of commitment to multicultural music education was adopted at the MENC Multicultural Symposium in 1990, leading to a broad world perspective for music education. The three MEJ special focus issues on multicultural music education epitomized each of these growth areas.*

> The confrontation of the cultures is the destiny of our times, and the bringing about of this confrontation in a meaningful manner is the great cultural-political task of our century. We, the music educators, can contribute significantly.—*Egon Kraus, secretary-general, ISME, 1966*

In January 1967, the *Music Educators Journal (MEJ)* published a speech given by noted German music educator Egon Kraus at the International Society for Music Education (ISME) conference the preceding summer. In that speech, Kraus argued that a one-sided view of music from either East or West was no longer appropriate, and that an open mind leads to better understanding and knowl-

For copies of this article, contact Terese M. Volk, 808 Woodstock Avenue, Tonawanda, NY 14150.

edge. He outlined eight problems that he challenged ISME and music educators in general to solve in the future. He asked for:

(a) proper regard for foreign musical cultures in music teaching at all education-al levels,
(b) methodological realization of the music of foreign cultures, past and present,
(c) renewal of ear training, rhythmic training, and music theory with a view to inclusion of the music of foreign cultures,
(d) reviewing of school music textbooks and study materials (also with regard to prejudice and national and racial resentments),
(e) preparation of pedagogically suitable works on the music of foreign cultures with special attention to authentic sound recordings....[1]

He also sought the establishment of international seminars and some way for all nations to share multicultural music education concerns, as well as continuing cooperation with the United Nations Educational, Scientific, and Cultural Organization (UNESCO).[2] He concluded with the quotation at the beginning of this article. Kraus's speech was a sign of the changes in music education at the end of the 1960s. Music educators had begun to see with a multicultural perspective.

INTRODUCTION

Throughout their existence, the public schools of the United States have pre-sented an essentially white, Eurocentric education. Therefore, it is not surprising that historical accounts of American music education have said little about multi-cultural perspectives in music in the schools. Edward B. Birge does not include references in his textbook either to African-American music or any musics that immigrant peoples brought to the United States.[3] Theodore A. Tellstrom has two paragraphs in which he tells of the rising interest in world musics and recom-mends that the well-rounded music program include such study.[4] James A. Keene and, more recently, Michael L. Mark and Charles L. Gary refer briefly to the study of world musics when summarizing the Tanglewood Symposium.[5] In addition, Mark and Gary mention "ethnic [music], rock, pop, and jazz" when discussing the changing music of urban classrooms.[6] This evidence seems to concur with George N. Heller's assessment that multicultural music education has been more practiced than documented in the published histories of music education.[7]

The following three publications deal specifically with the history of multicul-tural music education. In 1983, Heller wrote a broad retrospective discussing early Music Educators National Conference (MENC) involvement with musics from var-ious cultures through its conference sessions, describing the founding of ISME, and commenting briefly on the increased activity within the profession since the Tanglewood Symposium.[8] William M. Anderson provided a more detailed view of multicultural music education from 1916 through 1970, beginning with the work of Satis Coleman, a music teacher at the Lincoln School of Teachers College, Columbia University in New York and ending with the beginnings of research in multicultural music education following Tanglewood.[9] A recent study by Christine E. Brett focused on trends in multicultural music education from 1960–1989. The main thrust of her work, however, was not historical documenta-tion but rather the philosophical development of the movement and the imple-mentation of this philosophy in the Silver Burdett Music Series.[10]

Since there has been scant historical documentation of the development of multicultural music education during the last twenty-five years, one purpose of this research was to trace its history and development as documented in the *Music Educators Journal (MEJ)* from 1967 to 1992. A second purpose was to see, by studying this history, how well music education has approached solutions for the problems posed by Kraus. I hope that this will give music educators some perspective of how far they have come and of how far they may have yet to go in addressing these problems.

For the purposes of this study, "culture" is defined as learned ways of thinking and behaving that enable an individual to survive in a society.[11] If "music education" is the transmission of that part of culture that is expressed through music,[12] "multicultural music education" enables one to function effectively in multiple music cultures.[13] "Music" is defined as a human expression using patterned behaviors in sound that are agreed upon by the members of the society involved.[14] Therefore, the phrases "musics of many cultures" and "musics from a variety of cultures" will be used to mean the musics from any assortment of cultures, worldwide. Although this definition of music encompasses the art, folk, and popular traditions of any culture, this study will focus primarily on the global perspective in music education that developed through the addition of musics from many cultures to the music curriculum.[15]

The *MEJ* has been selected as the source for information for this study for the following reasons. First, it is the official journal of the MENC, the largest music teacher organization in the United States, and organizational activities can be traced through conference announcements and reports in the pages of the *MEJ.* Second, as Maureen D. Hooper noted, the *MEJ* is a means of communication between the leadership of the organization and its membership.[16] She also noted that

> Authors from outside music education play an important role in the communication of the concerns of society as they relate to the music program. ... [and] Officials of the Music Educators National Conference carry the major responsibility for the formulation and communication of the organized theoretical foundation for music education.[17]

In voicing both the needs of society and the views of the leadership of the MENC, the *MEJ* takes on the role of "guide" for the profession. Third, as John W. Molnar's study showed, looking at the *MEJ* in retrospect can reveal trends in music education, applicable at least to the membership of the MENC, and, as far as the MENC membership constitutes a representative sample of music educators in the United States, for music educators across the country.[18]

Evidence for this study was taken from articles, MENC conference program listings and follow-up reports, announcements and reports of MENC activities, advertisements, and monthly features such as the "Book Review" and "MENC Adviser" columns. It was beyond the scope of this study to include every article or report on the subject in the *MEJ.* A reasonable attempt has been made to identify those that seemed to point most toward the development of multicultural music education, and in particular those articles that would indicate direction taken in providing solutions for Kraus's problems. It is acknowledged that these are not all-inclusive. Articles that dealt with comparative music education (i.e., how music is taught in the schools of other countries) were omitted from this study, as were biographical and autobiographical articles.

OVERVIEW TO 1967

Music educators have long been interested in musics from around the world, and it has been the *Music Educators Journal* (and its predecessor the *Music Supervisors Journal*) that has documented multicultural music education in the music classrooms of the United States. As early as 1918, the *Music Supervisors Journal (MSJ)* carried the program listing for that year's annual meeting of the Music Supervisors National Conference (MSNC), which included a lecture-recital of folk songs presented by Walter Bentley and an address by Elizabeth Burchenal on "Folk Dancing."[19] In 1919, the *MSJ* published an article by John Wesley Work titled "The Development of the Music of the Negro from the Folk Song to the Art Song and Art Chorus."[20]

There was a stronger emphasis on world musics throughout the 1920s and 1930s. MSNC annual meetings often included folk songs and dances.[21] In 1928, the *MSJ* announced the formation of the MSNC Committee on International Relations,[22] and over the next decade music supervisors from Europe, the United Kingdom and the United States met during the summer to exchange information about music and music education.[23]

Interest in inter-American music education began through the cooperation of the State Department Division of Cultural Relations and the MENC in 1939,[24] and in 1944, the Advisory Council on Music Education in the Latin American Republics was established in cooperation with the Pan American Union.[25] Along with this, MENC developed a program called "American Unity Through Music." Through the *MEJ*, teachers were encouraged to include both American folk musics and Latin American musics in their classes.[26] A gradually widening world view in music education led to the establishment of ISME in 1953.[27] The interest in the musics of other cultures continued throughout the late 1950s and into the 1960s and was given added strength by the civil rights movement.

The impetus to include music from a variety of cultures as part of the curriculum in the music classroom began with the Yale Seminar in June 1963. Its call for a school music repertoire that included non-Western and folk musics[28] was answered by the Juilliard Repertory Project, begun in 1964.[29] The Repertory Project was reported in the pages of the *MEJ* and, although the Yale Symposium was mentioned only briefly, the anthology itself was considered a "welcome addition to our [music educators'] resources."[30]

The International Seminar on Teacher Education in Music took place at Ann Arbor, Michigan in August 1966. Along with issues relating to the education of music teachers, the musical training of general classroom teachers, and technical media for education, "Papers were presented and discussions held relative to the importance of the use in schools of the music of all cultures."[31] Egon Kraus gave his speech the next week at the ISME conference at Interlochen.

1967: THE TANGLEWOOD SYMPOSIUM

Spurred by the Yale Seminar and the Juilliard Repertory Project, MENC undertook a major self-evaluation of the profession and its goals for music in the schools. Meeting at Tanglewood in the summer of 1967, this Symposium was titled "Music in American Society." To stimulate national thinking on the Symposium's topics, a series of questions was developed for each area to be discussed, and these were published in the April 1967 issue of the *MEJ*. Music educators were asked to voice their opinions as input for the discussions at the symposium. Addressing

"Music in our Time," some questions dealt specifically with the issue of musics from a variety of cultures in the schools: "Polycultural curriculums are developing rapidly. Should music of other cultures be included? For what purposes? Few centers exist in this country for such studies. What are the implications?"[32]

The Tanglewood Symposium was fully reported in the November 1967 *MEJ*. The final declaration of the Symposium opened the door for all musics to be taught in the public schools with the statement: "Music of all periods, styles, forms, and cultures belong[s] in the curriculum ... including avant-garde music, American folk music, and the music of other cultures."[33] In the same issue, Charles Fowler's editorial supported the need for studying world musics. He stated, "Music education, by latching on to diversity, by being comprehensive in its coverage of the musics of the world, will insure that the tastes of the public are based on choices made from acquaintance with all that constitutes the art of music."[34]

David McAllester's speech at Tanglewood was printed in its entirety in the *MEJ* in December 1968. In it, he emphasized the fact that a rapidly shrinking world was one of the forces shaping music education. He asked, "How then can we go on thinking of 'music' as Western European music, to the exclusion of the infinitely varied forms of musical expression in other parts of the world?"[35]

During 1967, the *MEJ* carried articles by Zoltán Kodály and Kwabena Nketia both validating and advocating the use of folk song in music education. Lucius Wyatt's article included museum photographs of instruments from around the world.[37] This article is notable because it is the first in the journal to contain pictures of authentic instruments from a variety of cultures in the period under study.

From 1968 to 1972, there was an increase of articles on the musics from a variety of cultures in *MEJ*. The journal acted to encourage music educators to implement the statements of both Yale and Tanglewood. There was a special report on the use of popular music in the classroom, and the foundation of the National Association of Jazz Educators (NAJE), also reported in the *Journal*, gave impetus to jazz education.[38] Articles early in this period mainly gave information about various musical cultures, but gradually more were included on how to use these musics in the classroom. Many of these dealt with African-American music, hardly unusual in the light of the growing awareness of African-American culture in the United States.[39] Informative articles were published on the music of India and Hudson Bay Native Canadians, and another on Native American music in the classroom.[40] In an article based on her research, Elizabeth May reported "An Experiment with Australian Aboriginal Music" in the classrooms of Los Angeles, California.[41] A working collaboration between ethnomusicology and music education was suggested by Donald Berger,[42] and John M. Eddins[43] spoke of both comprehensive and cross-cultural trends in teaching music.

It did not take long for the MENC to include musics from various cultures around the world in its national conferences. At the 1968 conference in Seattle, the University of Hawaii presented a program of songs and dances illustrating the diverse heritage of the Hawaiian islands.[44] At this same conference, jazz concerts were introduced and quickly became a mainstay for all subsequent MENC national conferences. There was a series of sessions at the 1970 Chicago conference called an "Ethnic Musics Institute." These sessions all featured a lecture and demonstration by a specialist in the field and concluded with a special session devoted to teaching resources.[45] The 1972 conference in Atlanta included sessions on ethnic musics,[46] as did the 1974 conference in Annaheim. This conference featured sessions ranging from a demonstration by an African drum ensemble, to choral and instrumental performance practices in various parts of the world, to the implications for music education dealing with the "culturally different student."[47] The 1976 conference in Atlantic City offered ways to incorporate African and Native Alaskan musics in the elementary classroom. Discussions of the problems and perspectives of multicultural music education in grades K–12, as well as the role of multicultural music education in higher education, were also part of the program. Concert music featured a combination steel drum and wind ensemble, and a balalaika orchestra.[48] Members attending the 1978 conference in Chicago could choose from sessions focusing on musical concepts taught through the music of many cultures, or on African and Japanese musics.[49]

The name of the Ethnic Musics Committee of the MENC was changed by the 1978 Chicago meeting to the Ethno and World Musics Committee. The word "Ethnic" apparently was too limiting, as if the committee only represented an interest in various "ethnic" (folk?) musics, hence the addition of "and World," which would include the art and popular traditions of music systems worldwide. In 1974, the Minority Concerns Commission also sponsored sessions at the biennial conferences. Its name changed to the Minority Awareness Commission by the 1978 meeting. It became the Multi-Cultural Awareness Commission in 1979 to better reflect both the many musics found in the United States and around the world, and the committee's role in the MENC.[50] Although the commission was restructured in 1982, the name "Multi-Cultural Awareness Commission" remained.

THE FIRST MULTICULTURAL "SPECIAL ISSUE"

The *MEJ* has often devoted sections of individual issues to some specific topic. In November 1971, MENC published a special issue of the *MEJ* devoted entirely to African-American music. This issue covered research, the impact of music and African-American culture, and a program in African music established at Howard University.[51] The issue also included a selected resource list for studies in African-American music.[52] This is the first time such compilation of materials for any culture was made available to the *MEJ* readership.

OCTOBER 1972 SPECIAL FOCUS ISSUE: "MUSIC IN WORLD CULTURES"

Titled "Music in World Cultures," the October 1972 issue of *MEJ* was designed as a resource issue for music educators and was divided into three sections. The first section presented an overview of world musical cultures. Beginning with "Music is a Human Need" by Margaret Mead,[53] the articles proceeded through the musics of Northeast Asia, Southeast Asia, South Asia, West Asia–North Africa, and Africa south of the Sahara, European folk traditions, the Americas, and Oceania.[54] A unique aspect of this issue was the inclusion of two soundsheets with musical examples from cultures representative of each of these world regions. The soundsheets were accompanied by a listening guide that included pertinent information about the source, context, and content of each selection.

While the first section provided basic information about these varied musical cultures, the second section contained articles on the need to use these musics in the schools. Malcom Tait wrote "Increasing Awareness and Sensitivity through World Musics,"[55] Ricardo Trimillos said that musical experiences must be expanded to fit today's world,[56] and Charles Seeger put forth a challenge to American schools to use world musics.[57] Educators were also shown some ways to use musics from a variety of cultures in the classroom. Hawaiian and African-American musics could involve students in other cultures from within the United States. Rhythm concepts could be taught from a multicultural perspective, and a greater understanding of various ethnic musics could be obtained through movement experiences with the music.[58] The authors of the articles in this issue were, and still are, leaders in the field and experts on their particular area of musical culture.

The third section of this issue was a compilation of resources for classroom music teachers. With the exception of the resource list on African-American music compiled in 1971, there had not been another effort made like this one. The issue contained a glossary of terms, a bibliography/discography, and filmography of available materials for many cultures. Also included were nearly ten pages of pictures of musicians and instruments from around the world, as well as a list of the societies and archives for ethnomusicology and the names of colleges and universities offering courses in ethnomusicology.[59]

The "Book Reviews" column of this particular issue is worth noting.[60] Up to this point there were few, if any, books reviewed that had anything to do with multicultural approaches in music. This was due in part to the scarcity of books written, but also to the fact that the *MEJ* published reviews of books that its readership would find useful. Up until 1967, the musics from cultures around the world were simply not very high on the "useful" list for most teachers. All the books reviewed for this issue, however, dealt with some facet of these musics. These reviews became a further resource for the teacher looking for more depth on the subject of various cultures, or ethnomusicology in general. From this issue onward, the *MEJ* either reviewed publications about world musics, or listed them in the "Book Browsing" or "Study Shelf" columns.[61] In 1989, these columns were supplemented with "Video Views," which often included reviews of video materials on the musics of other cultures.[62]

Over the next ten years, the pages of *MEJ* continued to include articles about musics from many cultures. The topics were eclectic, ranging from "A Practical Introduction to African Music," to Eskimo string-figure games, to American popular and rock music.[63] Readers learned the joys of a Scottish pipe-and-drum band, about the folk music of Jamaica, and how to make a Tsonga xylophone.[64] The musics of Argentina, China, Tibet, and of Native Americans were brought to the attention of music educators,[65] and there were articles on Appalachian traditions, gospel music, and the training of Indian musicians.[66] Along with these more explanatory articles, there were some thought-provoking essays. Among them, Malcom Tait suggested keeping a balance between attitudes and strategies when working with world musics, and Albert McNeil wrote on the social foundations of the music of African-Americans.[67]

During this same period, the advertisements in *MEJ* for college and university summer study began to include notices of courses and workshops in multicultural music education. Although ads containing these notices were more plentiful in the magazine's pages during the 1970s than they are today, summer multicultural music education classes and workshops have continued to be offered at various locations across the country to the present.[68]

Other advertising also began to reflect a more global perspective. Advertisements included bilingual songs among new choral releases, the musical instruments from other cultures, and folk dance albums for educational use, as well as books dealing with the music of other cultures, or classroom applications of these musics.[69] MENC regularly announced its publications and resources for multicultural music education in the pages of the *MEJ*.[70]

By 1980, the study of musics from many cultures in the schools had increased, and educators became aware of the commitment that teaching these musics would require in the curriculum. The September 1980 issue of *MEJ* included a section on multicultural awareness. In his article "Teaching Musics of the World: A Renewed Commitment," William Anderson said, "Because of the ethnic diversity within our country, schools need to ensure that representative examples of a variety of musics are in the curriculum. ... There are a number of highly sophisticated musics in the world, and Western art music is just one."[71]

If educators were to implement music from a variety of cultures, multicultural training would be necessary, especially in graduate teacher education.[72] In October 1980, the Report of the MENC Commission on Graduate Music Teacher Education was published.[73] The MENC recommendations for minimal requirements for a master's degree now also included "Basic knowledge of music literature, including jazz, popular, ethnic, and non-Western music; An acquaintance with instructional materials for multicultural needs; Techniques for motivating and relating to students of diverse cultures."[74]

Although teacher education remained an issue, some educators were starting to make use of their new knowledge in their classes. Early in the 1970s, Paul Berliner had told of his methods of incorporating a world perspective in his music classes.[75] Now other teachers wrote to give their colleagues ideas about what worked for them.[76]

A multicultural perspective was starting to pervade other areas of music study as well. Along with articles on many forms of improvisation in the classroom and in jazz, the January 1980 special focus issue on improvisation devoted an entire section to world musics. Improvisation was addressed specifically in the musics of Latin America, West Africa, the Near East, and Korea.[77]

"THE MULTICULTURAL IMPERATIVE": SPECIAL ISSUE, MAY 1983

It had been ten years since an entire issue of *MEJ* was devoted to multicultural music education. While the 1972 special issue had focused on acquainting music educators with musics from around the world, the May 1983 special issue, "The Multicultural Imperative," emphasized the fact that music educators needed to teach music from a multicultural perspective. This issue had four main topic areas: the multicultural imperative, educational tactics, tools for teaching world musics, and selected resources. The articles in the first section all stressed the fact that no educator could ignore the cultural diversity in the classrooms of the United States.[78] The second and third sections of this issue offered assistance with classroom applications.[79] In addition, there were ideas for using the community as a resource,[80] and annotated resources for Hawaiian and Samoan musics.[81] There were especially pertinent reviews in both "Book Browsing" and "Study Shelf" columns.[82] The issue concluded with a selected resource list. This list was not as extensive as the bibliographical list found in the 1972 special issue; however, it also included reports, committee results, and upcoming events such as the ISME conference scheduled for 1984 in Oregon.[83] The MENC national conferences during the 1980s continued to offer sessions to assist music educators with the implementation of musics from various cultures. The 1980 conference in Miami Beach offered several sessions on African-American music as well as reading sessions devoted to the music of African-American composers.[84] String teachers began to focus on multiculturalism at the 1982 conference in San Antonio with an international round table of artists as well as a viola lecture/recital of music by Spanish and Latin American composers. In addition, one elementary session introduced oral tradition as a teaching practice in musics of various cultures, and another featured a student demonstration of folk dances.[85]

Many of the conference sessions at the 1984 conference in Chicago were, like the topics of the 1983 special issue, focused on teacher training, resources, and teaching methods. There were also groups performing Latin American chamber music and East European instrumental music.[86] *MEJ* did not announce the conference programs for the 1986 and 1988 MENC biennial conferences. Instead, this information was carried in the *MENC Soundpost* newsletter.

In addition to the national conference, MENC, Wesleyan University, and the Theodore Presser Foundation jointly sponsored in August 1984 the Wesleyan Symposium on the Application of Social Anthropology to the Teaching and Learning of Music. The emphasis of the symposium was "on exploring practical implications of research findings in other cultures for U.S. music teachers in their daily instruction."[87] Even though this symposium focused "principally on a transcultural approach" and did not deal specifically with curricula for classroom use, it was the first time the MENC sponsored a gathering of anthropologists and ethnomusicologists for the purpose of a face-to-face exchange with the music educators who would use the results of their scholarship.[88]

Although it was not a special issue, the March 1985 issue of *MEJ* had several articles dealing with musics from many cultures. Elsie Buck told of her successful approach to incorporating world musics in her general music class. In addition, Samuel Miller wrote about the blues, and Martha Giles discussed the improvisational techniques of Indian flute music.[89]

TEACHER TRAINING

The need for teacher training courses in multicultural perspectives for music education continued to be emphasized. René Boyer-White issued a call for teacher training in approaches to multicultural music education in colleges because of the growing diversity of students within America's classrooms.[90] Marvin V. Curtis was even stronger in his views on teacher training: "Educators cannot teach what they themselves do not understand. Schools of higher education must make multicultural music education a part of the training of teachers to prepare them to deal with the black aesthetic experience along with other cultural experiences."[91]

David G. Klocko advised not just a single course of study in multicultural perspectives in music, but an integrated approach including music history and literature courses for a better overall understanding. He said, "The Eurocentric world view is outdated; a more global perspective must replace it."[92] He pointed out the multicultural thrust of the newest resources developed by the MENC, and he also mentioned the fact that the MENC's Eastern Division conference to be held in Boston in March of 1989 would have an international theme.[93] (Although musics from many cultures had previously been included in divisional conferences in one form or another, this was the first time that an entire conference carried a multicultural theme.)

The emphasis during the late 1980s tended to be twofold. Multicultural perspectives in musics were studied not only to increase students' knowledge about the musics of other peoples, but to increase understanding about the people who made these musics. In addition to Klocko's and Curtis' articles on teacher training, which stressed a world view and the fact that teachers cannot teach understanding if they themselves do not understand, Patricia Shehan recommended using multicultural musics as "windows" to cross-cultural understanding.[94]

As teachers became more exposed to musics from many cultures through the pages of the *MEJ* and through MENC conference presentations, they became aware of their own shortcomings in this area. A questioner in the "MENC Adviser" column in February 1990 asked, "How can I incorporate world music into my classroom when I have never been exposed to it? I live in a rural district that has just started to emphasize global education."[95]   The need for teachers not just to know, but to experience and thereby be able to teach better, was growing.

SYMPOSIUM: MULTICULTURAL APPROACHES TO MUSIC EDUCATION, 1990

The Multicultural Symposium was presented by the MENC in cooperation with the Society for Ethnomusicology, the Smithsonian Institution's Office of Folklife Programs, and MENC's Society for General Music. It preceded the 1990 National Biennial In-Service Conference in Washington, D.C., and targeted the culture and music of four ethnic groups: African-American, Asian-American, Hispanic-American, and Native American. An ethnomusicologist, performers from the culture, and a music educator well versed in that musical tradition presented material from each culture.[96]

The speakers at the Symposium provided much for music educators to reflect on. Bernice Johnson Reagon's keynote address for the Symposium, as reported by Anderson, stressed the need to help students "understand the relationship between people and their music."[97] Along the same lines, David McAllester said, "We need to learn how to live together even though we belong to different cultures."[98] Perhaps even more powerful was the following statement by Edwin Shupman:

> I believe the potential role of a music educator has not yet been realized in terms of broadening the multicultural horizons of their students, of promoting human understanding, and tolerance for racial and cultural differences.[99]

The nearly three hundred music educators who participated in the Symposium sang songs and learned dances for both the Native American and Asian-American segments of the event. They had opportunities to perform in a Chinese percussion ensemble, play Andean raft-pipe instruments, see an excerpt of Chinese opera, and attend a dance party with salsa and other Latino dance music. Special concert performances featured Nguyen Dihn Nghia and his family performing on Vietnamese traditional instruments, and the Kings of Harmony, an African-American brass band.[100]

At the close of the Symposium, a Resolution for Future Directions and Actions was adopted by the participants. This resolution, quoted below, forms a statement of commitment to multicultural musics for not only the MENC as an organization, but for all music educators:

> *Be it resolved that:*
>
> We will seek to ensure that multicultural approaches to teaching music will be incorporated into every elementary and secondary school music curriculum,
>
> Multicultural approaches to teaching music will be incorporated into all phases of

teacher education in music,

Music teachers will seek to assist students in understanding that there are many different but equally valid forms of musical expression,

Instruction will included not only the study of other musics but the relationship of those musics to their respective cultures; further, that meaning of music within each culture be sought for its own value,

MENC will encourage national and regional accrediting groups to *require* broad, multicultural perspectives for all education programs, particularly those in music.[101]

In addition to the Symposium, the MENC 1990 biennial conference featured performing groups from Hungary, Australia, Taiwan, and Canada.[102]

Also in 1990, *MEJ* carried an article by Marsha Edelman that described ways to incorporate Jewish music in the music curriculum.[103] In a special issue on creativity, Patricia Shehan Campbell viewed the topic of musical creativity from a cross-cultural perspective.[104] In addition, Ellen McCullough-Brabson described a successful museum/school project.[105] One of the highlights of this project was allowing the students hands-on exploration with instruments from around the world. Demonstrations at the 1992 biennial conference in New Orleans included a similar hands-on technique with musical instruments, Native American dances for classroom use, and the musics of the various cultures from southern Louisiana. There were discussions on the philosophical implications of music education in a multi-value culture, and on multicultural concerns in music teacher education.[106]

1992 SPECIAL FOCUS ISSUE: "MULTICULTURAL MUSIC EDUCATION"

For the third time in twenty years, *MEJ* offered a special issue on multicultural music education. Teachers had learned about other cultures in 1972, learned of the necessity of classroom applications in 1983, and now were challenged to incorporate the music from many cultures into all their music classes—choral and instrumental as well as general music.

This issue had a slightly different format from the previous multicultural issues in that it was not divided into sections as were the past issues. Each article had an individual focus. Anthony Seeger presented an opening article that was an encouragement for multicultural music education. After commenting that "Music is an effective way to experience at least one aspect of another culture first-hand,"[107] he went on to say that the musical traditions students bring with them into the classroom should be welcome. These traditions can then be supplemented through exposure to others' musical traditions.[108]

Patricia Shehan Campbell offered several pedagogical techniques to foster the infusion of musics from a variety of cultures in the general music curriculum.[109] Practical lesson plans followed her article for Native American, African-American, Filipino, and Latin American musics.[110] Judith Tucker's multicultural resource list included texts, audiotapes and videotapes, and culture-specific books and recordings.[111] The possibilities of incorporating a multicultural perspective in the instrumental and choral programs were examined by Will Schmid and Joan Conlon respectively.[112] Selected lists of repertoire in these areas followed their articles.[113]

Anderson's article presented a view of multicultural music education in teacher training. He argued that if students are to be taught music from a multicultural perspective, then music teacher education also needs this perspective. Anderson suggested broadening the entire music curriculum for future teachers from theo-ry and history classes to methods classes and performance opportunities in such areas as Asian, Latin American, and African-American musics.[114]

CONCLUSION

In 1967, Egon Kraus challenged music education to become multicultural in its perspective. He left music educators with the goals of developing multicultural attitudes and classroom methodologies, integrating multicultural approaches in other music courses, reviewing textbooks and study materials for multicultural perspectives, providing source materials, holding international seminars, cooper-ating with UNESCO, and sharing multicultural music education concerns with other countries. How far has the music education profession come in meeting these goals?

Over the last twenty-five years, MENC, through the *MEJ*, has guided the profes-sion with many informative articles about the music of other cultures. This is espe-cially evident in the 1972 special focus issue on "Music in World Cultures." The *MEJ* also emphasized the need for a multicultural perspective in the music class-room. It is safe to say that all these articles were aimed at helping educators devel-op what Kraus called "proper regard for foreign musical cultures." The declara-tion of the 1990 Multicultural Symposium provides the clearest indication of the positive attitude many music educators now have toward the musics of other cul-tures.

MENC and the *MEJ* supplied various strategies and resources for applying the musics of many cultures, both through the publication of multicultural music arti-cles throughout the 1970s and 1980s (particularly in the 1983 "Multicultural Imperative" issue) and through the inclusion of sessions on musics from a variety of cultures in national conferences. The most outstanding of these were the ses-sions provided at the 1990 Multicultural Symposium. In addition, both MENC and the *MEJ* continued to voice the need for teachers trained in multicultural approaches to music, especially in graduate programs. The Multicultural Symposium provided a model for in-service training for music educators. "Methodological realization" has certainly been addressed.

Although there is little evidence in the *MEJ* of educators reviewing school music textbooks with the purpose of making improvements in multicultural per-spectives, the *MEJ* has, since 1967, regularly reviewed textbooks and study materi-als that deal with the musics of other cultures in the "Book Review" and "Video Views" columns. By bringing these resources to the attention of its readership, the *MEJ* kept music educators aware of current scholarship in the field and encour-aged further personal investigation. It is music educators who are knowledgeable about multiple music cultures who can demand more authenticity and less preju-dice from the school music textbook publishers.

Contributors to the *MEJ* assisted greatly with the preparation of multicultural resource lists for music educators. These included bibliographies, discographies, and lists of audiocassette and video recording. Although these were selected lists, they were also fairly comprehensive in scope. It seems that music education took Kraus's injunction to prepare "pedagogically suitable works" with "authentic sound recordings" to heart. The publications and films that MENC produced from the multicultural symposium are further evidence of this.

Integrating a multicultural perspective into other music areas such as ear train-ing and music theory is beginning to be more commonplace. The solution to the problem posed by this type of integration has not yet been found, although there is some progress to be seen. The 1992 "Multicultural Music Education" special focus section of the *MEJ* emphasized a global perspective in all aspects of music education—choral, general, and instrumental. In other issues, there have been articles about improvisation, and creativity in a variety of cultures. In addition, Klocko and Anderson both recommended that schools of music incorporate multicultural approaches in music history, music theory and teaching methods classes.

Work with UNESCO and "international cooperation and seminars" perhaps appear to be more the role of ISME than MENC; however, MENC did cosponsor the Wesleyan Symposium. International scholars were among the presenters at this Symposium, and music educators were afforded the opportunity to meet them and discuss the educational implications of their research.

The final resolution/declaration drawn up by MENC and ratified by the teachers at the Multicultural Symposium in Washington, D.C., is a culmination of the past twenty-five years' growth of multicultural approaches to music in music education. History will show if this declaration will have the impact on the profession that the Tanglewood declaration had in opening the doors of the classroom to greater implementation of musics from many cultures. The hope, at least as expressed by the educators at this symposium, is that these beginnings in multicultural music education will become the foundation for a global understanding of music.

Music educators today face an even broader diversity of students in their classrooms than they did in either 1967 or 1980. The need is even greater for teachers themselves to understand the musics these children bring with them into the classroom, to understand the various music systems in the world, and, as pointed out in the 1992 special focus on "Multicultural Music Education," to teach music from a global perspective. Only then can they help their students to understand music in its many forms, to see music as a mode of human expression, and perhaps to help them understand the people who make the music. The declaration of the Multicultural Symposium could be considered a report card for how far the profession has come since 1967. Music education has not solved the problems posed by Kraus, but it has come close on some and has begun work on others. The need for teacher training remains essential. If the past twenty-five years are an accurate indication, the *MEJ* will continue to publish articles and MENC will continue to sponsor conference activities that will assist music educators in accomplishing this task.

NOTES

1. Egon Kraus, "The Contribution of Music Education to the Understanding of Foreign Cultures, Past and Present," *Music Educators Journal* 53, no. 5 (January 1967): 91.

2. *Ibid.*, 91.

3. Edward B. Birge, *History of Public School Music in the United States* (Boston: Oliver Ditson, Co., 1928).

4. Theodore A. Tellstrom, *Music in American Education: Past and Present* (New York: Holt, Rinehart, and Winston, 1971), 280.

5. James A. Keene, *A History of Music Education in the United States* (Hanover, NH: University Press of New England, 1984), 362–363; Michael L. Mark and Charles L. Gary, *A History of American Music Education* (New York: Schirmer Books, division of Macmillan, Inc., 1992), 311–313.

6. Mark and Gary, *A History of American Music Education*, 366–367.

7. George N. Heller, "Retrospective of Multicultural Music Education in the United

150   VOLK

   States," *Music Educators Journal* 69, no. 9 (May 1983): 35.

8.   *Ibid.*, 35–36.

9.   William M. Anderson, "World Musics in American Education, 1916–1970," *Contributions to Music Education*, no. 3 (Autumn 1974): 23–42.

10. Christine E. Brett, "A Study of Trends and Developments in Multicultural Music Education (1960–1989) and their Manifestation in Silver Burdett Music Series" (Master's thesis, Florida State University, 1990).

11. Norris B. Johnson, "On the Relationship of Anthropology to Multicultural Teaching and Learning," *Journal of Teacher Education* 28, no. 3 (May/June 1977): 10.

12. Derived from J. H. Kwabena Nketia, "Music Education in Africa and the West," in Lusaka, ed., *Education and Research in African Music, 1975*. Cited in Barbara Lundquist, "Transmission of Music Culture in Formal Educational Institutions," *The World of Music* 29, no. 1 (1987): 67–68; and Kwabena Nketia, "The Place of Authentic Folk Music in Education," *Music Educators Journal* 54, no. 3 (November 1967): 41.

12. Derived from J. H. Kwabena Nketia, "Music Education in Africa and the West," in Lusaka, ed., *Education and Research in African Music, 1975*. Cited in Barbara Lundquist, "Transmission of Music Culture in Formal Educational Institutions," *The World of Music* 29, no. 1 (1987): 67–68; and Kwabena Nketia, "The Place of Authentic Folk Music in Education," *Music Educators Journal* 54, no. 3 (November 1967): 41.

13. This idea is derived from David Elliott, "Music as Culture: Toward a Multicultural Concept of Arts Education," *Journal of Aesthetic Education* 24, no. 1 (Spring 1990): 158; Barbara Lundquist, "Transmission of Music Culture," 75. For examples of different views of the purpose of multicultural music education, see Abraham Schwadron, "World Musics in Education," *ISME Yearbook* 9 (November 1984), 92; Keith Swanwick, *Mind, Music, and Education*. London: Routledge, 1988, 180.

14. Alan Merriam, *The Anthropology of Music* (Evanston, IL: Northwestern University Press, 1964), 27.

15. Though jazz is included in this definition, and does have its place in multicultural music education, this article is not intended to provide a history of jazz education. For a brief overview of the jazz education movement, see Bryce Luty, "Jazz Education's Struggle for Acceptance," *Music Educators Journal* 69, no. 3 (November 1982): 38–39+ and "Jazz Ensembles' Era of Accelerated Growth," *Music Educators Journal* 69, no. 4 (December 1982): 49–50+.

16. Maureen D. Hooper, "Major Concerns of Music Education: Content Analysis of the *Music Educators Journal*, 1957–1967" (Ed.D. diss., University of Southern California, 1969) *Dissertation Abstracts International*, 30 10A, 4479-80.

17. *Ibid.*

18. John W. Molnar, "Changing Aspects of American Culture as Reflected in the MENC," *Journal for Research in Music Education* 7, no. 2 (Fall 1959): 174–184.

19. Music Supervisors National Conference, Program listing for annual conference in Evanston, IL, *Music Supervisors Journal* 4, no. 4 (March 1918): 4–5.

20. John Wesley Work, "The Development of the Music of the Negro from the Folk Song to the Art Song and Art Chorus," *Music Supervisors Journal* 6, no. 1 (September 1919): 12–14.

21. Music Supervisors National Conference, Program listing for annual conferences in Cincinnati, *Music Supervisors Journal* 10, no. 3 (February 1924); in Detroit, *Music Supervisors Journal* 12, no. 3 (February 1925), 48; in Chicago, *Music Supervisors Journal* 16, no. 3 (February 1930): 19+.

22. Paul J. Weaver, "British and American Educators Plan Unique Meeting," *Music Supervisors Journal* 15, no. 1 (October 1928): 7–15+.

23. Percy Scholes, "An International Movement in Musical Education—Is It Possible?" *MSNC Journal of Proceedings, 1930)*: 96; William M. Anderson, "World Music in

American Education, 1916–1970," *Contributions to Music Education*, no. 3 (Autumn 1974): 25.

24. Charles Seeger, "Inter-American Relations in the Field of Music," *Music Educators Journal* 27, no. 4 (March–April 1941): 17–18+.

25. Hazel Hohavec Morgan, ed., *Music Education Source Book* (Chicago, Music Educators National Conference, 1947), 208.

26. For examples see: Music Educators National Conference, "Music for Uniting the Americas," *Music Educators Journal* 28, no. 2 (November/December 1941): 13–14; MENC Committee on Folk Music of the United States, "American Songs for American Children," published in each issue beginning with *Music Educators Journal* 30, no. 3 (January 1944) and ending with *Music Educators Journal* 31, no. 4 (February/March 1945); Harry E. Moses, "A Good Neighbor Policy for Appreciation Classes," *Music Educators Journal* 32, no. 1 (September/October 1945): 22–23; Hazel Kinsella, "Folk Music Aids," *Music Educators Journal* 38, no. 4 (February/March 1952): 52.

27. Hazel Hohavec Morgan, ed., *Music in American Education* (Chicago, IL: Music Educators National Conference, 1955).

28. Claude Palisca, *Music in Our Schools: A Search for Improvement* (Washington, D.C.: U.S. Government Printing Office, 1964), 11.

29. *Juilliard Repertory Library*, Reference/Library edition, (Cincinnati, OH: Canyon Press, 1970), 192–232.

30. Wiley Housewright, editorial, *Music Educators Journal* 53, no. 2 (October 1976): 76.

31. Vanette Lawler, "International Seminar on Teacher Education in Music," *Music Educators Journal* 53, no. 3 (November 1966): 55.

32. Robert Choate and Max Kaplan, "Music in American Society—Introduction to Issues," *Music Educators Journal* 67, no. 8 (April 1967): 77.

33. Robert A. Choate, "The Tanglewood Declaration," *Music Educators Journal* 54, no. 3 (November 1967): 51.

34. Charles Fowler, "Joining the Mainstream," *Music Educators Journal* 54, no. 3 (November 1967): 69.

35. David P. McAllester, "The Substance of Things Hoped For," *Music Educators Journal* 54, no. 6 (February 1968): 50.

36. Zoltán Kodály, "Folksong in Pedagogy," *Music Educators Journal* 53, no. 7 (March 1967): 59–61; Kwabena Nketia, "The Place of Authentic Folk Music," 41–42+.

37. Lucius Wyatt, "The Brussels Museum of Musical Instruments," *Music Educators Journal* 53, no. 6 (February 1967): 48–51.

38. See the several articles under "Youth Music—A Special Report," *Music Educators Journal* 56, no. 3 (November 1969): 43–74; Music Educators National Conference, "National Association of Jazz Educators," *Music Educators Journal* 68, no. 8 (April 1968): 57.

39. See, for example, Barbara Reeder, "Afro-music—As Tough as a Mozart Quartet." *Music Educators Journal* 56, no. 4 (December 1969): 88–91; and "Getting Involved in Shaping the Sounds of Black Music," *Music Educators Journal* 59, no. 2 (October 1972): 80–84; Dominique de Lerma, "Black Music Now!" *Music Educators Journal* 57, no. 3 (November 1970): 25–29; Kwabena Nketia, "Music Education in Africa and the West: We Can Learn From Each Other," *Music Educators Journal* 57, no. 3 (November 1970): 48–55.

40. Marie Joy Curtiss, "Essays in Retribalization: India," *Music Educators Journal* 56, no. 1 (September 1969): 60–62; Don DeNevi, "Essays in Retribalization: Hudson Bay," *Music Educators Journal* 56, no. 1 (September 1969): 66–68; Louis Ballard, "Put American Indian Music in the Classroom," *Music Educators Journal* 56, no. 7 (March 1969): 38–44.

41. Elizabeth May, "An Experiment with Australian Aboriginal Music," *Music Educators Journal* 54, no. 4 (December 1968): 47–56.

42. Donald Berger, "Ethnomusicology Past and Present," *Music Educators Journal* 54, no. 7 (March 1968): 77–79+.

43. John M. Eddins, "Two Trends in Teaching Music: The Comprehensive and the Cross-Cultural, *Music Educators Journal* 56, no. 4 (December 1969): 69–71.

44. Music Educators National Conference, "Seattle in Pictures," *Music Educators Journal* 55, no. 1 (September 1968): 46.

45. Music Educators National Conference, Program listing for biennial conference, Chicago, *Music Educators Journal* 56, no. 6 (February 1970): 38–40+.

46. Music Educators National Conference, Program listing for biennial conference, Atlanta, *Music Educators Journal* 59, no. 6 (February 1972): 25–33.

47. Music Educators National Conference, Program listing for biennial conference program, Annaheim, *Music Educators Journal* 60, no. 5 (January 1974): 30–39.

48. Music Educators National Conference, Program listing of biennial conference program, Atlantic City, *Music Educators Journal* 62, no. 6 (February 1976): 64–71.

49. Music Educators National Conference, Program listing for biennial conference, Chicago, *Music Educators Journal* 64, no. 6 (February 1978): 74–104.

50. Ella J. Washington, "Multi-Cultural Awareness Committee: New Directions," *Music Educators Journal*, 69, no. 9 (May 1983): 67.

51. Otis D. Simmons, "Research, the Bedrock of Student Interest," *Music Educators Journal* 58, no. 3 (November 1971): 38–41; Harry Morgan, "Music— A Life Force in the Black Community," *Music Educators Journal* 58, no. 3 (November 1971): 34–47; Beverely Blondell, "Drums Talk at Howard," *Music Educators Journal* 58, no. 3 (November 1971): 45–48.

52. Music Educators National Conference, "Selected Resources in Black Studies in Music," *Music Educators Journal* 58, no. 3 (November 1971): 56+.

53. Margaret Mead, "Music is a Human Need," *Music Educators Journal* 59, no. 2 (October 1972): 24–27.

54. See the *Music Educators Journal* 59, no. 2 (October 1972): 30–64.

55. Malcom Tait, "Increasing Awareness and Sensitivity though World Musics," *Music Educators Journal* 59, no. 2 (October 1972): 85–89.

56. Ricardo Trimillos, "Expanding Music Experience to Fit Today's World," *Music Educators Journal* 59, no. 2 (October 1972): 90–94.

57. Charles Seeger, "World Musics in American Schools: A Challenge to be Met," *Music Educators Journal* 59, no. 2 (October 1972): 107–111.

58. See the *Music Educators Journal* 59, no. 2 (October 1972): 73–84, 95–99, and 100–104.

59. Music Educators National Conference, Bibliographies and photography sections, *Music Educators Journal* 59, no. 2 (October 1972): 65–72 and 112–141.

60. Music Educators National Conference, Book Reviews section, *Music Educators Journal* 59, no. 2 (October 1972): 145–161.

61. Examples include: David Reck, review of *Teaching the Music of Six Different Cultures in the Modern Secondary School*, by Luvenia George, in *Music Educators Journal* 64, no. 9 (May 1977): 15–16; Will Schmid, review of *Lessons From the World: A Cross-Cultural Guide to Music Teaching and Learning*, by Patricia Shehan Campbell, in *Music Educators Journal* 78, no. 6 (February 1992): 64–65. Content descriptions were included in the "Book Browsing" and "Study Shelf" sections. Many were found in the 1983 special issue (see Note 82). Other examples include: Dena Epstein, *Sinful Tunes and Spirituals: Black Folk Music to the Civil War*, in "Book Browsing," *Music Educators Journal* 65, no. 1 (September 1978): 22; Jeff Todd, gen. ed., *Worlds of Music: An Introduction to the Music of the World's Peoples*, in "Book Browsing," *Music Educators Journal* 71, no. 4 (December 1984): 71; William Anderson and Patricia Shehan Campbell, *Multicultural Perspectives in Music Education*, in "Book Browsing," *Music Educators Journal* 76, no. 1 (September 1989): 60; C. W. McRae, *Sing 'Round the World: International Folksongs*, in "Book Browsing," *Music Educators Journal* 77, no. 2 (October 1990): 65.

62. See, for example, Jo Ann Baird, review of *Arabic Musical Instruments* in "Video Views,"

Music Educators Journal 76, no. 3 (November 1989): 11–14; William Anderson, review of *The JVC Video Anthology of World Music and Dance,* in "Video Views," *Music Educators Journal* 77, no. 7 (March 1991): 51–52. Content descriptions were also published. See *The Hawaiian Show,* in "Video Views," *Music Educators Journal* 76, no. 7 (March 1990): 16; *Pan in 'A' Minor: Steel Bands of Trinidad,* in "Video Views," *Music Educators Journal* 78, no. 5 (January 1992): 70.

63. Carleton L. Inniss, "A Practical Introduction to African Music," *Music Educators Journal,* 60, no. 6 (February 1974): 50–53; Thomas F. Johnston, Matthew Nocolai, and Karen Nagozruk, "Illeagosuik! Eskimo String-Figure Games," *Music Educators Journal* 65, no. 7 (March 1978): 54–61; for articles on popular/rock musics, see *Music Educators Journal* 66, no. 4 (December 1979): 26–34 and 54–59.

64. John C. Laughter, "Bagpipes, Bands, and Bearskin Hats," *Music Educators Journal* 63, no. 3 (November 1976): 66–69; Olive Lewin, "Biddy, Biddy, Folk Music of Jamaica," *Music Educators Journal* 63, no. 1 (September 1976): 38–49; Thomas F. Johnston, "How to Make a Tsonga Xylophone," *Music Educators Journal* 63, no. 3 (November 1976): 38–49.

65. Nick Rossi, "The Music of Argentina," *Music Educators Journal* 59, no. 4 (January 1973): 51–53; Fred Fisher, "The Yellow Bell of China and the Endless Search," *Music Educators Journal* 59, no. 8 (April 1973): 30–33+; Ivan Vandor, "Cymbals and Trumpets from the 'Roof of the World,'" *Music Educators Journal* 61, no. 1 (September 1974): 106–109+; Paul Parthun, "Tribal Music in North America," *Music Educators Journal* 6, no. 4 (January 1976): 32–45.

66. Randall Armstrong, "The Adaptable Appalachian Dulcimer," *Music Educators Journal* 66, no. 5 (February 1980): 38–41; Horace Boyer, "Gospel Music," *Music Educators Journal* 64, no. 9 (May 1978): 34–43; Michael Stevens, "The Training of Indian Musicians," *Music Educators Journal* 61, no. 8 (April 1975): 33–39.

67. Malcom Tait, "World Musics: Balancing Our Attitudes and Strategies," *Music Educators Journal* 61, no. 6 (February 1975): 28–32; Albert J. McNeil, "The Social Foundations of the Music of Black America," *Music Educators Journal* 60, no. 6 (February 1974): 47–49.

68. Examples are: New York University, Advertisement, *Music Educators Journal* 55, no. 8 (April 1969): 114; Indiana University and Wesleyan University, Advertisements, *Music Educators Journal* 58, no. 8 (April 1972): 116–118; Northwestern University, Advertisement, *Music Educators Journal* 64, no. 8 (April 1978): 92, and 71, no. 8 (April 1985): 58; Central Connecticut State University, Advertisement, *Music Educators Journal* 74, no. 8 (April 1988): 58; University of Hartford, Advertisement, *Music Educators Journal* 78, no. 7 (March 1992): 77.

69. For examples, see: Associated Music Publishing, Inc., Advertisement, new choral releases, *Music Educators Journal* 54, no. 3 (November 1967): 22; Inter Culture Associates, Advertisement, instruments of India, *Music Educators Journal* 58, no. 8 (April 1972): 17; RCA Records, Advertisement, *Music Educators Journal* 58, no. 8 (April 1972): 8; Kent State University Press, Advertisement, *Music Educators Journal* 69, no. 9 (May 1983): 77; MENC Publications, *Music Educators Journal* 78, no. 4 (December 1991): 68; Silver Burdett and Ginn, Advertisement, school music textbooks, *Music Educators Journal* 75, no. 4 (December 1989): back cover; Macmillan/McGraw-Hill, Advertisement, school music textbooks, *Music Educators Journal* 78, no. 7 (March 1992): inside back cover.

70. Although a particularly extensive listing of professional resources published by MENC is found in *Music Educators Journal* 52, no. 3 (November 1985): 47–54, *MENC Professional Resources* is now a separate catalog, published annually.

71. William M. Anderson, "Teaching Musics of the World: A Renewed Commitment," *Music Educators Journal* 67, no. 1 (September 1980): 40.

72. Bette Yarbrough Cox, "Multicultural Training," *passim.*

73. Chuck Ball et al., "Report of the MENC Commission on Graduate Music Teacher Education," *Music Educators Journal* 67, no. 2 (October 1980): 46–53+.

154   VOLK

74. Chuck Ball et al., "Report of the MENC Commission," 48.

75. Paul Berliner, "Soda Bottles, Whale Bones, Sitars, and Shells—A World Music Perspective," *Music Educators Journal* 59, no. 7 (March 1973): 50–52+.

76. Jerry and Bev Praver, "Barb'ra Allen, Tom Dooley, and Sweet Betsy from PS 42," *Music Educators Journal* 70, no. 5 (January 1984): 56–69; Patricia Shehan, "Teaching Music Through Balkan Folk Dance," *Music Educators Journal* 71, no. 3 (November 1984): 47–51; Martha Holmes, "Israeli Folk Dance: A Resource for Music Educators," *Music Educators Journal* 67, no. 2 (October 1980): 36–39.

77. See "Improvisation in World Musics," *Music Educators Journal* 66, no. 5 (January 1980): 118–147; and "Improvisation at the High School and College Levels," *Music Educators Journal* 66, no. 5 (January 1980): 86–104.

78. Anderson, "Teaching Musics of the World," 40–41; Jack P. B. Dodds, "Music as a Multicultural Education," *Music Educators Journal* 69, no. 9 (May 1983): 33–36; Robert Garfias, "Music in the United States: Community of Cultures," *Music Educators Journal* 69, no. 9 (May 1983): 30–31; Bess Lomax Hawes, "Our Cultural Mosaic," *Music Educators Journal* 69, no. 9 (May 1983): 26–27.

79. See "Educational Tactics," *Music Educators Journal* 69, no. 9 (May 1983): 39–51; "Tools for Teaching World Musics," *Music Educators Journal* 69, no. 9 (May 1983): 58–61.

80. Emma S. Brooks-Baham, "Collecting Materials in Your Community," *Music Educators Journal* 69, no. 9 (May 1983): 52–55.

81. Barbara Smith, "Musics of Hawaii and Samoa: Exemplar of Annotated Resources," *Music Educators Journal* 69, no. 9 (May 1983): 62–65.

82. Music Educators National Conference, "Book Browsing" and "Study Shelf," *Music Educators Journal* 69, no. 9 (May 1983): 22–25.

83. Music Educators National Conference, Resource Listing, *Music Educators Journal* 69, no. 9 (May 1983): 66–70.

84. Music Educators National Conference, "Miami Beach Conference Program Preview," *Music Educators Journal* 66, no. 7 (March 1980): 86–88.

85. Music Educators National Conference, Program listing of biennial conference, San Antonio, *Music Educators Journal* 68, no. 4 (December 1981): 58–62.

86. Music Educators National Conference, Program listing for biennial conference, Chicago, *Music Educators Journal* 70, no. 5 (January 1984): 62–64.

87. Music Educators National Conference, Advertisement for Wesleyan Symposium, *Music Educators Journal* 70, no. 8 (April 1984): 57–58.

88. David P. McAllester, project director, *Becoming Human through Music* (Reston, VA: Music Educators National Conference, 1985): 2.

89. Elsie Buck, "Mom, Pack My Bags for Music Class," *Music Educators Journal* 70, no. 6 (February 1985): 33–35; Samuel D. Miller, "Lessons in the Blues," *Music Educators Journal* 70, no. 6 (February 1985): 39–40; Martha Giles, "Improvising on an Indian Flute," *Music Educators Journal* 70, no. 6 (February 1985): 61–62.

90. René Boyer-White, "Reflecting Cultural Diversity in the Music Classroom," *Music Educators Journal* 75, no. 4 (December 1988): 50–54.

91. Marvin V. Curtis, "Understanding the Black Aesthetic Experience," *Music Educators Journal* 77, no. 2 (October 1988): 23–26.

92. David G. Klocko, "Multicultural Music in the College Curriculum," *Music Educators Journal* 75, no. 5 (January 1989): 39.

93. Klocko, "Multicultural Music in the College Curriculum," 40.

94. Patricia K. Shehan, "World Musics: Windows to Cross-Cultural Understanding," *Music Educators Journal* 75, no. 3 (November 1988): 22–26.

95. Music Educators National Conference, "MENC Advisor" column, *Music Educators Journal* 76, no. 5 (January 1990): 10.

96. Music Educators National Conference, Advertisement for Multicultural Symposium,

Music Educators Journal 76, no. 3 (November 1989): 15.

97. William M. Anderson, "Toward a Multicultural Future," *Music Educators Journal* 77, no. 9 (May 1991): 30.
98. *Ibid.*, 31.
99. *Ibid.*, 31.
100. *Ibid.*, 32.
101. *Ibid.*, 33.
102. Music Educators National Conference, "Conference Connection," *Music Educators Journal* 76, no. 7 (March 1990): 9–10.
103. Marsha B. Edelman, "Exploring the Rich Tradition of Jewish Music," *Music Educators Journal* 77, no. 1 (September 1990) : 35–39.
104. Patricia S. Campbell, "Cross-Cultural Views of Musical Creativity," *Music Educators Journal* 76, no. 9 (May 1990): 43–46.
105. Ellen McCullough-Brabson, "Instruments from Around the World: Hands-On Experiences," *Music Educators Journal* 77, no. 3 (November 1990): 46–50.
106. Music Educators National Conference, "1992 Conference Performing Groups and Education Sessions," *Music Educators Journal* 78, no. 6 (February 1992): 39–43.
107. Anthony Seegar, "Celebrating the American Music Mosaic," *Music Educators Journal* 78, no. 9 (May 1992): 29.
108. *Ibid.*, 26–29.
109. Patricia Campbell, "Cultural Consciousness in Teaching General Music," *Music Educators Journal* 78, no. 9 (May 1992): 30–33.
110. See *Music Educators Journal* 78, no. 9 (May 1992): 33–36.
112. Will Schmid, "World Music in the Instrumental Music Program," *Music Educators Journal* 78 no. 9 (May 1992): 41–44; Joan C. Conlon, "Explore the World in Song," *Music Educators Journal* 78, no. 9 (May 1992): 46–48.
113. See *Music Educators Journal* 78, no. 9 (May 1992): 44–45 and 49–51.
114. William M. Anderson, "Rethinking Teacher Education: The Multicultural Imperative," *Music Educators Journal* 78, no. 9 (May 1992): 52–55.

November 12, 1992

Name Index